"A PEOPLE'S CONTEST"

"A PEOPLE'S CONTEST"

The Union and Civil War

1861–1865

Second Edition, with a New Preface

PHILLIP SHAW PALUDAN

University Press of Kansas

© 1988, 1996 by Phillip S. Paludan
All rights reserved

Published by the University Press of Kansas (Lawrence, Kansas 66049), which was organized by the Kansas Board of Regents and is operated and funded by Emporia State University, Fort Hays State University, Kansas State University, Pittsburg State University, the University of Kansas, and Wichita State University

Library of Congress Cataloging-in-Publication Data

Paludan, Phillip S., 1938–
    A people's contest : the Union and Civil War 1861–1865 / Phillip Shaw Paludan. — 2nd ed., with a new pref.
        p.   cm. — (Modern war studies)
    Includes bibliographical references and index.
    ISBN 0–7006–0812–5
    1. United States—History—Civil War, 1861–1865—Influence.
    2. United States—History—Civil War, 1861–1865—Social aspects.
    3. United States—History—Civil War, 1861–1865—Economic aspects.
    I. Title.   II. Series.
    E468.9.P35   1996
    973.7—dc20   96-21303

British Library Cataloguing in Publication Data is available.

Printed in the United States of America

10   9   8   7   6   5   4   3   2   1

The paper used in this publication meets the minimum requirements of the American National Standard for Permanence of Paper for Printed Library Materials Z39.48-1984.

For Karin and Kirsten Paludan
and Cathy Haskell

Contents

PART III: FINDING WAR'S MEANINGS

Illustrations follow page 126

Preface

"THIS is essentially a People's contest," Lincoln declared on July 4, 1861. "On the side of the Union, it is a struggle for maintaining in the world, that form, and substance of government, whose leading object is, to elevate the condition of men—to lift artificial weights from all shoulders—to clear the paths of laudable pursuit for all—to afford all, an unfettered start, and a fair chance, in the race of life."

I have taken those words seriously in two major ways, and both are important for seeing this book in the context of previous histories of the war. First, I have accepted Lincoln's determination that the people of the North were the main actors in this conflict and that the story of the war is the story of their efforts and hopes and of what they revealed about themselves in the struggle. The vast majority of writing on the Civil War has focused on Lincoln, his administration, and the generals who led his armies. This is the first book since 1910 to describe in a single volume the multifaceted impacts of the war on Northern society.

Lincoln's words not only bring the people to center stage, they also suggest the broad dimension of this great civil war. A full fabric of life was at stake: not just a form of government but its substance —a polity, a society, and an economy all were challenged. The war was thus entwined with the forces that were shaping that fabric, forces born in the emergence of a modern industrializing nation. Between them, war and industrialization would significantly change the lives of the American people.

Both events were immensely complex, and historians have respected that complexity by treating the two in separate historiographies. The "new social and economic historians," who have been the most active in studying industrialization, often write as though the Civil War did not occur. Civil War historians usually return the favor. They write histories of leaders and institutions whose plans and policies float above the social and economic transformations of the age.

This book is an effort to introduce the "new social and economic history" to the more traditional political, constitutional, diplomatic, and military genre. It is an effort to show how the two great events of the age were interrelated, to demonstrate the fact that they happened at the same time in the same place to the same people.

Saying that is easy. But demonstrating it and showing the interrelationships between the great events of the age is a daunting task. The experience described here, the impact of the Civil War on Northern society, happened to over twenty million people who lived in a society divided by race, culture, occupation, age, and sex. It happened to people who felt the force of history with widely varied ability to respond. It happened to people whose perspective depended on the place from which they watched the world, whether they looked on as individuals, as members of a little community, or as participants in a national event. No one perspective tells the story, even about one person, for individuals viewed their lives at different times in all these ways.

This book, then, changes its angles of vision and uses every lens I can think of. The new social and economic history provides questions and generalizations about the costs and benefits of industrializing America and who gained and who lost. More traditional historiography also offers insights. Political and economic history describes the major legislation passed that shaped a more modern nation. It also assesses the role played by political institutions in keeping alive the ideals for which the North fought. Diplomatic history describes the place of the war in the international arena. Constitutional questions about dissent and the legal nature of war are inextricably part of the political dialogue. The history of religion explains an experience in which hundreds of thousands of Christian soldiers marched and died. The new historiography and the old thus combine to illuminate Northern society at war.

But there are other things to say as well. While the forces of history swept on, individuals still lived their private lives. Fathers, sons, husbands, and lovers tried to keep their ties to their loved ones, went into battle, were maimed and died. Mothers, wives, and daughters struggled to keep alive the ordinary world that soldiers longed and fought for, and these women sought a role that would have public meaning as well. Too often historians of the public war have left these kinds of stories untold. But this fiery trial seared private lives, and the scars shaped postwar perceptions and experience.

I am also concerned with what literary figures saw in the conflict. The insights of Harriet Beecher Stowe and Herman Melville help us to see how the forces of industrialization and war were linked. No one understood the subtle anguishes of death better than Emily Dickinson. No one felt the rising of the people more keenly than Walt Whitman. The Civil War in the North was their contest, too.

Of course military history is inextricably part of the war. But my desire to emphasize the impact of the war rather than to chart its course has led me to see the generals in terms of what they represented as well as what they did. McClellan's history is also the history of professionalization in a changing world. Sherman resonated an image that Melville could have drawn. Grant's reassuring climb from poverty to victory was not his alone.

All these divergent historiographies are part of the story of the war. Yet I am most sensitive to the fact that this book is not a narrative history. It follows as much of a chronology as possible, but there are too many sides to the war to permit a single story line to be followed. Furthermore, since this is a study of the war's impact on so many different Americans, no one plot can fit. They lived different stories, woven together by the passage of time, to be sure, but experienced in complex contexts that tolled the passage of time in varied ways.

This volume is part of the *New American Nation Series,* a comprehensive, cooperative history of the area now embraced in the United States, from the days of discovery to our own time.

In the course of the decade that I have been involved in this project I have been helped by many people. My colleagues at the University of Kansas Department of History have participated in various faculty seminars where many of my ideas have been presented. They enthusiastically accepted their roles as critics. I am now very grateful for that enthusiasm. Haskell Springer, Philip Kissam, and Richard Colyer brought friendship and the perspectives of other disciplines to my persistent descriptions of this project. I have benefited from insightful assessments and lots of hard work by graduate assistants William Young, Daniel Black, and John Lomax. Norman Saul and Don McCoy encouraged me in important ways. Harold Hyman got the whole thing started and has been an invaluable model.

Henry Commager and Richard Morris were demanding and hence excellent editors. Our discussions about angles of vision helped to make this work a better one. Eric Foner's comments were both encouraging and challenging.

Sandee Kennedy deserves a line to herself. She turned rough drafts into understandable copy, and also encouraged me with her enthusiasm.

Research support from the John Simon Guggenheim Foundation provided a year to begin writing. Summer support from the University of Kansas General Research Fund further advanced the project.

I have also been blessed with the support of Kari, Kirsten, Marsha, my mother, and Marty. They have kept me at it and believed in what was going on (only that ambiguity can suggest the many ways they helped).

Preface to Second Edition

" *A PEOPLE'S Contest": The Union and Civil War, 1861–1865* first appeared in 1988 as a volume in Harper & Row's New American Nation Series edited by Henry Steele Commager and Richard B. Morris. Two other large synthetic books on the Civil War came out that year, James McPherson's *The Battle Cry of Freedom* and Eric Foner's *Reconstruction*. Each of the three reflected in its own way the divided state of scholarship on the war era in the 1980s. Two streams of American history controlled the scene then. The first, which had dominated the profession for decades, was the traditional narrative, which emphasized the actions of leaders—usually generals, congressmen, presidents, and judges. These men shaped events, influenced history by their actions in moving armies, giving significant speeches, making crucial decisions, passing laws, deciding cases. This traditional form of history was well adapted to describing the awesome drama of the Civil War: attention to Lincoln, Davis, Lee, Grant, Sherman, Jackson, with supporting roles played by Alexander Stephens, Charles Sumner, Roger B. Taney, and associates, focused the sprawling disruptions of the conflict and gave rise to grand drama.

Meanwhile the other branch of history, the writing of "new" social and economic history, was expanding the cast of the historical pageant. Who built the pyramids? these historians asked, and noted that pharaohs did not do so by themselves. Who fought the battles? they asked, and noted that generals usually watched from a distance while the blood flowed on battlefields. Who shaped industrial America?

they queried, and investigated the workers who sweated in the mills and wove the textiles and laid down the rails and picked the cotton. These historians posed significant questions about how workers of all kinds, and families at home, had responded to the combined revolutions of the market, transportation, and industry that changed the nation in the central decades of the nineteenth century.

But while traditional historical narratives told the Civil War story dramatically, the new social and economic history seldom even tried to tell that story; the Civil War was almost entirely ignored. These works provided compelling discussions of the nature and costs of economic and social change in mid-nineteenth-century America, but, with few exceptions, they either stopped at 1860 or gave the war short shrift. When Maris Vinovskis asked, in a 1989 *Journal of American History* article, "Have Social Historians Lost the Civil War?" he was clearly concerned that they find it, not that they win it.

Why had so little attention been paid to the Civil War? I think one major reason was that the culture which produced the new social history was that of the Vietnam War, and almost every one of the new historians opposed that war. They rejected a historiography that made war glorious and noble. They were also trying to write a history that focused on ordinary Americans, and most histories of the Civil War spotlighted elites. Furthermore, the events and institutions that many social historians were attending to were of long duration—spanning decades, sometimes centuries—and the Civil War lasted only four years. As one social historian remarked to me, it was both foolish and futile to think of a topic like The Family in the Age of Franklin Pierce. In addition, in an environment in which some militant social historians were even blaming traditional historians for preserving and sustaining the culture that had led to the Vietnam conflict there was satisfaction in rejecting almost any traditional focus. Generational factors also shaped the attitude of the new social historians toward the established tradition. Traditional Civil War writing had been written by a generation that had served in World War II, and these works tended to extol the earlier war as the triumph of equal liberty and national union. In the aftermath of Civil War centennial activities (often sponsored by traditional historians), which glorified the carnage of the 1860s even as the body bags came home from Vietnam, it is not hard to sympathize with some of the new historians' feelings.[1]

McPherson and Foner dealt with the two worlds of scholarship differently. McPherson summarized the new social history's findings in a first chapter and then moved to a Pulitzer Prize–quality traditional narrative which wove together battlefield and legisla tive hall, Washington and Richmond with a skill unlikely to be surpassed. Foner also followed a traditional narrative form and paid significant attention to how national politics set the guidelines of reconstruction policy. In addition, he wove into his story the many and diverse findings of new social and economic historians about the lives of black Americans. This book, too, was a brilliant achievement.

In writing "A People's Contest" I tried to provide a variation on what Foner had done. I also was trying to integrate the new and the older forms of history, an effort that had personal as well as scholarly sources. Being of draft age myself in the 1960s the antiwar feelings of the new social historians had an impact on me. I also found appealing their questions about who benefited and who suffered from the decisions made by elites. On the other hand my mentor, Harold Hyman, was one of the traditional historians (he had been a marine during World War II), and I had a much admired uncle who had also served in the South Pacific. My antiwar feelings were more focused on Vietnam, not on all war, and especially not on the Civil War, which I found increasingly fascinating. Through the 1960s and 1970s I worked to balance the two perspectives.

Meanwhile traditional historians were adding to our knowledge of the Civil War's impact on society. Since the early 1960s economic historians had been debating the economic impact of the war, and in 1965 George Fredrickson produced his imaginative *Inner Civil War: Northern Intellectuals and the Crisis of Disunion,* which pointed to several new paths of scholarship. Under the auspices of the Civil War Centennial Commission, Allen Nevins began and Harold Hyman continued to edit a series, The Impact of the Civil War, and by 1985 that series included works on women, agriculture, the Constitution,

1. See W. J. Rorabaugh, "The Meaning of the Civil War," *Reviews in American History* 21 (1993): 51–56, for a slightly different explanation as to why the new social history neglected the war.

literature, public charity and philanthropy, and science. By the 1980s things were in place for some syntheses that would look at the Civil War as a social process. In 1988 not only did major syntheses appear, discussions of soldiers and society broke out all over. That year alone saw the publication of Reid Mitchell's *Civil War Soldiers,* Randall Jimerson's *The Private Civil War,* Earl Hess's *Liberty, Virtue, and Progress,* and James I. Robertson's *Soldiers Blue and Gray,* and Gerald Linderman's *Embattled Courage* had appeared only the year before. All these works explored war not as an exercise in tactics and strategy but as it changed the lives of soldiers.

But the battlefield was still in the foreground, and while those works accepted the social historian's preference for ordinary lives, the larger issues of economic and social change in the nineteenth century still had not been integrated into the story of the war. Over seven decades before, in 1910, Emerson Fite had published *Social and Industrial Conditions in the North During the Civil War,* but that work paid almost no attention to war making, to the fact that what happened on the battlefield had significance for social conditions. Besides, after seven decades some updating of the story seemed useful. That was where *"A People's Contest"* fit in, covering congressional legislation that helped create a modern economy; elections in which union and equal liberty were deeply at stake; outlining conflicts over military strategy, international relations, emancipation, constitutional change. But underlying these discussions were questions that the new social and economic historians had posed: who gained and who lost as the nation industrialized, where was power concentrated, how much control did ordinary people have over their lives. The book was, to this point, a mirror of Foner's approach.

But while I was providing this synthesis, questions even further afield occurred to me. I developed a curiosity about some things that few historians had talked about in discussing the Civil War. The meaning of death, the deaths of over 620,000 young Americans, had hardly been mentioned in books on the idea of death in America. It struck me that one way to consider that impact was to look at how ideas of heaven changed as a result of the war. What kind of place had those "hearty darlings," as Whitman called them, traveled to? This religious question led me to reach out and incorporate work on religion in the war, work that had generally been marginalized in traditional syntheses.[2]

The war threatened the personal and family relationships of ordinary life. I was delighted as well as saddened to find letters between lovers, soldiers and families, and fathers and children which described loves risked and lost, the trials of parenting from hundreds of miles away, the loneliness of soldiers, and the anxiety of their families. The letters helped give personal meaning to this people's contest.

People have often called war "insanity," and I wondered what people who ran the insane asylums of the age thought about that question. Medical journals of the war years include reports from such people, and the conclusions they drew were surprising.

America has often considered its generals as heroes, no more so than in the Civil War era and in the popular military histories of the war years. What kind of heroes did those works reveal? Since societies tend to create the heroes they want and need, what did Grant and Sherman and McClellan come to stand for in the public mind of the age? The images that these soldiers evoked fit remarkably well with the concerns the society felt, not only about battle but about the costs and consequences of economic change.

When finished, "A People's Contest" was a combination of things: a narrative of politics, constitutional debates, economic decisionmaking, diplomacy, and civil-military relations integrated with insights from the new social history. In addition questions about cultural impact found voice here. It is a pretty diverse ensemble, but I think that diversity is imperative to even begin to understand the impact of this great war.

I began the book sixteen years ago and published it eight years later. In the years since I have thought what I might add were I to write it today. Although I am generally satisfied with what I was able to say in the more traditional areas of scholarship, politics, economics, diplomacy, civil-military relations, I left unanswered many questions about the social history of the war—about women for one

2. See Drew Gilpin Faust, " 'A Riddle of Death': Mortality and Meaning in the American Civil War," Thirty-Fourth Annual Robert Fortenbaugh Memorial Lecture (Gettysburg College, 1995), for a recent and stimulating discussion of ideas of death in the war.

thing. I tried to incorporate the experience of women into the narrative, focused on Mary Ashton Livermore's responses to the beginning and the aftermath of the war, fell in love with Ellen Wright, and described Emeline Van Vleck's suffering when her husband left for war. Now I think that maybe a full chapter on women would have presented a broader and more well-focused picture of what war meant to them and their society. If I had done that, I would have been more sensitive to the role of gender in shaping how and why women contributed to the war effort and how men defined their manhood by fighting.

Children are another subject I might have said more about. I wish I had known and understood more about what the war meant to them. I did describe children in factories and in orphanages and even jails, but I confess not to have found, or looked hard enough for, the war as seen through children's eyes. Without testimonials by children themselves, without recollections of their childhood as adults, focusing on children would have been a more difficult task than it is with modern wars, but more might have been done if only in asking questions—what did it mean when armies destroyed the only home that a child had ever known? It may be the deepest tragedy of war that there are always children present; I wish I had been more on the lookout for them.

At one point I planned a chapter on what it felt like to be in combat; somewhere as the pages piled up and deadline after deadline was passed and then extended, that plan went awry. But that was hardly a loss to scholarship, for Mitchell and Linderman and Hess and Jimerson have all provided excellent pictures of that experience, and the ongoing flood of published reminiscences of war continues to supply the evidence for even more work. Perhaps because I was writing essentially about life at home, behind the lines, I found an excuse not to seek out the battlefield. Now I recognize that when the soldiers came home, as many did during the war as well as after, they brought their combat memories and nightmares with them. My discussion of the psychological impact of war now seems too cursory. The topic needs further study, perhaps in the records of hospitals and asylums after the war, perhaps in the records of temperance societies, perhaps in the fiction of the age.

More discussion of the African-American experience in the war should also be here. The work of Ira Berlin and associates as well as the ex slave narratives provide a great amount of material on how the black soldiers viewed the war. My rather weak excuse is that blacks comprised a small percentage of the Northern population, and Northern blacks were not the majority of the 180,000 who fought for the Union. I was predominantly concerned with how white Northerners understood and came to accept different views of the blacks so that emancipation and advances toward equal rights might take place. But the nearly quarter million blacks in the North formed a significant community, and they symbolized in many ways what the war was about—on its best days. Beyond Frederick Douglass, whose ideas I did explore (without the guidance of David Blight's fine *Frederick Douglass' Civil War*), there were other black men and women of other parts of the country and levels of society whose voices would have added something to this work.

But a litany of things not done can begin to look too much like a revision, and it is much too late to rewrite this book. Besides, perhaps immodestly, I think overall it stands up reasonably well. There has been only one similar synthesis of Northern society during the war since 1988, a short survey designed as a textbook, Matthew Gallman's *The North Fights the Civil War* (Richard Bensel's *Yankee Leviathan* is essentially economic history). The subject remains vital and promising enough that studies of particular cities and towns and counties have been ongoing and should continue. Iver Bernstein's excellent *New York City Draft Riots* is only the best of a group of fine work. I would like to see Northern counterparts to Daniel Sutherland's *Seasons of War: The Ordeal of a Confederate Community 1861–1865,* a chronological description of how a town lived through the war. Fordham University is beginning a series called The North's Civil War, and Maris Vinovskis's excellent collection of essays, *Toward a Social History of the American Civil War,* shows how fruitful narrowly focused essays can be in general social history. Catherine Clinton and Nina Silber's fine collection, *Divided Houses,* offers exciting directions in the history of gender and childhood in the war, and Reid Mitchell's thoughtful *The Vacant Chair* studies what he calls "domestic imagery," the relationships between home and the soldiers' experience, and provokes further questions about that fertile topic. These works show how much more there is to be said about Northern society during the war, and how well scholars are beginning to say it.

Those works also show how unnecessary it is for me to rewrite what I said about the North at war in "*A People's Contest.*" Like every author I hope that other writers will take up that responsibility for me: that as they create their own books they will think there is enough here to deserve that kind of rewriting; that they will consider this book to be a useful part of the conversation about what the nation's greatest war meant, and that the conversation will abide and get richer and better. I'm grateful to the University Press of Kansas for making this book available for new participants in that discussion.

Princeton, New Jersey
March 15, 1996

PROLOGUE

Anxious Conversations:
The North Confronts Industrialization

T HE Civil War began in darkness at 5:30 A.M. on April 12, 1861. A cannon roared on Cummings Point in Charleston harbor; an explosion shook Fort Sumter. Then, quickly, the brilliant thunder of encircling batteries joined the dawn to illuminate the first day of four years of conflict. The moment was symbolic. Before the guns spoke, Northerners lived in a world of change that they only dimly understood. The confusions and anxieties of that world made them ready for conflict, but it was not completely clear what they might be fighting for. The war wiped away their confusions, it revealed to them where they stood, and defined, for a time, the kind of people that they might be.

Vast and ill-defined social and economic changes were under way as the North slipped toward war. In the generation before Sumter the economy accelerated, increasing its output, generating greater wealth, moving products and people at higher speeds, transmitting information with startling rapidity, linking distant places by rail, telegraph, newspapers. New inventions, industries, and products sprang to life. And new populations invaded Northern shores; hundreds of thousands, then millions of immigrants arrived, bringing with them old customs, faiths, cultures. To some they were threatening strangers, to others they were evidence of the magnetic force of a growing nation.

On the surface most of these transitions bespoke progress and improvement. In the decade of the 1840s the economy had begun

to grow more rapidly than it had in the forty years before. The
nation experienced great outbursts of prosperity in nearly twenty-
five of the thirty-five years before the Civil War. Between 1800 and
1860 per capita income doubled. The population multiplied sixfold.
The number of towns and cities grew, and they were getting larger.
By 1860 there were almost 400 places with more than 2,500 people,
35 of these with more than 25,000. New inventions promised to ease
the labor of workers, farmers, and their families. The number of
patents issued in 1860 was five times the number issued thirty years
before. Steam and water power increased production and accelerated transportation. Railroad mileage tripled between 1850
and 1860. In the business world new and complex accounting
procedures were formulated to make sense of the burgeoning numbers of transactions. New industries like insurance provided greater
security in risk-taking ventures. New legal interpretations promised
greater protection for private contracting, for the release of economic energy. The multiplication of reform societies and utopian
communities in the antebellum years promised a better America.

The nation also expanded in size, swelling its possibilities. In
1845 Texas joined the Union, adding more territory than the original thirteen colonies. In 1846 the Oregon territorial boundary was
settled, and a region the size of the Old Northwest was secure for
settlement. That same year the Mexican cession, with its fabled
fortunes in gold and its seemingly inexhaustible land, provided an
area larger than both Oregon and Texas. These acquisitions were
so breathtaking that when, in 1853, the Gadsden Purchase brought
into the Union an area larger than many of the existing states, it was
almost ignored.

These events could be contrasted with conditions only two generations before. In the approximately five million households in the
nation there were over one million Americans over sixty who could
regale the "youngsters" with stories of a time when the nation's
boundaries stood at the Mississippi, when organized territory meant
Ohio, Kentucky, Tennessee, and Georgia, and when foreign powers
had held the land across the river. But that was past; part of old
people's stories, not young people's dreams. Now the United States
was unchallenged in one-half of the world. The party of hope had
much to be proud of.[1]

Yet almost every one of these accomplishments could be chal-

lenged by those who asked and worried about the costs. Undoubtedly the economy was growing, but who was benefiting? Per capita
wealth went up but real wages declined. Wealth concentrated in the
hands of a smaller and smaller percent of the population. In the
Northeastern cities the top 1 percent held almost half of the property by 1850. In the North overall an estimated 30 percent of the
population held 92 percent of the wealth. The year 1860 shares with
1929 and 1914 the dubious distinction of being one of the years of
greatest economic inequality in the nation's history. Periods of prosperity were punctuated with economic collapse. The failure of 1857
had seen over five thousand bankruptcies, thirty thousand people
unemployed in Philadelphia, forty thousand in New York City. With
urban growth came urban poverty. The railroads that began to
thunder across the land left mangled workers in their wake, and the
irresponsible owners were miles away, shielded by anonymity and
protected by courts that favored growth. The factories produced
goods faster but seemed to turn workers into machines. New financial devices obscured economic accountability and built fortunes by
cunning, not sweat. Immigrants in greater numbers seemed to increase crime and perhaps immorality. For all the promise of antebellum reformers, their existence illustrated just how much was
wrong. Utopian dreamers ran away from the new America; that was
hardly a promising commentary. While painters like George Innes
and more popular lithographers like Currier and Ives idealized the
new America, the very need for idealization made some wonder. By
contrast, Thomas Coles painted huge canvases depicting the rise
and fall of great civilizations, while other illustrators sketched the
costs of industrialization. Here were rebuttals for the doubters in
the party of memory who lamented what had been lost.[2]

Most Americans imagined the best, believed that the nation's
future was full of promise. Yet doubts persisted. They nagged even
in the midst of celebration. A dialogue was under way, a conversation alternately reflecting hope and fear. This conversation—not a
simple monologue of optimism or pessimism—characterized antebellum America. Promise rebutted anxiety. Nightmare answered
expectation.

The debate over slavery, which was tearing the nation apart, took
place in this context and could hardly escape being touched by it.
To be sure, antislavery arguments had a force of their own. Not

every issue was an obvious product of the larger transformation. Southerners had real fears of slave uprising; they feared losing the culture they had built to maintain their "peculiar institution." Seeking to maintain political power in Congress, they turned debates over slavery into arguments over the structure of the constitutional system.

Northerners eagerly accepted this constitutional challenge. American politics had been built on discussion over governmental power, from the days of the revolution onward. The rise of Jacksonian democracy simply added a multitude of voices to the discussion. Involvement in local self-government and national constitutional debate made almost every adult male a self-styled expert on legal issues of rights and power. The increasingly bitter argument over slavery gained passion because important constitutional questions were at stake for both sides. As Southern demands for protection escalated, Northerners believed that slavery would escape from Dixie and corrupt and possibly break down the political and constitutional system. Gag rules in Congress, the caning of Senator Sumner for making an antislavery speech, the Dred Scott decision, the endorsement by Presidents Pierce and Buchanan of electoral fraud and intimidation in Kansas, the mobbing of speakers, and the destruction of newspapers and presses all were vital issues in the North, just as violations of the fugitive slave law were in Dixie. This fight over the legal and constitutional order was a bitter argument in and of itself.[3]

But, inescapably, social and economic change shaped the debate over slavery. As early as the 1830s John C. Calhoun defended the peculiar institution by attacking the North's emerging industrial system. He gained support in Congress from men who represented urban workers. Intellectuals such as Orestes Brownson, who were sympathetic to the plight of such workers and their families, also found Calhoun appealing. Southern defenders rebutted abolitionists by accusing them of having "hearts as soft as butter toward the oppressed laborers in the South, but as hard as flint toward a large portion of the white laborers."[4]

By the 1850s George Fitzhugh set the North-South conflict in the context of a clash of two societies: one industrializing, chaotic, and brutal, the other agricultural, stable, and humane. Basing his arguments on his reading of accounts in Northern newspapers as well

as reports from England of the evils of industrialism, Fitzhugh
taunted, "Equality where are thy monuments?" and answered,

Deep, deep [in] the bowels of the earth, where women and children drag
out their lives in darkness harnessed like horses to heavy cars loaded with
ore. Or [in] some grand, gloomy and monotonous factory, where pallid
children work fourteen hours a day and go home at night to sleep in damp
cellars. It may be too that this cellar contains aged parents too old to work,
and cast off by their employer to die. Great railroads and mighty steam-
ships too, thou mayest boast, but still the operatives who construct them
are beings destined to poverty and neglect. . . . The sordid spirit of mammon presides o'er all, and from all proceed the sighs and groans of the
oppressed.[5]

Republicans took up the challenge. They responded with contrasting social visions that denied everything. "The interests of the
capitalist and the laborer are in perfect harmony with each other,"
Henry Carey claimed. To promote that harmony Republicans promised the benefits of economic change in party platforms. They argued for internal improvements, tariffs, a homestead act, all designed to take advantage of the emerging economy. Wrapping
themselves in the Constitution and Fitzhugh's vision of a superior
Southern civilization, Dixie legislators opposed such laws. The two
Democratic presidents, influenced by the party's dominant Southern wing, vetoed them.[6]

Thus the struggle between North and South became a struggle
over political economy and contrasting social visions. Republicans
insisted that the North was "a great beehive" of "progressive civilization" where "our paupers of today, thanks to free labor, are our
yeomen and merchants of tomorrow." Lincoln's picture reflected
the party formula: "The penniless beginner in the world labors for
wages awhile, saves a surplus with which to buy tools or land for
himself; then labors on his own account another while, and at length
hires another new beginner to help him."[7]

But for all the Republican claims that all was well in the North and
would be better but for Southern opposition, still the horrors that
Fitzhugh pictured could not be erased. The struggle over the territories revealed that Republicans knew of failures in the system.
One of their strongest arguments for keeping the territories free
was to keep the urban poor of the East from losing faith in the

system. "The public lands," Horace Greeley proclaimed, "are the great regulator of the relations of Labor and Capital, the safety valve of our industrial and social engine."[8]

The idea that a safety valve was needed in a system that they insisted worked so well suggested some dark corners in Republican optimism. Their political rhetoric often showed the same thing. The fundamental story they told to advance their cause was that somehow the purer republic of the founders had been corrupted. It had been corrupted, Lincoln said, because "we have grown fat... greedy to be masters." "Mammon" in addition to "ambition" justified a philosophy and even a theology that said that some men should own others, keep the fruits earned by the sweat of other men's backs. William Seward warned of the "demoralized virtue" of the entire nation that threatened to overturn the ideals of the past. One future Republican explained the passage of the Kansas-Nebraska Act by noting that "a gross materialism, the success of trade, the progress of gain, an external expediency is preferred to the lofty ideal aspirations and spiritual truth" that the founders of the nation had exemplified.[9]

These warnings of subtle corruptions were a staple of American political rhetoric going back to accusations against King George III. But as industrial and social change accelerated they took on added intensity. While every major party promised prosperity and liberty should its candidates win, it warned of dark and obscure conspiracies should voters choose wrong. Whigs spoke of tyrants elected by drunken rabble and foreign agents when attacking Democrats. Democrats conjured up oligarchic bankers and economic royalists. Meanwhile powerful third-party movements fed voters' fears of Masonic conspiracies against religion and democracy, of debauched nuns and priests directed by the pope leading alien immigrants to steal the nation from true Americans.

The slavery debate continued what David Davis has termed the "paranoid style" in prewar politics. Republicans charged that Dixie was dominated by the Slave Power conspiracy. Democrats answered that Republicans were abolitionists under the sway of British agents, maddened by a Puritan fanaticism and concurrently eroded by free love decadence. All parties believed in the political power of telling the people that their society was in danger of losing its abiding values, that disorder impended, and that salvation lay in returning

to a simpler and purer time when enduring truths and stable homo-
geneous communities characterized the nation. Clearly Americans
were troubled by the changes being unleashed in their world. Their
sense of anxiety gave special force to the clashes between North and
South.[10]

The anxiety was more than political rhetoric, although politicians
were sensitive to it. It reflected a broad-ranging concern about the
culture, and hence generated a search for answers as to what was
happening and how people's fears might be ended. The most sensitive thinkers and many of the most popular writers were troubled
by change. Even Ralph Waldo Emerson, once optimistic about the
New World, by the 1840s had turned dubious. Americans had been
offered an opportunity for fulfilling their destiny by devotion to the
highest ideals of spiritual fulfillment. Instead they had chosen to
devote themselves to making money. "Works and Days were offered
us . . . and we chose works." "Things are in the saddle and ride
mankind," he lamented. His friend Thoreau was similarly concerned at the costs of industrial change. "We do not ride on the
railroad, it rides on us."

Conservative ministers like New York City's Unitarian Henry Bellows and Congregationalist Horace Bushnell and Catholic laymen
like Orestes Brownson all urged respect for tradition and existing
institutions in the face of economic and social turmoil. The Brahmin
elites of New England began to deplore rule by the masses at the
very time that those masses began to huddle in the cities, working
in shops and factories, apparently bringing to the United States the
dangers of class conflict.

Growing numbers of Northern readers were introduced to the
dark side of the modernizing Anglo-American society. The most
consistently popular author of the 1850s in America was Charles
Dickens, whose novels graphically pictured the evils of industrialization. When Victor Hugo sent *Les Misérables* to the United States it
also became a runaway best-seller, with its descriptions of economic
inequality in a modernizing French society.[11]

The most insightful and complex of American writers also probed
the meaning of the new forces loose in society. Herman Melville's
investigation had begun with quiet speculation on the encounter
between civilized sailors and the natural world of the South Pacific.
But by 1851 these musings became the profound and complex

encounter with an evil genius captaining a seagoing factory, who ruthlessly pursues a mindless mutilating creature that one day turns to destroy its pursuers. *Moby Dick* has many levels, but one of its most important suggests a troubling force loose in the world that can lead to a society's destruction. "Swerve me?" Ahab says, "ye cannot swerve me . . . the path to my fixed purpose is laid with iron rails, whereon my soul is grooved to run."

By the late 1850s Melville's grappling with the costs of industrialization became more direct. He wrote for the popular monthlies a series of stories describing the amoral ironies of the business world, the conflict between the hypocrisy of the rich and the savagery of the desperate poor, the exploitation of the working class. Two stories best capture his vision. "The Bell Tower" links industrial change to black magic and finds huge clock chimes forged from molten iron and human remains, and the maker of the bell tower crushed to death by the very precision he has created. "Tartarus of Maids" takes readers to a freezing valley where virgins mindlessly serve relentless machines that manufacture blank white paper. Melville knew that the deepest region of Dante's Inferno was the icy realm of Lucifer, whose greatest sin was that he had betrayed others. Machines betraying humanity, an ominous image for a society confronting industrialization.

Like other authors of the period, Melville was also alert to the evils and dangers of slavery. He savagely attacked slavery and racism in *Moby Dick*, "Benito Cereno," "The 'Gees," and *The Confidence-Man*. But like other writers and orators, Melville understood that slavery was a metaphor for both chattel and wage bondage. He linked together these twin evils. The girls in Tartarus are the victims of "machinery—that vaunted slave of humanity—[which is] menially served by human beings who served mutely and cringingly as the slave serves the Sultan." "The Bell Tower" opens with a poem that begins, "Like negroes, these powers own man sullenly;/mindful of their higher master; while serving,/plot revenge."[12]

Melville's vision encompassed the complexity of the age in its ambiguity. It revealed the fact that the nation was encountering the transformations of industrialization at an early stage. The shape of things to come had not yet emerged into clear view. He had the integrity to let the ambiguity stand, and thus to tell the most complex truths about a most complex age. Whereas more common discourse demanded blacks and whites, and hence created conspiracies of evil men, Melville let the whiteness of the terrible and inspiring Moby Dick stand for the juggernaut that was inexplicably loose in the world.

Melville was the era's greatest American author. Harriet Beecher Stowe became its most popular. *Moby Dick* was an artistic masterpiece but a financial failure. *Uncle Tom's Cabin* became the largest seller of the age. Yet both authors confronted the changes of industrialization, linked them with the evils of slavery, and thereby defined the stakes in the Civil War.

Uncle Tom's Cabin remains the most telling attack on slavery of its time. But what has gone often unnoticed is that much of its power comes from the fact that it also criticizes the values of the emerging Northern economy. Stowe often attacks the same evils that Fitzhugh criticized. She differs in blaming slavery for many of them, but she agrees with him that the North has much to answer for. Certainly it shares responsibility for keeping slavery alive. The worst of slavery's evils is that it treats human beings as articles of commerce. The first title that Stowe proposed for the book was "The Man Who Was a Thing." The most evil people in the book are slave traders, and the greatest villain is the Northerner come south, Simon Legree, who uses his plantation, "as he did everything else, merely as an implement for making money." The work on the plantation is machinelike, "hour after hour, with unvarying, unrelenting sameness," and the slaves are treated like replaceable tools: "Use up and buy more, 's my way,—makes you less trouble, and I'm quite sure it comes cheaper in the end." The book also contains a discussion of wage and chattel slavery in which Augustine St. Clare says, "The American planter is only doing, in another form, what the English aristocracy and capitalists are doing by the lower classes, that is, I take it, appropriating them, body and bone, soul and spirit, to their use and convenience."[13]

Stowe is sensitive to the political and legal elements of the antislavery debate. But even here her critique reflects the social changes that the new economy generated. The burgeoning market economy separated the workplace from home. Men and many women entered an economic arena where getting ahead was the main virtue. Meanwhile home, ideally presided over by virtuous mothers, became the institution that taught religious ideals and hence preserved the virtues of caring, nurturing, and love. Stowe's book describes a world in which these role divisions symbolize the worst evils of slavery.

Men dominate the public sphere, they pass the laws, control politics, and manipulate the economy in ways that encourage the slave trade. Women provide culture's moral compass. *Mr.* Shelby sells Tom and Little George. *Mrs.* Shelby protests. *Senator* Bird passes a fugitive slave law. *Mrs.* Bird persuades him to help Eliza escape. Almost every admirable character in the book either is a woman or has feminine virtues. Every villain in the book with one exception is a man. That exception proves the rule: Marie St. Clare is a horror because her love is selfish. She does not nurture others; she loves only herself. Like the evil men in the book, she sees others only in terms of what they can do for her. Slavery in *Uncle Tom's Cabin* is two things: first a reality clearly deserving damnation on its own merits and second a metaphor to criticize a North in danger of losing its soul. Stowe's classic fused elements of Fitzhugh's sociology with the literary insights of Dickens and Melville. She combined these with the true horrors of slavery and interwove the political rhetoric of the 1850s to produce the most popular book of the age.

When war broke out the Union thus faced a complex series of challenges. It faced the danger to the physical union itself and to the ideals that nationhood represented. It faced a challenge to the polit-ical-constitutional system, which was probably the most common means by which Americans understood their nation. The secession challenge continued a Southern attack on the process of self-gov-ernment that seemed to Northerners to endanger Congress, the Supreme Court, the presidency, civil liberties, and constitutional government in the territories. Secession escalated the attack by asserting the right to break up the Union by gunfire if necessary when the electoral process worked unfavorably. The North also confronted the challenge of defending a social and economic system of free labor against the challenge of a slave society. That task was all the more impassioned for two reasons. It was not clear just what the new system was becoming; it had begun to change rapidly in recent decades, and it was yet not comfortably defined. Also, deep and widespread doubts existed about whether Northern society was losing its ideals in the search for wealth, whether it could control or even understand the awesome forces that industrialization seemed to be unleashing. The system clearly needed explanation and de-fense. The guns sounding from Charleston harbor announced that an opportunity for both had arrived.

PART I

LEARNING WAR

CHAPTER 1

Communities Go to War

T HE beginning of the Civil War touched society at every level. It changed millions of individual lives, requiring men and women to ask what was worth fighting for. In the nonborder regions of the North hundreds of thousands of small communities proved to be crucibles of loyalty. While a traditionally enfeebled Washington, D.C., stumbled in confusion, state leaders organized the young men of these communities and sent them off to war. Meanwhile border state communities and individuals had to make agonized and dangerous choices between national and state loyalties. The constitutional system played its usual role in all this: defining the limits of power where personal, community, state, and national loyalties struggled for supremacy.

Individuals of every class recalled the days when the war came. Forty-one-year-old George T. Strong came to the Sumter crisis comfortable and influential in the largest and wealthiest city in the nation. His social circle included governors, congressmen, entrepreneurs, who all had profited from the burgeoning wealth of the newly emerging colossus. He protected its wealth as a lawyer in one of New York's most respected firms. But he also deplored the evils of an economy where the profit motive overawed respect for life and security, and he worried about what the victims of industrialization might do. Tenement fires in Manhattan, the explosion of two factories in Brooklyn, led him to muse that "if a few owners or builders of factories and tenement houses could be hanged tomorrow, life would become less insecure." And the horrible fire on January 10, 1860, in a Lawrence, Massachusetts, factory that crushed and burned to death hundreds of women workers provoked a savage irony that Fitzhugh would have applauded:

Some one has murdered about two hundred people [he wrote] . . . in order to save money, but society has no avenging gibbet for the respectable millionaire. . . . Of course not. He did not want to or mean to do this. . . . He merely thought a great deal about making a large profit and very little about the security of human life. He did not compel these poor girls and children to enter his accursed mantrap. They could judge and decide for themselves whether they would be employed there. It was a matter of contract between capital and labor; they were to receive cash payment for their services. No doubt the legal representatives of those who have perished will be duly paid the fractional part of their week's wages up to the date when they became incapacitated by crushing or combustion, as the case may be, from rendering further service. Very probably the wealthy and liberal proprietors will add (in deserving cases) a gratuity to defray funeral charges. It becomes us to prate about the horrors of slavery! What southern capitalist trifles with the lives of his operatives as do our philanthropes of the North?[1]

But the secession winter focused Strong's attention on the flashpoints of the North-South struggle and fed a growing anger at Southern "brag . . . mob despotism . . . that shoots or hangs its enemy or rides him on a rail when it is one hundred men against one . . . and is utterly without mercy for the weak." In this environment it was "hard for any Northern man to keep himself from Abolitionism and refrain from buying a photograph of John Brown." Yet winter found him fearing that "the North is timid and mercenary. . . . Were we only united and unanimous . . . I should welcome the prospect of vigorous war on Southern treason. But we are discordant, corrupt, deeply diseased, unable to govern ourselves, and in most unfit condition for a war on others."

Lincoln's inaugural fired hope. It had "a clank of metal in it . . . characterized by strong individuality." But a week later came despair and anger when Strong heard that the government might abandon Fort Sumter. Perhaps it was "a stern necessity, but [it was also] a deep humiliation . . . a gross personal insult from Jefferson Davis and Governor Pickens and their crew of 'chivalric' bullies and braggarts." Early April—and a feeling of expectation—rumors of action by the administration mixed with doubts that "the spiritless money worshipping North" could even be "kick[ed] into manliness."

On the night of April 11 Strong attended a dinner at the Astors' honoring the judges of the state court of appeals—the governor had, of course, been there. There were rumors that Jefferson Davis had ordered the authorities in Charleston to permit provisions into Sumter. Friday, April 12, Strong spent downtown on business, and the papers said nothing about Sumter. After dinner at another friend's house he went to a meeting to decide how much money Trinity Church should give to support St. George's chapel. No one agreed, the meeting broke up, and Strong and two friends walked uptown. Newsboys were crying, "Extry—a *Herald!* Got the bombardment of *Fort Sumter!*" The men concluded that "it was probably a sell and that we would not be sold, and declined all invitations to purchase for about four blocks. But we could stand it no longer. I sacrificed sixpence and read the news . . . by the light of a corner gas lamp." Strong still doubted that the news was true. But the next day he wrote in his diary: "April 13. Here begins a new chapter of my journal entitled WAR."[2]

The treasurer of the National Iron Molders Union, thirty-three-year-old William Sylvis, came to that moment with fresh recollections of recent hard times. The recession of the secession winter seemed much like those of the 1850s, further proof that unorganized workingmen were powerless to control decisions made by economic and political leaders, helpless in the face of economic tides. Sylvis had been instrumental in forming the national union in 1859 and at its first convention told new members that "labor has no protection, the weak are devoured by the strong. All wealth and all power centers in the hands of the few and the many are their victims and their bondsmen." He had long thought that abolitionists were fanatics who paid too much attention to degraded blacks while ignoring the needs of white workers. He thought that the Republican party was the mouthpiece of abolition, eager to make political capital out of a manufactured crisis.

Sylvis was under a personal cloud as well. At the union convention in January he witnessed firsthand the jealousies that divided even skilled workers. He had to defend himself against charges that as treasurer he had embezzled union funds. He won the fight, but victory quickly lost its flavor. He was out of work, one of thousands of victims of declining economic confidence that came with the new year. Through February and March he traveled to Louisville and then to Philadelphia to attend workers' meetings that demanded concessions to the seceding states and the election of politicians who were "not . . . mere tools of rotten corporations and aristocratic monopolies," and focused attention on the true crisis: the suffering of workers.

Sumter's guns drowned out this protest. Sylvis thought of enlisting immediately and began recruiting a company of soldiers. But his wife wanted her husband alive. She told him to "go to the country and remain there until the war is over." He was saved the embarrassment of having to retreat from his military fervor. Authorities first rejected his company as not needed. Then the unit disbanded when the enlisted men refused to serve under a tyrannical officer. Sylvis took his family to Washington, D.C., where he got work as a teamster. A few months later he found a job in a foundry as the war began in earnest.[3]

Forty-four-year-old Frederick Douglass had escaped from slavery twenty-two years before. In the past twenty years he had become the best-known black man in the English-speaking world, denouncing slavery and racism from platforms in the United States and England. His newspaper spread the message of emancipation as well as women's rights and social reform. When the abolitionist movement split in the early 1840s, he joined the political abolitionists, believing that the constitutional and political system might be purged of slavery. But passing years brought discouragement, and when John Brown came to him for help he encouraged the old man's plans to overthrow human bondage in the South.

But Brown's raid failed, and public reaction to it highlighted the apparent power of proslavery feeling. Douglass contemplated emigrating to Haiti. The secession winter fed his despair. Angry and despondent at the way public apathy and conservative mobs suppressed abolitionist ideas, he declared, "These [are] cowardly and compromising times." The nation was "dumb and indifferent to . . . cries for deliverance."

Then the news from Charleston harbor promised to change everything. "God be praised!" Douglass cried. He understood early feelings in and out of government that "the North only strikes for government . . . against anarchy . . . for loyalty . . . against treason and rebellion." But the only true settlement of the conflict would be the destruction of slavery. "If the Government is not yet on the side of the oppressed, events mightier than the Government are bringing about that result." In a conflict where the South was fighting for a government "in which Slavery shall be national and freedom no where, in which the capitalist shall own the Laborer," the death of slavery was assured. Douglass knew that there was much prejudice to be overcome but he believed that now war had given freedom its opportunity. He prepared to make the most of it.[4]

Mary Ashton Livermore had been born in Boston forty-one years before. But she had married and moved to Chicago with her husband, a universalist minister. The mother of two young daughters, she was gradually awakening to talents and potentialities that would one day lead her into the woman-suffrage cause. She ran a monthly universalist newspaper as associate editor, volunteered at the Home for Aged Women and the Hospital for Women and Children. She wrote stories, poems, and essays, usually on temperance themes. She even managed to be the only woman reporter at the Wigwam in Chicago when Lincoln was nominated. Livermore was not yet an advocate of woman suffrage, even though her husband was, but she knew that the nation denied women the full exercise of their talents. Having spent three years teaching on a large Virginia plantation, she was a dedicated abolitionist. She also believed that slavery played a major role in corrupting the image of women.

The secession winter helped to politicize her. She recalled that during those months of crisis "women, who had never before concerned themselves with politics, took the daily papers to their rooms . . . and wept over them." She wrote of "Northern men driven from the South" and, perhaps worse, "Northern women . . . treated with shameless indignities." It was impossible to remain aloof from the public arena when the turmoil around her was so intense.

Livermore was in Boston that April caring for, perhaps saying a final good-bye to, her sick father. Then the news from Sumter struck the town like "a thunderbolt." Pulpits sounded with cries of "crush the Slavocracy . . . no more concessions." "Hosts of excited men" surged through the streets echoing these words. The excitement seemed to revitalize the old man. Within days he was asking to be taken out in his carriage to watch the volunteers rush into the town.

Mary Livermore returned to Chicago also fired with enthusiasm. The conflict promised the "regeneration" of women, she wrote, and she stepped forward to play her part. She hired a governess to take care of her children and a housekeeper to manage the house and soon found a position with the Chicago office of the United States Sanitary Commission. There was much to do.[5]

Theodore Upson was only seventeen. He had had little time to consider his life in its larger contexts, or wonder where he fit within the changing world. He knew of public events in personal ways. In 1858 relatives from the South came to his family's northern Indiana farm to visit and brought along cousins to play with. They had their slave with them, and he thought that she was awfully bossy to young men of fourteen. She said she wouldn't run away even though she was on free soil because she was treated well by the family. His cousins told him that their father didn't whip his slaves, but they knew a man down the river from them who did, and sometimes slaves deserved it anyway.

But abolitionist lecturers came into town from time to time, and folks got into arguments. In 1859 an uncle from Nashville came to visit, and when the preacher said that slaves should be free his uncle said, "My how you must love a Nigger!" Then he said that if the Republicans elected a president the South would leave the Union. His grandmother said, "For shame, and your Grandfather a revolutionary soldier and your father in the war of 1812." But his uncle said that the North didn't understand the South and just "begrudge us our Niggers." Upson thought that was "silly talk."

Still, in the summer of 1860, when he was sixteen, he was ready to vote for Lincoln. He marched in a nighttime parade held by the Wide Awakes. "I guess every girl in Coldwater was out to see us march by." After Lincoln's election his father got a letter from down south, and his uncle wrote that "the Gallant Sons of Tennessee will stand like a wall of fire around her to protect her homes, her families and her property." "I suppose he means slaves," Upson wrote. "I don't see what has gotten into these people. I don't believe anyone here wants their niggers. And I am sure I don't want to fight for them."

But then came the day when

Father and I were husking out some corn. We could not finish before it wintered up. When William Cory came across the field he was excited and said, "Jonathan, the Rebs have fired upon and taken Fort Sumter." Father got white and couldn't say a word. William said, "The President will soon fix them. He has called for 75,000 men and is going to blockade their ports and just as soon as those fellows find out that the North means business they will get down off their high horse." Father said little. We did not finish the corn and drove to the barn. Father left me to unload and put out the team and went into the house. After I had finished I went in to dinner. Mother said, "What is the matter with Father?" He had gone right up stairs. I told her what we had heard. She went to him. After a while they came down. Father looked ten years older.[6]

Personal fears soon were absorbed in the excitement, and horror, of war. Young men went off to fight and wrote back to say that "it was awful to see men shot down like cattle." Still, when a company from a nearby town came marching through town on the Fourth of July, "some of us boys had a fife and drum and a flag and marched behind them." Upson himself tried to enlist, but he was too young to be taken without his father's consent, and his father didn't give it. The captain told him he had to go home. "I was so mad I bawled." When some of the soldiers said that they thought he would be a good soldier, he got even madder and scribbled in his diary, "Well if they don't want me they can fight their old war for all of me. I don't care."

But when April 1862 came Upson was almost old enough, and another company was being organized. He went to a meeting at the schoolhouse with his cousin and told him that "I will [enlist] if you will." So they both signed up. But his father said no again.

Still, other men's sons were going and so they talked about it. His father wondered why he would want to go. He didn't need the bounty. Didn't he feel happy at home? Upson said he had been treated with more kindness than he deserved. It wasn't that. Then why? "I don't know what came over me. I was scared at myself," he recalled. "Father, we must have more soldiers. This union your ancestors and mine helped to make must be saved from destruction. I can go better than some others. I don't feel right to stay at home any longer." His father agreed that he should join the army. By August of 1862 he was in camp in Indianapolis. Soon he joined Sherman's army. He would return home almost three years later.[7]

In addition to the millions of private reactions to the outbreak of war, there were also more generalized reasons to fight. Northerners felt pride in the growing size and wealth of the nation. They recalled a history that wove together the "mystic chords of memory" that Lincoln hoped would bind the nation. Most believed that they benefited personally from the bounty that the nation created. And they understood that an integrated economy linking North and South was indispensable to continued wealth. Perhaps most compelling of all reasons was a twofold vision that entwined the form of government of the nation with the economic ideals of a free and open economy.

Lincoln explained this "People's contest" as "a struggle for maintaining in the world, that form, and substance of government, whose leading object is, to elevate the condition of men—to lift artificial weights from all shoulders—to clear the paths of laudable pursuit for all—to afford all, an unfettered start, and a fair chance, in the race of life." To win the victory, therefore, it was necessary to preserve the nation against the "anarchy of secession" and to maintain the peaceful processes of changing the government by election and not gunfire. The president here joined together the social and economic hopes of the North with the survival of democratic government. He thus projected the ideals that formed the image of the Union into the most compelling of all the personal experiences that mid-nineteenth-century Americans had—the experience of self-government within the tens of thousands of communities in which they lived.[8]

Communities large and small formed the fundamental unit of human experience in the Civil War years as they have done throughout human history. They were the places where individuals, friends, and loved ones grew up, worked, married, and lived. In times of peace people died there. Most important, when the time came to decide for war, Northerners had learned the meaning of self-government in these small places.

Small community life gave most Northerners personal experience with politics, law, and government. They were officeholders in the thousands of villages, towns, counties, cities. Since offices were rotated with great frequency, a high percentage of the eligible male population of any town was very likely to have been a member of the town council, commissioner of roads, mayor. Furthermore,

Northerners were actively involved in the judicial system and in the making and preserving of law and order in their communities. They served on juries, were members of posses. From time to time they formed vigilante groups when the officials of the town could not act.[9]

Northerners also learned the meaning of self-government in local schools. Students memorized the so-called "federal catechism" taken from Noah Webster's widely used spellers and geographies. There they learned that "the peculiar advantages of representative governments" were "that the men who make the laws are to be governed by them. . . . When men make laws for themselves as well as for their neighbors, they are led by their own interest to make good laws." Children also acted out the political process within their schools. Student monitors assumed minor leadership positions, and provided favors for younger students. Public declamations of patriotic ideas, especially the wonders of the constitutional system, further reinforced the values of the political culture, as did the peer pressure of classroom recitation. Horace Mann, founder of the Northern public schools movement, observed that "in a government where the people are to be acknowledged sources of power, the duty of changing the laws and rulers by appeal to the ballot, and not by rebellion—should be taught to all the children." Practically from cradle to grave Northerners were immersed in a political-constitutional culture that took life in their communities.[10]

Political activity mirrored ideals. At no other time in the nation's history was participation in elections so large as it was in the United States in the middle of the nineteenth century. Northern involvement was especially intense. Over 75 percent of the eligible voters voted in the presidential elections of 1848–72. And in non-Southern states the figures were amazing. Michigan voter turnout between 1854 and 1872 was almost 85 percent. Ohio almost hit 90 percent in these years. New York's figures were near 85 percent. Northerners voted in almost equal numbers in state and local elections, too. And they voted in almost as high a percentage for lesser offices as for higher offices. They cared about politics. They cared so much that very few Northerners would split their tickets and vote for members of parties other than their own. If they disliked their own party's ticket, they stayed home. They could seldom stomach voting for their political opponents.[11]

Such widespread involvement in the legal and political institutions of Northerners' communities gave special meaning to their patriotism. Perhaps the most consistent theme of the call to arms was that the laws of the nation had been assailed. The issue again and again was posed as testing "whether we have a government or not." The most terrible consequence of a failure by the North to respond to secessionist blackmail and then assault was declared by speakers and writers to be "anarchy." Congressmen echoed Lincoln's equation of secession with anarchy. They proclaimed that to give in to secession would result in "quarrelling and warring amongst . . . little petty powers which would result in anarchy"; newspaper headlines called secession "Lawlessness on a Gigantic Scale." Melville and Walt Whitman wrote poetry describing the conflict between order and chaos. The secession crisis saw the republication of *The Anarchiad: A Poem on the Restoration of Chaos and Substantial Night,* a 1787 satire against the disorder of the Confederation period.[12]

These warnings against disorder bespoke the anxieties of a society undergoing major economic and social change. They also arose from the fact that the vast majority of Northerners had personal experience with, and personal involvement in, the making of the order and the law of their communities. The structure of society, one of small communities and neighborhoods, meant that issues of order or respect for law were not abstract subjects. They were subjects with which Northerners were personally familiar. To preserve that order they were willing to lay down their lives—or at least, and more perceivable to them at first, to pick up their guns.

Vital community life contrasted starkly with a long tradition of weak national government. Citizens in Northern communities seldom if ever saw a federal government official other than the postmaster. They lived their lives without contact with Washington, D.C., and they felt happy in that fact. Constitutional prohibitions kept the national government from acting on anything but Indians, interstate commerce, raising armies, coining money, collecting taxes, and making international treaties. Before the Civil War, the national government levied no income taxes, coined no money, raised a volunteer army. Its treaties directly affected almost nobody away from the oceans. Its dealings with Indians touched only a minuscule part of the white population. There was no agency to regulate interstate commerce. As one observer recalled, "We hardly knew we had a national government except when the quadrennial contest for the spoils of office came around." Entrepreneurs called on state, local, and occasionally national governments to assist their enterprise, but such assistance did not get in the way; it cleared the way. Life in communities went on without contact with the govern ment in Washington.[13]

The sinews of national government power were weak. On the other hand, the national political system provided a unity that inspired devotion. The "quadrennial contest for the spoils of office" was simply the most obvious occasion that made parties ubiquitous parts of the public experience.

Political parties were the major national institutions. Their activities linked the nation in political ideals as well as mundane electioneering activities. A fundamental feature of political parties was to insist on one's own nationalism while decrying the sectionalism of the opposition. After the demise of the Whigs the Democrats made much of the fact that they were the one national party; they abided in the face of divided churches and the growth of rabid sectionalism by Republicans. The new party was accused of being controlled by New England Puritans and abolitionists who sought to destroy national unity in the name of sectional partisanship. Republicans answered in kind. They accused the Democratic party of being controlled by a tiny minority of slave-power extremists who warped the democratic ideal to protect and then expand human bondage. When war broke out, one of the first actions that Republicans took was to adopt a name, the Union party, which testified to their national commitment, and played down their actual sectional foundations.

Parties also engendered national unity by the political spoils system. Men got local government offices from national politicians. As early as 1849 Congressman Abraham Lincoln could write to the secretary of the Treasury, "Col. E. D. Baker and myself are the only Whig members of Congress from Illinois. . . . We have reason to think that the Whigs of that state hold us responsible, to some extent, for appointments which may be made to our citizens. . . . I therefore hope that I am not obtrusive in saying . . . that when a citizen of Illinois is to be appointed in your Department to an office in or out of the state, we most respectfully ask to be heard." By 1861 congressional influence on local appointments had reached the point that a Pennsylvania congressman protested to the quartermaster general over the appointment of a *shoe inspector* at the Philadelphia arsenal. The spoils system gave structural sinews to the political ideology of parties. Both added to the sense of national unity.[14]

By the mid-nineteenth century Americans had developed widespread devotion to the political culture of the nation. Reformers might attack the party system as insensitive to moral values, and Republicans especially had their share of antiparty rhetoric. But for the most part Northerners extolled their party system. "The distinguishing excellence of free institutions consists in their giving birth to popular parties. . . . Popular parties . . . are absolutely necessary to uphold and preserve" republican government, theorist Frederick Grimke declared. William Seward echoed the sentiment in 1860: "Solid, enduring, and consistent parties, inspired by love of country, reverence for virtue and devotion to human liberty, bold in conceptions of measures, moderate in success and resolute through reverses, are essential to effective and benevolent administration in every free state."[15]

Such involvement in, and devotion to, the political and governmental structure forged a powerful commitment to the survival of the system of government itself and to the law and order it was said to nurture. Attacks on the political system inspired passionate defense. Democrats charged Republicans with imperiling the national political system. Republicans claimed that Democrats sold out democracy to slavery. Lincoln used faith in the political system as an antidote to the Dred Scott decision. Stephen Douglas alleged that popular sovereignty offered the only democratic way to determine the slavery issue. The Kansas crisis revolved around the prevalent feeling that the electoral process had been assaulted by Missouri border ruffians and White House capitulation to slavocrat demands. These charges and countercharges, attracting the passionate attention of a populace that ate, slept, and breathed politics, laid the groundwork for the violent reaction to what seemed the most egregious attack of all on the political-constitutional system—the secession of the South, ultimately backed by gunfire, as the consequence of the lawful election of a president.[16]

While the wellsprings of loyalty and unionism lay within the small communities, the institutions for creating armies were at the state and federal levels. When Confederates opened fire on Fort Sumter, President Lincoln first called upon the states to defend the Union. "Combinations too powerful to be suppressed by the ordinary course of judicial proceedings," he proclaimed, were opposing the execution of the laws. The president, therefore, called forth "the militia of the several states of the Union, to the aggregate number of seventy-five thousand to . . . maintain the honor, integrity, and existence of our National Union."[17]

This call for the militia rested on a military necessity and a constitutional requirement. The army of the United States stood at about sixteen thousand men in April 1861, most of these scattered in the West, keeping watch over Indians. Secession reduced the number further as Southern officers resigned. So few men so far away had to be reinforced by volunteers for there to be any hope of success. The Constitution gave to Congress the right to declare war and to raise armies, but Congress had adjourned a month before Sumter. Lincoln's most immediate recourse was a 1792 militia act that gave him the power to summon the militia in case of insurrection or invasion.

The call for the militia unleashed the passionate patriotism of the governors of the states. State leaders had been organizing for war even prior to Sumter. By early 1861 Wisconsin provided $100,000 to raise troops; Massachusetts had been organizing its militia since the crisis in Charleston harbor began. Neighboring Connecticut did the same as the governor began to buy powder and weapons in the state—competing with Southern buyers seeking arms for the rebellion.

Every Northern state was in some degree ready for battle when the war came, and Lincoln's call was met with thundering enthusiasm. He asked for seventy-five thousand men—hundreds of thousands of troops came forward. States competed with each other to provide the most soldiers. Governors complained that their states were called on to provide fewer men than their neighbors were. To suggest that Pennsylvania would supply more men than Ohio was an insult to Buckeye manhood. States rushed to see who could send men fastest to Washington. Three days after Sumter two Massachusetts regiments stood before Governor John Andrew listening to a speech sending them off to war. While Andrew spoke, tailors were moving through the ranks sewing buttons on their overcoats. Within a week three thousand more men plus a battery of artillery were on their way. At the same time, Morton of Indiana was sending a thousand men and telling Lincoln that six regiments were available. Soon Ohio's Dennison was boasting of not just the thirteen regiments of his state's quota, but fifty regiments. Men were coming so fast that he could not supply them. He begged Washington to take these soldiers. The South must be shown, he argued, how aroused the North was. Such a display would make rebels realize that they could not successfully challenge the Union. It would also show the world the power of the nation. Every Northern state had the same story to tell: volunteers rushing to enlist, bankers and other private citizens offering hundreds of thousands of dollars, state legislatures voting appropriations to equip their state's soldiers.[18]

The most striking thing about this situation was how much it contrasted with events in the nation's capital. Commentators all over the nation were surprised at the minuscule size of the army Lincoln called for. A mere seventy-five thousand men, the *New York Tribune* complained; the president could get that many from New York City alone. But perhaps as remarkable as the disparity between these numbers was the comparison between the seemingly boundless energies of the states and the confusion and weakness of the national government. Governors begged Secretary of War Cameron for instructions on when and how and where to send the men. He replied with confused messages, or with pleas for delays.

There were several reasons for Washington's ineffectiveness. First, the capital city was a community, too, and local matters demanded immediate attention. Only the Potomac separated the capital of the Union from enemy territory. There was little reason to feel safe about the city's other boundaries either. Maryland, a slave state of dubious loyalty, surrounded Washington on its other three sides. Anxiety over conditions there had led the newly elected President Lincoln to sneak through Baltimore on Washington's birthday to take over the reins of government. On April 17 a small contingent of Pennsylvania troops passing through the city had stones thrown at them. Two days later, when the Sixth Massachusetts Regiment marched through the city from one train station to the other, a major riot took place. Four people were killed, thirty-one were wounded. The state and local officials pleaded with the administration not to send any more troops through the city. To guarantee that their pleas were effective, they let it be known that the bridges around the town should be burned. Prorebel enthusiasts responded eagerly and went further, cutting the telegraph lines from the North to Washington.

The capital was in a panic. Buildings in town were barricaded. Women and children were sent to places of safety. Administration leaders tried to placate Maryland authorities by receiving a delegation from Baltimore and by routing troops around the city. Hearing of the city's isolation, the governor of Connecticut sent his son-in-law to Washington. The young man reported finding hotels silent, streets deserted. When he met General in Chief Winfield Scott, the general raised all six feet six inches and nearly three hundred pounds from his chair and said, "Sir, you are the first man I have seen with a written dispatch for three days; I have sent men out every day to get intelligence of the northern troops. . . . Where are the troops?" The visitor found Lincoln in an upstairs room in the White House standing beside a telescope looking at Arlington Heights in Virginia. The president asked anxiously if the North knew of the isolation of the city. The day before, Lincoln had told a delegation of Massachusetts soldiers, "I don't believe there is any North. The Seventh Regiment is a myth. Rhode Island is not known in our geography any longer. *You* are the only Northern realities." This sense of isolation and panic endured until the first week in May.[19]

Lincoln and his party's assessment of the nature of the crisis also inhibited national action. Republican party leaders believed that Southern leaders did not actually represent the majority of the Southern people. An oligarchy of slaveholders was somehow manipulating opinion, but if the truth could get to the people, disunion sentiments would be defeated. When secession elections in the South demonstrated divisions among the voters, Lincoln saw what he hoped for—a true sentiment in favor of his ideals. As late as July 4, 1861, he could say that "it may well be questioned whether there is today a majority of the legally qualified voters of any state except perhaps South Carolina, in favor of disunion. There is much reason to believe that the Union men are the majority in many, if not in every one, of the so-called seceded States."

Given this belief, it is not surprising that the president tried to respond to Sumter with some restraint. He feared taking action that would extinguish Southern unionism. Hence his actions were initially restricted to defensive measures. He announced a blockade of Southern ports on April 19, and his call for 75,000 troops to serve for ninety days was a rather modest call in light of two factors: first, the enormous willingness of the North to respond to Sumter with overwhelming force, and second, the fact that he called these troops from Southern as well as Northern states.[20]

Whatever the sources of the delay in Washington, by early May the end of the isolation of the capital, and especially the awesome uprising of the North, pushed Lincoln into taking the war more seriously. On May 2 he called for over 42,000 volunteers to serve in the volunteer United States Army. They would serve three years unless sooner discharged. He also requested eight regiments of regular army infantry and one each of artillery and cavalry; 18,000 sailors, enlisted for one to three years, were also called. If these quotas were filled, they would bring the Union army to more than 155,000, the navy to over 25,000.

The quotas were never reached. But it was academic that they weren't, for while recruitment in the national army languished, the states provided an awesome tide of men. By December of 1861 when the regular army had only increased by 4,000 men over the 16,000 plus of April, volunteers from state recruiting sources had reached over 640,000 men.[21]

State activity clearly was the mainspring of the Union effort in these early days of war. The army was overwhelmingly comprised of state units, organized by the states, carrying state names. The vast majority of units were not, as in the twentieth century, designated as the "Forty-third United States" Division. They were proudly called the Sixty-ninth New York, the Fifty-third Illinois, the Sixth Kansas. Public opinion demanded it. Salmon Chase, secretary of the Treasury and later chief justice, declared that he would "rather have no regiments raised in Ohio than that they should not be known as Ohio regiments." As one 1861 writer explained, "Our soldiers in Virginia and in the other Slave States, have not only their own reputations to support, but that also of the communities from which they come. There must be a rivalry in generous efforts among the troops of different States. Shall we not now have our regiments which by their brave and honorable conduct shall win appellations not less noble than that of *Auvergne sans tache,* 'Auvergne without a stain'?"[22]

The men in the ranks were devoted state loyalists even as they formed and fought in the largest national army of the century—the most notable national institution in memory. Massachusetts private Samuel Nichols was embarrassed that his state's efforts lagged behind those of neighbors. "New York and Pennsylvania and New Jersey are alive, while I am ashamed to speak of the apathy in Massachusetts." Learning later that the Bay State had brought forth sixty regiments, he explained, "I think that perhaps I have been somewhat severe on my home state, but you must ascribe it to have my state outdo all others." Interregiment competition was frequent. An Illinois lieutenant declared that his cavalry "don't acknowledge the Michigander troops to be more than the equals of . . . scalawags, and the Michigan boys really seem to think that the 7th regiment is not equal to one company of theirs." Wounded men in hospitals shared this state pride. A Maine nurse reported that "one of the sick boys told me he was glad to see *Maine acting . . .* for while ladies from other States had been visiting the Hospitals he had been *ashamed* to say that no one looked after him."[23]

State action built state pride. But community loyalties also endured. Governors had the legal authority to call the troops, but it was the communities—the towns, villages, and cities—that would send the men. These places made demands even as they brought forth the enlistees. Governors used their power to appoint officers for the regiments to reward friends and weaken enemies. Indiana's Governor Morton tried to cement an alliance of Democrats and Republicans by giving colonel commissions to members of both parties. But pressures from elements in Indiana shaped his actions. When congressmen, subject to pressures from their home districts, pushed for commissions for local favorites, the governor appealed to Lincoln to respect his role as political leader of the state. Lincoln complied by asking Morton for recommendations. But Morton could not always have his way. Important figures of the Republican party throughout the state demanded consideration for previous favors. Morton listened. One man, denied a commission by the governor, enlisted as a private and was elected a captain by his regiment. He was soon commissioned by Morton as a colonel.[24]

In the East one finds the same story. In Connecticut, for example, Governor Buckingham was besieged with complaints when he appointed his first commander of a state regiment. People in New Haven and Hartford complained that the appointee was from Norwich. When the next two appointments of commanders went to each of the complaining towns, they were not placated. For the governor had given his initial appointee overall command for state forces. State legislators wrestled with Buckingham over control of the provisioning and equipping of the state soldiers, demanding investigation of contracts and camp conditions. State governors throughout the North were kept busy looking after troops as soldiers wrote home describing how they were treated.

The soldiers complained that their provisions were of poor quality and their food was worse. They complained about the spartan discipline imposed by a West Point trained commander. Angered that their boys were being mistreated, the towns and villages sent investigators to make sure that commanders behaved properly toward their sons. As the war progressed, soldiers of every state used the lash of hometown opinion constantly, writing to local newspapers about conditions in the field.[25]

The attachment of communities to their soldiers endured throughout the war—linking community to the war in very personal ways. State-inspired agencies operated through local branches to raise funds for assistance. Local figures and organizations provided their time and money to aid the war effort. Local bands played, seamstresses sewed, ladies cooked, painters painted, and craftsmen provided their bit. Even the nationally organized U.S. Sanitary Commission fairs that swept the country after 1863 gave people in cities throughout the North a chance to feel that they were doing something for their boys.[26]

While under law, governors called for troops, most of the actual recruiting took place away from the statehouse. In thousands of Northern communities the pattern was the same. Let Galena, Illinois, stand for the small town experience. Word arrived in this county seat in the state's northwestern corner on April 18 that troops were needed. Posters appeared everywhere announcing a meeting at the courthouse. All business in the town stopped. People could talk of nothing else but what to do about the Sumter attack. By evening the courthouse was filled. A former army officer named

U. S. Grant was asked to preside. He was thought to be a Democrat as well as a soldier, and people wanted the meeting to show their unity and determination to fight. Three orators, a Breckenridge supporter, a Douglas Democrat, and a Republican, gave speeches appealing to the people of the town to love and defend their country.

Then volunteers were called for to form a company. The men came forward, and before the night was over they had elected their officers and their sergeants and corporals. The next day the women of the town asked Grant what infantry uniforms looked like. They bought the cloth, enlisted local tailors to cut it, and in a few days had the uniforms ready to wear. Within a week the company was ready to leave for their rendezvous point at Springfield. Although Grant declined the election to captain, he offered his services to organize and drill the men and take them to Springfield. When he got there he was asked by Governor Yates to help introduce recruits from additional companies and regiments to military life. Thus began the service that led to Shiloh, Vicksburg, the Wilderness, Spotsylvania, and Appomattox.[27]

Neighborhood communities in the large cities of the North also brought forth their regiments. Every Northern state with a large Irish population contributed companies—staffed by Irishmen, with Catholic chaplains and decorated uniforms or flags with symbols of Ireland. The *New York Tribune* reported the organizing of New York's all-Irish Sixty-ninth Regiment. The soldiers-to-be showed up on Prince Street to receive their supplies of blankets, muskets, and cooking and eating gear. Friends and relatives watched and cheered. Irish civic societies formed honor guards carrying banners showing the harp of Ireland kissing the stars and stripes. By two in the afternoon the crowd had grown so large that no vehicle could get through the street. The honor guard and the troops marched to the docks through cheers and waiting flags. When they got to the ship the crowd pressed in upon them and soon mixed together civilians and soldiers in a churning, confused community celebration that mixed joy and patriotism and pride and anxiety in a crucible forging firmly the links between those who went to war and those who would wait. As these scenes echoed through the communities of the nation's largest city, Walt Whitman exulted:

(O superb!
O Manhattan, my own, my peerless!
O Strongest you in the hour of danger, in crisis! O truer than
    steel)
How you sprang—how you threw off the costumes of peace with
    indifferent hand,
How your soft opera-music changed, and the drum and fife were heard
    in their stead
How you led to war, (that shall serve for our prelude, songs of
    soldiers,)
How Manhattan drum-taps led.

Ethnic communities eagerly contributed soldiers. About 150,000
Irish-Americans would serve in the Union army. German-Americans totaled 175,000, and Scots and French and Welsh and Dutch
and Scandinavians and Hungarians also came, adding up to almost
half a million foreign-born men willing to fight for the Union. Like
the Irish, they formed companies and regiments of men who came
from the same place and shared the same values and experiences.
Like the native American companies, their war experiences would
be linked to the communities they came from.[28]

As communities sent forth regiments, observers were delighted at
what that seemed to signify. Throughout the 1850s one of the most
commonplace lamentations of politicians, editors, lawyers, and intellectuals had been that Americans were falling away from the
purity and patriotism of the revolutionary generation. But the post-
Sumter rising awakened the belief that the spirit of the revolution
lived. Once again the minutemen seemed to be setting aside plows
and hammers and rushing forth to defend the nation. Doubts about
the country's selfish avarice faded before a vision of the war purging
society of its corruptions.[29]

Newspapers throughout the North proclaimed the onset of war as
a chance to purify national character. Evansville, Indiana, declared
that the war was a punishment for pride and corruption and that
now order would conquer threatened disorder. Newburyport, Massachusetts, was ready to respond to a crisis produced by the "degenerate children" of the pure founders of the nation. "Inflated and
intoxicated by the overflowing cup of too great prosperity," the
nation had been brought to the test. The *New York Times* was delighted that not even "the thick insulation which the commercial

spirit puts between conscience and duty" had been able to overcome the surge of loyalty of the Sumter crisis. In Bangor, Maine, people were encouraged that "the clamour of greedy selfishness, the canker of patronage, growing more virulent," was now to be overcome in a struggle to resurrect patriotism. Horace Greeley summarized a widespread feeling in the midst of the Sumter crisis: "Let no one feel that our present troubles are deplorable, in view of the majestic development of Nationality and Patriotism which they have occasioned. But yesterday we were esteemed a sordid, grasping money-loving people, too greedy to gain to cherish generous and lofty aspirations. Today vindicates us from that reproach, and demonstrates that beneath the scum and slag of forty years of peace, and in spite of the insidious approaches of corruption the fires of patriotic devotion are still burning."[30]

The places in society where the most ominous signs of class conflict had appeared were as enthusiastic as the rest. Lynn, Massachusetts, had witnessed the largest strike in the nation's history— a strike in which police and the militia had been called in to crush riots (and had helped provoke them). But in the secession crisis, town shoemakers set aside their grievances and enlisted in the Union army. The Republican party, vanquished by the Workers party in 1860 municipal elections, took over the city in 1862, and by 1863 not a single vote was cast against the incumbent Republican mayor. Rockdale, Pennsylvania, which had witnessed industrial strife in the 1840s and had a well-organized labor movement in the 1850s, nevertheless produced a patriotic enthusiasm in support of the Union cause. In St. Clair County, Illinois, long-standing tensions between miners and mine owners were forgotten in the first days of the war. Indeed the opening of the conflict brought together all the occupational groups of the community in patriotic enthusiasm. Joining the men from the coal shafts were brewers, coopers, and railroad workers, all enlisting in local regiments. The miners were sufficiently large a group to create their own company, the St. Clair County Sappers and Miners. Quickly organized, the company joined the hullabaloo in the town, singing patriotic songs on street corners and raising a flag at the mine itself. The rising of the urban laborers spoke of a unity in the society that calmed fears. Designated "dangerous classes" by many critics, laborers showed their devotion to saving the nation by enlisting in the army in a percentage larger than any other group with the exception of professional men.[31]

Before the war, Southerners had claimed that Northern avarice was a potential weapon in the Southern arsenal. A popular joke began by asking, "How would a Southerner defeat a well-armed Yankee?" The answer: "Buy his gun from him." But with the rising of the populace after Sumter, many people took heart. Northerners developed their own reply to that joke. Yes, they said, maybe the Southerner would buy the gun. But only after the Northerner had first delivered its contents into the rebel. And intellectuals joined Northern editors in rejoicing in the fact that there was iron, and perhaps even purer metal, in the Yankee soul.

Small communities all over the North thus rebutted prewar fears of a society eroded by materialism. Walt Whitman gloried in hearing "a new song" in which the banner of war called the poet to capture the exalted spirit alive in the country. "No longer let our children deem us riches and peace alone," the banner declared. "Nor market nor depot we, nor money-bank in the city." A child is fascinated by the banner, but his father tries to divert attention to "these dazzling things in the houses, and . . . the money shops opening." But the child insists, "Oh Father I like not the houses, / They will never to me be anything, nor do I like money. . . . But . . . that banner I like, / That pennant I would and must be." And the poet announces, "My theme is clear at last"; the "houses of peace . . . full of comfort, built with money," would stand "not an hour except you above them and all stand fast." And the poet concludes, "Great as it is, it is nothing—houses, machines are nothing—I see them not, I see but you, O warlike pennant! O banner so broad, with stripes, I sing you only." "Long, too long America," he said in another place, "you learn'd from joys and prosperity only, / But now . . . to learn from cries of anguish . . . to conceive and show to the world what your children en-masse really are."[32]

Herman Melville, whose short stories had revealed so many of the prewar concerns about the corruptions of a modernizing society, was not transformed into an optimist by the war. He kept his sense of the dark side of human experience, but the conflict enlarged his theme. His short stories had targeted corruptions, deceptions, hypocrisies. But with the war the theme that struck him was cosmic. Using characters and ideas from the Bible and *Paradise Lost,* Melville interpreted the conflict as a reenactment of the Fortunate Fall—though a fall with cost to the victors as well as vanquished. As he put it in "The Conflict of Convictions":

> Power unanointed may come—
> Dominion (unsought by the free)
> And the Iron Dome,
> Stronger for stress and strain,
> Fling her huge shadow athwart the main;
> But the Founder's dream shall flee.

Still, great things, not mean corruptions, were at issue in the war.[33]

Abolitionists, once known for pacifism as well as militant antislavery, found, as had Frederick Douglass, new paths in the explosion of patriotism. Wendell Phillips had so despaired over Northern inertia that he had welcomed pre-Sumter secession. Other colleagues agreed. But the passionate outpouring following the Charleston harbor attack alerted Phillips to the capacity of his society to fight for the good. He had believed that Massachusetts, like the North, was "wholly choked with cotton dust and cankered with gold." But now he could "believe in the possibility of justice, in the certainty of union." "Abolitionists everywhere," historian James McPherson observes, "enthusiastically closed ranks behind him." The rising of the people portended the coming of age of a moral and militant democracy. By early 1862 Julia Ward Howe, visiting Washington, D.C., saw "the coming of the Lord . . . in a hundred circling camps," a rising that would "loose the fateful lightning of His terrible swift sword."[34]

Most Northern states and communities burst with unalloyed patriotism. But the border states housed ambiguity, and issues of loyalty had to be agonized over, tested, and ultimately fought out. Missouri, Kentucky, and Maryland felt the disunion crisis with schizoid force—slave states themselves, they were linked in sympathy for the peculiar institution with seceding sisters. But they also feared that the battles of any civil war would be fought on their soil. Patriots in Massachusetts and South Carolina could hardly conceive that cannons would shatter the peace of their communities. But border state citizens could easily imagine their farms and homes destroyed, their town squares filled with armies.

Populations and people within these states divided over the safest and best courses. Unionists looked at Northern economic and industrial strength, recalled the wealth and happiness of union, remembered links to family and friends in the North, and demanded union. Secessionists projected Southern advantages, recalled their kin, family, and hopes in Dixie, and claimed the right to secede.

The issue of loyalty in the border states was pregnant with heartbreak. Kinship ties linked families in Kentucky especially with an entire Midwest basin. The Lincoln family journey that took the future president from Kentucky to Indiana and ultimately to Illinois had been followed by thousands. Nearly 160,000 residents of Illinois, Indiana, Ohio, Iowa, and Kansas had been born in Kentucky. Almost 34,000 people born in the Old Northwest had moved to Kentucky. Lincoln's marriage to Mary Todd of Kentucky mirrored thousands of similar ties in the border states and states above and below them. Mrs. Lincoln lost three brothers who fought for the Confederacy. The two eldest sons of Kentucky senator John J. Crittenden became major generals in the contending armies. "I do not know of a single family," one Kentuckian later recalled, "where all the men were arrayed on one side." He may have been remembering the day at Gettysburg when the men of the Fourth Kentucky Confederate Regiment leveled their guns at the men of the Fourth Kentucky Union Regiment. Where choices might require betraying family or country, decisions were often anguished.[35]

But making the decision which side to join did not end the agony of the border states. Mixed loyalties meant that intermittent guerrilla war raged there until approximately the middle of the war. Then the advance of Union power led to the disbanding of prorebel partisans. These men reorganized as bank and stagecoach robbers who romanticized their activities in the name of their former flag. But while the guerrilla war went on, it was brutal and escalated easily into savagery when rebel and Union supporters met. The picture provided by one Union officer described conditions in the lives of thousands of border state citizens. Guerrilla soldiers "degenerated into assassins," killing not only soldiers but "their own neighbors. . . . They pillage, burn, destroy, and kill." Another observer wrote: "Persecutions are common, killings not rare, robberies an every day occurrence."

Throughout the border areas there were cases of towns being burned and sacked, of murders by uncontrolled soldiers, of hangings of guerrillas and by them, of soldiers taking reprisals against suspected guerrillas or friends of guerrillas. Families of suspects were driven from their homes, fined, arrested, banished. Officials attempting to control irregulars occasionally approached the brutality of their foes. After William Quantrill's raiders had murdered over 150 people in Lawrence, Kansas, in August 1863, General Thomas Ewing ordered the evacuation of 20,000 people from the entire region of northwest Missouri, forcing whole families to leave their homes at gunpoint. General Sherman recommended in Kentucky that "all males and females who have encouraged guerrillas and robbers" be gathered together and sent down the Mississippi River where they might be shot at by Southern partisans who had ambushed Union boats. These were the larger incidents, but thousands of smaller-scale official and unofficial reprisals continued the brutality against innocent and guilty alike. During the war and after, the problems posed by this type of warfare created some of the most difficult dilemmas faced by generals, judges, and government leaders. But its most terrible effect was on people in these contested regions who knew violence and terror firsthand.[36]

The personal involvement of Northerners with self-government on the community level, the dangerous and compelling choices of loyalty that people had to make in the border states, focused enormous attention on the constitutional issues that arose in 1861. Of course constitutional argument continued throughout the war, but it had a special quality in the beginning when people made their commitments to the struggle, told themselves what they were fighting for and why it was important. Later in the war Northerners would debate which constitutional posture would best protect the Union and its ideals. In 1861 the question was the extent to which defenders of the Union could claim much of the Constitution at all. The fact that constitutional arguments had helped to create the conflict in the first place showed the profound importance of being able to make that claim. Thousands had written, millions had read, that the war was a struggle to preserve the rule of law, the constitutional Union. People listened eagerly to the legal rhetoric.

The most compelling argument advanced by secessionists was that national power threatened their lives and liberty. That Northerners had become so disdainful of law, so obsessed with their crusade against slavery, that civil liberty was dead, and the Constitution a meaningless piece of paper. The constitutional justification of secession had awesome power, as witnessed by the fact that it was the most frequently used weapon in the Southern rhetorical arsenal. "Coercion in violation of the rights of states and individuals" was the cry that had forged a confederacy of eleven states from a protest by South Carolina.

The efforts of the national government to generate allegiance were judged in border states by how much power the national government exercised. Washington thus faced a paradoxical dilemma. If it repressed individuals who sought to destroy the Union, it validated the argument that the federal government was so coercive as to justify destroying the Union. It was a dilemma that haunted Lincoln all through the conflict's early stages and only diminished as war progressed. "Must a government be too strong for the liberties of its people, but too weak to preserve itself?" he asked. The case of John Merryman down in Maryland raised the question in stark terms. And what made Merryman's case matter so much was that it involved not just an obscure Confederate sympathizer but the chief justice of the United States Supreme Court.

In the weeks after Sumter as Washington, D.C., lived in apprehension that it would be captured by the rebels, Lincoln suspended the privilege of the writ of habeas corpus between Philadelphia and Washington. This action allowed the army to imprison anyone who threatened its operations and to keep them in jail so long as they were deemed a threat. No judge could demand the release of the prisoner so that civil courts could try him.[37]

John Merryman was caught burning railroad bridges and recruiting for the South. He was imprisoned in Fort Henry in Baltimore. Anxious, perhaps, about the legality of the act, and seeking to retain as much latitude for civil law as the war environs allowed, the commander at the fort allowed Merryman's lawyer to see him. The lawyer quickly drew up a petition for a writ of habeas corpus and sent it to the nearest and most prestigious federal judge he could think of. That turned out to be Roger Taney, who, in addition to being chief justice of the United States, was also the presiding judge of the federal circuit court of Maryland.

Taney was an old man (death was only three years away), but his passion for a fight remained intense. He meant to have a fight on this issue with the president of the United States. Rushing to Baltimore he issued a writ of habeas corpus to free Merryman and lectured the president and the nation on the meaning of the Constitution. The old judge told them both that the Constitution had been violated, that Lincoln was acting like a dictator, that Congress, not the president, had the legal right to suspend the writ. Since Congress had done nothing of the sort, Merryman must go free.

Taney's rhetoric rang with the principles of civil liberty that Americans cherished. Lawyers and many other Americans in the twentieth century have been charmed by that rhetoric. A popular tradition speaks of Lincoln's "dictatorship." But Taney's arguments were not indisputably constitutional law. Over forty pamphlets appeared to debate the issue, and the Lincoln defenders included two Harvard Law School professors, Joel Parker and Theophilus Parsons; Horace Binney, the patriarch of the American bar; and the most respected constitutional lawyer in Congress, Reverdy Johnson. Although Parker and Johnson later joined the conservative opposition, they were persuaded that the Constitution supported what Lincoln had done. Even before these champions had sustained him, the president, with the support of Attorney General Bates, decided to ignore Taney. Merryman stayed in jail. The aged chief justice was left to soothe his outrage by preparing opinions against every Union government action, opinions that court majorities ignored.[38]

Meanwhile, Lincoln spent almost a third of his first message to Congress defending the constitutionality of his actions: denying the constitutionality of secession, affirming the legality of the Merryman arrest. It was an answer in kind to rebel claims that secession had been blessed in the Philadelphia charter. The war stimulated a massive concern for constitutional issues, most of it focusing on the question of the adequacy of the original charter as a guidepost of war. Prior to Sumter, many had doubted that the Constitution fit the needs of the age. Some blamed the old document for precipitating the crisis. A visiting Frenchman captured many feelings when he wrote in December 1860, "I told you . . . that everything about the Constitution of the United States was wrong." But the rising of the people to defend their government, the energy Lincoln showed in responding in the beginning of the war, and his commitment to constitutional argument in behalf of his policies persuaded most of the doubters that the Constitution was adequate to the crisis.[39]

An adequate Constitution was a mixed blessing. In a nation called by Englishman Walter Bagehot "the most law-loving of Countries," fighting for a living Constitution surely energized and ennobled the cause. But the nation's Constitution imposed restraints as well. It was a written document with its double balances, states versus nation, legislature versus judicial versus executive, and its litany of national government "no-no's": the Bill of Rights. The Constitution limited government options. It defined the purposes of war, and formed the foundation for political opposition. It laid a basis for intragovernmental conflict between the president and Congress and the Supreme Court. And it recognized the vitality of state rights and responsibilities. All these matters would surface again and again, shaping the nature of the war.

This extensive and serious discussion of constitutional issues both revealed and defined the structure of the society. To embrace or to accept the constitutional system was to recognize the vitality of localism in the nation's experience. Commitment to respecting the rights of states under the Constitution was simply the rhetorical flourish that dressed up the political reality—states had been sources of action throughout American history. They clearly showed their importance in raising soldiers, and sustaining them through local community efforts throughout the war.

Respect for the constitutional process in civil-military relations conceded the American commitment to legal constitutional institutions, a commitment made personal and vital by the widespread involvement of citizens in making and enforcing the laws. That involvement would have been impossible without their ties to their communities. To respect the Constitution was to respect the most encompassing symbol of the ability of the people to govern themselves with the laws they had made. Of course the law was a compelling symbol. Americans were deeply devoted to the law, as observer Henry Flanders noted, because "in doing homage to law, they do homage to themselves, the creators and preservers of law."[40]

Although there had been doubters about the ability of these people to exercise self-control, to discipline themselves in their passion for wealth, they had shown that they knew how to organize communities, clubs, churches, schools, and even militias. While they clearly were the least governed people in the world, they had given indications that they had intense personal reasons to fight and that there might be more sinew in them than doubters guessed.

They had, of course, much to learn, more discipline to acquire, but as they began to march to their first great battles, there were reasons to believe that they had something compelling to fight for, and they were willing to do so.

CHAPTER 2

Forging Foreign and Domestic Weapons

NORTHERN people and communities had shown their willingness to fight. They had defined their goals and sharpened the meaning of loyalty in a society that united individuals and communities as well as states. But now they had to go to war—to find international support while they discovered what kind of an army they required.

While the communities of the North were the wellsprings of the war effort, the United States lived in a community of nations. The outbreak of Civil War posed vital questions as to how the world would react to one of its great powers engaged in a fraternal struggle. Northern leaders contemplated a blockade to strangle the South. What would that mean in the international economy where hundreds of thousands of French and English workers depended for their jobs on Southern cotton, where powerful capitalists earned millions in that same trade? Would the divisions in the United States permit the expansion of European interests in the New World? What would be the impact on the idea of democracy in the world if the Union remained divided, proving the claims of conservatives that people could not rule themselves? What would be the meaning of a war pitting the resources of Northern industry and free labor against slave labor in a world where chattel slavery was dying even as wage slavery became a subject of concern? When belligerents fought to preserve international lifelines, would neutrals become targets? Ironically, the first step in deciding how the war fit into the international arena required a domestic, legal decision: just what kind of war was this?

Theoretically, two major options presented themselves in that definition. The first was to see the war as an international conflict, with two nations, Confederate and Union, as antagonists. Such a view allowed one side to blockade the other's ports, to confiscate its property and that of its citizens, and to make whatever laws it chose for conquered territory. The only restraints on the behavior of the belligerents was international law, which dealt with generalities like being humane in warfare and the necessities of international politics. Although they would later repudiate the consequences of the position, Southerners insisted that the war was an international war, the Confederacy a sovereign nation.

There was never a chance that this definition of the war would prevail in the North. Accepting it repudiated all legal reasons to fight. If the Confederacy was a nation, on what grounds could the Union oppose secession? The Union view of the conflict was that the war was an insurrection against the legitimate government. Secession was a violation of the Constitution, opposing secession a constitutional duty. The Lincoln government refused to recognize the legal existence of the Confederacy, and they called Southern soldiers rebels, insurgents, and traitors.

But imperatives of the war forced the Union government into actions more suitable in an international conflict than a rebellion. Southern property was confiscated—most spectacularly in the case of slaves. Southern soldiers were treated as though they were soldiers of a sovereign nation. To deal with them as pirates and traitors, which permitted the death penalty, would have provoked reprisals against captured Union troops. In the first week of the war, as a matter of fact, Lincoln blundered into behaving as though the conflict were exactly what he insisted it was not, an international conflict. His blockade of the Confederacy was an act that, in international law, conferred belligerent status. Thaddeus Stevens pointed this out to the president and further explained that the same result could have been reached by closing the Southern ports through federal government control over international and interstate commerce. Lincoln admitted his error, explaining that he had had little experience with international law in his Illinois practice.[1]

The dual nature of the war was officially recognized by the Lincoln administration and given legitimacy by the Supreme Court in the 1863 Prize Cases. The facts of these cases were the following. Between the mobilization of troops, the blockade, and the congressional recognition of war neutral ships and cargoes had been seized. The owners claimed that they were not lawfully taken because a state of war could only be declared by Congress. In upholding the seizure, the Court declared that a civil war did not have to be declared, it was the product of events, and presidential recognition of those events constituted the beginning of the conflict. As to the nature of the conflict, the Court held that so far as foreign nations were concerned, it was a war that gave belligerent status to both parties. But it might still lawfully be considered an insurrection by the federal government.[2]

The Prize Cases definition established the official Union government position on the war. It provided immense flexibility for government action—at once justifying a vast war to destroy rebellion and keeping the conflict within civilized boundaries. The decision also told foreign nations what the United States would tolerate and thereby set guidelines for future relations. To have such limits was indispensable given the need to deal with the strongest empire in the world.

No issue in the war was of greater immediate importance than what stance England would take. British support for the rebellion could provide the Confederacy with a navy to sweep away the Northern blockade. It might bring the war in the cannons of British ships to the coastal cities of the North. It might provide an invasion from Canada to coordinate with thrusts from the South and involve the Union in a two-front war. All this was possible if England should ally herself with the South.

Even if England did not act as Jefferson Davis' military ally, the English might provide invaluable assistance simply by breaking the Northern blockade. This was something the world's greatest trading nation might be expected to do. Furthermore, the importance of Southern cotton to the British textile industry had been a fundamental canon of Confederate ideology. Southern leaders were positive that so much of the British economy rested on the processing of cotton that Her Majesty's government would have to defend the new nation, at least to the extent of keeping the Confederacy's links to the world open.

But the English position was more complicated than Southerners had forecast. While England did need cotton, in 1861 it had large inventories on hand. British manufacturers could wait and see. Some, in fact, might even benefit from a diminished supply. Prices for cotton goods would rise if a cotton shortage occurred. If the supply of cotton from America were cut off, there was also a possible recourse to the cotton fields of Egypt, India, and other colonies. Furthermore, while cotton might be a monarch in the world's trade, it was not an absolute monarch.

Wheat from the fields of the North was also a vital item in the Atlantic economy. Any decline in the harvests of Europe worked in favor of Northern traders and farmers. England also had other economic interests that might aid the North. Should war break out between the United States and England, the American navy could sink vast numbers of English ships before the power of the British navy brought ultimate victory. Insurance costs as well as losses in ships and cargoes could become enormous. And while Canada could be a staging area for action against the Union, that colony was also hostage to Union might. As Palmerston had put it in 1857, "These Yankees are most disagreeable fellows to have to do with about any American question: They are on the spot, strong and deeply interested in the matter; totally unscrupulous and dishonest and determined somehow or other to carry their point. We are far away, weak from distance, controlled by the Indifference of the Nation to the question . . . and by its Strong commercial Interest in maintaining peace with the United States."[3]

The realities of international power also strongly influenced the British position. England was the world's greatest imperial power. Her empire made her sensitive to the argument, advanced by the North, that a central government should be allowed to put down rebellions without the interference of other nations. England had put down rebellions in Canada in 1837, in Afghanistan in 1841, in India in 1857. Furthermore, international commitments could produce a domestic backlash. In the aftermath of the Crimean War, when a short conflict had escalated into an enormous drain on English lives and fortunes, public opinion turned suspicious of other foreign adventures.

England's naval power made her sensitive to the entire issue of blockades. Should she interfere with the Northern blockade of the

South, she would be setting a precedent that could return to haunt her. As the *London Times* observed, "A blockade is by far the most formidable weapon of war we possess. Surely we ought not to be overready to blunt its edge or injure its temper." Accordingly the British did not demand that the Union blockade be total for it to be lawful. Foreign Secretary Russell wrote to Ambassador Lyons in Washington that even if "various ships may have successfully escaped through it [this] will not of itself prevent the blockade from being an effective one by international law."[4]

On the continent of Europe only the position of France was significant. Emperor Napoleon III had international ambitions and sufficient naval strength to help the Confederacy. In addition, the nation had recently supported Italian independence. There was some hope that Napoleon might now come to the aid of the American rebels. His personal and political inclination pushed in that direction. He had ambitions in Mexico and, believing that the Confederacy would succeed, sought Southern friendship. France was heavily dependent on Southern cotton; over 90 percent of its imports came from the South. There was also pressure from workers in the cotton industries in favor of helping the South lift the Union blockade. But other pressures pushed Napoleon northward. If Northern power proved formidable Mexico would be a hostage to the Union. French industry had thousands of customers in the North, and French liberal opinion saw the issue in the contest to be the survival of republican government. After the nation's Italian adventures, public opinion was growing against dangerous foreign commitments. Napoleon could not risk taking individual action in this crisis. He saw the opportunity to gain English friendship by linking French foreign policy in this matter to that of England. Hence France would follow the English lead.[5]

Both nations, however, shared one overriding concern. War threatened international stability even as it generated hardships at home. Both countries thus made ending the war the highest priority. While the early prospect of quick Northern victory meant that public opinion and governmental attitudes in both England and France favored the North, after Bull Run both countries began to change their attitude. Throughout 1862 and 1863 and even into 1864 it seemed probable that the South would create its new nation, that Northern will would fail, that the costs of conflict would overwhelm Lincoln's government. Leaders in France and England in those years tried to persuade the North to end the fighting, because they perceived Southern victory inevitable. In mid-1862 Paris and London came near to demanding the right to mediate the conflict. Only the Union victory at Antietam restrained England from supporting the French initiative. As Union power began to tell, foreign governments faded in their fervor for the South, and increasingly took neutral, and hence pro-Union, positions. Then, too, admiration for emancipation enlarged the ranks of the Union's foreign supporters, as faith in the victory of republican government inspired liberal adherents; this momentum built increasing sympathy for the Union cause. But fundamentally support grew with successes on the battlefield.[6]

While these practical considerations influenced British policy, ideological concerns were also important. By their very nature these were balanced less easily. The war in the United States posed a confused set of dichotomies. It was by no means clear-cut which side liberals and conservatives in England would choose. For example, the North claimed to be fighting for the viability of free society against a slave aristocracy. But Southerners insisted that their struggle was for an inalienable right of all free people, the right of self-determination. The Northern position would attract Englishmen seeking the expansion of democracy in their own country; the Southern would appeal to men who sympathized with uprisings against aristocracies in Europe. But both causes had attracted the same Englishmen. So was the North or the South the preferable ally?

The North also claimed the liberal position of fighting for the rights of free labor, as Lincoln put it, for lifting "artificial weights from all shoulders." England's working class might be attracted to that ideal. A meeting in Manchester described the North as "a singularly happy abode for the working millions where industry is honored." But the North, too, was evolving a British-style industrial system that Dickens, Engels, Marx, and the novelist Disraeli had all excoriated. Could there be an easy choice for reformers and liberals here?

Further complicating things was the fact that Lincoln and his government at the beginning of the war insisted that they were not fighting for emancipation. Bowing to pressures from the border states and Northern conservatives, the government rejected pressures to attack slavery. Doing this cut them off from the profound antislavery sentiment of British liberals. It also subjected the administration to attacks from British conservatives who often supported the South.

Union defenders were forced to insist that, whatever Lincoln might say, in fact the war did pit the forces of free labor against defenders of slavery. As Karl Marx asserted, "The people of Europe know that the Southern slavocracy commenced that war with the declaration that the continuance of slavocracy was no longer compatible with the continuance of the Union. Consequently the people of Europe know that a fight for the continuance of the Union is a fight against the continuance of the slavocracy." But this was hardly as powerful a justification for supporting the North as a war against slavery would be. As one labor paper put it, "Now that it is clear that the Northerns are not fighting for the emancipation of the slaves, we are relieved from any moral consideration in their favor; and as the Southerners are not worse than they, why should we not get cotton?"[7]

Conflicting pressures in British popular opinion produced no consensus. The Palmerston government took the most prudent course available. On May 13, 1861, Great Britain announced its determination to remain neutral in the disunion conflict. However, neutrality did make a concession to the South. It recognized the Confederacy as a belligerent engaged in war. This allowed the rebels to solicit men and arms abroad, except where neutrality laws forbade, to seek loans, to engage in privateering, to search and seize ships carrying contraband, and to use prize courts where the right to take suspected ships and cargoes might be in question. The act of recognition provided a rule book for proper lawful behavior under the canons of international law, thus helping to eliminate confusion, ignorance, and anxiety about how to conduct business and diplomacy in a dangerous situation.

Not surprisingly, such "benefits" to international diplomacy were lost on the Lincoln government in spite of its own blockade. British action defied the official position about the nature of the war. To recognize the Confederacy as a belligerent seemed to concede the very issue between North and South, in favor of the rebels. Furthermore, this recognition took place before any major battle had demonstrated Southern power. It even occurred before the newly designated minister to England, Charles Francis Adams, had arrived in the country. Ominously, it also occurred at a time when the Confederacy did have representatives in London. Northerners were outraged that England had encouraged their enemy. James Russell Lowell caught the mood in his poem to John Bull:

> It don't seem hardly right, John,
>   When both me hands was full
> To stump me to a fight, John,
>   Your cousin, tu, John Bull!
> . . . .
> You wonder why we're hot, John?
>   Your mark was on the guns,
> The neutral guns, that shot, John,
>   Our brothers and our sons.

Several American leaders questioned whether Jefferson Davis' government could have survived without the British action. After the Civil War, Americans filed claims against the English that included half the estimated cost of the war. Without this recognition, they argued, there would have been no serious fighting.

However, there was a strong argument supporting the English action. Precedent and recent behavior by the United States government justified what London had done. The United States had been one of the first countries to recognize rebellions in Latin America. Washington in 1837 accorded belligerent status to Canadian rebels. And in proclaiming a blockade of the South, Lincoln took an action that in international law conceded belligerent status to the blockaded territory. These facts underscored the conclusions of the English legal authorities on May 5 that "we must consider the Civil War in America as a regular war . . . & apply to it all the rules respecting blockade, letters of marque &c which belong to neutrals during a war."[8]

These general policy considerations would have an effect ultimately, but the American secretary of state William Seward had to act immediately. When the British recognized Confederate belligerency, Seward sent Minister Adams an official dispatch protesting vigorously. Should the English persist in having discussions with the Confederate commissioners in London, Adams was told, he should end diplomatic contact. Furthermore, Seward spoke of the probability of war if England recognized the Confederate government. Seward also observed how English meddling in the American and French revolutions had led to international disorder and threatened the aristocracies of the world. He wondered if England had considered the consequences to its society of meddling again. Lincoln toned the dispatch down, but it still vehemently opposed any ties between England and the Confederacy.

When Adams received the dispatch he was stunned. It seemed to him "like throwing the game into the hands of the enemy." But there was a method in Seward's apparent madness. Fearing that England would move easily from recognizing belligerency to full recognition, he wanted to shock the English into considering the consequences. Threatening war, he hoped, would bring Britain to its senses.[9]

Seward's tactic worked; but not without cost to Anglo-American relations. English leaders had long been apprehensive about the secretary of state. His political career was filled with anti-British rhetoric. The large Irish vote in New York had inspired him to twist the lion's tail frequently. His belief in the inexorable and beneficial expansion of American territory marked him as a threat to Canadian independence. In late December 1860 he had publicly expressed his opinion that "there is no such thing in the book, no such thing in reason, no such thing in nature as any State existing in the continent of North America, outside of the U.S.A." Also in 1860 he had told a visiting English lord that he planned to insult that country should he become secretary of state. He had spoken in early 1861 of the benefits of a foreign war to keep the Union from dividing. In private he had urged Lincoln to provoke a conflict with England, France, and Spain, as a means of uniting the nation. By February 1861 Seward had convinced the British ambassador, Lord Lyons, that he was "arrogant and reckless against foreign powers." The stern quality of American protests against British dealings with the rebels only confirmed suspicions that Americans were rash, dangerous, and irresponsible. As late as September 1861 Prime Minister Palmerston remarked that Seward and Lincoln were "so wild that any act of intemperance may be expected."[10]

Still, the behavior of Washington had its effect. British foreign secretary John Russell told Adams that he would have no official dealings with the Confederate ministers. And the British kept the Confederate contacts to a minimum. They did reserve the right to extend recognition in the future, but they assured Americans that they were acting with caution. The Confederacy would have to prove that it could sustain nationhood. While this did not mean that all informal contacts would be ended, the British indicated that they would not precipitously recognize the rebels.

By June 1861 Seward had moderated his tone to the English, confident of a quick victory and pleased that diplomatic recognition of the Confederacy had been sidetracked. But relations remained tense. Incidents kept feeding suspicion. In May word came that Canadians were preparing to deliver an armed ship to the rebels for use as a privateer. Seward protested strenuously, only to discover that Unionists were buying the ship. An English counsel in Charleston became involved in behavior that suggested recognition of the rebels, and again Seward growled. Confederate ships were found provisioning themselves with arms and food out of British-controlled ports. The fact that this was legal did little to make Americans happy about it. Still, confidence in imminent victory allowed Americans to see such actions as minor irritations. Anglophobia could be allowed to simmer out of sight.

After Bull Run Northerners reawoke to the seriousness of the conflict they faced. Alert now that the war was likely to be long and perhaps desperate, they began to magnify irritations into life and death matters. As for the English, they had themselves been angered by Seward's public pugnaciousness. A widespread feeling emerged that standing up to Americans was the only way to cool them off. Foreign Secretary Russell told Palmerston, "The United States Government are very dangerous people to run away from." The stage was set for a crisis, and on November 8, 1861, the crisis came.[11]

The Confederate government had determined to send to England and France two ministers, John Slidell and James Mason, to plead the case for recognition and to ask for assistance. Word of their sailing spread to Union officials, who began to seek them out all over the Atlantic. One Union ship was told to go into the English Channel if necessary to stop them, but the ministers had not gotten that far on their journey. Captain Charles Wilkes, commanding the USS *San Jacinto,* found them only one day out of Havana, where they had boarded the British packet *Trent*. Wilkes stopped the *Trent* and forcibly dragged Mason and Slidell onto the *San Jacinto*. He sailed north for Boston harbor, with a stop among a Union fleet just outside Charleston harbor where Mason and Slidell could see the Confederate flag flying above Fort Sumter. Arriving in Boston, Wilkes was lionized by an almost hysterical American press. The House of Representatives voted him a gold medal, the secretary of the navy applauded "brave, adroit, and patriotic conduct." The *New York Times* suggested that the proper response was to "consecrate another Fourth of July to him." After losses at Bull Run and Balls Bluff, with McClellan spending his efforts getting ready to begin but not yet beginning, the Northern citizens were lavish in their adoration.[12]

But, ominously, Confederates were rejoicing, too. While her husband was being taken off the *Trent*, Mrs. Slidell had proclaimed, "Captain Wilkes is playing into our hands!" Rebel leaders were pleased at the insult their enemy had delivered to the world's strongest naval power. Such an insult might be just the thing to produce at least recognition, and possibly alliance.

In England the public outcry exceeded, if possible, that applause in the North. A highly respected journalist wrote to Seward, "There never was within memory such burst of feeling. . . . The people are frantic with rage, and were the country polled, I fear that 999 men out of a thousand would declare for immediate war." Eight thousand troops were readied for transport to Canada; a squadron of warships was prepared. The cabinet wrote a memorandum to Lyons in Washington that bristled with outrage. Toned down by the prince consort, Queen Victoria, and a more moderate feeling that swept the cabinet after the first rage was vented, the note still required that the United States release Mason and Slidell or face serious consequences.[13]

Meanwhile in the United States sobriety shouldered its way forward. Men began to consider whether Wilkes had, as he insisted, acted lawfully. It was lawful to take contraband off of neutral ships, it was lawful to seize dispatches, soldiers might certainly be taken, but what about enemy officials carrying dispatches? Probably the law stopped at that point, and such men might not be taken. Indisputably Wilkes had violated the law in one particular. He had not taken the *Trent* to a prize court to determine the legality of seizing the men. He claimed that he had let the *Trent* continue its passage so as not to inconvenience the passengers any more. It was a reasonable act of kindness, but it was bad law. And British authorities could fortify intense anger with legal authority in their demand that the United States release the men.[14]

Could the Union government back down? Starved for something to cheer about, angry at the British for their neutrality, some hoping for a war to justify taking Canada as compensation for Southern secession, the government felt strong pressures to show England American obstinance. Lincoln at first wanted to keep the men. Then he thought that arbitration might be a way to settle the issue—a third party to determine Mason's and Slidell's fate. But finally it became clear that the men would have to be given up, and administration leaders backed away from the precipice. Lincoln said nothing about the *Trent* crisis in his first annual message to Congress in early December. Seward wrote Adams in London that Wilkes had not acted under orders, and that Washington wanted to settle the matter peacefully. When it came to preparing the official message yielding Mason and Slidell, he took the opportunity to assuage American patriots by lecturing the English on Wilkes' lawful right to do what had been done. Seward also trotted out old British impressment wrongs and announced that in releasing the Confederate envoys they were simply adhering to long-cherished principles. Nevertheless, Mason and Slidell were released and sent to England to begin seeking support for their "nation."[15]

Still, the very resolution of the *Trent* crisis suggested how little success they would have. At the brink, both governments had sought conciliation, even as popular pressure shoved them toward war. The costs of conflict between the two nations were recognized. The ties of history, economics, and shared institutions worked together to demonstrate how much both sides in fact wanted peace. As soon as Mason and Slidell got to England they must have known how hollow a victory had been achieved. The *London Times,* no friend of the North, remarked, "They must not suppose, because we have gone to the very edge of a great war to rescue them, that therefore they are precious in our eyes. We should have done just as much to rescue two of their own Negroes."[16]

The *Trent* affair thus produced some beneficial results in Anglo-American relations. It demonstrated to both parties how public pressures might build up for war, and warned them to be cautious in stirring such feelings. This was an especially important lesson for Seward, who had been used to playing to political galleries while engaging in diplomacy. Whatever the necessity for doing so to pressure the British, he had learned the potential danger in the tactic. Lincoln was also alerted to the passionate feelings of the English and became even more eager to avoid hostilities.

The crisis had demanded that both nations consider their relations with each other, to ponder the spectacle of the two strongest republics in the world tearing at each other's throats. Both sides had backed away and now respected each other the more for the diplomatic battle they had shared. Other crises would appear, but now they knew that they could deal with each other in responsible ways. The English especially had learned that while democracies might encourage demagogues, they could also spawn courageous and responsible leaders. It was beneficial experience. As Ambassador Adams wrote, "I am inclined to believe that the happening of the affair of the Trent just when it did, with just the issue that it had, was opportune rather than otherwise." And Seward agreed that "with all its exasperations" it was "fortunate that the Trent affair occurred."[17]

The settlement of the Trent crisis and the subsequent decision by the English to keep hands off the American war did not mean that all was quiet on the diplomatic front. If the government of England could not help the rebels, private citizens might do so by providing the rebels with the weapons of war. The British government had the responsibility of making sure that such efforts would not be undertaken, for allowing ships to be built for a warring nation violated international law.

But there were ways around the law. Peaceful ships could be built, and once they left the shipyards, who could be held responsible for later outfittings? A Confederate agent took advantage of this loophole and contracted for the building of two large cruisers in the shipyards at Liverpool. Minister Adams got wind of this action and immediately began investigation and protests designed to show the British government that a violation of law was under way and needed to be stopped. But proof was slow in coming. Before it could be marshaled effectively one of the cruisers got off to sea, traveled to a Caribbean island, and acquired the guns that turned the benign sailing ship into an armed and deadly Confederate raider, the *Florida*. As the second cruiser neared completion, proof mounted that she too would become a ship of war. Adams gathered unmistakable evidence that this was the case and took it to the British authorities, but again too late. The British ministry agreed that the ship should be stopped, but the paperwork needed to authorize the stoppage sat in the law offices of the Crown for five days, as the senior official there had gone insane. During the delay the second cruiser took to sea, later to acquire the guns that made her the most feared rebel raider of all, the *Alabama*. Led by the *Alabama*, these raiders ultimately destroyed over 250 Northern ships, worth approximately $15.5 million.[18]

The escape of the *Alabama* along with the general climate of hostility to England led Americans to believe that the ships had been sent off with the connivance of the London government. Adams thus was both tense and angry when he received word that Confederates had contracted with the Laird Brothers for two powerful rams, armored with heavy cannon and large and sharp iron prows designed to pierce the wooden blockaders of the Union navy. Visions of the rams crashing through the blockade, of drowning crews, of Confederate ports open to world shipping, and hence of a protracted war and possible rebel victory shattered Northern calm. Adams told the British ministry that if the rams were allowed to leave British ports, "this is war." Concurrently the United States Congress began discussing unleashing privateers who would make their own decisions about which ships to prey on in defense of the Union cause and their own profit. Now it was time for British visions. The looming success of the *Alabama* made it possible to envision English merchant ships sinking after being plundered of their cargoes. London did not need threats by Adams to see ominous consequences should American hostility intensify. Even before the minister's threat, the decision had been made to confiscate the rams. From that point on, in September 1863, Confederate hopes of English shipbuilders nourishing the rebel navy faded. Other ships sneaked out of English ports, occasionally British sailors assisted Confederate raiders at sea, but the most powerful naval power in the world now was clear in its support for the Union cause.[19]

While the North found security in the international arena, the real fighting awaited. After Sumter both North and South gathered their armies and prepared for war. Since the South had adopted a defensive strategy, it remained for the North to take the offensive. If Northern forces did nothing, then the Confederacy would, by default, have established a new nation protecting slavery in a world where momentum had been running against human bondage. There were abiding questions about the ability of Northern society to marshal its resources to achieve victory.

Northern capacity to fight was based on many factors. The courage and commitment of potential soldiers was, of course, fundamental. But equally important was the need for an effective army. Without that, losses would undermine the willingness to fight. It was therefore crucial to determine what kind of army would be the most effective. But prewar Americans could not agree. Debate had been widespread over how war should be made. That debate had been marbled with doubts in important places about whether it could be made successfully by Northerners at all.

Two traditions existed in antebellum America as to the most effective and satisfactory structure for an army. The dominant one was described in the 1776 Virginia Declaration of Rights: "A well regulated militia, composed of the body of the people, trained to arms, is the proper, natural, and safe defense of a free state . . . standing armies, in time of peace, should be avoided, as dangerous to liberty."

George Washington expressed the other idea. Proclaimed as a Cincinnatus, his experience with citizen militia nevertheless appalled him. "Men accustomed to unbounded freedom, and no control, cannot brook the Restraint which is indispensably necessary to the good order and Government of an Army," he wrote. "To bring Men to a proper degree of Subordination, is not the work of a day, a Month or even a year."[20]

The insecurities of the Napoleonic era led American leaders to seek a balance between the citizen and the professional army. Washington, Hamilton, and even Jefferson came to agree on the need for a military academy to train officers. In 1802 Congress founded the U.S. Military Academy, providing a permanent military establishment for the nation. Throughout the pre–Civil War years the regular army grew, graduating officers from West Point, enlisting soldiers for a force that grew from about four thousand when Jefferson took office to sixteen thousand on the eve of the Civil War. These officers became advocates of a trained regular professional soldiery. With a small cadre of congressional supporters, they studied the battles of the past, problems of supply and engineering, and theories of strategy and tactics. Naturally, their ideas dominated the leadership of the Union army as war began.[21]

West Point became the focus of the professional army tradition. Meanwhile the minuteman ideal gained its vitality in thousands of Northern communities. Acting under state authority, towns, villages, and cities organized militia, which became an important part of everyday life. A combination of fraternal organization, police force, and public entertainers, these groups elected their own officers, chose their own uniforms, and regulated admission. They held picnics, balls, and contests, sponsored reading rooms and lecture series, and, of course, mustered for annual parades and for important town events.[22]

In more rural areas, that is, in most of the North, militia units served predominantly as social organizations. Their functions gave them prestige in their community and linked the community in their allegedly bellicose duties. Urban militia had social functions, too, but served more actively. The duty of preserving order often required that they put down riots against minority groups and gang warfare between ethnic communities, and occasionally suppress strikers who resorted to violence to enforce their labor demands. Rioting workers in New York City, Philadelphia, and Baltimore were crushed by the militia. In Boston, Brooklyn, Hoboken, Chicago, Philadelphia, and Ellsworth, Maine, and Charlestown, Massachusetts, as well, urban militias helped police or acted as police themselves against mob violence.[23]

But rural or urban, volunteer militia companies played an important role as the Union army gathered. Increasing in numbers throughout the antebellum years, more companies were in existence in 1859 and 1860 than ever before. These companies gave the young men some experience in military discipline, joined the community with them in their patriotism, and thus prepared Northerners for the contest to come.[24]

Preparedness varied from place to place. Western state militias ranged from nonexistent to, at best, disorganized. Eastern units were more ready for action. Massachusetts and to a lesser extent

Connecticut and New York were especially prepared. Under the direction of Ebenezer Stone, a Boston clothing merchant, the Massachusetts militia became the model for the North. Well equipped, trained in yearly encampments, the force was so popular that in 1854 Stone was forced to reject new regiments because the state limit had been reached. Furthermore, the militia helped train officers in large-scale warfare. By 1860 Benjamin Butler, as high-ranking officer in the Massachusetts state militia, had commanded more troops than any regular army officer.

Militia units built allegiance to the nation among ethnic groups. When foreign-born companies were disbanded in the Northeast during the Know Nothing fever of the mid-1850s, Irish, German, and Scottish militias simply began calling themselves literary societies and continued business as usual. But when war broke out they eagerly sought to prove their loyalty, rushing to be the first to enlist.[25]

Union volunteers from the militia companies of the Northern states became the Union's first soldiers. Often the companies joined as a whole, providing units experienced in giving and obeying orders, familiar with each other. They were, of course, not so well trained as regular soldiers, and certainly less well trained than West Pointers believed they had to be. Nonetheless, they were something more than an armed mob, if something less than battle-trained veterans. They were capable of becoming a powerful army.

While most of the prewar state militias became members of the United States Army, others stayed at home and played important wartime roles. They provided military experience for thousands of men and officers. Trained in local units, providing a security force behind the lines, ready for, and called into, service when Southern raids probed into Pennsylvania, the Ohio Valley, the Missouri-Kansas border, these men supplemented the volunteer and regular forces. Anywhere from 125,000 to 200,000 men served as home guards, and their presence in the communities of the North kept the war in the minds of the people at home. They also wedded state and local military experience to the national. Men from state militias joined the Union army units organized in their states. Union army veterans returned and served in the home guard. Home guard units called into federal service returned to their communities, proud of having shown the abilities of "Jonesville's" boys in saving the

Union. And, of course, they brought back with them memories of a world beyond Jonesville and purposes larger than those of Main Street.[26]

However active the militia had been before the war, many professional officers harbored doubts about citizen soldiers. The experience that some had had with volunteers during the Mexican War spawned suspicion. Volunteers had engaged in gratuitous brutality against the Mexican civilians. The enlistees in the regular army also carried a stigma. In the 1850s most of them were recent immigrants who either deserted or resigned as soon as possible. Professionals like Grant, in fact, thought that the regular "rank and file were probably inferior as material out of which to make an army, to the volunteers that participated in all the later battles of the war." But neither group seemed promising material for creating an army.[27]

Civil-military relations in the antebellum period also contributed to professional doubts about the armed citizenry. While many Americans admired the professional army, others attacked it. The traditional fears of a standing army were mixed with valid charges that West Point was a school for the children of the American upper class—that birth, not merit, was the key to admission. There were moves in Congress to abolish the academy, and while unsuccessful, they revealed a strong Jacksonian suspicion of the claims of privilege, and an enduring belief in the competence of the common man. Battles in behalf of military amateurism, of course, simply reinforced the commitment of the regulars to their ideals.

West Point kept emphasizing professionalism to its students. Inspired by the teaching of Dennis Hart Mahan of Virginia, encouraged by his writings and those of Henry Halleck and George McClellan, the academy emphasized again and again the need for intensive training, thorough knowledge of an extensive body of literature, organization, and discipline. "Modern nations," Halleck wrote, were "learning that military success depends more upon skill and discipline, than upon numbers." By contrast, "the peaceful habits of our citizens tend but little to the cultivation of the military character." The only hope of military strength for the nation would be the ability of the officers to make professional soldiers out of the material at hand—and that would take some doing. McClellan agreed that "mere individual courage cannot suffice to [bring military success]." Victory would come only "by discipline, and . . . by that consummate and mechanical military skill which can only be acquired by a long course of education . . . and by long course of habit."[28]

Strategy and tactics taught at West Point further emphasized that war was a professional's business. The most respected theorist was the Swiss-French writer Baron de Jomini. He had served with Napoleon, and his observations thus gained great force. His *Précis de l'art de la guerre* was extolled by McClellan and Halleck, and read admiringly by other generals. Even Sherman, in 1862, declared that ignorance of Jomini "would be a lasting disgrace." Jomini emphasized that the army on the offensive always had the advantage. He focused attention on the need for maneuver, for moving forces, and hence the need for discipline and a high degree of training among the soldiers. Jomini confined his discussion to the actual battlefield and preparations for fighting there. He thus further encouraged his readers to believe that war was a matter for experts with fixed rules and complex stratagems best understood by trained men. He found no argument in that quarter at West Point.[29]

But this main theme of Jomini's writings had also evoked an American counterdiscussion. While the French theorist had emphasized the primacy of the frontal attack, men like Dennis Mahan and James St. Clair Morton suggested that events since Jomini began his studies called for some rethinking. Two factors were of major importance. First, the advances in weaponry, and second, the nature of American armies.

The major advance in weaponry was the rifle. It fired more bullets longer distances and with vastly improved accuracy. The older muzzle-loading muskets had a range of about one hundred yards. The newer weapons had an effective range of almost five hundred yards. Furthermore, they could be loaded more rapidly. Troops making an assault on men with rifles would thus be under more deadly fire for longer periods of time. On battlefields where men had rifles, a frontal attack might become a death march. To cope with the rifle's firepower, Mahan increasingly emphasized the importance of entrenchments in battles, and these entrenchments suggested a crucial role for defense as well as offense. A man with a rifle shielded by a wall, felled trees, or a mound of dirt was more than a match for exposed attackers. The power of the rifle in the arms of an entrenched man was so great that 80 percent of all assaults attempted in the Civil War failed. While it would take the war itself to teach that gruesome lesson, prewar evidence raised doubts about Jomini's precepts.[30]

The other factor suggesting Jomini's limitations was the nature of American armies. Mahan and a few colleagues knew that their nation would hardly tolerate the large standing armies of Europe. To build tactics and strategy for Americans on the Napoleonic example was impossible. Some of Napoleon's soldiers were veterans of seven years of combat. The majority of Americans would be poorly trained militiamen. While experienced regulars might advance and maneuver skillfully, novices would fight best when protected. Again, the value of entrenchments seemed obvious, even to people who were not soldiers. George Strong commented in May 1861 that "in a contest between raw levies, the party that fights under protection of ditches and embankments must prevail."[31]

But the existence of these caveats to Jomini did not undermine the power of his major ideas: offensive armies had the advantage; massed forces, pushed against the weakest spot in enemy lines, were the means to victory. Mahan and disciples simply added to Jomini's offensive strategy the warning that armies should prepare fortifications while in the field. They might retreat to these if necessary, and fortifications would also prove to be places from which to launch attacks. Attack was still the key.[32]

Attack fit the mentality of some military leaders, and it certainly harmonized with overwhelming public sentiment. The uprising of the Northern people showed an eagerness to take the offensive. Editors began to clamor for an attack on the Confederate capital of Richmond, and governors insisted on the offensive. Lincoln himself joined in pressuring the military for victories.

But the reservations expressed by Mahan and his colleagues set up a conflict with serious consequences for the fighting of the war. The best students at West Point eagerly absorbed his ideas about the need for entrenchment. They also believed that soldiers would have to be very well trained for battle. They insisted again and again on taking the time to prepare the troops, to dig fortifications—to create, in short, a highly disciplined army, sustained by fortifications, prepared for any eventuality. Being good students, they insisted on applying their lessons thoroughly. George McClellan and Henry Halleck were two of the best students that Mahan had.

This combination of curriculum and professional ethos among the regular army officers also raised doubts about how to use the citizens' army that surged forward. Generals vacillated in their strategy. They either demanded that the volunteers perform intricate maneuvers they were incapable of, or they became tremendously cautious as a result of lack of faith in troops. They had failed to develop theories of warfare that integrated professional knowledge with the courage and commitment of the people at large. The war itself and the people would teach them better, but the lesson for both professionals and amateurs would be blood-soaked and painful.

The pain was increased considerably by the policy adopted in organizing the army. The regular and volunteer armies were kept separated from each other. Few trained and experienced soldiers were available to instruct the volunteers. Governors seeking officers for state regiments tried very hard to get men with military training. But more often than not they were forced to appoint men whose major qualification for command was an ability to raise a regiment, but not to teach it how to fight. In addition, governors too often rewarded political friends and punished enemies in granting commissions, perhaps believing at first that in a short war such politicking would not matter.

The sixteen-thousand-man regular army might have provided trained leadership for these volunteers. Indeed, Grant recommended that "the government ought to disband the regular army, with the exception of the staff corps, and notify the disbanded officers that they would receive no compensation while the war lasted except as volunteers." A few regular officers tried to transfer from the regulars to the volunteers, and Lincoln's cabinet agreed that up to one hundred regular officers could take commands in volunteer units. But powerful opposition against breaking up the regulars existed. General in Chief Winfield Scott hoped to make the regular army the spearhead of a quick offensive that would crush secession in the cradle. Volunteers would serve auxiliary roles and, of course, might observe the regulars as a model for their amateur efforts. The adjutant general Lorenzo Thomas stated that "if he had his way not a single officer of the Regular Army would go into the Volunteer service." Thus the regulars stayed together as a separate force. Regular officers rose to overall command of armies, brigades, divisions, and corps. West Point generals commanded on both sides in fifty-five of the sixty greatest battles of the war. In the other five a West Pointer was on one of the sides. But the officers with most direct contact with the soldiers had to learn about war preferably in front of, more often beside, and occasionally behind their men.[33]

There was more to assessing the ability of the North to fight than strictly military considerations. Involved also were beliefs about the nature of the societies that would go to war. Military leaders shared Northern anxieties about the social fabric. West Pointers were usually the children of the American establishment; it is not surprising that they had conservatives' doubts. They imagined a society made weak by the comforts of civilization, losing its healthy familiarity with the frontier, decaying in its respect for values beyond making money. By contrast, the South seemed well endowed with martial talents.

The rural nature of Dixie allegedly meant that Southern soldiers felt more passionate about their soil than did more urban Northerners. The image of the violent South, with its code deullo, the rude brutality of its poor farmers and backwoodsmen, the knives and guns carried for hunting or fighting, suggested a dangerous belligerence. Northern readers of the April 1861 *Atlantic Monthly* also read that the marksmanship of South Carolinians was the best in the world. Foreign observer Frederick Marryat had reported that Southern horsemen had no peers.[34]

Southern leadership also appeared superior to Northern. There was a widespread belief that West Point was dominated by the South and that the elite of the nation's generals had been Southerners. The experience gained as masters of slaves and rulers of poor whites allegedly bore fruit in the army. The military heroes that most Americans recalled were George Washington, Andy Jackson, William Henry Harrison, Zachary Taylor, and Winfield Scott, all from below the Mason-Dixon line. Scott's loyalty did not erase the image of the Southern martial heritage. Statistically the South did not dominate military leadership. In fact there were more Northern than Southern graduates of West Point as of 1860. But the statistics were overshadowed by the memories of Washington and Company. The linkage of West Point and the South was so strong that as late as 1863 Kansas senator James Lane got a quarter of the U.S. Senate to support a resolution abolishing the military academy. That linkage was also strong enough to give great impact to what Major Anderson told New York society just after surrendering Fort Sumter. "We must not underrate the rebel army. It is brave and desperate and well drilled. Ours includes some dead wood, but theirs is young and fresh and vigorous. Should Providence send them a great general, woe to the North." And this was before any-one had heard very much of Robert E. Lee and Stonewall Jackson.[35]

Further feeding Northern doubts was the contrast between the two presidents. On the Confederate side a trained West Pointer, a man of long and distinguished service in his state and nation. He had declined a brigadeer generalship to become a United States senator. From 1853 to 1857 he had served ably as secretary of war. Jefferson Davis by experience and reputation seemed the epitome of a wartime leader. The Union could only boast an Illinois lawyer-politician with one undistinguished term in the House of Represen-tatives, where he had opposed a Mexican War in which Davis had been wounded. His sole experience with anything military was as an officer of untrained militia in the so-called Black Hawk "War." Even Lincoln joked about that experience. It seemed unlikely that he would find much to laugh about now.

As war gathered around them, the Northerners witnessed a thun-derous outpouring of patriotism from a society that many had doubted. But if the unexpected patriotism numbed some of their fears, others remained. That they remained in the minds of military leaders was important, for these were the experts on how to conduct war—these were the men to whom the nation's leaders would turn. And, in their areas of expertise, they were correct in many of their opinions.

Enthusiasm was not enough. Mere enthusiasm charging en-trenched rifles produced dead enthusiasts. Well-trained soldiers, used to discipline, were more than a match for forces whose only asset was courage. But other professional judgments were open to question. The emphasis on maneuver and complex tactics as a dom-inant element in battle, a product of the encounter with Jomini, was surely questionable given the nature of American armies. The Jominian suggestion that war was a professional matter and should not involve all of society would hardly fit a conflict as passionate as civil war. To limit the goals of war to the goals of professionals was impossible given the nature of this conflict.

Had they understood this more clearly, the professionals would have been more sensitive to the meaning of the rising of the people after Sumter. They would have been more suspicious of their social theories. This war was too serious in the minds of Northerners to be left to professionals. The people's stake in the victory was immense. And, most crucially, without that continued devotion to the conflict, there could be no hope of success. Although discipline was crucial for any army, there first of all had to *be* an army. There had to be the men who would fight and the people to supply them and support them. The outburst of patriotism after Sumter showed the willingness of the North to provide soldiers and to endorse and sustain their efforts.

Between the opening excitement of secession and the first major battle at Bull Run both sides heard more calls for war than actual war itself. Southerners proclaimed their readiness to fight forever to retain their independence. Northern spokesmen demanded action and insisted that once rebels understood Northern determination, reunion would be swift. When the Confederate capital was moved to Richmond, just over ninety miles from Washington, D.C., it became certain that the first test of both perspectives would come in Virginia. "On to Richmond, on to Richmond," Horace Greeley's *New York Tribune* urged, and by mid-summer Union forces under West Point–trained Irwin McDowell were prodded into moving south.

The target for first action reflected an understanding of the modern character of the war. Manassas Junction was the meeting place for two railroad lines, one striking directly westward through the Blue Ridge Mountains into the rich Shenandoah Valley, the other heading southwest toward Culpepper, then on to Charlottesville and Lynchburg. Off of this line an army could turn in two places directly east on rails that ran to Richmond itself. Control of these tracks meant the ability to move large numbers of men, their weapons, and supplies against the rebel capital. A large Confederate force assembled there also provided a target for Union effort, an effort that would reduce the threat to Washington, D.C., as well as gain a strategic advantage.

The battle took place on July 21, 1861, and both armies revealed how unready they were for war. McDowell's plans to flank the rebels looked fine on paper, as did Beauregard's plans to flank McDowell.

But confusions among men not accustomed to giving, receiving, or comprehending orders in battle situations led to delays and misunderstanding. McDowell's early moves brought success; but then Thomas J. Jackson's Virginians and Wade Hampton's South Carolinians stood "like a stonewall" against Union charges, and the tide of battle turned. When reinforcements arrived for Beauregard, Union forces wavered and then retreated from the battlefield, giving victory to the Confederates. The Union army had suffered casualties of nearly 2,900 men; 460 killed, 1,124 wounded, 1,312 missing. Confederate casualties were estimated at over 1,900.[36]

The defeat at Bull Run disillusioned some Northerners, embittered others, and, surprisingly, satisfied still others. Furthermore, the Southern victory validated preconceptions about the two societies. To everyone, it taught the seriousness of the war and suggested the dimension of the conflict to come. Much of the early enthusiasm had come from believing that the Southerners would back down when faced with a determined and powerful North. Victory thus seemed assured merely by the demonstration of a willingness to fight. There were ninety-day volunteers because of widespread belief that ninety days would be enough.

In addition to its impact on civilians, this confidence limited the willingness of Northern volunteers to submit to military discipline and organization. Visitors to the encamped Union army reported that health and sanitary facilities were either neglected or quickly overwhelmed and then ignored. Soldiers submitted halfheartedly to military drill, believing that it was time to get fighting and stop the parades.

The nature of the Confederate victory shook Northerners out of their arrogant slackness. While most Northern troops had fought with courage and discipline, there were hundreds who had not. They panicked, threw away their weapons, defied officers who tried to turn them back to the battle. Worse, they did so in the presence of an audience of reporters and congressmen who rushed to judgments that all discipline had fled. The uniqueness of the conflict explains some of their impressions. It was the largest battle ever fought on the continent to that time. It took time for men to understand that what they personally had seen was only a portion of the field. But most were unwilling to wait.

Newspapers spoke alarmingly of the panic, the chaos, of the retreat. Senator Lyman Trumbull observed that "literally three could have chased ten thousand." Walt Whitman overheard a colonel talking to "a swarm of officers and gentlemen in a crowded room." This defeat had proved, the officer said, that the best course for the national government was to desist from any further attempt at stopping the rebels, and admit them again to the Union, on the best terms they were willing to grant. "Not a voice was raised against the gentleman," Whitman recalled. "We have sent in Virginia the best . . . of our grand army," another observer wrote. "We have fought the greatest battle ever fought on the continent, and we have been not only beaten, but our army has been routed, and many of its best regiments wholly demoralized."[37]

Despite the numbers of soldiers who had fought well, these criticisms gained a wider audience and called to mind the prewar fears about the North and the martial quality of the enemy. Even during the battle these fears had surfaced. As the Union forces began to retreat, the image of the violent, dashing expert horsemen terrified Northern soldiers. Rumors ran rampant that the rebels would now unleash the "Black Horse Cavalry." What this unit might be no one knew, and ignorance inspired further panic. English journalist William Howard Russell recalled that retreating men told of "blood running knee deep" and of how these stampeding men wailed as they ran "the dreaded cry . . . The cavalry! Cavalry are coming!"[38]

In the aftermath of the battle these fears of the martial South continued and helped to feed doubts about the quality of men that Northern society produced. Many newspapers spoke of commanders running away, or sitting comfortably behind the lines, ignorant of where their underlings were. Faulty strategy was targeted as another sign of failure of high commanders, and battlefield leadership was also said to be inept. General Scott himself told one lieutenant after Bull Run that the South had the best officers. "How we shall make head against them, or how it will all end I dare not say, but my heart is full of doubt and sorrow!" General McDowell was relieved of field command. General Patterson, who was responsible for permitting the Confederates to get the reinforcements that brought them victory, was roundly criticized.[39]

Officers were not the only targets. Although many newspapers insisted that the enlisted men, volunteers, and regulars had fought well, and only needed better leaders, the leaders themselves, unsurprisingly, had another opinion. A member of McDowell's staff told a reporter that "lack of courage and discipline among the troops" was one of the main reasons for defeat. General John Reynolds argued that "you cannot make soldiers of volunteers," and General George Meade told his wife in October that the men he commanded were not soldiers "in any sense of the word." William Tecumseh Sherman saw in the Bull Run failure confirmation of his doubts about the Northern ability to fight: "Democracy has worked out one result . . . brag, but don't perform." As late as January 13, 1862, General Philip Kearny wrote, "Every high officer distrusts (and with reason) our volunteer troops."[40]

But balanced with the mutual recriminations, more positive forces were emerging. Many Northern papers rallied around the flag with admonitions to be firm in the face of adversity. They drew analogies with previous wars to show that after initial defeat other nations had gone on to victory. Recognition began to grow that the war would be something more than a ninety-day romp. Big cities and small towns resounded with renewed dedication. Out in Belleville, Illinois, the local paper proclaimed, "The Grand army in its first encounter with the enemy has met with a decided defeat. . . . It is useless to attempt to characterize it as anything else; no softer term will answer. . . . But all of this will not affect the result; it will only tend to prolong and intensify the struggle. . . . It cannot make our cause less dear to us." The *New York Post* offered a poem to raise martial spirits: "Oh Northern men—true hearts and bold / Unflinching to the conflict press! / Firmly our country's flag uphold, / Till traitorous foes its way confess!" In Congress John Sherman, whose brother had been at Bull Run, pointed the direction of Congress facing the crisis: "We now begin to see the magnitude of the contest in which we are involved; and I believe every American citizen felt, when he read the account of the achievements of our army on last Sunday, and their repulse, only a deeper and stronger determination that, whatever might come, this rebellion should be put down; and with force of arms; and I have no doubt that it will be done."[41]

Action echoed words. Veterans of Bull Run returned home to recruit more volunteers. State governors telegraphed Washington offering new regiments: fifteen from Pennsylvania, ten from Indiana, seventeen from Illinois. New York called for twenty-five thousand new troops. Within two weeks after the defeat more than seventy-five thousand new enlistees signed up for three years of service, and reported for training.[42]

In the training camps and in the already organized armies a new spirit prevailed. Bull Run taught with crimson clarity the need for discipline and organization. Brave men lacking effective discipline had been able to stand only so much in their first day of battle. Only the best-trained units left the field in good order. While the army had insisted that disciplined men were imperative in battle, the opinion had been strong that only extensive training would produce that discipline. Army officials seemed to have assumed that "discipline could not, and need not, be enforced with volunteer troops." Bull Run taught them better. But it also taught that democrats were willing to accept discipline when persuaded of its necessity. Three months after Bull Run Frederick Law Olmstead reported that regulations were being enforced with increased rigor and that "even the demoralized regiments with but very few exceptions, are now in better condition, better spirit, in better health, than they were when they received their order for the advance on Bull Run." Measures that "it was said could not be enforced, would not be submitted to, and would be useless with volunteers, are now rigidly enforced, are submitted to with manifest satisfaction by volunteers and are obviously producing the most beneficial results, and this equally in the new and the older regiments."[43]

Even as the army moved toward greater discipline, social critics outside the military used the post–Bull Run environment to argue for the moral reform of Northern society. Influential Unitarian minister Henry Bellows argued that nothing but the disaster could thoroughly arouse the country to the efforts, the reforms, and the spirit essential to the proper and vigorous conduct of the war. Extolling the "advantage of defeat," Charles Eliot Norton said, "We are not to expect or hope for a speedy return of what is called prosperity. . . . we who have so long been eager in the pursuit and accumulations of riches, are now to show more generous energies in the free-spending of our means to gain the valuable object for which we have gone to war." New England conservative minister Horace Bushnell saw the extension of the war as "God's ordinance for sinners, and they want the schooling of it often. In a time of war, what a sense of discipline is enforced. Here at last there must and will be obedience."

For such men there was something to be happy about in the way that death and disaster turned men away from temporal things. On the last day of 1861 George Strong summed up this feeling that from tragedy might come a stronger republic: "It has been a gloomy year of trouble and disaster, I should be glad of its departure, were it not that 1862 is likely to be no better. But we must take what is coming. Only through much tribulation can a young people attain healthy, vigorous national life. The results of many years spent in selfish devotion to prosperous, easy moneymaking must be purged out of our system before we are well, and a drastic dose of European war may be the prescription Providence is going to administer."

The North was coming to understand what war meant and beginning to believe in its own capacity for victory. It was clear that the Union would find defenders, and there was no lack of advice as to what the lessons of war might be. But who would organize the victory? Who would unite the passion of patriotic amateurs and the knowledge and experience of professional soldiers—bonding them with the discipline necessary for ultimate success?[44]

CHAPTER 3

The Ways of Making War

T HIRTY-five-year-old George B. McClellan appeared to be the answer to a thousand prayers. His professional credentials were formidable. His West Point education had emphasized discipline, order, organization, and expertise. McClellan learned those lessons extraordinarily well, graduating second in his class. He was also an experienced soldier, having fought with distinction in the Mexican War. In addition, he was a respected student of warfare. The army had sent him to the Crimea to study modern tactics, and paid respectful attention to his observations. Civilian experience also validated McClellan's preparation for a modern war. He had been chief engineer and then vice-president of the Illinois Central Railroad. McClellan also spoke several languages, further evidence of his intelligence and discipline. He even looked like a commander with a broad chest and erect military bearing, sitting confidently astride his horse. Furthermore, he enjoyed being called "a Napoleon." William Sherman observed this rising star and called him "a naturally superior man" who had had the "finest opportunities in Mexico and Europe." McClellan seemed to symbolize the model modern professional soldier ready to lead the Northern armies to victory.[1]

But not all elements of Northern society were happy with the modernizing forces that McClellan seemed to represent. The professionalism that marked him as a savior to some inspired anxieties in others. The professional was a product of the transformation

61

of the American economy. Increasing economic and social complexity called forth men with organizational abilities who could direct these forces. The experts organized to separate themselves from that commonsensical world in which everyone could be doctor, lawyer, merchant, chief. Many respected their talents, for they promised direction and control of the vast changes and forces that society was unleashing. They offered discipline to a society whose most common call was for order.

But doubts remained strong. Jacksonian America had protested control over common lives by any elites. Most especially it was angered and frightened about the experts who seemed to be controlling the changing economy in complex and mysterious ways. Perhaps the most basic concern of the worriers was that experts would forget their allegiance to moral principles even as they forged their professional competence. "The interests or God" is the alternative that historian Daniel Calhoun sets forth. He argues that concern was strong that "if [the professional] faltered in devotion to the highest duty, then those other men who held worldly power—property or the means of coercion—might step in and use him as one of their more subtle instruments." But even without the action of others the expert might become not a *hired* gun but a man who simply used his talents for his own amoral selfish purposes. Emerson illustrated the concern in an essay on Napoleon Bonaparte. The great emperor exemplified the genius of modern man shaping his world, Emerson argued, but he was also a dangerous model to others because he lacked a moral vision.[2]

Such concern about powerful men who used their power to dominate others, of course, echoed attacks on slave owners and factory owners, as well as bankers. But military professionals seemed especially worth watching. And Lincoln fed suspicion by noting in his July 4, 1861, address that "in the government's hour of trial, large numbers of those in the Army and Navy who have been favored with offices have resigned and proved false to the hand that pampered them." By contrast, "not one common soldier, or common sailor is known to have deserted his flag."

Still, such anxieties only smoldered at first. Wrapped in the aura of victories in West Virginia, McClellan seemed the answer to meet the needs of the army and also the Union. Radical congressmen, likely to be most antiprofessional, reserved their doubts. The day after the Union loss at Bull Run, on the same day that the young general replaced McDowell as commander of the Federal Army of Virginia, Congress passed almost unanimously the Crittenden-Johnson Resolutions. The resolutions promised that the war was not being "waged . . . in any spirit of oppression or for any purpose of conquest or subjugation, or . . . of overthrowing or interfering with the rights or established institutions of . . . States." The goal of the war was to preserve, not change, the Union: "to defend and maintain the supremacy of the Constitution, and to preserve the Union with all the dignity, equality and rights of the several States unimpaired; and . . . as soon as these objects are accomplished the war ought to cease." They were resolutions that McClellan heartily endorsed and seemed to portend harmony between congressmen of all persuasions and the new army leadership.

But weeks and then months passed, and McClellan did not move the army against the enemy. He organized and reorganized, gathered supplies and equipment, drilled, drilled, and drilled again to discipline soldiers for their enormous duties. At first congressmen were fascinated by this emerging military colossus. They took excursions out to see the stirring spectacle of thousands of men maneuvering with startling precision. McClellan was gathering the largest army since Napoleon's 400,000 had invaded Russia: 190,000 well-equipped soldiers seemed poised and ready. But McClellan kept preparing and not advancing. The fall weather, optimum for marching and fighting, passed, and still the army marched in camp, not toward the enemy.

Growing frustration over McClellan's inaction awakened the anti-professional feelings. By December 1861 Senator Trumbull from Lincoln's state was saying that West Point attitudes could be blamed for the fact that the war "has languished as long as it has." Ben Wade argued that aristocratic West Point trained officers were vastly inferior to "men of genius" who were trained in the field. John Sherman, whose brother was a West Pointer, still asserted that he "did not believe that a military education at West Point has infused into the Army the right spirit to carry on this war." Horace Greeley chimed in: "However imperfect the civil appreciation may be as to military science, common sense is quite as competent as tactical profundity to decide questions of hastening or deferring operations against the rebels."

The attacks on McClellan also targeted the failure of professional soldiers to display any moral commitments. Senator Fessenden grumbled that "I think the military education at West Point is of greatest value to the country . . . but I believe the moral education is a very bad one." Secretary of War Simon Cameron reported on a visit by the Board of Visitors to the Point that warned about too much emphasis on obedience and not enough on morality. Zach Chandler picked up Lincoln's old inference about disloyalty among the officers and spoke of more treason at the military academy than in all the years since the time of Judas Iscariot.[3]

Intimately entwined with accusations about treason and amorality were demands that the war escalate beyond merely saving the Union. By December Congress was no longer satisfied with the Crittenden-Johnson Resolutions. When Democrats asked for a reaffirmation of those resolutions, the House, by a vote of 71–65, said no. Pressures increased to attack slavery, to turn the war into a moral crusade as well as a fight to preserve the Union. Moncure Conway spoke for many who had argued since Bull Run that the Southerners had won that battle because they had a cause, not just an army. "God is not on the side of the strongest battalions," he insisted. "The strongest battalions are on the side of God." Abolitionist speakers became increasingly popular in Washington. Congressmen attended lectures to hear abolitionist ministers denounce the sinfulness of slavery and extol the necessity for emancipation. Forty-three Republican legislators invited Reverend George Cheever to preach an abolition sermon in the House of Representatives in late January 1862. One abolitionist noted that "in Washington, where nothing of the kind has ever been attempted before . . . [abolition lectures given in November 1861] have been more entirely and triumphantly successful than the most sanguine of us dared to hope." There had been something morally arid in all the calculating and preparing and organizing, in treating war as a mere professional problem or legal struggle, Orestes Brownson noted. It was time to proclaim that "the Union is and must be sacred to liberty. Here man must be man, and nothing else."[4]

McClellan's inertia was a focal point for these attacks, but closely related was a fear about his apparent lack of a moral compass. Rumors circulated that McClellan was forging that juggernaut on the outskirts of the nation's capital for personal reasons. To demand that he use that army to attack slavery was in part to ask for reassurances that professional skills and power were morally trustworthy. But McClellan would not move south, and he bitterly opposed turning the war into a moral crusade.[5]

Frustration at inertia fed a more radical mood. Pamphleteers and editors began demanding not only emancipation, but the even more extreme doctrine of arming black men, perhaps even former slaves. And soldiers in the field began to strike out at slavery. In May Benjamin Butler decided to turn the Southern argument that slaves were mere property against Dixie. He announced that slaves coming into his lines were "contraband of war." They would be confiscated. Congress echoed the battlefield in an August law. The First Confiscation Act announced that property used "in aid of the rebellion" might be confiscated by Union armies. Slaves were specifically included. The administration endorsed this measure and supported Butler's actions.[6]

Congressmen began to itch for action. By the end of the first week of Congress' December 1861 session, they had organized the Joint Committee on the Conduct of the War. Comprised of three senators and four representatives, the committee seethed with impatience. It began an effort that would span the war, investigating not only military lethargy but also military contracts, trade with the enemy, hospitals and treatment of the wounded, and the employment of disloyal people in the government. But its greatest efforts were directed at pushing the government toward a more energetic prosecution of the war—toward emancipation, the use of black soldiers, and the appointment of fighting generals.

The committee often revealed its Republican partisanship. McClellan was its special target, and it vindictively harassed and prosecuted Democratic general Stone for months, making him the scapegoat for a minor defeat at Balls Bluff. But the committee also pursued more useful functions. It provided Lincoln with information, and the president used its outspoken criticisms to prod more conservative people toward greater action. The committee worked with Secretary of War Stanton to secure congressional backing for administrative appropriations, policies, and appointments. It served as a constant reminder to generals and the more conservative members of the North that powerful forces were pushing vigorously for taking whatever measures might be necessary to win the war.[7]

Deploring these efforts by politicians to turn the war into a radical crusade, McClellan tried to separate war making from revolution, strategy and tactics from partisanship. He sought to keep the war a business for the professional soldier. He asked the publishers of the *New York World* to "keep the papers and politicians from running over me." For his part, McClellan insisted that he would "pay no attention to popular clamor" but "quietly and quickly as possible, make this army strong enough to give me reasonable certainty that . . . I will win the great battle." In contrast to his own self-image of expertise and decisiveness, McClellan believed that Washington had no plans, and "sat in a state of indecision," pandering to shifting popular moods.

The general's opinion of Lincoln was similar. At first he thought of the president as simply another ignorant political meddler. Gradually his respect increased, but he went only so far as to explain that the president had succumbed to the influence of less principled men. He knew that Lincoln could be influenced because "he was always much influenced by me when we were together." But behind the general's back the radical politicians could work their spells.[8]

Disdain for amateur and conniving politicians led McClellan to keep Congress and the president at arm's length. On at least two occasions the general refused to see his commander in chief when the president came to call. McClellan joked patronizingly about Lincoln—"He will tell everything to Tad"—and he simply had no faith at all in his congressional critics.

McClellan's haughty secretiveness, his known opposition to endangering slavery, combined with this seemingly endless interest in preparing, preparing, preparing, fed congressional hostility. By the end of 1861 the members of the Committee on the Conduct of the War were persuaded that the "Young Napoleon" was incapable of leading anyone to battle. Some saw in him nothing but "infernal, unmitigated cowardice."[9]

For his part, McClellan's personal insecurity and professional pride led him to misunderstand most of his critics. Since he was the expert and they were mere politicians, he could only attribute their opposition to personal ambition. He accused them of, first, trying to rush him into battle so that his unprepared army would lose and he would be discredited. Then they allegedly changed their tactics and tried to deny him the means to attack once he was ready. Their goal in both cases was to prolong the war so that the public would accept in desperation the radical goals of political partisans. And their ambition knew no shame. "I do not doubt that more than half a million men were sacrificed unnecessarily for the sake of insuring the success of a political party," McClellan explained later.[10]

McClellan was not only a professional; he was a young professional, and his youth served him poorly. He was very conscious of the age difference between himself and the older politicians and even generals in Washington. He thought that General Scott was in his dotage and worked to have him removed. On several occasions McClellan noted how impressed the general public and national leaders were by his youth. He contrasted his vigor with that of the cabinet, whom he called a gang of "old geese." Not only were politicians unprofessional, they were also behind the times, and that further nurtured the thirty-five-year-old general's feelings that his perspective on war was unassailable.[11]

But his youth also seems to have unnerved him by the empathy it evoked with his soldiers. He identified with the young men in the ranks, referring to himself as "the young general" and noting how the soldiers called him "our George." With the exception of Lee, no other general in the war seems to have been so beloved by his troops. McClellan encouraged that devotion by calling the soldiers comrades and by the image he projected of this army seeking to do its duty while assailed by enemies on both sides.

He hated to send his comrades out to die. "I am tired of the sickening sight of the battlefield," he wrote his wife in early June 1862, "with its mangled corpses and poor suffering wounded!" And later that month he wrote, "Every poor fellow that is killed or wounded almost haunts me! My only consolation is that I have honestly done my best to save as many lives as possible." He felt "in [my] heart," he told Secretary of War Stanton, "the loss of every brave man who has been needlessly sacrificed." These deaths and his professional knowledge of the complexity of war encouraged McClellan's desire to conduct campaigns only after extensive planning, and to prepare strong defensive positions where soldiers might find some safety. It helped to fortify his feeling that the war must not drag on but should close with one massive irresistible offensive won with minimum bloodshed. While it is certainly true that all Northern leaders wished for such a result, McClellan believed that the most bloodless way to achieve it was not to attack and keep attacking day after day, but to prepare and prepare until with one blow the war would be over.[12]

McClellan's personal inclinations coincided with the dominant public mood at the beginning of the war. Despite the radical trumpets on the left, and impatience for invasions and quick victories, war goals remained conservative. As late as December 1861 Lincoln told Congress, "I have been anxious and careful that the inevitable conflict not degenerate into a violent and remorseful revolutionary struggle. I have therefore, in every case, thought it proper to keep the integrity of the Union prominent as the primary object of the contest on our part. . . . The Union must be preserved and hence all indispensable means must be employed. We should not be in haste to determine that radical and extreme measures, which may reach the loyal as well as the disloyal are indispensable." The delicate condition of Kentucky, administration hopes that Unionists in Dixie might be able to undermine the Confederacy, and the widespread belief that secession and warfare undermined the status quo, endangering order and threatening constitutional government, all argued for restraining potential revolution.[13]

McClellan, modern in his training and outlook but personally anxious and insecure, found security in adhering to a war strategy that focused on conservative goals. He was careful to define the enemy in limited terms. He was not fighting for "the subjugation of the people of any state," nor did he seek "at all a war upon population." His target was simply "armed forces and political organizations." He was careful to insist that his goals were both "constitutional and conservative." He would return the escaping slaves of loyal masters. He would take the property of civilians only in the most urgent cases of military necessity, and then the army would pay the owners. "Pillage and waste should be treated as high crimes; all unnecessary trespass sternly prohibited and offensive demeanor by the military toward citizens promptly rebuked." Above all, any "declaration of radical views especially upon slavery, will rapidly disintegrate our present armies." McClellan needed a war that was confined to the battlefield, a war that trained professionals would control.[14]

This political program was reflected in the general's overall strategy. Seeking to win more "by maneuvering rather than by fighting,"

McClellan planned a grand strategy that if executed might have given the Union precisely the victory he desired. His plan was to quickly take the major coastal and railhead cities of the South that predominantly lay close to rivers. These operations would allow him to use the almost unchallenged naval superiority of the North. Having taken these places, he planned to control the length of the railroads, thus making it impossible for rebels to supply their armies effectively. The rebels would be forced to choose between attacking the entrenched Union rifle positions at these vital places or resigning from the field.[15]

McClellan's caution was not only a product of his professional attitudes and his conservative goals. It was also an imperative born of the complexities of modern mass warfare. Even had McClellan been inclined to be aggressive, the dimension of his task would have restrained him.

He was the first general called upon to organize an army for the greatest war in the nation's history. Compared with any previous effort, the Civil War was gigantic in size, prodigious in complexity, and mind-numbing in its toll. McClellan's job was to create an army capable of conquering a population larger than most nations' in the world at the time, of defeating the largest gathering of soldiers that any American general had ever faced. Furthermore, he had to prepare perhaps the least militaristic society in the world to do so. He would have to teach men who gloried in their individualism to obey orders; teach them how to fight facing weapons that killed with high accuracy at a quarter of a mile; teach them utilizing a thin stack of knowledge as to just how one could fight such a war. The last contest of similar size, the Napoleonic Wars, had been fought with weapons with less than half the range of those of 1860, by experienced professional armies.

McClellan knew the size of his task. Furthermore, having been an observer of the first war using rifles, the Crimean War, he knew firsthand what such weapons could do. He also understood the importance of defensive warfare in such combat, and he understood that amateur armies fought better behind cover, well protected. A defensive strategy was not an ignorant choice in such a circumstance.

Logistics was a problem of equal complexity. The size of the armies made supply and transport almost as important as actual battles. Simply gathering resources was a major task. By mid-war, professionals and veterans were arguing that the best officer was not defined by courage under fire. He was characterized by the preparations he made before the battle, making sure that fighting men had the weapons, the food, the uniforms, the boots, the medicines, the ambulances, the doctors, on which battles turned. He had to make sure that there were enough mules and horses to haul the needed supplies, that the railroads nearby could be scheduled to bring troops and materials in on time. When General Sherman spoke of the military lessons of the war, he described at length the logistical lessons, and hardly mentioned tactics of battle. Sherman spoke of needing to know how many pounds a mule team could pull, the number of wagons needed by an army on the march, the number of men per mile that made for efficient and orderly marching, what foods were acceptable for the men and animals to keep them healthy, the proper types of pontoons necessary for bridges, the proper use of the telegraph, the ways of integrating land and water operations. War at times was, of course, hell, but it was also a huge, complex organizational, supply, and transportation problem.[16]

Furthermore, in the early days of the war the need for new solutions did not make them available. McClellan knew the importance of railroads and the telegraph to the making of modern warfare. But he suffered from the fact that the ways of using them had yet to be discovered. The most efficient telegraph for tactical use would not be developed until 1862. The railroad quickly became the basis for much supply and troop movement, but where McClellan fought he could not make as effective use of rails as could Western commanders. He did work out a very effective system of supplying the army by water, but this took time, for supply departments were as new to their jobs as soldiers were to theirs. The demand for speed also increased the pressure. As Quartermaster General Meigs observed, "A few days or weeks only have been allowed for the outfit of expeditions which other nations would spend months in preparing."[17]

McClellan also lacked maps and experienced intelligence. The maps that he had were so bad that they led armies into totally unexpected places and sometimes promised opportunities that never materialized. McClellan had the terrain surveyed as he marched, producing reliable maps, but later generals would get the greatest benefits from them. Similarly, McClellan's reliance on Allan Pinkerton's organization for enemy size and dispersal led to exaggerated reports. The Pinkertons were inexperienced in estimating such large masses of men. They often counted not only the armies immediately available but also troops that were in the entire theater and that might become available. This led to the belief that Southern forces outnumbered the Army of the Potomac throughout McClellan's tenure. It should be noted that other Union generals such as Fremont, Rosecrans, Buell, Hooker, and even William Sherman overestimated enemy army size, too.[18]

McClellan was the first Union general seriously to face these vast problems. And being "the firstest," he had "the mostest" of them. Grant recognized the enormous challenge that McClellan faced. "The test which was applied to him," he wrote, "would be terrible to any man, being made a major general at the beginning of the war. It has always seemed to me that the critics of McClellan do not consider this vast and cruel responsibility—the war, a new thing to all of us, the army new, everything to do from the outset."[19]

Ready or not, McClellan had to move. Doubts about his moral commitment would only grow while he delayed action. Concerns over his political loyalties could only be dispelled by action. And while anxieties about the ability of Northern society to make war were supplemented by the immense organizational challenges of making a huge modern war, that anxiety would fade only with action. McClellan may well have been right about all the professional elements of war making. But he would have to recognize that more than professional judgments were relevant to bringing Union victory.

Consumed by the great task he saw before him, McClellan delayed and delayed until finally the president ordered him to move. From the executive mansion came General War Order No. 1: "Ordered that the 22d day of February 1862 be the day for a general movement of the Land and Naval forces against the insurgent forces." In case McClellan didn't understand that, Lincoln was even more specific: "especially . . . The Army of the Potomac . . . be ready for a movement on that day."[20]

By March the Army of the Potomac headed into Dixie, beginning the invasion toward Richmond not overland but by sea. McClellan hoped to use the naval superiority of the Union to keep his supply lines open. He believed that by attacking up the peninsula between the York and James rivers he could more quickly move on Richmond. The plan worried the political leaders in Washington. They wanted the Army of the Potomac to move directly south toward the Confederate capital, always between the rebel army and themselves. Lincoln especially feared consequences to Union morale of losing Washington. McClellan argued that the need to counter his army on the peninsula would keep the Confederate forces away from the Northern capital. The proximity of naval support and supply, the massive army he was assembling, would bring a crushing defeat to the rebels in their capital. The war would thus end, the Union be restored, the nation advance unchanged toward its future.

As McClellan's forces were growing on the peninsula, fears were growing in Washington that somehow the enemy would attack the capital. Lincoln thus withheld forty thousand men who were heading for McClellan and kept them to defend Washington. McClellan had counted on these men to be a major part of his advance. Already cautious in his advance, he grew more so. In early April 1862 he began a siege of Yorktown, even though his army outnumbered the rebels by almost ten to one. He felt the loss of the men he had expected and asked for more and more men—he wanted to command a juggernaut. McClellan continually reported that he was outnumbered and would lose his army, and the war, if Washington did not support him. The difficulties of moving so massive an army were immense and he was their expert, so Lincoln backed the general despite doubts. And McClellan's plans and strategy did move him closer and closer to Richmond as the rebels retreated. But the political leaders in Washington grew increasingly upset at the care and caution with which "Little Mac" moved.

McClellan had been right about the need to organize and to discipline soldiers for modern war. And he understood better than the politicians the complexity of mobilizing battlefield victories and campaign success. But after all the plans were laid and the materials gathered and the soldiers made ready to respond to orders and face the terrors of battle, there remained the one indispensable thing— to fight. And in the West a man was emerging who was capable of doing that with such determination that one day he would lead all the Union armies and accept the surrender of Robert E. Lee.

U. S. Grant's contrast with McClellan is symbolically striking.

McClellan, the young professional, successful in civilian life, a leader in his West Point class, author, linguist, adored by his men, united all these talents and built only frustration in the East. Grant had graduated in the undistinguished middle at West Point and failed in civilian life. At thirty-eight he had been reduced to coming back home and asking his father for a job. But as the war began Grant found his genius, found the thing he could do with consummate skill and found it in the West, where that genius could be nurtured and could grow.[21]

In the East the pressures for success were intense, and commanders had few chances to learn from mistakes. The Army of the Potomac went through McDowell, McClellan, Pope, Burnside, Hooker, and Meade before settling on Grant. Western commands were more secure, and the caliber of Confederate commanders made a crucial difference. Lee, Longstreet, and Jackson were the cream of rebel generals; all fought in the East. The four finest Union generals, Grant, Sherman, Sheridan, and Thomas, made their marks in the West. Furthermore, Western geography fostered grander images of war. Campaigns ranged over hundreds of miles, state borders passed under the feet of Union armies, and whole regions, hundreds of square miles in size, passed into Union hands. Western winning streaks on such a grand stage fed the self-esteem of the Western army.

Westerners perceived themselves and the war somewhat differently than did their Eastern colleagues. Soldiers in the Army of the Potomac believed themselves facing the elite of the rebel armies, a feeling Lee and Stonewall Jackson did nothing to reduce. Furthermore, anxieties over Northern capacities to defeat such forces seem to have been stronger. Doubts about the weakening effect of city life and civilization were naturally stronger when armies from the more urban East faced allegedly superior material of an aristocratic and uncivilized South. This seems to have fed McClellan's natural cautiousness.[22]

But by a quirk of fortune Grant found his opportunity away from these influences. He had actually tried to get himself attached to McClellan's command when the younger leader was in Ohio. McClellan, however, was too busy to see his former West Point schoolmate, and so Grant took a different path. Gaining command of Union forces in Cairo, he moved across the Mississippi to his first major battle at Belmont, Missouri, and in a battle that proved every-one's inexperience he first won and then lost the town. While the action got little public attention, it was the first test of battle for his troops. Everyone learned the need for better control of themselves, and Grant learned to maintain a reserve force in case the enemy regrouped.[23]

Still, few people knew or heard much about Grant until he teamed up with the Union river navy and captured first Fort Henry and then on February 6, 1862, ten days later, in an action involving a Union force of about 27,000 men and over 2,800 casualties, took the much more important Fort Donelson. The manner of the taking was elec-trifying. Union forces backed Confederates into the fort, and rebel commander Simon Bolivar Buckner, a friend of Grant's from West Point and the Mexican War, asked for terms. The date was February 16, and McClellan's Eastern forces were still not moving. Then from the West Grant's answer to Buckner showed that somewhere a general understood the necessity for boldness. "No terms except unconditional and immediate surrender can be accepted. I propose to move immediately upon your works." Buckner caved in and 12,000 Confederate soldiers surrendered. Now Tennessee stood open to Union forces, Kentucky was securely in Union hands, and two arteries into Dixie lay exposed. Grant's initials came quickly to stand for "unconditional surrender," and the man himself emerged as an option to McClellan, a symbol of a new conception of the war.

Stanton suggested in a Washington newspaper that it was time for McClellan to show similar aggressiveness. Lincoln, though gripped by concern over the worsening illness of his son Willie, knew of Grant's success. After having spent much of his time badgering McClellan for action and even information, it was a relief to hear of a general who would fight. Charles Dana saw the Donelson victory as "the first significant victory over the rebellion" and contrasted the success of "this unknown man and undisciplined army" with the "perfect equipment and organization" of the Army of the Potomac, which "had not yet begun its forward movement."[24]

With eyes now on him, Grant met resentment from his profes-sional superiors. Henry Halleck had assumed command in the West. He worried about Grant and what the younger man's rise might portend. Halleck doubted that Grant understood the demands and complexities of warfare half so well as his commander did. Halleck was known as "Old Brains" in the army for his study and translation of foreign treatises on strategy, among them works by Jomini. Like McClellan, Halleck was concerned that aggressiveness might be pure rashness. He believed that campaigns had to be carefully planned and organized, and that drill and discipline were the foundations of success. The boldness of Grant threatened both Halleck's plans and his temperament. Grant was a comparatively ignorant upstart, whose civilian failures contrasted with Halleck's civilian successes, and a man known to resort to the bottle as well—the commander was not about to let Grant forget who was in charge.[25]

When Grant advanced after the Donelson victory, he lost touch with headquarters. Halleck grabbed the opportunity. He worked to have Grant relieved, listening to, and then spreading, rumors to supreme military commander McClellan that "General Grant has resumed his former bad habits." But Grant short-circuited Halleck's efforts. He sent Congressman Elihu Washburn a copy of his strong explanation to Halleck of why he had lost touch. Stanton and Lincoln were easily persuaded that they could not afford to lose an officer whose contrast to McClellan was very stark. They told Halleck to either supply particulars of charges against Grant or let him keep his command. Grant kept his command and began his expedition toward a place called Shiloh, Tennessee, near the Mississippi border.

He had also found a friend in William T. Sherman. Sherman had also seen prewar failure, and during the days when Halleck was undermining Grant, he offered encouragement and assisted in supplying his army. Sherman even offered to waive the fact that he ranked above Grant in the command structure should Grant need his aid at the front. And at a moment when Grant's despondency led him to consider resigning, Sherman persuaded him to stay in the army.[26]

With Sherman as his most trusted subordinate, Grant in March began a push down the Tennessee River as part of an overall plan to take Memphis on the Mississippi. But rebel forces, seeking to recoup from the losses at Henry and Donelson, gathered at Corinth, Mississippi, near the Tennessee. The two armies met in a two-day battle on April 6 and 7, which moved Grant further into the limelight at the same time that it brought home inescapably the true meaning of the war.

Although Confederates surprised the Union soldiers and carried the field on the first day, by the second, Union forces had been reinforced enough to drive the rebels back toward Corinth. But the fighting that surged back and forth near Shiloh church left such a scene of death, destruction, and agony that no one could ever again believe in swift victory.

The battle left 23,000 casualties, 1,700 dead on each side, a carnage that made the 4,700 casualties at the first Bull Run pale by contrast. A quarter of the men who fought were casualties. Confederates limped away from Shiloh, and the Union forces let them go, stunned, exhausted by the bloody work that had been done. Grant then knew and the rest of the nation was coming increasingly to recognize the great and awful task ahead. "Up to the battle of Shiloh," Grant later wrote, "I as well as thousands of other citizens believed that the rebellion against the Government would collapse suddenly and soon a decisive victory could be gained over any of its armies." But after Shiloh, "I gave up all idea of saving the Union except by complete conquest." Personal experience explained just what that would mean. "I saw an open field," Grant recalled, "so covered with dead that it would have been possible to walk across the clearing, in any direction, stepping on dead bodies, without a foot touching the ground."

It was in this context that the Union army expanded its targets as it advanced. Previously generals had tried to restrain men from living off the countryside as they marched. Now it became policy to consume everything that could be used to support and supply armies. In August 1862 Grant reported that he was now "ordered to live upon the country . . . directed to 'handle rebels within our lines without gloves.'" A new way of war was being born in the West.[27]

Meanwhile in the East McClellan was moving slowly, cautiously, but inexorably toward Richmond. By May 16, 1862, the Army of the Potomac stood within ten miles of the Confederate capital, and soldiers could hear the city's church bells. Confederate forces kept growing in the area, but McClellan still had twice their manpower. Still, the important thing on a battlefield is not the overall size of an army; it is how many face an enemy at a particular point. Terrain and weather were generating a problem for the Union forces on the peninsula. McClellan had divided his forces into two parts, one north of the Chickahominy River, the other south. Spring rains—

the heaviest in most men's memory—were swelling that usually docile creek into a rushing torrent. Mud and forests made rapid movement extremely difficult. The two parts of the Union force were thus divided. The rebel leader Joe Johnston chose this moment, May 31, 1862, to attack the smaller of the two Union groups at Seven Pines and bloodied it severely. Reinforcements arrived to save it, and the Confederates retreated toward Richmond.

A less cautious Union commander might have rallied his forces for a fast attack, but McClellan's juggernaut strategy prevailed—overwhelming, awesome, inexorable power organized and supported, with every eventuality prepared for, would bring a total victory. McClellan pushed forward slowly, carefully. He rationalized his caution with announcements that he was outnumbered. He fortified his demands for reinforcements by reminding Washington that if his army failed, the Union cause would fail. He dared not lose that army, for, professionally led and organized, it would bring victory, end the war here, now. He simply needed to have enough men and enough time to crush the rebels completely. He would move when he was ready.[28]

In Washington impatience and anxiety prevailed. Anxiety because Stonewall Jackson was engaged in a brilliant raid in the Shenandoah Valley to the northwest of the capital. Impatience because the largest and best-equipped American army that anyone had ever seen, or even dreamed of, had lain apparently idle throughout the fall of 1861 and had practically been ordered to move on the South after ten months of preparation, and now its leader was saying that he needed more of everything just to continue crawling toward the rebel capital. Suspicions grew among some in Washington that McClellan had political ambitions that would best be served by a stalemated war. Lincoln himself told the general that some considered him a traitor. Reasonable men did not go so far, but their frustrations mounted. Secretary of War Stanton was urging Lincoln to throw McClellan out and replace him with someone who would fight; militant Republican congressmen agreed at the top of their voices. The population of the North, never known for its patience about anything, suspicious of the so-called experts, was, in growing numbers, demanding action. It was still early enough in the war that they were not yet resigned to accepting ultimate victory. They wanted it now, and no excuses.[29]

On the peninsula professional concerns dominated. There McClellan faced a new adversary. Robert E. Lee replaced Johnston after the battle at Seven Pines. Lee had no intention of letting the Union commander fight the way he chose. Calling Jackson down from the Shenandoah Valley, he launched an attack on the still divided, if strengthened, Union forces. On June 26 nearly 55,000 Confederates hit a Union force of 25,000 at Mechanicsville. The bluecoats held for a day and then retreated across the Chickahominy, uniting the forces of the Army of the Potomac. But McClellan's communications with forces on the York River had been cut off, and in a masterly maneuver he shifted his entire base from the White House landing on the York to Harrison's Landing on the James. He had had a chance to move on Richmond with 60,000 men against only 25,000 defenders when the rebels hit Mechanicsville (delay had wiped out that opportunity), but the shifting of the base kept the army safe and kept it ready for whatever Lee now planned.[30]

Lee kept the offensive. In strikes at Gaines' Mill, Savage Station, Fraser's Farm, he battered away at the retreating Unionists. It was a strategy forced on him by the extreme danger to the Confederate capital, and he paid a heavy price for having to attack. The greatest of his losses came at Malvern Hill. When rebel armies reached this place they faced entrenched infantry supported by land and naval artillery. Attacking Confederates were slaughtered and Lee had to fall back, leaving McClellan's army safe at Harrison's Landing. The Seven Days campaign had bloodied the Confederates more brutally than it had the Union. Federal losses stood near 16,000: 1,734 killed, 8,062 wounded, 6,053 missing. Confederate casualties were over 20,000 in all: 3,286 killed, 15,909 wounded, and 946 missing. And McClellan's army of nearly 90,000 was still only twenty miles from Richmond.

But forces were at work to pull this army away. McClellan himself contributed by insisting constantly that he was outnumbered. Lee allegedly now had 200,000 men, and the Army of the Potomac must have reinforcements or all would be lost. In fact, Lee had closer to 80,000, and at least one Northern adviser looked in Southern newspapers to calculate the figure as 100,000 fewer than McClellan claimed. But Lincoln and advisers believed the higher figure and worried how they should ever meet McClellan's needs. The president told Attorney General Bates that if he should give the general his 200,000, McClellan would promise a quick advance, but the next day he would wire that Lee had 400,000 and that he could not move. Still, the safest course seemed to be to believe the general. And believing him, they did the very thing that McClellan feared. They ordered him to abandon the peninsula.

Fearing that Lee might pin McClellan's army down with some of his forces and attack Washington, Lincoln relieved McClellan of the overall command of the Army of the Potomac and called him back to the Potomac to reinforce General Pope, the army's new commander, near Manassas. McClellan pleaded against the move; he believed that the politicians were once again undermining potential victory and, worse, sacrificing his beloved troops. But finally he accepted the inevitable and prepared to abandon the peninsula. It was over two years before another Union general brought his troops closer to Richmond.[31]

The apparent stalemate on the Virginia peninsula helped feed the flames for change. McClellan deplored turning the conflict toward radical goals; his July 4, 1862, letter from Harrison's Landing implored Lincoln to reject "confiscation of property . . . territorial reorganization of States . . . forceable abolition of slavery." But his protests reflected the changing shape of the war. As he wrote, Congress was debating a second confiscation measure that directly attacked slavery by confiscating the slaves of anyone who supported the rebellion. In early March Congress had debated a measure to declare rebellious states territories, thus giving Congress complete control over them. The measure had been tabled, but any day might see it spring to life again. And slavery itself had been under siege for months.

Support for emancipation gained and lost strength, but the tide surged with increasing force as months passed. The August 1861 First Confiscation Act, Ben Butler's "contraband of war" order of May 1861, swept toward freedom. But political pressures and the need to keep Kentucky loyal dammed the flow. Lincoln revoked Fremont's proclamation freeing Missouri slaves in September, and deleted a section of a report by Secretary of War Cameron that endorsed freeing and arming escaped slaves. As late as May 1862 the president revoked the order of General Hunter in Georgia and South Carolina emancipating slaves there. But the emancipation tide, propelled by army victories at Forts Henry and Donelson, which drove rebel forces from Kentucky by March, rolled higher. In March Congress ordered Union officers to stop returning fugitive slaves to their owners, and Lincoln asked the border states to give up slavery in return for compensation paid by the federal government. In April 1862 Congress freed the slaves in Washington, D.C. May saw Lincoln still pressuring the border states to accept his emancipation plans. June saw Congress end slavery in the territories, and July witnessed Lincoln's continuing effort to persuade the border states for freedom. When they rejected Lincoln's plan, the time had at last come for the radical step of abolishing slavery by presidential fiat.[32]

On July 13, the day after he had failed to persuade border states to emancipate their slaves, Lincoln attended the funeral of Secretary of War Stanton's baby son. Only five months before, he had buried his own boy Willie, and he knew the meaning of such a death. Yet the pressures of the war were ongoing, and as he rode in the carriage with Secretary of State Seward and Navy Secretary Welles, Lincoln's thoughts turned to emancipation. He had decided to free the slaves, for slavery was clearly "the heart of the rebellion." Emancipation would be a just punishment for slave owners who had begun the rebellion, he told his companions. The time for clinging to the hope that the Constitution might still protect slavery was clearly gone. Furthermore, there would be a military advantage in that slaves would run toward freedom, thus depriving Dixie of needed labor.[33]

Nine days later the president told the full cabinet. He read to them a proclamation he had drafted declaring that all slaves in areas still in rebellion by January 1, 1863, would be freed. All the cabinet officers agreed with the measure's goals, but Secretary of State Seward raised objections that stayed Lincoln's hand. He worried about the timing. The public seemed depressed by recent reverses, and to emancipate now would seem "the last measure of an exhausted government, a cry for help." He urged that Lincoln wait until the measure could come to the country "supported by military success, attended by fife and drum and public spirit." Wait for a victory, he urged the president. Ironically, given his hatred of revolutionary goals, McClellan was to be the instrument of that victory.

While McClellan awaited orders at Harrison's Landing, Lincoln called in John Pope to command a newly formed Army of Virginia, with responsibility for the area around Washington, D.C. Pope came from the West with a reputation for aggressiveness that made him attractive to the president and to Secretary of War Stanton, both frustrated by McClellan's ponderousness. Others knew the new general also to be, in Allan Nevins' words, "a swaggering, muddleheaded egotist." And Pope quickly combined all these qualities in an address to his Eastern soldiers, bragging that the bold armies of the West had always seen the backs of rebels and that it was time to stop thinking about such callow things "as bases of supplies," "lines of retreat," "taking strong positions and holding them." He also issued general orders on foraging by his troops and against guerrilla fighters, which revealed that a more brutal stage of the war was emerging. Attacking McClellan's policy of "gentlemanly war," Pope announced that his army would subsist by foraging what it needed from the farms and houses of Virginians. Payment would be made after the war only if owners could prove their loyalty. Also, the people of northern Virginia were to be held responsible for the attacks by guerrillas on his troops—anyone firing on soldiers would be summarily shot, railroads damaged would be repaired by forced work crews drawn from populations near the ruined tracks. Every disloyal citizen in Virginia taken by the army would face the choice of a loyalty oath or deportation, and anyone who broke his oath would be shot. Threats of retaliation by the South stifled execution of these orders, but they did suggest that the wraps were coming off the war, that McClellan's and Lincoln's earlier hopes for a conservative war were being abandoned in Washington. The probability that the orders had been written by Secretary of War Stanton suggested just how serious a turn the conflict was taking.

As the Army of the Potomac withdrew from the peninsula, General Pope and his army were defeated at the second Battle of Bull Run. Lee and Jackson had outmaneuvered Union forces and, by attacking before reinforcements from McClellan could arrive, pushed Pope back across the old battlefield toward Washington. This time there was less panic and a courageous rear guard action in which two Union generals, Phil Kearny and Isaac Stevens, lost their lives. When Pope returned to Washington he found McClellan there to greet him, for Lincoln had given McClellan the duty of preparing the city's defenses. Soon McClellan was restored to command of all the Eastern forces and went after Lee.

The rebel commander had determined that the time had come to bring the war further north. Perhaps he might detach the slave state of Maryland from the Union even as he outflanked Washington, D.C., from the north. Surprisingly, McClellan moved with great speed to stop Lee's moves. In two weeks he restored the Army of the Potomac to fighting readiness. The men of that army welcomed him back with almost frantic enthusiasm. Now he went looking for Lee and found him with the help of a set of orders lost by a Confederate officer that described the rebel general's plans. Lee turned to meet McClellan, and the armies moved toward the bloodiest single day in American military history.[34]

On September 17, 1862, at Antietam Creek in Maryland, the two armies met. During the day over twenty-three thousand men fell, and almost twelve thousand of them died, either immediately or later from their wounds. More men fell on that single day than died in the War of 1812, the Mexican War, and the Spanish-American War combined. Four times more casualties resulted from Antietam than from the fighting on D-Day in World War II. The Eastern war now had a bloodbath that matched, indeed, that incredibly surpassed Shiloh.[35]

It might have been a total victory for the Union forces. For after the seventeenth, McClellan had almost twenty thousand fresh troops that he had not committed to the battle. Lee's army had been brutally mauled. His back was to the Potomac, and a Union advance would have crushed his forces. The death of the Confederacy was within sight. But the carnage was stunning, and McClellan's caution mastered him once more. Even as Lincoln, Stanton, and Halleck awaited news of the destruction of the Army of Northern Virginia, that army was slipping quietly across the Potomac, retreating onto friendly soil.

McClellan claimed a great victory. "I feel some little pride," he wrote his wife, "in having, with a beaten and demoralized army, defeated Lee so utterly and saved the North so completely." "I have the satisfaction of knowing that God has, in his mercy, a second time made me the instrument for saving the nation." He spoke of once more having to reorganize the army to prepare for a future campaign, of working to get the most complete and careful figures on losses at Antietam. He dared not go after Lee without preparation, for were he to lose, the entire North would be open to the rebel armies. He thought of everything, prepared for everything, and while he did, Lee's army had the chance to regroup and sustain the Confederate cause.[36]

The Union victory at Antietam allowed Lincoln to issue the preliminary Emancipation Proclamation, and that fact appalled McClellan. His position was already almost intolerable, what with Stanton and even General Halleck undermining his efforts. And now, "the President's late proclamation . . . render[s] it almost impossible for me to retain my commission and self-respect at the same time." Meanwhile, his opponents had other reasons for urging his retirement. Stanton in the War Department had given up on him long before, and the escape of Lee to fight again fortified his feelings. Furthermore, he was angered when the general publicly referred to the proclamation by saying that the "remedy for political errors . . . is to be found only . . . at the polls." Horace Greeley reported that around McClellan's headquarters one could hear a great deal of disloyal talk. The abiding hostility of radical congressmen and abolitionists added to the outcry that even this victorious general would have to go, if his victories were as halfhearted as his moral convictions.[37]

Lincoln dragged his feet for a while. The 1862 elections were coming up. He also wondered who was going to take his tarnished Napoleon's place. Perhaps he could push McClellan into aggressive action. But finally on November 7, 1862, elections behind him, he removed the general from command and replaced him with Ambrose Burnside. McClellan waited for another assignment, but it never came; and while he waited, he prepared to run for the presidency as a Democrat, the party whose motto was "The Constitution as it is; the Union as it was."[38]

As McClellan was relieved, important Northern papers agreed on an epitaph. "We think we can see plainly how his troubles all arose," the *New York Tribune* approvingly quoted the *Philadelphia North American.* "The primary dogma of West Point is the theory of adequate preparations, and the nation in this war, the first waged under West Point influence, is paying dearly for its whistle in the enormous outlay of money for matériel of war and the astounding levees and waste of human life. General McClellan naturally followed his mentor." But with McClellan removed, the natural wisdom of the people would make its way forward. "It is at length becoming felt that the practical education acquired in this war by our soldiers is worth infinitely more than all the teaching of the schools."[39]

But the epitaph was characteristic of epitaphs. It spoke not of complex reality, but of lessons writers and readers wanted to hear, appealing blends of truth and falsehood. The theory of adequate preparation was not a casualty of war. Practical soldiers were learning the importance of preparation; blood-gorged battlefields guaranteed that. But generals were also learning to trust their troops, learning that professional wisdom needed to be entwined with amateur courage in this stupendous conflict. These were lessons that Grant and Sherman would absorb and refine.

Behind the lines other lessons were being learned as well. New visions of just what practicality meant were being born. Reforming ideas, once considered extreme, were now sounding more like common sense. Rapid changes in the society and economy as a whole were now beginning to find a direction, a focus: forging victory, giving purpose to the lives, the limbs, the fortunes being lost. The conservative ideals McClellan hoped to use his modern talents to achieve were increasingly at risk. It was time for the political system to take upon itself the challenges of accommodating to the transformations of war, a time for Americans to debate what was so desperately at stake, to bring the world of abiding values and changing needs into meaningful dialogue.

CHAPTER 4

The Dialogue of Politics, 1861–1862

THE outbreak of war challenged the life of the national political system. Southern secession seemed to demonstrate the failure of politics to resolve fundamental issues. Within the North itself questions were also raised. In such an enormous struggle for the life of the republic, would political dialogue continue to produce responsible alternatives? Passion for politics remained, ingrained in the prewar experience. But what kind of politics would war bring?

Just after Sumter the answer seemed to be that political dialogue would become a monologue. Northerners rallied to save the system represented by the Union and the government. Partisanship all but vanished. Stephen Douglas rushed to Lincoln's side right after Sumter and emerged from the White House to say, "There are but two parties, the party of patriots and the party of traitors. [Democrats] belong to the first." In a widely circulated letter Douglas declared that "there is but one path of duty left to patriotic men . . . it is a question of government or no government, country or no country . . . we should never forget that a man cannot be a true Democrat unless he is a loyal patriot." Eastern Democrats agreed. New York City mayor Fernando Wood said, "I know no party now." New York State party makeweight Horatio Seymour, traveling in the West when war began, spoke at rallies urging unity in time of crisis. He helped to recruit a regiment and to pay part of its travel expenses to the East. In many Northern states local and state party conventions stopped meeting, and the Democratic party faithful set out to recruit regiments.[1]

Gratified by this support from old enemies, the Republicans still saw a chance to expand their constituency. To their way of thinking, the party and the nation would both benefit. Democratic policies had spawned secession. A unified section under Republican aegis would advance the fight for national survival even as it supported the other party measures. Efforts were begun to create bipartisan organizations under a "Union" party banner. While Republicans dominated these groups, they asked Democrats to join them. Lincoln assisted this effort, appointing Democrats and former Democrats to his cabinet and offering military commands to men of both parties. He also set conservative war goals that would appeal to Southern Unionists (his primary target) but might also attract conservative Democrats. The Union party appeared in the elections of fall 1861 and elected governors in Ohio and Rhode Island and major state officers in New York. Even some old organization Democrats like Daniel Dickinson supported this new party, saying that "all loyal men should enter it heart and soul."[2]

Many Democrats did join the Union party, continuing a prewar trend of desertion to Republican ranks that already included Salmon Chase, Hannibal Hamlin, Lyman Trumbull, Gideon Welles, and Montgomery and Frank Blair. Enlisting shortly after Sumter was Edwin Stanton, and a short time later came future president Andrew Johnson. Such defections were predictable in the early patriotic tidal wave. The Democratic party pulled in its horns, fearing that anything short of bipartisanship might sound like disloyalty. Nevertheless, the nation's oldest political institution stayed alive even while muting its trumpets. In fact, Democrats used the enthusiasm for popular rule to remind voters that a healthy party system promoted Union-saving efforts and that effective policies on nonwar questions required the crucible of political debate. While only Clement Vallandigham and a few other future peace partisans counseled obstruction to every Republican effort, party loyalty abided, waiting for the opportunity to express itself. The defeat at Bull Run was that opportunity.

The Union defeat alerted Northerners that the conflict would be more than a ninety-day romp. It confirmed Democratic predictions that Southerners were deadly serious in their commitment to their cause and that any war could disrupt nation and society. Republicans who had minimized the crisis were now proved wrong. Democrats now spoke up—attacking Republicans for the Bull Run debacle and for measures that promised to prolong conflict. On the other hand, defeat inspired Republicans to stronger efforts and intensified devotion to their goals. Such behavior in turn inspired Democratic partisanship, and political debate was reborn.

The most immediate impact of the renewed Northern efforts appeared as Union soldiers returned to their homes after Bull Run to recruit more regiments as well as to inspire increased patriotism. They arrived to find Democrats attacking the administration. Veterans responded by leading angry mobs that destroyed offending newspapers and threatened Democratic speakers. Republican leaders spoke out publicly against the violence but often were secretly pleased that "the people" had shown opponents the limits of wartime dissent. At times mob violence was replaced by government suppression. News began to reach Democratic readers of the intimidation of the Maryland legislature by army soldiers, and John Merryman's arrest, in which the army and the president defied the chief justice of the United States. Taney's opinion, an eloquent defense of civil liberty despite its legal confusions and practical ignorance, soon appeared regularly in Democratic organs and speeches. Party members began to mine the riches of the civil liberty issue.

Seriously concerned about the suppression of speech and press, since they were uniformly the targets, Democrats also saw the political value of defending constitutional liberty. Within three weeks of the Bull Run battle Ohio's Clement Vallandigham wrote gleefully of party rejuvenation:

Light is beginning to last to break upon us. The vindication of free speech in Congress and the Battle of Manassas—the two great events of the age —are opening the eyes of the people to the true origin, character and magnitude of the war. The maintenance of the organization and integrity of the Democratic party give us an ancient and still admirable machinery wherewith to rally the masses and to save the Constitution and public and private liberty and I hope—it is the desire of my heart—to restore the Union, the Federal Union, as it was forty years ago.[3]

Events in Congress, enmeshed as they were with growing opposition to Democrat McClellan's efforts, also renewed political rivalry. In July Congress passed by large and bipartisan votes the Crittenden-Johnson Resolutions, limiting the war to conservative goals: the preservation of the Union and the restoration of the rule of law ante-Sumter. Conspicuously absent, and thereby satisfying to Democratic leaders, was any threat to slavery. But by August moves to energize the Northern effort led to the First Confiscation Act, authorizing the confiscation of property used in the rebellion, slaves included. The measure split Congress on party lines. Only six Republicans opposed the measure. Only three Democrats favored it. By the time Congress reassembled in December 1861 the bipartisan spirit was gone. McClellan was under attack as a Democrat as well as a sluggard. Party politics as usual had revived. Democrats would fight Republicans throughout the war. While usually supporting bills that supplied and armed the soldiers, they maintained a passionate opposition to other Republican policies.[4]

Sheer numbers gave Republicans political dominance in Washington. Secession had cost the Democrats almost half of their voting strength. The Thirty-seventh Congress that sat first in December of 1861 had 105 Republicans and only 43 Democrats in the House and 31 Republican and only 10 Democratic senators. The Democrats had lost 49 House and 16 Senate seats since the last Congress. At the national level Lincoln's party would have its own way.

But these figures undervalue Democratic power. The persistent loyalty of voters to party endured throughout the war, and margins of victory for Republicans were narrow in crucial districts. In the 1864 presidential election Democrats received 45 percent of the popular vote, and their total vote in the North actually increased by almost 450,000 over 1860. It fell only 30,000 votes short of the combined Northern and Southern party vote in 1856. While Lincoln's 1864 margin was the largest in any election since Jackson, Democrats retained strength. In the central bloc of states from Connecticut to Illinois, where national elections were won or lost, the party actually increased its percentage of the vote between 1860 and 1864. In many crucial states a switch of only 5 percent of the votes could bring Democratic victories.[5]

The strength of the Democratic party during the war strengthened the Union effort. Republicans attacked their opponents as the party of "Dixie, Davis, and the Devil," but without their rivals the war effort could have suffered. Democrats protested Lincoln's "tyranny" and defamed the Republican party as "violent and revolutionary," engaged in a "reign of terror" guided by "malignant and bigoted intolerance," but the Union effort thrived on this passionate dialogue. Democratic strength molded Republican unity and energized party institutions, providing the benefits of party that had evoked so much admiration before the war.[6]

The Union had a political vitality and coherence the Confederacy lacked. Northern political parties kept dissent within limits and were rallying points for patronage. They organized divergent viewpoints into effective platforms. In the Confederacy disgruntled opponents of the government could neither channel their efforts into electoral politics nor fear that their activities would give power to political rivals. Alexander Stephens, vice-president of the rebel government, became President Davis' most vocal critic and ultimately helped the governor of Georgia to align the state behind a peace movement. Robert Toombs had been Davis' closest challenger for the presidency. After five months as secretary of state he resigned, tried a generalship without success, and then turned on Davis as "a false and hypocritical wretch." Davis could threaten neither man with loss of position within the party. He could not point out the political costs of a divided party. There were no parties in Dixie.[7]

By contrast, Lincoln's vice-president, Hannibal Hamlin, although representing a different wing of the Republican party, worked loyally for his president and then stepped down when political necessity and Lincoln called. He campaigned for the 1864 ticket of Lincoln and Johnson and received for his loyalty the collectorship of the Port of Boston, one of the patronage plums in party hands.

William Seward had been the favorite for the Republican nomination in 1860, but lost to Lincoln. The new president quickly awarded him the most prestigious cabinet post, secretary of state. Seward campaigned actively for Lincoln in 1860 and used his own party connections to advance Union efforts. He fought with more radical Republicans within the cabinet but kept his quarrels within the system, advising Lincoln on party as well as policy matters. He was rewarded with patronage and with the ear of the president. Seward knew that to break with Lincoln would have high political costs. He also knew that internecine war within his party would only help the Democrats. He kept his peace and his place.

State governors in both "nations" also demonstrated the political differences between the two sides. Northern governors were in large percentage Republicans. Ideologically committed to party goals, they also had the political obligation to support the leader of their party. Federal patronage spread into state realms and could be used effectively. Lincoln sustained Republican governors by allowing them to control the appointment of high military officers and by following their advice when possible on civilian appointments. When elections came in the North the administration was ready with furloughs for soldiers in the field, so that they could go back and elect Republicans. The president used the patronage to help party regulars at the state level. Federal arsenal and ordinance workers were expected to support Republican candidates. Cabinet officers appeared at political rallies to support state Republicans. The administration used the institutions of politics to sustain the war effort. The necessity for this political activity, the possibility of Democratic victories, served to bind together the state and national Republicans and thus to strengthen the political structure.

By contrast, Dixie's disaffected governors felt little or no pressure to obey Jefferson Davis. They might do so out of a shared sense of duty to the cause, but when they perceived the cause differently they turned on their national leader. No political opposition threatened Confederate governors. No political rewards could restrain them. Governors Brown of Georgia and Vance of North Carolina became bitter opponents of Davis, undercutting war efforts especially in the conscription area, publicly and privately denouncing him as a tyrant and working to defy his policies. Opposition became personal, fed by a long-standing Southern tradition of personal politics and passionately defended honor. Sharing the tradition, Davis fought within it and suffered accordingly.[8]

In the North a healthy, if often bitter, political diversity reigned, springing to life in the beginning of 1862. The Bull Run defeat had given the Democrats a rebirth, and the frustrations of the conflict fed its strength. Northerners had expected to win easily and did not yet understand, as they would in time, that the war would be long and demanding of their endurance as well as their patriotism. By 1863 they would understand this fact, but 1862 found them frustrated by the failure to gain an early victory, not yet reconciled to slugging it out. Furthermore, in the second half of the year the war took on such revolutionary dimensions that Democrats found it impossible to refrain from all-out and violent opposition. By late

1862, as they prepared for fall elections, they had reason to believe that such a posture pointed the path to victory.

Throughout the war the Democratic party stood for conservatism, for tradition, for restoration, for maintaining. They were the nay sayers who offered no new programs, no new policies, no new approaches to fighting the war. Emerson had once drawn the balance between "the Party of Hope" and "the Party of Memory." The dichotomy fit the Republicans on the one hand and the Democrats on the other. For every Republican yes there was a Democratic no. There were no notable Democratic yeses. Traditionally the Democratic party opposed government action; Democratic leaders proudly noted that their party was, in Horatio Seymour's words, "a let alone party," while Republicans were "a meddling party." One angry Democrat cursed the Republicans because they "look exclusively to the future. Their Policy is purely present and original. They are a band of reformers, with new schemes, new doctrines, and new purposes to promulgate and establish."[9]

History set the path of Democratic doctrine. From the time of Jefferson's opposition to the First Bank of the United States to Jackson's veto of the recharter of the second, dominant party rhetoric spoke of keeping government action at a minimum, allowing the people themselves to gain their goals on their own initiative. Democratic presidents had stopped not only banks but internal improvements and charitable reform activities as well as educational efforts by the government. With the very large exception of efforts in behalf of slavery, Democrats had lived on the ideals of laissez-faire.

Constituent concerns also nurtured Democratic negativism. Immigrants, especially Irish Catholics, were drawn to a doctrine that attacked the power of government. They were attracted to the rhetoric of revolution that had swept Europe from the time of the French Revolution and had proved the ideological foundation for liberalism in the Old World. Democrats gained allegiance also by contrasting their own tolerance for differences with a growing Know Nothing nativist spirit that attacked immigrant culture and ideals. They defended the right of immigrant ethnic communities to preserve their culture against the temperance and Sabbatarian ideals of Puritan reformers. In the white South this hands-off philosophy, of course, was especially appealing. Southerners joined Northern Democrats in deploring the Republican compulsion "to meddle with everything . . . to force their uncongenial puritanical creed down the throats of other men and compel them to digest it under pains and penalties." Pointing to the linkage between Republican allegiance and the temperance crusade, the Know Nothing movement, and abolitionism, Democrats cried "enough." In a highly pluralistic society they deplored "the evils of political meddling with morals, religion, and the rights of distinct communities." Imposition of cultural unity in such a nation was arrogant tyranny, Democrats charged. People in the North with family and cultural links to Dixie joined this alliance of immigrants and slavery supporters. Democrats also included wealthy men with economic ties to the enormously important national and international cotton trade, and people who simply were Democrats by the tradition of their families or communities. While the Democratic party shared with Whigs and Republicans a fuzzy commitment to liberty and the nation, it still was distinct. It was the party of conservative values. Democrats were supremely qualified for their role as opposition party during the war; some might say overqualified.[10]

Democratic conservatism took many forms. The one they were proudest of was their role as defenders of "the Constitution as it is; the Union as it was." Republicans, of course, also claimed the Constitution as their own. Throughout the war they sought and found legal precedent to support their programs. Republican platforms and leaders spoke to the people about constitutional commitment. Lincoln's first two major addresses spent about one-third of the time discussing constitutional ideas. The 1864 Republican national platform led off its eleven planks with four resolutions supporting the national charter.

But Democratic constitutionalism differed from Republican. Lincoln's party sought new directions, discovering in the Constitution meaning and principles that expanded national power and encouraged economic, governmental, and social change. Republicans were trying to weave constitutional sail. Democrats, however, were forging constitutional anchor. Their unwavering insistence was that, as one leader put it, "the Constitution is as binding in war as in peace." Another spokesman announced that "since its inception [the Democratic Party] steadfastly denied that circumstances should affect the application or enforcement of the cardinal doctrines it professed." The purpose of the war was not to change anything but "simply to subdue, destroy, and scatter the rebel armies, leaving the rights of northern citizens and the property of southern slaveholders just where the Constitution leaves them." Clement Vallandigham declared that both Southern secessionists and Northern abolitionist Republicans were engaged in a rebellion against the constitutional system. Anyone who wished to make war for any other purpose than to maintain the Constitution "as it is," he proclaimed, "will be guilty of a flagrant breach of public faith and of a high crime against the Constitution and the Union." The images Democrats used to depict the Constitution conveyed their belief in its unchanging nature: "a rock," "an ark of safety," "a sheet anchor," "our shield and protector." Their cartoonists consistently drew pictures of the Constitution as a pillar being shaken or crumbling under attacks by Republicans. By contrast, Republican cartoonists depicted Lincoln trying to fight off an attacking South with a shackle of Democratic constitutionalism wrapped around his leg.[11]

Constitutionalism expanded beyond legality to a sense of holding back the changes and transformation of war and society itself. In a long pamphlet attacking Lincoln's suspension of the privilege of the writ of habeas corpus, Edward Ingersoll declared that the issue between the parties was between revolution and stability. "Conservatism is our only chance of safety. Conservatism of our own American institutions; such as our forefathers gave . . . to attempt to throw them aside is as great administrative madness in the emergency as it is indicative of popular madness to be willing to relinquish them." War Democrat Samuel Cox drew the line between Democrats and Republicans in terms of strict and loose construction of the Constitution. But the two positions were more than legal perspectives, for "a loose construction of law tends to loose government. Loose government leads to loose morals."[12]

Seeking to be heirs of a tradition of republicanism in the United States, Democrats expanded their constitutional arguments to call forth the spirit of the American Revolution. Their attacks on military arrests and the draft echoed ancient arguments about the evils of standing armies. Their critique of Republican economic policy spoke of taxation crushing the people and further subjecting them to the power of a distant government that would use the taxes and the newly created federal bureaucracy for further intrusions on the lives of ordinary citizens. In S. S. Cox's words, Americans would be "crushed between perpetual debt and standing armies." Suspicious of power generally, Democrats had cried conspiracy against the "Monster Bank." They now alleged that Republicans conspired with wealthy, distant interests to make war for their own purposes. Alternatively, Republicans were allegedly guided by "high steeple . . . plotters and cabalists" from New England dripping with the "slime" of abolitionism. One Northern Democrat spoke of the "contest between the advocates of constitutional liberty on one hand and base conspirators on the other."[13]

Democrats had learned their past catechism very well. That catechism was in large measure a protest against the changes in society that the Republicans advocated. Democrats opposed national banks, higher tariffs, and internal improvements, indeed the entire second "American system" that constituted the Republican program for the war years. But Democratic opposition also was diffuse as well, reflecting the limited understanding of the transformations that were under way. Democrats simply did not want government action to control or direct change in any form. They wanted to be left alone.

These sentiments crystallized around the general Democratic hostility to "the Yankee"—a target for Jackson's party almost as frequent as the disloyal "copperhead" was for Republicans. The image of the Yankee not only included the Puritanical meddler and the moralistic fanatic, it encompassed images of Northeastern materialism and commercialism with its corrupting uncontrolled tyranny in economic matters. The Yankee image revivified the old Bank of the United States monster and spoke especially to Midwesterners of the dangers of Eastern dominance of the economy of the West. The same newspapers and politicians who deplored the moral tyranny of nativism, abolitionism, and temperance lambasted Republican economic measures as well. When Congress passed the Morrill Tariff in 1861 Democratic papers attacked this outreach of Eastern power. The *Cincinnati Enquirer* declared that New England was "determined that the whole country shall be subservient to the interest of her manufacturers; and having driven the South out of the Union, she wants additional burdens put upon the West to make up for the loss of the Southern Market." A similar litany was recited against the Republican-backed paper money and national banking legislation. The focus of their attacks was "Yankee shrewdness," "oligarchs of

New England privilege," "roundheads," "Puritan patriots who were fattening on the spoils of war," and "New England terrorism under Lincoln."[14]

The most compelling of the weapons in the Democratic arsenal was racism. While calls to preserve the Constitution unchanged and the Union intact might appeal to both head and heart, the racist appeal struck deeper. It enflamed sexual anxiety, played on economic insecurity, and fed fears of loss of control to people buffeted by the changes around them. Democrats circulated broadsides showing blacks as beasts embracing young white women. (The women in question were usually presented as acquiescing in this alleged horror, suggesting the depth of anxiety being probed.) Democratic editors and orators repeated endlessly the accusation that the "black Republicans" meant to unleash black workers who would rush north and take away laborers' jobs. The *Columbus Crisis* (Ohio) warned of the Republican attempt "to mix up four millions of blacks, with [our] sons and daughters." The *Chicago Times* complained of a flood of "two or three million semi savages" rushing north if Republican reformers had their way. The *Cincinnati Enquirer* spoke of "hundreds of thousands, if not millions of slaves [who] will come North and West, and will either be competitors without white mechanics and laborers, degrading them by the competition, or they will have to be supported as paupers and criminals at the public expense." The Society for the Diffusion of Political Knowledge, a Democratic National Committee organization, printed and distributed a pamphlet in 1863 defending slavery as blessed by the Bible. In 1864 another pamphlet entitled "Miscegenation Indorsed by the Republican Party" continued the theme. Democrats injected the race question into attacks on the tariff, higher taxes, greenbacks, and inflation during the war and carried the theme over into postwar measures such as the purchase of Alaska and the building of the Southern Pacific Railroad. Somehow, all these activities were allegedly either inspired by black Republicans' pro-Negro sympathies or would redound to the benefit of blacks but not whites.[15]

The use of the black as bugbear resonated as a potent emotional symbol of vague and ambiguous fears about a world out of control. In the mid-nineteenth century the minstrel show had flowered, bringing out millions of Americans to laugh and ridicule the blacks. These most popular of all American entertainments were entirely devoted to degrading Negro Americans, ranging in their targets from sexually aggressive and dishonest "Zip Coon" through tolerant and lazy old "Uncle Ned," happy in his slavery, to the violent "Nat the Brute." These symbols reinforced white ideas that degenerate blacks were incapable of either a personal or political self-government. They endorsed a permanent, secure racial universe where continuity could be assured by placing society's and nature's basest humans at the bottom. In areas of the nation with the greatest observable contrast between white classes—the South, big cities, southern parts of the Old Northwest—the racist argument sold best. This was Democratic country.[16]

In sum, the Democratic party, given new voice by the loss at Bull Run and provoked by Republican partisanship, by early 1862 relit the fires of party struggle and advanced its litany of conservatism. The old negative creeds found new echoes in a war atmosphere that to Democrats seemed pregnant with potential revolution. Their response was summarized in the party slogan: "The Constitution as it is; the Union as it was; the Negroes where they are." The words evoked a world that featured a restricted Constitution, a restored Union of slave and free states, blacks consigned to slavery in Dixie and inferiority in the North, governments keeping hands away from personal enterprise, reformers keeping their meddling to themselves. It was a world where things were let be, where men were left free, where things were left as they were, or had been, in some idyllic America.

But Republicans would not "let it be." They were the counterimage to self-projections by Democrats and hence another way for Jefferson's party to define itself. From its first days the new Republican party proclaimed itself "Wide Awakes," the party of action, energy, vigor. They spoke constantly of self-made men, controlling their own fate. Attacking Buchanan as "an old woman," deploring lack of backbone in the face of Southern demands, Republicans promised to stand up like men. As Ronald Formisano describes the new Michigan party, "Republicans talked ever of 'backbone.' Democrats and doughfaces lacked it; Republicans had it and would face up to the 'chivalry.'" Furthermore, the new party adopted active government support for economic growth, linking government and private energy to forge a richer and stronger nation. To Democrats, this ceaseless molding, shaping, pushing, controlling, like relentless, irresponsible machines, threatened the destruction of liberty and stability. And the war, the Republican war, spawned by irresponsible agitating, transformed from a fight to maintain into a chance to revolutionize, forging new potentials for tyranny with every outreach of power, now seemed to bring to fruition every Democratic nightmare. The party of Jackson reaffirmed its conservatism in this apparently revolutionary struggle.[17]

As 1862 proceeded, Democrats saw signs of revolutionary change everywhere. Congressional Republican majorities were passing legislation that Democrats had been able to defeat for years. Now the North was gaining paper money, specie payments to banks had been suspended, a homestead act assured the victory of free soil in the territories, and legislation outlawing slavery in the territories insured the victory. Popular sovereignty was dead. State sovereignty, which had expanded slavery, was buried. The government was offering support to the building of a railroad to the West, and a huge revenue act, taxing a vast range of commodities and even including an income tax, skipped through Congress. A high tariff seemed to benefit the manufacturers at the expense of ordinary workers. Out in Iowa Democrat Dennis Mahoney warned about "the Massachusetts school of politics which would raise the tariff, substitute paper money for specie and create the legal and social distinction of classes in community and society by which capital shall become the rule and poverty the serf." Ohio's Vallandigham spoke of a burgeoning power in Washington, ominous for liberty in state and community. "Every dollar more borrowed or collected and every dollar spent is just added to the power and value of the executive office." Lincoln was organizing a faith "whose priests are a hundred and fifty thousand and whose worshippers are a whole army of jobbers and contractors." "Shall we sink down as serfs to the heartless, speculative Yankee for all time," another student of feudalism asked, "swindled by his tariff, robbed by his taxes, skinned by his railroad monopolies?" Western Democrats, linked by the Mississippi River to Southern markets as well as by kinship to Southern relations, were most interested in this economic imperialism argument. Republicans challenged these Jacksonian attacks by asserting that Democrats had "a natural prejudice toward all modern forms of progress, particularly banks, corporations and even railroads."[18]

Eastern Democrats were less interested in protesting the power of Eastern economic interests, but they, too, targeted the "revolutionary" Republicans in the 1862 elections. Horatio Seymour and Samuel Tilden in New York took a rather high road in terms of constitutionalism generally. Their major fears focused on the growing power of the national government in civil liberties questions, the arbitrary arrests of anti-administration spokesmen, the closing of newspapers, all forecasting a transformation of national government that would revolutionize the federal republic from the domain of ordered liberty to an arbitrary despotism. As one Democratic partisan wrote to party wheelhorse Samuel Barlow, "As this war has progressed the many necessities of the case have so trenched upon the Constitution as to have done and to do more to make out a case for Revolution than all other causes combined since the formation of the government."[19]

But economic and even constitutional revolution paled beside the major issue of the campaign, the revolution in race relations portended by the September 22 preliminary Emancipation Proclamation. Here was an issue that Eastern and Western Democrats could play to the hilt with their constituencies and with it even hope to reach nonparty conservatives in the North. Western Democrat William Allen of Ohio proclaimed that "every white laboring man in the North who does not want to be swapped off for a free nigger should vote the Democratic ticket." New York Democrats unfurled visions of revolutions in Santo Domingo, describing the proclamation as a measure "for the butchery of women and children, for scenes of lust and rapine, and of arson and murder." The proclamation, another Democratic source insisted, "draws the line between those who wished to see the Constitution preserved and those [who] wish to see it destroyed." Another decried such "experimental legislation, ending no man can tell in what unforeseen disaster." Once again the broader Democratic theme of the destruction of the social order also echoed throughout protests against the proclamation. "The primal sin of disobedience is not only the immediate cause of this war, but its spirit has also sapped and weakened the foundations of our . . . authority in every part of our land. . . . Obedience is the basis of all family, political and religious organizations. It is the principle of cohesion that holds society together, without which it crumbles to atoms. Yet we have seen a disregard of this vital principle. . . .

We have heard disobedience to laws taught in our pulpits, and commended by the press."[20]

Republicans answered the 1862 charges of their foes with charges of Democratic disloyalty. They backed up these charges with a bold outreach of natural power. Two days after the preliminary Emancipation Proclamation Lincoln suspended the privilege of the writ of habeas corpus throughout the month. Republican candidates demonstrated the need for the suspension by releasing a report in Indiana on an alleged conspiracy by the Knights of the Golden Circle to give the lower Midwest to the Confederates. They insisted that the true issue was support for the government in its hour of crisis or abandonment of the Union cause. Nominee for governor James Wadsworth in New York asked, "What can any honest patriot do but sustain and strengthen Abraham Lincoln? Let him be sustained. . . . Gentlemen, I stand by Abraham Lincoln."

Most Midwestern Republicans responded to the racial arguments of Democrats by pandering to constituent prejudices. One Republican editor told Salmon Chase that the best strategy was to declare that "[blacks] don't want to come North and we don't want them unless their coming will promote the conclusion of the war. Our newspapers ought to advocate this view persistently, and demonstrate that even our free colored population would go South if they were secure from sale into slavery." Even radical governor Andrew of Massachusetts was quoted in the Midwest as opposing any influx of blacks into the North, since they would be "paupers or sufferers . . . to a busy community where they would be incapable of self-help —a course certain to demoralize themselves and endanger others. Such an event would be a handle to all traitors and persons evenly disposed." State Republican conventions in Illinois and Michigan endorsed emancipation as a war measure but ignored any humanitarian justifications.

A few Republicans in more radical sections and states did accept the proclamation as their war standard and fought directly for the end of slavery, but even these supporters emphasized the war necessity argument. Michigan's Zach Chandler spoke of the "use of all the elements which God and nature have placed in our hands to crush this rebellion." Even Charles Sumner spoke in favor of the proclamation by pointing to "Emancipation! Its Policy and Necessity, as a War Measure for the Suppression of the Rebellion," while radical governor Austin Blair in Michigan told a political gathering, "I am unable to see why it is not proper to use a rebel's sacred nigger."[21]

But the election results in the North as a whole showed a strong shift away from the Republicans. Democrats gained thirty-five congressional seats previously held by Republicans. They won the governor's post in New York and New Jersey and took the statewide races in Illinois, Pennsylvania, and Indiana. Republican vote totals dropped even where they won. While vastly outnumbered in New England, Democrats still got almost 45 percent of the vote in all the state races and nearly 50 percent in the congressional tally. In the central core of states running from Connecticut to Illinois their vote totals went to 50.8 percent, up 5.4 percent over the 1860 presidential totals. Since these states contained nearly 60 percent of the Northern population and 127 electoral votes with 117 needed to elect a president in the next contest, these gains were striking.[22]

Many observers blamed emancipation for Republican losses. Senator Sherman said that "the ill timed proclamation contributed to the general result." Editors of both parties throughout the Midwest explained that fear of the Negro was the cause of Democratic advances. Lincoln's old friend from Illinois, Orville Browning, told the president that the proclamation had revived opposition politics in the state. Horace Greeley explained that the president's emancipation advances had taken him too far ahead of the people. A losing candidate in Ohio noted that "I had thought until this year the cry of 'nigger' and 'abolitionism' were played out but they never had as much power and effect in this part of the state as the recent elections."[23]

Democrats jubilantly insisted that the elections were a repudiation of the revolutionary excesses of Republicanism. They saw a conservative coalition forming that would bring into the party fold disillusioned Republicans, many of whom had once been Democrats. In October Horatio Seymour described the conflict as "not merely . . . between the Democratic and Republican organizations, but a struggle between the conservative and radical classes of our citizens." Democratic editors spoke of how Lincoln policies were "drawing together conservative men in defense of the Constitution." Even conservative Republican papers reflected this opinion. The *New York Herald* blamed the party for yielding to extremists and declared that "the State of New York has given the finishing blow to our radical abolitionists." Inspired by this victory, the Democrats focused their subsequent wartime positions on preserving the Constitution and denouncing revolution. "The Constitution as it is; the Union as it was; the Negroes where they are" had been anointed with victory.[24]

But Democratic beliefs that the voters had come to their conservative senses were in part deceiving. The sections of the North with traditional Democratic loyalty had turned out to reaffirm old Jacksonian faith. Parts of the North with the least to gain from economic and social change stayed in the party column along with strongholds that voted party tickets from sheer instinct, no matter what their socioeconomic position. But other factors had influenced the election of 1862. These revealed not a retreat away from change but simply wartime malaise, dismay at the military situation, and possibly even feelings that the war had not produced revolution enough.[25]

Democrats had won because Republicans stayed home. While Democratic vote totals had increased slightly, Republican totals had fallen way off. Republican voters may have been protesting restraint as much as radicalism. In the districts of strongest egalitarian sentiments, those of New England and Michigan, vote totals were down significantly. Senator Trumbull of Illinois insisted that "hundreds of republicans who believed that their sons and relatives were being sacrificed to the incompetency, indisposition or treason of proslavery generals, were unwilling to sustain the administration which followed this policy." Carl Schurz told Lincoln that the loss was explainable because it "admitted its professed opponents to its counsels." Vermont's Justin Morrill told Chase that "the Democrats are making capital on the ground of our imbecility more than our radicalism."[26]

Democrats also had made their gains because of two other temporary factors, one regional, one national. In the Midwest, the election campaign was fought in the context of a major political blunder by the administration. Faced with a growing number of refugee freedmen gathering at Cairo, Illinois, Secretary of War Stanton on September 18, 1862, had authorized the commander to send black women and children to communities that would provide jobs, food, and housing. The Illinois Central Railroad began shipping these refugees throughout the state. Democrats publicly cried havoc, speaking of a plague of black locusts, the onset of miscegenation, crime, and pauperism. Privately they were delighted, while Republicans fired urgent telegrams to Washington pleading for a reversal of the policy. Within a month Stanton had forbidden further shipment of refugees away from Cairo, but the damage had been done. The administration had validated the racial doomsaying of Democrats. The Midwestern election results showed the consequences.[27]

Republican losses reflected most fundamentally the military situation as of the fall of 1862. The year had seen three great battles with unprecedented deaths and maimings. The victories of April at Shiloh and New Orleans mixed the horrors with hope, but the summer saw another Union loss at Bull Run following on the heels of the bloody and inconclusive peninsular campaign. Over a hundred thousand Union soldiers had stood within sight of Richmond and yet had been called back for a battle that ended in another defeat within sight of Washington. Whether one blamed McClellan or Lincoln for that episode, it certainly gave no one much reason to vote Republican. Even the "victory" at Antietam inspired little pro-administration enthusiasm, for the slaughter of that day brought no final victory, only the main Confederate army of Robert E. Lee retreating to reassemble and fight again. Ideas about the nature of battle and of victory still were cast in terms of earlier wars and types of warfare. Misunderstandings of the murderousness of modern battle, the complexities of moving vast armies, all built frustration. Even victories seemed to produce no enduring success. Amateur strategists, and there were millions of them in the United States, hundreds editing newspapers, a few running governments, kept demanding that after battles armies jump forth to pursue and destroy the enemy. All those deaths simply had to bring some definite triumph. These factors created the frustrations of the fall of 1862, which produced Republican losses at the polls.[28]

Still, these events had been perceived within the context of the political dialogue in which voters could choose between a party of movement, action, and modernization—a party of hope—and its opponent, a party of stability, conservatism, and tradition, a party of memory. The political structure and the constitutional system guaranteed the Northerners would continue the dialogue. And the economic and social changes that the war was unleashing set the agenda for that dialogue to give it further vitality.

PART II

MAKING WAR

CHAPTER 5

Congress and the Capitalists

T HE Northern economy at the beginning of the war had enormous advantages over that of the South. Industry for building the weapons of war, transportation for delivering those weapons into the hands of soldiers and for taking both to the battlefield, organizational skills for handling complex institutions on the large scale, all were concentrated in the North. Even agriculture showed a Northern advantage. Taking the last point first, in 1860 the North had more acres of improved farmland: two-thirds of the national total of over 163 million acres. The North had twice the cash value in farm improvements, machinery, and livestock. It produced over four times as much wheat, over twice as much corn, over six times as much oats, over fifteen times more white potatoes, five times more wool, almost three times as many horses, over three times as many sheep. The Confederacy led the Union in value of homemade manufactures, but that figure actually confessed Southern weakness, for it revealed Northern superiority in manufacturing. The loyal states even led Dixie in producing tobacco.

Northern superiority was even more striking in the industrial and financial realm. Of the over 128,000 industrial firms in the nation, the Confederacy housed only 18,026. New England alone topped that figure with over 19,000, so did Pennsylvania with 21,000, and New York with over 23,000. New York State manufactured four times as much in terms of the value of manufactured products as the entire Confederacy. The Northern states produced 96 percent of the locomotives, and as for firearms, more firearms were made in one Connecticut *county* than in the entire South. There were over ten times as many industrial workers in the North as in the South. The United States as a whole had the largest railroad network in the world, but the South contained less than one-third of the 31,256 miles. The major financial organizations, too, were overwhelmingly in the North; even Southerners of means did most of their banking in the North.

All these elements of Northern superiority reflected the tremendous growth of the economy of the nation in the twenty years before the coming of the war. In that period the United States had begun to demonstrate the sort of growth that marks modern economies. Yearly per capita income began to grow at about 1.6 percent, a major increase from the 1 percent of the premodern era. Commodity output increased 50 percent in the 1840s and went to 62 percent in the 1850s. The gross national product went from $1.62 billion in 1839 to $2.43 billion in 1849 to $4.10 billion in 1859, measured in 1860 dollars. Much of this increase in income was based on the profits from slavery, but slavery fueled Northern factories by providing the cotton that flowed through Northern textile mills. Slave-grown cotton also was marketed in such a way that many of the profits from it showed up in Northern financial and manufacturing pockets. While slavery and cotton kept the South from modernizing and diversifying its economy, it helped generate forces of a modern economy in the North.

Plummeting transportation rates were also vital in changing the Northern economy. They made it cheaper to ship farm products and thus stimulated both the growth of cities and the beginning of a cash crop agriculture. Nearly fifty thousand miles of telegraph lines, most in the North, allowed communication on a rapid scale over long distances, further lubricating the movement of goods. The so-called "American system" of interchangeable parts helped build the factory system, and the specialization of industry to include machine tool making was also in process. The North was also attracting a huge immigration that brought over three million people into the nation between 1845 and 1855. Public education built a better-trained work force. A burgeoning industrial sector attracted foreign investment. The opening of vast new lands in the West fed the growth of industry, producing markets and stimulating transportation and communication. The South, too, of course, benefited from the opening of the West and foreign investment, but in the North more elements of a modernizing economy ceaselessly reinforced each other. By 1860 the United States was second only to England in the world as a manufacturing country. And the North was where that status had been achieved.[1]

In Northern cities millionaires cropped up in growing numbers. New York City boasted 14 in 1846, 19 owning $500,000 in property, and 137 worth at least $250,000. Philadelphia in 1857 claimed 25 millionaires; Boston reported 18 in 1850. These were the extraordinarily rich people of the North, but even larger numbers were waiting to join them. Hundreds had more than $100,000—200 in Boston, 249 in Philadelphia. By 1870 there were an estimated 545 millionaires in the nation, most of them in the North. In a world where a man lived a life of leisure on $10,000, and where $150,000 was considered a fortune, these figures reveal the great wealth that the prewar economy had generated. These fortunes tended to stay in family hands, providing a strong foundation for further investments.[2]

But this vast wealth had to be mobilized for war; it had to be directed toward paying for weapons and men, it had to be organized to provide for a secure and regular payment of soldiers in the field, workers and owners in the factories, farmers in the field, merchants, and railroaders.

In contrast to the modern world, the direction of the economic resources of the Union did not come from the president. Lincoln articulated the purposes of the war. He recruited the armies, found the officers to lead them, and directed the emancipation effort. These actions were indispensably linked to his role as commander in chief. But he was far from commander in chief of economic resources. His Whig principles kept him from directing economy policy. Since the great conflict between legislators and "King Andrew" Jackson over the Bank of the United States, Congress ruled that domain. On his way to assume the presidency Lincoln had said, "My political education strongly inclines me against a very free use of any of these means by the Executive to control the legislation of the country. As a rule, I think it better that Congress should originate as well as perfect its measures, without external bias." Lincoln supported Congress. He recognized as well as did legislators that, in Senator Sherman's words, "the problem of providing money to carry on . . . a great war . . . [is] next in importance to the conduct of armies, and those who [are] engaged in solving this problem [are] as much soldiers as the men who . . . [carry] muskets or [command] armies." But Congress would lead in this realm.[3]

Before lawmakers could take hold they first had to clear away the financial structure that years of Democratic policies had built. As of 1861 there was no national banking system, no national currency, no federal income tax or excise tax. All this reflected a philosophy of government that emphasized what government was not to do. Jacksonians had attacked the national banking system created under the Bank of the United States as a monster that linked in corrupt brotherhood the national power and private concentrations of wealth. That bank had died in 1836, to be replaced by a system of thousands of the state banks. Whatever their advantages to the prewar economy, they did not provide the national resources to fight a major war.[4]

The money of the nation consisted of bank notes from approximately 1,600 banks. An estimated 7,000 different notes circulated, some from banks that had gone out of business. It was a counterfeiter's paradise. As late as 1863 approximately 6,000 bogus issues were floating around with the 7,000 legitimate bank notes. In New York notes of 303 banks circulated. Only 45 of these notes were legitimate.[5]

The national government did its financial business through an Independent Treasury through which the national government paid and was paid in gold and silver. This meant, among other things, that instead of paying and receiving through the quick and easy process of changing accounts in ledgers, tons of gold were hauled back and forth in and out of the Treasury on horse-drawn drays. It also meant that the ability of the government to pay its debts was limited to the amount of gold and silver that was available. When the government was a small-scale operation, as it was in times of peace, this system worked. But as of 1861–62 the government no longer fit that description. In the fiscal year that ended on June 30, 1861, national government expenditures were $67 million. One year later spending stood at $475 million, an increase of 700 percent. By 1865 government spending would reach $4 million per day. The national government was spending in two and a half weeks the entire yearly outgo of 1861.

Prior to 1861 the national government had used several devices for raising money. Customs duties and public land sales gave the nation the revenues it needed in ordinary times. When extra funds were needed the nation sold bonds with attractive interest rates. In the distant past excise taxes on the making and selling of various commodities, such as liquor, brought in additional income. But excise taxes had been unknown for almost a generation. The federal government therefore relied on customs and land and bond sales, which had generated in 1861 receipts of $41,510,000. That would be about enough to pay for ten days of the war by 1865. Action was clearly needed to change the prewar system if the North was going to fight.[6]

Secretary of the Treasury Salmon Chase responded first. His political influence and not his financial experience had placed him in that office. And his ideology was at first a handicap. He was a former Democrat, persuaded of the dangers of paper money, reluctant to forge a strong government with power to tax. Still, ideology did not blind him to an inescapable fact—the Treasury needed money to pay for the war, approximately $328 million, Chase estimated. But like most other Northerners, he knew only the guideposts of the past. The means he proposed to get the money were familiar ones: $80 million from raising import fees and from land sales, a revived excise tax to bring in about $20 million. The rest he would get by borrowing.

Chase sought to tap the powerful outpouring of patriotism that was sweeping the North. He asked Congress for $100 million in low-denomination Treasury notes that people could pay for in ten installments over a five-month period. To encourage their enthusiasm Chase wanted to have these notes earn interest at a penny a day on a $50 note—a higher rate than usually paid by the government. Average Northern citizens would thus link their fortunes to the success of Union arms.

But the secretary of the Treasury also wanted to tap the big money of the North. He asked for a $100 million loan in denominations of up to $5,000, paying 7 percent interest. Observers noted the value in making all the people a part of the war effort. One commentator declared that the "patriotic, united and rich" people of the loyal states would snatch up these notes enthusiastically and thus "show the world that a government dependent upon the people may be as strong and as rich in resources as it is free." For the larger notes the prediction proved correct. The government was swamped with offers to buy them. The value of government securities went up 3 percent in one week. But the lower-denomination bonds moved more slowly. The average person had no experience with government bonds and remained aloof.

Chase's early plans were also hurt by his abiding faith in hard money. He kept in force the requirement that the government be paid in gold or silver, and he expected specie to be delivered to sub-Treasury buildings. This requirement cut into bank reserves. The government spent the coin it received to pay debts all over the country, but coin was scattered so widely and passed through so many hands that it made its way back to the banks rather slowly. Should public confidence drop, gold might simply be hoarded. In mid-November the public confidence took several shocks. The *Trent* affair seemed to portend war with England. Doubts over military inactivity grew. Chase himself kicked out another prop with an annual report that revealed a large Treasury deficit. Gold fled into a million holes, and on the next-to-last day of the year the banks suspended specie payments. Government contractors ceased to be paid. Worse, the army, reaching nearly 576,000 men, also went unpaid.[7]

Something had to be done to pay for the war. Congressman Spaulding estimated in early January 1862 that "we will be out of the means to pay the daily expenses in about thirty days." By the end of the month Chase wrote in desperation that "immediate action is of great importance." He suggested that some rigid economy in government would be helpful, but that seemed almost laughable given the skyrocketing costs of war. He thought that if Congress would pass a confiscation measure, then the taking of rebel property might provide government revenues. But that idea would at best bring in revenue only in the future. Finally, from Thaddeus Stevens, chairman of the House Ways and Means Committee, came a proposal that attacked the financial commandments of hard money—print money, backed not by gold but simply by the promise of the government to pay.[8]

The proposal frightened the sound money men and terrorized the Democrats. Chase believed that "irredeemable paper currency" was the most "fatally certain expediency for impoverishing the masses and discrediting the government." The chairman of the

Senate Finance Committee, Republican William Fessenden, reported that he had been "tormented . . . day and night for weeks," for he believed that paper money was "wrong in itself." Democrat George Pendleton spoke the fears of people in both parties in reiterating his party's catechism: "The currency will be expanded; prices will be inflated; fixed values will depreciate; incomes will be diminished; the savings of the poor will vanish; the hoardings of the widow will melt away; bonds, mortgages, and notes—everything of fixed value—will lose their value; everything of changeable value will be appreciated; the necessaries of life will rise in value; the government will pay twofold—certainly largely more than it ought —for everything that it goes into the market to buy; gold and silver will be driven out of the country."

But the war unsettled much of the financial wisdom of the day. When Fessenden got Stevens' bill he contacted two of the leading financiers in the nation for their advice. James Gallatin wrote him that Stevens' plan would ruin the country. Morris Ketchem told him that the measure was indispensable to the nation's needs. With both letters on his desk Fessenden received a personal call from Gallatin, who had come to Washington to oppose the paper money plan. Fessenden handed him Ketchem's letter. Gallatin was stunned and left to think things over. The next day he telegraphed the senator to say he had reversed himself. He agreed with Ketchem. Relieved, Fessenden began to open the day's mail. He found a letter from Ketchem, who announced that he now opposed the greenback bill![9]

Recognizing that the war would not wait while financial experts figured out some answer, perhaps already grown dubious about experts, given McClellan's apparent lethargy, Congress acted. On February 25, 1862, it passed the Legal Tender Bill. The measure authorized the secretary of the Treasury to issue $150 million in notes that would pay no interest and would be legal tender for taxes, internal duties, excises, and personal debts. The government would accept these notes as payment for every obligation except import duties. These would have to be paid in specie. On the other hand, the government itself would pay its creditors in this paper money, too. The only exception was that it would pay the interest of people who bought bonds and notes in specie. Everyone else in the nation would have to accept the paper for debts to governments or to each other.

In many respects the act brought significant changes. It reversed a policy of the government in which it had never paid its debts or accepted in payment anything but gold or silver. In so doing, the national government took back a power it had allowed the states to usurp—the power to establish the currency for the nation. State bank notes circulated for a few more years now, but the national government had its own money, backed by the law and force of the central government. People now transacted their business in that national currency, literally linking their fortunes to the survival of that government. It could be argued that making paper legal tender violated the intentions of the authors of the Constitution, but the authors of the document were not engaged in a Civil War when they set forth that prohibition. It was at least probable that they considered the survival of the nation of greater importance than whether gold and silver were the only legitimate money or not.[10]

Despite the novelty of the Legal Tender Bill, vestiges of older faith still clung to it. In asserting that holders of the public debt would be paid interest in specie and that import duties would have to be paid in specie, the government debased its own money. It was an implicit recognition that specie was preferable to paper money, and that the resort to paper money was an expedient only the survival of the nation could justify.

To Thaddeus Stevens and a few supporters in Congress, this aspect of the bill seemed grossly unfair. Government bondholders were most likely wealthy bankers. Men who needed protection the least were going to be protected from the potential inflation. The common man would not have such protection. And soldiers would also be paid in depreciating currency. The people who could least afford the inflation would pay the most for it. There are "two classes of money," Stevens charged, "one for the banks and brokers and another for the people." But Congress was more impressed by the need of the nation to borrow, and people of wealth wanted gold. Failure to pay interest on government bonds in gold would reduce their value, and the nation needed to sell its bonds as a further element in the program to raise money to fight the war. Some of the people would have to pay the price.[11]

But if the older monetary faith survived, one thing changed irredeemably. The federal government exercised its powers in establishing a currency, and signs of its influence would now abide in the pockets of people throughout the North and later throughout the nation. In the struggle to save the nation, the national government extended its reach, becoming a fuller partner with the states in the exercise of sovereignty. "We the People of the United States" joined the people of the several states as active agents in saving their government. While they continued to see states and communities as vital to their needs and more easily accessible to their demands, they added a new dimension to their image of a government of the people, a new appendage, capable and willing, when called on, to meet their needs.[12]

The greenbacks rose in total volume to $450 million during the war as Congress passed two more bills, one in July 1862 and the other later in 1863, each one producing another $150 million. And even Chase came around to defending greenbacks while war raged. But while the bills got paid, there was still a cost for greenbacks. Inflation accelerated, reaching the highest level since the revolution. The overall cost of living almost doubled by January 1865. Real wages fell. In 1860 the purchasing power of annual wages stood at approximately $363. Five years later it had dropped to $261. Not all the fault for this loss in real wages can be put at the feet of inflation, but one estimate blames it for at least 47 percent. Inflation hit the poorest sectors of the economy hardest—wage workers and people on fixed incomes. They could not pass along their costs to anyone, could raise no prices, could not pressure the government to protect them by compensations in other areas such as tariffs. They suffered other costs in taxes as well. Their means of protest were few and limited. They sometimes exercised those means. But overwhelmingly they continued to support the war, despite its costs.[13]

While the creation of legal tender paper money marked the major innovation in the nation's financial system, greenbacks did not pay for most of the war. The government issued only $450 million in greenbacks. The cost of the conflict almost reached $13 billion. The largest source of money came from the traditional means of borrowing—from the sale of bonds to large and small investors, which took place on an unprecedented scale. As of 1860 the total national government debt was just under $65 million, or about $2.06 for every citizen in the nation. In 1861 there was only a modest rise to $90,582,000, or $2.80 per capita. But then the debt skyrocketed, increasing fivefold by 1862, growing by almost $550 million in 1863, by $700 million in 1864, by $800 million in 1865, until in 1866 it reached the tremendous sum of $2,755,764,000, or $75.42 for every person in the United States. This figure would not be matched until the nation entered World War I fifty-two years later.[14]

At the beginning of the war there was reason to wonder if the necessary money would be raised. The federal government had done its prewar borrowing through private dealings with bankers—predominantly those in New York. Few sources outside these financial centers had been tapped. The farmers and merchants of all the states bought state bonds sold by states through local bankers. The small-scale national government made the needs of Washington, D.C., little more than a rumor to most Americans. But the threatened destruction of the nation brought the needs of the army to the forefront. States issued bonds to pay state obligations, but the national government now sent a call throughout the country for money to pay for men and equipment.

The way that these bonds were sold illustrates a crucial fact about the nature of the war itself: the heavy involvement of the private sector of the economy in the entire war effort. As of 1861 the national government did not have the facilities, tradition, or public support to take up the effort to fight the war by itself.

Decades of Democratic administrations at the national and state level had reinforced a strong laissez-faire government philosophy. Although government and the laws often assisted private enterprise, in the vast majority of cases it was private management that directed economic effort. Fears about the use of government power for personal gains joined admiration for liberal capitalism to keep government from involvement in transportation, manufacturing, and banking. Small wonder, then, that when a vast government effort was needed, administration and congressional leaders looked for help to the experts, in the executive offices of banks, railroads, and factories, all over the North.

Such arrangements between wealth and politics were a common feature of the political system. In return for contributions legislators supported the interests of contributors. Law thus advanced the schemes of private enterprise. But in the mid-nineteenth century the arrangement also worked in reverse as well. Private knowledge, experience, and resources advanced the cause of government.

Given the diminished size of the government, who else could do it? The private sector thus fused self-interest with the sense of public service. Some used this fusion to rationalize self-serving. Others performed invaluable services for the Union cause even as they earned profits for doing so.

To market government bonds Secretary Chase turned to Jay Cooke of Philadelphia. The son of a prosperous Sandusky, Ohio, lawyer, Cooke moved to the big city in 1839, joined the banking house of E. W. Clark and Company, and built a fortune strong enough to allow him to retire and enter private banking on his own by 1857. In early 1861 the state of Pennsylvania had called upon Cooke to sell its bonds. Promoting both patriotism and self-interest, he managed to sell the entire $3 million loan.

Chase knew of Jay Cooke through his connection with the banker's brother, Henry, who ran an Ohio newspaper that promoted Chase's political ambitions. The Cooke family also had ties to other politicians in the state; they helped to finance the campaign of Senator John Sherman. Sherman would later support Jay Cooke and Company in the selling of bonds and the reformation of the national banking system.[15]

Cooke was already in Washington as the war began. He offered to help the government in transferring funds from private sources to public need, observing that the government officials should "keep on the right side of those capitalists who are disposed to dabble in the loans, etc. of the government, and if they do make sometimes a handsome margin it is not more than they are entitled to in such times as these." Yet while Cooke expected a "fair commission" from the government, he also felt strongly that the Union had to survive, and he offered his personal services to the secretary of the Treasury, telling his brother that "pay or no pay, I will do all I can to aid him."[16]

The failure at the first Bull Run accelerated Cooke's involvement. The day after the battle he rounded up subscribers in Philadelphia who promised to take nearly $2 million in 6.00 and 7.30 percent federal government loans. Impressed by what had been done in that city, Chase picked Cooke up on his way from Washington, D.C., to New York. Together they made the rounds of New York's bankers and capitalists. By August 1861 the nation's financial capital had subscribed $35 million. Boston financiers had provided $10 million and Cooke's hometown had subscribed an additional $3 million. The totals seemed awesome at the time. One New York City banker warned that "you cannot depend upon further aid from the Associated Banks."

But the sums of the summer of 1861 were but a trickle of the billions of dollars that the war consumed. And Cooke, having proved his talents, was appointed the official agent of the Treasury Department to sell further loans for the government. It was a job he did for little personal profit and with vast consequences for the nation. Of course, the most obvious one was the raising of money. But equally important was the way he managed to sell the bonds.[17]

Cooke used every known device to make bond buying a nationwide, patriotic act. He advertised widely in regular, foreign language, and religious newspapers. He provided editorials for busy editors to sign extolling the importance of buying government bonds. He sent wine and cases of food to editors and to agents. He gave editors special chances to sell bonds. He published lists of contributing patriots in the newspapers save for the few who asked to remain anonymous. He opened up night sales offices for workers. His agents visited clergymen and asked them to preach the bond gospel. Through nationwide salesmanship he made the buying of bonds an activity of the public, not just an enterprise of bankers.

Most of the bonds were bought by the wealthy. But newspapers described the involvement of people from almost every class. The *New York Tribune* described an evening at one of the bond agencies:

The machinery of the agency is simple—a few desks and tables—a corps of experienced clerks and tellers—the exchange of the registered 7.30 bond for each individual loan—and the applicant . . . becomes at once the nation's creditor and beneficiary. . . . A glance at the characters ordinarily encountered in a single night . . . will give some idea of the universality of this impartial money distribution. Out of the 100 bond buyers who crowd the office . . . at least 60 are mechanics or laborers, 20 are saloon keepers, small dealers and soldiers, and the rest are almost non-descript condition of vendors, clerks, and even boys, mixed in with a number of women in faded calico or mourning—toil, sorrow, wrinkled thrift, or the working woman's work-a-day written upon their features.

Most of New York City's races and nationalities appeared as well. "Ten colored men, two boys, 13 Irishmen, 16 Germans and Portuguese, Chinese and one Moor" bought bonds one evening at just one agency. Cooke claimed that it was the small contributor to the loan who built allegiance to the nation. Holding a handful of telegrams reporting on many small sales, he announced, "I hold in this fist the guarantee of permanent union between the east and west and the center and the extremes."[18]

Such publicity helped to build the image of a united people rising in support of the cause. Still, those who benefited most from the sales were the agents themselves. Those men, usually bankers in communities throughout the North, acted as Cooke's salesmen in the field. They could buy the largest number of bonds, and they also received a commission for any sales they made, apparently even to themselves. But they felt themselves engaged in a patriotic enterprise, and no one seems to have resented their profits in such an endeavor: using their business acumen in a cause that would bring the wealth of the Union inexorably down upon the Confederacy, crushing secession and saving the nation.

Both bonds and greenbacks helped to swell national feeling. They put people throughout the North in personal contact with symbols of national authority and wealth. They linked individual fortunes in shops, stores, and farms as well as in banks with the survival of the nation. And they provided the means to pay the soldiers and to buy the guns, supplies, and equipment to win victory. In doing this, of course, they also brought fully to light the awesome power, dedication, and resources of Northern society.

In a similar manner Congress called upon the power to tax in assembling the resources of the North. While Secretary Chase took the lead in using bonds as a resource and gradually reconciled himself to making greenbacks legal tender, he kept to the rear in the matter of taxation. Here Congress took the reins both because of Chase's conservatism and because of the powerful tradition that only elected representatives could decide how much wealth might be taken from the people's pockets.

In the summer of 1861 as it slowly became clear that the war would require an awesome commitment of resources, Congress projected a taxation package that mixed traditional methodology with innovation. In a tax bill of August 5, 1861, legislators asked states for $20 million through a direct tax on their landed property. The measure respected the fact that state resources for raising taxes far surpassed those of the national government. It also showed the sort of respect for constitutional traditions indicated in the Crittenden-Johnson Resolutions.[19]

But a new path also appeared. Contained within the bill was the first federal income tax in the history of the United States—a provision taxing all incomes over $800 per year at 3 percent. What inspired the measure was the recognition that a changing economy expanded the number of potential taxpayers. Lawmakers were concerned that nonagricultural wealth might escape paying its share of the taxes needed for the war. Therefore the income tax provision had been added to gather resources from all forms of income. The income tax was in the bill also to reassure potential buyers of national bonds that some revenues would be available to pay them for their investment.

The innovation was clear, but the willingness to implement the new tax lagged. When Congress adjourned its special session in August 1861, it still had no sweeping tax program, and no provisions for tax collectors appeared until June 30, 1862.[20]

But by the time Congress gathered again in December, legislators knew that action could not wait. After heated and long debates they wrote a comprehensive tax package that laid the foundation for a major change in national revenue policy. As of 1860 federal revenues were generated almost entirely by customs duties and land sales. Between 1839 and 1860, of the $897 million in federal revenue, $824 million had come from customs, $72 million from land sales. The remaining million came from other minor sources. By 1865 internal revenues in the form of excise and income taxes comprised $210 million of the total $334 million collected. The foundations for modern national taxation were in place.[21]

The excise tax was the major source of income. Congress taxed the manufacture, distribution, and purchase of practically every commodity made in the United States. It was a momentous shift for a government so unused to entering an increasingly intricate and complex economy. Congress struggled for three months in what the *New York Times* described as "a task of inconceivable magnitude. A thousand conflicting interests had to be consulted, local and sectional jealousies conciliated, the burdens distributed as equitably as possible between loyal and disloyal communities, and districts which depend upon agriculture and these which depend upon commerce add the more or less wealthy classes of society. Indeed, merely to enumerate the shallows and quicksands which had to be kept in view, would overtask him who catalogues the stars." When completed the measure was the largest bill ever to be introduced into Congress before the war. The description of the breadth and size of the July 1, 1862, law provided by Congressman James G. Blaine hit the mark:

Spiritous and malt liquors and tobacco were relied upon for a very large share of revenue: a considerable sum was expected from stamps. . . . Manufacturers of cotton, wool flax, hemp, iron, steel, wood, stone, earth, and every other material were taxed three percent. Banks, insurance and railroad companies, and all other corporations were made to pay tribute. The butcher paid thirty cents for every beef slaughtered, ten cents for every hog, five cents for every sheep. Carriages, billiard tables, yachts, gold and silver plate, and all other articles of luxury were levied upon heavily. Every profession and every calling, except the ministry . . . was included within the far-reaching provisions of the law and subjected to tax for license. Bankers and pawn brokers, lawyers and horse-dealers, physicians and confectioners, commercial brokers and peddlers, operators of theaters and jugglers on the street were indiscriminately summoned to aid the national Treasury. The law was so extended and minute that it required thirty printed pages of royal octavo and more than twenty thousand words to express its provisions.[22]

The excise tax brought in almost ten times more internal revenue than the income tax. But this latter provision was the greatest innovation, having the potential for a system of taxation that was the basis for future government financing. Still, men of the war era cherished older visions and moved grudgingly toward a federal outreach that would tax Americans. When the major income tax measure of the war, that of 1864, was debated legislators still complained at the unfairness of taxing the rich more than other people. Justin Morrill protested that "the very theory of our institutions is entire equality; that we make no distinction between the rich man and the poor man." But more persuasive were arguments on the side of the progressive tax. The majority of Congress accepted the idea expressed by Congressman Augustus Frank: "It is just, right and proper that those having a higher income shall pay a larger amount of tax . . . the larger tax we pay at this time the safer we are and the better will be the securities of the government."[23]

In fact the income tax measures of the Civil War were among the most popular of any taxes. Northern people could not escape taxation. The question was what form would it take. The income tax spread the burden of taxation widely, and onto people who had gained the benefits from being citizens. Proponents of the income tax successfully played upon the powerful forces of nationalism the war crisis evoked. The tax linked almost the entire population to supporting the war, participating in the burdens and successes of the Union, nurturing devotion to the Union.

The income tax also garnered support when balanced against other alternatives. Those who resented the favors to the manufacturing classes that the new tariffs brought, merchants and importers who would suffer from high tariffs, agreed that an income tax was free of class bias. The general populace, faced with higher prices as a result of both the excise taxes and tariffs, were naturally pleased that the income tax brought revenues that kept other taxes from going even higher. Writing in November 1863, the commissioner of Internal Revenue reported that "the present tax laws on the whole have not merely been endured, but welcomed by the people in a manner that is believed elsewhere unparalleled."[24]

The government collected the income tax in several ways, all new involvements of national power in daily life. Government employees never saw the taxes they paid. Their assessment was withheld from their pay. Large companies paid taxes by withholding from dividends and interest payments to stockholders. Private individuals picked up returns from federal revenue officials and filed the return with a payment of what they owed. If the federal assessors thought they were not paying what they should, the amount due could be demanded. In the first income tax bill citizens could defeat the assessors' claim by simply taking an oath that they had in fact paid the proper amount. But by 1864 the government had strengthened its hand. Now if an assessor demanded increased payment, the taxpayer had to appeal to the district assessor. The decision of this official was final.[25]

The tax burden on Americans had never been so great. No national power had ever reached so directly into the lives of citizens before. Some likened the tax to being held up. One imaginary figure named Growler proclaimed, "There it is! Just so much robbery! Stand and deliver, is the word. Pistols and bayonets! Your money or your life!" But the retort that silenced complaint was a form of the following:

Instead of being robbed . . . you have been protected in your property and person, and guaranteed all the high privileges of citizenship. . . . I know a man who has given his right arm in the cause; and another has given his right leg. Do they grumble? No sir! I never heard a word of complaint from their lips. Thousands and tens of thousands have given their sons, and wives have given their husbands—sons and husbands who will never more return! They are with the dead. Sir you are dishonoring yourself in the eyes of men. A grumbler over this paltry war tax, for shame.[26]

But if patriotism made taxation popular, it also obscured the serious imbalances of wartime taxation. The income tax was progressive; incomes under $800 and then $600 were exempt from payment. And William Aspinwal, reputedly the richest man in the nation, gained great applause when he presented a check for $25,-000. But the income tax was a comparatively minor part of the tax burden. Of the $210 million raised in taxes in 1865, the vast majority came from excise taxes. In fact, during the entire period of its operation between 1863 and 1865, only $55 million was raised by the income tax, less than 8 percent of the federal revenues.[27]

Meanwhile the vast excise taxation hit consumers hard. They paid higher prices for all their needs. And, unlike manufacturers who also paid these taxes, the average citizen could not raise prices to pass these taxes along. Consumers also paid higher prices for a large array of products protected under tariff increases that averaged 47 percent during the war. Furthermore, the tariffs were so designed that they raised the cost of consumer goods higher than the capital goods used by manufacturers. In addition to raising prices to pay the excise taxes, manufacturers were also able to further offset such taxes by the protection they got from the tariff. Given the unprecedented size of the wartime tax bite, organizations like the National Manufacturers Organization, the National Association of Wool Manufacturers, the National Wool Growers Association, the American Iron and Steel Association, and the New England Cotton Manufacturers were able to persuade Congress of the need for compensation through these higher tariffs.[28]

Greenbacks, taxation, and borrowing were all part of an integrated vision of the type of economy that the war made indispensable. All pointed to a more centralized and centralizing system. All signaled a reaction to the profoundly weak and inactive national government many believed had helped to precipitate the war. Linked with these other measures was a proposal made by Chase in 1861 for a national banking system to provide a uniform currency throughout the nation and hence reinforce public confidence in the economy. Furthermore, a national banking system would provide a guaranteed market for national government bonds and secure the value of those bonds.

At first this proposal found little support. While they generally supported the new national currency, strong banking forces in the nation's financial center, New York City, feared the loss of influence to national banks. Traditional anxieties about the power of the "Monster Bank" of Jacksonian years meant that Democrats would oppose it. Furthermore, state banks outside New York benefited from their note-issuing practices and feared the loss of control over this function. Even Jay Cooke was reluctant at first to support national banking legislation. He feared that it would cost him the support of the nationwide banking community, which sold and bought his bonds.[29]

But forces combined to weaken the opposition to some form of national bank. The escalating demands of war played the major role. As bills for the army mounted, pressures grew for more money to pay them. Greenbacks were, of course, a continuing option. But the idea of the government simply cranking up the printing press to pay its bills frightened most legislators, banks, and the general public. Chase's 1861 proposal had linked the national banking system with a national currency, and that idea promised a more secure currency. By late 1862 these needs and promises, along with the success of prior national economic measures, led to a push by the administration for a national banking system. Taking a rare active role, Lincoln included in his December 1862 speech to Congress a recommendation for a national bank. The next month he reminded lawmakers of the need for action. Sensitive of its prerogatives, Congress practically ignored this public prodding. But Lincoln persevered, lobbying Western Republican senators and legislators as well as Finance chairman Fessenden on behalf of the measure.[30]

These executive efforts were linked to pressures by Chase that helped convince Jay Cooke to support the measure. Cooke pushed

Senator John Sherman to champion the bill. In a powerful speech the senator defended the national banking system as a bulwark against inflation, an attack on the confusions of a system where 1,600 banks issued several thousand bank bills and counterfeiters thrived, a facilitator of tax collection, and a stimulus to bond buying. But most of all Sherman called forth the spirit of nationalism, which would unite classes together in defense of the Union. The bill, Sherman declared,

will make a community of interests between the stockholders of banks, the people, and the Government. At present there is a great diversity of interests. The local banks have one interest and the Government has another. They are brought into conflict. But . . . by the passage of this bill you will harmonize their interests; so that every stockholder, every mechanic, every laborer who holds one of these notes will be interested in the government —not in a local bank, but in the Government of the United States—whose credit he will be anxious to uphold. If this system had been spread all over this country, and these banks had been established as agencies upon the basis of national credit, I believe they would have done very much to maintain the Federal Government and to prevent the great crime of secession.[31]

The bill passed, but by the narrowest of margins: 23–21. Only 2 Democrats voted for it, and 9 Republicans were in opposition. An almost equally close margin appeared when the House supported the bill 78 to 64. Here again the vote followed party lines: 2 Democrats were for it; only 19 Republicans opposed. Opposition came from men who feared banks in general and from those who wished to protect state against national banking power. It had also come from lawmakers who feared generally an expansion of national power into domains it had not occupied for decades.[32]

The major features of the bill were simple. Five or more individuals could request a charter for a national bank from the comptroller of the currency, whose position had been newly created. To get their charter they had to provide at least $30,000 or an amount equal to one-third their capital in federal bonds. When they provided these bonds they would get, along with their charter, national bank notes in an amount equal to 90 percent of the market value of the bonds. To restrain the possibilities of inflation, only $300 million in these bank notes would be issued, apportioned to each state according to its population. These new national banks would also be required to keep reserves of 25 percent to pay their notes.

Opposition to the measure rallied around state rights fears and the defense of the state banks. Concession to such feelings were necessary to get it passed. The act did little to injure state-chartered banks. They could still issue their own currency. State banks could even issue the new federal currency, albeit at less advantageous terms than could national banks. The $300 million in new U.S. notes simply joined the stream of greenbacks and thousands of state bank notes. The counterfeiting of prewar years continued. Since the act did not compel anyone to join the new system, and offered few inducements for doing so, the most powerful banks in the nation, those of New York City, stayed outside and attacked it in public reports. They even threatened the extraordinary step of refusing to accept the national notes.[33]

The national government fought back with a carrot and a stick. The newly appointed comptroller of the currency, Hugh McCulloch, announced that if the new law should "prove to be too stringent, it is safe to expect that such amendments will be made to it as will accommodate it to the reasonable requirements of capitalists." In his 1863 report McCulloch also recommended changes in the act designed to gain the favor of opponents. But the banks remained adamant.

The stick was carried by Jay Cooke. Chase and McCulloch asked him to organize national banks in New York City. Calling on friends in Boston and Philadelphia, as well as in New York, Cooke was able to gather $5 million to capitalize a national bank there. Furthermore, he threatened to raise $50 million to capitalize another such bank. And he warned the New York opponents that this new bank would "receive the national deposits and enjoy every benefit that could be realized from a connection with the Treasury of the United States."[34]

Cooke worked on Congress in other ways, too. The bludgeon might encourage financiers to support the banking measure, but more subtle means were employed to bring the weight of "public opinion" on legislators. Cooke sold the new banking system as he sold bonds. He employed newspapers of every state to extol its virtues and to condemn the weaknesses of the state banks. He suggested ideas for editorials and wrote a few himself, but his brother

Henry dusted off his editorial talents and produced most of them. In a six-week campaign in which arguments were changed almost daily, the Cooke brothers sold national banking. The fact that they contributed large sums to newspapers in advertising bonds gave them influence with editors. When the local journalists published these editorials the Cookes took copies of "the opinion of your district" to legislators. To remind Congress of constituent feelings, they also had extracts from home papers printed in the Washington papers. Lawmakers could use such pressure to leverage large bank supporters into accepting the need for a change in the system.[35]

These late 1863 activities of Cooke generated congressional support and showed the New York City bankers the potential costs of continued opposition. Meanwhile McCulloch continued to offer compromise. This pincer approach brought a resolution of the problem in 1864. A new banking law was enacted after New York bankers had met with the House Ways and Means Committee in early March 1864. The major benefit to the big city financiers was a reduction of the reserve requirements from 25 down to 15 percent. This allowed banks outside the city to send more of their funds to New York, where they were paid interest on them. This provision concentrated the banking of the nation in that city. Further to assist that process, the requirement that the $300 million in national currency be distributed to states according to population was dropped. Now vast amounts of that currency could be allotted to the Northeast.

Additional economic power went to New York City and to Boston and Philadelphia bankers through a section of the act that, while setting up eighteen cities where country banks would redeem their bank notes, provided that par redemption was guaranteed only in those three cities. In return for these concessions the national government demanded that only national banks would issue the new national notes. By mid-November of 1864 the New York City banks dropped their opposition to the national banking system, and the national banks began to grow rapidly in size and number. In 1865 Congress effectively eliminated state bank notes by a tax of 10 percent on them, and the national banking and currency system was secured. But this result was only achieved after the power of local banking and finance had been shown in forcing compromise by the national government.[36]

The local banks that gained the greatest power were those in the Northeast. Capital concentrated there to such an extent that even Henry Carey, the apologist for most of the Republican economic program, protested against the "money monopolists" of New York. By 1866 the per capita circulation of national currency was $33.30 in New England and New York, while it stood at only $6.36 in the seven Middle Western states and in defeated Dixie was $1.70. The sections that needed credit and currency for their economic livelihoods had to rely on the Northeast to get them. Seeds were being planted that would be harvested after the war in passionate protests by rural regions against the economic power of the Northeast. On the other hand, the financial structure that made the great fortunes of the late nineteenth century was also in place. Rockefellers, Carnegies, Vanderbilts, Armours, and Morgans all had reason to thank the Civil War Congress for its banking measures. Lesser people had more reasons to be dubious.[37]

1. John Ferguson Weir, *The Gun Foundry*. A midwar image of the industrializing North. (Putnam County Historical Society and Foundary School Museum, Cold Spring, N.Y.)

2. Salmon P. Chase, secretary of the Treasury. (J. W. Schuckers, *The Life and Public Services of Salmon Portland Chase,* New York: D. Appleton, 1874)

3. Senator John Sherman at thirty-five, major spokesman for Republican wartime economic legislation. (John Sherman, *Recollections of Forty Years,* Chicago: Werner Co., 1895)

4. William Henry Seward, secretary of state. (Frederic Bancroft, *The Life of William H. Seward,* New York: Harper & Bros., 1900)

1776 LIBERTY

1861 UNION

PHILADELPHIA & TRENTON

MASSACHUSETTS VOLUNTEERS

THE BOSTON REGIMENTS EMBARKING FOR WASHINGTON IN THE JERSEY CITY CARS.

5. Massachusetts Volunteers board trains in New Jersey in early May 1861 headed for Washington, via Baltimore. *Harper's Illustrated Weekly.* (Kansas Collection, University of Kansas)

6. Theodore Upson; from an Indiana farm to Sherman's army. (Captain E. J. Sherlock, *Memorabilia of the Marches and Battles in which the One Hundredth Regiment of Indiana Volunteers Participated*, Kansas City Mo.: Gerard-Woody, 1896)

7. George Templeton Strong, diarist and organizer of the Sanitary Commission, 1860. (New-York Historical Society)

8. William Sylvis, labor organizer. (James Sylvis, *The Life, Speeches, Labors and Essays of William H. Sylvis*, Philadelphia: Clayton, Remsen & Haffelfinger, 1872)

9. Mary Ashton Livermore at seventy-five. (Mary Livermore, *The Story of My Life,* Hartford, Conn.: A. D. Worthington, 1897)

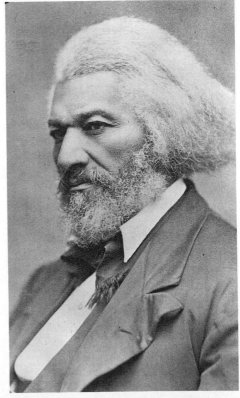

10. Frederick Douglass late in life. (Lincoln Museum, Fort Wayne, Ind.)

11. Recruiting office, 1863, *Harper's Illustrated Weekly*. (Kansas Collection, University of Kansas)

U. S. 7-30 LOAN.

The sale of the first series of $300,000,000 of the 7-30 Loan was completed on the 31st of March, 1865. The sale of the second series of Three Hundred Millions, payable three years from the 15th day of June, 1865, was begun on the 1st of April. In the short space of thirty days, over One Hundred Millions of this series have been sold—leaving this day less than Two Hundred Millions to be disposed of. The interest is payable semi-annually in currency on the 15th of December and 15th of June by Coupons attached to each note, which are readily cashed anywhere. It amounts to

One cent per day on a $50	note.
Two cents " " "	$100 "
10 " " " "	$500 "
20 " " " "	$1000 "
$1 " " " "	$5000 "

More and More Desirable.

The Rebellion is suppressed, and the Government has already adopted measures to reduce expenditures as rapidly as possible to a peace footing, thus withdrawing from market as borrower and purchaser.

This is the ONLY LOAN IN MARKET now offered by the Government, and constitutes the GREAT POPULAR LOAN OF THE PEOPLE.

The Seven-Thirty Notes are convertible on their maturity, at the option of the holder, into

U. S. 5-20 Six per cent.
GOLD BEARING BONDS.

Which are always worth a premium.

Free from Taxation.

The 7-30 Notes cannot be taxed by Towns, Cities, Counties or States, and the interest is not taxed unless on a surplus of the owner's income exceeding six hundred dollars a year. This fact increases their value from one to three per cent. per annum, according to the rate levied on other property.

12. Bond sale poster. (Historical Society of Pennsylvania)

13. "The Girl I Left Behind," 1860s style. (University of Kansas Music Library)

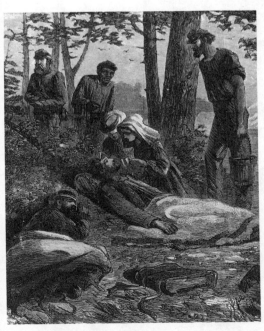

14. "Angels of Mercy," *Harper's Illustrated Weekly.* (Kansas Collection, University of Kansas)

15. General George B. McClellan, the "Little Napoleon." (Library of Congress, Matthew Brady Collection)

16. General William T. Sherman. (Lincoln Museum, Fort Wayne, Ind.)

17. General Grant and family at City Point, 1864–65. (Library of Congress, Matthew Brady Collection)

18. A few of the 620,000 dead in the war; these of the Iron Brigade killed on the first day at Gettysburg. (Library of Congress, Matthew Brady Collection)

19. General Ambrose Burnside: "The habit of declaring sympathy for the enemy will not be tolerated in this department." (Lincoln Museum, Fort Wayne, Ind.)

20. Clement Vallandigham arrested in his home. (Lincoln Museum, Fort Wayne, Ind.)

21. "Black Soldiers Will Fight," *Harper's Illustrated Weekly.* (Kansas Collection, University of Kansas)

22. "How to Escape the Draft," *Harper's Illustrated Weekly.* Irish thugs attack blacks in New York draft riots. (Kansas Collection, University of Kansas)

23. Private Cutler Rist, eighteen years old, 36th Wisconsin; wounded at Cold Harbor. (*Medical and Surgical History of the War of the Rebellion*, Washington, 1870)

24. Emeline and Mary Van Vleck, age five. Jacob Van Vleck was killed at Hatcher's Run, Virginia, in February 1865. (New York State Archives and Library, Albany, N.Y.)

25. Samuel Foster Haven, Jr., M.D.; killed at Fredericksburg at age thirty. (American Antiquarian Society)

26. Ellen Coffin Wright and her brothers. (Sophia Smith Collection, Women's Archive, Smith College)

27. Reverend Henry Ward Beecher at the close of the war. (Samuel Scoville, *A Biography of Reverend Henry Ward Beecher,* New York: Charles Webster, 1888)

28. Mass in the camp of the 69th New York. (Library of Congress, Matthew Brady Collection)

29. Lincoln and Tad. (Lincoln Museum, Fort Wayne, Ind.)

30. Winslow Homer, *Christmas 1865*, *Harper's Illustrated Weekly*. (Kansas Collection, University of Kansas)

CHAPTER 6

Congress and the Second "American System"

T HE pressing needs of the army and its suppliers for money generated national currency, lending, taxation, and banking. Congress marshaled the resources of the Union to push toward victory. The bankers and businessmen who had organized those resources in the rapidly growing Northern economy were the inevitable sources of wartime initiatives, and perhaps the inevitable beneficiaries. While average people gave the resources they had—the ability to fight, their votes, and their labor—the organizational elite gave what it had. The former gave their lives; the latter, if not their fortunes, at least the abilities that had made those fortunes.

While congressional majorities were molding an economic structure to finance the war, they were also enacting a program of internal improvements of enduring consequence. Like the financial measures, these policies were linked by advocates to fighting the war. Republican economics thus became part of wartime patriotism.

The foundation for such linkage had been laid in the prewar years. The clash between North and South generated conflicting economic and social visions of the two societies. Southern attacks on the North featured accusations of heartless brutality to workers, dangerous class divisions, mindless industrialism grinding away at human values. Such criticism had probed deep concern, but the evils of slavery had smothered much of this critique, branded it as hypocrisy, and helped a burgeoning Republican majority to forge its own vision. Republican writers and orators contrasted a stag-

nant, backward South where slavery degraded honest labor with a
North that was, in Eric Foner's words, "a dynamic, expanding capi-
talistic society, whose achievements and destiny were almost wholly
the result of the dignity and opportunities which it offered the
average laboring man."[1]

No man exemplified this theme better than Lincoln, whose personal experience and economic philosophy seemed to demonstrate
the opportunity of individuals to get ahead. Again and again "Honest Abe," the former rail-splitter become successful lawyer and politician, told listeners that he believed that men should be allowed to
rise to a position where they could keep all that they earned by the
sweat of their brow. This was the basic equality he asserted for the
blacks in his debates with Douglas, and it was "the leading object
of the government for whose existence we contend" when war
broke out. Union victory would preserve a government whose purpose was ". . . to afford all an unfettered start, and a fair chance in
the race of life."[2]

Concern for widespread economic opportunity had pervaded
prewar society, and opinions differed on how best to achieve it.
Democrats argued that the absence of government from all economic involvement would produce the best results. Concerned
about possible conspiracies between government and private economic power, they proclaimed a liberal capitalism that offered no
special advantages to any economic group—free banking laws, an
end to chartered monopolies, and a hard currency that common
people could trust.

But Republicans, while advocating the same general goal, emphasized the use of government support to advance enterprise and
develop the resources of the country. These were manifestations of
what Horace Greeley had called the "cardinal" Whig ideal that
"government need not and should not be an institution of purely
negative, repressive usefulness and value, but that it should exert
a beneficent, paternal, fostering influence upon the Industry and
Prosperity of the People." Party ideals were most clearly presented
in the 1860 platform. It advocated a series of internal improvement
and economic development plans for building a stronger, more
diversified, modern economy. Republicans promised a homestead
law opening public lands to settlers who could acquire them by dint
of their labor upon them, a federally assisted railroad to the Pacific

Ocean, federal funds for river and harbor improvements, and a higher tariff that would "secure to the workingman liberal wages, to agriculture remunerative prices, to mechanics and manufacturers an adequate reward for their skill, labor and enterprise, and to the nation commercial prosperity and independence."[3]

Democratic opposition had stifled these programs before the war. Fears of concentration of national power had awakened the constitutional scruples of many; so had concern about the impact on slavery of a stronger central government. Advocates of partnership between enterprise and government had also drawn the fire of Northern Democrats who believed that such assistance only concentrated wealth further in the hands of the wealthy. But Republicans convinced themselves that opposition was either misguided or, more likely, born of proslavery feelings. With the secession of the South and the beginning of war these economic ideals became more than a party platform. They became a program for victory over the South.

The Republican advocacy of a high protective tariff illustrates most clearly how party philosophy could become a banner for war. Before 1833 the United States followed a protective tariff policy. But in that year South Carolina threatened nullification of the so-called "Tariff of Abominations," and to resolve the crisis Congress agreed to lower the duties. By 1846 moderate duties were generally the rule, although importers of some articles such as iron and iron products, wool and woolen goods, along with cotton goods, paid duties of 30 percent.

The year 1857 saw a further reduction of duties, so that the most highly protected items were reduced to 24 percent and other duties were reduced, too. But Pennsylvania iron and wool interests, politically powerful in the state, remained dissatisfied. When the federal government began running a deficit for the first time in many years, pleas for higher duties gained support from other places. Even before the election of Lincoln enough people were beginning to share Republican economic ideals that the House of Representatives passed a tariff measure introduced by Vermont's Justin Morrill that increased duties. The measure focused on gaining Pennsylvania's votes in the presidential election, but it was sufficiently popular that other legislators could also support it. Once in power Republicans passed the 1861 Morrill Tariff Act, which began a trend toward higher tariffs that would not cease until the twentieth century.

War environments promoted burgeoning tariff rates. Need for revenue naturally inspired an effort to increase import duties. Initial efforts were not successful, but the distortions of the 1861 crisis were easily blamed. In 1862 legislators began passing tariff increases that, by 1864, averaged more than twice those of 1857. War also inspired tariff increases to offset the huge increase in taxes. Manufacturers, many of whom were initially neutral on the protection question, increasingly began to ask for higher tariffs that would compensate them for heavier taxation.[4]

But manufacturers were not the only advocates of protection. Men who had made legitimate reputations as defenders of workers also urged high tariffs. Horace Greeley published articles by Henry Carey arguing the benefits to workers of being protected from foreign competition. Important labor leaders like William Sylvis, Andrew Cameron, and Richard Trevellick agreed with the *Iron Molder's Journal* that workers would benefit from "a well regulated protective system, and . . . fair home competition." And farmers were to benefit from protection, too, for productive and prosperous workers bought more farm products, and that demand raised farm values. These opinions were endorsed and argued by well-known Republicans like Thad Stevens and William Kelley of Pennsylvania, Ben Butler of Massachusetts, and Ohio's Ben Wade. The president accepted them.[5]

Republicans were not unanimous in supporting a high tariff policy. Divisions between well-established New England manufacturers who operated highly profitable enterprises and men who were trying to build new industries in Pennsylvania and further west would become obvious after the war. Labor leaders also debated the merits of protection. But during the war the factions united behind raising the tariff walls so that the government might get revenues to pay for projected victory. Just as war necessity had brought together hard-money and soft-money Republicans, so it forged unity on the tariff as well. Patriotism diluted the potential economic divisions in the party even as it muted class divisions between labor and capital.[6]

Republican legislators also unified a range of economic constituencies in the creation of the largest grant ever provided by the national government to higher education—the Morrill College

Land Grant Act. The tradition of using land to fund education went back at least as far as the 1785 land ordinance. That law reserved one section in every township of the Old Northwest for common schools. New states entering the Union received a similar allotment for education. In 1850 the grant was increased to two sections per township. The tradition of assistance was there. Advances in agricultural knowledge also spurred government action. Pressures were growing to help farmers modernize, to utilize the growing science of agronomy being pioneered in Europe. The literature of scientific farming was also growing rapidly. In 1861 the leading agricultural newspaper in the country provided a list of eighty-seven books on farming that farmers should utilize.

In addition to pressures for some form of training in agriculture, manufacturers sensed the need for a more highly trained work force. Workers themselves began to see the advantages of education in a society of growing complexity. Furthermore, even some people in rural states were beginning to see the need for education as a means to help the "industrial classes" better their condition. In Jacksonville, Illinois, former New Englander Jonathan B. Turner called for national endowment of such universities.[7]

Beginning in 1857 a strong lobbying effort by the United States Agricultural Society also helped persuade Congress to act. In that year the effort had paid off as Congress passed a land grant bill by narrow margins. But the opposition of Southerners who spoke ominously of such an outreach of federal power, as well as Westerners who wanted full benefit from public lands to go directly to their states, combined with the constitutional scruples of President Buchanan, led to a veto.

But with the war on and with former opponents in Congress now retired to the battlefield, conditions changed. The outpouring of national support to railroads, banks, and industries made it hard to argue that farmers should not also reap a reward, that science and technology should not be organized in agriculture as well. Trained mechanics would prove also indispensable elements in the machinery of war.

Accordingly, Congress passed in June of 1862 the Morrill Act. It provided that each state would receive thirty thousand acres of public land for every senator and representative in Congress. States without large tracts of public land were given scrip that entitled them to tracts of land that they might sell. Proceeds from the sale of these lands would go toward supporting colleges "to teach such branches of learning as are related to agriculture and the mechanical arts." These colleges were also to teach "military tactics."

This federal grant unleashed political warfare in state legislatures. As was uniformly the case with wartime national government grants, little national direction or regulation attended these gifts. States decided which colleges or universities would receive the money from land sales. In state capitals, cities bargained and bribed for the right to house institutions of truth and wisdom. Furthermore, no one in Washington made an effort to make sure that states sold this bounty responsibly. The profits from land sales varied greatly. Rhode Island, which sold its lands fast, got about 40¢ an acre. States that waited for a better market could get much more, though the average was about 80¢. Since the act applied to states created in the future, the South, too, would benefit when the war was over, as would western states of the North. Idaho, for example, would get $900,000 for selling only ninety thousand acres.

The long-range consequences of this measure were profound. Twenty-two states added this new higher education onto their teaching systems. Some states gave the money to existing schools: Massachusetts divided the funds between MIT and the University of Massachusetts; New York gave its funds to Cornell; New Jersey to Rutgers; Rhode Island to Brown. But in the Western states great schools such as the Universities of Illinois, Wisconsin, Minnesota, and California were given birth.[8]

This expansion of higher education in the United States increased the trained leadership of the nation and thereby encouraged the continued growth for the economy. Both were endorsed by the deep patriotism shown in the existing colleges and universities of the nation. These places enthusiastically contributed to the war effort. Harvard sent 56 percent of its graduates in 1861 to serve in the Union army. Yale sent 42 percent of that same class, Dartmouth and Brown sent 35 and 50 percent respectively into the war. Over 24 percent of graduates of the Harvard classes of 1841–61 served in Lincoln's armies. Yale sent almost 23 percent of the graduates of the previous twenty years to join the Crimson. These figures were much larger than the percentage of the Northern population that fought on the Union side. There were between the ages of fifteen and fifty approximately 14.7 million white men as of 1860. About 2.6 million of these wore blue—or 17.6 percent.

Colleges and universities contributed so substantially to the war that enrollments declined during the conflict. Yale, Harvard, Union, Williams, and Amherst in the East and Dennison, Western Reserve, and Lafayette in the West all lost enrollments. Michigan was unique among larger schools in gaining students. Hundreds of former students never returned. Ninety-two Harvard scholars died at war; one hundred from Oberlin, forty-four from Bowdoin, twenty-two from Williams, gave "the last full measure of devotion" to the Union cause.[9]

The contribution of these men and other college graduates was manifold. The heroism of Harvard aristocrats validated the moral qualities of America's upper class. Thomas Higginson observed that the war had demonstrated that "there is no class of men in this republic from whom the response of patriotism comes more promptly and surely than from its most highly educated class. . . . It is surprising to notice [in the Harvard list of soldiers] how large is the proportion of Puritan and Revolutionary descent." In addition, the well-educated young men provided expertise in organizing Union forces. At times this influence was indirect: West Point trained most of the nation's engineers as of 1860, but the Point was overseen by a board that had Ivy League graduates in the majority. Graduates increasingly entered the ranks of lawyers and businessmen, bringing their skills to help organize the growing economy. Businessmen obviously practiced these skills, but the lawyers had begun to be intimately involved in business organization through their drafting of corporate charters and defending businesses in the courts. And, of course, the personal contacts that college men gained linked experts in all fields to each other in ways that spread knowledge and greased organizations with the lubricant of personal familiarity. Contacts grew between the wealthy families and organizational experts that would bind capital and expertise together in a force capable of energizing Northern victory.[10]

Not all of the organizational genius of Northern victory came from West Point or the higher education elite. The nation was still sufficiently the society of the common man that mechanics, or "skilled operatives," played vital roles in keeping the Union war machine in motion. Ben Butler recalled a moment in 1861 when a disabled railroad engine seemed likely to keep his Massachusetts regiments from saving Washington. Could anyone in the ranks repair it? Butler asked. An enlisted man spoke up. "Well, General, I rather think I can. I made that engine."[11]

A crucial part of the Republican philosophy of the prewar years had been the need for Western lands open to settlement. By offering a safety valve for workers in the East, the frontier was supposed to provide the hope and opportunity necessary to make Eastern workers continuing supporters of the new America that the party promised. The outrage against the expansion of slavery fed on fears that slavery would foreclose the hopes of free labor in the territories. Not every Republican supporter had favored the free soil idea. Henry Carey had argued that the migration of workers from the East would restrict national prosperity. But the majority of the party strongly favored homestead legislation.[12]

But by the mid-1850s frontier hopes became clouded. Opportunity seemed to be declining in the West. Individual and corporate speculators acquired millions of acres of Western land, between eight and twelve million acres in Illinois and Iowa alone. This land speculation drove prices beyond the reach of potential settlers, increased interest costs to 30 to 50 percent on the average, and inevitably led to foreclosed mortgages, sheriffs' fees, and a growing number of farm tenants and farm laborers. The old Jeffersonian ideal of a nation of yeoman farmers seemed in jeopardy, at the same time that President-elect Lincoln had promised supporters that he favored "cutting up the wild lands into parcels so that every poor man may have a home."[13]

Sentiment grew that the existing land policy had to be changed. A settler who "transforms by his labor a patch of rugged forest or bleak prairie into a fruitful, productive farm," Greeley wrote in June 1862, "pays for his land all that we think he ought to pay." The measure that resulted seemed to provide greater chances for settlers, allowing them to acquire land by working on it, not by simply holding it, waiting for value to increase. Any person twenty-one years or older, or a head of a family who was a citizen or had filed an intention of becoming a citizen, and who had never been disloyal to the country might claim up to 160 acres of land upon payment of a small fee. At the end of five years, upon showing the improvements made, and swearing that they neither were claiming the land for someone else nor had sold it, the land was theirs. The law, signed by Lincoln on May 20, 1862, was to go into effect January 1, 1863, the same day as the Emancipation Proclamation.[14]

The law did provide land and farms for thousands of actual settlers. Between 1863 and 1865 over 26,500 homesteads were claimed. In Minnesota, where most of the claims were made, the number of individual farms grew from 18,181 in 1860 to 45,600 in 1870. The law thus validated a Republican promise that free labor would benefit from free soil. There were some demographic consequences to the measure as well. New England's poorer rural regions lost population, a proportion of it to lands opened up in the West. Soldiers especially benefited from the act. If they served two years in the army the five-year residency requirement of the Homestead Act was reduced to one year. Many Northeastern soldiers took advantage of this provision. Combined with the inducements to go west provided by railroads selling their congressional bounty, the Homestead Act depleted New England of young men and their wives, who sought new futures in the West.

But limitations balanced benefits. Much of the land available for homesteading lay in the central prairies where drought might destroy a homesteader's future and where the 160 acres was inadequate for successful farming. Furthermore, the law did not replace the old system. It brought a new settlement policy into what Paul Gates has called an "incongruous land system." Congress had already embarked on a policy of land grants to railroads that gave them up to 94 million acres between 1862 and 1871. States had granted an additional 38 million. Another 140 million acres had been set aside for schools and universities and public buildings. An equal number of acres were designated for Indian reservations, part of which would be sold. And there remained the millions of acres of land already owned by railroads and speculators. The area not open to homesteaders was much greater than the land finally acquired by them. The hold of large investors on the frontier was hardly eliminated by the homestead law. Speculators continued to acquire up to 50 million acres between 1864 and 1869. And the numbers of tenant and farm laborers did not decline.[15]

The desire of the Republican party to build the wealth and power of the Union also led to strong support for the building of a railroad to the Pacific. At a time when the added wealth of the North was indubitably an element of Union strength, proposals that promised additional wealth and development of resources were hard to dispute. Just as the government spared no effort in defending itself, voices were strong that urged government support for the building of a railroad that would bind California to the Union and would open up the lands between the Missouri River and the Pacific Ocean to development. Minerals and timber as well as farm products would flow on rails to markets in the East. These markets would encourage further development of the West. Prosperous towns and rich farms would replace useless wilderness. Furthermore, the building of railroads would provide jobs to enrich the working classes as well, and might draw them to the West where they could settle. Not only would these steel sinews generate wealth, they would in fact save money. One California senator estimated that it would save $50 million per year if railroads replaced other methods of hauling between Eastern ports and San Francisco. Using all these arguments, Western railroaders like Leland Stanford, Mark Hopkins, and Collis P. Huntington lobbied passionately in Washington for government assistance in this gigantic enterprise. Their voices blended with a chorus of supporters who shared the visions of what railroading would mean to the nation's wealth and strength.

This combined support produced in June 1862 majorities of 35 to 5 in the Senate and 104 to 21 in the House passing the Union Pacific Railroad Bill. Lincoln signed the measure happily. Two railroad construction companies were to build a track and facilities between Omaha, Nebraska, and Sacramento, California. To pay for this enterprise the national government granted them a 400-foot right-of-way and ten alternate sections of land per mile, five sections on each side of the track. The resulting grant provided 6,400 acres of public land for each mile of track built. This checkerboard reached across the entire length of the route and included 15.5 million acres of land. But even this vast contribution did not prove inducement enough to begin the building effort from the Missouri. Two years later Congress doubled the size of the land grant. In addition to granting land, the government promised to lend the companies 6 percent bonds according to the type of terrain being built upon. The companies thus received $16,000 of those bonds for each mile built on the plains, $32,000 per mile in the hills, and $48,000 per mile in the mountains.[16]

Such generous grants to private corporations inspired some harsh criticism. But the practice of trading land for railroad building was not unprecedented and previously had yielded profitable results. The Illinois Central Railroad, beneficiary of the first such grant in 1850, had helped make Lincoln's state prosperous. During the war, the railroad hauled great quantities of men and supplies and did so for free. The only charge the government paid was for the use of locomotives and cars. The Western railroads would also later provide cut-rate hauling for the government. These companies also paid back the loans they had received at the end of the century, returning almost $167,750,000 on an initial loan of slightly over $64,600,000.[17]

The railroads received, however, an enormous bounty, land that would ultimately bring them almost half a billion dollars. It also gave them much control over the wealth of the West, control that one day would inspire a powerful protest from farmers who felt themselves at the mercy of this iron octopus. It was another mixed heritage of the war, reflecting the ambiguous nature of an economy just entering the modern age. Men during the war saw the power and the strength railroads could bring, the prosperity they fostered. The wartime mentality made it easy to equate the benefits that rails would bring to the nation with the profits to be made by government-encouraged private enterprise. The war marshaled the resources of the whole society. It linked elements of that society in a shared patriotic enterprise. Since government and private enterprise were engaged in the same crusade, it is not surprising that the majority of Northerners did not give extensive thought to the possibility that private gain was not necessarily public benefit. The war made it easy to avoid such suspicions.[18]

The railroad industry provides an illuminating example of the interrelationships between the Republican legislative program, the economic transformations of the period, and the success of the Union war effort. While the war did not give birth to these transformations, it did anoint them with a sanctity that obscured their darker potentials for high social cost. Railroading was the most compelling symbol of the new economic forces as well as the key factor in transforming the economy of the prewar years. Furthermore, it played the most public role in forging Union victory.

At the beginning of the war the North had unquestioned superi-

ority over the South in its railroad network: over 22,000 miles of
track to the Confederacy's 9,000. Such an extended network assisted not only the movement of troops and materials for the army.
It proved an indispensable element in maintaining the strength and
vitality of the Northern economy. Railroads helped enrich the farmers of the West who sold in Eastern markets, and the Eastern manufacturers marketing their products in the West. The railroad also
moved the people into cities and onto Western farmlands, building
such markets in the first place.[19]

The railroad industry in the North was also the strongest force for
transforming the economy from a small-scale local operation into
a mass-production, high-volume, well-integrated system. Combined with the telegraph, railroads made communication and transportation of goods faster, surer, and more reliable. While canals
would continue to carry millions of tons of cargo through the war
years, the railroads were rapidly overtaking them. They were swifter
than canal boats and not affected half as much by the weather. These
advantages permitted goods from manufacturers to be distributed
more quickly than ever before to buyers who could get what they
wanted on short notice by direct contact with the suppliers. They
also reduced advantages of many small-scale local suppliers who
could not easily compete with wealthier high-volume manufacturers
some distance away. Established firms had lower transportation
costs to go with the advantage of quick supply. The growing influence of larger economic units meant that communities could be
affected by decisions of companies far away. It also meant that the
wealthier enterprises would have more influence within the communities. This increasing wealth concentrated in the hands of certain companies had consequences both within those communities
and in distant places where they might do business. And, of course,
the railroad companies themselves were the strongest of such economic forces. Their power would soon produce protests from local
communities of farmers and small cities against decisions made in
New York, Boston, Philadelphia, and Chicago that shaped the lives
of people in small communities throughout the North.[20]

Railroads also made necessary the invention of modern business
organization, pushed by the imperatives of operating large-scale
enterprises involving the safety and money of thousands of passengers and shippers. Large roads like the Erie, the Pennsylvania, the

Baltimore and Ohio, began to specialize the functions of management, creating organizations that knew how to move vast quantities of people and materials in efficient and profitable ways. All these changes were in process before the war and would continue after it.[21]

It seems likely that the war did not accelerate these changes overall. But war did have an impact on the railroad system, just as that system shaped the nature of the conflict. While Northern roads were developed far beyond those of the South by 1860, they did not form an integrated rail network. Local imperatives and selfishness impeded that integration. Since railroads had been built initially to enrich individual cities, many urban officials and business leaders opposed integration of the system. They feared that their cities would become mere way stations and lose their importance as terminals for products. Railroad officials feared loss of business to competitors. Some roads did not allow their rolling stock to be used on other lines, thus requiring that long-range shipments be unloaded and reloaded onto new cars. Philadelphia for years fought the linkage of railroads through the city, and even during the war connections were only made by building rails around the city to connect New York and Washington. In addition to local prejudices, there were mechanical obstacles to integration. There were at least eleven different gauges of rails in the nation. While 53 percent of the total mileage was set at four feet eight and a half inches, trains might encounter track that ran from six feet wide to five feet to four feet ten inches. Different railroads had separate terminals in towns, making transfers difficult. There were also problems in track and bridges that had been too quickly built and were deteriorating.[22]

When war came these problems became not merely questions of inconvenience but instead matters of national survival. The Union loss at the second Battle of Bull Run was in large measure due to the failure of ten thousand bluecoats to be sent by rail to the battlefield. On the other hand, railroads were imperative to the success of major campaigns. At Gettysburg it was the ability of Herman Haupt to run fifteen to seventeen trains on track that usually handled three to four that kept Meade supplied and ready to meet Lee and Longstreet. General Sherman testified that his successes in Georgia rode on iron rails. A "single stem of railroad," he wrote, "supplied an army of 100,000 men and 35,000 horses for the period of 196 days. . . . To have delivered that amount of forage and food by ordinary wagons would have required 36,800 wagons of six mules each, allowing each wagon to have hauled two tons twenty miles a day, a simple impossibility in such roads as existed in that region."[23]

In helping bring the Union victory, railroad leaders learned how to integrate the efforts of different roads. Movement of troops over long distances involved the crossing of several lines, and railroad leaders learned how to cooperate. The four-foot-eight-and-a-half-inch gauge began to prevail over all others. The war years saw the establishment of uniform freight-handling systems, the unification of ticket offices in major cities, the creation of fast freight lines for emergency cargo, the establishment of a single superintendent for the vital lines between New York and Washington. The huge volume of mail to and from soldiers led to the establishment of a system of mail distribution that all the railroads adopted.

War necessities also engendered technological changes in the railroad industry. The heavy traffic in vital cargoes of men and supplies, moving at high speeds, wore out iron rails faster than the roads could afford to replace them. Steel rails, paid for by mid-war profits, began to replace iron, and their durability over the long haul made heavier and faster cargoes and traffic more and more profitable. Although most of this replacement took place after the war, the conflict had given it impetus. Steel also took the place of iron in locomotive wheels and fireboxes. Since most steel rails were imported from Europe, this technological change had an impact on the international economy as well. The war also accelerated the transition from wood to coal as fuel. As costs rose because of taxes and labor scarcity, and the need to repair depreciating equipment, the railroads looked for ways to economize and found that coal would drive trains farther than wood at less cost.[24]

Little of the activity of the railroads involved laying new rails. There was too much to do in maintaining lines that had already been laid and that were experiencing enormous traffic. In 1862 miles of track built fell below one thousand for the first time since 1848, and not until 1866 would that figure be reached again. But the approximately thirty-five miles that were laid were vital in connecting lines together. In 1862 the line between New York and St. Louis was completed. The Atlantic and Great Western linked the

Ohio and Mississippi rivers with the Erie Railroad and the East, and tapped the rapidly growing oil production in Pennsylvania.[25]

This growth was a sign of the most prosperous times that the companies had ever had. Prewar use had not reached capacity, but the war more than made up for that. Full-time operations brought immense profits to the lines, helping them to pay off old debts and to accumulate the funds necessary to the immense building programs that came after the war. Given the estimated $1,138,000,000 in commerce that flowed between East and West, it is hardly surprising that the railroads made so much money, even if they shared in this commerce with Great Lake shipping and canals. Between 1863 and 1865 railroads of the North paid dividends of $28 million, $41.3 million, and $36.2 million. They paid interest to bondholders of $18.6 million, $19.1 million, and $23.5 million.[26]

This vast activity and profitability of the railroads took place with little government control. Lincoln had been given the right to take over the railroads in case of military necessity, but chose not to exercise that right except in rare instances, such as during the draft riots in the Pennsylvania coalfields. Still, the possibility of government control could persuade railroads to cooperate. When the roads seemed to be charging excessive rates to the government, Secretary of War Stanton, General McClellan, and Quartermaster General Montgomery Meigs met in a Washington hotel in February of 1862 with leaders of the industry. Together they worked out a satisfactory rate formula. Stanton also urged that they standardize gauges, signaling systems, and the use of freight cars. Although concerned early in the war about government regulation, railroad leaders were beginning to note the surge in business that the war promoted. They accepted Stanton's suggestions, and the rails continued under civilian control throughout the war. Profits and patriotism were eloquent arguments.[27]

Yet even such minor intrusions into the domain of the civilian war makers were rare. As was the case with the creation of the banking system and the marketing of bonds, the government let the experts have their way. Railroads were indispensable to the waging of the war. The government had no experience in running a railroad. But men like Haupt and Thomas Scott of the Pennsylvania, John Garrett of the Baltimore and Ohio, Louis Parsons of the Ohio and Mississippi, and David McCallum of the Erie had been building the world's greatest industrial enterprise. They had learned how to organize widespread and vast resources and could apply their talents to war as well as to peace. Indeed, the line between what was needed in war and in peace began to be erased. Marshaling the resources of a nation to win a war by definition called forth that society's organizers and not just its generals. It had become impossible to leave war to the generals, and even the generals knew it.

Scott became the War Department's assistant secretary in charge of government transportation. Parsons managed river and rail transport in the Western theater from early in the war until summer 1864 when he replaced Scott. McCallum directed the military railroads in the crucial mid-war years of 1862–64 and was the architect of Sherman's transport system. Haupt brought his awesome talents in railroad construction, engineering, and operation to such refinement that Confederates allegedly believed that the Union army carried duplicate tunnels to replace any that might be destroyed. By 1865 these men were in charge of the largest single railroad in the world—a transportation network that was serving the army but was a civilian-run enterprise.

These experts worked intimately with the military and thus earned the respect of the country's future heroes and leaders. Linking themselves with the successful prosecution of the greatest event in the nation's history, they gained the right to point with pride at the service they had done the country. And they, of course, thus could justify to themselves and future critics the enterprises they would operate in peace. Mixed with the experience they had gained during the war, it was a potent legacy for the postwar years when railroads would achieve even greater power and wealth.

If there were prewar experts to be drawn upon, the war also gave invaluable experience to others who would later achieve prominence. General Grenville Dodge would go on to build the Union Pacific. Frank Thompson would direct operations of the Pennsylvania and Erie. Adna Anderson of the Northern Pacific, J. H. Devereaux of the Cleveland and Pittsburgh, E. C. Smeed of the Kansas Pacific, all built on their wartime service to shape peacetime railroading.[28]

The wartime experience also had significant consequences in the postwar relations between railroads and the government. After providing its huge grants to the railroads, the government stepped out of the way and let the roads and their operators build and administer as they chose. Although the government appointed inspectors for the building of the Western railroads, company clerks most often wrote their reports for them. Congressmen wrote to ask for direction about what federal laws should look like to the best interest of the company. Iowa's Senator Grimes, widely respected for his independence, told the president of the Burlington Railroad that "those who are disposed to be friendly to you do not know how to act, because they are ignorant of what you have concluded is the true policy for your companies and there is no one here to enlighten them." The Union Pacific was given control over the army in the West to get rid of the Indians that obstructed track laying. The company also used troops to remove squatters from disputed land and to put down labor trouble.

This subsidization without regulation led to confusion in the minds even of business leaders about government policy. They responded with incessant lobbying and not a little bribery to get the laws they wanted. One historian has argued that the government hands-off attitude helped to create the corruptions of the postwar era. Since government would not direct the economic efforts it was subsidizing, business efforts to shape policy in favorable directions became necessary. There is much truth in this assessment, but what needs to be made clear is that the war environment had seen supremely successful efforts by railroad leaders in winning the war. Government hands-off policy saw track laid, cargoes moved, and prosperity increasing. Furthermore, the profits made had immediately and clearly redounded to the defeat of the South, the arch antithesis to the free labor economy that Republicans extolled. The line between public and private interest was obscure in an environment where private expertise had been such an imperative instrument of national victory. Future corruptions found some excuse in the nature of the Union victory, and in the prosperity that attended it.[29]

While the war brought prosperity to the railroads, the rest of the economy boomed, too. Despite the statistical evidence that shows an overall nationwide reduction in prewar rates of growth, the war years saw vitality and important activity throughout the Northern economy. With a high proportion of the workers in the army, with resources going into destruction as well as growth, with efforts being devoted and directed toward the war and not into more venturesome peacetime activities, the North produced a wartime boom that astounded observers. Reporting to his state legislature in January 1863, Governor Richard Yates of Illinois noted, "In the three departments of industrial progress—agriculture, manufactures, and commerce—there has been a most remarkable development . . . not withstanding the war [which] has diverted so large a proportion of the most effective and most skilled labor of the country from its ordinary fields of usefulness." Speaking to the nation in his annual message of December 1864, Lincoln noted that after three years of war the Union was "gaining strength, and may if need be maintain the contest indefinitely. . . . Material resources are now more complete and abundant than ever. . . . The national resources are unexhausted, and, as we believe, inexhaustible."[30]

In 1865 a Southern visitor came north to discover the impact of war on the victors.

Currently with the enormous and unexampled expenditure of men, money and materials which the Federal States were subjected to for five years [he noted], every one of them increased its production and added to its wealth. And this increase of wealth was permanent and visible. It is to be seen in new furnaces, mills, factories, tanneries; in new mines of iron, coal, copper, lead, and zinc; in new railroads and countless oil wells; in the multiplication of machinery and the establishment of new industries; in the vast number of new vessels on lakes and rivers, and canals; in the extraordinary increase of elegant and costly dwellings in country and town.[31]

The first reaction to the outbreak of war had turned the economy downward. More businesses failed in the secession winter than had failed in several years during the recession of the mid-1850s. But by late 1862 a business upturn began that would lead to the boom of the mid-war years. Instrumental in this economic vitality were wartime orders from the government to build the war machine and the offshoots of those orders, which helped business and industry generally. In addition to increased orders came an increase in the money supply from the greenbacks, which made payment easier for manufacturers especially. Wartime inflation also helped. Many of them had been in debt throughout the prewar period to merchant creditors. Rising prices enabled them to pay off debts in cheaper dollars. One study estimates that manufacturers could pay off prewar debts from one-fourth to one-third more cheaply in 1863 than they could in 1860.

Furthermore, more cash and greater demand meant that buying and selling for cash became the norm. Interest charges became less and less a factor in draining capital from manufacturers. The result: increased profits to expand and strengthen their operations. Manufacturers gained greater independence in the economy. Their earlier indebtedness to merchants who would distribute their goods faded as debts were paid. Manufacturers were freed to make contracts with a greater number of dealers and, aided by better rail facilities, could expand their markets, thus increasing profits further. In the building of railroad locomotives and cars, woolen goods, watches, ships, machinery, and hundreds of other products, the war thus built economic independence as it generated profits. Small wonder that the owner of one Pennsylvania forge could declare, "I am in no hurry for peace."[32]

As merchants lost their position of major creditors financing manufacturing and other activities, banks gained. Helped by the wartime legislation, banks expanded their credit operations. This had further consequences for the growth of manufacturing in the North. Merchants had limited the investment options of manufacturers to activity directly helpful to merchandising. But banks specialized only in lending money, thus providing a wider range of investment options to borrowers. Some merchants chose to become bankers, accelerating economic specialization. While banks suffered a bit from wartime inflation, in the postwar period they benefited from this specialization and the growth of industry they fostered. The consolidation of economic influence was nurtured indirectly in the same way that the 1863–64 banking legislation had helped it directly.[33]

These structural changes underlay activity and success in many industries across the North. Of course some industries did suffer. The most prominent of these was cotton manufacturing, before the war the largest manufacturing industry in the nation. With cotton supplies cut off from the South, manufacturing of cotton clothing declined. The factory hands in this most factory-dominated industry left the large mills and sought work in other industries, or joined the army, or, if they had originally left farms to work in the mills, simply returned home. Still, stockpiled cotton was available in 1861, and most mills operated about two-thirds of the time. By 1862 dwindling supplies cut work to anywhere from one-half to one-fourth. But as Northern armies pushed south, new supplies flowed again, and some factories kept going by shifting to wool products —an industry that prospered greatly, doubling its output during the war. And even though production of cotton goods fell, reduced supplies still meant profits for mill owners.[34]

There were even better opportunities for profit in iron manufacturing. When war broke out England reduced its exports to the United States. Continued fluctuations in the price of gold kept British caution alive. This opened up markets for domestic producers. They expanded to meet these new markets, refurbishing old rolling mills and building new mills all over the country, especially in New York, New Jersey, and Pennsylvania. Pig iron production accelerated in the war years, reaching levels that broke previous records. Between 1854 and 1859 production had increased by 14 percent. In the next five years production increased by 32 percent, and, operating on war momentum, the next five years saw an increase in output of 68 percent. In real terms pig iron production jumped from 841,000 tons in 1859 to 1,136,000 tons in 1864. Fueled in part by iron output increases, the production of coal jumped from 8,756,000 tons in 1861 to 12,349,000 in 1865.[35]

The building of guns, rails, nails, bolts, stoves, locomotives, hundreds of thousands of horseshoes, and myriad other items encouraged a trend seen in most wartime industries toward concentration. Large, open-hearth steel making was just beginning and required more capital than could be generated by the operation of any small furnace. Iron companies thus began to combine to smelt and roll iron. Larger and more complex devices for making rails spread throughout the country, and big businesses were the ones who could make use of such equipment. Pennsylvania saw the building of three great rolling mills during the war. Pittsburgh witnessed the creation of six large iron mills in a single year, and in the last year and a half of the war that city produced $26 million worth of iron and steel. All this caught the attention of a young man named Andrew Carnegie, who had begun his career in railroads but shifted to Pennsylvania iron and steel to build his stupendous fortune.[36]

War also encouraged concentration and with it the rise of the factory system in other industries. In Lynn, Massachusetts, the shoe industry was on the way toward concentration even when the war broke out. Workers were losing control of their work environment, of the pace of their work, of individual ways of working. Production lines pushed workers from behind and pulled them from ahead. Concentrations of ownership reduced employment options. The huge strike of 1860 showed workers' feelings on this point. But the war accelerated the process. Relying on the invention of a machine capable of sewing soles to the upper parts of shoes, shoemaking moved from households to the factory where production increased to meet war demand.

And the numbers of workers needed to increase the output declined. Comparing 1855 with 1875, the number of workers in Lynn declined by two thousand while the number of shoes made increased by seven million. Since shoe prices also rose from $1.00 a pair in 1860 to $1.65 a pair in 1865, there was a vast increase in profits for the industry. In 1863 a local paper in Lynn described the changes war brought: "Of course the system is yet in its infancy—the business is yet in a transition state; but the wheels of revolution are moving rapidly, and they never turn backward. Operatives are pouring in as fast as room can be made for them, buildings for 'shoe factories' are going up in every direction, the hum of machinery is heard on every hand, old things are passing away and all things are becoming new."[37]

Concentration also appeared in the clothing industry and in oil. By the 1850s ready-made clothing was already being manufactured, but the war stimulated demand. The tariff cut off foreign competition. Boston, New York, Philadelphia, Rochester, and Cincinnati prospered by taking over the industry and introducing factory methods to meet extraordinary demands from the army for uniforms. One manufacturer got an order for $1,250,000. A process that had seen increased capital investment and a decline in the number of establishments as early as the 1850s was accelerated. A burgeoning oil industry whose products were used for illuminating the rapidly expanding cities was still in its early stages of disorderly growth, but men like John D. Rockefeller were learning the ropes that would one day bring awesome concentration to this industry as well.

Not all areas of the economy saw large-scale concentration. Coal mines, some of the oil industry, much manufacturing, still was in the hands of small firms, thus sustaining the vision of small entrepre-

neur farmers, mechanics, and laborers united in a free labor economy. But the signs of concentration flashed with increasing frequency, and even the *Commercial and Financial Chronicle* was troubled
at war's end by seeing "an increasing tendency in our capital to
move in larger masses than formerly. Small business firms compete
at more disadvantage with richer houses and are gradually being
absorbed into them . . . the power accumulating in the moneyed
classes for the concentration of capital in large masses is attracting
the attention of close observers of the money market. It is one of
the signs of the time and will probably exert no small influence over
the future growth of our industrial and commercial enterprise."[38]

If some economic statistics, such as cotton, went down, more, like
iron, went up. The latter numbers were more widely read and believed, further nourishing the climate of enterprise. Reflecting on
economic conditions as of January 1865, the *New York Times* reported figures by R. G. Dun and Company that proclaimed prosperity. Between 1857 and 1861 almost 19,000 businesses had failed,
ranging from about 5,900 in 1861 to 2,700 the year before. But the
war had changed things dramatically. A mere 1,652 businesses had
failed in 1862, down by over 4,000 from 1861, and the next two
years saw a total of only 1,000 failures. The *Times'* explanation
pointed to the health of an integrated economy. Agricultural prosperity "has augmented the wealth of the trading classes." Labor
scarcity in skilled trades had produced increasing wages and led to
"enhanced receipts of the operating classes." With both farmers
and industrial laborers enjoying increased income, the basis for the
success of the rest of the economy was laid. Retail merchants could
pay off the jobbers who supplied them, and jobbers could easily pay
importers and commission merchants. "The natural conclusion
must be that each, acting in harmony with the other, has produced
a more satisfactory result than could have been anticipated by even
the most sanguine."[39]

This Civil War boom in the North was part of a longer trend of
economic growth that began in the 1840s. The war years did show
a decline in the overall rate of growth of the national economy, but
once the devastation of the South was overcome, the nation continued a growth rate that would march upward until 1914. The real
GNP per capita increased about 2 percent per year. By World War
I it would be three times that of 1865. Real GNP itself would in-

crease nearly 4 percent per year, producing a GNP eight times bigger in 1914 than in 1865.[40]

The war itself demonstrated the awesome wealth and power of the Northern economy. The Union could send almost two million workers away to war and still increase its productivity in practically every area of national wealth. It could produce the food, the weapons, the clothing, the transportation, to supply the largest army in the hemisphere in almost profligate plenty and still unleash a civilian boom that raised a storm of criticism for its excessive displays of wealth. The explosions of war cast a brilliant illumination over the economic vitality of Northern society. Doing so, it helped to transform prewar anxieties into both paeans of praise and more realistic forms of criticism.

The literary offspring of the early stages of industrialization had spoken of vaguely defined monsters, of inexorable and ambiguous forces demanding the lives of men and the spirit and femininity of women. But the war clouded over the brilliant ambiguities of romanticism and brought forth a new realism to American literature. Like the antebellum writing, it, too, reflected a response to socioeconomic transformation. But now the targets were clear. Mark Twain would scald the immorality of business, industry, and politics in *The Gilded Age*. William Dean Howells could demonstrate the personal costs of business rapaciousness in *The Rise of Silas Lapham* and *A Modern Instance*. And literary utopians like Edward Bellamy could propose socialist alternatives to the blatant excesses of private enterprise. These efforts in fiction mirrored growing criticisms by farmers and industrial workers of clear and obvious flaws in the economic structure.

The massive efforts of the wartime economy also generated for the first time a volume of statistical data that provided guidelines for new government activity and offered ammunition for critics of society. The income tax innovation created the office of commissioner of Internal Revenue. The new commissioner, David Wells, provided a growing volume of data on income distribution and national wealth. The creation of a Department of Agriculture added to the data collected and distributed about farms and the movement and distribution of farm products. These facts made the picture of the economy and its impact on society more clear and more objective, laying groundwork for realistic critics and assessments. Even though the protesters of the early postbellum age still echoed preindustrial themes, they now had the basis for understanding and assailing a system whose costs were more clearly recognized.[41]

The "American system" of the wartime Republican party thus marshaled the resources of the nation to help save the Union. The Whig concept of enterprise assisted by government action received the mantle of patriotism. In the hothouse of war, prosperity and military victory walked hand in hand. The nature of the assistance provided did help the entrepreneurs who were already forging the modern economy of the prewar years. What was good for the General Motors of the day was linked inexorably to the good of the nation. But the Civil War was not unique in this linking of business benefit and winning wars. In both the world wars of the twentieth century government again promoted an environment that encouraged the concentration of economic power and did so in the name of patriotism.[42]

These results were mixed. Although prosperity was the most common result, there were segments of the economy where doubts became more clear about the emerging modern economy even as other sections experienced the best years of their lives. The impact of the war on the farmers illuminates the positive experience; its impact on industrial workers reveals the darker aspects of the conflict. Yet what needs to be recalled is the fact that the Republican program emphasized the integration of the economy, and the shared benefits of economic advance. In the growing economy, tinged with the aura of patriotism, Republican policy kept obscure for some time the winners and losers in the emerging modern America.

CHAPTER 7

Agriculture and the Benefits of War

A LTHOUGH the United States was moving rapidly toward its future as an industrial superpower, in 1860 it was still overwhelmingly a rural nation. Almost 75 percent of the population of the North lived on farms or in villages with a smaller population than the 2,500 required for urban status. Over 14.5 million Northerners were rural people, while slightly over 5 million were urbanites. This latter group included people in towns near the 2,500 cutoff point as well as people in New York, Boston, Philadelphia, Cincinnati, or Chicago.[1]

The degree of rural or urban life varied in the North. Rhode Island was over 60 percent urban and Massachusetts neared that figure, but for the rest of the region rural life predominated. Vermont was the most rural state east of the Missouri River. The Granite State's 98 percent rural population was surpassed only by the Nebraska Territory, which lacked any urban population at all. In the other regions of the North no state as of 1860 had even a 40 percent urban population. Not surprisingly, the farther west one traveled the more likely the population was to be rural: New England, 63.4 percent; the Middle Atlantic states, 64.4 percent; the Old Northwest, 85.9 percent; and the states west of the Mississippi, over 86.6 percent.

The work that people did and the products of their labor also reflected the rural character of the North. Out of a working population of approximately 10,533,000 in the nation as a whole, almost

60 percent did farm-related work. And nearly three-fourths of the nation's exports came from farms. In the North throughout the 1860s, the number of farm workers increased and so, too, the number of farms they worked and the volume of their products. The rural population increased by almost 2.5 million, the number of farms by almost 350,000, the number of farm acres by over 34 million. Between 1862 and 1864 alone the area under grain cultivation expanded by 2,659,000 acres. The contest between North and South is often pictured as one that pitted an agrarian South against an industrial North. However, the Union Lincoln led consisted preponderantly of farmers.[2]

Any generalizations about the over 1,300,000 farms in the North must respect their diversity. Different crops shaped the farmers' lives in different ways. The breeder of merino sheep in Vermont had little in common with the wheat farmer of Wisconsin. The beef cattleman from the Scioto Valley in Ohio had different problems from those of the dairyman just outside New York City, or the onion or tobacco farmer of Connecticut. While most raised some vegetables for their own use and hay for their livestock and often cut wood for sale in towns, climate and tradition led the farmers of different parts of the country to follow separate paths.

The primary goal of most farmers was self-sufficiency. They produced for their own needs, or sold enough of their output to buy land nearby that their sons could farm. The age-old ideal of a self-reliant, independent yeoman remained powerful, among those who actually lived that way and also among those who didn't. But changes had entered the rural world of the prewar United States just as they had urban America. Farmers experienced the results of those changes in many ways.[3]

The coming of railroads and the burgeoning of cities between 1830 and 1860 unleashed new forces in agrarian America. Railroads gave farmers access to markets outside their locale, more potential buyers for farm goods, while at the same time providing factories and shops that could supply tools, clothing, and other household and farmyard goods. Farmers close to transportation became part of regional, then national, and ultimately international economies.

By the outbreak of the war the farmer's world expanded beyond his county, state, or region. The *Prairie Farmer,* published in Chicago, carried advertising predominantly from Illinois, but also hawked products sold in St. Louis, Milwaukee, Toledo, Philadelphia, and Pittsfield, Massachusetts. It also published regularly the shipping rates to New York City, Boston, and Montreal.[4]

New consumer values also flowed from the involvement of farmers in the national market. Handmade furniture was replaced by the products of factories and shops in distant cities. Pennsylvania kerosene began to be used to light homes in Wisconsin. As farmers acquired reapers to help them in the fields, their wives got sewing machines to make their work easier. These products became an expected part of farm life. In a letter to the *Prairie Farmer* arguing that farm women did not need the fancy education of "city belles," one writer still insisted that to deprive country women of their sewing machines would be to "enslave" them. Faced with such inroads of the industrial world, immigrant English and Scottish farmers who had spoken in the 1840s and 1830s of farm life as an escape from industrialization began to drop that theme from their letters home.[5]

These changes also fostered a new image of the farmer as a businessman seeking profit, rather than self-sufficiency and independence. By 1868 one farm paper would say, "The old rule that a farmer should produce all that he required and that the surplus represented his gains is part of the past. Agriculture, like all other business, is better for its subdivisions, each one growing that which is best suited to his soil, skill, climate and market, and with its proceeds purchase his other needs."[6]

Along with an expanding transportation network, mechanization also helped the transformation. A man with horse-drawn equipment could harvest five times as much wheat as could a man on foot. That machine-assisted farmer could bring in a harvest faster, thus responding more successfully to vagaries in the weather. Aided by horse-drawn reapers, mowers, and cultivators, the output of Northern farms outstripped even the dramatic increase in population. During the 1850s population increased 35 percent, while acreage in improved land increased by 44 percent. Mechanization played a large role in such growth. By the end of the 1850s the McCormick Company in Illinois was selling an average of twenty-five thousand reapers annually throughout the nation. By 1859 the nation's farm equipment was valued at $18 million, an increase of 159 percent from 1849.[7]

The changes in agriculture induced by the transportation revolution and mechanization had consequences beyond increasing productivity. They helped to make farming generally profitable. While it was not the most profitable way to make money, for large numbers it still produced good returns on the money and labor invested. Not only were successful farmers able to purchase machines, they also hired laborers to help them, further increasing the productivity of farms and thus helping to raise land values.[8]

But progress also brought problems. As Western lands began to fill up, farming costs increased. The average farm, including land, tools, and livestock, cost over $1,000 for 40 acres in the Midwest, over $2,000 in the Northeast. An 80-acre Midwestern farm cost approximately $1,700 to get started. A similar place in the Northeast could be begun for about $3,000. If one could find a 160-acre farm, it would cost nearly $3,000 in the Midwest and nearly $4,700 in the Northeast.[9]

As of 1860 the possibility of owning a farm began to stand further on the horizon. The earlier ladder of farm acquisition had been fundamentally two-stepped. Farm laborers, frequently the sons of farmers, moved from laborer to owner. They inherited a farm, were given one by their father, or, if employed outside their family, saved money to buy land themselves. But by mid-century there was a new step on the ladder—farm tenancy was inserted between laborer and owner. Men had to work longer to save the money before they could buy. Many took to renting, hoping to accumulate enough money to later buy that farm or land somewhere else. But rising land and operating costs kept tenants in their position longer and made it more difficult for farm laborers to acquire farms. One estimate, based on seven counties, suggests that in two of the counties only one-fourth of laborers had enough money to buy a farm. In the other five the number of potential buyers was closer to one out of ten. Tenancy increased throughout the mid-nineteenth century. Edmund Morris, in his 1864 book *How to Get a Farm and Where to Find One,* explained: "A young man will have to work out a great deal more than seven years, in most cases from twice to three times that length of time before he can even pay half down for a good farm, to say nothing of the money that will be needed to begin farming with." This description was overly gloomy, but it still dramatized the declining reality of the yeoman farmer of the American dream.[10]

Many farm owners had a hard time making ends meet. The *Rural New Yorker* for 1860 noted that "persons owning good farms and free from debt, can ordinarily not only secure a good living, but lay aside yearly a considerable surplus—perhaps from two to five percent; but this is not making money by farming. . . . It is really receiving a low rate of interest on his capital." And as for buying a farm, "We doubt very much whether any man could take a farm at present prices . . . and pay for it from the proceeds after paying for the help, stock and machinery necessary to carry it on properly. On the contrary, we know many persons who have paid from one third to one half of the value of their farm, who can barely raise the annual interest money on their debts, and in bad years not even that."[11]

The changes in agriculture that tied farmers to the larger economy through dependence on railroads and the need for equipment generated resentment. Although the widespread protests by farmers came later, even before the war anger grew at railroads for rate-setting practices that hurt small shippers. Concern was growing also about monopolistic agreements between some railroads and warehousers that made farmers dependent on the whims of aquisitive middlemen. The increasing complexity of the agricultural market also increased the suspicion of middlemen whose profits seemed consistently to be much larger than what they paid the farmers. During the war resentment of the power of railroads continued to surface. Even while boasting that Illinois was the leading railroad state in the nation, Governor Yates still complained that the closure of the Mississippi River gave railroads an improper advantage. "Our flour, corn, cattle, and hogs are taxed with such rates for overland transportation as materially to reduce the prices at home. Once remove the monopoly enjoyed by the railroads, by bringing the Mississippi into competition with them, and every article of western produce would probably command twice the price it now brings."[12]

While the changes in agriculture attracted most of the attention and generated concerns that would one day fuel major protest, farmers in general were content. Most of them were not yet directly involved in the national commercial economy. They remained subsistence farmers, content to make enough to feed the family, sell a little surplus at the town market, set aside a little money perhaps to buy more land in the neighborhood or maybe to speculate a bit in Western lands. Living on farms that ranged from an average of 109 acres in New England to 113 in western New York and Pennsylvania, to 125 in the Old Northwest, to 169 acres in Iowa and its neighbors, Northern farmers saw themselves the backbone of a nation in which they did "middlin' well."[13]

The onset of war overwhelmed even latent discontent. Enlistments in the army took away large numbers of farm laborers, who did not own farms themselves. And the needs of the army and the nation during the war increased demand for farm goods and helped raise prices. The good luck, for Americans, of poor European harvests during the war pushed farmers to new peaks of prosperity. Economically the war brought most farmers the best years of their lives.[14]

The rural North echoed the patriotic enthusiasm that resounded after Sumter. The farmers' majority in the nation was reflected in their proportion in the army. Almost half of the soldiers were farmers or farm workers. Interestingly enough, the farm laborers formed the majority of those enlisting. In 1863 the Ohio Board of Agriculture pointed with pride to the contribution of its rural warriors by declaring, "At least from one-third to one-fourth of the ordinary farm laborers were transferred to the battlefields, and in many instances the farmers themselves." Fewer dependents and smaller resources encouraged farm laborers to enlist. Furthermore, with declining chances in peacetime to get farms, many saw the enlistment bounties as instant down payments. They might also have foreseen being paid in land for their service, a long-standing practice in the nation.[15]

The fact that farm laborers were the predominant enlistees in the Union army had several consequences. It increased wages for workers who stayed home. Thus Ohio's worker wages escalated from $120 to $150 per year plus room and board to $200 to $250 by 1865. Farm owners themselves stayed home to maintain the level of farm production needed to fuel the war machine. Many women and children went into the fields to replace absent husbands, but this colorful fact should not obscure the large numbers of farmers who served at home in "rural regiments."[16]

Still, the number of men who went away to war was immense. In the five states of the Old Northwest, Ohio, Indiana, Illinois, Michigan, and Wisconsin, an estimated 680,000 men left the fields to fight. At least 47 percent of the men ages 18–45 left the work force.

And in many towns the proportion was much larger. One Wisconsin community reported that 111 out of its 250 voters had volunteered. An Illinois township reported that 117 of its 147 healthy men between 18 and 45 had enlisted. New England sent off a similar proportion of its youth. Fifty-five percent of Vermont's men between 18 and 45 served in the army. One-tenth of New Hampshire's population left for war.[17]

It was natural for women to step into tasks left behind by departing soldiers. Women have always been the "invisible farmers," comprising over half of the agrarian population and performing at least half of the farm labor. Cooking, washing, cleaning, sewing, weaving, and rearing children within the farmhouse, women also worked in garden plots providing food for the table and cared for domestic animals. In addition, their labor was there when needed in the fields, when husbands planted and harvested the main crop.

In a schedule that abided throughout the century, farm women often rose at four in the morning, set breakfast on the table by five-thirty, fed and watered the livestock, turned to straightening the house and cleaning, got the children up, fed, dressed, and out to play or to school, began churning the butter for an hour or two, went outside to hoe the garden, stopped to prepare lunch, cleaned up the kitchen, went outside to hoe again and perhaps make a flower bed, stopped to chase livestock out of gardens and play with the children, picked up the hoe again, put it down to prepare dinner, watered the horse and milked the cows and put grain out for the chickens, joined the family for dinner, cleaned up the kitchen, got the children ready for bed, then got things ready in the kitchen for the morning. Bed at 9:00 P.M. usually brought quick sleep.

These days came and went throughout the war years and throughout the century. They were the constant rhythm of life for millions of women. The war made few changes in these days, except perhaps to add men's chores to those women had to perform regularly. The 1862 report of the Department of Agriculture observed, "In plain language, in the civilization of the latter half of the nineteenth century, a farmer's wife, as general rule, is a laboring drudge . . . on three farms out of four the wife works harder, endures more, than any other on the place; more than the husband, more than the 'farm hand,' more than the 'hired help' of the kitchen."[18]

The involvement of women in field work increased the hours they worked harvesting, mowing, and reaping, while seldom reducing household responsibilities. One New York family of a mother and seven daughters brought in a hundred acres of wheat, milked twenty-two cows, made butter and cheese, and still had time to lath and shingle an addition to their house. They, of course, also kept up with the usual chores of caring for the children, doing the housekeeping, and feeding chickens and tending the house vegetables. Some social critics voiced concern that male tasks would degrade and coarsen the fairer sex, deform their bodies and lower their social position. Women responded that the needs of the war took precedent, and that such exertions were temporary.[19]

The social environment in which these tasks were performed varied. On the Western frontier women faced an isolation that provoked profound loneliness. They were deprived of the support that came from the ethnic communities that were part of rural as well as urban America. They were away from mothers, sisters, and friends who provided the networks of affection, sympathy, and domestic assistance. The divergence of gender roles in the nineteenth century meant that women often found their greatest emotional support from other women whose life-styles they shared and to whom they often expressed their love and caring. It was easier for Eastern farm women to keep these bonds alive. Indeed, by generating women's aid societies and by taking so many young men away, the war may have reinforced the interconnections within the world of women. The world of Louisa May Alcott's *Little Women* may have been common in many Northern communities.[20]

Rural women were also isolated from public events. Men elected other men to office. The men were the judges and lawyers and juries who responded to the needs for public order and to the changing claims of the economic system. Men were the family bargainers and the buyers and sellers of products in the wider market. Hence it was often the men who represented the forces of economic change that the war era brought to rural regions. The divided roles of men and women might thus produce clashes between the more traditional culture and new impressions of a modernizing world. Urban women were frequently strong critics of the new commercial values that signaled the growth of modern industrialized society. Rural women could also protest the specialization in agriculture that undercut the contributions they could make to the farm as an economic unit, and that might destabilize their lives.

During the war, however, some modernizing forces freed women from their drudgery and were welcomed. Enlistments by male clerks in growing country towns opened some opportunities for farm girls. So did the expansion of government and business. Sewing machines made life easier for those who could afford them. The war years saw the development of changes in cheese making, traditionally a household task that might take several hours for two or three days. But the new cheese factories that sprang up to meet growing foreign and domestic demand centralized the cheese-making process and took it out of the homes. The factories picked up milk from the farms and processed it themselves. In 1864 a leading cheese manufacturer extolled his new system, which had replaced "the old system of family cheese making [that] has done more to injure the health of our wives and daughters than any other cause."[21]

Still, the transformations brought about by the war and the larger economic changes were background for the more enduring private lives that meant much more to the women and men of the war years. Women of rural America generally sought to live up to what was expected of them, no matter the hard work and weariness they often experienced. Young Rachel Bowman finished reading Martha Stone Hubbell's *The Shady Side; or Life in a Country Parsonage, by a Pastor's Wife* and vowed that "I should desire just such labor, however hard. I have been trying to show more of a Christian spirit at home. I feel like that Mother is wearing herself out, while we are going to school, I know that . . . I have resolved to live more effectionate [sic] toward my parents and the rest of the family . . . I desire very much to be real good and to get a better heart. I feel that I am prone to think too much of my own happiness." She took up gladly the role of farmer's wife when called to it and maintained her love for her husband, and her husband's love. Even reformers like Martha Coffin Wright could admonish their daughters to perform their expected roles and duties of wives and mothers. And farm wives such as Lucinda Casteen might care for domestic duties on her and her husband's farm, raise five children, occasionally do some sewing for her bachelor brother, suffer from abscessed teeth, lose a child to cholera, and quickly follow that child in death yet still see herself not as a victim but as a woman doing her duty. She was Henry Casteen's wife, Isham's sister, mother to the children, Mary Peters' daughter, and she had done the best she could. Other women found that doing their best meant fighting for women's rights, but more of them, the vast majority of rural women, measured their lives by the duties their society imposed.[22]

While women made up for the lost labor of perhaps one million men, they were helped enormously by the burgeoning use of farm machinery that war encouraged. Already growing rapidly throughout the 1850s, the farm machinery industry advanced even more rapidly by the mid-war years. On the average each farmer had invested about $7 in new equipment in 1850. By 1860 he was investing $11 a year, and by 1870 the figure stood at $20. Overall there was a 300 percent increase in the amount of capital invested in manufacturing farm machinery and a 359 percent increase in the value of that farm machinery. During the war decade the rate of farm mechanization reached its peak. Mechanization made it possible for harvests to remain large despite labor shortages. As the *Belleville Democrat* (Illinois) put it, "If not for reaping machines not one half of the county's harvest could be reaped."[23]

Agriculture papers spoke in early 1864 of the "immense proportions of business" in the selling of reapers. The 33,000 that were made in 1862 had risen to an estimated 70,000 for the coming year. At a price of $130 each, that would mean sales of over $9 million in a single year, and adding repair parts raised the total to $11 million. "Never in the history of the world," an editor declared, "was there such a supply of labor saving, and therefore money saving implements." Since these machines could be "delivered to your very doors," he urged farmers to invest in reapers. In mid-1863, the savings in labor and time provoked the *Scientific American* to gush, "Farming is comparatively child's play to what it was twenty years ago, before mowing, reaping, and other agricultural machines were employed. The severe manual toil of mowing, raking, pitching, and cradling is now performed by machinery operated by horse power, and man simply oversees the operations and conducts them with intelligence."[24]

Manufacturers could not keep up with a demand stimulated by the fact that inflation made farmers more willing to go into debt to pay for the machines. Concurrently, the national currency laws increased the money available to buy equipment. Anson Buttles farmed just north of Milwaukee in the war years, and his experiences illustrate the ways that mechanization made its meaning felt. In 1860 he bought a threshing machine and not only did his own threshing but also helped the neighbors. The next year, reflecting the impact of refinements in other areas of the economy and his access to them, Buttles began to light his house with kerosene. The next year saw the purchase of a new cultivator, which he again used to help neighbors as well as himself. By 1865 the old threshing machine was worn out. But new ones cost so much that he joined with two neighbors to buy the needed replacement. Two years later he traded a wagon for a reaper to complete his collection of farm machines.

But once again the new farming methods exacted a cost. The growing mechanization raised the ante for successful farming, especially in the Western states where conditions favored the adoption of machines. Farmers with machines could hire fewer farm laborers. Aspiring landowners had to go to the cities to earn wages. While the numbers of farmers and farm workers increased throughout the coming decades, fewer farmers were needed to feed an increasingly larger proportion of the population. The proportion of the farm population to the overall population began to fall with increasing speed.[25]

Two foreign factors also helped Northern farmers during the war. European harvests fell off, placing a greater demand on American farmers to meet the needs of English, French, and German populations. While the percentage of farm products exported remained at 4 percent, the volume of exports increased, which was felt at grain distribution centers and on grain-carrying rails and canals. The Chicago Board of Trade reported in 1862 that five thousand more vessels moved to the Eastern terminus at Buffalo than in any previous year. Erie Canal usage doubled. Before 1860, Chicago grain shipments had never exceeded ten million bushels. Each year of the war an average of twenty million bushels were shipped. These figures represented a vast increase in domestic consumption. They also signaled a major increase in foreign use, which led many to believe that "King Wheat" had replaced "King Cotton" as a major force in international relations.

The burgeoning shipments of grain and other foodstuffs reverberated in other industries. More ships and railroad cars had to be built to carry these cargoes, elevators were needed to store shipments, more railroad workers had to be employed, and greater organization was necessary to handle new magnitudes of shipping.

The increased size and complexity of the trade in food products made necessary more middlemen between farmers and consumers, and helped to extend the influence of Eastern grain sellers by multiplying the need for credit. Also magnified were the opportunities for speculation in grain futures and other gambling. These activities encouraged private regulatory efforts by merchants in Chicago and other major cities. They also encouraged farmers to organize, to cope with the ever more complex rural world. The postwar world found farmers increasingly active in politics, supporting laws to bring order and honesty to the grain elevators, railroads, and middlemen. While these changes had been sighted in the prewar world, the Civil War brought them inescapably into view.[26]

The continuing wave of immigrants also influenced wartime agriculture. While most immigrants settled first in cities, thousands continued on and took up farms or, more often, supplied the labor needs generated by enlistments. During the war eighty thousand immigrants arriving in New York City listed the prairies of Illinois as their ultimate destination. Twenty-three thousand looked to Wisconsin, and a single railroad carried over eighty thousand people to the West. The Homestead Act played a major role in stimulating European interest in the United States, and efforts of railroad companies to recruit immigrants helped to spread the word about the free land and other benefits of going to the New World.[27]

By the use of machines and with the help of immigrant farm laborers, aided by the fortuitous foreign demand, Northern farmers of both sexes maintained their productivity and experienced a widespread prosperity during the war. But in addition to the general hidden costs of commercialization of agriculture, there were temporary economic difficulties that war imposed. So much effort was extended in productivity, in planting and gathering crops for marketing, that farm improvements, other than machines, were neglected. Many farmers gave limited attention to such matters as repairing fences or roofs, rotating crops, or carrying manure to the fields. In 1867 the U.S. Department of Agriculture deplored such practice as a "blind, senseless and suicidal system." But the war helped excuse it.[28]

One important impact of the war on Northern farmers was that it generated so much market activity that it pulled greater numbers of them into the commercial economy, increasing the pressures on those wishing to remain self-reliant yeomen. Farmers in the United States had always been interested in making money, in improving their economic position, but the growth of the market system meant that they could control fewer and fewer of the forces shaping their lives. Success more and more lay with colleagues who bought the machines, concentrated on cash crops, shipped large amounts of their produce to markets far away. These were the people who could buy more land and more machines and when necessary hire more help, thus increasing their dominance in the country. They could acquire the things from the city that made farm life more pleasant, and that neighbors might envy.

The war era also witnessed further integration between rural and urban America. Growing urban populations increased the demands for farm products. Farmers with access to railroads found larger markets for their products. But large-scale health problems in cities also affected farmers. Urban consumers demanded milk, and suppliers sprang up to meet their demand, but from dangerous sources. The largest milk suppliers within cities were dairies that sprang up as offshoots of breweries. The processed grains left over from brewing provided a usable feed for cattle, who were supplied this swill and then milked. But such feed produced weak and watery milk, and the unsanitary conditions in which the cows were milked magnified dangers. As early as the 1840s swill milk was discovered to be germ-ridden, threatening the health of adults and children who drank it. But not until the late 1850s did urban newspapers take up the cry. They sent out investigative reporters, who often risked beatings and death to get their stories, but also created public demands for better milk.

The campaigns for purer milk would not achieve major success until late in the nineteenth century, but two wartime solutions did emerge. The first was the growth of milk trains into the countryside to bring cities purer milk. In 1861 the Harlem Railroad hauled nearly 28 million quarts of milk into New York City, and the Erie nearly matched that figure. Farmers from surrounding counties were sending up to 201,000 quarts per day into the city. Countrysides around other large Northern cities also increased their milk output, and farmers benefited even as their bonds to cities grew. The growth of dairy business made up for the loss of grain sales to Western farmers.[29]

Farmers' horizons also expanded when local and state government responded to outcries against adulterated milk. Massachusetts passed in 1862 an anti-adulteration statute, and New York in the same year and in 1864 passed similar laws. Urban dairies, brewers, and many farmers fought these laws. Agrarians were not above watering their milk in order to increase profits. Such public health measures forecast postwar activity by states and the federal government that regulated cattle shipments to soldiers in the field and city dwellers.[30]

Gail Borden's response to the milk crisis illustrated in another way the growing linkage of industrial and rural America. In 1851 Borden, a Texan who moved to Connecticut, patented a method for finding the impurities in milk and for condensing it. By 1859 two factories were producing Borden's milk, and doctors began recommending it to urban families. But it was the war that fueled the success of Borden's enterprise. Armies in the field presented an obvious market for milk that could be canned and shipped long distances while maintaining its purity. Borden's fortune was made, and canned products became a growing part of the food industry. The needs of the army also connected farmers to industrialized processing in the meat, fruit, and vegetable industries. Processes developed by the French during the Napoleonic Wars and used by the British to feed their armies and navy found acceptance in the United States in similar circumstances.[31]

The Civil War's impact came as much because of increased production of old and new products as because of distribution. Armies in the South required tons of food and thousands of draft animals. Millions of uniforms had to be made, and this fiber had to be shipped to distant cities, where the clothing industry grew rapidly. Hides had to be sent to towns like Lynn, Massachusetts, where shoemaking moved from cottages or small shops into large factories. And foreign needs reverberated in an increasingly national market. It was becoming more and more difficult for the farmer to remain independent of these forces. It was also difficult for him to control them.

The war also brought other immediate demands. Secession deprived Northerners of cotton, sugar, and especially tobacco. Farms saw quick profit in providing substitutes. The greatest success came from Connecticut, Illinois, New York, and Ohio tobaccos, which were reasonably adequate substitutes. Efforts to raise cotton shivered in Northern cold. Wool manufacture at least provided an alternative fiber for clothing, but the lightness of cotton was sorely missed, especially in the summer heat. Still, wool growers increased their production on a scale never seen before. The number of sheep in the contiguous Northern states jumped from just over 15 million in 1860 to over 32.5 million in 1866. Growers experimented increasingly with higher grades of wool and generally succeeded in growing heavier fleeces. Attempts to find a substitute for sugar from sorghum were considerably less successful. One Ohio agricultural paper reported, "Of all the humbugs that have been foisted on honest people, sorghum . . . stands preeminent: It requires an immense amount of labor and care to plant it properly and look after it during its early life. . . . When cut, pressed and boiled, the yield is large enough, but the yield is only sorghum; nobody knows what to do with sorghum syrup." And efforts to get sugar from beets floundered because of a lack of good machinery and skilled workers.[32]

The war brought an enormous demand for farm animals for every use. Lincoln's armies were not mechanized. Hauling the supplies for vast armies, carrying the cavalry, transporting the artillery, were jobs for horses and mules. The need drove prices up from about $110 in 1860 to $185 by war's end. The army used so many of these animals, destroying an estimated 500 per day by the last months of the war, that the number of horses in the loyal states dropped from almost 4,200,000 in 1860 to just over 3,700,000 by February 1865. The mortality of mules was similarly high. Still, it was another sign of the economic wealth of the North that there were very few reported cases where lack of horses interfered with the domestic production of the wheat and corn that fed America and Europe.[33]

While soldiers worked their horses and mules to death—or had them killed on battlefields—they took more satisfaction in the cattle and hogs that the North produced. The Commissary General of the Army bought thousands of tons of beef and pork to feed Billy Yank and his officers. In the boom of the mid-war years some wage earners were also able to buy more meat products and lard and tallow as well. Foreign, battlefield, and civilian demands bit ravenously into the supply of cattle and hogs. Ohio's cattle population dropped by over 600,000 from 1861 to 1865, hogs declined to 1,460,000 from over 2,760,000 in 1862. In all the loyal states except those of the West Coast the hog population fell by over 3 million from 1860 to 1865. Cattle rose in numbers between 1860 and 1864, but by early 1865 the total of 12,841,000 stood 800,000 below the 1860 figures. An early frost and a hard winter in 1863–64 played an important role in the reductions of 1864, but increased consumption was a major factor.[34]

Farmers also felt the force of events in Washington, D.C. Three major laws emerged from Congress that shaped the future of agriculture in the United States. In May 1862 a Department of Agriculture was established as a full-fledged part of the national government. Opponents had argued against the measure on state rights and antibureaucracy grounds, but large legislative margins overrode such concerns. The new department continued an older practice of distributing seeds to farmers. More important, it increased the number and quality of statistics on weather and crop yields, foreign and domestic. Through its widely distributed monthly bulletin the department kept farmers abreast of farm conditions and helped them make sales and planting decisions. In doing so it encouraged the growth of the image of the scientific farmer, alert to new trends, involved in the larger world. These understandings and sensitivities opened channels for future demands for state and later national action to protect them. No longer able to avoid the larger world by absorption in the independent yeoman ideal, farmers began to wonder if unified action might give them control of their destiny.[35]

The passage of the land grant college legislation also challenged farmers with a complex future. The establishment of new universities focusing study on "agricultural and mechanical pursuits" further expanded knowledge of a wider world. The graduates who returned from Urbana, Ithaca, and Minneapolis brought with them understanding of new techniques and crops that would increase yields, thus making fewer farmers necessary. They also learned of national trends, further alerting farmers to an increasingly interconnected world. Although early educational efforts had limited success, the foundation for more modern farming was laid. Civil War legislation, like the war itself, shoved farmers into a newer America.

The Land Grant Colleges Act and the establishment of the Department of Agriculture swept farmers into a modern, national economy. The Homestead Act had more mixed consequences. In some ways it served traditional values. The founding of a land distribution system that created thousands of new farms gave people hope that they might escape the problems of an industrializing society and find independence by simply going west. It helped Northerners to look away from the problems of an industrializing society. By retaining the image of a safety valve, it gave critics of the urban poor a means for blaming the victim. With all the free land in the West, why didn't the urban poor simply pack up and get themselves a farm?

Some critics of the law argued that in giving away the major source of the nation's wealth the country deprived itself of vast revenues that would have come from selling the land. A point made infrequently at the time also raised doubts about the law: opening the West via Homestead increased the pressures to dispossess the Indians. It guaranteed that there would be Indian wars, massacres of innocent people on both sides, and the further destruction of tribes and cultures.[36]

But the critics were overwhelmed by the proponents, and the consequences transcended the impact on Indians and industry. The bill encouraged the trend toward specialization and integration of the marketplace. It opened to settlement lands where crop specialization was more of a necessity because of restrictions of soil and climate. Furthermore, railroad lines followed on the heels of the opening of homestead lands, and brought new farmlands into the national market. Few farmers fought such trends. Access to markets decreased transportation costs and raised land values. The land speculators who had managed to buy millions of acres of homestead land, of course, profited greatly from these benefits. But actual homesteaders also benefited, and the nation as a whole expanded its income-producing land.[37]

In sum, the Civil War years accelerated trends already firmly established in Northern agriculture: growing mechanization, greater integration of the market system, increased specialization. With these had come the need of machines for successful farming and higher costs for land, conditions that made land acquisition more difficult by 1860. The Homestead Act brought partial relief. It opened up millions of acres of land to farmers who paid predominantly in sweat to acquire a farm. The measure fulfilled the commitment of the Republican party and the Union to its fundamental principle of free land for free labor. Fulfilling that promise undercut concern that the days of the independent yeoman were passing. The Homestead Act seemed tangible evidence that the world envisioned by Republican orators, a world of free, hard-working moral men and women, was still viable.

Despite general prosperity, rural America was not free from protest or even violence. The antidraft riots that drew so much attention to New York City had their parallel in the farmlands, too. The older Middle West especially saw riots and individual protests. The provost marshal of the United States, James Fry, noted that "in almost every house" draft officers encountered "numerous and weighty obstacles." Thirty-eight of these officers were shot, sixty wounded. Others found their families threatened or their property destroyed by midnight vandals.[38]

Other draft resisters substituted escape for violence, practicing the so-called "skedaddle quickstep," to Canada or the West. In Ohio alone one estimate put the numbers of "skedaddlers" at "tens of thousands." Canada received nearly 90,000 Americans during the war, nearly 30,000 of them deserters, others trying to dodge being enrolled in the first place. There were so many young men in Canada that farmers there could hire laborers for room and board alone. The national government urged states to stop this bleeding of the manpower pool. Iowa's Governor Stone responded with an 1864 proclamation cutting off emigration from the state without a valid pass signed by the provost marshal. Washington pressured Canada to restrict immigration by regulating passports. But the tide rolled on, as young men and families went west where they would be harder to find while they sought new futures for themselves. Over a quarter of the 776,829 called in four drafts between the summer of 1863 and spring 1865 failed to report, an additional 200,000 deserted. Although large numbers of deserters were from ethnic and urban communities, the majority of the men who escaped from service were farmers.[39]

This protest against war service was, however, only a small dark cloud over the prosperous landscape of agriculture during the Civil War. Prosperity further served to encourage the belief in the success of free labor society, a success that fugitive soldiers wanted to live to enjoy. Many farmers could share the story of John Griffiths in

Appanoose, Illinois, on the Iowa border. The war had called his son to the army, but the young man received a $450 bounty when he enlisted, and would earn $25 a month during his service. Much of that money was used on the farm. Griffiths had difficulty finding hired men to help in the fields. With labor costs so high, he did most of the work himself. Still, he was able to build a new house two stories eighteen by thirty-four feet in size with an eighteen-by-twenty-seven-foot kitchen attached and a "good cellar under the large porch." Small wonder that he could tell the brothers and sisters he had left in Shropshire, England, "It has been a good time for making money in the north since the war began. Everything was so high." No wonder he believed what Northern leaders had made into a motto for the Union. "Any industrious man can make a good living in this country."[40]

CHAPTER 8

Industrial Workers and the Costs of War

T HERE were more than 9 million workers in the North. Almost 3,500,000 of them, farmers and farm laborers, directly benefited from the boom in agriculture. Another 5,600,000 workers found employment off the farms or engaged in professional or domestic service, trade, transportation, manufacturing, mining, and mechanical industries. These were domestic servants, laborers, teachers, clerks, railroad workers, middlemen, blacksmiths, boot and shoemakers, carpenters, cotton mill workers, miners, tailors. Those linked to the farm economy experienced good times, too. But a growing proportion of Northern workers lived in the growing industrial world, gathering together in increasing numbers in shops and factories and on work gangs. In this population about a million people were self-employed and/or company officials, but the majority worked for someone else. These were the workers who forecast the future structure of the economy. They were also the workers whose fate had caused so much prewar attention.[1]

Although their work experience forecast a modern industrial society, that society was not yet in place in the war years. Older localistic contexts endured side by side with a burgeoning industrial environment. Workers experienced this new world in that older context. While nationalizing forces moved in the land, local communities were dominant in the lives of almost everyone. Few workers were organized. A reasonable estimate puts the number at approximately 300,000, less than 10 percent of all industrial workers in the 1860s belonging to local or regional organizations. As of 1860 there were only five national unions: the Printers, the Stonecutters, the Hat Finishers, the Iron Molders, and the Machinists. When workers sought protection or progress they formed local mixed trade assemblies—uniting delegates from workingmen's clubs, trade unions, and general reform societies that were interested in workingmen's problems. Such assemblies usually sought political power, but occasionally they supported boycotts and strikes by member organizations or acted as bargainers in settlements.

Most organizations were weak. In a one-industry town, workers could control politics. Shoemakers in Lynn, Massachusetts, created the Workingman's party in 1860 and took over town government. But in larger cities assemblies lacked the numbers for political clout. When workers tried to oust a Republican mayor of Philadelphia in 1865, they failed. Efforts to organize national trade assemblies during the war were equally unsuccessful. When Robert Gilchrist, president of the Louisville assembly, called for a July 1864 meeting of all the trade assemblies in Canada and the United States, the response was so poor that he issued another call, this time for September. "There are 200,000 mechanics now represented in protective unions in the United States and Canada," he proclaimed. Twelve delegates showed up representing eight cities in eight states. After writing a constitution and planning an organization they disbanded, calling for a second conference in 1865. This meeting never took place.[2]

The National Iron Molders—perhaps the strongest of the national unions—suggests the puny power of organized labor. Membership in the eighteen locals was mixed. Some locals consisted of skilled workers only; others mixed skilled and unskilled. Some had only a handful of members; others, like that at Troy, New York, hundreds. Dues ranged from ten cents a month in Philadelphia to fifty dollars a year in Troy and Albany. Some locals could spend hundreds of dollars to carpet meeting halls; others had trouble paying rent. Some of the locals were quite businesslike, focusing on economic issues and discussions; others resembled secret lodges with mysterious initiation ceremonies, secret passwords, and even public silence about being union members.

The driving force of the national organization was William Sylvis, who became secretary of the Philadelphia local in 1859 and helped found the national organization. Defeated for the presidency, he was chosen national secretary and by 1863 took over as president, a post with no treasury and no control over the locals. Sylvis set out to create a national union in fact. Throughout the winter of 1862–63 he begged and borrowed his way from city to city. Some locals paid for his visits, others didn't. Some promised to and never did. At some stops he raised money for the next leg of his journey. At other stops he met local police and employers who put him quickly back on the train. Sylvis created an impressive number of new locals. But the national body remained frail.

There were strong locals that might win strikes at times. The number of locals grew under Sylvis' activity. But even at the end of the war in 1866 Sylvis could still deplore "the selfish and senseless croaking and opposition of some whose vision is so contracted that they cannot see beyond the narrow limits of the little village in which they live."[3]

Sylvis foresaw the shape of a national economy to come. But the immediate situation saw local communities confronting the early inroads of a national economy. Conflict of interest between labor and management was often difficult to visualize, as small communities engendered social and personal relationships between employer and worker. Even in a good-sized place like Lynn, Massachusetts, where the process of industrialization was unmistakable, workers still called for harmony of interest between owners and workers. During their great strike of 1860 workers applauded some of the factory owners even while protesting against others. And the outrage that most disturbed these workers was an effort by some of the larger owners to bring outside police into the community to enforce order. Other communities witnessed alliances between local workers and local merchants and businessmen against the efforts of national companies, usually railroads, to put down worker demands for better pay, shorter hours, and improved working conditions.[4]

The generally small size of the workplace also restrained labor militance. The most outspoken criticism of the industrial system targeted factories where masses of men and women swarmed like machines serving other machines. But the average manufacturing establishment as of 1860 did not look like that. There were about 19 workers per manufacturing establishment in New England, slightly over 10 in the middle states, and a little under 6 in the West. The whole North as of 1860 found an average of 9.34 workers in each of the approximately 140,433 manufactories.

But these figures hid signs of growing industrialization in the United States, and the growth of labor consciousness in certain pockets in the North, especially in textiles, shoes, iron, and machine manufacture. While most factories in the cities were not large by modern standards, every large city had factories of considerable size. By 1870 Cincinnati had about 4,400 manufacturing establishments employing some 61,000 workers—an average of about 14 hands per firm. But 17 of those firms employed over 5,250 of Cincinnati's workers. This small number averaged 310 hands. In New York City the average number of hands employed in the city's leading manufactories was 24.4, but almost 40 percent of the employees worked in the clothing industries where shops averaging over 70 were the rule.[5]

The factory work force reflected the concentration of industry, which had been going on for several years. The work force grew in size, but the number of places people worked diminished. This concentration worried observers. The *New York Times* headlined an 1869 story: "Concentration of Capital in the Hands of Few—Employers Becoming Fewer and Laborers More Numerous—the Rich Richer, the Poor Poorer." The *Times* suggested that if more workers would decide to live outside the big cities, this trend might be reversed, but the figures kept on going the other way, and the paper caught the analogy that had become common throughout the war era: "The capitalists or masters are becoming fewer and stronger and richer. . . . the laborers or slaves are becoming more numerous or weaker and poorer."[6]

These forces were at work in the country as it moved into the Civil War. But their effect varied from place to place, and attitudes about how permanent they were, of course, also varied. Practically nowhere was there complete despair. Even in New York, Boston, Philadelphia, where things were worst, stories could be told in workers' neighborhoods of men who had escaped poverty. Newspapers and politicians reiterated endless rags-to-riches tales. Few people could in fact exchange their rags for better clothing in one generation, but even among the poorest classes incremental improvement in conditions could be seen: unskilled laborers whose sons became semiskilled and whose grandsons became skilled workers and then foremen. In industries that recent immigrants dominated, laborers took orders from their countrymen and could visualize moving up. Workers were more likely to be impressed by the personal instances they encountered of success, however modest, than with a statistical pattern showing the odds against them. Statistics on such matters were, in fact, a phenomenon of the postwar world.[7]

Opportunities varied according to industry and job situation. Benefits existed alongside disadvantages. In larger shops where worker influence was limited, wages might be higher than in smaller shops. Industries that were growing offered greater opportunities for advancement than more attractive craft occupations. And within the larger factories, which employed increasingly larger percentages of the work force, a range of jobs existed that produced a labor aristocracy of higher paid, more highly skilled workers laboring alongside lower paid and less skilled counterparts. Common laborers in these conditions might learn skilled jobs by observation, and so move up.[8]

This confused diversity was reflected in the very language with which people spoke of economic occupation and class. Newly emerging manufacturers sometimes said that they were capitalists and called their workers "labor" or "workingmen." But they more frequently called themselves part of the "producing classes" or even "workingmen" and/or "labor." They called the older merchant elite "capitalists." The term "middle class" was just starting to make its appearance and was used in quotation marks when it was used at all. And when people spoke of the economic system as a whole they did not call it capitalism, they called it the "free labor system."

Social communities and traditional work patterns often softened the power of economic forces over workers. Friends helped with food and clothing when times were hard. Churches provided economic assistance and focused attention on spiritual matters. Ethnic-religious communities also provided the basis for effective organization to protest against the power of their bosses. Unions often served social as well as economic roles, especially among the Irish and Germans. Workers in factories often demanded respect for their traditional work habits and styles of living. They offset the forces of industry by taking days off work to celebrate traditional holidays. Owners protested but throughout much of the nineteenth century could do little about it. Workers also shortened their work week. "Blue Monday" was a constant irritant to owners, but the practice of not coming back to work on the first day of the week persisted. "King Friday" also provoked owners. Workers frequently left one job for another, especially in larger cities when jobs were plentiful and times good. And, of course, there could be strikes over specific grievances.[9]

Workers' cultural values thus helped soften the impact of industrialism. They also hindered widespread organizing. The dominant power of religion in their culture divided workers as it did the larger population. In the mid-1850s Irish Catholics, who comprised a large percentage of the unskilled workers in the larger cities, were the targets of nativist attacks by Protestant workers who burned and vandalized Catholic schools and churches. Catholics for their part feared the quasi-religious fraternal orders that attracted many Protestant workers. Priests warned about the potential corruption of the faith in workers who joined such groups. Catholic fears that public schools threatened the religious values of their children led to demands for public assistance to parochial schools. Protestants responded by proclaiming the separation of church and state and expressing fears about public money paid to support "popish" indoctrination. The great Protestant revival that swept the cities in 1858 hardly diffused this religious antagonism.

Workers were also divided by political allegiances, which were interwoven with religious values. Republican leaders such as Henry Wilson and Nathaniel Banks had many supporters among the workers and also had been prominent in the nativist American party. Democratic politicians played on the Catholic allegiances of their working-class supporters by insisting that the meddling Republicans wanted to destroy the rights of others to drink and pray and simply be let alone. Both parties claimed to be the party of the workingman, and gained the allegiance of workers and further divided them. It is no wonder that a leading labor newspaper observed that two iron molders from the same shop might be political enemies, and proclaimed that parties were "the curse of workingmen."[10]

The power of labor was further limited because many workers refused to see themselves as imprisoned in an industrial working class. Immigrants came to the United States hoping to buy farms in the nation with the largest open frontiers in the world. Native citizens who worked in the cities kept their rural ties. Most of them had been born in the country, even more had relatives living on farms. They retained their rural memories and their self-image as something other than hopeless prisoners of urban toil. They moved from the cities back to the farms for harvests and other jobs. Winter factory workers were often summer farmers. Unemployed mill workers became hired hands and plowboys. Even those forced by circumstances or temporarily attracted to industrial work might keep family farms. Many a worker, both immigrant and native, followed the admonition that Irish-American Mark Sullivan recalled his immigrant father giving him: "Never sell the farm: no matter what happens to you in the cities, this will be a shelter to you."[11]

On the eve of conflict the workers of the North lived in a world of conflicting and contrasting experiences, of local community attachments, with an economy predominantly rural but one where industrialization was a force of growing size and potential danger. Class consciousness was a fact in some places but mitigated in many others by hopes, by strategies, by options kept open, by lack of experience with the evils that called it forth. There was widespread concern about the shape of things to come, but that concern focused inevitably on the controversy over slavery, which symbolized so well the anxieties they felt.[12]

The secession crisis found labor divided in its sympathies, though more inclined to peace. German laborers in the Midwest offered their staunch support to Lincoln as he traveled to Washington. Troy, New York, workers pledged loyalty. Milwaukee workers resolved that if the crisis were not solved peacefully, "revolutionary" means would be justified since the South was responsible for the crisis. In Cincinnati Lincoln was told that

we, the German free working men of Cincinnati, avail ourselves of this opportunity to assure you . . . of our sincere and heartfelt regard. . . . Our vanquished opponents have in recent times made frequent use of the term workingmen and workingmen's meetings in order to create the impression that the mass of workingmen were in favor of compromise between the interests of free labor and slave labor. . . . We firmly adhere to the principle which directed our votes to your favor.[13]

But if some labor organizations supported Lincoln at this time, signs of opposition were more frequent. Just recovering from the impact of the mid-1850s depression, many workers feared that disunion would bring economic disaster. They also knew that they would be the ones on the battlefields of any war. Pro-Southern factory owners had helped foster opposition by closing their factories. Other businessmen had nurtured fears by retracting activity in the face of the crisis. Workers in all parts of the nation thus joined large antiwar rallies. Meetings in the East, in Philadelphia, Newark, and Boston, were balanced with Western gatherings in Reading, St. Louis, and Louisville. Sylvis of the Iron Molders was in Louisville and then in Philadelphia publishing a call that brought five thousand worker representatives to that city to demand compromise. The future founder of the Knights of Labor, Ira Stewart, joined in attacking the extremists who had spawned the crisis. The Louisville meeting damned "disorganizing traitors" and "congressional extremists" and insisted that both were disloyal and enemies to labor.[14]

But wishes for peace could not withstand the Confederate attack on Fort Sumter. Workers throughout the North surged forward to crush an attack on the nation and to punish the slave power. Industrial conflicts were quickly submerged in the rush to arms. The ironworkers of Troy were organizing a strike when the news from Sumter came in. Large numbers of the membership enlisted. The weakened union lost more ground when management used the opportunity to hire nonunion workers, required that these workers not join any union, and brought charges against the union for conspiracy. By early fall 1861 Troy ironworkers were largely disbanded, meeting only three times in five months. One Philadelphia local ended its 1861 meeting in this way: "It having been resolved to enlist with Uncle Sam for the War, this union stands adjourned until either the union is safe or we are whipped." Throughout the North the story was the same. Workers of all sections and all ethnic groups flocked to the army. In proportion to their percentage of the population, more industrial workers served in the Union army than any other group except for professionals. Looking at military service after the war, statistician Benjamin Gould noted that for every 1,000 soldiers there were likely to be 487 farmers or farm workers, 421 mechanics and laborers, 35 workers involved in commerce, 16 professionals, and 41 from a range of other occupations.[15]

But if the workers were willing to fight for their country, the war also gave them the chance to fight for their own interests as well. The ideology of the conflict had a strong impact on them. Lincoln's description of the war as a people's contest, a struggle to remove burdens from the backs of labor and give to everyone an equal chance in the race of life, spoke directly to their feelings. Furthermore, the president made clear on several occasions a sympathy for the workers. As early as his speech at Cooper Union he applauded a system where workers could strike. In the aftermath of the great Lynn strike, when a delegation of machinists and blacksmiths came to see him at the White House, he allegedly told them that "I know in almost every case of strike the men have just cause for complaint." He told another delegation, "I know the trials and woes of workingmen. I have always felt for them." A believer in the labor theory of value, Lincoln commented that labor "deserves much higher consideration" than capital. "I myself was a hired laborer," he reminded several audiences. Such words suggested that the war might directly benefit workers. From being a single group contesting others for support, the cause of labor became linked to the cause of all loyal Northerners.[16]

And yet this same phenomenon also might undercut labor's advancement. Workers' special needs and aspirations might be absorbed into the general, ill-defined free labor cause. With the North united under this banner all classes could lay claim to the patriotic ideals of the Union, and worker protest might lose its strength. More tellingly, the workers themselves fell prey to this patriotic homogenizing. Many began to identify their cause with that of the Republican party. They thus fell into bed with the very businessmen that they had been challenging. Lynn offers an example of this phenomenon at work in the most striking way. The Workingmen's party had won city elections in 1860 and 1861, but by 1863 the Republican party was in control, and by 1864 no votes at all were cast for anyone but the Republican candidate. Small towns growing into cities, like Springfield, Massachusetts, were often Republican strongholds, and workers in most of the major Northern cities throughout the war voted Republican.[17]

Experienced Republican party politicians with reputations as friends of the workers, such as Henry Wilson, argued that his party was the free labor party. "We have made labor honorable," Wilson declared, "even in the rice swamps of the Carolinas and Georgia; we have taken the brand of dishonor from the brow of labor throughout the country and in so doing that grand work we have done more for labor, for the honor and dignity of laboring men, than was ever achieved by all the parties that arose in this country from the time the Pilgrims put their feet upon Plymouth Rock up to the year 1860." Such appeals were frequently persuasive even to working-class leaders. Samuel Gompers cast the first vote of his life in 1872 for Grant in the belief that the Republican struggle against slavery showed party dedication to the cause of free labor. But Democrats also tried to collect labor votes by a similar appeal to the general and widely popular idea that the end of slavery was a victory for the working classes. In early 1865 the party published a pamphlet, "America for Free Working Men!" collecting material from the *New York Evening Post* to show how Democrats fought slavery for years, thus earning the support of free workers of the North.[18]

The credo of the war offered both promise and problems for the workers of the North. The actual experience of life behind the lines was similarly mixed. The war expanded the number of jobs available, providing work for the unemployed. The large number of enlistments in the army opened up jobs, and workers were there to fill them. Unskilled workers filled in for skilled enlistees, and that justified some pay reductions, but workers were glad to get whatever jobs were available. Employers began to complain that they could not fill all the openings they had.

Similarly, workers' families benefited from the bounties and wages paid to soldiers. Lacking opportunities to spend their pay, the young men sent millions of dollars home; as much as $400,000 might be shipped north in a single payday. The national government paid approximately $300 million in bounties for enlistment; state and local authorities paid an additional $285 million. These funds went into the hands of hundreds of thousands of working-class families. But they hardly brought the families a life of ease. Practically every community in the North had its organization to care for the families of soldiers.[19]

The economic suffering of the war years was only partly the product of inflation and men being away at war. When war broke out the

United States was experiencing a period of growing economic inequality. This phenomenon had begun somewhere around the 1820s, just as industrialism made its presence felt. By 1860 the top 10 percent of the Northern population held an estimated 68 percent of the total wealth, an increase of nearly 15 percent from 1774. Nearly 95 percent of the wealth of the nation was held by 30 percent of the population—a figure applicable to both North and South individually. When the war began, inequality of wealth distribution may have been at an all-time high.[20]

Wages reflected inequality, too. Skilled workers' pay rose much faster than that of unskilled workers. Between 1840 and 1850 the wages of New York bricklayers rose 18 percent faster than did the pay of common laborers. Carpenters and joiners gained increases that were 37 percent better than those gained by unskilled men. Machinists in New York City achieved the same improvement, while Massachusetts iron molders gained 13 percent more in the decade than did common laborers. These differences remained constant with only slight variations from 1820 to 1880.[21]

In some minor respects the war reduced the gap between the standard of living of the lower and upper classes. While gains in overall wealth in that period are not easily measured, the cost of living seems to have gone up less for lower- than for upper-class people. This was because expensive items rose more in price than did common goods. Increasing fuel, light, rent, and food costs hurt the lower classes, but prices of clothing, house furnishings, and other nonessentials were higher.[22]

But war helped the comfortable more than it did average folk. Increased profits in the wartime boom, the protection provided by the tariff, the tax system in which excise taxes carried most of the freight, all assisted people at the top. Newspapers carried frequent editorials on the ostentations and vulgar display that the wartime boom called forth. William Cullen Bryant echoed many:

Extravagance, luxury, these are the signs of the times; are they not evidence of a state of things unhealthy and feverish, threatening to the honest simplicity of our political life; and threatening not less evil to the ideas and principles of which that life has hitherto been a fair exponent? What business have Americans at any time with such vain show, with such useless magnificence? But especially how can they justify it to themselves in this time of war? Some men have gained great fortunes during the past two or three years, but that does not excuse their extravagance. Is there nothing worthier than personal adornment in which to invest their means? Are there no enterprises open to these men of fortune which would benefit the country and their fellows as well as themselves? One man spends two hundred thousand dollars on a dwelling house; but he might build with this sum a long row of decent cottages to rent to people in moderate circumstances; he might enable fifty or one hundred families of working men to live cleanly and respectably in New York, and thus make himself a public benefactor, that without sinking his money where he can never recover it. Or instead of dressing a few children in silks and jewels, and robbing them of the freshness and charm of youth by these vanities, why not spend the money in sending the homeless children of the city to comfortable farm houses in the West, where they will be trained to industry and virtuous conduct, and grow up good citizens?[23]

Suffering a decline in their already precarious living standard, and angered at the ostentation of war-made millionaires, workers were further threatened by hundreds of thousands of immigrants who surged into the country during the war. While many became soldiers, most went looking for jobs, competing with native laborers and driving wages down. When the Congress passed and Lincoln signed the 1864 Emigrant Aid Act permitting private businesses to bring immigrants to the United States, workers were bitter. Sylvis called the American Emigrant Company "the most infamous in America," and even the mayor of New York protested: "At a time when nearly 50,000 operatives in this city alone are contending against the oppression of capital, and the wages paid are inadequate for their support is it just to them or to the European laborers to bring the latter into conflict for existence with the former, for the benefit of employers, through the agency of societies called into existence by this act of Congress?"[24]

Some protests were misdirected. Despite the hostility that they faced, the wartime immigrants quickly integrated themselves into the mainstream labor movement, increasing its numbers. English immigrants often became leading figures in American unions. Irish and, to a lesser extent, Germans joined existing unions or more frequently formed their own local organizations. These groups provided the same social support for members that native locals did. They worked for the same economic goals of higher wages, shorter hours, less competition from machines, union control over apprenticeships, and occasionally even restriction of immigration. Most important, foreign-born regiments augmented the Union army and shared the deadly cost of conflict. Such behavior helped diffuse the nativism that had often marred relations between foreign and domestic workers.[25]

But the other target of workers' wartime hostility could do little or nothing to escape hatred. The black contribution to the Union army was minimized by workers who were frightened by the specter of cheap labor competition and afflicted with racial hatred. Encouraged by a Democratic party press, urban workers again and again took out their frustrations on Negroes. As early as 1862 New York City Irish longshoremen attacked black strikebreakers, and the police had to be called in. In August between two thousand and three thousand people from a predominantly Irish neighborhood in Brooklyn threatened to burn down the factories of a local firm unless the black women and children employees quit or were fired. In early 1863 the docks of that city again witnessed clashes between black and white workers. Such fights mirrored similar ones in Buffalo, Chicago, Cincinnati, and other cities in the North.[26]

Most wartime workers saw their standard of living decline. While skilled workers stayed a short step ahead of inflation, the larger number of unskilled workers saw a steady decline in real wages. While their wages increased by perhaps 50 to 60 percent, prices went up by almost 100 percent. Eggs rose from 15¢ per dozen in 1861 to 25¢ in late 1863; potatoes rose from $1.50 per bushel to $2.25 per bushel in the same period. Bread prices almost doubled, and rents and fuel also increased markedly. A New York newspaper in July 1864 estimated that a family of six in the city needed $16 per week for necessities and that the average wage in the city was just at the $16 figure. This left no money for clothing, medicine and doctors, transportation to and from work, or luxuries of any kind. The next month the paper observed that the cost of these same necessities stood at $18.50.

The wages of men workers at least kept commodities within their extended reach, but women workers, who did about one-fourth of the manufacturing work in the country, suffered even more. On the average, their wages increased by less than half that of men. In some businesses their pay actually went down as costs skyrocketed. Seamstresses in New York saw wages go from 17.5¢ per shirt in 1861 to

8¢ per shirt in 1864. Women who worked a fourteen-hour day at this job received on the average $1.54 per week. "The sewing women in Cincinnati" wrote to President Lincoln in March 1865: "We are unable to sustain life for the prices offered by contractors, who fatten on their contracts by grinding immense profits out of the labor of their operatives." Women umbrella makers in New York worked from 6:00 A.M. to midnight and received 6–8¢ for each umbrella they made. They could earn from 72 to 94¢ a day. In the fall of 1863 they struck, and won the concession from owners of 2¢ more per umbrella.[27]

The economic effect of the war also struck children. Tens of thousands lost their fathers in camps and battlefields. Family income dwindled or vanished. The number of children in New York City almshouses rose 300 percent. Even in the years of "the great war boom," from late 1862 to 1865, children suffered. The New York City Newsboys' Lodging House between 1861 and 1866 provided homes for 27,249 boys, and the yearly figures rose from 3,875 between 1861 and 1862, to 6,325 in 1863–64, to 7,256 in 1865–66.

Tens of thousands of children were drawn into the labor force to replace men at war. By the end of the Civil War it is estimated that 13 percent of the labor force in Massachusetts textile mills consisted of children under sixteen. In Pennsylvania almost 22 percent of the textile mill workers were sixteen or younger. By 1872, when the plight of child laborers began to be noticed nationally, there were an estimated 11,000–13,000 of them in Philadelphia. In August of the next year Charles Loring Brace claimed that over 100,000 were steadily employed in New York City factories, while between 15,000 and 20,000 drifted from one factory to another in search of work. In a brief survey of child labor in New York City Brace found the following:

There are from one thousand five hundred to two thousand children, under fifteen years of age, employed in a single branch—the manufacture of paper collars. . . . In tobacco factories in New York, Brooklyn, and neighborhood, our agents found children *only four years of age* sometimes half a dozen in a single room. Others were eight years of age, and ranged from that group up to fifteen years. Girls and boys of twelve to fourteen years earn from four dollars to five dollars a week. One little girl they saw, tending a machine, so small that she had to stand upon a box eighteen inches high to enable her to reach her work. In one room they found fifty children; some little girls, only eight years of age earning three dollars per week. In another, there were children of eight and old women of sixty working together. In the "unbinding cellar" they found fifteen boys under fifteen years. Twine and artificial flow manufacture, and hundreds of other occupations, reveal the same state of things.[28]

In Massachusetts, child labor, on the increase before the war, accelerated during the conflict. The state legislature in 1866 produced a special report that looked at working conditions in the state. It found children as young as seven working nearly fourteen hours a day in the cotton mills of Lowell, Fall River, and New Bedford. One witness said, "Small help is scarce; a great deal of the machinery has been stopped for want of small help, so the overseers have been going around to draw the small children from the schools into the mills; the same as a draft in the army." A legislator asked another witness, "Is there any limit on the part of the employers as to the age when they take children?" The man answered, "They'll take them at any age they can get them, if they are old enough to stand. . . . I guess the youngest is about seven. There are some that's younger, but very little."[29]

Homefront hardship showed up in the jails and prisons of the North as well. General disorder increased as the number of arrests went up in cities. The peak for wartime arrests came in 1862, a figure built in part on growing homicide statistics but also including burgeoning numbers of arrests for disturbing public order. The number of women arrested increased notably. In Massachusetts women had comprised slightly over 20 percent of those in jail in 1860. Four years later over 60 percent of the prisoners committed to county jails were women. By 1865, 233 women and 286 men were placed in the Detroit House of Correction. At Sing Sing in New York in 1860, the average number of inmates during the year was 1,173 men and 137 women. By 1865, 689 men and 188 women spent some part of the year there. Only at the state prison in Albany did the number of women decline from a high of 373 in 1863 to 249 in 1865. But this latter figure may indicate that more women were being kept in local jails. Observers were especially struck by the fact that so many of the women in prison were related to soldiers who had gone to war. Authorities at the time argued that the main reasons for this were an increase in money from bounties, which "makes these women idle and exposed them to temptation. . . . [and] the absence of their sons, husbands and fathers leaving them without restraint or protection." More likely economic need played a larger role.

The number of children arrested also increased. In New York City the juvenile delinquency rate climbed throughout the war. Beginning with 363 children admitted to the House of Refuge in 1861, the numbers rose to 538 by 1863 and hit 710 by 1865. In 1866 the impact of war was still being seen as the number of children admitted rose to 750. The inspector of prisons in Massachusetts observed, "I have talked with many boys in Jails and Houses of Correction who were either sons or brothers of soldiers or sailors in the service. It may not be extravagant to say that one out of four of the many children in our prisons have near relatives in the army."[30]

On the other hand, efforts to help the needy increased. Northern states funded new institutions for the insane, the deaf, the sick. More people in the North began to contribute to charities that helped the urban poor. In mid-war, the New York Children's Aid Society stated that "it seems easier for people to support charitable institutions now . . . than before the war." The receipts of the major benevolent societies of the North increased, and one student of wartime philanthropy argued that in time of war the desire of people to "taste the luxury of doing good" was on the rise. The New York Society for the Improvement of the Condition of the Poor saw its relief recipients fall from eight thousand families in 1860 and 1861 to four thousand in 1863 and 1864.[31]

Yet with all the assistance that was beginning to flow under the impetus of war, there was still great need. Orphanage facilities, while doubling during the conflict, still could not meet the demand created by battlefield carnage and economic dislocation. Efforts to send these children to the West where they would find work on farms and thus be free of the evils of city life still fell short. And this plight of the children was only the most heartrending of the economic pains that war inflicted. The fall in real wages, the suffering of women workers, and the growing casualty lists among workers all entwined to persuade labor leaders and workers of the need to speak out in word and in deed.

As the war dragged on, the initial patriotic enthusiasm of workers began to diminish. Soldiers' letters home, newspaper reports, revealed war's horrors. Labor spokesmen began to question the alleged unity of labor and capital in the war against slavery. Speaking to the National Iron Molders meeting in January 1864, Sylvis catalogued the suffering of workers and declared that "nothing can be more absurd" than to believe in the natural unity of labor and capital. While capital was "selfish, haughty, proud, insolent," wallowing in the luxury of wartime prosperity, labor was "reduced to the lowest possible condition of wretchedness." In New York City thirty thousand sewing women worked day and night to earn between one and three dollars a week to sustain not only themselves but children and parents. Thirty thousand people lived in Manhattan cellars "literally buried alive, huddled together like cattle in a pen," wrapped in a "mental and moral darkness" that would make "angels weep."

In cotton mills it required "the combined labor of . . . husband, wife, and every child old enough to walk to the factory, [working] from twelve to fifteen hours a day to earn sufficient to keep body and soul together." "Anyone who will take the trouble to investigate and study" the conditions of the nation's industrial workers would "find thousands sunk to a degree of mental, moral and physical wretchedness horrible to contemplate, whose very soul are crushed within their living bodies." And the capitalists, "the worst enemies of our race, . . . make commerce of the blood and tears of helpless women and merchandize [sic] of soul. In the poverty, wretchedness and utter ruin of their helpless victims they see nothing but an accumulating pole of gold. In the weeping and *wailing of the distressed* they hear nothing but a 'metallic ring.' "[32]

Feelings like these, the greater activity of the economy, and the needs of the war helped to create hundreds of new labor organizations. In 1863 the leading labor newspaper, *Fincher's Trades Review*, listed 79 local unions. Within a year the list had grown to 270. By March of 1864 *Fincher's* had reported on strikes around New York City by "Slate and Metal Roofers," "Segar makers," "Long shoremen," "Jewellers," "Bricklayers," "House Carpenters," "Printers," "Dry dock practical painters," "Plumbers," "Blue Stone Cutters and Flaggers," "Piano Forte makers," "Iron Moulders," "Cabinetmakers and Tailors," "Carvers," "Shipwrights," "Brush makers," "Wheelwrights and Blacksmiths," "Coopers," "Coach painters and coach trimmers."[33]

The number of tradewide strikes in New York City alone continued to rise from thirteen in 1862 to twenty-nine in 1863 and hit a high of forty-two by 1864. During this last year there were also forty-six single-shop strikes. For the most part, workers struck for higher wages, as when seven thousand machinists went out in the winter of 1863. But sometimes workers protested the use of machines to do the work of men. In June 1862 the surge of wartime orders led the owners of port facilities in New York City to use grain-unloading machines. Five thousand workers struck at this time, but lost their protest. Shop, factory, and mine workers throughout the North struck during 1863 and 1864 when work stoppages reached their peak. Most of these strikes were successful, since war needs and profits encouraged owners to give in. But, after mid-1864, as ultimate victory seemed assured, management became more determined to prepare for projected postwar retrenchments and workers backed away from militance. By the end of the war labor leaders were urging members to consider strikes as a last resort and speaking more often of mutual interests between capital and labor.[34]

By the early 1870s the percentage of workers belonging to unions reached its nineteenth-century peak. As the number and membership of local unions increased, so did the number of labor newspapers. Between 1863 and 1873 120 journals appeared, publishing monthly, weekly, or daily the opinions and activities of workers. The largest of these was the Philadelphia-based *Fincher's,* which grew from a circulation of about five thousand in 1863 to over eleven thousand by 1865, reaching into thirty-one of the thirty-five states, three Canadian provinces, and eight English cities. Major labor papers also appeared in Chicago and Boston.

These activities in the main were local activities. While fifteen new national unions did appear between 1861 and 1865, several of these were temporary. None carried the impact of local unions. Citywide trade assemblies, the major organizations of labor above the local union, engaged in a wide range of activity. They set up co-op stores and reading rooms and libraries and generally fostered a sense of community among the workers in a city. They provided advice and publicity to strikers, collected money to help them, and counteracted efforts by employers to recruit strikebreakers in nearby cities. They also occasionally tried to persuade assembly members to boycott shops and businesses that refused to yield to worker demands. Some assemblies also wielded political clout in local elections. New York City politicians often had to promise sympathy with union goals to get elected. Lobbying was another function they engaged in, and in at least one case the assemblies helped to kill an 1864 New York State antipicketing bill. These increased activities during the war laid the foundation for a postwar labor movement, but the foundation consisted of locally made bricks.[35]

On the other hand, the local nature of mid-nineteenth-century industry produced harmony between workers and owners in some areas. The Waltham Watch Company became a model for other industries in the nineteenth century, with its combination of manufacturing efficiency, good profits, and labor/management harmony. Employing between 157 in 1860 and 541 in 1866, the company increased its productivity per worker by nearly 77 percent without spawning protest or conflict. The company managed this in several ways. It kept Irish out of the work force as much as possible. The resulting cultural homogeneity of the workers seems to have engendered a sense of community. The company policy of hiring family members of workers reinforced these feelings. Worker benefits were also very good. Waltham provided loans to purchase company land and to build houses. The company itself also built housing, a policy followed by other industries as well. Employees could garden unused company land without charge. Death benefits were also paid to workers at times, and workers who joined the army had their jobs guaranteed upon return.

This commitment to soldiers manifested a strong patriotism that thrived in the company and the town of Waltham during the war. In 1863 the Watch Factory Soldiers' Aid Society was founded. It raised money through community activities such as strawberry festivals, dances, sleigh rides, and lectures. The same year saw the creation of a Factory Brass Band with a hired instructor and a uniform and instrument purchase fund. The band provided free concerts, played in town parades, and accompanied the workers to the polls on election days. By 1864 workers had organized a cooperative store, and just after the war there emerged the Watch Factory Relief Society to help all employees meet medical emergencies and the loss of loved ones.

These activities helped to balance the fact that growing profits went primarily into the hands of owners, not workers. Wartime profits, built on a strong demand for watches during the war, increased by 164 percent. Wages did go up for the workers but only by 52.6 percent, while prices increased by 96 percent. The result was a drop in real wages while company profits soared. But the watch factory was the highest-paying company in the region, with the exception of munitions makers, and the company kept the rent for its housing at the 1860 level throughout the war. Worker turnover was thus very low during the war and after. There was only one minor dispute between management and workers during the entire nineteenth century.[36]

The feelings of the working class were often complex and contradictory. They included a powerful patriotism, shown in the overwhelming response to the Sumter attack, and continuing throughout the war with strong enlistments and reenlistments and large Republican majorities in many elections. But there was also unrest and anxiety and, in many places, growing anger as the war continued. As workers' enlistments had been extraordinary given their percentage of the population, so were their casualties. They were experiencing the most heartrending of the costs of war in proportions larger than almost any group in the population. At the Battle of Fredericksburg, Meagher's New York Irish Brigade lost all but 280 of its 1,200 men. The 116th Pennsylvania Regiment suffered bitterly at Fredericksburg and Gettysburg. Similarly, large Irish losses in other battles alienated many at home and in the field. Some believed that commanders intentionally risked Irish lives in dangerous situations.[37]

War losses combined with economic suffering, racial hostilities, and cultural antagonism to the modernizing forces of industrial society all combined to fuel an explosion by workers in New York City in the summer of 1863. Still mourning Fredericksburg, the Irish community of New York, overwhelmingly the largest group of New York City workers, were infuriated over the Conscription Act passed by Congress on March 3. Declining enlistments had provoked legislators into passing this major bill, but its provisions demanded far more of poor than of wealthy Americans. The requirement that all men between twenty and forty-five be enrolled for potential conscription portended an intrusion by government into the daily lives of citizens, but it could be understood as a war necessity. The provision for calling up single men from twenty to twenty-five and married men from twenty to thirty-five before calling older married men seemed more debatable. Older married men were likely to be better off and their children more capable of caring for themselves, but at least some attention was paid to family needs. But the provision allowing draftees to hire a substitute or to buy their way out of service with a $300 commutation provoked outrage.

Three hundred dollars was at least half a year's wages, and substitutes would hardly be available for anything less. "A rich man's war and a poor man's fight" was the cry that rose up against the draft law. The *New York Copperhead* parodied a popular recruiting song with the words "We're coming Father Abraham three hundred thousand more. / We leave our homes and firesides with bleeding hearts and sore, / Since poverty has been our crime, we bow to the decree; / We are the poor who have no wealth to purchase liberty." Another paper offered a simpler parody: "We are coming Father Abraham, 300 dollars more." Labor spokesman Fincher urged that the $300 fee be repealed so that "rich men" could fight their own war. Opposition to such injustice was not disloyalty to the government, he argued, it was loyalty to the working class.[38]

Protests against the inequities of the draft and the economic suffering of workers broke out into violence in New York City on three sweltering days, July 13–15, 1863, just after the Gettysburg and Vicksburg victories. Encouraged by the protests of Democratic newspapers in the city, and to some extent by a speech given by Governor Horatio Seymour, tensions exploded when the names of draftees were drawn. Early controlled protest by union artisans was replaced by mobs of unskilled workers, including women and boys, who surged through the city attacking draft officials and policemen, turning on soldiers set against them. They burned draft offices, pro-administration newspapers, and the homes of known abolitionists (including the composer of the recruiting song "We Are Coming Father Abraham"), beat up well-dressed gentlemen whom they called "$300 men," and sometimes turned their fury on street-sweeping machines or mechanical grain elevators.

But their greatest hatred focused on the city's Negroes. Rioters burned a Negro orphanage to the ground, and black men and women were hunted in the streets and murdered when caught. At the height of the rioting economic activity almost completely stopped in the city, and fears grew that the mob might rule the city.

When order was finally restored an estimated 119 people were found to have been killed and over 300 to have been wounded or injured, making these riots the largest civil disturbance in the nation's history to that time.

The composition of the mob at the peak of its fury showed the frustrations of the poor. The rioters were overwhelmingly Irish and predominantly unskilled workers. While a few criminals took advantage of the disorder, the large majority of the rioters had no previous criminal record. Of the over 350 later identified, 92 were not themselves eligible to be drafted. These were the people at the bottom of New York City's society, angered by their suffering, fearful of further inroads on their lives, resentful of both those above them, whose money protected them, and those below them, who seemed potential beneficiaries of the war now that emancipation was a goal. Sufferings, envy, hatred, all served to spark the uprising.

The draft riots advanced the rioters' cause after the violence was crushed. Blacks fled New York City in large numbers, reducing labor competition. Those who stayed suffered even after the riots were over when private charity ran out. The city council voted $2 million to buy substitutes or pay commutation money for any policeman, fireman, or member of the militia who might be drafted. And any other poor New Yorker who could prove that induction would impoverish his family received the same benefits. Furthermore, few of the rioters were ever punished. Grand juries refused to indict them, and under neighborhood pressures, few victims chose to press charges.[39]

New York City was not the only place where workers reacted to war and the pressures of industrialization with antidraft violence. The Tenth Congressional District of Pennsylvania also saw bitter resistance. Irish-American miners there experienced conditions that reminded them of English oppression at home. They had to rent their homes from company officials, buy provisions at company stores, and work under the supervision of the more highly skilled English and Welsh miners. Targets of nativism in the mid-1850s, suspicious and bitter over Republican puritanism, they forged their community ties all the more strongly for self-protection and identity. When the draft began, their anger crystallized, and almost three hundred miners gathered to stop the process. Troops came to help the government and for a time kept the lid on. But when the troops left, a well-known mine owner who had given a lavish party for the soldiers was murdered, and community pressure blocked prosecution of the killers. In the meantime opposition to the draft had become so bitter that Pennsylvania governor Curtin feared using more troops to enforce the law. Lincoln told him that the law either had to be executed or at least appear to have been executed. Curtin took the latter course. The quota of draftees from the miner's district was filled by crediting previous enlistees who had once lived there to the district.[40]

Parts of the country as urban as Chicago and as rural as Vermont also showed the hostility of foreign-born communities to the imposition of the draft. Chicago's Third Ward was called "the Patch" by Republican newspapers, the home of "the very lowest, most ignorant, depraved and besotted rabble that can be found in the city" (a typical description of immigrant communities by outsiders). Here a mob of between three thousand and four thousand men, women, and children first obstructed draft procedures with mass protests, then attacked the police when they tried to arrest protesters. Bricks, stones, and bottles rained down upon the authorities, and ultimately the police had to release their captives. Vermont's approximately one thousand protesters were Irish workers in marble quarries in Rutland. Their protests were answered by the local provost marshals calling in soldiers to teach them a lesson. Counterforces from the quarry met the soldiers with stones and clubs, and order was restored only with great difficulty. Similar opposition, varying in intensity, took place in every section of the country from Boston to Portsmouth, New Hampshire, to Troy, New York, to Milwaukee, Wisconsin, to St. Paul, Minnesota.[41]

Worker protest against the draft was not just economic in nature. Workers were attacking an economic environment that had limited their chances for success, indeed that threatened them with at least military service and possibly with death because of their poverty. Men with $300 could stay home, those without it had to serve. But beyond the obvious economic elements of their condition workers were also protesting the transformations of a society that intruded on their community life. They were fighting the long reach of the registration and draft official whose loyalties were to a vague national ideal and who reported to officials of the distant national government. Local upper-class elites often enforced national draft laws. Workers protested not only with violence against the draft, but with evasion by running away to Canada or the West, or simply vanishing into their local communities. At the beginning of the war the over 160,000 men who dodged the draft tended to be poor immigrant Catholic Democrats from the cities. Other portions of the population followed their lead, especially border state men with family and cultural ties to Dixie. Protest against conscription marked another example of the cultural divisions that characterized the political environment of the North, divisions that often found antagonists to Republican-generated economic modernization seeking to protect traditional cultural life-styles.[42]

Official reactions to this protest moderated federal policy. In the aftermath of the draft riots many New York cities wrote and adopted ordinances to pay commutation for any drafted man. While the *New York Times* charged that this was a "scheme for propitiating the mob," towns like Utica, Brooklyn, Albany, Troy, Syracuse, and Auburn passed such measures in the summer of 1863. Other states didn't follow this method, but they did increase the bounties to volunteers.

Occasionally special circumstances elicited special treatment, perhaps with officials recalling the bloody July days. In late July 1864 rebel Jubal Early raided Southern Pennsylvania with destructive success. Residents of the region petitioned for exemption from the draft because they had suffered from the war already, and presumably because there they were needed at home to repair the damage. Former Secretary of War Cameron wrote Stanton in support of their request, and it was granted.

Companies also gained leverage from the 1863 protests. During the 1865 draft the president of the Pennsylvania Railroad, Thomas Scott, arranged a deal that permitted the company to furnish substitutes for any employee drafted. The railroad would raise the substitutes in the big cities of the state—Philadelphia, Pittsburgh, and Harrisburg—to replace employees drafted from all parts of the state. Scott reminded Stanton that while draftees would serve only one year, substitutes were liable for three years, "quite a good trade for you." Stanton agreed.[43]

The riots also had larger consequences. In the Confederacy, reeling under the losses of Vicksburg and Gettysburg, such violent protest nourished hope for ultimate victory. The Democratic party of the North, however, housing the vast majority of pro-Southern voices, was put on the defensive and took pains to disassociate itself from violent opposition.

In the realm of ideas the riots also had their consequence. The vision of the war as a struggle for order was reinforced but took on added dimension. Conservatives had hoped that the discipline of war would purge society of its anarchic ways. But apparently there were elements in society who, after over two years of fighting, remained dangerous. It was difficult to believe that men might easily be made moral citizens through calls to their selflessness. Sterner forces would now be necessary, and optimistic visions of the American people would have to be revised. As Melville put it:

> All civil charms
> And priestly spells which late held hearts in awe—
>   Fear-bound, subjected to a better sway
> Than sway of self; these like a dream dissolve,
> And man rebounds whole aeons back in nature.
> . . . .
> Wise Draco comes, deep in the midnight roll
> Of black artillery; he comes, though late;
>   In code corroborating Calvin's creed
> And cynic tyrannies of honest Kings;
> He comes, nor parlies; and the Town, redeemed,
> Give thanks devout; nor, being thankful, heeds
> The grimy slur on the Republic's faith implied,
> Which holds that Man is naturally good.
> And—more—is Nature's Roman, never to be scourged.

Along with the mountains of battlefield dead, the riots helped to undercut any easy faith in recapturing the purity of the old republic. They signaled a growing realism and in some cases cynicism about the quality of the nation.[44]

While the antidraft rioting captured the headlines and did reveal serious suffering among the working class, the majority remained loyal to the Union cause. The Sixty-ninth New York Regiment, an all-Irish unit, marched from the battlefield at Gettysburg and helped to crush the mobs in New York streets. Labor leaders like Sylvis and Fincher damned the riots, even as they demanded a repeal of the major inequities of the draft law. Most of the rioters were unskilled workers, and organized labor in New York City was almost unanimous in condemning the riots. Most of the fire companies, composed of lower-class workers, courageously stood up to bricks and stones and fought the city's fires. Trade unions in the city organized the Democratic-Republican Workers Association to demonstrate their loyalty by propagandizing for the war effort.[45]

Workers continued to vote for the Republican party in most places. In 1864 Lincoln carried twelve of the largest urban centers, while McClellan carried only seven. And just before the draft riots, as Lee invaded Pennsylvania, the coal workers of Philadelphia organized six companies to repel his invasion. New York City and Brooklyn stayed Democratic, but even in the metropolis Tammany Hall, led by prowar factions, was gathering power and dominated the antiwar Mozart Hall faction.[46]

The increasing number of strikes and of unions produced a reaction by employers. They, too, began to organize associations to advance their cause. Usually meeting in secret to avoid charges of monopoly, these associations protested, as the Ohio Founders and Machine Builders Association put it, against "every combination which has for its object the regulation of wages. . . . We desire the utmost individual liberty both for employers and employees. The demand for and the supply of labor, the merits of each individual workman, and the cost of living, are the natural causes which should regulate wages." To be sure that "natural causes" worked, these organizations often set maximum rates of pay, worked to blacklist any allegedly dangerous worker, lobbied for anti-union legislation in state capitals. Several states responded by passing "anti-intimidation laws" that proscribed efforts to prevent someone from working.

Other laws that the associations successfully urged challenged union activities as conspiracies, and allowed companies to evict strikers and their families from company-owned housing. Operating in the iron industry, building trades, shipbuilding, and railroads, these organizations gave businessmen the opportunities to get to know each other better and to thus further the integration of the economy. Of course, the competitive business spirit still remained vital, and members of the associations sometimes refused to be bound by the rules of the organization, but the associations gave industry experience with the benefits of organization and combination that they would later use to advantage.[47]

Labor newspapers and organizations kept a sharp eye on the employers' organizations. Their own nationalizing efforts were further stimulated by such employer enterprise. War experience would find use in some postwar labor organizing. But in wartime workers could do little but protest in response to the military support of employers when strikes seemed to affect the war effort. When workers struck an ammunitions factory in Cold Spring, New York, the army was called in and the strike leaders were first thrown in jail without a trial and then driven out of town. Striking dock workers in Brooklyn were locked in the yards and had their pay taken away. Troops ran the Reading Railroad when engineers struck. The strikers gave in and went back to work. Workers at a government arsenal in Nashville went out when promises of overtime pay were broken. The army marched them back to work at bayonet point and gave the workers half pay. Commanding General George Thomas exiled two hundred of these men as "untrustworthy." In St. Louis in April 1864 union workers striking against nonunion labor met the wrath of General William Rosecrans. The general outlawed strikes, provided the names of the strikers to army officials, and threatened a military tribunal for transgressors. This "attack upon the private rights and the military power of the nation by organizations led by bad men," Rosecrans declared, would be stopped. The next month General Burbridge in Louisville copied this order and also used bayonets to drive the strikers back to work. All in all, worker protests against soldiers' intimidating workers in a struggle for free labor had no effect. Lincoln did intercede indirectly by telling officials at the Brooklyn navy yard to return workers' pay. The president may also have been responsible for telling army leaders not to "interfere with the legitimate demands of labor." But usually military necessity overrode labor protests. The general public and even some labor leaders supported the hierarchy that put military success first, labor advancement second.[48]

In sum, during the war the urban working classes on the whole suffered greatly from inflation and from military support used to crush strikes. They provided an enormous number of soldiers for the Union army, given their percentage of the population, and this patriotism served to seriously weaken the power of nativism in the nation. The war also provoked an outburst of organizing of local and national unions and workingmen's associations, although by far the greatest activity took place on the local level. Ideologically the war gave support to the ideals of free labor and demonstrated the utility of organizing resources to achieve its goals.

But a major element in the ideology of the North also served to diffuse the claim of workers for special attention. Since all of society was linked in the free labor struggle, owners, industrialists, capitalists, might equally assert their devotion to free labor goals, thus weakening the special force of labor's claim to the idea. In a society not yet clearly industrialized, a society just beginning to develop the clear divisions between wage earners and independent owners, it was, in fact, easy to deny the permanence of the growing gap. By its emphasis on unity and loyalty the war helped hide this distinction. On the other hand, the war, with the economic costs it exacted from labor and the organization it stimulated, with the contrasts between free labor ideology and wage slavery reality, provoked many labor leaders to greater efforts. These would have their impact in fostering a stronger labor movement after the conflict. One of the reasons for the endurance of the labor movement and its growth after the war was the fact that the war did very little, if anything, to decrease the actual economic inequality in the nation. Possibly Northern labor made minimal gains overall, but the gap between rich and poor and between wage earner, hired laborer, and the owners of shops, factories, and farms narrowed hardly at all. The war taught labor the need and efficacy of organizing to achieve its goals. It did little to bring those goals much closer.[49]

CHAPTER 9

The Meanings of Emancipation

THE Northern economy proved its vitality during the war, producing prosperity at home and victory in the field. Inequities remained, perhaps were even encouraged by wartime economic measures, but general prosperity combined with the patriotic efforts of both capitalists and laborers muted criticism of the system as a whole. War clarified the problems of economic change, making labor protest more well focused even as it linked successful capitalism to a successful nation.

Despite economic achievements, Northerners paid more attention to emancipation. Economic changes lay below the surface, forging institutional and structural imperatives whose impact would be long-range and complex. Emancipation, by contrast, crystallized thought, focused attention, sparked heated debate, boldly symbolizing the ideals and goals of the war.

If emancipation had the advantage of clarity, it did not lack complexity. Freeing the slaves was an issue with meaning for both races, and that fed the complexity. Emancipation pushed whites to new definitions of what the nation stood for and of the type of people they were. Integrating new visions with old would not be simple. Black citizens found themselves for the first time in traditionally white arenas. Whites would have to accommodate themselves to these new intruders, while blacks learned new roles.

Even the first steps of this transformation were filled with question marks. Could blacks gain freedom without the Union losing

Kentucky and the border regions? Could they gain freedom when the legal-constitutional system defined them either as slaves or as second-class citizens? If and when emancipation came, the complexities endured. What would freedom mean if the victories of the North were seen to endorse a free labor system that valued virtues traditionally linked to white enterprise? What would freedom mean if the war were seen as demonstrating the viability of a constitutional system that had traditionally limited protection of minorities? All these questions were affected by the fact that emancipation and equal rights were war issues.

War pitted the North against an enemy that had long served as its counterimage. Just as slavery crystallized the evils of American society as a whole, the South was perceived as the antithesis of what the North at its optimum could be. Prewar visitors had described the South as enslaved by the slave system, with an image of work that kept it economically and morally backward. As Horace Greeley said, "Enslave a man and you destroy his ambition, his enterprise, his capacity. In the constitution of human nature is the mainspring of effort." Lincoln described the ideal Southern laborer as not the intelligent and self-reliant yeoman, but "a blind horse upon a treadmill."[1]

The Northern counterimage to this South featured independent yeomen and mechanics, shopkeepers and businessmen, joined together in a bustling, vigorous, prosperous society where work was cherished as the highest ideal. To the image of the lazy South Northerners contrasted a work ethic that built self-discipline as well as fortunes. This ideal existed in dialogue with anxieties about the actual realization of these goals, but it endured unsullied as a motivating vision in the North. Arising as early as Jackson's fight against the Bank of the United States, preceded in fact by Jefferson's yeoman farmer, this ideal was shared by Democrats and Republicans alike.[2]

The contrasting views of society of the North and South helped explain the conflict between them, and in the vision of most American nationalists unity required that one overwhelm the other. Prewar debate had described a house divided between rival economic and moral visions. When war broke out Northern leaders spoke of a victory that would transform Dixie. In late April 1861 the *New York Times* called for the "redemption of Virginia" by the "settlement of free white men . . . who will manfully and loyally labor for her regeneration." Others argued that war might bring the South into the modern world, as had been the case with Britain, Prussia, and France. China, too, was being modernized by "the redeeming influence of force," in the words of one writer.[3]

Some hopes for this transformation reflected white opportunism, dreams that Southern resources might bring prosperity to hardworking Northern farmers, shopkeepers, and entrepreneurs. But integrated with selfish ambition was the hope that the freed South would advance in general prosperity, providing benefits for all of its citizens. With slavery gone, the economic power of the great lords of the lash would be broken. A free society alive with progress and opportunity, with labor dignified and education nurturing improvement in every field of endeavor, would take its place. The Union would become one in its society as well as its politics and law.[4]

Contrasting images of the societies at war undergirded the conflict. Achieving these ideals depended upon the specific actions that Northern leaders would take, and obstacles to freedom loomed large. Lincoln was president of a government whose Constitution protected slavery. He was trying to preserve a union that included loyal slave states, and one of those states, Kentucky, occupied the pivotal position in the war. "To lose Kentucky," Lincoln said, "was to lose the whole game." Ideals might argue emancipation; law, politics, and strategy complicated things immensely. Lincoln overcame these obstacles to emancipate the slaves. Abolitionist oratory, congressional pressure, losses in the field, the securing of Kentucky for the Union side, rejection by border states of Lincoln's plan for gradual compensated emancipation, all led to the freeing of the slaves. First had come the September 22, 1862, proclamation giving the South until January 1, 1863, to return to the Union or face emancipation. Republican reverses in the fall elections had indicated the depth of opposition to liberating blacks. But on the first day of 1863 emancipation came and along with it the declaration that blacks might become Union soldiers.

Emancipation did not free the slaves everywhere. Those owned in places not in rebellion as of January 1 remained chattel. But after that day every step forward by Union armies into the Confederacy was a step toward freedom. Furthermore, turning the war into a struggle for equality as well as union loosened the shackles of prejudice everywhere. Freed blacks in Dixie had the opportunity to demonstrate their capacity for self-disciplined liberty. Black soldiers staked claims on equality by their sacrifices to save the Union. Blacks everywhere demanded, in the name of officially endorsed ideals, their rights to equal justice under law. And white Americans, or at least those of the Republican party, worked for liberty for all slaves in the Thirteenth Amendment and challenged state discrimination with the Fourteenth and Fifteenth.

Still, as of mid-war these were only promises. If they were to become realities, blacks had to prove to white majorities that they could become part of the new society that Union victory was supposed to bring. Given the limitations of traditional law, of the long-treasured images of the meanings of a free republic, of abiding racial phobias, the proving ground was predictably challenging.

The Northern encounter with the slaves thus took place in a context full of complexities, and alive with a range of goals, hopes, and concerns. Depriving the Confederacy of its loyal labor supply and acquiring troops for the Union was one strong motive, and received most of the attention. Reformers and political leaders sought to justify emancipation in terms of its immediate wartime benefits. But allied with this immediate goal were feelings expressed continually and forcefully by abolitionists that freedom was right, not just expedient. And underlying these goals was a widely shared conception that the society that was proving itself viable, healthy, and strong in this awesome struggle was the proper model for an entire nation once the war was over.

The Negro's place in this picture was equally complex. His condition hardly reflected the goals of a free labor society. Slavery and a poverty that withstood emancipation validated ideas about his innate inferiority. Only a few whites saw his circumstances alone as producing this result. Few were willing to blame themselves for what the black man was. While humanitarians strove with true dedication to improve the status of blacks in America, the blacks themselves had to prove their adaptability to this ideal society. Soldiering helped, for the war demanded their services and provided frequent opportunities to earn the respect and gratitude of whites. Evidence of the capacity to survive in peacetime was equally crucial. Everyone knew that one day peace would come, and the longer war lasted, the more guaranteed it was that blacks would be free in that day.

As the war unfolded, two major stories of black experience emerged. One spoke of the poverty and disorder of slave society as war moved into Dixie. For decades Northerners heard of a decadent Southern system that nurtured moral anarchy among blacks and whites, destroying the self-discipline and hence the prosperity of the South. Southern whites insisted that blacks would not work unless enslaved. As Union soldiers moved into the South, destroying slavery in their wake, that hypothesis would be tested. The crucial issue would be, could a self-disciplined laboring people arise out of the heritage of slavery and the disruptions of war?

The other story focused on the blacks as soldiers. Here was a much more promising environment for improving the condition of black Americans. If young Negroes could prove their courage, their discipline, their willingness to fight for their country and their race, white prejudices would be under siege. Blacks would have demonstrated their capacity to be part of the Northern society that many hoped would sweep away the moral and economic backwardness in Dixie and unify the nation in culture as well as in law.

War's devastation hardly gave blacks a promising platform from which to gain white admiration. Colonel John Eaton, appointed by General Grant to care for the Mississippi Valley freedmen, described the impact of war and the collapse of slavery on the freedmen he met in mid-1863, near Vicksburg:

The scenes were appalling: the refugees were crowded together, sickly, disheartened, dying on the street, not a family of them all either well sheltered, clad or fed; no physicians, no medicines, no hospitals; many of the persons who had been charged with feeding them either sick or dead. . . . The only industry found among twenty thousand—there were ten thousands more scattered on the opposite bank of the river—was that performed by twelve men with axes. . . . The ideas of the people had not been improved by idleness and association with the army. The great multitude were unprepared to work beyond supplying their immediate necessities. As laborers they came and went regardless of their agreements or the wishes of their employers. . . . Their minds were not adjusted to the new situation. Laborers were so abundant, Southern prejudice against paying blacks was so great, that it required almost superhuman efforts on the part of my officers to secure payment and trustworthiness in service.

A year later Eaton was proud to say that some improvement was notable despite continued problems. The artisans were gathering in the cities and seemed "manageable, and susceptible of improvement. Many more of them have learned to read and write than among the whites." While these people were "not so far an exception to the rest of humanity as to be free of vice and crime," they were "sloughing off the evils of slavery," and with the help of "government and benevolence" they were moving toward "intelligence, virtue and industry."[5]

This context troubled the North throughout the war. Emancipation did not terminate the effect of slavery. Blacks suffering under bondage had to learn how to be free laborers. Two days after the Emancipation Proclamation became final the *New York Times* targeted that question as "vast and difficult," a subject "which will in time challenge universal attention." The newspaper was pleased to see that Lincoln had admonished the newly freed blacks to continue to work for wages despite the end of bondage. But could he reasonably expect that a people who had never bargained for their needs, who had never been consulted about their wants, who had never provided for themselves or had to provide for their families, could easily become free laborers? The *Times* was dubious. Perhaps they might pass from slavery to free labor quickly, take up their work as free men. But if they did not, then "they must be compelled to do it—not by brute force nor by being owned like cattle and denied every human right, but by just and equal *laws*—such laws as in every community control and forbid vagrancy, mendicancy and all shapes by which idle vagabondage preys upon thrift and industry."[6]

The focal point for understanding if the freedmen would work or not became the Port Royal region of South Carolina. Occupied by Union forces early in the war, these sea islands surrounding Beaufort and spreading out between Savannah and Charleston were inhabited overwhelmingly by former slaves. A group of New England reformers came soon after the army arrived to educate and assist the freedmen in transition to freedom. They pushed for land to be provided, established schools and medical facilities, side by side with churches. The freedmen welcomed them, and the two races worked together to demonstrate how well blacks could accommodate themselves to being free people.

The nation was watching. Reporters from the North came to report the outcome of the experiment. The national government used the Port Royal experience as a model for its treatment of the emancipated slaves all over the South. No area of Dixie had been so overwhelmingly black and so powerfully entwined with slavery. If freedom could work here, there was hope for its victory everywhere.[7]

The story that emerged was mixed and marred by white prejudice but overall showed the freedmen diligent in their work, and especially eager to learn. The New England reformers who managed the enterprise described self-supporting blacks who had no interest in going north, but rather wished to stay in their homeland as free farmers and laborers. They occasionally reported that the blacks, like all "degraded races," would take some time to elevate to full citizenship, but they assured the Northern public that blacks had the capacity.[8]

But if the overall lesson of the Port Royal experiment was that blacks would work, things were complicated by debate among Northern reformers as to *how* they should work. The more religious reformers argued that freedmen should immediately be given land and make their own decisions about how and what to grow. Freedmen themselves strongly supported this view, and their success on private lands certainly disproved claims of innate laziness. But it also raised the possibility that the new Dixie might resemble the more traditional pockets of Northern agriculture, where farmers sought self-sufficiency and isolation from national and international market pressures.

A more progressive alternative argued that blacks should continue laboring to produce cotton, demonstrating the superiority of freed labor by producing more of it. Edward Philbrick, spokesman for this perspective, insisted that "as a general thing, the amount of cotton planted will always be a pretty sure index to the state of industry of the people." The cotton South would continue to import foodstuffs, tools, and machines but would contribute to the economic integration and hence the wealth of the modern nation. Ironically, this argument shared the fears of postwar white Southerners. As one Alabama newspaper put it, if blacks controlled their own land, they would "raise corn, squashes, pigs and chickens, and will work no more in the cotton, rice and sugar field . . . their labor will become unavailable for those products which the world especially needs."[9]

Davis Bend, the plantation on the Mississippi owned by Jefferson

Davis, also attracted attention. General Grant hoped that the place might become "a negro paradise" on the very spot owned by wealthy slave owners. Reformers planned to use the place in such a way that "the good results of our beneficence would incite others to do the same good work, and . . . the ability and good conduct of [the freedmen] would silence and put to shame the calumnies against this unfortunate race." At the end of 1863 a Northern reporter told his readers about "Jeff's Plantation Turned into a Contraband Camp," where freedmen would prove slavery unnecessary and demonstrate black abilities as free laborers.[10]

As in Port Royal, the message that emerged was complex. Blacks who originally lived in the area established a successful new community. But thousands of refugees who sought a haven from the destruction of war gathered in poverty and sickness. Northern and Southern white cotton speculators swarmed into the region. When possible they exploited black labor, as did Northern men to whom the Treasury Department leased abandoned plantations. Meanwhile, Northern reform societies sent their schoolmarms into Davis Bend, where they met freedmen passionate to learn, but sufficiently obstreperous in their newfound freedom to resent excessive bossing by the teachers. Economic necessity also sometimes kept freedmen away from school. The new and often unhealthy environment of the deep South wilted teacher patience and enthusiasm. Despite some private doubts, however, most teachers reported that the success of their black charges matched white pupils' in Northern schools.[11]

The experiments at Port Royal and Davis Bend brought economic success. Freedmen produced cotton crops that, if not equal in quantity to the days of slavery, still provided profits. Near Port Royal one large cotton-planting operation provided a clear profit of more than $80,000. Reformers there who gained such profits were embarrassed that doing good had paid so well. Nevertheless, news spread rapidly into the North that freed labor might pay as well as slave. In Mississippi the story was similar. Despite the disruptions of war, and the absence of many able-bodied workers, profits marked the experiment in free labor. Blacks gained only a small percentage of these profits, most of which went to whites who leased and managed the operation. But the lesson was clear: former slaves had the capacity to emulate the free labor society of the North. By December 1864 the *New York Times* could write, "The nest in which the rebellion was hatched is the Mecca of 'The Freedmen.' The home of Jeff. Davis who represents the rebellion for slavery, is consecrated . . . as the home of the emancipated. . . . [This experiment] will strike an answering chord in all the loyal North, as it points out the fitness of the place for humane and economic work of elevating thousands of an oppressed race."[12]

Other smaller-scale efforts to hold former slaves to the standards of white economic virtue illustrated the complexities of the problem. Union chaplain Joel Grant took over contraband duties in February 1863 in a rural area outside Memphis. His commanding officer was James W. Denver, a Democrat who had been born in Virginia and was, according to Grant, "a regular Copperhead." The general opposed emancipation, often telling the chaplain that "he would send them all back to their masters if he could." For six weeks Grant stayed out of Denver's way.

But Denver resigned in March 1863, and General William Smith took over. At first Smith seemed as bad as his predecessor, but Grant worked on him and soon the general backed the chaplain's efforts to provide a satisfactory answer to the widespread question "What shall we do with the Negroes?" For Grant the answer was to demonstrate black diligence by replicating an ideal Northern community. He got his charges to plant five hundred acres of cotton, and to build a community of about six hundred cabins, laying out streets, building a church, a schoolhouse, a store, a carpenter's shop, a tool and harness shed, and a commissary. The New England town he and the freedmen managed to create seemed to him an almost perfect symbol of a regenerated South.

But Smith got orders to report to Vicksburg, and Major General Richard Oglesby took over. Grant's hopes died. Although the Kentucky-born general was a loyal man, his wife was "a secessionist." Grant believed that her influence had pushed Oglesby to a new position. He "took it into his head that he did not want so many niggers (we had about 1,300) about and ordered them all transferred." The chaplain was also transferred. Grant begged and argued, but the best he could do was to get an agreement that fifty men could stay and look after the cotton. The rest were sent to Memphis. "I felt at the time much as you and I have felt at the death of a child," Grant wrote his father. He tried to keep up the community by traveling fifty miles each way from the city, but his other duties proved too much. He hoped that he might get another contraband camp to reinforce the example, but seemed to have had his spirit broken by the turn of events. With some understatement he remarked that "the contraband question is involved in a good deal of uncertainty."[13]

Communities like Joel Grant's and those at Port Royal and Davis Bend demonstrated black capacities for work and economic success. But the successes came framed in a war context that often made freedom ambiguous. While the army freed and protected slaves, it had other roles to play that restricted freedom. As soldiers invaded Dixie and met the hundreds of thousands of freedmen, the first need was to bring order to the conquered region. One imperative was to stop slaves from seeking revenge on former masters. The number of slaves inclined to do so was small, but the few incidents of reprisal put the army on alert and made them conscious of the need for controlling freedom. Fighting rebel armies was the major task of bluecoats. They could hardly afford to be stamping out partisan warfare.[14]

Second, the army could not afford to provide supplies for the blacks over any extended period of time. It was imperative that they be put to work caring for themselves. Accomplishing this would, in addition to providing rations, also demonstrate black commitment to self-discipline and order. Northern philanthropic organizations were called upon to help in the immediate needs of regions disrupted by war, but it was obvious that blacks should care for themselves as a matter of policy and necessity. General Grant recalled the need to somehow provide for the huge numbers of refugees by putting them to work under army supervision, paying them wages for harvesting cotton, cutting firewood. "At once the freedmen became self-sustaining. The money was not paid to them directly, but was expended judiciously and for their benefit. They gave me no trouble afterwards."

The implementation of these goals brought some strange forms of free labor. Some soldiers impressed black workers into service, offering alternatives of being soldiers or laborers, but nothing else. Blacks got wages for their work, but deductions taken out for equipment, rations, and medical care often reduced wages to a pittance. Northern investors leased many plantations and worked freedmen especially hard despite occasional uprisings and protests. Army officials had the duty of securing "continuous and faithful service, respectful department, correct discipline and perfect subordination," and they enforced those rules when called upon to do so. Blacks became increasingly restless under these circumstances; freedom looked much like slavery.

But there were great differences. Free black protesters did not met with death at the hands of a master who could depend on the law to find him innocent if he killed to enforce discipline. Families were not torn from each other to meet white economic needs. Blacks negotiated contracts with white help and might thereby gain some rights. The whip vanished almost everywhere as a means to compel obedience. And the army at times also stopped planters from abusing blacks. If freedmen were restless, their restlessness was perceived not as demanding stern repression, but as a problem to be somehow circumvented. And the poverty and disruption that the trail of war left behind demanded supervision and a paternalism by whites if widespread want was not to result. This was especially true since the army had taken thousands of the men away from their fields and families, leaving only women, children, and the aged behind.[15]

Black refugees posed an equivocal picture. Black soldiers offered a purer view. To win its victories, the North increasingly called upon its "sable arm." First used in unofficial capacities around the camps into which they streamed as the Union army advanced, blacks were officially accepted into the army on August 25, 1862, when Rufus Saxton in South Carolina gained approval to "arm, equip, and receive into the service of the United States" up to five thousand black volunteers. From the first days of the conflict James Lane had enrolled blacks in his Kansas armies, but that had been done unofficially, as Lane did most things. Stanton had been quietly supporting other uses of sable soldiers, and the Second Confiscation Act had permitted doing so. The January Emancipation Proclamation announced nationwide that the nation was calling on black men to fight for the Union. It thus focused a spotlight on black soldiers that made their service more than simply military.[16]

Doubts had existed that blacks had the capacity to be soldiers. Lincoln himself had worried that they would somehow lose their guns to the rebels. Other white prejudices were more precise. Some viewed the Negro as a docile child, too ignorant and irresponsible to obey orders, too cowardly to fight. Others objected that to arm blacks was to arm savages who would rampage, rape, and destroy, turning war into unrestrained barbarism. Any action taken by black soldiers would be scrutinized with these prejudices in mind.

Many white troops refused to serve with Negroes in the Union-saving struggle. Seeing themselves involved in a noble enterprise, sharing the camaraderie that binds soldiers together in intimacies as well as suffering and death, whites feared that the presence of black soldiers would debase the cause and bring them down to the level of "niggers." A corporal in a New York regiment announced, "We don't want to fight side by side with the nigger. We think we are a too superior race for that." In 1862 a correspondent to the *New York Times* asserted that "I am quite sure there is not one man in ten but would feel himself degraded as a volunteer if Negro equality is to be the order in the field of battle." Even after black troops began to be used, Northern soldiers disliked the idea. When Adjutant General Lorenzo Thomas told Theodore Upson's brigade of Lincoln's order arming the blacks, the Ninetieth Illinois Regiment hissed and the brigade was hastily marched back to quarters. "The truth is," Upson wrote, "none of our soldiers seem to like the idea of arming the Negroes. Our boys say this is a white man's war and the Negro has no business in it." While the men favored emancipation, "we don't care to fight side by side with them." When Upson himself was offered a captain's commission if he would lead a black regiment, he exploded, "Not any Niggers for me! Thank you, Uncle Sam, but if it is all the same to you, No! *No! No!*"

Still, some soldiers intensified their will to fight after seeing slavery firsthand. In February 1863 an Iowa regiment met its first contrabands escaping from rebel lines. Among them was "a bright little girl whose hair fell to her shoulders and was just a little wavy," Cyrus Boyd recalled. "Her features were sharp and clear while her eyes were dark blue." The mother of the girl told the Union men that she had had two other girls by her master and that all three were kept slaves. "A soldier who stood by and heard the Mother tell this story exclaimed, '*By God I'll fight till hell freezes over* and then I'll cut the ice and fight on.'"[17]

The participation of blacks in the Union cause served to mitigate but not to destroy the predominant racism of the North. Few gave up the idea that blacks were somehow a distinct and inferior race, but new understandings emerged. In the early days of the war, when slaves failed to rise up against their masters, many whites saw blacks as a docile, peaceful people, whose freedom would not threaten them. When blacks began serving as soldiers even their white officers retained images that denied equality. Thomas Higginson saw his black soldiers as "the world's perpetual children, docile, gay and loveable . . . I feel the same degree of sympathy that I should if I had a Turkish command—that is, a sort of sympathetic admiration, not tending towards agreement, but towards co-operation." Another writer conjured up the image of the English in India commanding natives, taking up the white man's burden. Black soldiers were "American Sepoys without any disposition to treachery." Still, this was a stronger foundation on which to build equality than the image of the stupid and/or savage "darky" that had been strong before the war. And once the Negro soldiers moved into action, minds would be changed in significant ways.[18]

The battlefield courage of the Negroes weakened prejudice in the full spotlight of the Northern press. Dramatic evidence that blacks had the capacity for freedom and citizenship emerged early in 1863 as regiments of former slaves began to advance against rebel positions. Even minor expeditions received intensive newspaper coverage.

In February a detachment led by Higginson pushed up the St. Mary's River on the Georgia coast, fought its way through rebel soldiers, and captured a large quantity of supplies. "A complete success," a *New York Times* reporter proclaimed. "Our colored troops are more than a match for an equal number of white rebels." But the first serious fighting that black soldiers engaged in took place at Port Hudson in Louisiana on May 27, 1863. Confederates besieged in their garrison built rifle entrenchments, commanding the only possible approach. They backed these rifles with cannons and then felled trees in front of their lines to slow down attackers. Two regiments of black troops attacked these fortifications. Six and then seven times they charged and charged again. Every time they failed, but in the face of failure they kept attacking. "Heroic conduct," General Banks was quoted as saying in the *New York Times.* "No troops could be more determined or more daring." The general's entire report to Washington was reprinted, and the *Times* added, "This official testimony settles the question that the Negro race can fight with great prowess."

Shortly thereafter at Milliken's Bend blacks were defenders and fought off rebel attacks with bayonets and swords, and the entire North was told that "it is impossible for men to show greater gallantry than the Negro troops in that fight." By midsummer people were reading and thrilling to scenes like that played on a New Orleans levee: a black regiment embarking to fight former masters, a crowd of wives and children and friends saying their good-byes, and the whole of them united in singing "John Brown's Body." By the next year books appeared describing black courage, intelligence, and dedication not only on the battlefield, but on farms and in workshops and in schools that the army and Northern philanthropic organizations had founded. James McKaye in *The Mastership and Its Fruits: The Emancipated Slave Face to Face with His Old Master* and George Hepworth in *Whip, Hoe, and Sword* told fascinated readers what blacks could do and thus helped newspapers educate white readers on the inadequacies of racist accusations.[19]

The recruiting of black troops in the North further fed black claims to citizenship. Since the first days of the nation, citizenship and soldiering had been entwined. Frederick Douglass spoke with the force of history in observing, "Once let the black man get upon his person the brass letters, US; let him get an eagle on his button, and a musket on his shoulder and bullets in his pockets and there is no power on earth which can deny that he has won the right to citizenship in the United States."

In January 1863, with emancipation now Union policy, Governor John Andrew in Massachusetts got the authorization he had been seeking for months. He began seeking black regiments. Wartime prosperity that gave blacks jobs, rumors that the army would pay them less and that only whites could be officers, slowed early recruiting efforts. But Andrew called in prominent black abolitionists to stir up patriotism and to point up the opportunity. By the end of May, the black Fifty-fourth Massachusetts led by Brahmin colonel Robert Gould Shaw marched through Boston on its way to South Carolina. Following the same route that had witnessed the return of fugitive slaves a few years before, they passed cheering crowds that lined the street. On Essex Street on a balcony of Wendell Phillips' house, William Lloyd Garrison stood beside a bust of John

Brown, waiting. As the troops passed, they paused, Shaw and his officers lifted their hats, and then moved on to embark for the South.[20]

Similar scenes took place in Ohio, Rhode Island, Connecticut, New York, Pennsylvania. All served to weaken some of the prejudice whites held while strengthening black claims to equal citizenship rights. But even that came slowly. Until 1864 black troops received less pay than did whites, the government fearing too long strides in the face of enduring racism. Throughout much of the war black soldiers got poorer medical care, owing in part to the absence of black doctors in regiments. And, of course, there was no integration of enlisted men. However, the educational power of black soldiering helped shift the mood of the North, undermining much of the prejudice that stood as obstacles to black soldiers. Not only had black courage challenged racism, but for every black that went to war, a white man could stay home. Even the militantly Democratic Irish, long known for bitter prejudice, could say, as one Irish journalist put it, "I'll let Sambo be murthered instead of myself / On any day of the year."[21]

But the strongest claim that blacks could make in the eyes of most whites was that they were fighting for the ultimate goal of the war in the eyes of whites and many blacks as well—the saving of the Union. Even abolitionists agreed that the Union must be saved. To help in such an enterprise strengthened crucially the claim to white protection and support. In a widely printed public letter to Congressman James Conkling of Illinois, Lincoln made perhaps the strongest case that most whites could accept for the black soldier. First, "some of the commanders of our armies in the field who have given us our most important successes, believe the emancipation policy, and the use of colored troops, constitute the heaviest blow yet dealt to the rebellion." His goal, the president repeated, was to save the Union, and he believed that "to whatever extent the Negroes should cease helping the enemy, to that extent it weakened the enemy. . . . I thought that whatever Negroes can be got to do as soldiers, leaves just so much less for white soldiers to do, in saving the Union." Yet how could he enlist black help without earning it? "Negroes like other people, act upon motives. Why should they do anything for us, if we will do **nothing** for them? If they stake their lives for us, they must be prompted by the strongest motive—even the promise of freedom." And the contrast between blacks who fought to save "the great republic . . . the principle it lives by, and keeps alive—for man's vast future" and those who stood on the other side was stark: "There will be some black men who can remember that with silent tongue, and clenched teeth, and steady eye, and well poised bayonet they have helped mankind on to this great consummation; while, I fear, there will be some white ones, unable to forget that with malignant heart, and deceitful speech, they strove to hinder it."[22]

While blacks sacrificed their lives and proved their courage, they also gained sympathy by outrages they suffered, both on and off the battlefield. The savage anti-Negro violence of the New York City draft riots generated a reaction among shocked white employers. Irish workers were fired, blacks hired. Efforts were made to expand opportunities for employment and for the exercise of rights. The *Atlantic Monthly* advocated equal rights for blacks by contrasting them with the Irish of New York City. "The emancipated Negro is at least as industrious and thrifty as the Celt, takes more pride in self-support, is far more eager for education, and has fewer vices. It is impossible to name any standard of requisites for the full rights of citizenship which would give a vote to the Celt and exclude the Negro."[23]

In the field, atrocity also spawned sympathy. When Union armies began employing Negro troops, the Confederate government threatened to execute or enslave captured blacks and to try their officers for inciting insurrection. Lincoln checkmated this threat with the announcement that a rebel prisoner would be executed for every one killed by rebels and that every enslaved prisoner would find a counterpart in a Confederate prisoner placed at hard labor. But an outrage in Tennessee showed that the issue could not rest. On April 12, 1864, Nathan B. Forrest, later to found the Ku Klux Klan, attacked the Union force at Fort Pillow. Blacks formed over half the defending force, and when the rebels overran the fort, scores were killed, after surrendering. Others were given to masters as slaves. News of this atrocity rocked the North. "Indiscriminate Slaughter of . . . Prisoners," "Butchery," "Murder," newspapers trumpeted. Sympathy grew for blacks and their sacrifices, linked with increased willingness to punish Dixie by expanding the so obviously needed protection.[24]

These sporadic atrocities against black troops were matched by enduring grievances, too. The Confederacy refused to exchange any captured black soldiers or their white officers until late 1864. In retaliation, Union officials refused to exchange rebels they had captured. The result was an increasing prison population in which soldiers suffered terribly, and in which blacks were sold back into slavery.[25]

By the time the war ended, almost 180,000 black soldiers had fought for the Union. By 1865 over 12 percent of the 1 million men in blue uniform were Negroes, having comprised between 9 and 10 percent of the soldiers who actually served the Union cause. They were indispensable to the North. On September 12, 1864, Lincoln noted that to fight without the help of the blacks "is more than we can bear. We cannot spare the hundred and forty or fifty thousand now serving us." Their service produced an abnormally high percentage of casualties, although most of these came from disease— the greatest killer of white troops as well. Because of the suffering from the poorest medical care and extended garrison duty which led to bad water and unsanitary conditions, the over 68,000 casualties were predictable though immense. Over one-third of black soldiers were casualties of the conflict, with from 2,700 to nearly 3,220 killed in battle. While their service had not destroyed prejudice, it had helped destroy slavery in 39 major battles and 449 engagements, with 21 black Medal of Honor winners. Close to 119,000 former slaves had hammered off their own chains. The fighting by all the blacks had produced claims on white sympathy, linked them with an admirable cause, and laid the groundwork for changing some of the nation's racial ideas.[26]

Black soldiers and black laborers helped to persuade Northern whites that blacks generally might be part of the transformed nation. The struggle for equality also had an impact on white self-images. The articulate upper class of the North found in the war revitalized confidence in their own capacities, a new faith in their role in society. Before the conflict there had been deep concern that in the selfish stampede for wealth, society was forgetting the nobler qualities of self-sacrifice, attention to duty. Conservative intellectuals like Charles Eliot Norton, Francis Parkman, and the immensely popular Oliver Wendell Holmes, Sr., had argued, in Norton's words, that without the leadership of the "intelligent and prosperous classes," America was doomed to decay, corrupted by "lavish abundance."

The war brought conspicuous opportunities for that leadership. Leading black troops was perhaps the most spotlighted of the positions the young elite held, and Robert Gould Shaw became the symbol of his class's dedication. Assuming the leadership of the Fifty-fourth Massachusetts, Shaw took his troops to Battery Wagner where he died on the barricades urging his men forward. He immediately became the martyr who had shown in death the meaning of aristocratic nobility. Both Lowell and Emerson wrote poems about him, and Henry Ward Beecher, Henry James, Sr., John Lathrop Motley, as well as abolitionists Garrison and Lydia Maria Child, sent their condolences when he died. Emerson wrote of the meaning of Shaw's death in "Voluntaries":

> In an age of fops and toys
> Wanting wisdom, void of right,
> Who shall nerve heroic boys
> To hazard all in Freedom's fight
>
> . . . .
> And quite proud homes and youthful dames
> For famine, toil and fray?
> Yet on the nimble air benign,
> Speed nimbler messages,
> That waft the breath of grace divine
> To hearts in sloth and ease,
> So nigh is grandeur to our dust,
> So near is God to man,
> When duty whispers low, *Thou must,*
> The youth replies, *I can.*

Shaw was not the only noble upper-class hero. *Atlantic Monthly* carried an article in 1863 proposing a chapel at Harvard to commemorate the young men who had fought for "culture, generous learning, noble arts, for all that makes a land great and glorious." An 1865 article in the *North American Review,* "Our Soldiers," contained letters, sermons, and recollections of elite young men who had given up lives of ease to sacrifice for the nation, thereby demonstrating that the nation's wealthy class believed in, and were dying for, the same causes as the more common people. Fraser Stearns, son of the president of Amherst College, Walter Wymonds Newhall of Philadelphia, "one of the best and most noted cricketeers in the country," John Hanson Thompson, son of a New York minister and student at Yale, were but three young men who "might have lived absorbed in illusions, in the ignoble round of petty cares and selfish interests." But they had answered the call of war and so demonstrated "the spirit of manliness . . . obedience . . . absolute self-sacrifice," showing that their "strongest motive is duty." These men overcame "the temptations of prosperity [which] had already misled us; the love of ease [which] had already begun to work corruption." A nation that was "stagnating in selfishness, and losing the sense of virtue" now could see that its sons still cared for higher things. The most important was respect for laws demonstrated in obedience and service to others. The nation was learning the virtues of those ancient Spartans at Thermopylae whose monument read, "O stranger, tell the Lacedaemonians that we are lying here, have *obeyed* their laws."[27]

Not all these young men were associated with raising the blacks to freedom, but they did display the same sense of "earnest and martyr-like spirit" attributed to Stearns as well as to Shaw. It was in the aftermath of emancipation that Northern writers increasingly spoke of the nobler qualities that war was inspiring among the masses as well as the elite. Only three days after the September 22 proclamation the *New York Times* observed that the Northern populace was now demonstrating the nobler qualities of its character. "The working, pains taking, money getting white male laborers of the North, whom the secession filibusters believed would be so craven and selfish that they would never go to war are shaping into the fiercest and readiest martial temper that the war has brought to them." A year and a half later the comments of another writer were similar: "One of the more immediate results [of the war] has been . . . to disabuse the Southern mind of some of its most fatal misconceptions as to Northern character. They thought us a trading people, incapable of lofty sentiment, ready to sacrifice everything for commercial advantage. . . . They are not likely to make that mistake again."[28]

For all the talk of improving character and high and noble ideals, the fact remained that the young men were dead, and that fact had a private meaning that swept through family and friends with deep sadness. James Russell Lowell, who lost three nephews and was on intimate terms with the Shaw family, caught that personal meaning:

> Why, hain't I held 'em on my knee?
>   Didn't I love to see 'em growin',
> Three likely lads es wal could be,
>   Halmsome an' brave an' not tu know'?
> I set an' look into the blaze
>   Whose natur', jes like theirn, keeps climbin',
> Ez lon 'z it lives, in shinin' ways,
>   An half despise myself for rhymin'.[29]

The talk about the sacrifice and building of character and the social and public meaning of the deaths did serve a purpose. It helped give meaning to a carnage that touched almost every Northern family. It asked of them a certain height and public involvement. And because it was their sons' lives that were the motivating force, the ideals became formidable ones, justifying whatever causes and efforts that later might be connected with the war. Reconstruction reforms carried the force they did in part because of the larger meaning given to the many tragedies. And, of course, less noble activities could also wrap themselves in the sacrifices of war.

While emancipation and the courage of black soldiers had an important symbolic impact, more concrete results also ensued. Significant changes occurred in patterns of prejudice in the North. At the beginning of the war free blacks in the North suffered discrimination both by law and by social custom. Only Massachusetts let black and white children into the same schools. In every other state north of Dixie blacks attended segregated schools that were poorly heated and furnished, and supplied with the worst educational materials. Some blacks were kept off tax rolls so that they could not even pay into funds to establish schools. Local school boards almost uniformly made sure that blacks and whites did not gain equal educational opportunities.

Only five Northern states let blacks vote equally with whites, all five in New England. Still, Connecticut kept its ballot boxes lily white. New York allowed blacks with $250 in property to cast ballots, but Ohio denied the right to vote to any man who looked more Negro than white. Only one state, Massachusetts again, allowed blacks to be on juries, but everywhere else they were kept off by custom that was so effective that only five states officially denied black testimony. Iowa, Illinois, and Indiana adopted laws in the 1850s making it a crime for blacks to settle there, and Oregon spread this bias to the Pacific. Michigan, Iowa, and Wisconsin turned down equal suffrage in prewar referenda.

Not all barriers that blacks faced were legal ones. Custom kept Negroes in segregated seats at lectures and theaters, kept them out of hotels with white clientele, put them in Negro pews in churches, threw them into segregated prisons, cared for them in segregated hospitals, and buried them in their own cemeteries. In public they faced insults on the streets, caricatures in the press and magazines, and parodies in popular minstrel shows of the age. And, of course, white children everywhere learned that to be "like a nigger" in anything was a terrible insult.[30]

But the war generated changes. No revolution ensued, but changes came in the van of battlefield courage and discipline as well as with the reassurance that emancipation would not threaten white society. Lincoln had tried his hand at calming white fears as early as December 1862. In his last public message before emancipation the president urged colonization, but also spoke of an America for both blacks and whites. To be sure, Lincoln envisioned a nation where blacks lived predominantly in the South, but whites there would benefit too. Freedmen would take on the tasks of the years of bondage. They would probably do less work, no longer being driven to it. This would mean jobs for white laborers. And should colonization work to even a limited extent, the rise of wages would be "mathematically certain" and whites would benefit.

Yet Lincoln also sought to calm concern about a black tide sweeping northward. Already in the country, they would hardly increase in numbers by being free, and if they were, in the worst case, to spread throughout the North and be "equally distributed among the whites of the whole country . . . there would be but one colored to seven whites. Could the one, in any way, greatly disturb the seven?" Many communities already had even larger populations of free blacks and lived without trouble—Washington, D.C., and the whole states of Maryland and Delaware illustrated that a biracial society would work.[31]

But the greatest efforts to move the North toward equality came from abolitionists, and from blacks themselves. The struggle against the South allowed orators like Wendell Phillips to give a national meaning to the struggle for equality. Early in 1862 he said, "I hold that the South is to be annihilated. I do not mean the geographic South. . . . [I] mean the intellectual, social and aristocratic South—the thing that represented itself by slavery and the bowie knife, by bullying and lynch law, by ignorance and idleness." Phillips' associate Stephen Foster insisted that the real enemy was "not merely the . . . form of slavery . . . but the spirit of oppression." Susan B. Anthony indicted racial discrimination in the North as akin to slavery in the South. "While the cruel slave driver lacerates the black man's mortal body, we, of the North, flay the spirit." The regeneration of the nation that the war made possible had to operate in the North. "Let us open to the colored man all our schools. . . . Let us admit him into all our mechanic shops, stores and offices, and lucrative business avocations, to work side by side with his white brother; let him rent such pew in the church, and occupy such seat in the theater, and public lecture room, as he pleases; let him be admitted to all our entertainment, both public & private; let him share all the accommodations of our hotels, stages, railboats and steamboats. . . . Extend to him all the rights of citizenship. Let him vote and be voted for; let him sit upon the judge's bench, and in the juror's box. . . . Let the North thus prove to the South by their acts, that she fully recognizes the humanity of the black man."[32]

Some advances toward equality were private: white ministers asking black colleagues to preach from their pulpits, black laborers hired to work alongside whites. Arriving in the capital to serve as a nurse, Louisa May Alcott was surprised to see blacks performing a range of jobs she had not seen them perform before. There were "draymen, hack drivers, oystermen, carpenters, even some shopkeepers." Charles Sumner led the legal profession in opening its doors. In 1864 he sponsored John Rock as the first Negro to practice before the United States Supreme Court. Eight years before, that same court had ruled that blacks could not be citizens of the United States. Congress followed the Massachusetts senator's urgings also in permitting blacks to testify in federal courts, allowing them to deliver the mails, and admitting them to the galleries of Congress so that they could watch the laws being made. They would be on hand when Congress passed the Thirteenth Amendment ending slavery forever in the United States.

But the states controlled most of the rights blacks sought. Here progress was slower, although definitely an advance over the conditions of 1860–61. Prodded by the courage of black soldiers in the field and persuaded by reformers at home, Northern states repealed some of their laws barring equality. Illinois and Iowa threw out their exclusion laws. Ohio and Iowa began granting poor relief for both races. Illinois and Ohio gave blacks the right to testify in court, and the Buckeye State also wiped out its law that had made voting impossible for men looking like Negroes. New England, already the most advanced in equality before the war, moved a bit further. Rhode Island passed a law at the end of 1865 eliminating segregated schools in the state. Agitation begun in the war bore fruit in 1867 when Connecticut desegregated her schools. Jim Crow in public transportation also suffered setbacks, as New York City, Washington, D.C., and Philadelphia integrated streetcars.

The streetcar battle focused national attention over the struggle for equality, for such transportation was part of daily experience, and quarrels there were very public. In New York and Philadelphia black soldiers or their wives, widows, and families were thrown off streetcars, sometimes by company workers, sometimes by gangs of toughs, frequently Irishmen. After one such incident the powerful *New York Tribune* roared, "It is quite time to settle the question whether the wives and children of men who are laying down their lives for their country . . . are to be treated like dogs." In the aftermath of the draft riots, public pressure forced the privately owned companies to integrate their streetcars by mid-1864. The Philadelphia struggle took longer, but ultimately the city with the largest black population in the North yielded to mass meetings, petitions, and private lobbying efforts. In 1867 the state legislature of Pennsylvania ended Jim Crow streetcars in the City of Brotherly Love.[33]

The streetcar struggle in Washington, D.C., produced an incident that symbolized the human side of the movement toward equality. Sojourner Truth, an aged former slave and abolitionist, found herself working in Washington, D.C., in 1865 and one day decided to take a streetcar with a white friend. Congress had passed a law forbidding discrimination on the cars, but not everyone was inclined to comply. As Truth and her friend entered the car a man getting off turned to the conductor and asked if "niggers were allowed to ride." The conductor grabbed the old black woman and ordered her to get out. Her friend said, "Don't put her out." And the conductor asked if she belonged to the white woman. "No. She belongs to humanity." Unimpressed, the conductor shoved her against the door and ordered both women off the car. The black woman warned him that he could not "shove me about like a dog" and told her friend to take down the number of the car. The conductor backed off and they rode on, to get off at the hospital. Truth's shoulder had been slightly dislocated, and she complained to the president of the line. He told her to sue the conductor. She got a lawyer from the Freedmen's Bureau and won the case. The conductor was fired. Word spread everywhere, and even before the trial was over, "the inside of the cars looked like pepper and salt." Within a few days conductors were stopping their cars for blacks and whites, and were saying politely to them, "Walk in ladies."[34]

Another incident also symbolized the changes that the war had brought. It was the custom after the inauguration for the White House to be open to all callers. People were allowed to come and shake the president's hand. A band played and the president and some of the other national officials presided. Frederick Douglass, having heard the second inaugural address, determined that he would attend the reception. He asked several friends to go with him, but they made their excuses. Finally one man agreed to go. As they approached the White House, police stopped them. Douglass insisted on going in and declared that if Lincoln knew he was outside, he would permit blacks to enter. The officers disagreed, and Douglass had to run past them into the building itself. Two more policemen stopped him and did their best to get Douglass out of there. Seeing a friend, Douglass asked him to tell Lincoln what was happening. Within half a minute the black leader was ushered into the crowded East Room. Lincoln spotted him coming and in a loud voice announced, "Here comes my friend Douglass." He reached out and took his friend's hand and asked what he had thought of the inaugural speech. "There is no man's opinion I value more than yours; what do you think of it?" Douglass protested that there were thousands waiting to shake his hand, but Lincoln wanted the process to stop for a moment. He asked again for his opinion as the crowd watched. "It was a sacred effort," Douglass said. "I'm glad you liked it," Lincoln replied, and the handshaking ceremony was allowed to proceed.[35]

But there were defeats as well as victories in the struggle. Blacks could not vote outside New England during the war. Movements to give them the vote failed in every state in the Union until 1868. Then only Iowa and Minnesota agreed to black voting, and in the latter state voters were tricked into approval. The issue on the ballot did not mention black suffrage. It stated only that they should vote to "amend Section 1, Article 2" of the state constitution. Six Northern states turned down black voting. Racist campaigns by Democrats blocked it and frightened Republicans away from equal voting rights. While Illinois repealed its antiblack civil rights laws and took pride in being the first state to ratify the Thirteenth Amendment, other states still kept blacks from serving in the militia and sent them to segregated schools. Indiana stood as a bastion of anti-Negro sentiment. Blacks there could not vote, testify, go to public schools, make valid contracts, or even enter the Hoosier State. The Democratic party fought effectively against almost every equality measure with accusations of race mixing and other portents of miscegenational doom.[36]

Yet if prejudice against blacks endured at the end of the war, it was not the overpowering force that it had been. By 1865 substantial numbers of Northerners supported Negro suffrage. Three states had elections in the fall of that year in which the voters were asked to permit blacks to vote by amendment to the state constitutions— Connecticut, Minnesota, and Wisconsin. The amendments failed in all three states, but the margins of victory were small. Equal suffrage lost by 6,272, 2,670, and 9,003 respectively. Over 27,000 voters in Connecticut favored black ballots, as did over 45,500 in Wisconsin and over 12,000 in Minnesota. Half of the ten Republican conventions held in 1865 passed resolutions favoring black voting, three in New England and two in the Old Northwest.[37]

Within black communities impetus for hope and action was stimulated by the claims they could now make on white power. Black community solidarity was also strengthened, cohering around the black regiments that had served with valor during the war. Just as in white communities, black veterans would provide leadership and strength for future black enterprises. Negroes made strong showings in advancing the equality measures of Reconstruction and were effective voices in ratifying the Fifteenth Amendment, which ended blatant racial discrimination at the ballot box.[38]

By 1870 sentiment on behalf of black equality grew to such an extent that thirteen of the twenty-one states that fought for the Union ratified the Fifteenth Amendment, and three of those that refused to do so were former slave states. Still, prejudice endured, Ohio, New Jersey, California, and Oregon rejected the amendment. Yet if there were dissenters, the war had advanced the cause of black rights profoundly. In 1861 a constitutional amendment guaranteeing slavery forever in Dixie had passed the Congress and gone to the states. Within five years after the war three constitutional amendments advancing equality had been ratified. The war had written promises of freedom, and not slavery, into the nation's fundamental law.[39]

War had made emancipation possible. Without it slavery might easily have endured into the twentieth century. But the conflict also limited the meaning of emancipation and the struggle of equality. Since freedom came only in the storm of war, it was justified more as a military necessity than an end in itself. Since the fight against slavery was born of the passion of Northerners to save their constitutional Union, implicit conflicts between securing equality and respecting the Constitution had to be compromised. Since the war goals envisioned the triumph of free labor society and culture, war gains like black freedom were measured by that culture's definitions of freedom, not necessarily by freedmen's needs.

The military necessity argument was imperative for emancipation. In 1864 abolitionist John Jay told Charles Sumner that "the most expedient manner of proceeding against slavery in all its phases, has been . . . grounding our actions on military necessity." Lincoln constantly insisted that he was saving the Union in his emancipation efforts and believed that military necessity was the only legal basis for his freeing of the slaves. Leading intellectuals like Emerson and James Russell Lowell extolled Lincoln's emancipation efforts as combining idealism with the deep wisdom of realizing that mere humanitarian motives lacked power to bring freedom. As Lowell put it, the president had made "a somewhat impracticable moral sentiment" into "the unconscious instrument of a practical moral end." Contrasting Don Quixote, who "was incomparable in the theoretic and ideal statesmanship," with Sancho Panza, who "with his stock of proverbs and the ready money of human experience, made the best practical governor," Lowell put Lincoln in the latter category and applauded him for being there. Lincoln thought so highly of this article that he recommended it to members of the cabinet as a fine assessment of his policies. The president also wrote to the publishers of the journal to thank them, saying that he hoped the article "will be of value to the country."[40]

Abolitionists deplored and feared the military necessity argument. To free men because of military necessity rather than because it was right was "the most God insulting doctrine ever proclaimed," Parker Pillsbury argued. Lydia Maria Child decried "this entire absence of a moral sense on the subject. . . . Even should [slaves] be emancipated merely as a 'war necessity' everything must go wrong if there is no heart or conscience on the subject." And Frederick Douglass caught the danger in specific terms: "A man that hates Slavery for what it does to the white man, stands ready to embrace it the moment its injuries are confined to the black man, and he ceases to feel those injuries to his own person." The postwar struggle for equality would validate Douglass' prophecy.[41]

Respect for the Constitution was also a two-edged sword. The Union created by the Constitution was the prize of war. Both Republicans and Democrats debated in constitutional terms. The whole military necessity argument arose because Republicans justified emancipation under the Constitution's war powers. Reconstruction debates rang with definitions of congressional power, under the Constitution, to turn states into territories so "needful rules" would protect black liberty. This argument lost out to another, which rested Reconstruction on the power to "guarantee to every State in this Union a Republican Form of Government."

The fundamental element in this revered constitutional structure was the federal system linking vigorous states with a viable national government. The American Union was not unitary, it united the states. Saving that Union meant purging the nation of its corrosive impurity, slavery, and of slavery's constitutional corollary, state sovereignty, which permitted secession. Both died in the war. But state rights endured and gained respect. The huge contributions states made to fighting the war increased devotion by citizens. Increasing state budgets during and after the conflict reflected state government vigor in facing problems of public welfare and economic growth. Furthermore, the very concept of republican government, which secession had challenged, rested on local self-government where responsible citizens established and operated their communities, their states, and ultimately their nation.

All these factors combined to constrain the extent of freedom blacks could gain. The constitutional Union that was the prize of war would be a Union where states would control most of the daily lives of all citizens, especially the new black ones. When Congress wrote the Fourteenth Amendment, on which black protection would rest, John Bingham, author of its key clause, could say, "I have always believed that the protection in time of peace within the States of all the rights of person and citizen was one of the powers reserved to the States. And so I still believe."[42]

"Saving the Union" was one definition of victory, a complex concept that sparked both freedom and limitations on that freedom. But Northern victory meant more than that. In a war pitting one social vision against another, free labor had defeated slavery. Self-mastery had been proved superior to the rule of masters. Four million slaves moved from one society to another. Wartime demonstrations at Port Royal, Davis Bend, and elsewhere had suggested that they were ready for that new environment. But their success was deceptive. For blacks were free in a world that defined freedom by the ideal of the self-reliant, nondependent yeoman, mechanic, capitalist, or laborer. They were, however, also free in a world where their color, their poverty, and their heritage disadvantaged them far more than white competitors. A slave system that endured for centuries had been wiped away. Most whites optimistically ignored the impact of those centuries in determining what freedom required.

Dominant Northern descriptions of freedom spoke of challenge to character, not of compensation for black disadvantages. "Freedom is not bread and butter," the *North American Review* said, "it is not comfort, it is not house and clothes, it is not a happy life, it is not a certain heaven." The laws of "supply and demand" operated unrestricted in freedom. "We have never said that the black man's life should be raised above suffering. We have said that he should be free to choose between inevitable hardships." In March 1865 Congress established the Bureau of Freedmen, Refugees, and Abandoned Lands to respond to the destruction and disruption of war. But the director of this Freedmen's Bureau, O. O. Howard, insisted that the operations of his bureau were temporary and were designed to teach independence and self-reliance, to give nothing to the blacks that they could not earn by hard work. The definition of what such things were was broad. "It is better for the freedman to begin at the bottom and work up, that he may learn how to preserve the property he acquires." Northern investors in Southern lands also argued that they were teaching the freedmen the need to work and the self-discipline of freedom by making the freedmen buy lands from them. Even the thousand and more New England schoolmarms and -masters who went south to teach the freedman spoke of an education devoted to teaching "industry, economy, and thrift" and "the Puritan doctrine of the dignity of labor." Both avarice and humanitarian reform revealed the ideal Northern political economy where labor that earned its keep earned the label "free." To be beholden to others for gifts meant the failure of the character necessary for freedom.[43]

Land distribution formed the major testing ground for the meaning of liberty in the new Southern economy. Northern reformers knew that abiding freedom required economic security. In late 1863 Wendell Phillips observed, "While . . . large estates remain in the hands of the slave oligarchy its power is not destroyed. But let me confiscate the land of the South, and put it into the hands of the Negroes and white men who fought for it, and . . . I have planted a Union sure to grow as an acorn to become an oak. . . . Plant a hundred thousand Negro farmers and by their side a hundred thousand white soldiers, and I will risk the South, Davis and all."[44]

The prospect of providing lands for the freedmen intrigued Northern leaders, but their approach was cautious. When government agents confiscated lands in South Carolina and Georgia for the failure of rebels to pay taxes, Lincoln told them to give preference to freedmen in subsequent land sales. In January 1865 General Sherman set aside the lands thirty miles inland from Savannah to Jacksonville for blacks. Up to forty thousand freedmen settled there in response to this order. Blacks helped themselves to land abandoned by fugitive rebels or confiscated from the disloyal, with or without government approval. Talk that the government would give them forty acres and a mule was widespread and based on the former slaves' beliefs that they had earned that land by their years of "unrequited toil." Blacks gained the use of large tracts of land. In addition to Sherman's forty thousand settlers, a large number settled on abandoned Port Royal lands, and a thriving colony took over Davis Bend.[45]

But Congress would not guarantee this land ownership. In early 1865, after narrowly defeating a confiscation measure, the lawmakers settled on the 1865 Freedmen's Bureau Bill, which Charles Sumner argued for by urging that the blacks be placed on the land "for a few months" so that they could benefit from the labor they had put into the current crop. The bill itself allowed freedmen to farm forty-acre allotments, but did not give them the land. It promised that one day they might purchase "such title as the United States could convey."[46]

The government also allowed private entrepreneurs to bid for and buy large tracts in the Port Royal area and hence to employ blacks as wage laborers to cultivate the land. Here was the Yankee desire to turn a penny, but giving power to that materialistic goal was the morality that rationalized it in ways that persuaded Lincoln and important portions of Northern sentiment. Blacks would allegedly learn the true meaning of free labor by first being wage laborers. As one supporter argued, "To receive has been their natural condition. Giving them land and a house, and the ease of gaining as good a livelihood as they have been accustomed to would keep many contented with the smaller exertion." Promising to sell part of their land once blacks had learned the meaning of free labor, entrepreneurs mixed materialism and morality in a persuasive blend that symbolized the power of Victorian ideas of what freedom meant.[47]

The promise of permanent ownership faded before the conservative pressures of the war period, ironically also before the self-reliant free labor idea. The constitutional provision of Article III, Section 3, that confiscation could not affect heirs of the rebels, left land legally in the hands of the government. A lenient pardoning policy by Lincoln and especially by his successor, Andrew Johnson, gave back to former rebels lands they had lost. And this policy could be justified by an ideology that warned against the moral costs of giving things to people without being sure they had earned it. Lincoln's provision for giving blacks first chance to buy abandoned lands in South Carolina had been hedged with the urging that those with first claim would be freedmen who were "examples of moral propriety and industry to those of the same race."

In an age in which the adjective "self-made" was applied to almost every American of stature, an age in which Frederick Douglass' most popular lecture was not on slavery but on "Self-Made Men," after a war that had been fought with the image of free and independent labor before all eyes, it is hardly surprising that freedom was seen as the right to struggle for survival, the right to enter the race of life, not to have enduring protection for economic well-being. Douglass himself in widely quoted words declared in April of 1865 that the answer to "What shall we do with the Negro?" was "Do nothing with us! If the apples will not remain on the tree of their own strength, if they are worm-eaten to the core, if they are early ripe and disposed to fall, let them fall. . . . If the negro cannot stand on his own legs, let him fall also." A Southern black leader echoed Douglass and optimistically set forth the most transcendent promise of the nineteenth century in talking about what freedom required: "This is the panacea which will heal all the maladies of a Negrophobia type: Let colored men simply do as anybody else in business does, be self-reliant, industrious producers of the staples for market and merchandise, and he will have no more trouble on account of his complexion than the white men have about the color of their hair or beards." The liberty that blacks had gained by 1865 reflected these ideals.[48]

But failure to achieve full equality or justice should not obscure the advances from slavery to freedom. In slavery no black man had significant control over his labor. What, when, and how to plant, cultivate, and harvest were decisions made by masters. The full fruits of slave work went into the hands of whites. In slavery, the whip, threats of separating families, stimulated black enterprise and effort. Freedom produced significant changes in the labor of the freedmen. Blacks rejected whenever possible a wage labor system because it kept all decisions in the employers' hands. They chose sharecropping, which permitted them freedom to work in their own way and let the forces of the marketplace, influenced, to be sure, by racist assumptions, affect them in the long run. Such forces were profoundly different from the white man with the whip and the force of the law behind any decision he made to secure obedience. Blacks did acquire land even in this environment, their incomes increased, and certainly their share of the fruits of their labor skyrocketed. None of these improvements compared with white advances, but blacks who compared freedom with slavery knew how much had changed.[49]

By the end of the war, the peculiar institution was dead. A war to save a Union that had housed slavery in 1861 had been transformed into a war to save a more perfect Union—one in which slavery no longer contradicted ideals of the nation, no longer seemed to be undoing the hopes of the nation's founders. As strategic and political necessities declined in importance, as loyal slave states revealed the tenacity of slavery's hold upon Americans, the North had come to recognize what abolitionists had seen for years. There could be no free Union with slavery within it. Their understanding was not always pure. Millions in the North supported black freedom to achieve white men's purposes. But whatever the motives underlying emancipation, it had come, and moves toward equality advanced in its wake.

Blacks played vital roles in the process. Their courage as soldiers undermined some racist hypotheses. Their diligence as free laborers undercut others. Their contributions as orators and petitioners and writers illustrated further flaws in the ideology of slavery. Pricking white consciences, challenging white assumptions, serving white needs, blacks had begun their move forward. Northern racial exclusions lost power. New claims under the law linked devotion to the Constitution with freedom in 1865. Four years before, such devotion protected slavery. Blacks proved their capacities to be free laborers, demonstrated the validity of their claims to legal protections.

The results flowed naturally from the war's goals. A constitutional system threatened by a slave-based Confederacy had been saved. A constitutional system founded in equal justice under law was the obvious trophy. A free labor society had defeated its antithesis and in so doing had validated its worth and quality. The expansion of a free labor economy was the obvious device for enduring unity. But the victorious Constitution and economic system provided the contexts that would limit the extent of the freedom blacks had gained. The end of the war saw them as free, self-reliant laborers protected by the laws of a constitutional Union. If it could be demonstrated that their status required increased national protection, if it could be argued that an enduring Union depended on the same thing, then for a time blacks might hope for special protection. But respect for a revitalized federal system and admiration for the validated free labor ideal might one day deprive them of that protection. By 1865 they were free as they had never been before. The postwar years would determine if they would be as free as they should have been.

CHAPTER 10

The Dialogue of Politics:
Loyalty and Unity, 1863–1864

W AR validated economic transformation and the destruction of slavery. The conflict also shaped the political debate over these changes. Republicans justified them in the name of saving the Union, and since Democrats fought against them, the argument raised questions of loyalty. Debate over loyalty and dissent concurrently provoked an encounter with abiding concerns about the structure of the political-constitutional system itself.

The question of disloyalty among Democrats was complex. Contemporary Republicans, for political and personal reasons, charged their opponents with disloyalty to the Union cause. Since it was a Republican administration whose election had precipitated the war, matters of political and national loyalty were easily entwined. Republicans made the most of the linkage, branding political opponents as traitors at worst and as misguided comforters of the enemy at best. Their accusations had some force because rebels undoubtedly took comfort from Democratic criticism of the war. Confederates hoped for Northern war weariness. They prayed that anti-administration voices would sweep Lincoln and Republicans from office, replacing them with officials who would recognize the futility of maintaining union by force. Dissent in the North did help the Confederacy continue its fight.

There were Democrats whose opposition went beyond speeches and newspapers. Northerners with family and economic ties to the South did attempt to interfere with the war effort. In the first months of the war men like John Merryman in Maryland tried to recruit regiments to fight for the Confederacy. Men like Lambden Milligan in Indiana kept at this activity well into mid-war. Plots were hatched to release prisoners so that they could rejoin rebel armies. Efforts were made, meager though they were, to create a Northwest Confederacy that would make a separate peace and perhaps a separate nation. Desertion from Union armies was encouraged, and speeches opposing enlistments into the army were frequent in Democratic regions. Border states witnessed actual gunfights between pro- and anti-Union forces, and the legislatures of Indiana and Illinois proved so obstreperous to Republican war efforts that Yates in Illinois prorogued his, and Morton of Indiana ran the state without benefit of fund-raising by Hoosier lawmakers.[1]

Within the regions of Democratic loyalty antiwar feelings were intense, at times leading to violence. In a society enthusiastically devoted to keeping and bearing arms, political passion could turn to gunfire. A "Butternut Mass Meeting" in Indianapolis in 1863 brought several thousand Democrats into the city; some had pistols. While most of the men kept their arms under control, many didn't, and the police were kept busy arresting people for bearing concealed weapons or for firing guns in the general hoopla. As one of the trains left the town hundreds of shots were apparently fired out the windows, many directed at a soldiers' home outside town. Other trains leaving the meeting were stopped by military authorities who confiscated up to 1,500 guns and numbers of knives. Similarly, soldiers on leave and Republicans of the town of Charleston, Illinois, exchanged gunfire with the town's antiwar contingent in March 1864. Several men were killed before organized army units restored peace. Riots against the draft in the summer of 1863 also featured violence against enrolling officers, violence that came from the poorer regions of the North, regions that were overwhelmingly Democratic territory.[2]

In a population of twenty million, including many with strong personal ties to Southern family and friends, deep convictions about the futility and illegality of using force to maintain unity, and deep fears about the loss of loved ones on distant battlefields, actions against the war effort were clearly going to occur. Nevertheless, the Northern war effort took place without any organized guerrilla protest in the rear, without significant sabotage efforts against military or civilian supplies, with only one significant assassination plot against civilian or military leaders. The conspiracy against Lincoln and his cabinet was unique throughout the war years. Rumors circulated of assassination plots against national leaders, but proved to be unfounded. Ward Lamon, even after the assassination of his beloved friend, asserted that "the crime of assassination was . . . abhorrent to the genius of Anglo-Saxon civilization . . . foreign to the practice of our republican institutions."[3]

Opposition to the war effort was political opposition, expressed within the political structure, utilizing traditional political-constitutional rhetoric, urging predominantly political alternatives. Opponents of the administration urged listeners to believe something, rather than to break the law. Rhetoric could reach extremes. A few county Democratic meetings spoke of "resist[ing] to the death all attempts to draft any of our citizens into the army." A few editors spoke of a potential counterrevolution by the people should Lincoln and the Republicans persist in their "lawless" course. Brick Pomeroy in Wisconsin breeched decency and legality in 1864 by declaring that "the man who votes for Lincoln is a traitor because Lincoln is a traitor and a murderer. And if he is elected to misgovern for another four years, we trust some bold hand will pierce his heart with a dagger point for the public good." Cheers for Jefferson Davis were heard when men gathered to protest the conflict. Passionate rhetoric characterized political protest. Poems and songs appeared in Democratic papers reciting Lincoln's efforts to kill young soldiers in the interests of a mad partisanship. One Democratic paper in Pennsylvania offered a poem called "Abe's Visitor," in which the devil asks the president:

> How are you my Abe? Is the list nearly filled
> Of sick men and dying of wounded and killed,
> Of widows and tears, or orphans unfed
> Of poor honest white men struggling for bread?
> "Dear devil," quoth Abe, "I'm doing my best
> To promote the interest of you and the rest."[4]

Antiwar words coincided with actions that hindered the war effort. Democratic districts saw much more desertion from the army than did Republican. Democratic counties were overwhelmingly the places of antidraft violence. Leading army officials charged with enforcing the draft in the North targeted Democratic newspapers as the prime cause of the violence. One official pointed a finger at the *Chicago Times* as "chief among these instigators of insurrection and treason, the foul and damnable reservoir which supplied the lesser sewers with political filth, falsehood and treason." When the Democratic majorities in the Illinois and Indiana state legislatures threatened to pass measures that would have withdrawn state troops from the conflict, Republicans understandably linked Northern and Southern enemies.[5]

Despite these authorities, Democratic opinion preponderantly favored the maintenance of the Union. Even while criticizing administration means, party leaders asserted constantly that they, too, sought a restored union. It was their belief that Lincoln's efforts divided the Union more surely than they secured it. In the summer of 1863 Seymour insisted that the Republican party not only had divided the North and the South by its revolutionary doctrines, it had also divided the North. How could there be unity in the North, Seymour asked, when the Republican government was engaged in "infringing upon our rights . . . insulting our homes . . . depriving us of cherished principles for which our fathers died and to which we have always sworn allegiance"? Furthermore, the very political tactics of the Lincoln party, the rejection of the idea of a loyal opposition, undermined unity. Instead of seeking a harmony of party interest in saving the Union, Republicans "stigmatize . . . true and honest [men] whom experience has proven to have been wiser, as men who do not love their country and who are untrue to her interests." Constantly insisting on their loyalty to the constitutional Union, Democrats argued that loyalty to that hallowed institution would band together Northerners of all persuasion. But Republicans, Democrat Daniel Voorhees of Indiana alleged, attacked the very Constitution that was the basis of union. "What is there to America worth preserving of the principles of liberty, the doctrines of the Constitution shall perish . . . does mere land and water, mere extent of soil, constitute the life of a nation? No, sir; immortal liberty is its life."[6]

Voorhees' abstractions might lead to evasions about continuing the war to save the Union, but New York's Samuel Tilden and many of his friends spoke unequivocally. In the fall of 1862 before an audience that included state party chairman Dean Richmond and candidates for highest state offices, Tilden provided a peroration full of iron.

If my voice could reach the Southern people . . . I would say to them that in no event can the triumph of the conservative sentiment of New York in the election mean consent to disunion, either now or hereafter. Its true import is restoration, North and South of that Constitution which had secured every right, and under whose shelter all had been happy and prosperous until you madly fled from its protection. . . . Within the Union we will give you the Constitution you profess to revere, renewed with fresh guarantees of equal rights and equal safety. We will give you everything that local self-government demands; everything that a common ancestry of glory—everything that national fraternity or Christian fellowship requires; but to dissolve the federal bond between these States, to dismember our country, whoever else consents, we will not. No; never, never never!

And Western Democrat David Turpie was similarly fervent less than a year later. Deploring Republican efforts to change the meaning of the Union, Turpie nevertheless insisted, "If you mean by the Union, the restoration of national authority upon every foot of the national soil; if you mean by the Union the preservation of national fame and of the national flag the flag which waved at Bunker Hill, at Saratoga . . . at Chepultepec, at Shiloh and at Donelson—that flag with not a star undimmed, not a stripe obliterated; the only flag in the world which floats over a limited government and a free people—if you mean that by the Union, I am for it now and forever."[7]

Democrats also demonstrated loyalty by enlisting in the army (in larger numbers than Republicans, so they claimed), in the support that even Vallandigham and Voorhees gave for obeying despised laws such as the draft, and in the reactions of Democratic areas to Southern invasions. Both times that Lee entered the North, especially in Pennsylvania, he met not rebel sympathizers, but either apathetic neutrals or angry defenders of home and farm. When John Morgan raided the butternut strongholds in Southern Indiana and Ohio in midsummer 1863, even as draft riots were breaking out all over the North, there was no welcoming committee overt or covert. Northerners turned out to drive him back to Dixie. Morgan lost all but 300 of the 2,500 men he had started out with.[8]

Such demonstrations of loyalty fed Democratic charges of Republican excesses. Distinctions between degrees of support were often ignored by local, state, and sometimes national Republicans. Lincoln's party, and some of his generals, manufactured the image that political opposition masked sedition. The Knights of the Golden Circle, the Sons of Liberty, the Order of American Knights, all minor and poorly organized antiwar societies, were turned into treasonous Democratic conspiracies by Republican editors and officers. Local Republican mobs destroyed Democratic newspapers, attacked Democratic speakers. The army removed judges from their courtrooms in Maryland and preachers from pulpits in border and more Northern states. Republican schoolchildren fought with Democratic schoolchildren over the wearing of badges signifying unconditional loyalty or dissent from the conflict; Republican editors urged that opponents of the war be denied the right to wear badges unless they were prowar badges. Republican generals issued orders behind the Union lines threatening military arrest to anyone who persisted in "the habit of declaring sympathy for the enemy." The administration suspended the privilege of the writ of habeas corpus throughout the North just two days after Lincoln announced the preliminary Emancipation Proclamation. Democrats saw in that action a clear message that dissent from even controversial measures would be punished.

The operation of the draft was put in the hands of Republican favorites and narrow-minded partisans totally lacking in tact or judgment. The provost marshal's office was so entwined with the Republican party of Iowa that the central committee assessed district provost marshal boards $100 each for the 1864 presidential campaign. A strong Republican wrote to Stanton that the provost marshals in Cleveland were "as corrupt as Hell." General John Pope complained from Milwaukee that "federal officers should learn to hold their tongues and do their duty without making counter threats of blustering about the use of military force, which probably would not be required if they did their duty quietly and discreetly." At the national level the War Department adopted a definition of suspected disloyalty that swept in those civilians who kept silent while being questioned about the draft. Lincoln himself in a widely distributed letter of June 12, 1863, had said, "The man who stands by and says nothing when the peril of his government is discussed cannot be misunderstood. If not hindered he is sure to help the enemy."[9]

Acts of repression and intimidation took place in the context that further gave them a political tone and led Democrats to believe that their politics was their crime. By early 1862 local groups were organizing Union Clubs to rally Republicans and Democrats favorable to the war into local organizations that took loyalty as their special province and sustained every administration effort as legal and necessary. These clubs also were not averse to intimidating Democrats who opposed the administration by branding them traitors and by tolerating mob violence against antiwar protesters.

The formation of the Union League Clubs among the upper-class Republicans in the North also linked the war effort with party-organizing activity. From these roots came an outpouring of pamphlets by the Loyal Publication Society, whose very name tinged opponents with alleged disloyalty. Among the most popular pamphlets of the society was Francis Lieber's April 1863 effort, *No Party Now, but All for Country*, which measured loyalty by a test that demanded support for the draft, emancipation, suspension of civil liberties, support for the government from "unfriendly and mischievous neutrality," and the total conquest of the South. All these were anathema to most Democrats, even to those who supported the war to save the Union. To have matters of dissent over means condemned as disloyalty persuaded Democrats that administration goals included more than military victory in the South.[10]

Yet for all this debate about threats to civil liberty during the war, the actual number of people arrested by the army for speaking against the war was remarkably small. Historians traditionally have spoken of Lincoln's dictatorship and of an "incredibly harsh" policy against dissenters. From 35,000 to 40,000 are usually said to have been subject to arbitrary arrest. However, Mark Neely's careful study of individual arrest files shows a major reduction in those numbers. About two-thirds of the people that the army arrested were in Confederate territory. The remaining one-third included those taken in the border states for a range of reasons having nothing to do with dissents against the government. Many were detained when they presented themselves to Union pickets claiming to have legitimate business behind Union lines or claiming to be deserters from Dixie. The army held them in order to check their stories. Others were arrested when they tried to cheat soldiers in business deals (horse trading was a major source of deceit) or tried to deceive the government in collecting the bounties due allegedly dead soldiers. The total number held for these reasons as well as for protesting the war Neely puts at around 4,400. But he argues that the numbers jailed for dissent are a tiny percent of even this reduced figure.[11]

But the debate over loyalty and the restriction of civil liberty touched bedrock. Even the few arrests for dissent created an outcry that sounded throughout the nation, and adding fuel to that debate was the fact that history had produced no clear guidelines about the limits of dissent in the nation. The First Amendment's noble phrases lacked the clarity that comes from large numbers of cases where freedom of the press and freedom of speech could be legally defined.

As early as 1800 the distinction had been made between words that advocated ideas and words that advocated unlawful action. The former were lawful, the latter unlawful. Still, there existed much ambiguity of what in fact constituted the borders of lawful and unlawful advocacy. The passionate intensity with which politics was pursued guaranteed that language would be used up to and beyond the limits of civility, and even beyond the limits, at times, of public safety.[12]

The war environment added complexity and passion to these issues. Loyalty to the Confederacy or the Union was not precisely defined by geography. Varying degrees of support for the Southern cause could be found throughout the North, from occasional acts of sabotage to publicly expressed hopes for rebel victory, from talk of obstructing conscription to impassioned attacks on governmental legislation believed by the party in power to be imperative for winning the war. Which expressions were unlawful, which protected? Administration opponents asserted that the utmost loyalty consisted in pointing out misguided, ignorant, or malicious policy by the government. Republicans insisted that in time of peril to the life of the nation, the limits of political opposition had to be constricted. The crucial question in determining the propriety of repression of speech and press was just how much actual danger continued freedom constituted, a matter on which honest men could differ, depending on their knowledge or ignorance, their hopes or their fears.

Theory does little to show actual limits. The best understanding of the state of civil liberty in the nation during the war comes from discovering which words evoked repression and which were tolerated. Even here the picture is blurred. Words offered in one place might be tolerated, while the same words could inspire repression in another. Context made a difference, too. Fears for the security of the cause could evoke repressive acts. Victory on the battlefield could argue for government restraint.

With these caveats in mind, consider some examples. In October 1861 Superintendent Kennedy of the New York City police sent to Washington his prime candidate for supression: a German-language newspaper known as the *National Zeitung*. The strongest language in the material sent was "Who has eyes must see that our calamity, this satanic civil war, springs from the unholy intermeddling of the Northern abolitionists with the relations of slavery which pertain exclusively to the South, and which they cannot forgo but with which the North has no more to do than with Russian Laplanders." The *Zeitung* urged a convention (one that would exclude abolitionists) in Indianapolis to solve the crisis. This got the newspaper excluded from the mails by Postmaster General Blair.[13]

Furthermore, the press did not have to be disciplined by exclusion from the mail or by seizing and silencing the printing presses. A more subtle means existed. Superintendent Kennedy wrote to Seward that "the seizure of a printing office or of the papers printed is not the best way of correcting the evil . . . under the present circumstances the only sure way is to put the editors and publishers out of harm's way. . . . The arrest of one of the most active of these men would lead to a modification of its tone." Seward replied that he would be willing to arrest "one or two persons whose arrest would be likely to produce a proper effect upon the course of that paper." The policy of arresting dissenters and protesters had another advantage as well. Arrests did not have to proceed to trials. Indeed the administration chose a policy of arresting and then dropping charges once the suspects had been held for a time. Government leaders feared that trials would only produce martyrs and might in fact lead to acquittals that would further inflame anti-administration opinion. They thus chose the policy of arbitrary arrest followed by arbitrary release typically requiring an oath of loyalty from suspects. This allowed the president to maintain an image of concern for individuals, a reputation not undeserved but perhaps inflated. It also got results. Fearing arrest and imprisonment and not particularly comforted by a prospect of ultimate vindication, dissenters often moderated their outcries.[14]

The cause célèbre of civil liberties was the Vallandigham case of 1863. The arrest at Mt. Vernon, Ohio, on May 5, 1863, of the former Ohio congressman by General Burnside reverberated throughout the nation, symbolizing to Democrats and not a few Republicans the excesses of internal security activity in the North. Careful consideration of the arrest and aftermath provides an understanding of the civil liberties issue that no generalization can encompass.

Vallandigham had been a thorn in the side of the administration since the war began. He had protested every act of the new Congress that smacked to him of excessive and illiberal expansion of power. He protested having West Point cadets take an oath that ignored their allegiance to their states, he was outraged by measures excluding Jews from the military chaplaincy, and he opposed almost every effort of the government to advance the war effort. Furthermore, he did so eloquently, speaking with a sarcasm and irony that made him a fascinating and compelling spectacle. Self-righteous to a fault, he was also an eager martyr for his ideals, willing to take to extremes his belief in Jeffersonian government. His opposition knew some limits. He opposed antidraft violence and toured the Midwest after the draft riots, counseling opposition at the ballot box and not in the streets. Vallandigham walked a thin line between sedition and dissent but preponderantly stayed on the lawful side. It was his reputation and his eloquence more than his advocacy of the rebel cause that marked him in the eyes of many soldiers and Republican politicians.

The case arose when General Ambrose Burnside issued General Order No. 38 on April 13, 1863, announcing that "all persons found within our lines who commit acts for the benefit of the enemies of our country will be tried as spies or traitors and, if convicted, shall suffer death." Burnside added that "the habit of declaring sympathy for the enemy will not be allowed in this department. Persons committing such offenses will be at once arrested, with a view of being tried, as above stated, or sent beyond our lines into the lines of their friends. It must be distinctly understood that treason, expressed or implied, will not be tolerated in this department." What made the order notable was that Burnside was not at or near a battlefront. He commanded in the states of Ohio, Illinois, Indiana, Michigan, and the part of Kentucky that lay east of the Tennessee River. Of equal interest is the fact that Burnside equated spies with people who openly declared sympathy for the enemy and targeted something called "implied treason" as intolerable and subject to a potential death penalty. Furthermore, since Lincoln had suspended the privilege of the writ of habeas corpus throughout the North in late September 1862, violators of Burnside's order would be tried by military, not civilian, courts.[15]

Within less than three weeks Vallandigham, seeking his party nomination for governor, saw an opportunity to stand up for his civil libertarian ideals, and to fuel the enthusiasm of the party faithful by giving them a martyr. On May 1 at Mt. Vernon, Ohio, with Burnside's plainclothes agents taking notes in the crowd, the copperhead speaker challenged Order No. 38 directly, insisting that it was in violation of the Constitution itself. "General Order #1, signed by General Washington," was superior to any order of Burnside, Ohio governor Tod, or even Abraham Lincoln. Vallandigham charged that the administration was trying to suppress political meetings, that "military marshalls [sic] were about to be appointed in every district who would act for the purpose of restricting the liberties of the people." The administration, he insisted, had rejected opportunities for peace in order to pursue "a wicked abolition war." Insisting on his unionism, Vallandigham hoped the people would vigorously oppose war for other purposes. He focused directly on the usurpation of constitutional rights implicit in Burnside's order. Still, even witnesses for the prosecution admitted that he did not counsel violent resistance to the law, but specifically said that the people should "come up united to the ballot box and hurl the tyrant from his throne." Vallandigham also denounced cheers for Jefferson Davis that members of the crowd had given before he spoke.

He ended his speech to general applause as Burnside's agents retired to reconstruct the speech and to report to their commander. Four nights later, as he was asleep, a military unit gathered around Vallandigham's home. Just after midnight they knocked on the door to announce that he was under arrest. With his wife, sister-in-law, and two children watching, Vallandigham denied their entrance and was chased into the house, where soldiers ultimately succeeded in dragging him away for trial before the very military commission that he had attacked. When tried, Vallandigham denied its jurisdiction, even though he did conduct his own defense before the tribunal. The commission, despite evidence showing no direct advocacy of violent disobedience of the law, convicted Vallandigham anyway of "publicly expressing in violation of General Order No. 38 . . . sympathy for those in arms against the Government of the United States, and declaring disloyal sentiments and opinions with the object and purpose of weakening the power of the Government in its efforts to suppress an unlawful rebellion."[16]

The arrest and conviction raised tremendous excitement both in Ohio and throughout the North. The day after Vallandigham was taken, a mob of enraged Democrats stormed the office of the Republican newspaper in Dayton and burned it down. Only the efforts of party leaders stopped attacks on the homes of Republican leaders. Reverberations echoed in Washington as well. Vallandigham and his party spread nationwide the congressman's protest against the government that had jailed him in "a military bastille" for "speeches made . . . in denunciation of the usurpations of power, infractions of the Constitution and laws, and of military despotism. . . . I am a Democrat," Vallandigham proclaimed from jail, "—for constitution, for law, for the Union, for liberty—that is my only crime."

Lincoln quickly saw the power of the protest, although earlier he may have encouraged Burnside's prosecution. The president conferred with cabinet members. They advised backing off while Stanton drafted a special suspension of the writ applying specifically to Vallandigham, in case doubts existed about the general suspension of September 1862. Lincoln told Stanton to withdraw that order and prepared an extended defense of his civil liberties policy that appeared throughout the North. Likening Vallandigham to a "wiley agitator who induces a simple-minded soldier boy . . . to desert," Lincoln affirmed his belief that standing silent while others discussed the peril of the nation was sure to help the enemy; "much more," Lincoln continued, "if he talks ambiguously—talks for his country with 'buts' and 'ifs' and 'ands.'" In extraordinary times, extraordinary remedies were required, and the Constitution itself allowed action in rebellions that were not allowed in peace. The issue, Lincoln said, scolding Democrats, transcended party and involved the "battle for the country we all love." Furthermore, Burnside himself was a Democrat, and thousands of Democrats were "shedding their blood on the battlefield [and] many approve the course taken with Mr. V."[17]

Such declamations set the intellectual tone of politics and insured a vital debate. The actions of the two sides gave it the framework of events on which to play. Ohio Democrats, in a surge of outrage that troubled some party leaders, gave the governor's nomination to Vallandigham. Meanwhile Lincoln symbolically cast further doubts on the Democrat's loyalty by changing the sentence of the military commission from imprisonment to banishment behind Confederate lines. The Ohioan stayed as short a time as possible in Dixie and went quickly to Canada, where he conducted his campaign, constantly playing the theme of civil liberty besieged by administration tyrants. While this refrain played well with the party faithful, it failed to move the authorities. When Vallandigham appealed his trial by military commission to the United States Supreme Court, the justices danced aside. Taking their opinion directly from the brief of the government, they denied their own jurisdiction to rule on the activities of a military commission, a position they would later change once the war was over.[18]

Suspensions of civil liberty did not, however, weaken significantly the ongoing passionate and vital political process. In fact they may have ironically enlivened it. As the party most noted for its constitutional purity, the Democrats found in their martyrdom new passion for the cause. As Horatio Seymour put it on July 4, 1863, "My friends, we have not now a mere intellectual knowledge of the Constitution; we do not give it now a mental support; we accept it with a vital living piety that makes us better men and better patriots." And members of the party rode the constitutional liberty issue as hard as any other, with the possible exception of the racial one. The party motto put "The Constitution as it is" in the forefront, and the party circulated as its major campaign documents of 1864 a book-length collection of speeches and articles called "The Constitution" and the "Handbook of the Democracy." These publications contained speeches from every spectrum of the party, ranging from outspoken defenders of a war to defend the Union like Seymour and Samuel Tilden and S. S. Cox to noted copperheads like George Pendleton and Richard O'Gorman. The opinions of former Supreme Court justice Benjamin Curtis and his kinsman, constitutional historian George Ticknor Curtis, were noted prominently. The message was clear: the Democratic party was the party of the Constitution. Vallandigham had rushed to martyrdom in defense of that document.[19]

Even Republicans criticized administration policy on dissent. After the arrest of Vallandigham Horace Greeley proclaimed, "Freedom of speech and of the press are rights which like everything else have their limitations. The license of speech and of the press which men like Vallandigham indulge in, calls for the abridgment of neither. . . . Leave everyone free to proclaim his sympathy with the Rebellion up to the point of overt, indictable treason. Let everyone speak or write as to him shall seem good, up to the point which shall bring him into direct and punishable collision with the laws of the land." George William Curtis, who earlier in the year had supported administration policy, broke with Lincoln on the Vallandigham arrest. "The mistake of the government," Curtis wrote in *Harper's Weekly,* was in "not trusting the people sufficiently." They had "quite enough courage to bear any amount of misfortunes and quite sense enough to understand any amount of seditious nonsense, be it uttered ever so glibly."

Jurists who had been supporters of early suspension of the privilege of the writ in military areas withdrew their support when civilian areas lost the privilege, too. Harvard's Joel Parker, professor of constitutional law, had written a tough-minded and telling defense of Lincoln in the Merryman encounter. By early fall 1862 expanded executive power, manifested in both emancipation and extended military authority in the North, led Parker to call Lincoln's government "a perfect military despotism." Ex–Supreme Court justice Benjamin Curtis and congressional constitutional expert Reverdy Johnson took the same path. Clearly the civil liberties issue touched bedrock.[20]

These mid-1863 protests echoed earlier Republican sensitivity to civil liberties issues. Congress had reluctantly acted to put itself on the record on this delicate question. Legislators waited until March 1863, almost two years into the conflict, before passing a law that sustained presidential suspension of the writ in the previous years. The measure straddled major issues of law about who had the right to suspend it, even though the struggle over that question, the focus of the Merryman argument, had found Lincoln opposed by the despised Justice Taney. The measure itself also respected the civilian judicial process by requiring that the government release arbitrarily arrested civilians if local grand juries could find no grounds for indictment. The act was one more illustration of the powerful strength of constitutional devotion that suffused the Congress and was a reflection of the import of ongoing constitutional discussion in the North.[21]

This ongoing dialogue over the civil liberties question revealed the health of a political system that existed because of the guarantees of those very liberties. Free speech, press, and assembly meant that politics would thrive. Economic alternatives, new social directions, would be matters of deep concern. The race issue inspired profound passions. But civil liberties issues kept in the public eye the health and security of the process of debate itself and guaranteed that such matters would not be taken for granted.

In 1862 and 1863 the process had been linked in various degrees to concerns about racial revolution and modernizing economic measures. But the crucial test for the process was the presidential contest of 1864, nationwide in scope and issues, challenging the national administration, which was directing the most sweeping, the most encompassing of all American wars. The election of 1864 demonstrated in the most wide-ranging and unequivocal way the goals for which the nation was struggling.

One sign of the importance of that political-constitutional process was the fact that the 1864 election was going to take place at all. In England major wars, especially civil wars, had justified suspending politics in the interests of national unity and security. But in the United States no one considered for a moment suspending the electoral process. The Civil War tested whether the bullets could replace ballots whenever one side lost an election. The process demonstrated the ideals for which the nation fought. Suspending it for the duration of the war was, thus, unthinkable. The constitutions of the nation and the states clearly set up election timetables. The electoral clock went on ticking unless someone wrenched the hands or impeded the mainspring. Such an action would have been an act of revolution. Conservatism counseled that Americans risk the electoral process in the midst of Civil War.[22]

Constitutional imperatives were not alone in demanding politics as usual. The passion of the culture was its politics, and even the army itself was thoroughly inoculated with political sentiments and commitments. Election laws in eighteen of the twenty-five Northern states recognized the political interests of the soldiers, and permitted voting in the field. In other Northern states the soldiers themselves would show their commitment by taking advantage of furloughs to return home to cast their ballots. The citizen soldiers were inescapably connected with the process of citizenship. Privates and generals involved themselves in partisan debate around campfires throughout Dixie, arguing over issues that divided the parties at home. A correspondent noted that "the great questions of the age —confiscation, with the employment of blacks in government service, and Emancipation—have been thoroughly discussed." Another journalist echoed sentiments that rang throughout the North. "A volunteer army, accustomed to vote at home, on going to camp yet remain citizens. We do not like the common phrase which speaks of citizens and soldiers as if the two were distinct . . . they are intelligent citizens, wearing for a while a dress of war which they will gladly at any day throw off to reclothe themselves with the garments of peace—never for a moment ceasing their interest in the civil affairs of the country."[23]

Democrats faced the elections of 1864 with confidence. The political history of the years since Andy Jackson had forged a minitradition of one-term presidents. Some believed that this thirty-four-year experience established good policy. Of greater significance, the continuation of the war built growing frustration, and the lack of major victories in over a year fed that frustration. Grant stood before Richmond, and the blood flowed and the young men died and the Confederacy survived. Over 52,500 casualties had been endured between the beginning of May and June 15 in Virginia alone. Sherman stood before Atlanta, but the town remained in rebel hands and so did the heartland of Dixie. And the draft continued and soldiers left their homes to go to the battlefield and inflation continued and so did the arbitrary arrest policy of the administration, and the commitment to the blacks endured and still there was no peace. Lincoln worried about his future. Six days before the Democratic convention he wrote, "It seems exceedingly probable that the Administration will not be reelected." "Old Abe is quite in trouble just now," Cyrus McCormick, Chicago industrialist and Democratic party makeweight, wrote. "The Democracy must defeat themselves if now defeated."[24]

Party divisions threatened Democrats with defeat. On one side stood what Joel Silbey has called the "purist" wing, predominantly Westerners but represented well in large Eastern cities. Here were Vallandigham, Daniel Voorhees, William Allen, and George Pendleton joined across the Appalachians to Fernando Wood in New York City. Opponents of practically every administration measure, they insisted that only immediate peace could preserve the Union and an unchanged Constitution. "There can be no such thing as a War Democrat," Wood insisted, "because when a man is in favor of the war he must be in favor of the policies of the war as it is prosecuted by the party in power, with its unavoidable tendency to destroy the Constitution and the Union." They wanted their party to repudiate the war and affirm prewar party values.[25]

On the other side stood men termed "legitimists" by Silbey. Predominantly Easterners, such as Horatio Seymour and Samuel Tilden, both future nominees for president, they had Western allies like David Turpie and Samuel Cox. Sharing the purists' conservative constitutional and social philosophy, they recognized that ideological purity required the ballast of realism if ideals were to be executed by an elected administration. They wanted to go before the electorate as patriots supporting war ends while rejecting Republican means.[26]

There was little doubt about the Democratic candidate. Since 1862, George McClellan had been the obvious choice. His leadership of the Union armies in the early years of the war gave him a national reputation. Furthermore, it linked the Democratic party with the war effort, undercutting Republican charges of disloyalty. The timing of "Little Mac's" leadership was also crucial. He was the symbol of the time in the conflict when the war goals were predominantly conservative. McClellan had led when the Union and the Constitution were institutions to be preserved, and not transformed. His leadership coincided with a time before emancipation, before the outreach of civil liberty restrictions throughout the North, before the draft, before Republican economic legislation threatened to transform the society. While clearly a modernizer in his military leadership, McClellan the politician epitomized opposition to the war's transformations.[27]

Purist Democrats for a time opposed the general's nomination, fearful of blessing the war by offering a general as candidate. But McClellan reached out to them in 1863, supporting purist gubernational candidate Judge George Woodward in Pennsylvania. And he managed to offer that support while retaining a commitment to saving the Union "with all possible decision and energy." This balancing act of 1863, supporting a peace candidate on a war platform, was reversed in 1864.

The 1864 national party convention meeting in Chicago chose McClellan as its candidate. But its antiwar element was appeased with the nomination of noted purist George Pendleton of Ohio and the adoption of a platform that, in addition to attacking the alleged horrors of emancipation and arbitrary government, demanded that "immediate efforts be made for a cessation of hostilities." Declaring that Lincoln's war had trampled on the Constitution and made peace impossible, Democrats called for a convention that would meet "to the end that at the earliest practicable moment peace may be restored on the basis of the Federal Union of the States." Peace first and then a restoration of the old Union. That platform satisfied the Vallandighams of the party. Meetings between the two factions brought agreements to unite efforts and restrain rhetoric. Even in New York City, where Tammany and Mozart Hall fought bitterly for party control, harmony was achieved. Democrats forecast victory.[28]

But their platform housed potential disaster. At first the legitimists were as satisfied with the platform as were the purists. After all, it had promised the soldiers and sailors "all the care, protection, and regard that [they] have so nobly earned." It had promised "unswerving fidelity to the Union under the Constitution," reiterated that "the aim and object of the . . . party is to preserve the Federal Union." But Republicans attacked the Democratic platform as a sellout of the war. "The Copperheads of the country, speaking through their Chicago Convention and elsewhere, have virtually proposed to surrender the country to the rebels in arms against it," a widely distributed party pamphlet charged. The success of this accusation pushed Democrats to a rebuttal. Fearing the label of "appeasers," Democratic legitimist leaders urged McClellan to "explain" the platform when he accepted the nomination. He did. The explanation nailed together the fragile linkage of peace and union that the platform had provided and put the Union first. It was "the one condition of peace," it "must be preserved at all hazards." "No peace can be permanent without Union." Purists felt betrayed, threatened reprisals, grumbled, stormed, and yet in the end fell in behind McClellan.[29]

War unified the Democrats. They had not had a party convention without a major split in eight years. The war generated one. Furthermore, the conflict generated a series of issues that all Democrats could unite around. National party platform and rhetoric avoided the economic questions that had rallied supporters in the past. No mention was made of the bank or the currency, issues that could potentially feed sectional divisions. An Eastern presidential candidate and a Western running mate balanced sectional concerns. There was little interest in opening them up again. Besides, all agreed that the war issues overshadowed all other concerns. Civil liberties, the Constitution, the rights of states preserved, ultimately a reunion without rancor with the South—these issues forged party unity in the campaign and promised that after the conflict a national party with restored strength in Dixie might regain national political dominance. Democrats could legitimately claim that they were trying to be the one truly national party, bound together to defend the old constitutional system.

Furthermore, unity was achieved by a phenomenon that struck Republicans, too. The national election pulled party extremes toward the middle, reinforcing the growing national party influence. National issues dominated state campaigns, further uniting the party around an ideological core. Despite the real repression many Democrats suffered, press, pulpit, and rostrum remained relatively open, further securing an enduring and intense discussion of those national ideals. In fact, repression gave an urgency to those discussions that strengthened party commitments. Although the postwar period would find intraparty divisions on economic issues, Democrats never forgot, never lost, the sinews of unity that war fostered. The national party organizations of the postwar years grew around the passions of the war.[30]

Republicans forged political unity in the fires of war, too, but only after bitter struggle. War frustrations grew among more radical party members even as they were growing in the populace at large. With the war at an apparent stalemate in early 1864, forces within the party began to believe that Lincoln was expendable, that the time had come for a man of boldness and vigor to take over and wage war in earnest.

The first standard-bearer who came to mind (especially his own) was Salmon Chase, who had managed to keep people thinking of his availability even as he sat in Lincoln's cabinet. The Chase movement got under way in February 1864 when Kansas senator Samuel Pomeroy and some associates distributed a pro-Chase pamphlet, "The Next Presidential Election." Several radical congressmen sent out this document under their franking privilege, and it circulated widely. Lincoln's reelection, it claimed, would be a "national calamity." The nation now needed "an advanced thinker; a statesman profoundly versed in political and economic science . . . who fully comprehends the spirit of the age." Shortly after this missive began to circulate, Pomeroy himself sent out a private circular to leading politicians emphasizing the strength of a Chase candidacy.

But the whole effort backfired. The private circular became public. Letters of outrage poured into the offices of congressmen who had franked "The Next Presidential Election," and the congressmen began dodging. John Sherman was told that he couldn't get ten votes in the Ohio legislature if it were proved that he actually believed in the Chase activity. The senator lamely explained that he had been tricked into using his mailing privileges. Chase himself protested innocence of the whole affair, even though he had been secretly courting financial backers and had used Treasury workers to begin organizing. He offered to resign, but Lincoln refused to accept the resignation. Chase stayed in the cabinet, a position that crippled his ability to interfere with Lincoln's renomination. Meanwhile Lincoln lined up state party delegations, earning public declarations of support from fourteen states (Chase's Ohio especially), as well as from the Republican National Committee. By early spring the Chase movement was dead. The president's strong control of the party organization and a combination of spontaneous and manufactured public enthusiasm kept most Republicans in line.[31]

But another challange awaited Lincoln from the left in the form of the 1856 party candidate John C. Fremont. A hero to the militant antislavery people since his 1861 proclamation freeing Missouri slaves, Fremont also was popular among the influential German-American community. He attracted the disappointed Chase supporters as well. By late May Fremont backers had gathered together in Cleveland, rallying around a platform that proposed confiscation of rebel land and a constitutional amendment ending slavery and guaranteeing "all men absolute equality before the law." Other constitutional changes were a one-term presidency and an end to the electoral college. The radical voices of the political spectrum formed around the Fremont cause. Wendell Phillips, the voice of uncompromising abolitionism, endorsed the Fremont candidacy, carrying with him a narrow majority of both the New England and the American Antislavery societies. The leading figures of the woman's movement, Elizabeth Cady Stanton and Susan B. Anthony, enlisted in support of Fremont. Frederick Douglass lent the power of his position as spokesman for black Americans. They named their organization the Radical Democracy to symbolize their focus on an expanded electorate and a government more directly sensitive to popular opinion.[32]

Yet, indicative of the ambiguity of ideas about liberty and power at the time, the Radical Democracy also incorporated themes from the Democratic litany. The platform condemned the excesses of the government against civil liberty: "The rights of free speech, free press, and the habeas corpus [should be] held inviolate, save in districts where martial law has been proclaimed." Furthermore, old Democratic ideas of "integrity and economy . . . in the administration of the Government" also were included. Modern radicalism finds harmony in appeals to power to the people, condemning the electoral college and government interference with free expression, and urging the broadest participation by all races and sexes in the political process. The Fremont candidacy forged such a linkage as early as 1864. Yet at that time the appeal was at war with itself. Expanded freedoms for blacks required expanded national government power, but the power could also be used to stifle opposition. Economy in government as a basic principle would have killed the ability of the government to wage the very war that made black freedom a reality.

The ideological contradictions reflected political facts of life. Rallying around Fremont were not just radicals who thought Lincoln too lukewarm in pursuing equality, but also War Democrats who feared that their party might be captured by peace extremists. In addition, regular Democrats saw the chance to weaken the Republicans by promoting divisions. The platform had to be broad enough to reach its wide range of supporters. That breadth undercut the power of the radical cause that had called the movement together in the first place. Republicans who might have been attracted smelled copperhead influence and stayed with their old allegiance. The narrow abolitionist majority which at first had backed Phillips returned to the Garrison camp. There awaiting them was the pragmatism that kept the old liberator and former allies like Phillips at war with each other from mid-war into the Reconstruction period. Agreeing that Lincoln was not perfect, Garrison still proclaimed that "a thousand incidental errors and blunders are easily to be borne with the part of him who, at one blow, severed the chains of three millions, three hundred thousand slaves." Furthermore, Garrison and allies believed, the only beneficiaries of the Fremont splinter would be the rebels and the copperheads who would surely win if the Republicans were divided. In the interest of political power, the abolitionists moved right.[33]

But pressures of politics also moved the Republicans to the left. Fremont's candicacy pressured Republicans to include in their platform support for a constitutional amendment ending slavery. Even as the Fremont movement dwindled through the summer, Republican leadership spoke and acted to appease radicals. Garrison and other abolitionists came to the White House for publicized discussions. In September 1864 a revealing conjunction of events took place. Montgomery Blair, long a target of radical criticism, resigned his position as postmaster general on September 23, the day before Fremont published a letter withdrawing from the race and urging support for Lincoln. A few militants who had rallied to Fremont clung to their positions, but the majority now wheeled into line behind the Republican party, inspired also by the Democratic party peace platform and by the resurgence of general optimism in the North aroused by Sherman's taking of Atlanta on September 2.[34]

These intraparty quarrels revealed an ongoing conflict over the much more complex and potentially divisive issue of Reconstruction. Here again, the Republicans forged unity.

The constitutional structure built in potential for division. Lincoln's duties as commander in chief required him to develop a policy for governing conquered rebel territory while the war continued. Congressmen were obligated to make rules for governing territories and for admitting representatives and senators into Congress, as well as passing laws for the nation as a whole. Both branches of government were presumably included in the mandate that "the United States shall guarantee to every state in this union a republican form of government."

Lincoln acted first. In 1863 he offered a Reconstruction program that guided rebel states back into the Union. All who had joined the rebellion, except for high-ranking government and military leaders, would be pardoned upon taking an oath of future loyalty, and agreeing to emancipation. When a number equal to 10 percent of the voters in 1860 took that oath they could form a state government. That government had to be republican in form and had to support all existing legislation and proclamations on emancipation. There were no provisions for blacks to vote. There was a promise that after the state had provided for freedom, and (it was hoped) had opened schools for the freedmen, legislators could pass laws "which may yet be consistent with their present condition as a laboring, landless and homeless class."[35]

The first congressional response to Lincoln's program was generally positive. It was viewed as a beginning, an outline that permitted Congress to fill in details. The president himself had spoken of congressional responsibilities in seating new legislators and had also noted that other Reconstruction schemes would be acceptable.

In February 1864 Congressman Henry Winter Davis and Senator Ben Wade began filling in Lincoln's broad framework. They agreed with many of the presidential ideas. They excluded from pardons almost the same people that Lincoln had. They agreed that oaths of future loyalty would be acceptable for testing the loyalty of the population in forming new governments. They did not require that blacks be voters.

But there were differences that congressmen believed the situation demanded. They wanted 50 percent, not 10 percent, to take the original oath of loyalty. They worried about such a small minority acting for the rest. They also were more suspicious of having delegates to new state conventions take only an oath of future loyalty. Congress required of new lawmakers an oath of past loyalty as well. And congressmen wanted some ironclad protections for the freedmen, too. Lincoln had been pretty vague about legislation that would recognize the economic dependency of freedmen. Congress insisted that any person who tried to use that dependency to keep blacks subservient could be fined and sent to jail. Any freedman who was "restrained of liberty under pretense of any claim to . . . service or labor" would be freed by federal courts. The Wade-Davis measure made greater demands for Southern loyalty and provided greater security for the freed slaves.[36]

The two policies abided side by side for some time. Republican congressmen, believing or wanting to believe that Lincoln would agree to their modifications, backed the bill almost unanimously. Lincoln, meanwhile, was trying to get Louisiana and Arkansas back into the Union while providing equal opportunities for the freedmen. Doing so meant persuading long-term slavery supporters that emancipation would not unleash economic and moral chaos. The last thing the president needed in this delicate situation was a public debate with congressmen over details. He kept silent about his reactions to Wade-Davis.[37]

But finally the time came for Lincoln to sign the bill, and it coincided with the time when the Republicans were looking attentively at the upcoming election. The president refused his signature. He explained that he had first seen the measure one hour before he was asked to sign it. More fundamentally, he was "unprepared by a formal approval of this bill to be inflexibly committed to any single plan of restoration." He didn't want to "repel and discourage" the people in Louisiana and Arkansas who were trying to establish loyal governments.[38]

The veto came as a shock to his party, and its timing posed intriguing choices as to how to react. The sponsors of the bill hit the ceiling. Wade and Davis issued a manifesto criticizing Lincoln for "dictatorial usurpation." Warning him that their "support is of a cause and not a man," they forecast that "the people" would turn against anyone who lacked the courage to follow their path. Several other radical colleagues added their signatures to this declaration, and Horace Greeley printed it in his widely popular newspaper.[39]

But the majority of Republicans in Congress backed Lincoln. They weren't happy that he wanted to keep Reconstruction policy in his own hands, but they had reasons to stick by the nominee of their party with an election two months away. (States in the North voted in October and November in the nineteenth century.) The manifesto was a product of the Fremont schism, and they concurred with the *New York Times* that it was "by far the most effective Copperhead campaign document thus far issued." Even noted abolitionist Gerrit Smith attacked the manifesto, and Greeley editorialized against it.[40]

The president mended fences also. Lincoln's request for Blair's resignation delighted the more radical wing of the party. The chief executive took the trouble to explain that the Wade-Davis plan might be a guideline for any state that wanted to use it to return to the Union. That was an unlikely prospect, but it did soothe congressional egos. Furthermore, he reemphasized his commitment to permanent emancipation, speaking of his expectation that the constitutional amendment abolishing slavery would soon be passed. This was no mere sop. For Lincoln's actions against slavery had all along been undertaken with the constitutional justification that, given state inaction, only the president could free the slaves without a constitutional amendment. With that amendment passed, Lincoln could step back and Congress step forward as protector of black freedom. At that time measures like the Wade-Davis bill could replace presidential proclamations as the path to Reconstruction. In short, Lincoln's plan was a war measure, while congressional plans focused on the postwar world. There would be a season for each.[41]

Political pressures and presidential compromising smothered the disunity threat on the left. Party strategists reached out to gather support from the more conservative side. Eschewing the name "Republican," the party advanced under the "Union party" label. This clever rhetoric implicitly painted the opposition as anti-Union. But more than this, it presented border states and Northern conservatives with a name they could embrace. Further indicative of the Union emphasis was the replacement of Hannibal Hamlin of Maine with Andrew Johnson of Tennessee in the vice-presidential slot. Johnson, a former Democrat, had been the only Southern senator to stay in Congress as his colleagues departed in 1860–61. Furthermore, he had administered Tennessee's government as a military governor during the war and had been uncompromising with Confederate elements there.

But if the name suggested a conservative emphasis, recalling the early aims of the conflict, the platform showed how far the party and the nation had come. In 1860 the party platform had confined its attacks on slavery to discussion of the territories, a reopening of the slave trade, and a vague declaration of principles of devotion to the ideals of the Declaration of Independence as "essential to the preservation of Our Republican institutions." Republicans had condemned John Brown's use of violence to free the slaves and had declared in favor of "the maintenance inviolate of the rights of the states."

By 1864 the party platform called for a constitutional amendment to "terminate and forever prohibit the existence of Slavery within the limits of the jurisdiction of the United States." It praised the Emancipation Proclamation and the black soldiers who were marching to the tune of "John Brown's Body." Lincoln was working in Louisiana for the rights of freedom, including the right to vote, and Congress was rallying around legislation that would protect former slaves from the power of their masters. Congress and Lincoln might exchange hot words, but the party stood as one in favor of measures of equality that were outside the discourse of responsible politics four years earlier.[42]

Lincoln also took care to see that the intraparty conflict remained civil and that he kept ties to his more radical colleagues. No one was more well known for his radicalism than Charles Sumner, the Harvard-educated Massachusetts senator. Though frequently taxing his congressional associates with his pompous and uncompromising rhetoric, Sumner was the Senate's most notable and notorious spokesman for left-wing party views. Lincoln cultivated Sumner with invitations to social events, when the two of them might be seen together as personal friends. Sumner had access to the president in the White House whenever he thought it necessary. Mrs. Lincoln reported that the two of them would sometimes "laugh together like two schoolboys." Even after Sumner had helped to defeat Lincoln's Louisiana government, the president invited the senator to accompany Mrs. Lincoln and himself to the inaugural ball on March 6, 1865. As Lincoln entered the ballroom accompanied by the Speaker of the House, observers noted just behind them Mary Lincoln on the arm of Charles Sumner. Sumner later observed that the president "seemed to take this very conspicuous way of assuring the senators, representatives and people present that he still claimed me as a friend, and that a conscientious discharge of what I thought my duty, although directly opposed to what might be his favorite projects, would not sever or weaken our intercourse."[43]

Such efforts to maintain personal ties with the radical wing of the party supplemented the necessities of party politics and helped maintain the unity necessary to win elections. Victory in 1864 was the product of many forces, but party unity was crucial. By voting time both Wade and Davis were giving speeches supporting Lincoln, as was Sumner. Chase joined in and so did Montgomery Blair on behalf of party conservatives. A united party met the Democratic challenge successfully. Lincoln received 2,213,665 votes, McClellan 1,802,237. Lincoln carried every Northern state except for New Jersey, and two border slave states, Kentucky and Delaware. His electoral college majority was 212–21. Congressional elections saw major party victories, too. The next Senate would have a 42–10 Republican majority; the House would be 149–42 Republican. Only New Jersey chose a Democratic governor, and Republicans gained control of all the state legislatures they had lost two years before.

The Republican party kept the allegiance of all spectrums of the party. Party vote totals remained at or near levels of prior elections, and states and counties that had established themselves in the Republican column in the realignment of the mid-1850s tended to stay where they were. The best predictor of how a county would vote on election day remained how it had voted in the previous election. That was a testimony to the ability of Republicans to stick together when they had to, despite antagonisms over policies and quarreling between branches of government. It was also a testimony to the way in which the war helped to engender party coherence and loyalty.[44]

The quarrels within the Republican party tended to fade in the aftermath of the 1864 squabbles. By December 1864 Lincoln and Congress were even more clearly in step. Lincoln and radical James Ashley agreed on a Reconstruction bill that mirrored Wade-Davis, except for recognition of the Lincoln government in Louisiana. Three days before his death Lincoln was speaking publicly of giving the vote to blacks who had fought for the Union and "the very intelligent." He was applauding the newly created school system for both races in Louisiana. He was also expressing pleasure over the fact that his own earlier idea of turning freedmen into apprentices did not appear in the new Louisiana constitution. He was even suggesting a change in his policy in a more radical direction.[45]

These steps toward radicalism did not denote full party harmony. This last public address, so full of concessions to advanced measures, still sought to persuade Congress and the nation to accept the presidential Reconstruction policy of Louisiana and Arkansas. Lincoln was speaking to reply to critics, answering the enduring opposition within his own party. Those critics remained adamant. A few of them believed that Lincoln's death would end the obstacle to a truly liberal reconstruction. Ben Wade told Andrew Johnson upon his taking over the government, "By the gods there will be no trouble now in running the government."[46]

But simply viewing the conflict between Lincoln and his more radical party opponents as a question of total victory ignores a vital fact: the *process* of politics, the dialectic of ideals, was the crucial beneficiary of the argument. It was not a fight in which Lincoln or the radicals had to be victorious. Lincoln's movement in their direction does not mean that they won or that the conservatives lost. The process of political argument that generated both dialogue and controversy opened options, sustained the vitality of the political system, and in so doing helped unite parties even as they warred among themselves over options, methods, means. True party division would come once the dialogue stopped. With Andrew Johnson in the White House, that is what happened, and the result was a major constitutional crisis. But the resolution of that crisis revealed the political vitality Lincoln and the war had forged. Johnson's challenge to the dialogue of politics produced Republican unity around a Reconstruction program that reflected a vast measure of agreement with Lincoln's early military governments as well as with his and his party's egalitarian goals.

The election of 1864 brought the parties together in the unifying spectacle of the presidential contest. Within each party, factions struggled for influence and control, but those intraparty rivalries themselves brought a balancing of views, forming a consensus that reached out to the largest number of potential voters for each party. No faction had dominated, no group of voters had been alienated from the process. Party regulars and the electorate found the nation's political institutions alive and vital, sustaining the dialogue over where the Union should go and how it should get there. The war, begun to defend a process that promised peaceful, orderly change, had not overcome the process. Conceptions of security, notions of loyalty, had limited political debate, but had also inspired fervent discussion of such limitations. Even repression had enlivened the national political conversation. And as the conversation was ongoing, so, too, was the constant reminder to the people of what was at stake, so, too, was the personal involvement in the arena, so, too, was the commitment to the culture of politics.

Specifically, the war had killed off the most divisive, most life-threatening of issues in the political process. Slavery would no longer endanger politics by making some issues uncompromisable. Secession was dead as the threat that intimidated dialogue over paths to the nation's goals. No challenge to politics would ever again be credible. An expanded electorate was also in the offing. By the conclusion of the war Republican leaders were suggesting giving ballots to black soldiers. Republican radicals were demanding that all black males receive the franchise. Within two years Republican congressmen demanded black suffrage in Dixie. Within five years slavery and race were no longer lawful reasons to deny the right to vote to anyone. A little further in the future the women of the nation would find the power to bring to life the ideals of equal suffrage that war and the struggle for equality had spawned.[47]

PART III

FINDING WAR'S MEANINGS

CHAPTER 11

World Images of War

B Y late 1863 the major crises in foreign policy had been settled. Although the war was obviously going to be protracted, it was clear that the Union was creating an awesomely powerful army and navy, and an economy to supply them. No nation in Europe wanted to challenge this new giant directly. Russia had indicated its support by sending its navy on an apparent goodwill mission to Northern ports. France still had some hopes of persuading Seward to accept Napoleon's Mexican ambitions, but that project grew increasingly precarious as Union power burgeoned. Irish leaders turned toward the Confederacy in the aftermath of the draft riots. The crushing of the New York City protests seemed to reveal the same Anglo-Saxon brutality that Northern generals had shown in sacrificing Irish lives on the battlefield. But Ireland was an English colony; its antipathy to the Union could harm no one directly. Furthermore, the rising strength of Prussia began to demand European attention. There was enough to do nearby without reaching overseas.

England, the fulcrum on which European reactions to the Civil War rested, had determined not to help the Confederacy. Queen Victoria's nation conceded the fact that the rebels were a belligerent, but recognition was now a virtual impossibility. The blockade continued to strangle Dixie even as Union armies prepared to follow Lee's and Johnston's bloody trails. The trip to the precipice over the *Trent* affair and the Laird rams made both England and the Union eager for stability and goodwill. By November Henry Adams could write, "Our affairs are quite in the background." His father echoed the refrain half a year later: "America is not talked of here. Never so little since I first came."[1]

International politics no longer played a leading role. But international perspectives remained crucial in defining the meaning of the war. Northerners often used the mirror of foreign events and opinion to define what they were fighting for. Lincoln insisted throughout the conflict that the United States was the last, best hope for free government in the world. Foreign opinion could either accept that claim or deny the attractiveness of the American model.

England provided the nation's most compelling mirror. As Howard Temperly observes, "What Americans believed about Englishmen had much to do with what they believed about themselves. Often, too, they expressed not what people's senses told them, but what they wished or needed to believe about one another." As Americans observed the English reaction to the Civil War, they often saw what they needed to see. They revealed something about themselves in the process.

It is hardly surprising that this should be so. American intellectuals looked to England as what Hawthorne called it, "our home." English thought and letters were wellsprings for our legal and political thought. English literature informed and incited most American writings. Emerson might protest the need for the new nation to strike out on its own, but he knew the impossibility of the enterprise. Seven years after his intellectual Declaration of Independence he wrote, "Our civility England determines the style of, insomuch as England is the strongest of the family of existing nations and as we are an extension of that people." Melville, Hawthorne, and Longfellow as well as Emerson joined lesser American thinkers in traveling to the mother country to learn and to introspect. Americans might damn the English, insist on English decadence, highlight English hypocrisy, rage against criticism by English travelers, even insist that the New World was defined in contrast to the Old. But all of this was done with an obsession about what England was and said about her offspring.[2]

When Great Britain recognized Confederate belligerency, therefore, most Northerners were outraged. Dependent as they were on the good opinion of England, sharing so many traditions, men like George Strong and Charles Sumner railed against the betrayal of the Union, "with sorrow unspeakable and astonishment of her course." The outrage of the intellectuals was supplemented by the hostility of the populace, which readily accepted the anti-British postures whenever the two nations were at sword's point.

While much, perhaps most, of this anti-British feeling was unambiguous, reflecting considerations of power politics, some important elements of the feeling were more complex and revealing. The range of British opinion about the Civil War was wide and varied, but Americans generally accepted and promoted an almost polar picture. Two evil forces were combining against one good one. It was widely believed that the British conservative class and its wealthy leaders favored the South, while the working classes favored the Union. Northerners explained this fact in obvious ways. The aristocrats of England were attracted to the aristocratic pretensions of Southern slavocracy, and repelled by what they saw as egalitarian mobocracy. Since these aristocrats had opposed the expansion of liberal ideas in their own country, they were delighted to see them fail in the United States. The other allegedly sinister group was an ill-defined conglomerate of avaricious merchants, traders, and capitalists, "pharisaical shopkeepers and bag-men," Strong called them. The nation that had once fought against slavery was now allegedly supporting a slave owners' rebellion. The South, Sumner asserted, was a "bordello . . . [a] mighty house of ill fame which the Christian nations are now asked for the first item to license." But the avarice of England's merchant class pushed the nation to condone license. And the profit to be gained from the weakening of an economic rival was sufficient motivation for the hostility. The aristocrats were thus anti-Union because they hoped that democratic government would fail. Merchants were anti-Union because they could see a profit in it.[3]

Part of this picture was true. The most widely read English newspapers in the United States were noisy proponents of the Davis government, mocking the amorality of the Union position, insisting on the hopelessness of Lincoln's cause. Those Americans who got their information about English public opinion from the *London Times,* for example, would harbor no doubts about upper-class support for the rebellion. Readers of Lord Acton knew of his belief that the South sought liberty from democratic tyranny. But more thorough examination of parliamentary debates, public speeches, and correspondence of British conservatives would have revealed another picture. On the whole this class opposed helping the Confederacy. Their major focus was on staying out of American affairs, avoiding actions that would unstabilize the Western Hemisphere. Thus they backed a firm position on the *Trent,* but were pleased with the peaceful resolution of the crisis. Despite the fact that conservative neutrality was a matter of public knowledge, however, Americans clung tightly to a belief in the enmity of the aristocracy, and accepted evidence that supported such a satisfying view.[4]

While Northerners believed that conservatives and "shopkeepers and bag-men" were their enemies, they insisted that their supporters were the forces of reform in England, and more important, were the workingmen of England. As we shall see, half of this vision was correct. Many of the proponents of reform in England were pro-Union.

But it was the position of the workingmen of England that played a vital role in forming the Northern self-image. They represented the common people to an America that prided itself on equality. Of more compelling importance was the fact that the workingmen of England were consistently seen in the United States as industrial workers. To a nation anxious about the future of industrialization, the attitude of other industrial workers was important.

Americans, apprehensive about the condition of industrial workers in the United States, had been shocked by the plight of such people in England. Frederick Olmsted visited Liverpool in 1850 and was "astonished to observe with what an unmingled stream of poverty the streets were swollen." Horace Greeley the next year described "the outcasts of London . . . no family ties, no homes, no education . . . born to wander about the docks, picking up a chance job now and then, but . . . often compelled to starve." Emerson had seen in English cities "children . . . trained to beg, until they shall be old enough to rob." Melville had described old women picking through garbage for food and rags. While all these men had believed things better in the United States, they were well aware of parallel American scenes, and a colleague of theirs, Nathaniel Hawthorne, spoke of linkages that must have occurred to them.

Hawthorne looked at industrial poverty, saw its horrors for the innocent, and was reminded of hell, "a place 'with dreadful faces thronged' wrinkled and grim with vice and wretchedness; and thinking over the line of Milton here quoted, I come to the conclusion that those ugly lineaments which started Adam and Eve, as they looked back to the closed gate of Paradise, were no fiends from the pit, but the more terrible foreshadowings of what so many of their descendents were to be. God help them, and us likewise, their brethren and sisters."[5]

When war began, Americans eagerly sought reassurances from European observers of the justice of the Union cause. Frederick Douglass noted how the people "watched eagerly to see what the London *Times* had to say—what Lord John Russell had to say—and what Davis Napoleon had to say." Works by foreign authors—Edouard de Laboulaye and the Count de Gasparin in France, John Elliott Cairnes and John Stuart Mill in England—received effusive praise and wide distribution by Northern opinion makers. The French authors wrote to assure American readers that in Europe the forces of popular rule and democracy were watching the Union effort and being inspired by it to keep alive the spirit of liberty, equality, and fraternity. Cairnes and Mill reassured Northerners that the cause in the North was clearly the cause of free labor against slavery's despotism. Mill wrote that the North was fighting the Southern doctrine "loudly preached through the [Confederacy] that slavery, whether black or white, is a good in itself and the proper condition of working classes everywhere." All this good opinion overwhelmed Thomas Carlyle's impatient epigram that Americans were "cutting each other's throats, because one half of them prefer hiring their servants for life, and the other by the hour."[6]

The attitude of the English workers to the Civil War was an especially important mirror for Americans of the nature of their war. If those workers refused to endorse the Union cause, doubts would be inescapable about whether the war was to save democratic government. More important, the fundamental ideology underlying the North-South conflict itself would be challenged. Slavery and Southern society had come to symbolize the evils afflicting free labor in the United States. Slavery had become the lightning rod for the anxieties that existed about the cost of industrialization in the United States. But if British workers refused to accept the Union position as defender of free labor, if instead they aligned themselves with the section that had proclaimed the failure of free society, that image would be tainted. And if British workers raised the questions, as some of them did, about Northern links to English factory owners and Northern devotion to Manchester economics, the ability of the war to subsume prewar anxieties would be jeopardized. People might have to consider the possibility that Northern success would serve not free labor, but the world of Liverpool, Manchester, and Birmingham. Given the growing power of wartime industry, such thoughts would have been disturbing indeed.[7]

The evidence that many British workers supported the South was very strong, especially in the first years of the war. Liverpool was notorious for its pro-Southern feelings. The county of Lancashire found many workers who opposed the Union effort. The more successful the Union blockade the stronger their hostility grew. Nine out of ten workers' newspapers opposed the Lincoln administration throughout the war. Scores of workers' meetings were held throughout the conflict, demanding everything from mediation of the conflict and recognition of the South to naval action against the blockade.

Many of these workers were not dissuaded from their views by the Emancipation Proclamation. They argued that the measure was designed simply to raise more soldiers to help the North win the war. Given the strong anti-Negro sentiment of the North, they believed that the proclamation would not bring liberty to blacks in peacetime. In fact, they insisted that emancipation would come more surely, and be more meaningful, if the South won the war. Furthermore, they argued that emancipating the slaves simply increased the supply of laborers and thus drove wages down, to the advantage of employers.[8]

Such sentiment reflected both the economic hardship imposed by the blockade as well as criticism of the Northern society. The blockade hit Lancashire with brutal force. By December 1862, 247,230 people were jobless; 485,434 were on relief. Women and children as well as men suffered. Though many British labor leaders were appalled by this scale of suffering, the deprivations of the laboring classes were not new to them. They blamed not just the war, but the industrial system itself. Given the fact that Northern industrial might was growing, they wondered about the benefits of supporting an economic system as well as a nation that could inflict such suffering. As Royden Harrison observes, "Working class leaders, journalists and advisors who . . . thought of the industrial capitalist as the main enemy, or who treated the propertied classes with an impartial and indiscriminate hostility tended to favor the Confederacy." Given a widespread belief, especially after Bull Run, that the South would gain independence, workers and such leaders sought a quick end to the struggle. As *Reynolds News*, with 300,000 subscribers, put it, "Better fight Yankees than starve operatives."[9]

Further drawing such people to the Southern side was the nature of pro-Union support. Richard Cobden and especially John Bright were vociferous and visible supporters of Lincoln, writing articles and public letters, calling meetings, and giving speeches. While these two fought against the Corn Laws, thus bringing bread prices down, they also opposed Chartism and especially factory reforms. Bright had attacked the ten-hours law for women and children as "a delusion practiced on the working classes." Cobden similarly opposed interfering in the economic arena to improve working conditions or to support trade unions. He boasted that he would not "please the people by holding out flattering and delusive prospects of cheap benefits. . . . Mine is that masculine species of charity which would lead me to inculcate in the minds of the laboring classes the love of independence, the privilege of self-respect, the disdain of being patronized or petted, the desire to accumulate and the ambition to rise." These were the sorts of speeches to be expected of wealthy factory owners. They gave little comfort to the children, women, and men who worked up to twelve hours in mines and factories for a pittance. The support of such men for the Union cause, the suffering imposed by the blockade, and objection to the industrial system combined to engender worker hostility against the Northern war effort. It thus had the potential for undercutting the ideology of the Union effort.[10]

But English industrialization was not monolithic. While large numbers of workers decried the costs of the process, others were beginning to accommodate themselves to it. More highly skilled workers were able to organize more effectively and gain some of the benefits the new processes were creating. And such men were more likely to be attracted by that side of Bright and Cobden that had led fight against the Corn Laws, which was, after all, also a fight for free trade, which helped industrial exports. They were susceptible to the argument that whatever the evils of factory work, they were less than those of human slavery, Dixie style. They especially found appealing the idea advanced by the Republican party, that the fight against slavery was a fight in favor of the dignity of free labor, a labor that built character as it built fortune, created discipline as it fostered self-reliance. These were the people that Bright and Cobden called together in large rallies to support the North. They symbolized the hopes of the burgeoning industrial world and the belief that the working classes might find entry into the bourgeoisie.[11]

This latter segment of opinion satisfied the need of Northerners for approval. Northerners eagerly highlighted it at home and overseas. Henry Adams, acting as secretary to his father, the minister to England, in 1861, doubted the sentiments of the Lancashire workers. As soon as the first pro-Union meetings began, however, he embraced them as the salvation of democracy in both England and the United States. Such support, he believed, would keep England from helping the Confederacy and might in fact bring democracy closer to realization in England. "I never quite appreciated the 'moral influence' of American democracy nor the cause that the privileged classes in Europe have to fear us, until I saw how directly it works. At this moment the American question is organizing a vast mass of the lower orders in direct contact with the wealthy." "We have strength enough already," the twenty-three-year-old wrote, "to shake the very crown on the Queen's head if we are compelled to employ it." While, of course, the United States would not try to cause trouble, a force was loose in the world that would challenge aristocracy, and the United States led that force.[12]

Lincoln was intensely interested in the opinion of the English workingmen, and hoped to enlist them in the Union cause. He also knew the value in the North of describing the war as a workingmen's struggle. He wrote resolutions he hoped would be adopted by them at mass meetings throughout England. When a group at Manchester passed similar resolutions he responded publicly with a recognition of "the sufferings which the workingmen at Manchester and in all Europe are called upon to endure." These were, he insisted, due to "the actions of our disloyal citizens" who sought to "overthrow this government, which was built on the foundation of human rights, and to substitute for it one which should rest exclusively on the basis of human slavery." The "sublime Christian heroism" these sufferers had shown "has not been surpassed in any age or in any country."[13]

Comfortingly for the Union, manifestations of support did increase as the war went on. Although in the immediate aftermath of the Emancipation Proclamation there was little growth in Union support, by late spring 1863 much more of it appeared. Workingmen's meetings grew in number, and it was, of course, these meetings that Northerners paid most attention to.

The outstanding illustration of such an event and the American press reaction to it took place at a town near Manchester named Staleybridge. There, on October 1, 1862, pro-Union workers took over a meeting organized by Southern sympathizers; they passed resolutions proclaiming that "the distress prevailing in the manufacturing districts is mainly owing to the rebellion of the Southern States against the American Constitution." Other meetings in the same region had passed pro-Confederate resolutions, and the English press gave the Staleybridge meeting only passing notice. But the American press trumpeted the victory of the "laboring classes" over the forces of aristocracy in England and Europe. The *New York Herald* saw the Staleybridge incident as a symbol of the clash between the "frightened despots" of Europe who hoped that a democratic government would fail and "the masses" who "judge our present struggle correctly," seeing in it a test of popular government and the ability of the people to rule themselves. When the inevitable Northern victory was achieved the masses throughout the Western world would overthrow the tyrants who oppressed them. The *New York Times* noted that "the British laboring classes are not blind to the fact that the interest of labor and of democratic institution is identified with the success of the North, and that the South is a simple embodiment of the veteran domination and tyranny which the capitalist has always struggled to maintain over the workman."[14]

The efforts of the British Emancipation Society began to pay off in increased numbers at enthusiastic rallies proclaiming the victory of liberty over slavery. In late January 1863 the *London Spectator*, long a supporter of the Union effort, asserted that "the masses of people all over England—including especially the districts suffering most heavily from the war—are nearly unanimous in sympathizing with the North." And two labor newspapers switched sides. Both *Reynolds* and the *Bee Hive* adopted pro-Union stands and began insisting that the wealthier classes were the supporters of the slave state cause. The *Bee Hive* printed a labor leader speech declaring, "This American war has made apparent the profound chasm between upper and lower classes. The struggle for political rights on the part of English laborers will be worthily inaugurated by their disinterested and generous protest on behalf of the enslaved laborers of America." Such endorsements pleased Americans immensely, validating the perception of the war as a free labor crusade. Lincoln, as noted, replied gratefully to a resolution of support from Manchester extolling the "heroism" of supporting the North in the face of suffering caused by the blockade. Notable in Lincoln's answer is this fact. While the resolutions of support had come from "citizens of Manchester," including not only workingmen but others as well, Lincoln's reply was presented "to the *Workingmen* of Manchester" (my italics), highlighting the idea that the industrial classes of England favored the Union cause.[15]

Northern newspapers exulted over growing proof of the loyalty of English commoners and the working class. There was much to celebrate in declarations and resolutions that told the North that the cause of freedom in England and America were linked; that English Tories knew "that if the black labourers got their rights, the next thing would be that the white labourers would be wanting theirs." There was also much comfort in believing that the world might be improved by Northern victory. In the heat of war it is hardly surprising that such a view prevailed.[16]

The end of the war brought final endorsement. In 1865 Little, Brown and Company published John Bright's *Speeches on the American Question,* a collection that the editor had taken the time to assemble to permit Americans to receive the applause of "their old home." Singled out for attention were Bright's remarks "upon free labor, upon the social advance of the working men." These ought especially to attract the "careful attention," the editor said, "of merchants and statesmen." Northern victory would demonstrate the triumph, Bright argued, of a section where "Labor has met its greatest honor and . . . reaped its highest reward," where "labor is honored more than anywhere else in the world." In vanquished Dixie labor was "not only not honored . . . it is degraded." Comforting words indeed.[17]

English opinion was the most important mirror for the United States. But France also attracted attention. The great popularity of

Hugo's *Les Misérables* in 1861 guaranteed an audience for Gallic ideas. Alexandre Dumas had thirteen works published in the United States during the war. Four works by Jomini were published, reviewed, and discussed, further testifying to American interest in French opinion. American writings on Napoleon I continued in military and popular journals. And, of course, Napoleon III was a subject of some fascination both for his personality and because of his power in France. The *New York Times* provided weekly reports on events in that country, and every two or three weeks editorials discussed French policies and reactions toward our war.[18]

The North's initial outrage at English neutrality made French perspectives even more appealing. American writers concluded that the English observers of the United States were often blinded by jealousy. The similarity between British and American institutions made the English too sensitive about their own frailties. But Frenchmen allegedly stood at a distance that gave them a more objective view. There was truth in the observation. Alexis de Tocqueville clearly was the most insightful commentator on America, but Michel Chevalier's observations were also keen.

Wartime French writings gained widespread attention. Despite a French population that was mostly apathetic about the United States and a press divided in sympathy between North and South, Northerners most frequently read the good news. When Agénor de Gasparin published his two volumes on *Les Etats-Unis* one reviewer suggested that Americans should feel "gratitude to a friend who sends us such words of lofty cheer in a time of need." Gasparin wrote of the rising of "a great people" who by accepting war were saving themselves from the evils of slavery. Apathetic churches and the temptations of commerce had kept the nation from realizing its destiny, Gasparin argued. But now, by championing liberty against slavery the Union would gain both military victory and the salvation of its soul. Edouard de Laboulaye's *Paris en Amerique* paid little attention to the war, but its essays extolling Yankee culture went through thirteen editions in two years. Americans also admired Laboulaye's writings on the virtue of the American Constitution and his argument in favor of making war for liberal nationalism. American counsel John Bigelow had these printed as pamphlets and circulated.[19]

Pro-Union French writers were predominantly part of the liberal opposition to Napoleon III. In the 1850s some Americans had welcomed the second Bonaparte for bringing order to a chaotic society. But the majority regretted the end of the Second Republic. And as the emperor restricted freedom of speech and the press, Americans rallied almost unanimously behind the liberals of France. These liberals in turn used American ideas and institutions as standards to challenge Napoleon. Such mutual admiration further enhanced the self-image of the North, and validated Lincoln's claim of worldwide mission. Here again Americans ignored contrary evidence. The French textile workers especially were as hard hit by the blockade as their compatriots in England. They reacted the same way, opposing in large numbers the Union position. But Americans highlighted those Frenchmen who proclaimed the rightness of their cause.[20]

American feelings about France were shaped by power politics as well as wishful thinking. Had Napoleon III been a liberal, Americans would still have passionately opposed his offer in November 1863 to mediate the Civil War. The emperor tried to get England and Russia to join him in this effort, but they left him on his own. The North cheered Seward's reply that there was nothing to mediate, since the only issue in such a meeting would be the destruction of the United States.[21]

The most compelling question of Franco-American relations was Napoleon's involvement in Mexico. The emperor originally had high hopes for a French-dominated Mexico. He wanted to maintain a Catholic state in the New World and to serve his European ambitions by offering a throne there to Maximilian of Austria. Perhaps envy of England fed hopes that Mexico would prove to be his India. Furthermore, he believed that a disunited states of America would serve him well. He hoped for, and expected, a Confederate victory. If he could ingratiate himself with the rebel government, it might trade toleration of French involvement in Mexico for French recognition of the new nation. He might also get the Union government to leave him alone by threatening recognition of the Confederacy.

The emperor's hopes had to be very strong, for they clashed with reality. Napoleon's enemies in Europe were happy to see him wasting effort and resources abroad. His own people were divided on the question. The Latin American states felt threatened by any monarchical regime returning to the region. A victorious Confederacy would have its own expansionist goals in the Caribbean. These predictably would overcome any gratitude to France for help in gaining independence. The Union government whether victorious or not would still have powerful reasons not to forget French coercion. That government would also be strong enough to make France pay for its misdeeds. The Monroe Doctrine and the passion and history that lay behind it guaranteed trouble for France whichever way the war turned out.

Many of these factors should have been obvious to Napoleon. But in the early days of the war, the crucial factor, the possible reach of Union power, was problematic. Faced with the immensity of the Civil War, even William Seward doubted that the Union could directly challenge the first French steps. France assured the United States that it was going into Mexico only to collect debts that the Juárez government owed. Furthermore, at first England and Spain joined in sending troops to collect. Seward accepted Napoleon's word as a diplomatic necessity. The United States continued to recognize the Juárez government in Mexico, and Seward explained that we "could not view with indifference" any effort by European powers to interfere in Mexico's internal affairs. Nevertheless, words were our main weapon. Even when England and Spain withdrew from the expedition Seward avoided a confrontation. As he explained to Minister William Dayton in Paris, "Why should we gasconade about Mexico, when we are engaged in a struggle for our own life?"[22]

But by August 1863 Union power began to tip the scales, and Seward could hint at the folly of French involvement by lecturing on recent history. He sent a long letter to all the legations in Europe. In the past, he noted, foreign governments had responded to Union protests about their actions by mentioning the likelihood of Confederate victory. But Vicksburg and Gettysburg surely demanded a reconsideration of that prospect. Furthermore, the blockade was increasingly effective, and Northern armies were now utilizing black troops to add to existing numerical superiority. The letter focused on persuading European governments to withdraw all recognition and support for the rebels, but it clearly had implications for Mexico as well.[23]

At first Napoleon ignored those implications. The French army took Mexico City even as Seward's memo began to circulate. In April 1864 Maximilian accepted the Mexican throne. But now

American devotion to the Monroe Doctrine sounded forth. If Seward had to be diplomatic, congressmen didn't. They, too, were deeply involved in fighting the South, but they kept alert to events in Mexico. Even as Maximilian became emperor the House of Representatives spoke out. The new monarch was "the arch dupe" of Napoleon, and congressmen wanted the world to know that their previous "silence on events in Mexico" did not mean indifference. "It does not accord with the policy of the United States to acknowledge any monarchical government in America erected on the ruins of any republican Government in America under the auspices of any European Power." The vote on that resolution was 109–0.[24]

Meanwhile Napoleon's position began to erode in Europe, too. Elections in France revealed strong opposition to the Mexican venture. Austrian relations deteriorated. The Hapsburgs rejected a proposed agreement with Napoleon over land cessions in Italy, Silesia, and Danubian provinces. Bismarck and the Austrians formed an alliance to invade Schleswig-Holstein, revealing Prussia's growing power. Napoleon determined to abandon the monarch he had brought to Mexico. Maximilian would have to hang on to his crown by himself.[25]

Burgeoning Northern power revealed that he could not do it alone. In 1864 the surety of victory increased the strength of Seward's hand. Northern newspapers began to roar with demands that the Monroe Doctrine be enforced. In public the secretary of state joined the commotion. The United States could no more tolerate an emperor in Mexico than she could accept one in Washington, D.C., he told the French chargé d'affaires. Privately, he reassured the French government that Union intentions were not warlike in Mexico.[26]

But sabers were rattling. The end of the Civil War found thirty thousand Union veterans under General Sheridan looking eagerly into Mexico, spoiling for action. Many soldiers probably shared the feeling of a colleague who had written as early as 1863, "I mean to go to Mexico and fight the French after this war is done. It . . . would certainly be good fun to cut off those little red-legged sinners, who have been swelling about their fighting and victory." Grant had advised immediate action, but Seward persuaded President Johnson that diplomatic leverage, backed by that thirty thousand, would work as well. It did. In April 1866 Napoleon announced that his troops were going home; the experiment in monarchy and empire on this nation's border ended ingloriously. Without the troops, Maximilian and his empress, Carlota, were helpless. She rushed to France to beg Napoleon to help. Maximilian stayed, was captured by the Mexicans, and executed in June 1867. The horror of her husband's death soon drove Carlota insane.[27]

Mexico provoked Union concern because of its contrasts to the United States. It was an unstable Catholic country populated by people Americans considered racially inferior. Napoleon threatened to alienate it further by replacing its republican government with a monarchy. The Union affirmed its ideals and protected its security by checkmating the scheme of a foreign autocrat.

On the Union's other border Canada presented a different situation. It was so similar to the United States that Northerners constantly took it for granted. Canadians insisted on differences, but Americans ignored that, too, and learned little about themselves by looking northward. As a British colony, Canada lacked a unique foreign policy that could force the Union to consider its special qualities.

London made the foreign policy of Canada. The vulnerability of its last American possession made England unwilling to challenge the status quo. As Cobden had said, the British could no more defend Canada than the United States could defend Yorkshire. Furthermore, the British by mid-century had adopted a policy of holding colonies by what Gladstone called "silken ties of affection." This policy gave Americans less reason to fear foreign interference in Canada. The Union turned its attention to other places.[28]

Nevertheless, the potential for trouble in the North existed. Canadians were by no means automatically friendly to the neighboring giant. They remembered invasions during the revolution and the War of 1812. They heard the comments that Canada one day would drop "like ripe fruit" into the United States. The outbreak of war increased the suspicions about Union intentions. Seward's anti-British outbursts and past ambition for Canada came back to mind. Rumors circulated during the secession winter that the United States would, in either victory or defeat, turn to Canada and shake the tree. If the South were lost, what better place to find compensation than in the north? If the South were held, then the military material and spirit would find useful employment in taking over a grand new empire. Another alternative was that the Lincoln government might respond to secession by picking an international fight, thus uniting North and South in a foreign war. Canada watched the American Civil War carefully.

Opinion there was divided as it had been in England. The British press helped shape Canadian views. Conservatives in both countries took their slogans and arguments from the anti-Northern *London Times*. John MacDonald and George Cartier, leaders of Canada's ruling party, had previously used the United States, with its disdain for tradition, its devotion to mobocratic democracy, as a negative example. A week after Sumter fell MacDonald gave one of his most impressive speeches on "the failure of the American system." Cartier and MacDonald did agree that a strong central government was indispensable for Canadian nationhood and prosperity, but both men insisted that nationhood could be built by learning the weaknesses of the United States, not aspiring to copy her.[29]

The friends of the Union were led by George Brown's "Clear Grits," or Liberals. They combined demands for an American-style popular representation in the legislature with support for abolition. For decades before the Civil War began many Canadians had sympathized with the abolitionist cause. *Uncle Tom's Cabin* was wildly popular. Presses in both Toronto and Montreal printed copies, and the major Toronto newspaper also carried sections of it. By 1860 approximately sixty thousand blacks lived in Canada, many of them arriving after 1850 in the heart of the disunion crisis. Their choice of sanctuary complimented Canada on its tolerance and respect for liberty. While blacks were segregated, they still were free, and some of them prospered.

American abolitionists looked north and saw the support of the cause. John Brown visited in 1858, meeting with several blacks and whites to plan revolution in Dixie. Other abolitionists believed that in any conflict between the forces of slavery and those of emancipation, Canada would oppose slavery.[30]

But the beginning of the war saw a shift in Canadian opinion. Lincoln's early unwillingness to make the war a crusade against slavery drove Canadian abolitionists from the Union cause. By the summer of 1861 moral issues faded from view, to be replaced by fears about Northern imperialism. Even *DeBow's Review,* which attacked "the vile, sensuous, criminal, brutal, infidel, superstitious

Democracy of Canada and the Yankees," could not shake Canadian suspicion of Union intentions. The *Trent* crisis saw opinion strongly on the side of England, where it tended to stay through most of the war. A very vocal conservative press fed general discontent with Union policy. The majority of Canada's newspapers supported the Confederacy, unaffected by even the Emancipation Proclamation.[31]

The North was unconcerned about Canadian opinion. To be sure, some editors noted Canadian hostility, and abolitionists were surprised at the shallowness of Canada's antislavery opinion. But the Lincoln government was so uninterested in what Canada thought that, aside from sending Joshua Giddings as counsel general, it sent no one to advocate its interests. In fact, Canadian officials had to request some of the materials that the United States government distributed to other nations promoting the cause of union. On the other hand, Confederates actively propagandized the idea of independent nationhood and struggle for self-government. These ideas had appeal among those pushing for Canadian autonomy.

As their situation became more desperate Confederates spread more than propaganda. They tried to create a clash between the Union and Great Britain in Canada. England's neutrality required that Canada stop any Confederate intrusions into the United States, but the long border was hard to patrol. Rebel agents were active despite official disapproval. In November 1863 Canadian authorities discovered a plot to release prisoners held near Lake Erie. This time the governor general notified the United States government. Quick action by Seward and Secretary of War Stanton alerted the border and stopped the plan in its tracks.

But Canadian officials could not catch everything. A month later Confederates captured a steamer named *The Chesapeake* and took off with it toward Nova Scotia. There American gunboats cornered the rebel pirates in Halifax harbor and took them prisoner. But one of the men was a British subject and had friends in the town who demanded his release. Local authorities agreed with that demand, and their shore batteries looked threateningly down on the Union boats. Union officials backed away. Secretary of the Navy Welles told his sailors to give the ship to Canadian authorities. The prisoner was also released and tension subsided. Seward explained that the United States had not authorized the invasion of Canadian waters.

But even while settling this incident, Seward insisted that Canadian authorities enforce neutrality with greater vigor. Meanwhile Americans prepared to take matters into their own hands. In October 1864 another breakdown occurred. This time twenty armed Confederates jumped out of Canada and raided the Vermont hamlet of St. Albans. They robbed the town's three banks and tried to set the place on fire. They also managed to kill one man and injure several others before heading back to Canada. Vermonters were in no mood to wait for Canadian action. A posse chased the rebels across the border and captured them. At that point they did turn the rebels over to Canadian authorities, but tensions remained high.

American authorities were ready for action. General John A. Dix told his soldiers to go into Canada whenever necessary to catch Confederate raiders. A Canadian judge gave him a reason to believe that it would be necessary. The judge released the St. Albans raiders on a technicality so blatant that even the Canadian press protested. Dix then sent soldiers with orders to either kill the rebels or bring them back for military trial in the United States. General Hooker down in Cincinnati added to the tension by blurting out that "somebody shall be hurt if I have to go into Canada." Congress escalated things further by calling for the termination of the Rush-Bagot agreement, which had previously settled issues between Canada and the United States. Seward set up passport regulations that slowed travel between the two countries to a crawl, and asked for extradition of the raiders.

These pressures worked. The British government asked the Canadian legislature to pass an alien law that expelled all foreigners suspected of hostile acts toward foreign governments. The law also permitted the seizure of ships and arms that might be used in such acts. Meanwhile Lincoln rescinded Dix's orders and Seward revoked the strict passport system. The secretary of state also announced that the Rush-Bagot agreement would remain in force.[32]

The end of the war found Canadian-American relations quiet as usual. War had shown that differences could be reconciled. The assassination of Lincoln inspired an outpouring of sympathy for the United States. There remained voices in the United States that called for using American armies to take over Canada, but these were a minority. Some argued that Canada might be proper compensation for the losses the United States incurred as a result of British recognition of the Confederate belligerency. But these voices, too, were not persuasive. While Americans might fantasize a republic reaching to the North Pole, they relied on time to bring that about. In 1867 Britain established the Dominion of Canada, recognizing its independent status and the union of all Canadian possessions under one government. Congress grumbled that this dominion somehow violated the Monroe Doctrine. But this protest reflected political posturing rather than serious concern. The United States had found Canada to be a friendly and very familiar neighbor even in the midst of the greatest test in its history. Temptation was strong to take Canada for granted once again.

The Union people and government looked at the world and saw their ideals affirmed. The foreign opinions they listened to were most often the ones they wanted to hear. One reason for this limited vision arose from the huge foreign-born population in the United States. Almost 20 percent of the population of the North was foreign born as of 1860, the largest percentage in this nation's history. Their presence suggested the truth of Lincoln's assertion that the United States exemplified ideas shared by right-thinking people everywhere. The nearly 500,000 foreign-born soldiers who fought for the Union surely endorsed that idea.

Scots, Welsh, Hungarians, Mexicans, Danes, Swedes, Poles, Frenchmen, all fought in Union ranks. Approximately one-fourth of the Union army, in fact, was made up of foreign-born soldiers. But the most prominent were Germans and especially Irish. Although Germans, with about 185,000, were the largest group numerically, the approximately 144,000 Irish-Americans who fought received the most attention at the time. Irish ethnic identity was more obvious than that of other groups. Their Catholicism especially distinguished them, and their loyalty was a subject of serious debate. Their place among the lower classes of the North also made them the object of special attention to a culture concerned about economic inequity.

The Irish did nothing to hide their heritage. Like the Germans, they insisted on forming their own units and proudly gathered in their neighborhoods to march to war wearing shamrocks, escorted by the Hibernian Benevolent and other societies, blessed by their priests. They demanded recognition as Irishmen as well as Americans. They protested loudly when one of their own did not receive the recognition he deserved, complaining to Lincoln at the low number of high-ranking Irish officers. They also experienced their sacrifices as Irishmen. Individual units built legends in and outside the Irish community by their sacrifices. T. F. Meagher's Irish Brigade in the Army of the Potomac gained national admiration for its courage and its great losses, especially at Fredericksburg and Chancellorsville. The 5,000 men that Meagher started with had been reduced to 520 after Chancellorsville.[33]

The largest number of Irish soldiers came from the Northeast, New York providing 51,000, Pennsylvania over 17,000. Most of these men came from the working classes of New York City and Philadelphia. Their motivations for fighting were diverse. Some men needed the money and enlisted for the bounties provided by the state and the city. Others were inspired by the enthusiasm of the moment or shamed into it by the pressure of public opinion.

When they looked beyond immediate personal motives many saw the opportunity to claim respect as American citizens, to undo the stigma that nativism had attached to them of being aliens unfit for this society. A flag carried by the Ninth Massachusetts Volunteers spoke the sentiment: "As aliens and strangers thou didst us befriend. As sons and true patriots we do thee defend." When in 1868 John Francis Maguire described the service of the Irish in the war, he used the opportunity to insist on the loyalty of Irishmen to their American homeland, whether North or South, and to note especially the cleanliness of Irish soldiers and their gallantry toward beaten foes. These were respectable citizens, not untrustworthy rabble. In the Midwest as well, the Catholic hierarchy urged parishioners to prove their loyalty to "the first country the Irishman ever had that he could call his own country." Newspapers there echoed the message that these Irish sought to deliver. One said, "Let the nativist bigot think and say what he will, the Irish element in America is giving conclusive evidence of devoted attachment to the Union."[34]

But pressures to join the mainstream met counterpressures. After the first enthusiasm many Irish withdrew from their advanced patriotism. Some were repelled by abiding nativism. In the Midwest especially old prejudices endured. Newspapers and politicians declared that they did not want aliens to corrupt the struggle. Furthermore, the Republican coalition in the Midwest rested on pietistic groups who disliked the Irish for their faith and their nationality. Lincoln's party often used anti-Irish rhetoric to split the traditionally Democratic German and Irish Catholics and to frighten other voters away from the Democrats. Such name-calling helped erode Irish patriotism.[35]

Even more persuasive was the Irish belief that poor men like themselves were making larger sacrifices for the war than native Americans. The draft offered poor urban workers few loopholes. The carnage among Irish regiments, especially the bloodbath of Fredericksburg, inflamed hostility to the Republican party and "its" war. The Emancipation Proclamation exacerbated feelings further. It commited the Union government to freeing blacks, thus benefiting the group most despised by the Irish. By 1863 among the general Irish population support for the conflict was minimal. Irish communities continued to be bastions of Democratic votes and draft resistance. The draft riots only made more vivid their reputation for disloyalty.

And yet the image of the Irish as alien suffered a heavy blow. Election propaganda about Irish disloyalty endured. But on the battlefield, where most hearts and minds were focused, the sons of Erin demonstrated their courage and commitment to saving their adopted nation. After Antietam one admiring corporal wrote, "They fight like tigers & no rgt. of Rebs can stand a charge from them. They have a reputation which our Regt. will never get." Union generals shared these feelings. Sherman admired their courage. Fitzjohn Porter spoke of being "kindled into rapture" at Malvern Hill at the sound of an Irish charge.

Even rebel generals spoke of them with respect. Colonel Richard Taylor reported that if he could choose men on which to rest his military reputation, he would choose Irish soldiers. The six Fredericksburg assaults on Marye's Heights became a legend of the war. Robert E. Lee reported how A. P. Hill had cried, "There are those damned green flags again!" George Pickett wrote his wife of his heart standing still watching "those sons of Erin . . . rush to their deaths . . . we forgot they were fighting us, and cheer after cheer at their fearlessness went up all along our lines." Longstreet called that assault "the handsomest thing in the whole war." Generals like

Meagher, James Shields, and especially Philip Sheridan further spread Irish fame and testified to Irish faith in the Union mission.[36]

The service of the almost 150,000 Irish troops crippled nativism. And on the home front there were signs that these immigrants claimed America as their home. Irish children began to learn the patriotic speeches of Webster and Patrick Henry. New York City's archbishop Hughes flew the flag over his cathedral and told parishioners to "be patriotic . . . do for the country what the country needs, and the blessing of God will recompense those who do their duty." Even in the aftermath of the draft riots an attempt to revive the old Know Nothing party fell apart. George Strong, who personally mused that "I would like to see war made on the Irish scum as in 1688," wrote in late July 1863 that "a mere anti-Hibernian party would have no foundation on principle, would seem merely vindictive and proscriptive and would lead to no lasting result."[37]

Before the Civil War, and in many places after, the term "Irish Democrat" was practically redundant. But by the end of the war the Republicans were appealing for Irish votes. In 1868 Grant's party sent out a special campaign sheet for the Irish voter. The *Irish Republic,* a Republican paper, changed its headquarters from Chicago to New York to campaign for Grant, and a few prominent Irish leaders urged Irish veterans to vote for their old commander. Here was further evidence that immigrants found in the victorious Union ideals they could fight and die for.[38]

Immigrants from every nation, in fact, found the Union a magnet even in the midst of the war. While immigration dropped in the first two years of the conflict, by 1863 and 1864 it had reached prewar levels. Even from Ireland, where bitterness was widespread over Fredericksburg and other bloodbaths, came more immigrants in 1863 than had been seen since 1854. Over 800,000 people arrived between 1861 and 1865. The Union army gained an estimated 183,440 soldiers from the young men who arrived here from all overseas countries. Few probably came to serve in the army, but they seldom ran away from service. Most came because the wartime boom meant jobs, and enlistments added to the openings. Men who joined the army left vacancies behind that immigrants gladly filled. And immigration was encouraged by legislation that supported private capital's demands for more and more men to meet the war economy's needs. The Homestead Act also called foreigners to the

United States with its promise of land where free labor could realize the promises that Republicans had been making for years.

Wartime perspectives reinforced the belief of Northerners that theirs was the cause of free labor, democracy, and liberty. Foreign countries and immigrants endorsed the view. Events immediately after the war added to it. England in 1867 passed its Electoral Reform Bill, which expanded the right to vote to new thousands of Englishmen. Although domestic issues were most crucial, supporters of the bill gave credit to the example of the United States, which had recently shown that a democracy might preserve stability while expanding liberty. French liberals gained inspiration, too, for Napoleon's plans had gone awry and nationalism in the United States had survived without crushing liberalism. The creation of the Third Republic would benefit from the American lesson.

Canada's new commonwealth status also reflected the impact of America abroad. Here the lessons were not likely to be as pleasing to Americans. Fears of an American military power argued that Canadian unity was imperative. Interruption of trade between the two North American nations pushed economic cooperation between Canadian regions. Civil War in the United States showed Canadians potential dangers should they not create peaceably a strong constitutional system. Canada's acquisition of independent commonwealth status did not prove the power of America's example. It demonstrated the need for a unique path, and thereby further established Canadian nationalism. But, of course, Americans were experienced in ignoring the Canadian alternative.

Yet in a larger sense both North American nations demonstrated to the world the viability of liberal nationalism. Before the conflict that ideal was under a cloud. Napoleon built French strength by stifling liberty there. Italy achieved its unity at cost to its liberal ideals. Bismarck was building Germany, not by linking liberty and union but in the crucible of "blood and iron." Austria and Russia stood ready to stamp out liberalism wherever it might appear. But after the war the United States was indisputably strong and slavery was dead and the process of changing government by ballots was alive and well. A free labor society had in fact defeated one based on slave labor. The self-serving quality of much of the Northern worldview had considerable facts to endorse it, and an awesome and bloody triumph to help explain it.[39]

The victorious North thus left the war behind, secure in its self-image, and unchallenged in power in the Western Hemisphere. The background had been laid for reaching out into the larger world. Seward, always the expansionist, was ready to move fast and did. An American squadron occupied Midway Island in the Pacific; Denmark agreed to sell the Virgin Islands to the United States, but the Senate refused to ratify the agreement. Still, the biggest prize of all, Alaska, was acquired in the warm afterglow of a visit to the United States of the Russian fleet in 1863, a visit Northerners interpreted with gratitude as Russian support for the war effort. The lingering effect of that visit and the immediate effect of some vote buying by the Russian minister led Congress to provide $7,200,000 for what critics at the time called "Seward's icebox" and "Seward's folly."[40]

It would be much later in the century that a new expansionism would overtake the United States, one that focused more on manifest destiny to gain more and more power abroad. But the Civil War had shown the strength of the nation, endorsed its vitality and the worth of its economy and society. If quiet gains were the immediate rewards of the conflict, the foundation had been laid for a world power to proclaim its duty, assert its strength, and try to shape the world in its own image.

CHAPTER 12

Frankenstein and Everyman: Sherman, Grant, and Modern War

NORTHERNERS were sensitive about their world image. Politics was an obvious and ongoing passion. Economic transformations surged in and out of view, and emancipation compelled attention, but the battlefield held their hearts. Too many sons and loved ones were out there, their fate dependent on what generals might do. The ideals of their culture were also at risk, challenged to justify the deaths, to explain the promise, that would make it all worth it, and to shape the often chaotic images that the war unleashed. The generals and their plans, the symbolic qualities of who they were and what they did, became crucial ways to determine what this war meant.

The early years had been McClellan's war. Both in his virtues and his failings he had shaped the conflict's meaning. The modernizing professional had organized what his successor, Joe Hooker, called "the finest army on the planet." Yet McClellan was undone by his own conservative strategy and the fears of his critics that he exemplified every ominous aspect of the professional soldier. His political insensitivity had deprived him of the support of the reformers in the North at a time when reform in matters of race moved inexorably forward. His excessive understanding of the complexities of modern warfare had nurtured a natural caution that was fortified by anguish over the carnage of battle. McClellan was at home in a world before war began to engender a major transformation in moral perspective as well as in economic, institutional, and organizational structures. He had suffered because he could master only the organizational elements of the modern world. He could not comprehend or adapt himself to the demands for a similar change in moral perspective that the fight against slavery was also evolving.

McClellan had left the national scene as military commander after his failure to pursue Lee aggressively after Antietam. Lee took his army back into Virginia and awaited the next Northern move. Lincoln replaced McClellan with Ambrose Burnside, and the result was the slaughter at Fredericksburg and a new Union commander, "Fighting Joe" Hooker. Chancellorsville was Hooker's chance to defeat Lee and Jackson. Instead, the Confederates defeated the Army of the Potomac in the late spring of 1863 and turned again toward the North. The goal: persuade the people of the North and their leaders that they were not immune to battle and that the Confederate commitment to nationhood was unrelenting.

Lincoln replaced Hooker as commander of the Army of the Potomac in late June 1863 even as Lee pushed into Pennsylvania. George Meade took the reins just in time to gather his forces at Gettysburg to meet Lee. In three days of the greatest battle ever fought in the Western Hemisphere, nearly forty-six thousand men fell as casualties: dead, wounded, or missing. Lee staggered south, his army defeated in its courageous insanity of attacking entrenched rifles and cannon. But Meade's army reeled, too; the vast bloodletting drained it of the will and ability to rush after the retreating rebels. Lincoln hoped, as he had hoped after Antietam, to hear of the rout of Lee's army. Instead the telegraph spoke only of reorganizing, reinforcing, resupplying. The explanations somehow all made sense in an outrageous, frustrating way. The Union generals were, after all, on the scene, they knew what the battles had done to their men and supplies, and yet surely there was some way to energize the vast resources of the North to destroy the rebellion. But finally Lincoln accepted the reality of an ongoing struggle. The Eastern front ground downward into a frustrating inertia of huge armies glaring at each other menacingly, occasional brief encounters, and then "all quiet along the Potomac" as a new song taunted the administration and its Eastern generals.

In the East it was a stalemate. But in the West a different story unfolded. The momentum gained at Fort Donelson, Fort Henry, and Shiloh rolled onward. People heard increasingly the names

Grant and Sherman, names that meant movement, action, perseverance, and, above all, victory.

Like Grant, Sherman had known hardship and failure. Orphaned when he was very young, Sherman had been adopted by the powerful Thomas Ewing family. They obtained his entry into West Point, but after graduation Sherman met only defeat in civilian life. He tried banking in California and failed. He tried lawyering and real estate in Kansas and failed there, too. By 1860 he had been reduced to accepting the headship of a Louisiana military academy. In an America where making it on your own was every man's ideal, Sherman moved downward. I am "a dead cock in the pit," he told his wife Ellen. It was not something he could accept stoically. He was a profoundly ambitious man whose ambitions had been denied. "Life is a race," he would write in the war. "The end is all that is remembered." But in 1861 he found himself forty years old, the father of five children, with no place, no career, little promise. He seemed destined to be "a wanderer," he wrote, "a vagabond."[1]

This rootlessness made him extraordinarily sensitive to the flux and disruption of prewar America. Like millions of others, Sherman fought that anxiety by focusing on the need for law and order. The prewar struggle between North and South seemed to symbolize a clash of the forces of order and anarchy. He was not bothered about slavery, but by disrespect for law in both sections. In San Francisco he had encountered the vigilance committee of 1856 as it took over the city and hanged two opponents. In Kansas he had seen firsthand the consequences of a Civil War that had broken out between pro- and antislavery forces. He even saw in the efforts of the underground railroad a disrespect for law and the disruption of order. And he protested a world in chaotic flux:

The law is and should be our king; we should obey it, not because it meets our approval but because it is necessary to every system of civilized government. For years this tendency to anarchy has gone on till now every state and county and town through the instrumentalities of juries either regular or lynch masks and enforces their local prejudices as the law of the land. This is the real trouble, it is not slavery, it is the democratic spirit which substitutes mere opinions for law.[2]

The war brought Sherman an opportunity to bring discipline to that society and to build a career doing so.

His wartime work began without much fanfare. He was at the first Battle of Bull Run, commanding his portion of the field well, but around him the Union forces disintegrated and he had to join the retreat. Then came a transfer to Kentucky and an environment that unnerved him. Forecasting a war that might last decades, Sherman got raw recruits in meager numbers while McClellan seemed to receive everything he asked for and more. Sherman's territory was vastly larger than McClellan's, but requested reinforcements went east rather than west. Furthermore, Kentucky seemed to him to be swarming with disloyal and dangerous civilians. Sherman took to fretting publicly about his plight and firing off letters to McClellan and Lincoln demanding support, telling the world that he was vastly outnumbered and that the war might last thirty years. Concurrently he was alienating the press by ordering them away from his soldiers. The mixture finally exploded when a Cincinnati newspaper proclaimed, "General William Sherman Insane!"

Sherman was relieved of command and sent home for a rest and then, gradually, under the solicitous eye of his family and General Halleck, regained his health. Halleck slowly increased Sherman's responsibility until once again he was ready to resume a major role in the war. Grant emerged as the major influence on Sherman. The friendship, begun when Halleck and Grant had quarreled after Donelson, now began to flower. The two men, whose childhood and early maturity had seen loneliness and economic disaster, now found an empathy that strengthened their mutual respect. Late in the war Sherman summed up the friendship: "He stood by me when I was crazy and I stood by him when he was drunk; and now . . . we stand by each other always." That friendship would one day forge victory.[3]

The first union of their talents took place at Shiloh. Sherman's divisions took the first shock of the Confederate surprise attack on the first day. Four horses were shot from under him; he was grazed twice by bullets. But Sherman's men held, and by the next day Grant had brought in reinforcements and the bloody, brutal victory was won. The generals agreed about the meaning of that battle. After Shiloh Grant said, "I gave up all idea of saving the Union except by complete conquest." Both understood that to successfully wage this war required constant offensive; pushing, forcing the South to use up men and resources. Sherman would add a dimension to that strategy that would link him inextricably with words spoken long after the war was over: "War is hell." He would bring the war to the homes and farms of Southern people, tearing through the stomach of the rebel nation.

But that event lay in the future. After Shiloh Sherman moved to a command in Memphis. There his theater included the Mississippi River and its banks, and he met war at its most brutal. Not all of his enemies were organized troops. Partisan bands preyed upon traffic in supplies and troops. They ambushed patrols, fired on boats from trees and bushes along the riverbanks. Reports came in of guerrilla brutalities in the Unionist regions of Appalachia, where divided loyalties led to ambushes and atrocities: hangings, reprisals against civilians. Sherman increasingly understood that his enemy was not just the armies of Dixie. The populace itself sustained enemy will, he believed, and were responsible for the consequences of the war they nurtured.

Sherman struck back. For every boat fired upon, he ordered, ten known pro-Confederate families would be expelled from Memphis. When guerrillas near Randolph, Tennessee, fired on riverboats Sherman's men burned that village down. Should such partisan attacks continue, Sherman warned, he would fill riverboats with captured guerrillas and use them for targets of Union cannon. These were threats he never carried out, but they showed the broadening brutality of the war. Taken in the context of the July 1862 Confiscation Act and Grant's August order that his troops live off the enemy countryside rather than rely on supply trains, Sherman's threats helped announce the coming of total war. He proclaimed this new day in October 1862: "We cannot change the hearts of the people of the South," he wrote Grant, "but we can make war so terrible that they will realize the fact that however brave and galant [sic] and devoted to their country, they are still mortal." And this lesson was not only legitimate as a tactic, it was also justified on moral grounds. To people who submitted "to rightful law and authority, all gentleness and forbearance," but for "such as would rebel against a Government so mild and just as ours was in peace," Sherman envisioned the fate of "Satan and the rebellious saints of Heaven."[4]

Grant was not inclined to discuss the meaning or purpose of the war so garrulously as his friend Sherman. Grant's deeds bespoke his philosophy. But while Sherman acted, battling frustrations and brutalities of the river's partisan war, Grant had to wait before continuing his war making.

He waited because Halleck geared the Western campaigns down to a steady crawl into the South, fortifying occupied territory, organizing the army, gathering supplies. The tactics resembled McClellan's in the East, but Halleck got away with it. His generals could point to past victories. McClellan could not.

Meanwhile, with most Americans looking east, there was major Western action in late 1862. At Corinth Rosecrans had further tightened the Union grip in northern Mississippi. "Old Rosey" and Don Carlos Buell secured Kentucky and most of Tennessee for the Union in battles at Perryville and Murfreesboro as the year changed to 1863.

In the East as McClellan pulled away from the peninsula the second Battle of Bull Run demonstrated the skills of Lee and Longstreet, and Stonewall Jackson showed his genius. He kept a force two and a half times larger than his own tied up in the Shenandoah Valley and then turned to join Lee at Bull Run. Only the bloody stalemate at Antietam gave Union supporters a modicum of hope. But McClellan's inertia led to his removal, and then the slaughter at Fredericksburg and Hooker's defeat at Chancellorsville brought grief and desperation to the North. But Grant was beginning to move toward Vicksburg, where he would manifest the qualities that helped him become the North's most admired general and its most compelling symbol.

Vicksburg dominated the Mississippi River between Memphis and New Orleans. Passage up or down the river was next to impossible without the consent of the rebels. With Vicksburg in rebel hands the western Confederacy, including Arkansas, Louisiana, and Texas, was still linked to the East. Vicksburg symbolized a united Confederacy and blocked huge shipments of Midwestern products overseas and to the East. The Illinois president worried so much about Vicksburg that he set General John McClernand to work recruiting a new army to take the city even as Grant was moving on it.[5]

Grant's taking of Vicksburg combined dogged determination, a quiet willingness to subordinate military to political leadership, plus tactical and strategic brilliance that his other qualities somehow managed to obscure. The campaign took almost half a year, and even that delayed victory worked to Grant's advantage, endorsing the vision of a man undaunted by delay, defeat, or disappointment.

The campaign began late in 1862 with two repulses. By early January 1863 the Federals began to dig a canal across from Vicksburg to divert the Mississippi and thus gain a more secure basis for attack. This failed, and so did an attempt to go around the city in a four-hundred-mile detour, an effort to slog through the Yazoo Delta northeast of the city, and a move through Steele Bayou directly to the north.

Weeks and months slipped by and still Grant hung on. He believed that the canal-digging efforts were misdirected, but he pursued them because Lincoln urged him to do so. Then it was Grant's turn to take charge. Audaciously and brilliantly, in the face of arguments even by Sherman that he was wrong, Grant moved his army west of the river, marched down the Louisiana shore below Vicksburg, recrossed the river, and cut the city off from the eastern Confederacy. Two armies stood ready to stop him, one at Jackson, the other in Vicksburg itself. But at Port Gibson he defeated the first, then moved toward Jackson where he drove away the second. In eighteen days his forces marched two hundred miles, won four battles, and inflicted eight thousand casualties upon the enemy. By mid-May 1863 almost thirty thousand Confederates were under siege within Vicksburg. In a month and a half it was all over. Vicksburg surrendered on July 4, 1863. The "father of waters goes again," Lincoln said, "unvexed to the sea." The Confederacy was cut in half, and the North found the military hero it had been seeking.[6]

After Vicksburg Grant's star drew all eyes. Although Meade had commanded at Gettysburg and won his victory on the same day as Vicksburg fell, Grant was the man who fascinated the people. Biographies flowed from the presses, ranging from *Grant and His Campaigns* to *Our Great Captains* to *The Boys' Hero.* Newspapers celebrated him in almost every issue; so did magazines. The ladies of Rochester, New York, asked for a lock of his hair to auction off at their Christmas bazaar. By 1864 he was probably the most popular man in the United States, and even received twenty-two votes nominating him for president at the Republican convention. "The great man of the day—perhaps of the age," Strong called him.[7]

Grant the hero did not look heroic; that was one of the reasons he became one. He was five feet eight and weighed only about 135 pounds. He walked and sat with a slight slouch and so looked smaller than he actually was. "Thin in flesh and very pale in complexion," O. O. Howard described him, "and noticeably self-contained and retiring." A correspondent of the *New York Herald* thought he looked like "a little old man" during the battle of Chattanooga. Personality matched unpretentious looks. "The most modest, the most disinterested, and the most honest man I have ever known," Charles A. Dana wrote. His dress was constantly described as at best casual. He did not glorify himself or seek publicity. After Vicksburg he and his son visited St. Louis and quietly registered at a hotel as "U. S. Grant and son, Galena." The gesture suited him. When called to Washington in 1864 to assume command of all the armies, he registered as "U. S. Grant, Chattanooga," walked to a White House reception without an entourage of aides, and stood in the lobby waiting to be seen by the president.

By the time that Grant emerged the nation had had enough of the paladins of war's early days. Crisp uniforms and Napoleonic bravado lay submerged in the blood and the death. Declarations of impending total victory had been drowned out by gunfire and the cries of the wounded and dying. The war had moved out of the hands of the peacocks and into the hands of the people, hundreds of thousands of citizen soldiers whose heroism consisted in simply hanging on and slugging it out. Grant was the general for that kind of war.

He seemed such an awesomely common man, little interested in theories of warfare, determined to fight with brutal practicality. An officer in the Vicksburg campaign caught how time had changed the war in changing commanders. "Here was no McClellan, begging the boys to allow him to light his cigar by theirs, or inquiring to what regiment that exceedingly fine marching company belonged. . . . There was no nonsense, no sentiment; only a plain businessman of the public there for the single purpose of getting that command over the river in the shortest time possible."[8]

The aura of averageness pervaded Grant's relationships with friends and family. His staff was generally efficient and able, but included no allegedly brilliant military commanders or strategists, no philosophers of war and tactics. They were practical common men like himself, businessmen, lawyers, engineers, in peacetime. And closest of all to the commander was John Rawlins, a poor farmer's son who had made it to the post of Galena city attorney. Most were friends as well as colleagues, comrades a man would want to make camp with.[9]

And Grant was publicly, obviously, unabashedly a family man, reliant on his strong wife Julia (who actually outweighed him), and devoted to his children. He took his son with him on official business and brought the family to camp when there was no campaigning to do. Photographers delighted in taking pictures of the family and spreading them throughout the country. Lithographs of Grant and his daughter Nelly were popular items at county fairs and in city shops.[10]

Perhaps the most striking sign of Grant's commonness, his image as the simple earthy workingman, was his drinking. When alone or despondent Grant drank too much. Once or twice during the war this happened. But when actively campaigning he stayed sober and won victories. Here was a man that ordinary men could understand. He liked his whiskey but could do a job when he had to. At a time when patrician reformers had attacked liquor as the curse of the working classes, Grant stood as living proof (maybe even 100 proof) of the ignorance of that arrogance.[11]

The rise of Grant, the acceptance and approval he had won, spoke not only of the inherent strength of the American people. His victories endorsed the economic and social system. The material resources that the nation was able to bring to bear against the South were a factor in that validation. Lincoln boasted in his last message to Congress that the North was stronger and more wealthy than it had been before. But equally impressive, the war had shown that common, ordinary, hardworking, persevering people could achieve success.[12]

The North best saw Grant in the myriad popular biographies that his success inspired. In describing and creating a cultural hero, his admirers affirmed and revealed the culture's values. In 1864 Colonel Theodore Lyman said of Grant, "He is the concentration of all that is American." His story, told to fascinated readers, revealed what being American meant to people of his age.

The life that pulp writers described (and often made up) was one from boyhood to supreme command, where dogged perseverance, and not natural brilliance, was constantly rewarded. While a child in school, one biography "recalled," Grant "had a difficult piece of work placed before him by his teacher, and it seemed to puzzle poor Grant's brains more than any other of his preceding studies." The teacher told him, "You can't master that task." Grant asked what "can't" meant. The teacher simply repeated, "You can't." Grant then went to the dictionary to find the word "can't," and it wasn't there. Grant boldly told the class that "can't" was not in the dictionary. The announcement delighted teacher, students, and Grant himself, and the future general never forgot that lesson. Of course, he mastered the original difficulty, too. The moral was repeated when Grant entered West Point. There he slowly and tenaciously studied material that the other students seemed quickly to grasp, for "having nothing of that dashing brilliance which is thought so much of," Grant needed to work harder. But he learned lessons better and built a better foundation for himself, a foundation that would lead him to command over every classmate at West Point who served in the war. These stories were paradigms for his future success, for "for true talent will ultimately make its way, no matter how modest the possessor may be and notwithstanding all the opposition that may be placed in its way by others."

And, of course, the biographers insisted that the not too brilliant general had risen from poverty. At a time when the nation was growing increasingly aware of poverty and frustrated dreams, it was indispensable that its heroes seem to be poor men who had fulfilled their hopes. So it had been with Grant. His early failures were mentioned but explained away; they were not due to personal weaknesses but because other, less scrupulous men did not pay him the debts they owed. Grant paid all of his debts faithfully but was not himself a good successful collector of debts. Unlike many debt collectors, Grant had "a truthful and honest soul," and when he was told that a debtor had no money he believed the poor man and did not trouble him again.[13]

Grant the man explained and justified Grant the general. His way of war reflected his character, and as that character was symbolic of the nature of the war, Grant's war making has come to stand for the American way of war. For one thing, that image is one of total war demanding unconditional surrender. The happy conjunction of his initials with his phrase "unconditional surrender" guaranteed that no one would easily forget the character of the war he was waging for the Union. Nothing would stop him as he moved inexorably toward victory. He would not negotiate, he would not retreat. Once aroused, the American people were supposed to be like that, too, implacable as they moved toward the ultimate and total defeat of the enemy.[14]

Grant, like Sherman, reflected that total commitment. He also fought like him. He was willing to have his men make war on the South and not just its armies, to shoot Southern partisans who bushwhacked his men, to wage a war of annihilation every day, day after day, in campaigns that ground out casualties and set crosses row on row. As Russell Weigley has observed, "He developed a highly uncommon ability to rise above the fortunes of a single battle and to master the flow of a long series of events, almost to the point of making any outcome of a single battle, victory, draw or even defeat, serve his eventual purpose equally well." Nothing could stop Grant's hammering toward success.[15]

As he had fought at Vicksburg, he fought at Chattanooga. Like Vicksburg, the city of Chattanooga had inestimable strategic value. Guarding a gap in the Cumberland Mountains, it dominated the Tennessee River. As the junction of the two east-west railroads that the Confederacy had, it was a gateway to Atlanta's industry, to the rich farmlands of Georgia. It also guarded the Southern approaches to the mountains of east Tennessee. Even as Gettysburg and Vicksburg were falling, Rosecrans, through brilliant maneuvering, was backing Braxton Bragg toward Chattanooga, and by September 1863 Bragg was forced to abandon the city.

Confederate leaders recognized how vital the city was and gathered forces to turn the tide. Two divisions came from Joe Johnston in Mississippi, and 12,000 soldiers under Longstreet were transported from Lee's army to reinforce Bragg. On September 19 and 20 these forces met the Union army in battle at Chickamauga and drove Rosecrans' army from the field. Only the generalship of George Thomas, who held off several Confederate attacks as other bluecoats retreated, saved the army from a complete rout. He gained the nickname "the Rock of Chickamauga." But the Union army found itself almost under siege back in Chattanooga, and the 16,170 Union casualties tinged the early hopes of mid-1863 with grief. The defeat at Chickamauga set some people wondering once again whether the Union should be preserved at such a cost. With the Union forces now bottled up in Chattanooga, greater loss impended. Thomas had said that they would stay there until they starved, and that seemed a possibility.

On October 23, 1863, Grant arrived in Chattanooga as supreme commander of the Western armies. He had earned that for Vicksburg. He found his position the reverse of that in his Mississippi campaign. He was on the inside looking out. Only a single supply line stretched out of the city; horses were dying and soldiers were on quarter rations. But with Grant on the scene, as one officer observed, "we began to see things move. We felt that everything came from a plan." Taking reports from his officers one evening, Grant dismissed them all and began writing orders that turned Chattanooga from a city besieged into a staging area for action.[16]

The vast resources of the North were waiting to be used. In the last days of September, just as Rosecrans had settled into the city, Secretary of War Stanton pulled off the most remarkable feats of transport and organization in the entire war.

Seeing the need to reinforce Rosecrans and to do it fast, Stanton had called a council of war on the night of September 23, 1863. Lincoln, Seward, Halleck, and Chase were there, and Stanton told them his plan—send thirty thousand men from the Army of the Potomac to Chattanooga in five days. The president and Halleck doubted it could be done. It would take five days to get the men out of the Washington area, they argued. Still, they agreed to let him try. By two-thirty in the morning Halleck was telling General Meade to get fifteen thousand men ready to move in twenty-four hours. By noon the secretary of war had assembled the presidents of the railroads to determine the route. Although maps of the railroad system indicate a fully integrated railroad system in the North as of 1860, the maps deceive. Different gauges on different lines, lack of track through some cities, absence of bridges over rivers, all meant that unbroken travel between point and point was an illusion. Stanton and the presidents had to plan the best way to get reinforcements to Chattanooga, and the route was complicated: from Culpepper, Virginia, to Washington, D.C., on to the Baltimore and Ohio to Benwood on the Ohio River, northward across the Ohio by ferry to the train via Columbus to Indianapolis, then to another railroad line and down to Jeffersonville, Indiana, across the Ohio again, this time going south, then by train to Louisville and on to Nashville, and then from Nashville south finally to Bridgeport, Alabama. From there it would be a twenty-six-mile march across the mountains into Chattanooga.

Two and a half days after the first meeting Stanton wired Rosecrans that twenty thousand men were on the way. Soldiers were busy building a bridge across the Ohio to get the men over the river. Eight thousand blacks were impressed into service in Kentucky to change the gauge of the Louisville and Nashville Railroad, station masters rerouted traffic and marshaled the other rolling stock to carry the vast array of men and supplies. At 10:30 A.M. on the last day of September the first men from the East joined the Western armies. Three days later twenty thousand reinforcements, ten batteries of artillery, horses, and ammunition, joined Rosecrans. From Chattanooga General Hooker wired Stanton, "You may justly claim the merit of having saved Chattanooga for us."[17]

The Northern economy and leadership had shown what it could do, but it needed a soldier to utilize these resources. Even after receiving all these men Rosecrans could not change his situation, while the added numbers merely gobbled up supplies. The arrival of Grant changed this, and now the movement forward began. Opening up a better supply route along the river was the prelude to organizing a strategy that would lead to victory in the Battle of Chattanooga on November 24–25.[18]

Once again Grant showed his tactical skill. Confederate forces held a seemingly impregnable position along Missionary Ridge—four hundred feet high along a six-mile front. To the south of the ridge stood two-thousand-foot Lookout Mountain, also covered with gray-coated soldiers. Grant and everyone else knew the almost impossible odds against taking an entrenched position by frontal attack. He sent Hooker to flank the Confederates from the south and Sherman to flank from the north. Thomas was assigned the center so that the enemy could not send reinforcements to the primary points of attack. Hooker's advance was successful; Sherman bogged down. At this point, Grant ordered Thomas to advance up the center, and take the rifle pits at the foot of the ridge. His soldiers took them, but refused to stop. On and on they moved up the ridge. Grant demanded angrily, "Who ordered those men up the hill?" but then, along with Thomas, watched thrilled as the men advanced to the top, sending the rebel army in headlong flight. At the top of the ridge the scene was "as wild as a carnival. . . . Men flung themselves exhausted upon the ground. They laughed and wept, shook hands, embraced; turned round and did all four over again." Their commander general Granger made it to the top shortly after and shouted, "Soldiers, you ought to be court-martialed every man of you, I ordered you to take the rifle pits and you scaled the mountain." But there were tears in his eyes.[19]

Chattanooga insured Grant's elevation to leadership of all the Union armies and built the image of Grant the unconquerable. The battle also linked Grant's name with the victory of the common soldiers. The apparently unplanned charge by Thomas' men up Missionary Ridge so clearly illustrated the courage of the soldiers in the ranks that even if Grant had been reluctant to let the men go, they had shown that armies under him took seriously the ideals of a people's contest, which he had come to symbolize.

Grant went east to take over the supreme command of all armies in the field. The rank of lieutenant general was resurrected, and he became the first man since George Washington to hold it without brevet. His popularity was at a peak, and hope rose that the West might come to the Potomac and bring its ways of victory. But a different kind of war and Robert E. Lee were both waiting. It would be in the East where Grant's image of tenacity would be tinged with the image of Grant the relentless butcher. And the nation would learn the true costs of unconditional surrender as it lost many of its illusions.

With Grant gone, Sherman took command in the West, poised looking south toward Atlanta, and then moved inexorably into Dixie's heartland. Rebel commander Joe Johnston stood in the way, and Johnston knew every trick of defensive warfare, but Sherman moved on. Every mile was costly, but Sherman advanced. He knew the skill that Johnston was employing, admired and hated it at the same time, and he wished that somehow someone less capable faced him. Then, remarkably, Sherman's wish was granted. Jefferson Davis wanted a victory, and "Retreating Joe" Johnston could only give him stalemate. John Bell Hood was called in to replace Johnston. Hood took the offensive and demonstrated again the murderous advantage that defending riflemen had in battle. By August 1864 Atlanta, the second largest city in the Confederacy, was almost surrounded by Sherman's army. Hood's lines contracted further to the outskirts of the city. Sherman determined that he did not have enough men to garrison the city. He wrote Hood to announce that he planned to send all the civilians out of Atlanta. He asked Hood to help him with the evacuation process.

Hood howled in protest. In a letter sent both to Sherman and to the Southern press the rebel general declared, "The unprecedented measure you propose transcends, in studied and inglorious cruelty, all acts of war ever before brought to my attention in the dark history of war." Since both Northern and Southern armies had removed people from their homes to maintain control of a territory, Hood was wrong. Furthermore, in the context of a conflict that had already witnessed William Quantrill's murder of over 150 men in Lawrence, Kansas, in August 1863 and the murder of black and white prisoners at Fort Pillow in April of 1864, Hood's charges rang rather hollow. Sherman had made every effort to provision and transport the approximately 1,600 Atlantans to safety and asked Hood's help in doing so.

But more was at stake than the disposition of Southern refugees. Hood tried to make propaganda points out of the military situation. Sherman knew that game, and he responded to Hood's letter with a propaganda blitzkrieg of his own. In words targeted to Northern observers and Southerners in greater Dixie, the Union general scolded Hood: "In the name of common sense I ask you not to appeal to a just God in such a sacrilegious manner. You who in the midst of peace and prosperity have plunged the nation into dark and cruel war. . . . If we must be enemies let us be men, and fight it out as we proposed to do, and not deal with such hypocritical appeals to God and humanity. God will judge us in due time."[20]

When the mayor and city council of Atlanta filed their own protest to Sherman, the answer also resounded in the press. "You cannot qualify war in harsher terms than I will. War is cruelty and you cannot refine it, and those who brought war into our country deserve all the curses and maledictions a people can pour out. . . . You might as well appeal against a thunderstorm. . . . I want peace, and believe it can only be reached through armies and war, and I will ever conduct war with a view to early and complete success. But my dear sirs, when peace does come, you may call upon me for anything."

Both letters also catalogued Southern outrages: removal of Union families, destruction of unarmed ships, confiscation of property, attacks on soldiers who had been in the South in 1861 to protect the populace against "Negroes and Indians." Sherman also accused Hood of defending Atlanta from positions so close to the city that Atlanta could not but suffer destruction in the fighting. But his main point was that Hood and the entire South had attacked the noblest government on earth and thus had threatened the stability and order that were the foundation of peace. "You cannot have peace and division of our country. If the United States submits to a division . . . it will not stop but will go on until we reap the fate of Mexico, which is eternal war."[21]

The North cried, "Amen!" "A model of condensed history," the *Cincinnati Commercial* declared. Charles Francis Adams, Jr., wrote to his brother Henry in London, "What do you think of Sherman's letter to Hood? What a 'buster' that man is. He really seems to be the most earnest and straightforward of the whole war. In him and in him alone we seem to get a glimpse of real genius. Here is the most scathing exposition of rebel nonsense . . . which has yet enlightened the world."[22]

The essence of Sherman's message was not that men as soldiers might do whatever they wished to punish their wartime enemies. Contrary to philosopher Michael Walzer's view, Sherman's idea of war was more description than doctrine. It expressed the recognition that modern war is a horrible thing and that those who unleash it would learn the extent of the crime they are guilty of. To learn this lesson they must experience the pain that they have set in motion. Once they see that war is cruelty and not glory, they will cease to support it, and peace will follow. The path of retribution was the path to peace.[23]

Sherman the bringer of retribution echoed in Southern minds as he had hoped. But there was another Sherman, scalded by accusations of alleged barbarity. "Hood knows as well as anyone that I am not brutal or inhuman," he told a Southern minister. The carnage of war affected him deeply. He would say sincerely to an old Southern friend:

Your welcome letter . . . came to me amid the sound of battle and as you say little did I dream when I knew you, playing as a schoolgirl on Sullivan's

Island beach that I should control a vast army pointing . . . toward the plains of the South.

Why, oh, why, is this? If I know my own heart it beats as warmly as ever toward those kind and generous families that greeted us with such warm hospitality in days long past. . . .

And yet they call me barbarian, vandal, a monster. . . . All I pretend to say, on earth as in heaven, man must submit to some arbiter. . . . I would not subjugate the South . . . but I would make every citizen of the land obey the common law, submit to the same that we do—no more, no less—our equals and not our superiors. . . . God only knows how reluctantly we accepted the issue, but once the issue joined, like other ages, the Northern races, though slow to anger, once aroused are yet more terrible than the more inflammable of the South. Even yet my heart bleeds when I see the carnage of battle . . . but the moment when the men of the South say that instead of appealing to war they should have appealed to reason, to our Congress, to our courts, to religion, and to the experience of history, then I will say, peace, peace.[24]

But the public Sherman was not a man of peace. By his own efforts as propagandist and by the military role he was destined to play, he became the image of the stern uncompromising general, his army a terrible swift sword, inexorably sweeping toward Union victory. That army swept into Atlanta on September 2, 1864, and he telegraphed Washington, "Atlanta is ours and fairly won." The fall of the city helped to produce victory in the elections of 1864, and it also provided the staging area for the great sweep through Georgia that has forever been associated with Sherman.

Here Sherman's army lived up to the reputation he had built. They took what they required for supplies from the farms and plantations of the South. They destroyed what they did not need. His march went down in Southern annals as perhaps the most brutal act of the conflict. But it needs to be understood that the brutality of the march was asserted in the context of Hood's accusations and Sherman's widely broadcast threats of the terrible consequences of continued opposition to Union rule. There is no doubt that the march was devastating, but whether it deserves to rank with the most horrible deeds of modern war is questionable.

Vast amounts of property were destroyed. Guerrillas who fired on the army were hunted down and executed. But destruction of enemy property and execution of guerrillas fell within the existing rules of warfare. Civilians suffered undoubted hardship, but there were no documented cases of unarmed civilians being murdered. Rape was similarly almost unheard of. From time to time the Union soldiers got out of hand in their foraging, but their excesses did not even approach the horrors of more modern wars. Victims of the war in Vietnam, for example, would have been grateful indeed if their war had been as restrained as this one was.

The march of Sherman's army stood at the beginning of modern warfare, a warfare in which the will of societies and not just the army in the field became the target. The purpose of the war was not just to conquer enemy troops but to undermine the will of the nation. Southern hopes for victory rested upon war weariness in the North. Northern hopes similarly rested on teaching the rebel society the cost of making a rebellion. Once societies became targets, war would be experienced not only by soldiers but by those they left behind. To that extent the Civil War raised the level of war's brutality.[25]

On the other hand, the Civil War actually advanced the international law of war toward more humane standards, even while nurturing new concepts in war. This was the first war in which rebels were considered to be within the restraints of international law. Previously the laws of war permitted rebels to be killed indiscriminately. Prisoners of war, even women and children, were all legitimate victims if they were rebels. Sherman's army expanded the destruction of war, but fought under a new code of conflict developed by German-American Francis Lieber that protected rebels and helped to restrain the impact of war. In addition, of course, restraint was necessary because rebels might retaliate. But Sherman's army, faced with small danger of such retaliation at this stage of the war, almost unanimously respected that code and waged total war against the property, not the lives, of Confederate civilians.[26]

They wreaked havoc in Dixie. Setting out from Atlanta on November 16, 1864, Sherman's sixty thousand men destroyed everything that might be useful to rebel armies. Their target went beyond physical destruction. If a Union army could march unimpeded through the belly of the Confederacy, no foreign nation could think of aiding the disemboweled South, and growing numbers of rebels would escalate their demands for peace.

As the army brought victory to the Union cause, however, it also generated new perceptions about the meaning of the conflict. People of the North followed the progress of Sherman's army. They could see the surging of the tide of victory. But they understood the meaning of that victory through the type of story that the media of the day told about Sherman and his army.

The progress of that army generated an outpouring of books, articles, and editorials creating Sherman's story. It was a story that told the people what their heroes were, what the people were capable of, what they were fighting for, what war was doing to their society. By 1865 Northern readers would be able to choose from half a dozen instant books and countless newspaper and magazine articles on Sherman, full of stories of his life, descriptions of his battles, excerpts from his dispatches and correspondence, all parts of a portrait of what the war meant.[27]

The army showed realistically what the war meant. Sherman's words articulated ideas and images that showed Northern power and justified its wrath. The popular literature supplied descriptions that gave these actions a tone that resonated with the self-image of the North as it sped to victory. Descriptions of the army spoke of speed and boldness, the unstoppable advance of a locomotive clearing the way for a modern America crushing the backward and traditional South. Images of railroads being built, of bridges being constructed, of mountains of supplies being organized for victory, emerged from the words and pictures of this popular literature. Even humor added to the picture. A story made the rounds that some rebels had despaired of blowing up a tunnel to stop Sherman's advance, for "Uncle Billy" allegedly carried spare tunnels in his supplies. Newspapers and books proudly spoke of America teaching the world the ways of modern warfare, proving the superiority of the American way. Sherman became one of the major symbols of the superiority of the modern North.

He looked the part. "The concentrated quintessence of Yankeedom," a Massachusetts soldier described him, ". . . tall, spare, and sinewy, with a very long neck, and a big head . . . all his features express determination." Sherman promoted the picture, insisting that his victory was being won by Northern hard work as well as military know-how. He reveled in the exercise of the very Yankee cleverness that critics north and south had blamed for causing the war. He boasted that he had outfoxed Hood by "a Yankee trick" and explained the fall of Atlanta by contrasting the raw courage of Southern soldiers with the ultimately irresistible force of Northern persistence. "You can beat us fighting," he told a Southern critic, "but we can outmaneuver you, your generals do not work half enough; we work days and nights and spare no labor nor pains to carry out our plans." Combined with the widely recognized success of Northern farms and factories in supplying Billy Yank, the growing discipline of the army, the utilization of complex railroad operations, the coordination with Grant across hundreds of miles, Sherman's analysis validated a Northern society that many had doubted before the war.[28]

But there may also have been a feeling of ambiguity as well about the victory of industrialized society. Prewar literature had contrasted the Southern cavalier, genteel in manner, noble in character, with the irresponsible Yankee sharper, wealthy but amoral in his economic power. Ahab had come from New England, and his relentless will had led the *Pequod* to its doom. Simon Legree had come to Dixie and crushed all humanity and human feeling in his drive for wealth. The stories and images of Sherman's victory also suggest some of the anxieties of the age. There is often applause for the destruction of the rails of Dixie, as though the iron horse itself was at once an instrument of victory and a worthy object of destruction.

The image of Sherman himself perhaps best reveals the ambiguities of Northern victory. In this popular literature his genius is constantly extolled, his fiery, unrelenting sternness is often discussed, but often with some concern about what restraint there might be on all that power. Genius in the nineteenth century often provoked fear. Greatness inspired awe, but greatness might spawn madness as well. And stories of Sherman mentioned the insanity charge in the early days of the war, picturing the man as "nervous, irritable, rude, speaking in short jerky sentences." Writers were at pains to reassure readers that he was disciplined and self-controlled. Yet even then readers could be told of his leading the western armies of the North, characterized by their rudeness, roughness, uncivilized manner. Sherman himself was described by a friend as "a man of immense intellectuality, but his brain is like a splendid piece of machinery with all the screws a little lose [*sic*]."[29]

Balancing this dark picture yet entwined a bit with it were the stories repeated again and again of the religious quality of this army,

stories of hymns being sung on the march, swelling from regiment
to regiment, reaching an army spread over miles. These stories
stood side by side with descriptions of ruthlessness and cruelty.
Melville might have drawn a picture of Sherman and his army:
"Swerve me? ye cannot swerve me, else ye swerve yourselves! man
has yet there. Swerve me? The path to my fixed purpose is laid with
iron rails, whereon my soul is grooved to run. Over unsounded
gorges, through the rifled hearts of mountains, under torrent's bed,
unerringly I rush! Naught's an obstacle, naught's an angle to the
iron way."[30]

Sherman's image was forged in the expanses of the West where,
a roaring locomotive, his army could thunder across the land un-
swerved from its purpose. That was one image of the war, one
suggestion of what it meant to the North. But in the East there was
a different war and a different lesson to be learned, one that would
add another facet to the meaning of the conflict. It, too, would
validate the Northern victory, it, too, would diminish doubts about
the strength and the power of the emerging industrial North. But
where the enemy was Lee and the battlefield was the constricted
bear pit of Virginia, the image would not be one of Frankenstein's
monster, but of Everyman demonstrating a capacity to prevail by
enduring, a heroism born not of genius but of determination.

The Eastern campaign began in earnest in early May 1864 when
Grant and the Army of the Potomac, numbering almost one hundred thousand men, met Lee's sixty-five thousand in the Battle of
the Wilderness. In two days of the most horrible fighting that anyone had seen, Northern forces again and again rushed against
Southern fortifications and were bloodied and mangled. Rebel abilities to quickly prepare defensive positions showed the inappropri-
ateness of optimism that the new commander would bring the war
to a close. The Battle of the Wilderness was fought on the very
ground of the Battle of Chancellorsville in 1863. Soldiers in the
second battle found old decaying skeletons mixed with fresh dying
bodies. After that earlier battle the Army of the Potomac had staggered back to the North, leaving Lee master of the field. What would
Grant now do?

The men were ordered to move out of their camps away from the
battlefield. The past seemed to be replaying itself; Potomac veterans
marched past places they had retreated from before. But when they

approached a fork in the road where they expected to turn north, they discovered that they were to write a different history from that of 1863. Their officers told them to turn south. Word went back along the marching line that they were advancing, even after a terrible mauling. They were not giving in to lick their wounds; they were being given the chance to show their courage, their doggedness, their devotion to fighting if it took all summer, as Grant promised Halleck. Some regiments began to cheer, others to sing. They had to be ordered to keep quiet lest the Confederates plot their movements. They quieted down and moved south.[31]

The cheering would have stopped had they known what lay ahead. They had taken over 17,500 casualties in that two-day battle, and ahead lay the most grisly slaughters of the war. In the days between May 5 and 7 and mid-June 1864 the Army of the Potomac would take over 60,000 casualties, a number equivalent to Lee's total army. Included were over 12,500 at Spotsylvania, and nearly 15,000 at Cold Harbor, where, before assaulting rebel lines, soldiers pinned their names on the backs of their uniforms so that their bodies could be identified. The press and the War Department tried to put a good face on these figures and some believed them, but gradually the facts dripped out and the image of Grant and of the army took a new shape.[32]

In a strategic sense the cheering was justified. For three years the Eastern army had been reacting to what the Confederate leadership might do. Believing in the superiority of Southern troops and generals, and having their beliefs endorsed by rebel victories, Union generals had been on the defensive. Lee was able to frighten his Union counterparts, thus controlling both armies. During the Battle of the Wilderness one commander revealed Lee's power by rushing to Grant in a panic, saying, "General Grant, this is a crisis that cannot be looked upon too seriously. I know Lee's methods well by past experience; he will throw his whole army between us and the Rapidan, and cut us off completely from our communications." But Grant revealed the attitude that would prevail in the midst of the bludgeoning to come. Standing up and removing his ever-present cigar, he answered the general firmly, "Oh, I am heartily tired of hearing about what Lee is going to do. Some of you seem to think he is suddenly going to turn a double somersault, and land in our rear and on both flanks at the same time. Go back to your command,

and try to think what we are going to do ourselves, instead of what Lee is going to do."[33]

What Grant and his generals could do in this theater was, however, limited. The proximity to the Union capital, the enduring force of Lee's army, the restricted topography, all meant that the war in the East would become one of grim and dogged slogging, even as Sherman was marching to Atlanta, then sweeping across Georgia. Both armies had a role to play. Grant, Lincoln, and Sherman agreed on a two-front war, Grant keeping Lee in Virginia while Sherman ran loose. But in that strategy the Eastern army had to fight a war that became a brutal struggle for survival. If Grant's earlier successes had shown that the common man might hope to rise as Grant had risen, if Grant had shown what such men were made of, he now would show the grim reality of that common man's struggle. People had admired Grant for his quiet determination to move forward. They would now discover the cost such movement required. The common man would become a hero for the commonest of virtues—holding on, sticking to the ghastly business, never giving up. One correspondent had described Grant by saying that "he habitually wears an expression as if he had determined to drive his head through a brick wall and was about to do it." This was the Grant that now embodied the quality of the war, and led the men around him.[34]

The war also sculpted new visions of military virtue. By the end of June 1864 most of the hundred thousand men in Grant's army had not had a change of clothes in a month. They fought and marched and sweat and slept and bled in the same uniforms. Correspondents were now describing scenes for their readers such as those pictured in the *New York Tribune*. One corps marched all one Monday with no rations. That night they formed their battle line, digging entrenchments and gathering rations. They had no time for sleep. The next day they were in battle, and in the evening, "on 30 minutes notice, they marched at midnight, marched till morning, marched till noon, marched till 4 o'clock, and then set to work with all their might entrenching." The day had been brutally hot and dry, the dust hung in the air, "yet these . . . veterans, hungry for two days, sleepless for three days, fatigued with relentless marching day and night, all streaming with perspirations, grim and bleary eyed, their hair dusted with whiteness . . . grasped shovels and axes . . . and

sprang to work with never surpassed vigor, and an hour later exchanged tools for weapons and fought with unequaled spirit and
tenacity."[35]

And new conceptions of courage emerged from their experiences. Grant's friend and aide, Horace Porter, noticed new meanings as he campaigned with Grant during the last year and a half of
the war. True courage was not the bold recklessness that had led the
amateurs off to war. In fact, the courage born of passion was sus-
pect. True courage was the courage of 2:00 A.M., when lonely and
exhausted men still found a way to face danger. The greatest courage he had seen was at Cold Harbor, and those men pinning their
names on their backs. True courage manifested common sense; not
needlessly exposing yourself to danger, but rather doing what had
to be done, with discipline and determination. Men were frightened
in battle, they flinched when the bullets flew (the only two men he
had ever known who didn't were a company bugler and Grant himself), but they set their jaw and went forward. Oliver Wendell
Holmes, Jr., wounded three times himself, was also defining courage as almost the opposite of bravado: "That faith is true and
adorable, which leads a soldier to throw away his life in obedience
to a blindly accepted duty, in a cause which he little understands,
in a plan of campaign of which he has no notion, under tactics of
which he does not see the use." John DeForest was learning that a
soldier was a man stoical and grim, who learned "patience and
fortitude under discouragement." And the quiet heroism of the
army, exemplified in the "meekness and grimness" Melville saw in
Grant, found echoes in religious and political thought as well. Horace Bushnell, writing in 1866 of Christ's "vicarious sacrifice," described giving one's life for others as a quiet act that all men might
aspire to. It was "the simple duty of Christ, and not any superlative,
optional kind of good, outside all principles of virtue."[36]

With Lincoln's agreement, James Russell Lowell was defending
Lincoln's cautious policy on emancipation when he wrote: "The
only faith that wears well and holds its color in all weathers is that
which is woven of conviction and set with the sharp mordants of
experience. Enthusiasm is good material for the orator, but the
statesman needs something more durable . . . the deliberate reason
and consequent firmness of the people."

And throughout the North intellectuals were with increasing volume urging on the nation the virtues of endurance and discipline in contrast to what they deemed the simple-minded enthusiasms of earlier days. Holmes contrasted his prewar involvement in abolitionism with a more mature aristocratic code that featured "courage and courtesy . . . high breeding restraining all needless displays of bravery." Young Charles Russell Lowell wrote home of his growing feeling that heroism consisted of something different from involvement in "crude and stupid theories." The true hero was "mighty unpretending" and devoted himself to the practical effort to be a useful citizen. Others were looking to having a practical effect on society by doing jobs that needed doing, and turning their backs on the more self-centered pursuits of the prewar years. They became more interested in service than in self, at least that is how they defined it, although their abandonment of ideals cut them off from attention to causes that went beyond the pursuit of careers and personal fortune.[37]

These images of the courage and grim determination of the Northern armies were molded in an environment of growing discouragement and horror at the costs of victory. The sixty thousand Union casualties in the East in 1864's bloody summer shocked the North, which had once seemed confident that Grant would bring swift victory. Now every day for a month two thousand Yankee casualties were reported, and two thousand homes in the North were thrown into anguish. Opposition was growing from the home front to do something. No one was too sure what that something should be, except that that horrible river of casualties somehow would have to stop. Some Democrats were offering an alternative, a negotiated settlement of a war that they were persuaded had been a bloody failure. And Republicans were feeling that pressure. Some, like the mercurial Greeley, were saying that more radical leaders were necessary, others were saying that anyone other than Lincoln was needed to show voters that the Republicans could respond to the grief manufactured in Virginia and sent north. And Lincoln himself, who had been reading political currents for years, looked at the growing pain and unrest in the North and wrote a private note to himself. "This morning, as for some days past, it seems exceedingly probable that this administration will not be re-elected. Then it will be my duty to so cooperate with the President-elect as to save the Union between the election and the inauguration; as he will have secured his election on such ground that he cannot possibly save it afterwards."[38] But in the army where it really mattered the soldiers maintained their morale. A New England soldier heard some continuous firing and wrote home, "I suppose it's skirmishing, as they don't call anything a battle now without the whole army is engaged and a loss of some eight or ten thousand." He wondered what would happen to them if such action kept on but then said, "But this army has been through so much that I don't know as you can kill it off."[39]

When Sherman's taking of Atlanta reinvigorated Unionist feelings, the election showed determination to hang on till victory. Lincoln was re-elected by the largest margin of any president since Jackson. Indispensable in providing this margin were the votes of the soldiers. Lincoln got at least 75 percent of the soldier vote, and even McClellan's old Army of the Potomac (albeit with many new faces since 1862) gave the general only 29 percent. The army gave a stronger endorsement to the war effort than did civilians. And in so doing, it symbolized to the nation the depth of commitment to the policy of battle that Grant and his armies symbolized. As the correspondent of the *London Daily News* put it, the election showed the North to be "silently, calmly, but desperately in earnest . . . in a way the like of which the world never saw before. . . . I am astonished the more I see and hear of the extent and depth of determination . . . to fight to the last."[40]

As these words were written, Grant's forces were holding Lee's army on the defensive at Petersburg. While Grant would, of course, have preferred to crush Lee in mid-1864, he had achieved a major goal even while discovering the courage and intelligence of Lee and the Army of Northern Virginia. As commander of all Union forces, Grant's strategy encompassed lower Dixie as well as the East. And down there, Sherman's terrible army was loose, revealing to the South that it could never hope to win. While Sherman ran loose, the lessons of war would be inflicted on the rebels. Grant's strategy was to make sure that Lee did not, could not, get loose to stop what was happening in the deep South. Lincoln had described the overall strategy by saying, "Those not skinning can hold a leg." Grant was holding considerably more than a leg, but he was executing the strategy by pinning Lee in Virginia. His relentless assaults meant that the rebel military leader had to stay there, on the defensive, while the unstoppable tide of Northern men and materials finally took their toll. As Lee recognized, once he had to stand and take the pounding, it was only a matter of time. He had once been able to make vivid Northern assumptions about the innate superiority of Southern generals and fighting men. He had been able to raise and nourish doubts about the ability of Northern society to prevail. But now he was facing finally a man, a general, who had triumphed over doubts and who was revealing what Northern industrial might could accomplish and what its people were capable of.[41]

Except for a few sharp skirmishes, the winter of 1864 brought most fighting on the Eastern front to a close. Both armies dug in and waited for spring to thaw the fighting. But when spring came it brought only the ultimate recognition of the inevitable: Lee accepted Grant's April 7, 1865, invitation to discuss surrender terms. Two days later the two men met in a ceremony pregnant with symbolism of the war. Lee was dressed immaculately in a new uniform, carrying an English leather scabbard with gold inlay that held a ceremonial sword. His clean, relatively unmarked boots had handsome spurs with large rowels. He was every inch the Southern gentleman, born in a magnificent plantation manor house in cavalier Virginia. Grant's dress was similarly calculated. He might have dressed with equal pomp, but chose to come to the McLean house in Appomattox Court House directly from the field, wearing mud-spattered trousers and an unpressed jacket. He didn't have a sword or a sash or spurs. Except for the shoulder straps of a general, he wore the uniform of a private soldier. The engineer of victory chose to make very clear the simple Republican character of the victorious Union. Victory would be for the people of the North as Grant had come to see them, and himself as their symbol. It is doubtful that McClellan would have come to such a ceremony dressed like this, but McClellan's war had ended in 1862.

After Grant and Lee left McLean's house, the Union officers began to bargain for the furniture in the room where the surrender had taken place. Sheridan bought the table where the terms of surrender were signed and gave it to Custer as a present for Mrs. Custer. Ord bought the table where Lee sat; General Sharp bought candlesticks; General Capehart, Grant's chair; Captain O'Farrell, Lee's; a child's doll was taken by a Colonel Moore. Almost everything in the room went home with the victors.[42]

One day, long after the war was over, Grant would be forced to write his memoirs. Bad investments had almost wiped out his fortune, such as it was; he was dying of throat cancer, but his family had to be taken care of, and so he took on the job of telling people what the war had been like. The work summarized the man, not just the life. He described what had happened to him and what he thought about it all, from West Point to the end of the war, in direct unadorned language. William Dean Howells described it:

There is no more attempt at dramatic effect than there is at ceremonious prose; things happen that tell of a mighty war as they happened in the mighty war itself, without setting, without artificial reliefs, one after another, as if they were all of one quality and degree. Judgments are delivered with the same imposing quiet; no awe surrounds the tribunal except that which come from the weight and justice of the opinions; it is always an unaffected, unpretentious man who is talking; and throughout he prefers to wear the uniform of a private, with nothing of the general about him but the shoulder straps, which he sometimes forgets.[43]

The *Memoirs* was a great piece of literature, Howells thought, "because great literature is nothing more or less than the clear expression of minds that have something great in them." The *Memoirs* taught that genius was a false idea that consisted "chiefly in the fancy of those who hope that some one else will think they have it." The idea of genius was a "doctrine wholly opposed to the spirit of free institutions," and the world, at least the nation, would be better off without it; for Grant had shown something better, "the mastery that comes to natural aptitude from the hardest study of any art or science." Grant had told his story "as unconsciously as if it were all an every-day affair, not different from other lives, except as a great exigency of the human race gave it importance." But in so doing he had revealed mastery of language as well as of war. And the general had thereby shown the true power and quality of the American people themselves. A people could reveal itself authentically in its literature as well as in the making of war. Grant synthesized both. "We have heard a lot about what the American was to be in literature when he once got there," Howells concluded. "What if this were he—this good form without formality, this inner dignity, this straightforward arrival, this mid-day clearness."[44]

Howells' Grant revealed changes wrought by the generals, the soldiers, and the war beyond the battlefield. The editor's realism undercut the exalted romanticism that took so seriously its arrogant, if awesome, heroes. Like Mark Twain, Howells lived in a world that was destroying the "Sir Walter Scottishness" of prewar days. Twain did his part by having his hero in *A Connecticut Yankee in King Arthur's Court* literally blow up both Arthur's cavaliers and his world. Howells avoided Twain's bitter cynicism by finding heroism in a commonplace Galena tanner. A world that had produced Ahab and Hollingsworth was gone. The alleged brilliance of McClellan and even of Lee and Jackson faded before Grant's simple, deadly perseverance. Even Sherman's genius had been absorbed, domesticated by his friend's overwhelming commonality. Sherman avoided the public arena after the war, went west to fight the Indians, then returned to a comparatively quiet though extended term of fourteen years as army commander in chief. Grant stayed in the public eye, kept his place in Northern hearts. He served eight years as president, and gave his name to an age. "My family is American," Grant had begun his memoirs, "and has been for generations, in all its branches, direct and collateral."[45]

CHAPTER 13

The Scars of War

T HE generals stood as public symbols of the meaning of the conflict. They organized victory, shaping the choreography of the war, and no one more so than Grant. But Grant's image was entwined with the common soldier's experience. And it was the common man's experience that etched the meaning of war indelibly into the lives of millions. The soldiers and those who knew and loved them felt the deaths, the wounds, the anguish. They provided the Civil War with a staggering and grisly toll.

This war killed more men than were killed in almost all the subsequent wars in American history combined. An estimated 405,000 Americans died in World War II, 117,000 in World War I, 58,000 in Vietnam, 54,000 in Korea, a mere 2,000 in the Spanish-American War. An estimated 623,000 men died in the Civil War. There were almost 500,000 wounded. In the North nearly 360,000 died, and over 275,000 received nonmortal wounds. Confederate totals were similar. One out of 11 men of service age was killed in the war. About 1 out of 6 was either killed or wounded. One out of every 9 soldiers in the Union army died in service. These casualties and deaths took their toll in a population much smaller than in later wars. Had World War II produced the same proportion of casualties as did the Civil War, over 2.5 million men would have died.

Individual battles killed more men than whole wars had done. At Antietam on a single day an estimated 4,800 Americans died. The entire Revolutionary War killed perhaps 4,000. The War of 1812, in approximately eighteen months of war, killed less than half the men who died on September 17, 1862. In the three-day Battle of Gettysburg 7,058 men died, a larger number of battlefield deaths than had occurred in the Revolutionary War and the War of 1812 combined. The Battle of Shiloh killed over 3,400 Americans in the two days of battle. About 2,000 would die in the aftermath. As of April 1862 it was the bloodiest battle ever to take place in the Western Hemisphere. By the end of the war Shiloh was reduced to seventh place among Civil War battles.[1]

The huge numbers of deaths and casualties are striking in themselves, but they obscure a crucial contextual fact. These vast numbers accumulated over the four years of war. Only after the war was over was its full cost known. But it had a more human scale. The war consisted not only of the story of the nation or the Union. There were smaller stories as well. The death reports came in day by day, and they came not to the nation as a whole, but to the thousands of towns and communities that made up the nation. Death notifications did not arrive as numbers but as names in small communities that had known these young men, seen them as children, placed community hopes in them, defined themselves by what these young men might one day be.

The people of the nation did not live the war on a national scale; they lived it from the perspective of their communities. They counted losses in more telling ways. The communities in Worcester County in Massachusetts tolled their dead in small numbers. Phillipston, population 764, sent 76 young men to fight; 9 never came home. Seventy-eight young men left New Braintree out of its population of 805 shopkeepers, farmers, laborers; 10 died in a faraway place. Most of Auburn's 914 people had watched its 97 soldiers go off to war. They knew by name and by personal experience the 15 who were killed in battle, missing, or dead of disease. Worcester, the county seat, had sent 4,227 young men out of its population of 24,960; 398 of these men died. Of the entire county population of 159,659 there had been 19,024 young men sent to fight, and 2,316 of them were either killed, missing, or dead of diseases.[2]

But the story of the war consists of even smaller units: the experience of individuals, who, either ignorant or careless of the larger forces at work, found meaning in their lives within the everyday joys, pains, and abiding comings and goings of their own personal stories. To know the human meaning of the war we need to look at the experience of individual soldiers and of the lives they left behind. Each story was unique, but it echoed hundreds of thousands more.

Sam Haven, Jr., from Worcester, Massachusetts, was almost thirty when the war broke out. He stood at the beginning of a full and promising life. The early tragedy of his mother's death when he was only five was almost forgotten in the advantages that came to sons of well-to-do doctors. His father had sent him to Harvard, following three generations of Havens there. He rounded out his education with two years of medical study in Europe. A small article he published in 1860 suggested perhaps a budding scholar.

The war interrupted any such plans, and Haven was not disappointed. "I hold myself in readiness to start at a moment's warning," he wrote, "and to serve for any length of time." He asked his father's help in securing a commission, and by August he was wearing a new uniform and enjoying it. Apparently he looked impressive in that uniform. Within a month after enlistment an inexperienced unit mistook him for a general. "The whole regiment was turned out, drawn up in a line and made to present arms," he chortled, "all of which I received with becoming dignity."

The early months of army life were busy and enjoyable. He was proud of being solely responsible for the health of his regiment when the other doctors were sick. He reported a little sheepishly that he had been waited on by a slave and remarked casually that a bullet that whizzed by him while making rounds had probably been accidental. One of the things that kept his life comparatively pleasant was the Worcester community, which surrounded him in camp and kept strong the ties to home. People came and went from camp in Virginia to Worcester carrying messages and packages. The chaplain went to Worcester and other towns in the county to give a few speeches about the boys in the field. When requisitions to Washington failed to produce needed supplies, Haven and his compatriots wrote home and had family and friends send what was needed. He got some of his favorite Manila cigars. And the community in Worcester intruded sometimes when it wasn't wanted. One of Haven's letters home got into the hands of the Reverend Dr. Hill, who proceeded to print it in the local newspaper.

But ties to home were increasingly counterbalanced by military matters as the demands of war crowded more and more onto center stage. By fall of 1861 Haven was increasingly absorbed in and admiring of the disciplined army that McClellan was forging. He boasted that the men could march and maneuver splendidly. This seemed to compensate for the fact that "Little Mac's" passion for every detail of drill extended to the medical officers, too. He had ordered "the regular surgeons to drill the attendants in setting up and dismantling stretchers, putting them in ambulances—taking them out—carrying men—making sure that the leading bearer starts on the left, the rear bearer on the right."

Haven saw action, too. At Balls Bluff "the bullets flew like hailstones," and the young doctor worked long hours on lines of wounded men. He described to his father the details of the battle, comforting those at home with warnings against believing exaggerated reports of losses. He was all right, and his father had no need to come to see him. He was proud of himself, and disparaged the work of a fellow doctor who was no help at all when things got rough. He boasted that he was "busier than anyone else there . . . but I stand it very well and feel that I am perhaps doing as much good as I may ever have the opportunity of doing again."

Haven was at Fair Oaks on the Virginia peninsula, too, and escaped death there only when a bullet struck his knapsack instead of his back. He was at Antietam carrying the wounded, working seemingly endless hours to save lives. And then when McClellan was removed Haven's anger was intense—after all the fighting and the dying, after all the work that the general had done to build the army. "There is a strong feeling in the army among men and officers that we are no longer fighting for a noble cause, but are acting as the tools of a set of intriguing politicians."

The new commander of the Army of the Potomac, Ambrose Burnside, determined to be bold. McClellan's caution had doomed him to removal. The press and the public, as well as the politicians who had brought McClellan down, insisted on action. Burnside aimed the 120,000-man army at Fredericksburg and began to move. What Sam Haven thought about his new commander is not known. It didn't matter, for the huge force was under way, and Haven was going wherever it took him.

By late November they were opposite that city, and Haven looked at a scene with a veteran's interest in tactics and his next meal. "The rebel pickets and ours [are] within walking distance. The movement

of the people and soldiers in the city can be distinctly seen. We have
been expecting a great fight every day but in the meantime the
rebels have erected some more batteries and are largely increased
in numbers—and I do not see how we can cross the river without
great loss of life. This is Thanksgiving day and the pleasantest
weather we have had for some time. It is hard work to get any
eatables here but we have been saving a turkey for some time."

Haven had been ordered to hospital duty just before the army
moved to Fredericksburg, but got his orders changed. He wanted
to be with his regiment when the expected action occurred. He was
not far away as the day of the battle approached. He had gone down
to Falmouth to assemble with his men. On December 9 Sam sat
down to write another letter to "My dear father." It was very cold.
The men were building log huts for protection. His regiment was
increasing in size every hour, and that portended action soon. He
had written a "private letter of condolence to Mrs. Spurr on learning of Tom's death." He worried about the irregularity of the mails.
Then, in the middle of writing, an interruption. The regiment had
just received orders to be ready to leave. They were to have three
days' rations and sixty rounds of ammunition. "This looks like moving," he concluded, "and it remains to be seen what will be done."

General Burnside moved out of Falmouth on the eleventh; his
engineers began to build pontoon bridges across the river. For this
and the next day the army advanced into Fredericksburg under the
guns of the Confederate forces on the heights behind the city. On
the thirteenth the battle began—masses of Union forces moved
through the town and outside it, attacking again and again the
entrenched enemy. Four, five, six times the young men charged and
fell, "like the steady dripping of rain from the eaves of a house," in
Longstreet's words. In the safety of his headquarters Robert E. Lee
observed to his colleagues, "It is well that war is so terrible—we
should grow too fond of it." On the battlefield itself there was less
romance. One Union soldier exclaimed, "It was a great slaughter
pen . . . they might as well have tried to take Hell." By the end of
the day the Army of the Potomac had suffered over 12,650 casualties. Among the 1,284 killed was Sam Haven. His regiment had been
shelled while they maneuvered in the town. He had died instantly.

Six days after the battle Samuel Haven, Sr., received the first
condolence letter: "If anything could add to his claims on our grati-

tude," a well-meaning friend wrote, "it is the fact that he fell in the midst of the most sacred of duties—that of alleviating the suffering of his fellow men. Among your consolations in this hour of your heavy visitation is this—that you had such a son to lose. A striken [sic] and heart saddened community mourn with you." They buried Samuel Haven, Jr., the day before Christmas 1862. He was thirty-two.[3]

Austin Whipple was twenty-one when he enlisted near Concord, New Hampshire, in September 1862. He, too, was bound for Fredericksburg. He had been in the army only ten days when he got his first understanding of war as his regiment marched where Stonewall Jackson had fought near Antietam. The contrast between home and war was telling. "Oh, Brother," he wrote, "when we are away in quiet New England our imaginations of horrors of these scenes are nothing but dreams . . . dead horses, mules, and beeves' heads lay by the wayside, fields of corn grain, orchards had been ransacked and destroyed . . . we found some houses vacated, in others were found women, children, and negroes. . . . As we called for drink the women would say they doubted the existence of a God, then they would implore that if there was a God in Heaven he would release them."

The impact on Whipple and his colleagues was demoralizing. "They feel they are held here to be slaughtered, and they see no good coming from it, they see no end. . . . They hate the negro and so do I. . . . Don't enlist!" Whipple began to feel sorry for himself, a victim of immense forces that tossed him mindlessly aside. "A man here," he wrote, "is a mere machine to move when the power is applied. . . . John, was I mad or crazy that I came out here, that I put myself in this bondage. . . . Take heed and stay home, and when you are well enough off be quiet."

Yet even though he hated the army, Whipple was coming to believe that he might survive. In the last days of October he was cut off from his regiment and chased by rebel cavalry, and he could even joke a little about that experience. "What did I think while being chased?" he said. "Well all I thought was come up old horsie, come up!" The fact that he had escaped relieved him. He thought, "There is providence in it," and that he would survive.

Still, he hated "this damned institution" and bawled to his brother, "Oh William I am sick of this life . . . I tell you I am sick of it." He begged for contact with home. "Tell Mother I wish she would send me a word for oh mother I can tell you there is no one left behind who is thought of more than a mother, not only by me but by thousands of poor boys who miss a mother's kind advice and kind care." Yet despite the fact that the army life was ruining his health, and that the soldier's life was "the hardest in the world," "don't worry about me, I have good faith that I'm not to die out here."

Austin Whipple did not write again. A friend sent word that he had been taken prisoner at Fredericksburg. A month later Whipple had to dictate a letter describing a life in Libby Prison, sleeping in a room holding over 170 other men, with lice crawling all over them. He had taken a chill and his lungs were bothering him. On January 19, 1863, a woman visiting sick soldiers in Annapolis wrote to say that she was helping him write a letter to his mother. She thought that the family should know that she had asked Austin his thoughts about dying and he had replied that "whatever the Lord knew was best for him he was ready to acquiesce in." He died three days later. He had served in the army for just over four months.[4]

Whipple, an enlisted man, hated the army, complained constantly of how poorly he was treated, and died after little service. Albert Ames of Oswego, New York, had a different experience. He enlisted for three years in his hometown in the early fall of 1861. The governor commissioned him a first lieutenant in the First New York Cavalry. Every week he sent a letter home to "Dear Family Circle," describing a tour of duty that took him to Malvern Hill, Antietam, Fredericksburg, Chancellorsville, Gettysburg. He wrote about the need for better officers, about hating copperheads, and sometimes about "hot action." Once he recalled "mowing down the enemy like grass." He hoped that Northerners would never see such things on their soil. More often, however, mundane things were on his mind: not changing clothes for weeks, the dampness of the winter, missing letters from home, gratitude for family prayers. And as the war dragged on and the end of his enlistment drew near, he began to resent how the army pressured men to re-enlist after they had served so long and in such places. He was looking forward to coming home. But he did not get out at the end of three years. Military necessity kept him in the ranks before Petersburg a few days beyond his term. Too many. He was killed by a Confederate sharpshooter on September 26, 1864. He had served three years and eight days.

His commander wrote to console the family. He was not a brilliant officer, he told them, but was "so conscientious, industrious . . . implicitly to be relied on under every circumstance." The Sunday School of the Oswego Congregational Church, where he had taught children's classes, passed resolutions in his honor, and sent them to Albert's parents. Someone gathered together compositions he had written as a boy on "Railroads," "Gases," "School Days." His mother and father put these with his letters home and the Sunday School resolutions. And they buried him.[5]

Jacob Van Vleck enlisted near Lansingburgh, New York, in late 1863 and joined a regiment that brought him to the Army of the Potomac near Petersburg, Virginia, by January 1864. He left behind a wife, Emeline, and a young daughter, Mary, about five years old. Emeline missed Jacob terribly. She wrote letter after letter urging him to get a furlough so that he could come back to them at least for a while. She used every excuse that she could think of. They were running out of money; they didn't have enough warm clothes; sometimes little Mary didn't have anything to eat but bread and butter. And there was the loneliness. She begged for longer letters, she wanted to know everything that happened to him.

Sometimes these letters upset Jacob. He had gone to the captain asking for a furlough, but the rules said that they would be granted only for the "very urgent cases." "So I don't know when I will get one—So don't bother me any more about getting one until I get it for it is no use talking about all the time." And he was a little angry with that talk about not having enough money and not having enough to eat. "It is rather queer how you are allawys [sic] complaining of having nothing for [Mary] to wear . . . you have enough money to keep you comfortable in every way. So I want you to get all you both need anytime but I do not mean that you are to waste anything—and I don't believe that you will, but I don't like to have you send me such kind of news every letter—that's all." She could sell the house if she needed to, but "I want to hear nary more about dressing or eating, for I want you to be just like other folks."

Still, he always signed himself "your affectionate husband" and promised that he would make up for short letters with "long stories to tell you at the fireside when I get home again." And he assured her, "You must not fret as I think I will come through anything after what I have come through." And he urged her to "keep up your spirits for I think I will soon be home again." He hoped she would send him very soon some pictures she had had taken.

Jacob relied on his wife, too, for news from home, of course, but also for tobacco and writing paper—no one ever seemed to have enough writing paper. Emeline sewed him a shirt and sent it to him, and he was grateful for it because the winter even in Virginia was cruelly cold and damp. His wife was also his contact with the rest of the family, for news and good wishes, for lending money when they needed it, for little jokes about how Henry was to go down to Kizer's and drink a little rye for him.

In early February 1865 Grant decided to extend the Federal line south of Petersburg, to stretch Lee's already extended defenses even further. The Second and Fifth Federal Corps with cavalry support moved out to Hatcher's Run, and there some of the cavalry got themselves in a fix and were being driven back by the rebels. Van Vleck's brigade went to relieve the cavalry and a bitter fight ensued, Union troops rushing on the Confederates, hiding behind the rails, charging and yelling, firing until their ammunition ran out, then falling back themselves. Just in time relief arrived, but in the confusion they fired not only into the rebels but into their own troops. Federal cavalry crashed through Union ranks, adding to the chaos. But the Union soldiers held on and finally drove the rebels from the field. "I don't know what the papers will say about it," an officer wrote, "but I call it desperate."

Sometime during the retreat of his regiment, around 4:00 P.M., just as relief forces arrived, Jacob Van Vleck was hit. Comrades carried him off the field, rushed him to an ambulance, and started toward the hospital. When they arrived, Van Vleck was dead. The regimental doctor was there when he died and took some letters off his body, along with a piece of writing paper Jacob had been saving to write home on. An officer in the regiment used the paper to write to Lansingburgh the news of his death. "This is part of his paper," he observed, "*this is Jacob's blood* on it—I could get no other to send."[6]

The deaths were only part of the story of battle. In addition to the nearly 313,000 who died of wounds and disease, there were another approximately 250,000 wounded on the Northern side alone. These men carried their physical scars with them for the rest of their lives. The most gruesome reminders of the battlefield were the amputations.

Medical opinion was divided as to the efficacy of amputation. While American surgery relied for guidance on the British experience in the Crimean War, the guidance was equivocal. The surgeon general of England recommended against amputation except in extreme cases. But several other British and French sources urged quick removal to save lives, and the *American Journal of Medical Science* supported this latter view. "The sum of human misery will be most materially lessened by permitting no ambiguous cases to be subjected to the trial of preserving the limb," the editor declared. Although this might at first glance appear to be the most brutal of responses, the journal argued, it was in fact the most humane act. "If the surgeon hesitates in cases that appear doubtful, or if he places himself a little too much on the ground of what is called conservative surgery, he will not be long in repenting of it, and will often see wounded men die in consequence of wounds whose lives might have been saved had amputation been employed."[7]

Doctors in the field often followed this advice. After Gettysburg, Stewart Brooks says, "for an entire week, from dawn to twilight, some surgeons did nothing but cut off arms and legs." Perhaps the most grisly sights that struck soldiers, nurses, and general observers were the piles of arms and legs they encountered outside hospital tents in the aftermath of battles. Theodore Upson recalled seeing such a pile about the size of a small haystack after the Battle of Missionary Ridge. By the last years of the war army opinion had moved toward a more conservative view on amputations, but surgeons had still created a gruesome toll. Gross statistics give some idea of the mutilation that the war brought. The *Medical and Surgical History of the War of the Rebellion* listed the cases of amputation reported during the conflict: 6,229 amputations of the thigh; 5,452 amputations of the leg below the knee; 1,518 amputations of the foot alone; 7,161 amputations of the hand; 5,456 amputations of the whole arm; 1,734 amputations of the forearm; 852 at the shoulder; 189 at the knee; 161 at the ankle. There were almost 30,000 amputations in the four years of war.[8]

Here again, the meaning of such figures can only be understood by meeting individual cases. Private S. H. Decker, age twenty-four, of Company I of the Fourth U.S. Artillery, was ramming his cannon at the Battle of Perryville when the weapon exploded. Half of his right forearm and part of his left forearm were blown off, and his face and chest were badly burned. Five hours later both of his forearms were amputated. He was taken to the field hospital and then to Louisville where he was finally discharged when, after almost three months, the stumps were healed. In the fall of 1864 Decker began to devise some artificial arms for himself, and by March of the next year he had succeeded. He later boasted that "with the aid of this ingenious apparatus he [was able] to write legibly, to pick up any small object, a pin for example, to carry packages of ordinary weight, and to feed and clothe himself." He lived on his pension and through his job as a doorkeeper at the House of Representatives. His presence reminded legislators of the costs of war.[9]

Private Cutler Rist, Company A, Thirty-sixth Wisconsin, age eighteen, was shot at Cold Harbor on June 1, 1864. The bullet broke his tibia, shattering it down to the knee joint. Two days later doctors operated, taking the leg off at the knee. But something went wrong with the operation. By December he was still leaking fluid from the wound and gangrene was feared. Rist asked that they take more of his leg off. On December 15, 1864, the doctors complied, cutting the leg off above the knee. In three months Rist healed, and he was transferred to the hospital near home in Madison, Wisconsin. By May 1865 he was discharged. His doctor provided a picture of him to the surgeon general, looking well, his stump apparently healthy. Rist's pension was paid to him in 1879.[10]

The war seared the memories of the doctors who had spent seemingly endless hours surrounded by its wreckage. S. Weir Mitchell, perhaps the most influential physician of the postwar generation, recalled the months surrounded by "epileptics . . . every kind of nerve wound, palsies, choreas, stump disorders. I sometimes wonder how we stood it." Mitchell coped with the experience by writing the major treatise of the nineteenth century on nerve damage, by writing novels that focused on the psychology of people under stress, by formulating a rest cure for patients suffering from mental depression. But he never purged the war from his mind. As he lay dying in 1913 his family heard him whisper, "That leg must come off—save a leg—lose the life."[11]

As the young men went off to war they left behind private stories, too. And even though the boys' lives were at risk, these home front stories were not filled with constant worry over the possibility of death. Life had to go on in its normal rounds. This was both a practical and an emotional necessity for men in the field as well as women at home. Soldiers writing home demanded information on the routines of life. Their letters asked for a respite from the grim conditions they faced in camp and in battle. They wanted to carry with them a sense of an abiding "real" world to which they could return. Like Edwin Weller from the small town of Havana, New York, they reminisced about skating parties and "Sabbath evenings" and "our ride over to Trumansburgh" and "another excursion to Cayuga Lake," and they thought, even while hearing "heavy cannonading and musketry on the right of us," how they "should very much like to participate in some of those gay times you are having."[12]

In homes and communities of the North practical considerations controlled the routines of life, but even the mundane was entwined with the war. The historian reading letters of Northerners is struck by the rounds of activity that seem innocent of war experience. Letter after letter speaks of visits to neighbors and relatives, new buildings in town going up, harvests good or bad, weddings, efforts at school, practicing piano, trips to the dentist or doctor, work done or planned. Yet as the months and years pass, the war knifes through this correspondence, revealing the dialectic of common daily life in an uncommon time.

Ellen Wright of Auburn, Massachusetts, daughter of feminist Martha Coffin and antiresistant leader Henry Wright, wrote often to her friend Lucy McKim down in Philadelphia. Initially her letters spoke predominantly of domestic activities even as she noted the boys going off to war. But she was finding a wartime purpose even at home. For she felt her role as a woman in the conflict: "Away with melancholy is the tune for us women nowadays—Chirp up . . . stir the fire—relish your lemonade and 'make believe' a little longer." Still, the facade of domesticity sometimes dropped, only to be snatched back again. She longed to be with friend Lucy so that they could have "a good cry together." And sometimes the cry could not be held back. "After I fill this page I shall get quiet again," she wrote once, "and then life as usual. . . . This [outburst] is my 15 minutes indulgence . . . I want to do something tumultuous—I am undecided whether to turn a series of somersaults, or play the funeral march. . . . Good, the page is filled. I turn over with a sigh of relief." Augusta Noyes in Worcester felt the same way. Her letters spoke sorrowfully of soldiers killed: young Charles Norton engaged to a girl in Rome, New York, shot down leading his regiment: "His poor mother . . . his brother has made his coffin. . . . Oh when will it end," she cried, and then quickly, "but I will leave this dreadful war picture and come back to a little more town news."[13]

But the war ground on, and there was no real escape for those back home. Local papers carried battle stories and descriptions, written not just by reporters but by the young men who had fought in them. Soldiers wrote millions of letters home, and hardly a day went by anywhere in the North in which someone failed to get a letter from the men in the field. Single letters often carried news for many members of a community. Soldiers wrote constantly to say that they had seen friends from home, had helped fellow townsmen in preparing for battle, passing on messages to relatives, friends, acquaintances. And such letters frequently carried the first news that a young man had died, was seriously wounded, or was going into action. Letters from the soldiers were community as well as private events. Although few parts of the North would experience the war firsthand, it was constantly in their hearts and minds. There were hundreds of thousands of personal tragedies here. Every man killed was someone's son, and the men were also fathers and husbands and brothers and lovers.

One story from a hundred thousand others: Ellen Wright had come to know Dick and William "Bev" Chase very well. They were her cousins, but also dear friends. Along with Lucy McKim they had enjoyed many happy evenings together, sitting sometimes in the family library in front of a blazing fire. Although at eighteen Bev was about three years younger than Ellen, a romance seemed to be growing between them in the delicate, tentative way of romances of the time. When war broke out, Dick and Bev did not rush to enlist. Dick began work making gunboats, and Bev also found work outside the army. But by August 1862 they had made up their minds to join up. Bev asked Ellen for her approval and she agreed, "not exactly by telegraph, but right away and unconditionally," as she wrote Lucy. It seemed so sudden, but she was sure that "there is nothing that Dick will not dare to do, and nobly, like a hero, & Bev will follow him anywhere." But she worried about these young men and was concerned about how the boys' mother would grieve, "especially for B. her baby." She wrote asking Lucy to join her in becoming a nurse.

Apparently Bev asked Ellen to marry him just after enlisting, but something happened to make Ellen back away. The difference in their ages seems to have been one reason; perhaps the fear of committing herself and then losing him in war made her hesitate. Ellen's older sister apparently argued convincingly against accepting Bev's offer. Whatever the reason, Ellen wrote him asking that they not see each other until he was twenty-one. If they should meet accidentally, she told him, they, of course, would be friendly, but they must not risk a courtship.

Still, Ellen cared about Bev. She wrote Lucy often for news of him. When she heard that he had been wounded and was convalescing in Philadelphia, she asked Lucy to "look at Bev for me, and notice everything and tell me in March. I wish you were coming here with him—What evil genius put that moonshine into my mind?"

Meanwhile Dick and Bev were campaigning in the West. While Grant was beginning his long struggle to take Vicksburg, Confederate armies had advanced into Kentucky, only to be beaten back at Perryville in early October. Union commander Don Carlos Buell had proved so sluggish or so careful, depending on one's perspective, that Lincoln replaced him with William Rosecrans, providing the Chase brothers and 45,000 other soldiers with a new commander. Rosecrans was as professionally cautious as Buell had been but began his movements into Tennessee in early November and then the day after Christmas advanced toward a Confederate force known to be gathering near Murfreesboro. On the last day of 1862 that battle began. For three days of pounding, regrouping, and attacking again, the armies mauled each other brutally: 31 percent of the Union army and 33 percent of the Confederate were casualties. Finally on January 3, two days after Lincoln had signed the final Emancipation Proclamation, Southern forces retreated. The armies could begin to count their losses: 1,677 Northern soldiers dead, 7,543 wounded, 3,686 missing; 1,294 Southern soldiers dead, 7,945 wounded, nearly 2,500 missing. The casualty list for this battle equaled the entire population of Worcester, Massachusetts, Auburn's nearest big city.

Ellen's family surely celebrated Lincoln's proclamation. The news had flashed across the country even as the battle in Tennessee raged. Decades of abolition activity intimately involving her parents and friends had at last brought emancipation. But a few days later the private fears that lurked in the shadows of public celebration became realities. Word came that Dick Chase had been killed in the first day at Murfreesboro, and Ellen cried, "There is nothing earthly worth the life of a young man like Dick." Still, she had heard that Bev was alive and felt "it is so sweet, so bitterly sweet to know of this dear boy safe." But her gratitude was short-lived. Unknown to the people of Auburn, Bev had also been fatally wounded. Shortly he would join his brother among the fifteen young men that Auburn lost in the war.

Ellen's letters after his death say nothing about him. It is almost as if she could not bear to remember him and her letter to him. She writes Lucy of her increasingly active social life and then of meeting William Lloyd Garrison, Jr., of their growing affection, and finally of their marriage, about a year after Bev's death. She would bear the younger Garrison five children, involve herself in the postwar women's rights cause, and live to be ninety-one years of age. But she remembered Bev. When he died the family returned to her the letter she had written, interrupting their courtship. She kept the letter and sometime after Bev was gone she wrote a penciled addition asking for his forgiveness and declaring her love.[14]

War destroyed young loves that might have grown. It also challenged men and women to work out new relationships. Women seem to have been better able to play their expected roles, even while suffering the loneliness of separation. They could extend love and understanding, prepare boxes of food, clothing, medicine, and loving mementos of home. Nursing sick soldiers also provided an outlet for the household and maternal duties that the culture expected of them. A few, like Louisa May Alcott, may have been relieved to avoid their sexual feelings by playing this maternal role.

But men could not easily play their role as providers, and could not easily protect their wives from the little oppressions that women without men could suffer in this society. When Samuel Cormany went to war, for example, Rachel and baby Cora had to move in as boarders with a Mr. Plough, who made things very unpleasant for her: "Mr. P. was to get me what I need but he does not do so," she lamented in early 1863. "I asked him this morning for corn meal but he could spare me none he said. At first he seemed anxious to provide for me & overcharged me so shamefully. Of course I told him of it—since he sees he can make nothing off me he does not have it to spare. He has been treating me more like a dog than a human being with human feelings." When Samuel got a furlough he "had a long talk with John Plough, discussed some of Darling's difficulties, owing to some of his forgetfulness or neglects—am quite certain matters will now and hereafter be more satisfactory." But Samuel had to go back to war, and Rachel was again left on her own.[15]

Yet with all the strains, marriages survived and perhaps were strengthened by the events that husbands and wives shared. Rachel and Samuel lived on together until her death at sixty-two in 1899. Samuel survived her by over twenty years and remarried, and yet when he passed on in 1921 was buried beside Rachel. Edwin Weller, who had courted Nettie Watkins throughout the war, even while she stayed in Havana and he marched with Sherman, married her in November of 1865, and they lived together until his death forty-three years later. She lived on, alone, for twenty years more, and then was laid to rest beside him.

The roles of mother and father were also tested by war. Some women moved in with their families and shared child-rearing roles with their parents and sisters. Others tried to raise their children alone and often feared that their youngsters suffered from lack of the father's authority and discipline. Fathers lost contact with their children for months at a time, and even though occasional visits to the winter quarters by wives and children rebuilt some ties, they could only be tenuous one. In some urban places these separations resulted in a growing amount of delinquency. Fathers lost the ability to control their children. But concern about control and guidance did not vanish when the fathers went to war. From distant battlefields fathers tried to play their role, though the obstacles of distance interfered and the threat of death distorted it.

Even from hundreds of miles away, some fathers tried to provide advice and admonition. There may have been a sense of apprehension involved in this effort. Some were concerned that if they were killed, their children would have lost the guidance and examples they needed to become responsible adults. They hoped to leave a record or regimen for their children, and perhaps even to use their mortal peril as an impetus to build character.

It is hard to imagine a more conscientious father in this regard than New Englander John Cooper. In the three and a half years that he served with the Second New Hampshire Volunteers, Cooper sent daughter Ada a torrent of letters advising her on everything from handwriting to maintaining "a spotless character." She was to write him weekly, visit grandmother Cooper, correct her spelling ("Bad spelling in a letter is *horrid*"), keep a weekly journal, maintain an account of her expenditures, distinguish between hurting her knee "dreadfully" and hurting it "severely," learn what the capital of Turkey was and who was France's greatest general, learn how to begin a letter "properly and neatly and to close in good taste," be diligent in school, and "one thing above all others my darling daughter. Preserve your character unsullied. *Never, Never* do that which will bring disgrace upon yourself. A Woman's character gone! She had better be in her grave or it would be better if she had never been born." All these things she was to remember, for "suppose I should get killed in battle and never see you again, would it not be a pleasant thought to reflect upon, that you had been a dutiful child, and carried out all your father's wishes? And on the other hand if you *had not* how your little heart would be filled with remorse & in the agony of your soul you would exclaim why Oh! why did I not do as my father wished—You would have to regret it all your days."[16]

Individual family relationships were thus tested and at times twisted by the war. The enormous loss of lives, the mutilations, the distortions of distance and absence, all took their toll. Yet despite these personal pains and pressures, observers of the period more often saw a healthy society being spawned by the fiery trial. Nowhere was this more true than in the wartime discussions of insanity.

Although war has often been considered to be a sign of insanity in mankind generally, professionals in mental health during the Civil War did not see much evidence for that hypothesis. There were some who feared that the insecurities of war would unbalance the minds of the unstable. And some early reports claimed as did the Mount Hope Institution, near Baltimore, that in most of the admissions after April 1861 "excitement of the times has entered more or less directly into the causation of every attack." Four cases there indicated to the director that the war unleashed insanity. One patient claimed that people believed him a spy. Fearing apprehension, he would not sleep. A second worried that the government would punish him for disloyalty. A third tried suicide when he believed that he would be held responsible for the beginning of the war. A fourth heard the sounds of armies fighting, groans of the wounded, the shrieks of captive women.

A New York asylum in Kings County agreed that war provoked insanity but was more direct and concrete in documentation. Seven soldiers who were probably incurable had entered the asylum in 1862. However, most of the inmates were not soldiers but civilians, usually women who collapsed when loved ones were threatened: a mother with one son already in the Union army driven insane when she heard that two others living in the South had been impressed into the Confederate army; a young girl distraught at discovering her brother in danger at the front. Throughout the war there continued to be assertions that war and insanity fed on each other. An 1864 essay on malingering tossed off the aside that "the number of cases of insanity in our army is astonishing."[17]

But most of the evidence suggests that the amount of insanity was not affected by the war. Some doctors argued that the discovery of insanity among soldiers was a reflection of the examinations that preceded induction into the army. The army was sweeping in mentally disturbed people in about the same proportion as it was other elements in the population. Certainly the official statistics of discharges for insanity suggest this to be the case. During the entire war only 819 men were dismissed because of insanity. Between Sumter and Appomattox only 2,410 mental illness cases were reported.[18]

From all over the country came reports from mental hospitals arguing that the war had in fact reduced the amount of mental illness in the nation. Asylums in Maine, New York, Illinois, Connecticut, Ohio, the District of Columbia, and even the turbulent border states of Missouri, Kentucky, and Tennessee reported admissions down during the war. "Notwithstanding the destitution and devastation of armies," the director of the Tennessee Hospital for the Insane wrote, "the aggregate population of citizens and soldiers has probably not furnished during the war a larger number of insane than would have occurred independently of war." A Dr. McFarland in Illinois not only believed that the war had made little difference but actually believed that the war had reduced the amount of insanity.

The hardships and sufferings of warfare have made themselves strikingly felt, while the excitements, anxieties, and sometimes overwhelming bereavements of those whose all has been pledged, have hardly made a trace in our records . . . the same devotion which gave fathers, brothers and sons to the chances of the conflict have so nerved all hearts to the consequences of the sacrifice, that even the terrible disclosures of the battlefield bulletins, have carried a few beyond the bounds of temperate grief. Indeed, it may be claimed that the "war excitement"—limiting its phrase to its true meaning—has been healthful in its operation.[19]

Opinions varied as to why the war had reduced insanity. One belief was that men who might suffer from mental weakness found relief by joining the army. The new scenes to which the army exposed them generated new possibilities and directions, which restored health. Furthermore, the discipline of army life ordered their thinking, structured their lives, and engendered self-control. In the struggle between the pressures of insanity and the power of the will to control those pressures, the ordered army life brought victory for sanity.

But the impact of the war reached beyond the army and, in the eyes of observers, contributed to the overall mental health of the society. Prior to the war, it had been an almost unchallenged hypothesis that Northern society engendered mental instability. Advancing into the modern world with breathtaking speed, Northern society gained greater civilization at the price of increasing insanity. "All agree," wrote Edward Jarvis, a leading authority, that mental disorder was "a part of the price we pay for civilization." Isaac Ray, perhaps the most respected expert writing on the subject, declared that "insanity is now increasing in most, if not all civilized communities." When Dorothea Dix fought her campaign for humane treatment of the insane, she appealed to common assumptions by asking rhetorically, "Is it not to the habits, the customs, the temptations of civilized life and society" that America owed its mental health problems? This consensus endured through the mid-nineteenth century as George Beard blamed "American Nervousness" and "Nervous Exhaustion" on the "diseases of civilization . . . of modern civilization, and mainly of the nineteenth century, and of the [northern] United States."[20]

These vague anxieties about civilization had more specific focus in concerns about the ways in which the endless pursuit of wealth fostered an ambition that could lead to madness or at least instability. In this search for wealth, ambition could lead to "mental powers . . . strained to their utmost tension and labor" which could cause "minds [to] stagger under a disproportionate burden," as Edward Jarvis put it. Or in the words of a popular guide to mental health, "The demon of unrest, the luckless offspring of ambition haunts us all. . . . All are equally restless, all are straining for elevation beyond what they already enjoy . . . we go on toiling anxiously in the chase . . . until death administers the only sure opiate to our peaceless souls."

The constant turmoil of politics with its endless cycle of elections, its struggle for spoils and office, also took its share of responsibility for disturbing American minds. So did the involvement of people in testing and challenging the ideas of the past. Both suggested a lack of certainty in an environment where nothing was known for sure. Society fostered an endless diffuse debate with no answers for the seekers. A panting race for goals either impossible to achieve, even to define, or unworthy of devotion—this was the picture painted by critics of prewar society. A disordered society gave birth to disordered minds.[21]

But the war made many things very clear, focused attention on clearly defined and eminently worthy ambitions. It demanded a discipline that not only built mighty armies but gave steel and purpose to minds previously distracted.

During the war observers saw indications that the conflict engendered beliefs and commitments that counteracted the discontents of civilization. The decline in insanity in the North, the director of the District of Columbia asylum argued, suggested that "the mind of the country was raised by the war to a healthier tension and more earnest devotion to healthier objects than was largely the case amid the apathies and self-indulgences of the long-continued peace and prosperity that preceded the great struggle. . . . It is but a slight license to say that the nation laid down its life to save it; and that the national mind rapidly acquired a firmer strength and a higher tone amid the harrowing incidents of such a gigantic and all pervading strife and sacrifice." The director of Ohio's facility also pointed to the "wholesome influence of the diversions of the popular mind into new channels of thought, and popular activity into new and important spheres of labour." "Higher and nobler influences have been called out to antagonize and overcome those natural tendencies to mental disturbance and insanity which ever attend all great social convulsions," the head of the Hartford Retreat for the Insane wrote. "Whatever makes us better or wise, gives us more or correct views of our duty to God and our neighbour, and at the same time gives us more strength, courage and willingness to do that duty, places us so much beyond the reach of . . . insanity, and gives us also the greater ability to resist successfully the attacks of this disease." From Maine's Mental Hospital came the opinion that the decline in admissions "may be owing in part to the new and unusual occupation which has so thoroughly possessed the American mind since 1861. The awakening . . . of that wholesome principle in man—love of country which was slumbering in the heart has seemed to check for a time the onward flow of insanity."[22]

Significantly, when George Beard catalogued the elements of civilization that engendered "American Nervousness" and mental disorders, he did not include war. He did include the rapid development and acceptance of new ideas, increased amount of business, buying on margin, increased capacity for sorrow, love and philanthropy, repression of emotion, domestic and financial trouble, politics and religion, along with liberty itself.[23]

Northern observers were clearly linking their social philosophy with their medical expertise. To large numbers of Northern intellectuals the benefit of the Civil War was that it was bringing needed discipline and high ideals to a society grown materialistic and notably lacking in self-control. Comments on war and insanity also reflected the concerns held in the prewar world over the costs of industrialization and the growth of the economy. In this discussion, too, there appeared the contrast between a rapidly growing, bustling, almost frenetic North and a South that was deemed relatively free from either nervousness or insanity. The discovery that the war on the whole was reducing insanity suggested the possibility that this society was admirable when organized for a noble cause. The vitality of the North was not merely a cause for concern. Northern society apparently harbored within it values capable of uniting strength, action, and sanity.

Some observers did worry that the end of war might unleash an outbreak of insanity when people had leisure to reflect on their losses. Others were concerned that the "unavoidable results of overwork, exposure, excitement and gradual exhaustion necessarily associated with the long continued discharge of military duties in camp and field" would lead soldiers to postwar instability. The large amount of killing, the excesses often spawned in wartime enthusiasm, these elements meant to some that a bitter harvest might await the end of war. But while the war went on, most people involved in the care of the insane saw it as a stabilizing factor, and the statistics they offered tended to support their conclusions.[24]

Inescapably the war did leave mental scars. Some of it was suggested in articles on soldiers malingering. Desertion statistics as well as missing in action figures surely included men whose minds had cracked in combat. A condition called "irritable heart" showed up in hospitals. Dr. J. M. DaCosta followed over three hundred such cases where soldiers experienced dizziness, heart palpitations, and even pain, despite being apparently healthy. The syndrome had a long history from other wars. He concluded that the cause was likely to be that young recruits were forced into strenuous marching before they were ready for it. But modern authorities argue that "irritable heart" was probably an anxiety neurosis connected with combat.[25]

The mental costs of war remained hidden in other places as well. Opium addiction increased markedly after Appomattox, a consequence of a widespread use by doctors of the drug and of morphine to treat pain and even diarrhea. One authority suggested that in the Turner's Lane Hospital alone over forty thousand morphine injections had been given during the war. Although the drug had been given to reduce physical pain, its use also helped to hide emotional and mental scars as well. Not only ex-soldiers, but women as well began to take the drug for the comfort it provided. In 1868 Horace Day, in his treatise *The Opium Habit, with Suggestions as to the Remedy,* spoke of "maimed and shattered survivors from a hundred battlefields, diseased and disabled soldiers released from hostile prisons, anguished and hopeless wives and mothers, made so by the slaughter of those who were dearest to them, [who] have found, many of them, temporary relief from their suffering in opium."[26]

But writers of the war era were not sensitive to the condition of the mind as explaining the wounds of war. The physical carnage provided so many visible scars that only after the conflict was over did it occur to writers to explore the impact of conflict on mental health. S. Weir Mitchell would later develop a sophisticated understanding of the relationship between physical trauma and mental suffering. In 1867 he wrote a short story about the psychological scars suffered by a wartime amputee. He engaged in studies of the mind that illustrated the connections between mental and physical health. He even claimed that he had gained his insight of the mental aspects of disease from his war experience. But during the conflict, Mitchell and his professional associates focused their efforts on studying the neurological damage wounds inflicted. They studied palsy that seemed to follow wounds to remote parts of the body, soldiers who had collapsed after being near explosions even though they were apparently not physically hurt by the blast, and insisted on physical explanations of these symptoms. Before he began writing on "American Nervousness," George Beard described neurasthenia as somehow connected to war experience, but the majority of students of the medical aspects of the war insisted on explaining all the wounds of war as physical. In an environment that insisted on the benefits of war in improving the mental health of society, it was easy to overlook the mental costs. In a society so profoundly familiar with external wounds, the interior remained for a time hidden.[27]

CHAPTER 14

The Coming of the Lord:
Religion in the Civil War Era

N O FORCE shaped the vision that Northerners had of the war more forcefully than religion. Concerns about politics, free labor, the survival of the constitutional system, the continued health of the economy, were vital to them. But religion struck at matters of ultimate concern. It justified their accomplishments, explained their tragedies, consoled and inspired them. Their politicians merged the metaphors of theology with the words of partisanship. Reformers sanctified their efforts by appeals to Christian imperatives. Conservatives counseled prudence in warnings about overvaluing this world. And, of course, soldiers and their families found comfort and strength by looking to heaven.

On the eve of war the nation was the world's most populous and powerful Christian nation. Visitor Philip Schaff observed in 1855 that "there are probably more awakened souls and more individual self-sacrifice for religious purposes, proportionally, than in any other country in the world, Scotland alone perhaps, excepted." He was echoing de Tocqueville's 1830s observation that there was "no country in the whole world in which the Christian religion retains greater influence over the souls of men than in America." Between the two comments the nation had experienced a powerful revival movement that increased the number of professing Christians enormously. Between 1800 and 1850 membership in religious organizations grew from a low of one out of fifteen Americans to a high of one in seven. By one estimate there were over four million church members out of a population of twenty-seven million, and the religious population was rising fast. Between 1832 and 1854, while the population had grown by 88 percent, the number of clergymen had gone up by 175 percent. Nearly seventeen thousand full-time Methodist ministers spread the faith, and another eight thousand did so part-time. Organized religion grew throughout the war era. Between 1855 and 1865 the number of Northern Methodists rose by nineteen percent. Northern Baptists and Presbyterians increased by 28 percent. While membership figures are not exact, they do indicate a powerful surge of religiosity in mid-nineteenth-century America. And membership figures alone do not tell the whole story.

Revivalism increased the impact of religion beyond the church door. Home missionary societies spent half a million dollars a year to pay nearly three thousand missionaries to spread the faith and to teach Christian discipline. Thousands of Protestant Sunday School teachers went to work in Sunday Schools they organized to teach urban children (often Catholics) the moral values they deemed imperative for order and salvation. Hundreds of religious newspapers flooded the land, reaching millions of readers. In 1865 Methodists alone had 400,000 subscribers. Most of the higher education in the country was under religious sponsorship, and at least 20 percent of the students were training for the ministry. Even the popular fiction of the age was dominated by "that damned mob of scribbling women" who wrote endlessly on sentimental religious themes.[1]

The power of religious ideas transcended the pulpit, the tract society, and even the literature of the age. Religion was an inextricable part of the political process. Voting blocs often crystallized around religious and ethnic commitments. Catholic and Lutheran voters were overwhelmingly Democrats. In the North Republican voters were frequently Baptists, Methodists, and Presbyterians. Few Congregationalists and Unitarians ever voted for Jefferson's party. While political questions like tariffs, internal improvements, and constitutional interpretation could be discussed with some detachment, religious and social issues struck home. Fears of alien Catholicism had inspired a massive Protestant reaction in the wake of the huge Irish immigration of the decade from 1845 to 1855. The resulting turmoil cemented Democratic loyalties of the Irish. It helped midwife the Republican party as the Whigs dissolved in part through a failure to respond to such religious forces. While slavery and fears of declining republican virtue also inspired intense political feelings, partisan politics clearly reflected religious distinctions among Americans.[2]

The definition of the nation itself, subscribed to by both major parties and by minor parties as well, had at its core a set of religious values and ideals. So powerful was religious sentiment connected with national identity that G. K. Chesterton could describe the United States as "the nation with the soul of a church." Underlying the image of the nation had always been a belief in a higher and transcendent purpose for America. Puritans had argued that in the New World the Old might see a "city upon a hill" where God's purposes would be realized on earth. Even in the rationalistic environment of the American Revolution the Declaration of Independence spoke of self-evident truths emerging from the laws of nature and nature's God to which this nation pledged its faith. The enduring power of the republican ideal of virtuous and moral citizenship also testified to the religious impulse in American politics. Every presidential inaugural address from Washington to Lincoln (and since) invoked God's blessing and guidance. Lincoln spoke frequently of a nation "under God," which was "the last best hope" for mankind to achieve freedom and self-government.

Prewar revivals gave religious fervor to the American goal of living up to God's purposes. Concern for personal salvation increasingly became linked with saving the world. The success of this second Great Awakening encouraged a belief that the Second Coming was near. While a few churches took that as a sign to retreat further from society, the vast majority of Americans, especially those of the North, were inspired to reform the nation to prepare for the new kingdom.

Targeting the evils of drink, the sufferings of prostitutes, the insane, even the criminals, religious reformers worked to alleviate their pain. New institutions were built to provide the mentally ill with medical care instead of treating them as wild animals. Newly built prisons aimed at the rehabilitation of criminals, not retribution by the society. Especially in the revival activities of the 1850s, urban reformers began to provide actual assistance to those suffering from the economic downturn. Motivated in part by their concern to turn the lower classes into disciplined Christians, these reformers nonetheless opened the door to a concept of Christian charity that would appear in full view after the war in the form of the Social Gospel movement. During the war these concerns would also be seen in monumental efforts to help both the white poor of the North and South and the millions of freed slaves.[3]

Yet as revivalism and reform called the nation to live up to its professions, they could also undercut criticism. In part, revivalism operated as a conscious means of bringing lower-class workers under the influence of those above them. In Rochester, New York, for example, the middle-class leaders of the community required their employees to attend revival meetings and to join churches. They set up churches that were easily available and then went to the churches with the employees. This religious integration encouraged workers in the faith for practical reasons—known churchgoers got available jobs and developed the contacts that would allow them to improve their status. The Lynn, Massachusetts, Society for the Promotion of Industry, Frugality, and Temperance linked the business and religious leaders of the town in an emphasis on the junctures between worldly success and the salvation of the soul. In Rockdale, Pennsylvania, manufacturers promoted a similar Christian religiosity to undercut the freethinking radicalism that had united workers in their town. Revivalism undercut criticism of the basic structure of Northern society and could take pride in the improvements it brought to the nation.[4]

The consciences of the emerging middle class might still be touched by accusations that greed and selfishness brought punishment. When the war broke out, religious leaders joined the chorus of other upper-class intellectuals who spoke of the onset of battle as God's judgment on men who abandoned the Christian Sparta to feast on the fatted calf. Henry Bellows, leading Unitarian and later director of the Sanitary Commission, decried the excesses of individualist materialism. Boston Catholic Orestes Brownson and Henry Ward Beecher demanded that the nation ask forgiveness for the "luxury, extravagance, ostentation, and corruption of morals . . . the grinding of the poor, the advantages which capital takes of labor . . . the spread of vice among our people . . . the intense eagerness to amass wealth; the growing indifference as to methods of acquisition."[5]

But while Beecher and others blamed the excesses of Northern materialism for the crisis, a clearer target was in view. Slavery epitomized so many of the general evils of society that it became the major focus of Northern prophecy and judgment. Human bondage was "the most alarming and most fertile cause of national sin . . . a fountain from which have flowed so many sins," Beecher proclaimed. Because of the combination of greed and slavery, "the whole nation is guilty. There is not a lumberman on the verge of Maine, not a settler on the far distant northern prairies, not an immigrant on the Pacific shore that is not politically and commercially in alliance with this great evil. . . . Our body politic is pervaded with this deadly injustice." And for one sin above all, slavery was most reprehensible. It corrupted the word of God itself—in behalf of slavery ministers had opened the Bible "that all the fields of fiends of hell may . . . walk through it to do mischief on earth."[6]

The sinfulness of slavery was widely recognized by abolitionists. But not every Northern church determined that the proper response was to cry out against the sinners. The imperatives of national church institutions restrained them for some time. The Presbyterians and Baptists attempted to maintain a national church even up to the Civil War. This fact muted antislavery oratory. So reticent was much of the Northern clergy that abolitionists turned their guns on the churches. Some disrupted church services to give impromptu sermons against slavery. Stephen Foster took to calling the New England clergy "thieves, blind guides and reprobates, a cage of unclean birds." The attacks on slavery within the Methodist church led to a split in that church in 1845 between Northern and Southern branches.[7]

The question of the sinfulness of slavery had enough complexities that churches could justify their silence in conscience-calming ways. Some Presbyterians tried to distinguish between the system, which was admittedly fraught with the possibility for sin, and the slaveholders themselves. A slaveholder might still be a Christian if he practiced slavery with humanity, love, and concern for the souls of his slaves. Others argued that slavery per se, being mentioned and accepted in the Bible, was within the pale, but that the system of slavery in the South was sinful. Presumably this might allow a practitioner of "acceptable" slavery to escape condemnation if he could be distinguished from the general Southern system. There was the further argument that to scald the sinner would be to drive him from the church—the very place where he might learn a truth that would one day set his slaves free. Catholics divided over the issue of slavery, but not evenly. Most church authorities accepted slavery as potentially sinful, but not a mortal sin. The introduction of so many heathen to the faith mitigated its evils. Furthermore, Catholic focus on the redemption of the individual soul and a general fatalism about the human condition further undercut declarations of "sinner." The fact that so many antislavery voices were often anti-Catholic further diminished enthusiasm for the cause.[8]

Abolitionist and antislavery ministers and believers might also be rebutted with the insistence that "my kingdom is not of this world." Critics warned that Christians who tried to change the world might confuse Christ's message with their own secular interests. The editor of *Harper's* wrote in 1854 that "the tendency of the present day is to magnify the political, the social, the secular, or what may be called the worldly-humanitarian aspects of professedly religious movements." He worried that the continuance of this trend might enable the world to corrupt the church instead of the church redeeming the world. Speaking against Beecher's political commitments, Adam Badeau complained, "I do not think the pulpit is his sphere; he seems to me a stump speaker who has mistaken his way and stumbled into a church . . . he preaches politics, temperance, abolitionism . . . more than religion. . . . The influence of religion itself is injured, its sacredness lessened, its effect curtailed by such a course." While such ideas could and did justify silencing antislavery critics in order to protect slavery, they were also part of serious concerns that reflected changes in the religious thought of the nation.[9]

But doubts about using the cross to bless the sword were submerged in the outpouring of public feeling when the South fired on the flag at Fort Sumter. The already limited ability of the ministers of the North to distinguish God's purposes from those of the American society gave way to the call to arms. The obvious evils of slavery as practiced in Dixie overcame the skepticism about the purity of Northern ideals. The integration of revivalism with dominant secular values united preachers with politicians in at least a harmony of goals. A religion of the heart swept aside the claims of skepticism. The ideal that man could both know and do what God wished diluted doubts that God and the *United* States were practically co-partners.

The dilemma of the Presbyterian church illustrates the nature of the challenge Christians of the North faced. In 1837 the Presbyterian church had divided into an Old School and a New School. New School forces linked up with New England influences and nurtured an alliance with Congregationalism in the Northeast. These Presbyterians increasingly spoke the antislavery feelings of their flocks. The so-called Old School branch stuck to more conservative paths. While their more liberal brethren urged new church organization, they insisted on the old ways. When revivalism influenced New Schoolers to doubt the Calvinist creed, the Old School forces denounced them as heretics. Not surprisingly, Old Schoolers kept ties with Dixie even as their fellow Presbyterians opposed slavery. Approximately one-third of conservative membership resided in the South as of 1861, and the Northern majority was sensitive to that element.[10]

But with the outbreak of war Old School leaders were unable to withstand the demand for pro-administration resolutions at the national meeting in Philadelphia in May 1861. "Mr. Moderator," one leader said when the time to vote came, "I want to say no, but I must say yes." And the most powerful magazine of the Old School faith revealed just how far even conservative Christians might go in the face of war: "We shall keep the sacred desk free from the discussion of ordinary politics," the *Presbyterian* announced, but "we have never wavered in the belief that there are national crises in which it is required to speak." "It may be well enough to assert that politics should be kept out of the pulpit, but it is carrying the principle too far to shut out the revealed doctrine of government, an ordinance of God, and the iniquity of causeless rebellion."

Individual ministers risked their jobs by being lukewarm about the rebellion. When the associate pastor of a New York church insisted on praying for the governors of both the Union and the Confederacy, he was forced to resign. The minister of the Brooklyn First Presbyterian Church risked his position when he refused to preach in a church that flew the flag and objected to lending church support to the efforts of the Christian and Sanitary commissions. A trustee accused him of disloyalty, and only the threat of a slander suit forced retraction. On the other hand, a few pastors risked their posts by being too worldly. When the pastor of the Chicago church dominated by Democrat Cyrus McCormick got too political in a

Thanksgiving sermon, he felt the disapproval of "some six families to whom God has given wealth." The minister soon sought another church to preach in. But the most common means of dealing with the pressure to link religion with the state was to stifle doubts about that linkage. Even Old School congregations heard one or two sermons every year upholding the Republican government and its war policies.[11]

While most of the faithful had powerful feelings about the evils of slavery, other ideas also made them into crusaders for the Union cause. To endanger the nation that God had ordained with a special mission was to obstruct God's purpose for all of mankind. The *Independent* suggested that the text for the war come from Romans 13, "Let every soul be subject to the higher powers. For there is no power but of God; the powers that be are ordained of God." With that scripture as guiding light, the editors went on to characterize the war in terms that were resounding throughout the entire Northern society. "All other questions are now merged in one: Have we a Government? Is the Union of these states a solid reality or only an airy vision?" A. L. Stone of Boston's Park Street Church also linked human and divine government as the purpose of the fight. "Strike for Law and Union, for Country and God's great ordinance of Government." If free institutions "cannot be maintained here, in the midst of a Protestant population, with a Bible in every house, and education as free as air and in the enjoyment of 'perfect liberty in religious concernments,' " Francis Wayland observed, "then it may be reasonably believed that they can be sustained nowhere. Crushed and degraded humanity must sink down in despair, and centuries must elapse before this experiment can be made again under so favorable auspices."

Even the Catholic church, which had kept aloof from the antislavery discussion, could join in a crusade to maintain the rule of law and a stable society. New York's influential bishop John Hughes announced that Catholics would "fight to the death for support of the Constitution, the Government and the laws." He flew the flag from the top of his downtown cathedral, urged the city's Irishmen to enlist, and ultimately advocated a draft when enlistments lagged. The American Baptist Union saw the connection between God and the Union and hoped the war would link them in greater purity. "The doctrine of secession is foreign to our Constitution, revolutionary, and suicidal, setting out in anarchy and finding its ultimate issue in despotism . . . the wondrous uprising in strangest harmony and largest self-sacrifice, of the whole North . . . is a cause of grateful amazement and grateful acknowledgement to God . . . this resurgent patriotic . . . may in God's judgment correct the evils that seem growing and chronic and irremediable in the national character."[12]

New School Presbyterians gravitated to the imagery of Lucifer's rebellion against God. Believing that "we . . . Americans . . . are here by the ordering of Providence in charge of the final theater and the final problems of history," the general assembly in Cincinnati in 1862 resolved its prayer that "the last sad note of anarchy and misrule may soon die away." When Herman Melville examined the parallel between heavenly and earthly rebellion, he evoked the grandeur of *Paradise Lost.* But few Northern divines saw any correspondence between Jefferson Davis and Milton's hero.[13]

Describing the rebellion as an attack on law and order gave even proponents of peace reason to make war. Before the sectional crisis heated up, pacifists debated the role of the police in a society. Many argued that a peaceful society depended upon the order that police provided. The need for order had helped peace men like Gerrit Smith to make the transition from rejecting all violence to justifying it when the expansion of slavery seemed to make war on Northern moral and legal order. The elements in abolitionist thought that targeted the moral anarchy of bondage, that accused masters of making of war on the slaves, also justified making soldiers out of pacifists. In 1861 New School Presbyterians showed their awareness of such feelings in a call that "those of their followers of the Prince of Peace who have no swords should sell their garments and buy them."[14]

The most impassioned of the religious supporters of the war were the Methodists, at almost 1.5 million, the largest of the Northern Protestant denominations. While Presbyterians revealed varied reactions to war, Methodists were unwavering. They backed the Union effort with such fervor that the slogan "Methodism is loyalty" was born. "The cause of the country is the cause of God," one of that faith's preachers declared, and the message echoed in various forms throughout the land. At the New York Eastern Conference in 1863, the entire gathering took a loyalty oath from a United States district judge and a major general in the army. Bishop Matthew

Simpson became known as "the evangelist of patriotism" for his itinerant revivals throughout the North. The *Western Christian Advocate* in August 1862 stated the Methodist vision of the conflict. The faithful read that their choice was between "Union, Peace, Brotherhood, Liberty, Freedom, and equalizing, humanizing Christianity" on the one hand and "disunion, war, selfishness, slavery and a besotted, barbarous, brutalizing, bastard corruption, and the perversion of our holy religion" on the other. The Methodist *Quarterly Review* was more succinct: "They fight for anarchy; we fight for government. They fight for lawlessness; we fight for law." Northern leaders recognized the power of the Methodists in aiding the war effort. Salmon Chase noted that "I have thanked God that the Methodist church . . . knew only one sentiment, that of devotion to . . . our country." And Lincoln reportedly told a group of White House visitors in 1864, "We could never have gotten through this crusade without the steady influence of the Methodist Episcopal Church."[15]

This rhetoric was matched by action. Ministers became recruiters. Archbishop Hughes took special pride in recruiting the all-Irish Sixty-ninth New York. At the same time Hughes hoped that Hibernians would not ghettoize themselves into purely Irish units, but would use the opportunity of war to prove their patriotism and thus to destroy the stereotypes of the nativist movement. Beecher took an active role in the formation of the Brooklyn Phalanx, a regiment that formed around the community served by his church. He spent some of his own money to equip the unit in addition to giving impassioned declarations of the need for patriotism untinged with doubt or cavil. "God hates lukewarm patriotism," he declared, "as much as lukewarm religion and we hate it too. We do not believe in hermaphrodite patriots."

Local ministers presided over meetings at which the soldiers left their communities to march off to war, assuring all listeners that, as one Episcopal divine put it, "your country has called for your service and you are ready. . . . It is a holy and righteous cause in which you enlist . . . God is with us. . . . The Lord of Hosts is on our side." The linkage between the war effort and religion worked from the other direction as well. Politicians reached out to religious leaders for help. When Lincoln wanted someone who might persuade the Catholic emperor of France to support the Union cause, he thought of Hughes and sent the archbishop to Paris.[16]

Religious efforts were not confined to the home front. Approximately two thousand chaplains enlisted, one per regiment, and went south with their charges. Given the rank of private and eleven dollars per month, they were hardly there for the pay. They believed that their services would be needed and that religion was an imperative part of the soldier's life. Methodists led the way with some five hundred chaplains, but other faiths were represented, too, ranging from the more radical Baptists on the left to more stately Catholics, Unitarians, and Old School Presbyterians on the right. Conservatives alleged that abolitionist divines were favored by the governors who supported the war, although their larger numbers more likely reflect the religious commitments of antislavery people generally.

Whatever the denomination, all the chaplains had work to do. Immorality and death and suffering would require their presence. And while the army contained its share of reprobates, the soldiers wanted them there, if not to watch for purity, at least to help them face death. Generals encouraged the chaplains and suggested that troops attend the services that visiting religious leaders provided. Some generals like O. O. Howard, called "the Christian Soldier," were known for their piety and gave their own sermons and testimonies. Claims of conversions were large and unconfirmable: one hundred thousand, two hundred thousand saved souls, depending on the source. But it does seem safe to say that religion mattered profoundly in the army and that the dedication among the denominations at home to meeting soldiers' needs was intense. In addition to providing consolation and moral guidance, the ministers also helped strengthen resolve and commitment to the fight. Ironically, they thus probably contributed to the conditions they were alleviating. But they would surely have answered that continued war in the service of the Lord made their ministries both imperative and just.[17]

Religious activity among the soldiers was not confined to the chaplains. Volunteers from Northern churches spent several weeks in army camps at various times through the war. Soldiers showed their interest by building churches in their winter camps to provide places to worship. There were sixty-nine such structures built by the Army of the Potomac alone in the winter of 1863–64. The Bible and Tract societies also saw both need and opportunity in the gathering of the armies. With "the flower of the country" assembled in large numbers, the opportunity to spread the gospel was unparalleled. These organizations along with the Temperance Union sent millions of tracts on the evils of drink and millions of New Testaments and other spiritual guides to the Union soldiers. Sunday School contributions were used to help pay costs of printing and mailing. Old School Presbyterians distributed nearly 300,000 copies of "The Soldiers Pocket Book." The New School distributed "The Soldier's Friend," containing 123 pages of 31 religious readings, 31 hymns, 31 psalms, the Ten Commandments, the Apostles' Creed, some prayers, and a section called "Hints on Preserving Health." The same group also sent out "A Word to the Soldier, by a Lady," "The Young Soldier," and "The Soldier's Scrapbook." Some of this activity was directed at Southern soldiers as well. The Tract societies managed to get hundreds of thousands of Bibles to Confederates. But the major targets wore blue and learned from this tidal wave of religious literature the linkage between their faith and saving the Union. And, of course, this general religious involvement by Sunday School children, ministers, and congregations strengthened the bonds between home and camp.[18]

Nowhere was the connection between military and religious goals more clear than in the songs that the war found everyone singing. The popular Presbyterian hymn "Stand Up, Stand Up for Jesus" rang with martial images, addressed as it was to "ye soldiers of the cross" who were to "lift high His royal banner, it must not suffer loss." "Forth to the mighty conflict, in this His glorious day . . . Put on the gospel armor, Each piece put on with prayer . . . This day the noise of battle, The next the victor's song." These words resounded in churches at home and in the field, linking the God of battles with the Union cause. And, of course, the hymn that swept all was Julia Ward Howe's "Battle Hymn of the Republic," which became the anthem of the Union forces. The first lines of the first four stanzas rang with martial Christianity: "Mine eyes have seen the glory of the coming of the Lord . . . I have seen Him in the watchfires of a hundred circling camps . . . I have read a fiery gospel in burnished rows of steel . . . He has sounded forth the trumpet that shall never call retreat." Only in the last stanza does the childlike aspect of the faith appear: "In the beauty of the lilies, Christ was born across the sea," but that thought is absorbed in the final "As he died to make men holy, let us die to make men free, While God is marching on."

The "Battle Hymn of the Republic" borrowed its music from

"John Brown's Body," which promised that although that warrior's body was in the grave, "his soul goes marching on." Both pieces were immensely popular wherever Northerners marched or gathered. Stories of the power of the song spread its impact. In Libby Prison in July 1863 hundreds of Union prisoners heard from their jailers that Gettysburg had been a disaster for the Union. Stunned, they huddled together wondering what had happened. Then a Negro who was bringing food to the men told them the truth. Word flashed through the prison, and the men stood and cheered and hugged each other. When they had quieted, Chaplain James McCabe of Ohio's 122d Volunteer Infantry raised his voice and sang, "Mine eyes have seen the glory of the coming of the Lord." Soon all the prisoners were singing, "Glory, glory hallelujah!" When McCabe was released from Libby, he spoke in Washington and told his story to an audience that included Lincoln. The chaplain concluded by singing the song, and the whole audience joined in, then cheered and applauded; and as the noise died down, the president was heard to call, "Sing it again."[19]

Northern armies gained a useful reputation by being linked with religious ideals. Despite the great destruction and death that followed the Union armies across the South (or perhaps because of it), the public found comfort in seeing these killers and destroyers as angels. Stories made the rounds in the popular books and newspapers of the day about the religiosity of the soldiers. According to a popular account of Sherman's march, one morning the army heard a brigade band playing the favorite hymn known as "Old One Hundred." From brigade to brigade the men took up the song until five thousand voices could be heard singing, "Praise God from whom all blessings flow." Then there was quiet as the men ate their breakfast, broke camp, and fell into line ready to continue their march through Georgia. This image apparently comforted Sherman even as it was intended to comfort the nation. "My army, sir," he told a visiting minister, "is not demoralized—has improved on the march —Christian army I've got—soldiers are Christians if anybody is— noble fellows—God will take care of them—war improves character."[20]

The war thus encouraged religious imagery, and the churches of the North justified and energized the war effort. The conflict also brought to life vast organizational efforts to advance the Christian crusade. Here the Christian Commission and the Sanitary Commission played the central roles. The former of these organizations had the most thorough commitment to religious ideals and gloried in the fact. As their initial circular proclaimed, they sought to promote "the spiritual good of the soldiers in the army, and incidentally, their intellectual improvement and social and physical comfort." In competition with the Sanitary Commission for funds and support, members of the Christian Commission distinguished their efforts by noting the direct and personal nature of the help they provided. They were there to help the dying soldier meet his Lord, to bathe his wounds, and to provide gifts and supplies directly to individual soldiers. Deriding the impersonal Sanitary Commission for its arid professionalism, they emphasized their own individual direct compassion and Christian caring.

Still, the two commissions were distinguished by tone and emphasis more than by actual operation. The Christian Commission had been born of the immense need to organize charity as the war expanded in size. Before Bull Run, it was possible to believe that hometown groups could be effective sending aid to the boys of their communities. But after that vast and complex battle, a new structure was imperative. A special meeting of the YMCA was called to organize efforts of local groups. A national committee led by Philadelphia merchant George Stuart was set up to direct efforts. A Board of Directors and a national treasurer were appointed, and the business of saving lives and souls in wartime began. In large measure the new organization simply continued prewar benevolent efforts. Stuart had been a leader in the Temperance and Sunday School unions. The national treasurer had a parallel background, and the Board of Directors looked like an assemblage of the prewar reform society leaders. Still, new faces appeared as well and they illustrated the merger that the war encouraged between faith, wealth, and charity. Jay Cooke, organizer of Union finances, sat on the board. So did William Dodge, known as "the Christian Merchant." Government was represented by Congressman Schuyler Colfax of Indiana. The Lincoln administration gave its blessing as well. Annual meetings were held in the House of Representatives hall, and justices of the Supreme Court, cabinet members, and the president himself attended.[21]

Christian Commission activities grew to enormous proportions and fostered prodigious feats of organized charity. By 1863 each of the armies in the field had its own director who coordinated the activities of over 2,000 "delegates." By 1864 there were 2,217 delegates giving nearly 80,000 days of service and distributing over 47,000 boxes of supplies and publications worth over a million dollars. In that year alone, nearly 570,000 Bibles and Testaments, 500,000 hymn and psalm books, 4,300,000 "knapsack books," 94,-000 bound library books, 347,000 magazines and pamphlets, nearly 8,000,000 copies of religious newspapers, and over 13,000,000 pages of Tracts were distributed. Supplies were gathered at the major distribution point in Philadelphia and then sent out to places where the next battles were likely to take place. The railroads and telegraph companies helped by providing free passes and free use of the telegraph. Special appeals after battles brought in thousands of dollars to the commission. During the Battle of the Wilderness, Pittsburgh contributed $35,000, Philadelphia $50,000, and Boston $60,000. In all, the Christian Commission had total receipts of over $6 million.[22]

Although the spiritual needs of the men were allegedly the main target, delegates involved themselves in any activity that comforted the soldiers. They wrote letters for the wounded after having helped carry them from the battlefield. They visited the sick and delivered gifts, both spiritual and temporal. While Tracts and Bibles were their major gifts, they also provided clothing, food, sweets that families at home had sent. And the commission itself gathered coffee, writing paper, and "farina, oranges, lemons, onion, pickles . . . shirts, towels," which as one observer recalled were "given and distributed in the name of Jesus [and] though designed for the body, gave strength to the soul." This charity was augmented by the frequent prayer meetings and the Sunday services that the Christian Commission delegates either led themselves or assisted chaplains with. The widespread linkage of spiritual comfort with serving earthly needs helped to inspire men like Washington Gladden, a commission delegate, to develop a Christianity focusing on help in this world that would become known as the Social Gospel movement.[23]

The Sanitary Commission was also strongly religious at its base, but the top was controlled by men with different ideas about charity. Like the Christian Commission, it was organized as a means for integrating the efforts of many local societies, the main one being the Women's Central Association of Relief for the Sick and Wounded of the Army. Like the Christian Commission, its work was done at home overwhelmingly by women. It also was enormously successful, almost matching the $6 million in receipts of the Christian Commission. Its passion for organizing the relief efforts of the North efficiently made the Sanitary Commission a vocal supporter of McClellan in the early days of his command. His professional demeanor evoked their admiration, as they shared his doubts about the ability of the masses to respond with discipline to the needs of war.

The leadership of the Sanitary Commission focused on a tough-minded realism about the immense task to be done. It deplored the "vague sentiment of philanthropy," as one supporter put it, and dedicated itself to "obedience to duty divinely commanded." An annual report announced that "its ultimate end is neither humanity nor charity. It is to economize for the National service the life and strength of the National soldier." Such hard-nosed protestations led some members of the Christian Commission to see it as wicked, mechanical, and heartless in its approach. Certainly, its methods often featured more efficiency and bureaucracy than did the person-ally oriented Christian Commission. Withholding medicine until doctors had released it produced scenes that few nurses could toler-ate. The use of paid agents rather than volunteers, the utilization of professional canvassers to raise money, bespoke the coming of the professional who placed efficiency and control at the head of the virtues. Walt Whitman was only one among many who deplored the "hirlings": "the men as they lie helpless in bed turn away their faces from the sight of the Agents . . . they get well paid and are always incompetent and disagreeable."[24]

There were differences in style between the commissions, but a fundamental consistency underlay their efforts. Both were well or-ganized and interested in efficiency. Both relied on the prewar reli-gious societies for local participation and leadership as well as helping soldiers. Both kept extraordinarily good records of materi-als delivered and controlled distribution effectively. They even shared leadership; William Dodge sat on both Boards of Directors. And both were too well organized for someone like Clara Barton, whose suspicions led her to set up her own charity operation for the soldiers.

Backed by the powerful Massachusetts senator Henry Wilson, Barton solicited help in direct and personal ways, writing letters all over the country emphasizing her own personal experiences in helping the soldiers, calling them her boys, imagining the young men as former students in her public school, and speaking of them and herself as part of a family. Barton's effort, cast in these terms, reinforced the image of woman as mother that the social and economic changes of the age had fortified. The hospital experiences of women like Dorothea Dix, Louisa May Alcott, Jane Swisshelm, and the thousands of nurses (most of them tied to the Christian Commission) who attended the wounded boys similarly served to engender images of the angel of mercy mothering her boys.[25]

Swisshelm had helped organize Minnesota's Republican party and throughout her life fought for women's rights as an editor and journalist. When she went to work in Civil War hospitals she fought vigorously against the gruesome heroic medicine (featuring bleeding, purgatives, leeching) and the quick recourse to amputations by the doctors. Her protests to newspapers got her fired and also intensified a fight she had been having with Dorothea Dix, who, among other things, disliked having attractive women in field hospitals. But when she described her war experiences in her autobiography, she described how she had brought mothering into the lives of the wounded:

"What is your name?" a wounded soldier at Fredericksburg asked.

"My name is mother," she replied.

"Mother. Oh my God! I have not seen my mother for two years. Let me feel your hand."

In a hospital she comforted a young man, who responded and then pulled back. "Oh you will think I am a baby!"

"Well, that is what you ought to be," she answered. "Your past life is sufficient certificate of your manhood; and now has come your time to be a baby, while I am mother."

When she met veterans after the war they continued to call her "mother," and she treasured the word.[26]

These wartime efforts linking religious idealism and ambition with service to the needy found fruit in efforts to assist the freedmen. As the army moved into Dixie and millions of slaves found freedom, concern grew that the former slaves needed the self-discipline that came from Christian instruction in the duties of self-reliance and the sanctity of work. It was hoped that the gospel would perform the same civilizing task it was performing in the North. But for every desire to bring potential disorder under control there was also an honest concern for the needs of the impoverished and ignorant blacks. Thousands of Northern women and men went south to help the freedmen learn to read and write and to assist by providing clothing and, in the early stages, food to help them survive. These Yankee schoolmarms risked ostracism from Southern whites, as well as injury and death, to perform what to them was a religious duty. They sacrificed their own comforts to help others, reflecting a religious commitment of admirable magnitude. They also were examples of a social Christianity that the war had ennobled in the stories of the young men who did risk and lose their lives. Future involvements by religion in the reform movement on behalf of the needy built on this strong foundation.[27]

The success of all these efforts, their unprecedented nature, combined with the parallel destruction of slavery linked the religious impulse to the patriotic enthusiasm of the time. The success influenced and colored both. The war was culminating the reform efforts of the mid-nineteenth century. Focused predominantly on the soldiers, charity and moral reform also spilled over into activities that helped the needy behind Northern lines, first the families of absent soldiers, but then also the wayward children, the insane, and simply the poor men and women who could not make it in the wartime inflation. They gave further reason to believe that a Christian commonwealth would be born of the sacrifices of war.[28]

While most of the elements of prewar reform found new strength or culmination in the war, the cause of pacifism died. Even before the conflict it had been staggering. Pacifists had been unable to reconcile devotion to peace with the fact of slavery. Originally they had hoped that by convincing masters that violence was evil and that slaves had sacred souls they could achieve both emancipation and peace. But by the 1850s patience with meekness was wearing thin. Years of argument and agitation had freed no slaves and brought no peace. Indeed, the Mexican War and the Ostend Manifesto suggested slave owners' willingness to use force to expand bondage.

By the late 1850s pacifists were more than ready to confront the question that challenges the nonviolent everywhere: was violence that ended violence justified? What made the question more compelling was the fact that the answer affected not just pacifists but, in Wendell Phillips' words, the "millions of Christian slaves, standing dumb suppliants at the threshold of the Christian world who have no voice but ours . . . to demand justice." Slaves seemed to have no hope if men of peace kept turning the other cheek.[29]

John Brown's raid at Harper's Ferry found pacifists emphasizing the old man's motive and his willingness to sacrifice his life for emancipation. Lydia Maria Child wrote Brown, "Believing in peace principles, I cannot sympathize with the method you chose to advance the cause of freedom. But I honor your generous intentions —I admire your courage, moral and physical . . . I reverence you for the humanity which tempered your zeal. I sympathize with you in your cruel bereavement, your sufferings, and your wrongs. In brief, I love you and I bless you." Garrison, while protesting that he remained "a nonresistant—a believer in the inviolability of human life under all circumstances," still declared that "I thank God when men who believe in the right and duty of wielding carnal weapons are so far advanced that they will take those weapons out of the scale of despotism, and throw them into the scale of freedom. It is an indication of progress and of positive moral growth." Small wonder that Henry David Thoreau could admire the "sort of violence . . . that . . . is encouraged, not by soldiers but by peaceable citizens, not so much by laymen as by ministers of the gospel, not so much by the fighting sects as by the Quakers, and not so much by Quaker men as by Quaker women."[30]

American pacifism suffered a blow in the Civil War that it would not recover from until the outbreak of World War I. The linkage of patriotism with the Christian crusade surely played its role. The humble and meek Jesus who had served as the benchmark for pacifism had been replaced by the Christ who brought the sword to purge the nation. The almost universal endorsement given to the war effort from the pulpits of every faith overawed declarations of peace. Even a man like Moncure Conway, who eagerly and passionately sought peace throughout the conflict, could declare that although "war is always wrong," it was "not a thousandth part so bad as a false peace."[31]

Yet if the cause of pure pacifism suffered in the war, the dialogue of pacifism was nurtured by the conflict's challenges. Even before the war, pacifists had debated, in the luxury of peace, the meaning of their ideology in practice. But the coming of the war raised questions that demanded answers in immediate terms.

Some pacifists retained their purity. All war was wrong, old pacifists like Joshua Blanchard and Ezra Heywood argued. Let the South secede, they insisted, and slavery would wither away. The "law of benevolent persuasion" would conquer, while the "malignant law of force" would only build increasing hatred. It was especially dangerous to wrap war in any noble cause, for that gave killing a sanction that emasculated the testimony of peace. The proper role for true men of peace was to recognize that neither North nor South was wholly perfect or wholly evil and to stand outside the sectional strife witnessing for the love of Jesus, who had promised that faith would move mountains.[32]

But if some cried for pure peace, others were challenged to wonder how to apply the doctrine to this war. When pacifist critics in England reprimanded American brethren for deserting the faith, Charles Whipple replied with an appeal for thought, not slogans. "Does no thought enter your mind but the official and technical one —How wicked they are to be fighting? . . . Is Peace the one thing needful when it leaves one party established as a tyrant and the other as slave?" The prospect of ending slavery, what Gerrit Smith had called "the most cruel and horrid form of war," led former pacifists to support the conflict. Other pacifists squirmed as they sought to justify their feelings that this war was right, whatever the evils of war in general. Some followed Smith in insisting that this was not a war at all; it was a police action, maintaining order, which, of course, was the foundation for peace in any society. Others argued that while war between Christians was anathema, proslavery people could not be Christians, and hence war against them was not contrary to Christ's teaching. Others responded less sophistically.

The war unleashed awesome temptations for Quakers especially. Some tried valiantly to cling to pacifism, especially after 1863 when the government announced emancipation as a war aim. One author described their dilemma and the true faith. There was danger, he insisted, that emancipation would cause the Quakers to abandon their testimony for peace. Certainly they should rejoice that the war "begun by slaveholders more firmly to secure themselves in authority over their slaves" had led to overthrowing their authority. Still, Quakers must mix their rejoicing with the recognition that "it is done by a means that we as Christians cannot recommend or up-hold."[33]

But if they still rejected war as a tool, the Quakers in all branches of the society still supported the war makers in everything but the choice of weapons. Quakers had no sympathy with the rebellion. They insisted on their loyalty to the government and expressed their desire to serve as good citizens in all other duties save that of fighting its battles. They repudiated any connection with the cop-perhead movement, publicly declaring that "we cannot do or say anything calculated, even to identify our members with these men." Recognizing that the Friends' antiwar feelings were grounded in principles much different from those of the Peace Democrats or the rebels, the Lincoln administration did little to obstruct Quaker per-suasion. Quaker tracts were allowed to circulate in the army, Quaker speakers were permitted to argue their ideals to recruiting officers. Lincoln met with a group of Friends in the White House in October 1862. He prayed with them for peace. And he recognized the di-lemma that the war placed them in. "Your people," he wrote to one, "have had and are having a great trial. On principle and faith op-posed to both war and oppression they can only practically oppose oppression by war." He promised to do all he could to aid Quaker conscientious objectors should their principles place them in con-flict with authorities.[34]

Presidential understanding made Quakers Lincoln's friends. Eliza Gurney wrote to say that "there are very few amongst us who would not lament to see any other than Abraham Lincoln fill the Presiden-tial chair." And whatever their voting behavior, large numbers of Quakers supported the conduct of the war. One branch calling themselves Progressive Friends testified both to its peace principles and to its antirebellion feelings. Condemning the evils of war, they nevertheless attacked the "barbarities and crimes of [Southern] conspirators" and supported a draft of soldiers so long as the scru-ples of conscientious objectors were respected. Every branch of the society reported that many of its young men had either rejected or reinterpreted pacifist teachings of their childhoods and joined the army. And their families often cheered their decisions. One former Quaker wrote just after Sumter, "Quakers are drilling, contrary to all the peace principles of the sect; indeed, from all appearances we may suppose their hopes are based on war. I'm opposed to war—

to cutting men down like grass—but if ever a war was holy, this one in favor of the most oppressed, most forbearing, most afflicted, downtrodden, insulted part of humanity is a holy war."[35]

The reactions of the Quaker local meetings throughout the North varied, but most were not quick to disown young men who fought for the Union cause. The long-standing respect for private conscience allowed many meetings to put off action or to accept the confessions of veterans that they had strayed from their principles. These admissions might range from absolute confession of error to a more moderate pleading for forgiveness and permission to return to fellowship. Some simply expressed regret for having to deviate from the ideal and asked to rejoin the meeting. All these responses reflected sensitivity to the dilemma described by one young Quaker soldier: "I think that Peace is holy and should be encouraged constantly—and that an unjust war is only legalized murder. But the inner light made it very plain to me in the summer of '61 that I should enter the army."[36]

The government sought to recognize their position. The draft law of February 24, 1864, provided that authentic members of pacifist churches might be assigned to hospital duty or to care for the freedmen. They might also pay commutation money into a fund that went to care for the sick, not to some direct military purpose. But some Friends continued to reject these options. They believed that the government had no right to "oblige the subject to violate his conscience" by performing military service in any form. Furthermore, many objected to doing any kind of service that was connected to the military. They, of course, would help the sick and needy as a matter of conscience, but helping soldiers get ready to return to fight again hardly advanced the cause of peace. While not every Quaker subscribed to these objections, enough did to set them clearly apart from the vast majority of Northerners who supported the war effort without qualification. These objections served as an alternative vision of peace in the middle of the war. And they kept the mainstream of pacifist thought flowing clearly in a conflict that sorely challenged its course.

Members of a faith that encouraged private conscience, individual Quakers found themselves tested in diverse ways: what one could not do, others could. With this caveat in mind, however, the story of Cyrus Pringle does convey the meaning of being a devotee of the

Prince of Peace during war. In July 1863 Pringle, a twenty-five-year-old farmer in Vermont, got his draft notice. Aware that other Quakers had yielded, he determined that he would not. Friends urged him to pay the commutation, but he refused. He had "higher duty than that to country," he told them. The provost marshal came and took him into the army, to Brattleboro, then to Long Island in Boston harbor. Surrounded by war preparations, Pringle and two other Quakers still found sympathy; ordinary soldiers accepted the position that Quakers could not drill or perform any military duties. But officers were less tolerant. The Friends found themselves in the guardhouse and threatened with death.

Matters of conscience arose in subtle ways. Should they wear uniforms? Yes, but they would not sign for them. (Other Quakers had insisted that they would not themselves put the clothes on, but that others might dress them.) Should they help clean the camp and fetch water? Pringle agreed to try it, but "as we worked, we did not feel easy." When the sergeant then told them to "police the streets," they said no and were punished. Should they accept an offer to be assigned to hospital duty? A difficult test. The yearly meetings of New England and New York and individual Friends from New England and New York urged them to perform such duty. But Pringle and his two colleagues refused: "We cannot purchase life at cost of peace of soul."

Now the authorities were getting angry. To refuse hospital duty when other men faced battle, maiming, and death seemed mere obstinacy and perhaps cowardice as well. Pringle and his two associates were sent south to Camp Culpepper, Virginia, to get a taste of real soldiering. When they refused to carry rifles, soldiers strapped the weapons to them. They were threatened with court-martial, with execution, if they refused to accept hospital duty. Again older Quakers counseled hospital service; and as they looked around, they saw "around us a rich field for usefulness in which there were scarce any laborers." The question arose whether they might be better Christians by easing the sufferings of soldiers than by merely standing passive witness for a concept. Pringle and his friends agreed to try the hospital, but warned the authorities that they might change their minds.

"At first a great load seemed rolled away from us," Pringle recalled; "we rejoiced in the prospect of life again. But soon there prevailed a feeling of condemnation, as though we had sold our Master. And that first day was one of the bitterest I ever experienced. It was a time of stern conflict of soul." They told the colonel they could not do it. Their testimony against war would have to be pure, uncompromised by alternatives. The officer lost patience, and when Pringle later refused to clean his gun he was taken into the field, placed face up on the ground, his legs and hands tied so that he was spread to the elements, and left there. "I wept," he later wrote, "not so much from my own suffering as from sorrow that such things should be in our own country . . . and I was sad that one endeavoring to follow our dear Master should be so generally regarded as a despicable and stubborn culprit."

But even as Pringle endured this punishment, the authorities were relenting. Orders from Washington arrived to send back to the capital the Quakers who had been sent to Virginia. The men were released on parole and returned home. Four months of testimony to pacifism before the soldiers brought Pringle back to where he had started but fortified in his faith that Christ had been his guide.[37]

At home, other Quakers faced dilemmas that also tested their consciences. What should be done about the voluntary helping of sick and wounded soldiers? Most seem to have felt that if the care was given freely and not as a compensation for other required military service, it was accepted. Was sending clothes to soldiers in the field a proper act for a Quaker? Here more of them were concerned that the act could be mistaken as support for the war and not the men. They feared compromising their witness for peace. Taxes posed another problem. Rendering unto Caesar the taxes necessary to run the country was a long-standing obligation accepted in the faith. But taxes in wartime posed more difficult issues. Still, the most common resolution was to pay all taxes that were not unmistakably marked for war. Yet when some of the Friends refused to pay taxes at all, the meetings accepted the decisions of their consciences. Also accepted were private decisions to pay only the amount of tax not necessary for war expenses. Some deducted from their tax payment the percentage used for the war. Local tax collectors usually accepted these symbolic protests if they knew the man of conscience to be of firm religious scruples.[38]

But the Quaker response to war expressed the feelings of only a tiny portion of the Northern population. In overwhelming numbers the faithful united in their belief that the war was a Christian crusade, preserving the nation that God had chosen to advance His cause in the world. As the news of Lee's surrender came to Roxbury, Massachusetts, Caroline Barrett White spoke the mood of many Americans who saw God's handiwork: "I can be grateful to the Lord who has made bare his arm to save this people and who has brought them through great *tribulation* through suffering not to be described . . . to see this blessed day—step by step has He led this people up ever higher and higher—on to the great plain of righteousness, justice and freedom." Defeat of the South, Northerners insisted, would maintain order in God's special nation, restore an awareness of duties to enduring spiritual goals, regenerate moral discipline, and punish both the South and the nation for the sin of slavery. Most Northern preachers agreed with the Northampton, Massachusetts, preacher who proclaimed, "It is the will of God. It is the will of God." And that divine will would forge from the conflict a nation with a duty to mankind. "All this national power and greatness which God has so marvellously produced for us out of our national calamity," the *Independent* declared in April 1864, "is the property of the Lord Jesus Christ and is to be employed under his direction for the advancement of his Kingdom in this world. This nation is solemnly bound to exist for the glory of God. It is a covenant obligation that no power can repeal."[39]

Such holy bombast typified the religious ideology that ennobled the Union war effort. But there was another, more personally vital, purpose for it. Exaltation about the triumph of God's purposes met the need to confront the most profoundly felt fact of the war: the hundreds of thousands of dead young men, sacrificed for the cause. Ministers offered comfort by constantly speaking of the vast gains that war had brought. Preachers of all faiths told congregations that great losses would engender great gains. In 1861 Octavius Frothingham of Boston likened dying soldiers to Christ whose death regenerated society. Speaking after the carnage of Antietam in September 1862, Philadelphia Unitarian minister Henry Furness promised that at the conclusion of the conflict "distinctions of race . . . shall be obliterated, and men shall live together in the relations of a Christian brotherhood." Henry Ward Beecher looked at the three-day holocaust at Gettysburg and promised that "a pitiful God" was like a "midwife in the throes and groans of the Mother" who "heeds not the pain but waits for the child that shall bring joy out of woe." The child would be "peace, concord and universal intelligence . . . every death now, a thousand lives shall be happier. Individuals suffered; the nation revived." By insisting that God's plan was to wash the nation clean through the blood of its soldiers, Northern ministers gave some meaning to the thousands of deaths that grieved empty homes.[40]

Of course, in hundreds of such homes, even these words must have provided little comfort at those moments when they heard that a son, a husband, a father, a kinsman, or a friend had died. "There is nothing earthly worth the life of a young man like Dick," Ellen Wright had cried. "I feel how weak and fruitless must be any words of mine which should attempt to beguile you from the grief of a loss so overwhelming," Lincoln wrote Lydia Bixby as she grieved over the loss of two sons.[41]

Americans of the mid-nineteenth century were very aware of the fact of death. Widely perceived childhood mortality compelled sensitivity to it. Losses of children just after birth were feared, but also expected. Some families would not name their newborn infants until a reasonable time had passed in which they could be expected to survive. Parents who had lost infants warned others not to become too attached to newborn children. "O how heart-rending it is for us to be told that we must call off our affections from these dear second selves," one man wrote to his brother and sister, "and yet if we do not in some degree turn our affections away from them, we sharpen the Arrow that is to pierce our vitals."[42]

But while the deaths of children were the most stabbing reminders of the danger of attachment, death generally was seen in the prewar years as providing lessons for both the dying individual and the survivors. The most common lesson was not to covet this world too much. A dying man in Sterling, Massachusetts, asked his wife to tell others "that my being about to be cut off in the midst of my years may prove a warning to dear friends to be ready." The death of his wife reminded another that "the world is not our home." The metaphor of Matthew 25 rang through much of the period. "Watch, therefore, for ye know neither the day nor the hour wherein the Son of Man cometh."[43]

Antebellum Americans were not content with abstract generalizations about the meaning of death. They were interested in particular deaths of individuals in their families, not just as a matter of natural family significance, but also as "privileged moments" in which they might both help and learn. It was expected by most Americans of the time that the hour of dying would involve family members and friends as participants in the process. Loved ones would comfort the dying individual, but they would do so not by denying death, but by affirming it and by making sure that the victim knew of his condition.

Man was to know that he was facing God and eternity and to be ready to face his death with knowledge and acceptance. When his father died in 1855, a Missourian wanted to have his mother assure him "dear old pappy" had accepted his fate. "That gives me ease if he was perfectly resined to gow mother in that triing ower if he was prepared to gow what sweet thoughts to himself and all of his children." To accept death was to show that the human being gave up worldly things and accepted God's will. If a person died with such knowledge and acceptance, it would be, as one Connecticut woman put it, "not only my duty but my great privilege" to witness the death. Death thus was a social process, a dialogue in which loved ones comforted the dying person and, on his or her part, that person could teach others how to give up the world and move toward the Lord.[44]

The nurse in Baltimore who wrote to console Austin Whipple's mother in New Hampshire illustrated well the standard ideas of the age. She made sure to ask Whipple how he felt about dying and was comforted with the answer that "whatever the Lord knew was best for him" he would yield to. When the young man died, she went on, "he looked as calm and peaceful as if in sleep. . . . It seemed to me that death for him had no terrors . . . he was willing to live or die as it seemed best to the Lord. . . . The departed one has made a happy exchange and is safe with his savior, in whom he trusted." Whipple's commander also wrote to comfort the family and assured them that "his spirit has passed into the Spirit world and he now rests from all his labour."[45]

The war brought death into the foreground of life. Newspapers, personal letters, word of mouth, brought home to every community the growing mountains of dead that the war was exacting. English visitor James Burns testified to the presence of death in New York City in a very mundane way. The funeral business was thriving, he observed. Competition between merchants was inspiring increasingly elaborate coffins. Transparent lids, gilded coffins, hearses with glass sides so that people could see the coffins within as they passed, hearses themselves, were becoming works of art enlisting the craftsmanship of cabinetmakers and upholsterers. Baby coffins were especially attractive, Burns noted, "with their pure white satin linings, fringed with lace, plate glass panels with lids, French polished fancy wood and silver plated mountings." Matthew Brady's photographs displayed in his studios in the city also brought the battlefield death into inescapable focus. Almost every community in the nation witnessed some parallel to the moment described by Rebecca Harding Davis at a small station in the Pennsylvania hills: "Nobody was in sight but a poor thin country girl in a faded calico gown and sunbonnet. She stood alone on the platform, waiting. A child was playing beside her. When we stopped, the men took out from a freight car a rough unplaned pine box and laid it down, baring their heads for a moment. Then the train steamed away. She sat down on the ground and put her arms around the box and leaned her head on it. The child went on playing."[46]

Many of the dead never came home. There were thousands of unknown soldiers buried through the South. Outside Salisbury, North Carolina, the unknown dead numbered over twelve thousand. The War Department estimated that nearly twenty-five thousand died and were never buried at all. All these deaths lost the power directly to instruct anyone. There was only the shock, the sorrow, and the empty spaces in so many homes. And even with the bodies that came home, the moment of death had been unwitnessed. No one could tell with certainty that these men had welcomed or at least accepted the fact that their time had come. The hundreds of thousands of dead were all young men cut down in the middle of their lives. There was reason to doubt that they accepted death. The only thing their deaths could teach anyone was the sorrow of a life ended too soon.

Emily Dickinson spoke the anguish of millions in late 1862, just after the bloody day at Antietam: "At least to pray—is left—is left / Oh Jesus—in the Air— / I know not which thy chamber is— / I'm knocking—everywhere— / Thou settest Earthquake in the South— / And Maelstrom, in the Sea— / Say, Jesus Christ of Nazareth— / Hast thou no Arm for Me?" In at least a quarter of a million Northern homes were mothers and fathers and children and wives and other loved ones who had felt this terrible loss. They failed to be satisfied by sermons about the greatness of the nation, the victory of God's purposes, ultimate good arising out of personal loss. These people and the society around them looked to heaven for an answer.[47]

Antebellum America had not been obsessed with the afterlife. Once a year, perhaps twice, a book would appear that discussed the nature of the afterlife, such as the early 1850s work *Heavenly Home —the Employments and Enjoyments of Saints in Heaven.* But such works were without special concern to the reading public. Between 1852 and 1860 only seven books on heaven were published in the United States. Even in the midst of the war, the afterlife remained a rather uninteresting subject; only two books on the subject appeared between 1861 and 1866. But after the war, the flood began. The next five years almost matched the output of the previous fourteen. And between 1871 and 1876 over eighty volumes appeared.[48]

Some of this literature reflected a general trend in the nineteenth century toward domesticating death, robbing it of its terrors, sentimentalizing it. Whereas death in the early days of our history was a terror and a reminder of mortality, by the early nineteenth century a movement was under way which undercut that idea. Puritans had emphasized that God brought death in His own time and for His own purposes. Man was to learn to live with the thought of death so that he would focus attention on obligations to God. But the Enlightenment had begun to challenge these ideas even as it integrated death into the orderly processes of nature. Serene and stoical death replaced an image of anxiety about the hereafter.

By the second and third decades of the nineteenth century, the romantic movement had taken two paths in dealing with death. One, characterized by Edgar Allan Poe, focused on death as "an awe-inspiring event that elevated human emotions to peak sensitivity." But the more influential focused on death as part of the natural process of the world and likened dying to the necessary decay of plants in a forest, which brought forth life once more. To contemplate death was to contemplate God's involvement in the natural process, with judgment after death only slightly of concern. The beginnings of the rural cemetery movement reflected the feeling that death should be contemplated in lovely natural surroundings where family plots allowed relatives to be near each other in death, and the living might visit and talk with the deceased.[49]

Part of this process included an emerging interest in an afterlife that would reflect the serenity and naturalness of death itself. Instead of fearing an afterlife, voices began to be heard that argued, as did Beecher, that heaven was a homelike place that any person who agreed to be saved would inherit. It was a heaven that was "too good to be believed." Death was the passageway through which people moved from mortality to immortality. In the 1870s a debate began among American clergymen over whether or not hell existed at all, even as heaven was being transformed into a place for family and friends to treasure each other in an atmosphere of felicity and joy.[50]

The Civil War amplified this process of transforming the afterlife into a place of human contentment by the terrible toll it took in the lives of young men, so often called boys, or "our hearty darlings," as Whitman called them. The most popular of all the postwar books on heaven, Elizabeth Phelps' *The Gates Ajar* (1868), was inspired by contemplating the grief of the families who had lost their brothers, sons, and fathers in the war. The novel begins with the heroine receiving a telegram announcing the death of a dearly beloved brother in the Civil War. The plot reveals the ways in which she learns through various encounters with death and dying of the wisdom and the love of God and of the fact that her brother is still near her. While much of the subsequent literature on death and heaven deals with the deaths of young children and mothers, the parallel with the young boys of the war was clear. To imagine a heaven much like home was to be able to believe that, in one sense, the boys had come home, that they had not had their lives cut off before they had lived. In the heaven to which the young women, the mothers, and the children ascended, they would be assured of meeting the men whose deaths in such vast numbers had unleashed the cataract of new literature on heaven.[51]

The personal grief of loved ones thus had several impacts. Among other things, it called forth the efforts of preachers to proclaim that the war was worth the cost in that it would bring God's kingdom to earth. Northern victory allegedly would signal the beginning of a truly Christian future for America. Such hopes would help fuel reform efforts of the Reconstruction years. Furthermore, that grief turned a meager literary stream of the prewar years—the literature of heaven—into a flood. Stricken loved ones were reassured that their private worlds, shattered by war and death, would be reborn. They would rejoin their loved ones around the familiar family hearth.

But the personal tragedies held also the possibility of public vision as well. In wrestling with the most profound of all losses Americans might discover a humility that would answer the overweening pride implicit in equating God's goals with Northern victory. A God inscrutable enough to allow their children to be killed might have purposes for the nation equally beyond their comprehension. Not many Northerners could acquire such humility, but their leader did. His experience provided a spiritual meaning for the war that would deserve respect long after the trumpets of glory had ceased to echo.

The president and Mrs. Lincoln had three sons when he entered the White House. Robert, the oldest, went off to study law at Harvard, but two younger boys, Tad and Willie, lived at home and made the executive mansion into a full-sized playhouse. They used the roof as their battleship from which they could spy on rebels, the attic as a playroom, and all the other rooms for whatever took their fancy. Their parents indulged them fully. When Tad ate all the strawberries that had been set aside for a state dinner, the steward pulled his hair, but Mary only hoped that he wouldn't do such a thing again. The boys broke into cabinet meetings, once aiming a toy cannon at the assembled officials. They interrupted discussions in the Oval Office, and Lincoln laughed and played with them while he conducted business.

Tad was the slower of the two, a boy who did not read very well and who disliked studies enough that tutors came and went with regularity. Mary worried about him, but Lincoln believed that Tad would learn soon enough. Willie was the bright one. He liked to go off to his mother's room and read quietly with her there. He also read while his father worked and showed him proudly what he had learned and became the favorite of both his parents. In February of 1862 Willie took sick and so did Tad. But while Tad recovered, Willie got worse and, after four or five days of delirium and suffering, finally died on February 20.

Lincoln's encounter with the deaths of soldiers now took on an added profound personal meaning. With this death he was simply

a father, not the president, and he responded like parents all over
the nation. He did his best to console Mary, who had practically
gone out of her mind, and sought some consolation for himself.
Heaven became more than a poorly defined abstraction. He needed
there to be some place where his boy abided and was happy. He told
Elizabeth Keckley, Mary's personal servant, "My poor boy, he was
too good for this earth. God has called him home. I know that he
is much better off in heaven, but then we loved him so. It is hard,
hard to have him die."

When the Reverend Francis Vinton of New York's Trinity Church
came to console the grieving mother, Lincoln talked to him. "Your
son is alive in Paradise," the minister assured the president. Lincoln
then asked Vinton for a copy of a sermon recently preached on
immortality, and the minister complied. Visitors to the White House
reported that the president read the sermon many times and, in fact,
had a personal copy made of it.[52]

But Lincoln's understanding of the religious element in the Civil
War transcended his private tragedy. Personally comforted with
thoughts that Willie was in heaven, Lincoln nevertheless used his
private experiences to deepen his understanding of the religious
and theological nature of the war. Religious themes increasingly
began to appear in his public messages. He paid more serious attention to public ceremonies with religious overtones. In April of 1863
he endorsed the wish of Congress for a day of national prayer and
humility. In July he responded to the urgings of Sarah Josepha Hale
and proclaimed Thanksgiving a national holiday.

The Thanksgiving message set forth clearly his growing theological understanding. There was gratitude for "the blessings of fruitful
fields and healthful skies." There was an awareness of how the
bounty of the nation had increased even in the midst of war; "the
plough . . . the shuttle . . . the ship; the axe . . . the mines . . . have
yielded more abundantly than theretofore. Population has steadily
increased, notwithstanding the waste that has been made in the
camp, the siege and the battlefield; and the country, rejoicing in the
consciousness of augmented strength and vigor, is permitted to
expect continuance of years with large increase of freedom." Yet
this prosperity was not the work of man. "No human counsel hath
devised nor hath any mortal hand worked out these great things.
They are the gracious gifts of the Most High God, who, while deal-

ing with us in anger for our sins, hath nevertheless remembered mercy."

One could expect that a day of thanksgiving would be attended with evocations of God, but the religious strain surged steady and powerful through the other important speeches of the rest of the war. In style and in substance Lincoln poured forth a vision of the war reflecting a sensitivity to the power of the divine in human affairs. Biblical language and imagery characterized the Gettysburg Address, from the opening "Four score and seven years ago" to the image of a birth filled with promises that would have meaning for all people on earth, to the idea that death could consecrate the ground on which they stood and, more important, the cause for which the soldiers had died, to a final image of a nation "under God" that could have a rebirth because the young men had died. Of course, the means whereby the nation would fulfill its promise was a government of, by, and for the people, and the address therefore can be said to be about the preservation of democratic government. But Lincoln believed that such government was best suited to fulfill God's purposes on earth for the United States so far as men could understand them. His faith in democracy and in God were thus entwined.[53]

Lincoln's understanding of the theological meaning of the war was not mere patriotic piety. Unlike the majority of the ministers of both sections, Lincoln found a greater meaning in the war than could be reconciled with "Onward Christian Soldiers." And it may be that his personal tragedy, the death of his most beloved son, brought forth a more subtle and complex assessment that has led Reinhold Niebuhr to call Lincoln the "greatest theologian of the war years."

Willie's death confronted Lincoln with an inexplicable God. Although he had always been intellectually inclined to accept a doctrine of necessity, as he called it, which reconciled men to incomprehensible death and misfortune, that thought now acquired heart-wrenching endorsement. At such a time many abandoned a callous God entirely. Others, exhausted by their sorrow, stopped their search for understanding and adopted a heaven like home in which the dead still lived and were happy and watched over loved ones on earth. At an emotional level, one part of Lincoln stopped his search here, too. But Willie being in heaven was not enough.

Lincoln's spirit was weary, but his mind continued to seek a larger meaning for death and for suffering. He took the road of reconciling himself to the will of God and to finding peace in believing that the divinity of God was demonstrated by the fact that His purposes could not be facilely understood by men. It was a humbling kind of vision, but it offered at once an antidote to the predominant ministerial explanations and an expanded subtlety to the religious thought of the age.

No message shows Lincoln's understanding better than the Second Inaugural. The address built on the recognition that slavery was the cause of the war but expanded responsibility for the evils of that institution to both North and South. Challenging the desire of Northerners to see themselves as angels of light, Lincoln linked them with the enemy under a divine judgment that focused on both sections. Both sides read the same Bible, Lincoln noted, prayed to the same God. And while "it may seem strange that any men should dare to ask God's assistance in wringing their bread from the sweat of other men's faces . . . let us judge not that we be not judged." Whatever people might feel to be right and just, there was a higher and more complete understanding than any human could hold. "The Almighty has his own purposes," and if God determined that the time had come to end slavery and to use the long and bloody war to do so and to continue the strife "until all the wealth piled by the bondman's 250 years of unrequited toil shall be sunk and until every drop drawn by the lash shall be paid by another drawn with the sword, as was said 3000 years ago, so still it must be said 'the judgments of the Lord, are true and righteous altogether.' "

Lincoln urged the Union to be firm in its dedication to the right, but noted that only God himself fully knew the right, and thus the proper attitude for men was humility and tolerance, "malice toward none . . . charity for all."

In the burgeoning excitement over impending victory, Lincoln's comments were especially appropriate. A Union that had been dominated by images of Armageddon and good defeating evil walked dangerously close to the hubris of believing that God wore blue. Reunion was hardly auspicious in such an environment. During the war one Northern preacher wrote Lincoln to assure him that God was on the Union side. The president answered that his prayer went the other way, that he hoped the Union would be on God's side. These words spoke the understanding of a providence transcending earthly victories, one that performed the prophetic function of teaching humility even as it motivated action toward higher things. A nation that believed in its special mission and that, with slavery destroyed, seemed on the verge of fulfilling that mission needed reminding about the dangers of pride. When Thurlow Weed wrote to compliment Lincoln on the Second Inaugural, the president replied, "I expect [it] to wear as well as—perhaps better than—anything I have produced; but believe it is not immediately popular. Men are not flattered by being shown that there has been a difference of purpose between the Almighty and them. To deny it, however, in this case, is to deny that there is a God governing the world." Lincoln felt the need of reminding Americans that they were an "*almost* chosen people."[54]

Still, the genius of Lincoln's religious vision was that it did not reconcile men to God in a way that led to simple resignation. For the president believed in the ideals for which the Union fought and accepted the rightness of the victory over slavery. His recognition of the sovereignty of God still had a place for the efforts of man. And the war had clearly offered Northerners the chance to end slavery, to expand their efforts of charity, and to preserve the most democratic and the freest government of the age.

But the continued vitality of the nation, its ability to expand on the gains that war had brought, demanded not self-satisfied smugness, but a humbler recognition that there was still work to do, and that man needed constantly to keep in mind his own limitations while retaining faith that God would move him toward vistas broader than those he understood at the moment.

The war had seemed to most Northerners the fulfillment of a religious mission that destroyed the most incarnate evil of the nation, slavery. It had also entwined religious imagery with political ideals. Government of the people, the rule of law, the necessity of order, all became religious themes. The destruction and carnage of the war also brought forth a chance to exercise charity and to extend it to freed slaves as well as to the soldiers in the field. While the gospel of peace had been muted in the vast butchering of the battlefield, the destruction of slavery had ended for four million people the murdering of spirit and body. The vast majority of Northerners might well believe that they had done justice and loved mercy.

Lincoln's message completed the thought from the prophet Micah, however. They must also remember to walk humbly before their God.

It was not hard to remember, given the hundreds of thousands of dead young men. In the midst of the glory there was weeping as well. And the murder of Lincoln on the very eve of victory presented the North with a stunning reminder of the sins of pride. By example as well as precept, Lincoln had taught that lesson. The jingoistic Christianity of the war years quickly faded, not to be revived for a generation. The reforms of Reconstruction and the later growth of the social gospel suggested a dedication to helping those in need as well as admonishing them to salvation. The message of Social Darwinism, that somehow economic and social inequity were part of a cosmic plan, was answered by the fact of a growing social relief movement. There was an enduring arrogance in the behavior of some of the welfare reformers, but side by side went a growing willingness to help the urban poor as well as the freedmen. Many Americans took refuge from the pain of losing their young men in a sentimentality that turned God's heavenly kingdom into the little house on the prairie. But their pain was profound and personal, and not every American could use grief to achieve a vision for the nation.

Conclusion

THE end of the war, like its beginning, was a milestone for Northerners. They had once thought it would end quickly. It had lasted for four years. The deaths and the mutilations mounted day after day, month upon month, becoming first personal calamities, then community afflictions, then national tragedy. Each enlargement of perspective added the balance of gains as well as losses, triumphs as well as tragedies. Great events lay behind them now: stupendous battles killing more men in a day than had died in years of earlier wars; four million slaves freed, now facing unknown futures instead of generation after generation of bondage; laws passed in distant Washington, D.C., that organized great armies and swept the unwilling as well as the bold toward the fighting; new banking systems; transcontinental railroads; new currency; new taxes; new systems of education; homesteads for farmers—all were born of a day and sounded the reveille of a changing nation. But Lee's surrender at Appomattox, followed by that of Joe Johnston to Sherman on April 26, and the capture of a fleeing Jefferson Davis sandwiched between the capitulations of the last two Confederate armies in May meant the intense and passionate environment of conflict was over. Lincoln's shocking death, the first assassination of a president, quickly muted the trumpets of glory, and the two-week funeral journey from Washington back to Springfield swept the North toward somber mourning.

Some wartime passions abided. The assassination conspirators were hunted down, the net sweeping wide to include even those who helped the fleeing assassins. Booth himself was shot by soldiers as he attempted escape. Four of his accomplices were hanged on July 7, 1865; another four were sent to prison on Dry Tortugas off Key West, Florida. The horrors of Confederate prisons did not encourage forgiveness. Captain Henry Wirz, commandant at Andersonville, where thirteen thousand prisoners had died, was convicted of war crimes and hanged on November 10, 1865. Jefferson Davis went to jail for two years. War memories were legitimately kept alive to provide protection for the freedmen, and the Thirteenth, Fourteenth, and Fifteenth amendments strengthened the Constitution, while civil rights acts of the early 1870s offered promises of equality.

But the dominant voice said the war was over. Besides Wirz and Davis, no other Confederate leader lost anything other than a temporary right to vote and hold office. By 1872 all but 500 had regained these rights. In 1867 Davis himself went free, and no treason trials were held, an unprecedented show of magnanimity after a rebellion. An army of over a million men in May 1865 lost 80 percent of its troops by June, a year later stood at 38,000, and by October 1866 was, at 17,600, only 1,600 men larger than the pre-Sumter army.

The lives of all Americans had been touched with the most intense fire in the nation's history, sweeping from battlefield to governmental halls, into communities and homes, and thoughtful people wondered how the victory had been achieved. It was a large question, but certain elements were clear.

The North won the Civil War because in the largest sense it had the economic, institutional, intellectual, and social resources for victory. The economic resources are obvious: more men, more shops and factories, more tools, more railroads, more ships, even more farms, food, and fiber. Furthermore, it had the knowledge to organize those resources and employ them in the war. Prewar industrialization both required and created men who developed the necessary tools of finance, business, and industry. The growing equation of private advancement with the public interest encouraged public officials to rely on these men to mobilize resources. Private industry for its part believed in its obligation to preserve the nation. The North also relied on workers educated by the public school systems and work experience. They made and repaired the guns and the locomotives, harvested the crops with the new machines, supplying civilians and soldiers with what they needed.

Northern generals knew how to use material advantages. Most West Pointers did not stay in the army in the antebellum period. They went into private business, where their training in engineering and organization could be used profitably. McClellan especially had learned as a railroad executive how to forge an efficient and powerful organization, whether that was a railroad or an army. Henry Halleck and Montgomery Meigs similarly had learned in peace how to organize modern war. Grant and Sherman and other Union generals absorbed in prewar experience the nature and potentialities of Northern resources. Southern generals, of course, also knew of those things, but lacked sufficient resources to use the knowledge to mobilize for victory. Northern generals had the means and knew most of the ways.

The large and diverse Northern population also provided vital advantages. It supplied over 2 million enlistments and produced an army of nearly 1 million men by mid-1865. The North, which had welcomed immigration while the South had discouraged it, could call on 500,000 foreign-born troops who were ready to fight. Xenophobia still existed. But the North had sufficient tolerance to accept these 5,000 regiments. While most Northerners considered blacks inferior, they were not afraid to put guns in their hands: 45,000 free blacks from the North were added to the army. And 134,000 more stepped from slavery into soldiering, further swelling Union ranks. Northern needs overcame racial and nativist anxieties.

The North also developed self-images that set the stage for victory. The ideal of social mobility allowed its armies to generate new leadership in the midst of war. The Confederate generals who began the war as leaders kept their positions until the end. The architects of Northern victory sat in comparative obscurity in the conflict's early days. But as the war ground on, Grant and Sherman and Thomas and Sheridan emerged to take the reins. They had a commander in chief who knew from his own experience how to watch for and reward men on the make. The fact that war allowed such men to climb, of course, further endorsed the strength of Northern society.

Politics contributed another sign of vitality and built self-confidence. Lincoln initially called upon the North to defend the right of changing governments by elections, not secession. The electoral process continued throughout the war. Every election showed that self-government worked in the North. The system was strong enough that in the midst of a challenge to their survival as a nation, they could tolerate, indeed had to tolerate, the turmoil of the election process.

That turmoil strengthened the government. Winners pointed to the support of the people and undercut opposition. Losers by participating showed they believed in the process if not the result. The existence of the ballot box option made defiance appear as disloyalty. The vital two-party system kept opposition within bounds by requiring platforms that spoke to the broad middle of the political spectrum, not to the extremes. It also opened careers and patronage to those ambitious men who played by the rules. A strong opposition, in addition, kept the ruling party unified enough to win elections despite interfamily quarrels.

Lincoln played a vital role in strengthening faith in the political system. He spoke of the principles of self-government constantly—keeping the goal before the people. While there were abuses, Lincoln and his government generally exercised restraint in curbing dissent. Most of his critics were free to damn him for his "dictatorship," and he took pains to provide persuasive constitutional justifications for limiting civil liberties. Example as well as rhetoric persuaded Northerners that their system was worth fighting for.

The constitutional system also proved its strength and helped the Northern war effort. While Lincoln provided a constitutional presidency adequate to defend the nation, congressmen rediscovered the Hamiltonian heritage that used power to defend liberty. Jeffersonian/Jacksonian traditions that denied national power lost influence. A national currency, a national banking system, a national tax structure, all emerged during the war, linking ordinary people to their government in tangible ways, proving that national power paid off for those who had, or aspired to, economic influence. The war emergency both justified and obscured consequent economic inequities. These measures allowed the North to mobilize its wealth to save the nation. That wealth paid the armies, bought the supplies, built the transportation systems, and fed homefront faith in the system.

The War Congress satisfied factions in the private economy that had been ignored by Democrats with their laissez-faire theories. A Homestead Act opened lands to settlement, providing farms for those with little cash and much hope. The Pacific Railroad Bill linked the West Coast with the rest of the nation and in the process fulfilled white dreams of national grandeur and personal prosperity. Higher tariffs in fact benefited the capitalists who needed protection for infant industry and, theoretically, their workers. The war environment made it possible to believe that their interests were the same. Congress also funded a system of higher education that undeniably helped all segments of the society. Here were signs that the people's government might be their instrument, not their enemy.

Organized resources, emerging generals, a vital political and constitutional system, all built Northern strength that protected the Union in the foreign arena. England and France, the only powers that mattered, became less and less interested in challenging the Union blockade or assisting the Confederacy. The Union might provoke a crisis by challenging foreign powers directly, or by intransigence in settling inevitable disputes. But Seward and Lincoln were wise enough to balance the protection of Union prerogatives with a willingness to negotiate. The secretary of state alternated bombast and reasonableness, while Lincoln watched Seward to make sure that bombast did not dominate. Both men knew when to back away from confrontation and thus gain support by retreat. The strength of the North meant that they would not have to back away too far.

The North also had the advantage of fighting for ideals that the vast majority of the population agreed with. In Dixie internal opposition to the economic power of slavery produced a fault line running along the Appalachians that could unleash disruption at any time. Some in Dixie doubted the morality of slavery itself. Military defeats and/or the war measures of a desperate government could unleash these feelings and erode the will to fight. The Confederacy was potentially further divided by its abiding state sovereignty philosophy. Differences in Dixie not only were questions of policy; they were matters of the very structure of the republic.

There were also divisions in the North. The great divide was over how much the war cost in lives and in changing the society. Democrats argued against expansion of national power over civil liberties, the alliance between government and the economic power, changing the status of blacks. The draft riots showed how passionate such protest might be. But even though they interpreted liberty and equality and the Constitution in different ways, Northerners still were united by general agreements about their system. Even Vallandigham insisted he was for saving the Union, and every antiwar politician stayed in politics and insisted on his respect for the constitutional system. State sovereignty as a motto was heard in the North, but aside from an occasional state judge who lacked jurisdiction beyond his courtroom, no responsible Northern official ever used the doctrine to restrain national government action. The fact that the rebellion was based on that principle effectively weakened its force in the North. Northerners were nationalists, state rights nationalists in the majority of cases, but still believers in the right of the government to find the means to save itself.

All parties generally agreed on the validity of the economic system, too, and the war strengthened that agreement. Democrats denied that Republican direction of the economy was fair to the ordinary people they claimed to represent. They did not doubt that a Democratically guided economy would prosper. Laborers protested the power of capital in order to gain the right to be capitalists themselves. Northerners did not have to explain or rationalize away their free labor system. Both parties claimed to represent it. As the struggle for the Union and for the free labor system intensified, it stifled most of the latent class consciousness that did exist.

Opposition to slavery also was powerful in the North. In an environment already sensitive to loss of control and morality, the Republican party came to life out of anger that slavery reached out to imperil the Union, erode constitutional liberties, and corrode ideals of equality that had defined the nation in the first place. Racist fears combined with other constitutional imperatives, and love of the Union protected slavery. But the war undercut those protections. Sumter damaged arguments that slavery was the price of union. Securing Kentucky disarmed strategic opposition to emancipation. Black soldiers and laborers undercut racist fears. In this environment Republicans interwove abolitionist arguments about the justness and Christian duty of emancipation with arguments from expediency. Lincoln's eloquence kept alive principles he had spoken in the 1850s: the Union rested on the "standard maxim for a free society," the equality of all men.

As the war continued, therefore, saving the Union and ending slavery were integrated as harmonious goals. Those inclined to separate them began to recognize that their purposes were the same. By 1863 abolition was a popular unifying goal, and that unity increased until, by 1865, Democratic congressmen were voting for the Thirteenth Amendment.

Racism did not die. Its purposes could be sustained by constitutional and social ideas that gained power during the conflict. Nevertheless, during the conflict Northerners built the will to continue fighting in large measure out of the growing consensus that liberty and union were "one and inseparable."

The North also gained strength because its fears and anxieties were focused in positive ways. War answered the doubts of many that the system could produce moral citizens. It proved that men would risk their fortunes and their lives for an unselfish purpose. War provided answers to prewar worries that inequality was growing, opportunity for poorer men contracting. The wartime boom illustrated economic vitality. Its inequities could be explained away as imperative sacrifices for the cause. The widely publicized humble origins of wartime leaders argued that the paths of opportunity were open to hardworking, honest men. Lincoln, Sherman, Grant, and their well-supplied and unrelenting armies of farmers, laborers, and mechanics showed what the industrializing nation was capable of.

The South played an important role in the Northern victory. Southern strategy essentially left the North alone to discover its vitality and strength. Jefferson Davis and his military advisers understood that they lacked the ability to invade the North. Their best strategy was to defend Dixie until Northern will wore out. An occasional foray above the Mason-Dixon line might be employed in the service of this "offensive-defensive" strategy, but fundamentally the Confederacy could not bring the war to Northern farms, communities, and cities.

The deaths of thousands of young men reminded Northerners constantly that they were engaged in an agonizing, bloody business. But because rebel armies stayed in Dixie, Northerners could stir their fires, send their children off to school, go to work in busy shops and factories, plant and harvest their crops, and, as Ellen Wright said, "make believe a little longer," living the normal lives that the supranormal times both demanded and allowed. The thousands of communities that made up the Union were left alone to generate loyalty and nurture the daily affirmed faith that self-government was worth preserving. Northerners recognized the possibility of temporary military defeat, but the South never challenged the Northern belief that it had the strength to win if it only retained the will to win.

None of these factors alone explains the Northern victory. All worked together to create the will to continue the fight and the means to make that will irresistible. The economy that provided the resources to bring Northern victory generated at the same time anxieties that justified, and at times seemed to demand, war. The shared values of the North were preserved by the fact that fighting and destruction never seriously threatened Northerners' day-to-day lives. Unity thus came with success and success with unity.

Overall the system itself remained open, energetic, strong, and vital. Diversity and discussion generated faith that government of, by, and for the people could and should endure. The booming economy fostered further faith in what free labor could accomplish. And above all the nature of the enemy guaranteed that passion for the Northern cause would be intense. Slavery had challenged the system of government, it had been successfully labeled as the North's economic antithesis, it had earned the moral outrage of large segments of the Northern population. It had become the metaphor for almost every Northern self-doubt and external evil. Determined to destroy all that slavery meant, the Northern people rushed unswervingly forward upon their iron way.

But individual lives as well as the grand movements of the people continued onward, too, shaped by forces the war unleashed. Soldiers brought home war memories and were different men because of what they had seen and done. Civilians, too, had been "touched with fire." They also had to live in the world the Civil War had made.

Theodore Upson was with Sherman's army near Raleigh when he heard the news: Lee had surrendered to Grant. At first the men couldn't believe it, but then General Woods dismissed the guards around the camp, grabbed Upson and two comrades, and pulled them into his tent, and they began drinking punch and making speeches and a band came in and drank, too, while they played. General Woods took a shine to Upson, promoted him to lieutenant, then to captain, "and I might have got higher than that if the general had not noticed that the band wasn't playing." Woods picked up the big bass drum and other officers got horns, and all of them marched around the camp with the general in the lead, "and some sang or tried to sing. But when 'Johnny Comes Marching Home Again' and 'John Brown's Body' or 'Hail Columbia' and the 'Star Spangled Banner' are all sung together they get mixed up so I don't really think the singing was a grand success from an artistic point of view."

Then came the "terrible news that our loved President Abraham Lincoln was assassinated last night." Feelings of outrage and revenge replaced celebration. Woods gave orders to keep a sharp eye on the men. When word came that a citizen in Raleigh had fired at General Kirkpatrick and almost killed him, soldiers on the spot grabbed the man and hanged him. That night two thousand men started for Raleigh to destroy the place. General Logan ordered them to stop but they wouldn't do it, and so Logan threatened to fire grape canister into them. The angry men returned to camp.[1]

Upson was sent ahead to Washington, D.C., and found himself a hero, the first of "Sherman's bummers" that the people there had seen. He had free meals whenever he was hungry, everyone wanted to give him a cigar, the "darkies," as he called them, pointed him out in restaurants and on the street, and strangers gathered near to hear his stories. He showed civilians what a rifle could do, hitting a target five hundred feet away twelve straight times, and "didn't half try."

When the rest of Sherman's army caught up with Upson, he marched in a grand parade in May there in the capital. The Army of the Potomac led the way the first day with "polished shoes and brass trimmings . . . their rifles burnished til they shone . . . new uniforms, and nearly all with white gloves. Their marching was machinelike." Then came Sherman's army, wearing uniforms they had worn in Dixie, guns "clean but not burnished . . . our men did not try to put on any extra style." And as they marched "our boys fell into the long swinging step, every man in perfect time . . . and it seemed to me that the men had never marched so well before." The sidewalks were jammed and the cheering never stopped and the torn flags of the regiments fluttered, displaying the names of battles they had fought in.

Then the soldiers went home. The railroad took them most of the way west. They took a boat along the Ohio and got back on the train to Indianapolis. When they arrived the women of the town had made them a huge breakfast. Governor Morton welcomed them with "a grand good speech and gave us some excellent advice which I hope we shall all take to heart." Then they went to their old quarters at Camp Morton and a few days later were discharged.

But the war remained in Upson's thoughts. A thousand men had left that part of Indiana, he recalled. Four hundred and sixty-four did not come back. They had died in hospitals and on battlefields "far from home and friends." They had "given all they had to give."

Upson returned to find his parents living in Lima. They had moved off the farm. Restless, he, too, looked for a life someplace else. He went to Morristown, New Jersey, and became a successful carriage maker. He met a girl named Anna Beach and got married in May 1867. They had six children, two sons and four daughters.

They moved back to Indiana, and by the early 1880s Upson was known in his old hometown as a respectable businessman, with a busy shop making carriages and wagons. He was known also as an inveterate tinkerer and mechanic, always interested in how the machines of the thriving industrial age worked. The old-timers later recalled that he had made the first horseless carriage in town and then traded it in for a Stanley Steamer.

His war memories abided. He never outgrew his dislike of blacks, and had a peculiar aversion to shovels, probably because they reminded him of digging trenches. For many years he commanded one of the local Grand Army of the Republic posts. He wrote letters and poems for publication in the local paper. And he told his children about the history he had lived. They wanted to know more, and so he gathered his old letters home, his pocket journals and notes, molded them together with the memories they inspired, and wrote his recollections of the greatest experience of his life. Upson lived to be seventy-six and died in January 1919.

William Sylvis left no recollection of the days the war ended. While most Americans believed that the salvation of the Union and the death of slavery ended the disunion crisis, Sylvis kept another conflict in mind. He rejoiced that the Union endured, for its survival "settl[ed] forever the great problem of man's capacity for self-government." He was also happy that Negro slavery was dead.[2]

But these achievements did not satisfy him. For one thing, people linked them to the Republican party. Sylvis believed Lincoln's party was responsible for an inequitable draft, for an immigration policy that drove wages down, for generals who crushed strikes in the name of military necessity. For another, focus on the victory of union and emancipation obscured the abiding needs of industrial labor. Northern celebration, he told the 1865 Iron Molders convention, allowed people to ignore the continuing danger of "a war of classes . . . a collision between capital and labor." His postwar experience was shaped with that conflict in mind.

Sylvis had private demands on his life. His wife died in 1866 and left him with four young children. He remarried and then fathered another child. But he remembered his own grinding poverty and was never happy away from his work. Unlike Upson, Sylvis stayed in the public arena fighting.

One tactic he used in his fight for class equality was bold rhetoric, threats of class struggle. In theory he believed in that conflict, but day to day Silvis was a pragmatist. More organizer than ideologue, he had built the Iron Molders to seven thousand members and 122 locals by 1865, and though postwar economic decline cut into membership, Sylvis remained a power in the movement. He worked endless hours to strengthen and create postwar labor organizations of every variety. He ignored his personal prejudice and worked to bring blacks into the labor movement. "The negro will take possession of the shops," he warned, "if we do not take possession of the negro."

He also challenged personal bias as well as that of his membership to support women's involvement in the labor movement. He believed that ideally women should be "the presiding deity of the home circle." But when capitalists kept wages so low that women had to work, Sylvis set aside his ideals. His iron molders raised money to support striking women in Troy in 1868, and blacklisted the owners. Sylvis went to meetings of women's unions all over the nation, bringing advice on how to organize as well as encouragement.

He joined the eight-hour movement in 1865, supporting Ira Stewart's argument that reduced hours of work would allow laborers to learn skills so that they could move up the labor ladder. He helped organize the National Labor Union in August of 1866, urging a moderate platform. The NLU wanted greater access to the Western lands, an end to convict labor, amelioration of the evils of tenement housing, strict enforcement of apprenticeship regulations, and Stewart's eight-hour day.

Sylvis himself reached out to manufacturers even while representing the iron molders. He wrote letters sympathizing with their need to cut wages in the postwar recession. He said that he hoped their national organization would generate increased understanding between labor and management. While occasionally supporting strikes, he generally deplored them, urging arbitration instead. He also endorsed worker cooperatives that allowed laborers to become foundry owners.

In 1867 Sylvis joined thousands of other workers in following Alexander Campbell's panacea of currency reform. The fundamental reason why workers suffered, Campbell argued, was the influence of a "monster monied aristocracy" made more powerful by the wartime banking laws. The solution was simple: national greenback currency, payment of national bonds in greenbacks, and a legal limit on interest rates. "When a just money system has been established," Sylvis proclaimed, "there will no longer exist a necessity for trade unions."

Greenbacks, eight-hour days, cooperation, a Western safety valve, blacks and women in solidarity with white workingmen, better urban housing, union shops—Sylvis tried everything to bring the benefits of Northern victory to industrial workers. He tried cajoling manufacturers, moderation in strikes, threats of class warfare. None of these brought the power to organized labor that Sylvis struggled for. It remained for men like Samuel Gompers to narrow the targets and limit the tactics and thus create a stronger movement. But Silvis came to maturity at a time of total war, a time when evils were clearer than answers. His labors were inevitably restless, and ultimately he lacked the strength for them, though never the will. William Sylvis died in the summer of 1869. He was forty-one.

Mary Livermore discovered her talents during the war. Organizing the Chicago branch of the Sanitary Commission, visiting hospitals and armies, lecturing to large audiences on her experiences, she demonstrated what women could do for the Northern cause. These activities set the stage for her continued commitment to women's rights after the war. She organized the first women's suffrage convention in Chicago in 1868 and became the Illinois chairperson of the Woman Suffrage Association. By January 1869 she was publishing a newspaper to advocate the twin causes of temperance and suffrage.[3]

But she made her living on the lyceum circuit, the nation's first commercially viable lecture bureau. Its chief organizer, James Redpath, took to calling her "the Queen of the Platform." She traveled across the nation speaking on women's issues, her days as a governess in Dixie, her war experiences, her travels, interesting moments on the platform. She gave her most popular lecture, "What Shall We Do with Our Daughters," a combination of health suggestions, admonitions about women's public and domestic roles, and a call for suffrage, over eight thousand times "from Maine to Santa Barbara," she later recalled.

Livermore played an important role when the postwar women's movement divided between Elizabeth Cady Stanton and Susan B. Anthony on one side and Lucy Stone on the other. Immediately after the war, Stanton and Anthony cast off their wartime allegiance to the abolitionist cause. They said that it was time for women to claim the rights they had subordinated to the antislavery crusade. They pushed for the vote, for divorce law reform to allow women to end unhappy marriages. They advocated national legislation to protect sexual equality.

This platform challenged Republican and abolitionist reformers who still focused on racial equality and feared losing support by challenging traditional sex roles. Stanton and Anthony widened the gap between themselves and former allies by enlisting former copperheads in the cause as well as the notorious Victoria Claflin Woodhull, who not only spoke for, but publicly practiced, sexual free choice for women.

Livermore agreed that women's suffrage was vital as well as right, but she kept faith with the Republican party. She had come to recognize her full powers in the struggle for the Union and emancipation. She refused to abandon the party that had presided over her awakening. She was equally conservative in her views of women's proper sphere. In 1869 Lucy Stone called her to Boston to edit the *Women's Journal*. This paper answered the Stanton-Anthony platform of equality of the sexes with an assertion of the uniqueness of women. It opposed liberalizing divorce laws and supported state rather than national legislation to secure the vote.

The conservative position flowered in two postwar reform movements that enlisted Livermore's devotion. In the mid-1870s the Women's Christian Temperance Union was born, responding to the envisioned evils of urbanizing America and increased drinking, especially among ex-soldiers. Livermore quickly joined the movement to restore restraint and abiding virtues to the nation. She lobbied successfully to persuade the Boston City Council to hold a dry reception for President Hayes in 1877. She fervently endorsed Francis Willard's goal of bringing women into the public sphere in order to cleanse it of the evils that male perspective and practice produced. "Woman," Willard claimed, "will make homelike every place she enters."

By the 1880s Livermore had found a new focus for her energy. She took up the ideals of Edward Bellamy's best-selling *Looking Backward* and joined in the Nationalist movement, a nationwide organization of clubs devoted to restoring the virtues of self-discipline and patriotism, combining them with economic equality and women's suffrage. Both sexes, she asserted, would join in a society where "patriotism, passion for humanity impel the worker as in [the Civil War era] the soldier." Livermore became the president of the Boston Nationalist Club and proclaimed Bellamy's "nationalism" to be "applied Christianity."

"Nationalism" combined the basic ideals that Livermore fought for throughout her life, equal rights based on the special qualities of women, united in a moral crusade. It echoed her wartime experiences in which the women of the North "exerted a greater moral force on the nation than the army that carried loaded muskets." At the end of her life she still believed the crusade should go on. She wrote her memoirs in 1897 dedicated to "the Victorious Soldiers of the Union Army." Her memoirs sold over sixty thousand copies. When she died in 1905 at eighty-five, the editor of the *Boston Transcript* called her "the foremost woman in America."

During the war Frederick Douglass had played a major role in leading Lincoln to emancipation, then to the use of black troops, then to providing them equal pay. As the conflict wound down he was lobbying with some effect for the ballot so that the freedmen could protect their other gains. Lincoln promised him "over and over again," Douglass remembered, that at least soldiers and literate blacks would be enfranchised.[4]

But then Lincoln was dead, and Douglass lost access to the White

House. President Andrew Johnson now sat in Lincoln's chair, and from being "my friend Douglass" the black leader became "just like any nigger" who would "sooner cut a white man's throat as not," as Johnson snarled to his secretary. Douglass turned to Congress to secure freedom and equality for his people.

The task was not easy. Before and during the war freedom was a simple idea, understood in terms of its contrast with the horrors of slavery. But Appomattox found war's simplicity replaced by the more subtle struggles of peace.

Obstacles to equality loomed large. Racism remained a powerful force in the nation. To take one telling example, the New York City Common Council excluded blacks from the funeral cortege that accompanied Lincoln's body through the city. Respect for federalism potentially restricted the outreach of national power necessary to protect freedmen from former masters. Belief that self-reliant free labor provided the backbone of Northern strength and personal character could also limit the struggle for equality.

Racism had always been Douglass' enemy, and he had little respect for a federalism that allowed whites to oppress blacks. These commitments pushed him ahead of Congress, demanding civil rights and suffrage protected by national power, unhindered by claims of state rights and local self-government. Still, when Congress passed laws that provided equality while respecting federalism, Douglass supported them, all the while demanding more protection for black equality.

Even as the Republican party shed its mantle as the party of emancipation to become the party of the Gilded Age, Douglass continued the fight. He welcomed the 1875 Civil Rights Bill and deplored Grant's failure to protect blacks from white violence in 1875 and the removal of troops from Dixie in 1877. He was outraged by the 1883 Supreme Court decision that denied federal protection for equal accommodations.

Despite his disagreements with the Republican party about the extent of protection for freedmen, Douglass remained a loyal party man. Some asserted that he had abandoned his old radicalism and lost his moral authority as agitator. His appointments to political office did nothing to undercut those charges. He was President Hayes' marshal for Washington, D.C., Garfield's district recorder of deeds, and Harrison's minister to Haiti. But Douglass believed that he was the symbol and spokesman for his people. His offices, he insisted, illustrated what other blacks could achieve. Furthermore, he believed he was a more effective conscience for the party when he could speak directly to men who made the laws. The Democrats were never an option. "If we are slighted by the Republicans," he wrote, "we are murdered by the Democrats."

Racism and federalism posed obvious obstacles that Douglass could challenge unequivocally, but the free labor ideal was more complex. He retained a commitment to that ideal, damned slavery as "more than all things else [robbing] its victims of self-reliance." Freedom meant to Douglass that blacks could now prove themselves. When freedmen became "noted for enterprise, industry, economy and success, we shall no longer have any trouble in the matter of civil and economic rights."

Yet while Douglass used the old free labor ideals to advance equality, others found in them justification for retreat. Even as Douglass spoke, Booker T. Washington was developing his philosophy of accommodation. Washington urged blacks to earn equality quietly, through hard work, serving the economic needs of whites and the nation. Speaking for a growing number of blacks who despaired of getting full equality from whites of the late nineteenth century, he promoted industrial arts schools where former slaves could learn the trades that would make them economically indispensable to the society. He urged blacks to pull themselves up by their own efforts.

Douglass' vision for his people included self-help, but also transcended that free labor ideal. Unlike Washington, Douglass had learned the meaning of freedom in the Civil War world. He recalled a time when self-help meant heroism, defiance, a commitment to equality on every front. Out of that struggle had come abolition, citizenship, and the right to vote. Blacks had known then that "liberty won by white men would lose half its luster." In taking up arms blacks shattered doubts about their courage and strength.

Douglass could afford to be bold. He lived in a fifteen-room house in Washington, D.C. He moved on the national and international stage, promoting reforms like women's rights as well as racial justice, representing his country in Haiti as well as lecturing in Europe. He felt free enough to marry a white woman when, in 1884, his first wife died. He could parry the resulting white outrage with the comment that his marriages proved his impartiality. His first wife "was the color of my mother, and the second, the color of my father."

But if Douglass' arena allowed him a latitude that Booker T. Washington could not claim, he also understood things that the founder of Tuskegee could not. Increasing violence in Dixie against blacks led Washington to muffle claims to civil and political equality and to emphasize economic gains. By contrast, Douglass reduced his arguments for economic initiatives as oppression escalated. The contrast between the two men was symbolized in two interviews a young black reporter had with them. When the reporter asked Washington for his advice to his people, the leader replied, "Work! Work! Work! Be patient and win by superior service." Douglass' answer was "Agitate! Agitate! Agitate!"

When Douglass died in 1895 the nation stood on the brink of two symbolic events. Within seven months Washington spoke at the Atlanta Exposition. "The wisest among my race," he announced, "understand that the agitation of questions of social equality is the extremist folly, and that progress in the enjoyment of all the privileges that will come to us must be the result of severe and constant struggle rather than artificial forcing. . . . It is important and right that all privileges of the law be ours, but it is vastly more important that we be prepared for the exercise of those privileges. The opportunity to earn a dollar in a factory just now is worth infinitely more than the opportunity to spend a dollar in an opera house." Upon the conclusion of Washington's speech the white governor of Georgia walked across the platform to shake the black man's hand. A year later the Supreme Court showed what Washington's accommodation meant. Relying on precedents stretching back to the 1883 Civil Rights Cases, it declared that segregation did not violate the Fourteenth Amendment.

Washington knew that Douglass' life and words stood as a protest against accommodations. Personally and politically the new black leader had to confront the old. He did so by writing Douglass' biography. He admitted that Douglass had spoken eloquently for equal justice, but the message that he emphasized was Douglass the self-made man. He chose as a coda Douglass' comment that "neither institutions nor friends can make a race to stand unless it has strength in its own legs; that there is no power in the world which can be relied on to help the weak against the strong, or the simple against the wise; that races, like individuals, must stand or fall by their own merits."

And Washington tried to make Douglass a man for a different

season. "Frederick Douglass's life fell in the period of war, of controversy, and of fierce party strife. The task which was assigned to him was, on the whole, one of destruction and liberation, rather than construction and reconciliation." Washington sought a different peace than Douglass had. For him the war was over, best forgotten. For Douglass war's message and spirit abided. It would not truly be over until its promises, not only of the victory of free labor and self-help, but of equal justice under law, were kept.

For George Strong the war ended in jubilation and anguish. First a celebration on Wall Street when Lee surrendered as a huge crowd listened for three hours to speakers and sang "One Hundred" and "John Brown" and the "Star Spangled Banner," "repeating the last two lines . . . over and over." He walked through the crowds shaking hands with everyone and watched as "men embraced and hugged each other, *kissed* each other, retreated into doorways to dry their eyes and came out again to flourish their hats and hurrah."[5]

Then, too quickly, the horrible news. Lincoln shot, dead, and every building of every street in New York City draped with the bunting of mourning, "even in second- and third-class quarters, people who could afford to do no more [displaying] at least a little twenty-five-cent flag with a little scrap of crape annexed." All classes were united in their grief.

Outrage at the assassination, his desire to punish the South, his abiding unionism, kept Strong in Republican ranks, supporting congressional Reconstruction, urging the impeachment of Andrew Johnson. He wanted to preserve the results of war. But gradually he lost his fervor for equality. With the passage of the Fourteenth and Fifteenth amendments, he thought the struggle was over.

He turned away from national affairs and devoted attention to his law practice and to his city. He lost interest in the plight of the poor. He began comparing the blacks with the despised Irish "rabble." He looked now to protecting the upper-class beneficiaries of the war, accepting cases defending clients against the income tax laws. He doubted that they could win, but he took the cases anyway. With no war to inspire national economic efforts, he took to calling the tax laws "odious, inquisitorial, demoralizing, inequal, unconstitutional."

With no Sanitary Commission to consume his time, he focused on Trinity Church, and worked to establish Columbia's school of mines so that complex technology could be used to expand national wealth. He had always loved music and spent more time attending concerts, working as president of the Church Music Philharmonic Society. Economic troubles caught up with him in the depression of 1873. He had to economize and could not afford to be as involved in the social whirl as he had been in the past. A liver ailment sapped his strength. A quarrel with his son took an emotional toll, and he slid toward death. Old friends dropped in to say good-byes, and on July 21, 1875, George T. Strong died.

His funeral brought together leaders who had played central roles in the great events of the age. John Jacob Astor was a pallbearer. War governor John A. Dix attended. And President Grant himself, who had led Union armies to victory and now presided over the Gilded Age, joined the mourners. All paid their respects to the role that Strong had played in organizing the wealth of the nation's richest city in the interest of saving the Union.

As they stood there honoring him, perhaps these men, maybe many others as well, would have shared a thought that Strong had had a decade before as Kirby Smith surrendered the last rebel army. "We have lived a century of common life since [1861]," he wrote. Looking back to prewar America made him think of "records of some remote age and of a people wholly unlike our own." And yet for all the talk of change there still remained an undercurrent that flowed quietly and strong. Great events of war shook society, but mundane life endured. The contest had been a fiery trial, but while the fire burned the people's ordinary lives abided. "As I look back now to Bull Run, Fort Donelson, the Seven Days, Antietam, Gettysburg, Chancellorsville and other battles," Strong mused, "I wonder my thoughts have not been more engrossed by the developments of the great tragedy, that I have been able to pay any attention to my common routine and to be interested in anything outside the tremendous chapter that history has been taking down in shorthand."

Notes

Prologue. Anxious Conversations: The North Confronts Industrialization

1. Merle Curti, *Roots of American Loyalty* (New York, 1946); *The Statistical History of the United States* (Stamford, Conn., 1965), 10.
2. Lee Soltow, *Men and Wealth in the United States, 1850–1870* (New Haven, 1975), 24, 67, 99–103; Edward Pessen, *Riches, Class and Power before the Civil War* (Lexington, Ky., 1973), 31–45; Pessen, *Jacksonian America* (Homewood, Ill., 1978), 81–82; Robert Gallman, "Professor Pessen on the 'Egalitarian Myth,' " *Social Science History* 2 (Winter 1978): 194–95; Jeffrey G. Williamson and Peter Lindert, *American Inequality: A Macroeconomic History* (New York, 1980), chap. 3.
3. Phillip Paludan, *A Covenant with Death: The Constitution, Law and Equality in the Civil War Era* (Urbana, 1975).
4. Quoted in Bernard Mandel, *Labor, Free and Slave: Workingmen and the Antislavery Movement in the United States* (New York, 1955), 76–95.
5. George Fitzhugh, *Sociology for the South* (Richmond, 1854), 243–44; John Hope Franklin, *A Southern Odyssey: Travellers in the Antebellum North* (Baton Rouge, 1976), passim; Harvey Wish, *George Fitzhugh: Propagandist of the Old South* (Baton Rouge, 1943), 174–88; Eugene D. Genovese, *The World the Slaveholders Made* (New York, 1969), 165–94.
6. Wish, *George Fitzhugh*, 280–87; Eric Foner, *Free Soil, Free Labor, Free Men* (New York, 1970), 66–67; Stephan B. Oates, *With Malice Toward None: The Life of Abraham Lincoln* (New York, 1978), 137–38; Henry Carey, *The Harmony of Interests, Agricultural, Manufacturing, and Commercial* (New York, 1856); George Winston Smith, *Henry Carey and American Sectional Conflict* (Albuquerque, 1958); Charles G. Leland, "Have We a Principle Among Us?" *Knickerbocker* 58:154.
7. Foner, *Free Soil*, 15–18, 27–29, 55–58; Roy P. Basler, ed., *Collected Works of Abraham Lincoln* (New Brunswick, 1953), vol. 3, 478–79.
8. Foner, *Free Soil*, chaps. 1 and 2, conveys the overall sense of Republican opti-

mism. Foner believes that it was relatively easy for the party to dismiss the criticisms of the North that came from Fitzhugh and his ilk; see 66–69.

9. *Collected Works of Lincoln*, vol. 1, 108–15; vol. 2, 318, 403–4; vol. 3, 29. On Lincoln's concern about corruption, see Phillip S. Paludan, "Lincoln, the Rule of Law and the American Revolution," *Journal of the Illinois State Historical Society* 70 (February 1977): 10–17. George Forgie, *Patricide in the House Divided* (New York, 1979), 150–51; Anonymous, "The Kansas Question," *Putnam's* 6 (October 1855): 431–33.

10. David Davis, *The Slave Power Conspiracy and the Paranoid Style* (Baton Rouge, 1969); Robert Weibe, *The Opening of American Society: From the Adoption of the Constitution to the Eve of Disunion* (New York, 1984), 367–77.

11. Frank Luther Mott, *Golden Multitudes: The Story of Best Sellers in the United States* (New York, 1947), 122–42, 307–9; Susan Geary, "Scribbling Women," Ph.D. diss., Brown University, Providence, 1976; Helen Papashvily, *All the Happy Endings* (Port Washington, N.Y., 1972). George Fredrickson, *The Inner Civil War: Northern Intellectuals and the Crisis of Disunion* (New York, 1965).

12. William B. Dillingham, *Melville's Short Fiction, 1853–1856* (Athens, Ga., 1977), 1–17; Marvin Fisher, *Going Under: Melville's Short Fiction and the American 1850s* (Baton Rouge, 1977), ix–xii. I cannot agree with these authors that Melville masked his criticisms and insights into U.S. society in these stories. Although he does not announce that he is dealing with the problems of his time, the themes Melville explored are not obscure, except perhaps in the case of his travel story "The Encantadas," which is on the surface a natural history of these islands. Yet even here his language resonates with allusions to the evils of industrialism. See the reference to a land that looks "like the dross of an iron furnace—occupied by turtles in a changeless state of hopelessness." A hermit on these islands enslaves sailors through the use of deception and illusion. These latter themes of deception and illusion have been described as a major concern of the prewar period. See Davis, *The Slave Power Conspiracy*, 3–31. Davis does not explore the fictional allusions to deception. See also Carolyn Karcher, *Shadow over the Promised Land: Slavery, Race and Violence in Melville's America* (Baton Rouge, 1980); Beryl Bowland, "Melville's Bachelors and Maids: Interpretation through Symbol and Metaphor," *American Literature* 41 (1969): 389–405; Michael Paul Rogin, *Subversive Genealogy: The Politics and Art of Herman Melville* (New York, 1983), 201–8.

13. Harriet Beecher Stowe, *Uncle Tom's Cabin* (New York, n.d.), 249, 364, 369, 372.

Chapter 1. Communities Go to War

1. George Templeton Strong, *Diary: The Civil War, 1860–1865*, Allan Nevins and Milton Halsey Thomas, eds. (New York, 1952), vol. 3, 4–6.

2. *Ibid.*, 117–19.

3. James C. Sylvis, *The Life, Speeches, Labors and Essays of William H. Sylvis* (Philadelphia, 1872), 42–46; Jonathan Grossman, *William Sylvis, Pioneer of American Labor* (New York, 1945), 42–49.

4. The Frederick Douglass Papers, Yale University, New Haven, series 1, vol. 3 (1985), 412–35; Philip S. Foner, *The Life and Writings of Frederick Douglass*, vol. 3 (New York, 1952), 11.

5. Mary Ashton Livermore, *The Story of My Life* (Hartford, 1897); Robert Reigel, "Mary Ashton Rice Livermore," in *Notable American Women* (Cambridge, Mass., 1971).

6. Oscar Winther, ed., *With Sherman to the Sea: The Civil War Letters and Diaries and Reminiscences of Theodore F. Upson* (Bloomington, 1958).

7. *Ibid.*

8. *Collected Works of Lincoln*, vol. 4, 262–71, 421–41.

9. *1860 Census of Population*, 88–101, 220–26, 329–44, 373–96; *The Northern United States, 1820–1870* (Cambridge, Mass., 1969), 3–4. Daniel Boorstin, *The Americans, The National Experience* (New York, 1965), 3–168; and Page Smith, *A City on the Hill: The Town in American History* (New York, 1966), discuss the ideas and activities of communities and towns in the nineteenth century, but provide no evidence of the extent of popular involvement in these places. Stanley Elkins and Eric McKitrick, "A Meaning for Turner's Frontier," *Political Science Quarterly* 69:321, emphasize the importance of communities and towns in the settlement of the West but focus attention on the early stages of development. For a thoughtful discussion of the local nature of American society, see Robert Weibe, *The Segmented Society* (New York, 1976).

10. Jean Baker, *Affairs of Party: The Political Culture of Northern Democrats in the Mid-Nineteenth Century* (Ithaca, 1983), 87–106; Horace Mann, *Report of the Massachusetts Board of Education 1848*, as quoted in Daniel J. Boorstin, ed., *An American Primer* (New York, 1968), 367–69; Stanley K. Schultz, *The Culture Factory: Boston Public Schools, 1789–1860* (New York, 1973); Carl F. Kaestle, *The Evolution of an Urban School System: New York City, 1750–1850* (Cambridge, Mass., 1973). Writing in 1855, an essayist in *Putnam's* demonstrated the interrelationship between education and the larger political culture. What made the nation unique was its institutions: "It is the jury, the ballot-box, the free public assemblage, the local committee, the legislative assembly, the place of trust, and as a result of these, the school and the newspaper, which give such a spur to our activities, and endow us with such political competence." Quoted in Rush Welter, *The Mind of America, 1820–1860* (New York, 1975), 296. See also 276–97 on the relationship between education and democratic process; Lawrence Cremin, *American Education: The National Experience, 1783–1876* (New York, 1980), 104, 482–83; Marvin Lazarson, "Lawrence Cremin's Democracy in America," *Reviews in American History* 9 (September 1981): 382–86.

11. Walter Dean Burnham, "The Changing Shape of the American Political Universe," *American Political Science Review* 59 (1965): 7–21; Elkins and McKitrick, "Turner's Frontier," 333–36; William E. Gienapp, "Politics Seem to Enter into Everything," in Stephan Maizlish, ed., *Essays on American Antebellum Politics, 1840–1860* (Arlington, Tx., 1982).

12. Alexis de Tocqueville, *Democracy in America* (1835; reprint, New York, 1966), 147; Morton Grodzins, *The Loyal and Disloyal* (Chicago, 1956), 29, passim; Harold Guetzkow, *Multiple Loyalties* (Princeton, 1955), 37–39; David Potter, "The Historian's Use of Nationalism and Vice Versa," in his *The South and the Sectional Conflict* (Baton Rouge, 1968), 48. Phillip S. Paludan, "The American Civil War Considered as a Crisis in Law and Order," *American Historical Review* 77 (October 1972): 1013–34.

13. Paludan, *A Covenant with Death*, 15–18; James Willard Hurst, *Law and the Conditions*

of Freedom in the Nineteenth-Century United States (Madison, 1956); Robert Lively, "The American System: A Review Article," *Business History Review* 29 (March 1955): 85–96; Harold M. Hyman, *A More Perfect Union: The Impact of the Civil War and Reconstruction on the Constitution* (New York, 1973), 67–69; Daniel Elazar, *The American Partnership: Intergovernmental Cooperation in the Nineteenth-Century United States* (Chicago, 1962).

14. *Collected Works of Lincoln*, vol. 2, 32; Leonard White, *The Jacksonians* (New York, 1954), 104–18, 122–23.

15. Baker, *Affairs of Party*, 133–37; Garry Wills, *Explaining America: The Federalist* (New York, 1981), 177–264; Richard Hofstadter, *The Idea of a Party System* (Berkeley, 1972), 223–69. Antiparty ideology is explored in Ronald Formisano, *The Birth of Mass Political Parties: Michigan 1827–1861* (Princeton, 1971), and Robert Kelley, *The Cultural Pattern in American Politics* (New York, 1979). Descriptions of party importance are seen in Dale Baum, *The Civil War Party System: The Case of Massachusetts* (Chapel Hill, 1984), and Stephen E. Marglisk, *The Triumph of Sectionalism: The Transformation of Ohio Politics, 1844–1856* (Kent, 1983).

16. Paludan, *A Covenant with Death;* Harry Jaffa, *Crisis of the House Divided: An Interpretation of the Issues in the Lincoln-Douglas Debates* (Chicago, 1959).

17. *Collected Works of Lincoln*, vol. 4, 331–32.

18. Fred R. Shannon, *The Organization and Administration of the Union Army* (Cleveland, 1928), vol. 1, 23–25, 27–31; William Hesseltine, *Lincoln and the War Governors* (New York, 1948), 153–60; John Niven, *Connecticut for the Union* (New Haven, 1965), chap. 3; Allan Nevins, *The War for the Union*, 4 vols. (New York, 1959–1971), vol. 1, 169–71.

19. Niven, *Connecticut*, 52–53; Margaret Leech, *Reveille in Washington* (New York, 1941), 54–65; James G. Randall, *Lincoln the President* (New York, 1945), vol. 1, 363–67; Nevins, *War for the Union*, vol. 1, 79–84. For story of the riot from the viewpoint of the Baltimore mayor, see George William Brown, *Baltimore and the Nineteenth of April, 1861* (Baltimore, 1887).

20. *Collected Works of Lincoln*, vol. 4, 437 (July 4, 1861). Lincoln and his party's enduring faith in Southern unionism is persuasively argued in David M. Potter, *Lincoln and His Party in the Secession Crisis* (New Haven, 1942), 232, 247, 317–18, 375.

21. Shannon, *Organization*, 47.

22. Chase quoted in Nevins, *War for the Union*, vol. 1, 169; "The Advantages of Defeat," *Atlantic Monthly* 8 (September 1861): 362–63.

23. State pride of troops emphasized in Shannon, *Organization*, vol. 1, 15–50. Soldier comments quoted by Randall Jimerson, "A People Divided," Ph.D. diss., University of Michigan, Ann Arbor, 1977, 262–67.

24. Emma Lou Thornborough, *Indiana in the Civil War Era* (Indianapolis, 1965), 130–34; *Collected Works of Lincoln*, vol. 4, 402n.

25. Niven, *Connecticut*, 55–58; Thornborough, *Indiana*, 169–80; Eugene Roseboom, *The Civil War Era* (Columbus, 1944), 396, 426–27, 443; Arthur Charles Cole, *The Era of the Civil War, 1848–1870* (Springfield, Ill., 1919), 273–84. See Gerald Linderman, *The Mirror of War: American Society and the Spanish-American War* (Ann Arbor, 1974), for similar behavior in a later war.

26. William Y. Thompson, "Sanitary Fairs of the Civil War," *Civil War History* 4 (March 1958): 51–68.

27. *Personal Memoirs of U. S. Grant,* E. B. Long, ed. (New York, 1962), 116–19. See also Anthony Wallace, *Rockdale* (New York, 1978), 112, 459–61, for similar scene, and George Winston Smith and Charles Judah, eds., *Life in the North during the Civil War* (Albuquerque, 1966), 41–52, for first days of conflict.

28. Ella Lonn, *Foreigners in the Union Army and Navy* (Baton Rouge, 1951); Victor Hicken, *Illinois in the Civil War* (Urbana, 1966), ix, 7–8; Shannon, *Organization,* vol. 1, 42–43; Niven, *Connecticut,* 65; Stuart Blumin, *The Urban Threshold* (Chicago, 1976), 182–83; Florence Gibson, *The Attitudes of the New York Irish Toward State and National Affairs, 1848–1892* (New York, 1951), 122–23.

29. On concern for loss of revolutionary purity, see Forgie, *Patricide.* See also *Collected Works of Lincoln,* vol 1, 112–15, vol. 2, 318, 403–4; Fredrickson, *Inner Civil War,* 65–78.

30. *New York Tribune,* April 17, 1861; Cecil Perkins, ed., *Northern Editorials on Secession* (New York, 1942), 732–36, 757–59, 811. George Templeton Strong, despite suffering financially from the onset of war, still declared that "I welcome it cordially, for it has shown that I belong to a community that is brave and generous, and that the City of New York is not sordid and selfish." *Diary,* vol. 3, 133 (April 23, 1861).

31. Alan Dawley, *Class and Community: The Industrial Revolution in Lynn* (Cambridge, Mass., 1976), 103–5, 194–96; Dawley and Paul Faler, "Working Class Culture and Politics in the Industrial Revolution," *Journal of Social History* 9 (June 1976); Wallace, *Rockdale,* 454–60; *New York Tribune,* November 27, 1860; Benjamin Apthorp Gould, *Investigations in the Military and Anthropological Statistics of American Soldiers* (New York, 1869), 208–17; J. Mark Lambertson, "Belleville Illinois and the American Civil War," seminar paper, University of Kansas, Lawrence, December 1983.

32. Walt Whitman, "Song of the Banner at Daybreak" and "Long Too Long America," in *Drum Taps,* section of *Leaves of Grass* (New York, 1958). See also "Rise Oh Days from Your Fathomless Depths," in *Drum Taps.* For Emerson's similar views, see Emerson, "Works and Days," in *Collected Works* (Boston, 1885), vol. 7, 166; *The Journals and Miscellaneous Notebooks of Ralph Waldo Emerson,* William T. Gillman et al., eds. (Cambridge, Mass., 1973), vol. 7, 518; James E. Cabot, *A Memoir of Ralph Waldo Emerson* (New York, 1887), vol. 2, 600. See also Fredrickson, *Inner Civil War.*

33. See John P. McWilliams, Jr., " 'Drum Taps' and *Battle Pieces:* The Blossom of War," *American Quarterly* 23 (May 1971): 181–201; Richard Hart Fogle, "Melville and the Civil War," *Tulane Studies in English* 9 (1959): 61–90.

34. James McPherson, *The Struggle for Equality: Abolitionists and the Negro in the Civil War and Reconstruction* (Princeton, 1964), 29–51.

35. E. Merton Coulter, *Civil War and Readjustment in Kentucky* (Chapel Hill, 1926), 6–12; Edward Conrad Smith, *The Borderland in the Civil War* (New York, 1927); James Rawley, *Turning Points in the Civil War* (Lincoln, Neb., 1966), 11–45; N. S. Shaler, "Border State Men of the Civil War," *Atlantic Monthly* 69 (February 1892): 255; Nevins, *War for the Union,* vol. 1, 131; Richard Curry, *A House Divided: A Study of Statehood Politics and the Copperhead Movement in West Virginia* (Pittsburgh, 1964).

36. Curry, *House Divided,* 74–78; Coulter, *Civil War in Kentucky,* 228–36; William Parrish, *Troubled Partnership* (Columbia, Mo., 1963), 155–58; Smith, *Borderland,*

366–75; Frank Freidel, "General Orders 100 and Military Government," *Mississippi Valley Historical Review* 32:541–56; "Instructions for the Government of Armies of the United States in the Field," *Official Record of the War of the Rebellion* (Washington, 1869), series 3, vol. 3, 150–63; *Digest of the Opinions of the Judge Advocate General of the Army* (Washington, 1868), 196–97. For an interesting exchange of letters between Union and Confederate generals on guerrilla activity see *Official Records*, series 1, vol. 13, part 2, 648, 660–61, 742, 749–50. For legal issues of guerrilla warfare, inspired by Civil War behavior, see Francis Lieber, "Guerrilla Parties," in *Miscellaneous Writings of Francis Lieber* (Philadelphia, 1881), vol. 2, 277–92. Don R. Bowen, "Guerrilla War in Western Missouri, 1862–1865: Historical Extensions of the Relative Deprivation Hypothesis," *Comparative Studies in Society and History* 14 (January 1977): 30–51, assesses the socioeconomic background of Missouri guerrillas. Michael Fellman, "Inside War: The Guerrilla Conflict in Missouri during the American Civil War," in progress, provides an imaginative reconstruction of the torment of that state.

37. Leech, *Reveille*, 54–65; G. W. Brown, *Baltimore and the Nineteenth*; Nevins, *War for the Union*, vol. 1, 80–84.

38. Hyman, *A More Perfect Union*, 81–98; Alfred Kelly and Winfred Harbison, *The American Constitution* (New York, 1970), 439–41; Paludan, *A Covenant with Death*, 129–34; Sydney G. Fisher, "The Suspension of Habeas Corpus during the War of the Rebellion," *Political Science Quarterly* 3 (September 1888): 454–88. Carl B. Swisher, *History of the Supreme Court of the United States: The Taney Period, 1836–1864* (New York, 1974), 841–54, links events in Maryland to the decision. See Harold Hyman and William Wiecek, *Equal Justice Under Law: Constitutional Development, 1835–1875* (New York, 1982), 238–42, for recent assessment.

39. Hyman, *A More Perfect Union*, 34–64, 99–123; Paludan, *A Covenant with Death*, 186–97; E. L. Godkin, "The Constitution and Its Defects," *North American Review* 99 (July 1864): 117–45; James Russell Lowell, "Loyalty," *North American Review* 94 (January 1862): 145–59.

40. Flanders, "British Stricture on Republican Institutions," *North American Review* 91 (July 1859): 104–7. See also Andrew Preston Peabody, "Mill on Representative Government," *North American Review* 94 (July 1862), 232.

Chapter 2. Forging Foreign and Domestic Weapons

1. James G. Randall, *Constitutional Problems under Lincoln* (Urbana, 1951), chap. 3; Richard Current, *Old Thad Stevens* (Madison, 1942), 147.

2. *Prize Cases*, 2 Black 635 (1863): Stuart Bernath, *Squall Across the Atlantic: The American Civil War Prize Cases and Diplomacy* (Los Angeles, 1970).

3. Quoted in D. P. Crook, *The North, the South, and the Powers* (New York, 1974), 3. Robin Winks, *Canada and the United States: The Civil War Years* (Baltimore, 1960), 1–2, 28–29, 113; Kenneth Bourne, *Britain and the Balance of Power in North America* (Berkeley, 1967), 207–13.

4. *Times* and Russell both quoted in James B. Baxter III, "The British Government and Neutral Rights," *American Historical Review* 34 (October 1928): 9–29.

5. Serge Gavronsky, *The French Liberal Opposition and the American Civil War* (New York, 1968); David H. Pinkney, "France and the Civil War," in Harold Hyman,

ed., *Heard Round the World: The Impact of the Civil War* (New York, 1969); Donaldson Jordan and Edwin J. Pratt, *Europe and the American Civil War* (Boston, 1931).

6. Lynn Case and Warren Spencer, *The United States and France: Civil War Diplomacy* (Philadelphia, 1970); Thomas Sancton, "The Myth of the French Workers' Support for the North in the American Civil War," *French Historical Studies* 11 (Spring 1979): 58–80; Frank Merli and Theodore Wilson, "The British Cabinet and the Confederacy, Autumn 1862," *Maryland Historical Magazine* 65 (Fall 1970): 239–62; Crook, *North, South, and Powers,* 9–14.

7. *New York Daily Tribune,* November 7, 1861; D. G. Wright, "Bradford and the American Civil War," *Journal of British Studies* 8 (May 1969): 69–85; Crook, *North, South, and Powers,* 274–75. See also John Stuart Mill, *The Contest in America* (Boston, 1862), in Frank Freidel, ed., *Union Pamphlets of the Civil War,* 2 vols. (Cambridge, Mass., 1967), vol. 1, 326–44; J. R. Pole, *Abraham Lincoln and the Working Classes of Britain* (London, 1959), 10.

8. Julius Pratt, *A History of United States Foreign Policy* (Englewood Cliffs, N.J., 1972), 98–99, 156; Crook, *North, South, and Powers,* 75–80; Norman Ferris, *Desperate Diplomacy: William Seward's Foreign Policy, 1861* (Knoxville, 1976); Martin Duberman, *Charles Francis Adams, 1807–1886* (Stanford, 1960), 259–60; Bernath, *Squall Across the Atlantic,* 19–20. James R. Lowell, "Jonathan to John," *Poems of Lowell,* as quoted in Henry Steele Commager, ed., *The Blue and The Gray: The Story of the Civil War as Told by the Participants* (Indianapolis, 1950), 532.

9. Ferris, *Desperate Diplomacy,* 6–14; Glyndon Van Deusen, *William Henry Seward* (New York, 1967), 301; Gordon Warren, "Imperial Dreamer: William Henry Seward and American Destiny," in Frank Merli and Theodore Wilson, eds., *Makers of American Diplomacy* (New York, 1974), 203–4.

10. Duberman, *Adams,* 274. Peter Parish, *The American Civil War* (New York, 1975), 404–5, assesses Seward's behavior as "controlled truculence."

11. Nevins, *War for the Union,* vol. 2, 243–44. Ephraim Douglas Adams, *Great Britain and the American Civil War* (London, 1925), vol. 1, 178–201, discusses British reactions to first Bull Run. Brian Jenkins, *Britain and the War for the Union* (Montreal, 1974), vol. 1, 158–59, notes British preparations to increase troops in Canada in the weeks after their battle.

12. Norman Ferris, *The Trent Affair* (Knoxville, 1977), 18–31; Crook, *North, South, and Powers,* 99–107; Rawley, *Turning Points,* 78–81; *Official Record,* series 2, vol. 2, 1076–1115; John Niven, *Gideon Welles: Lincoln's Secretary of the Navy* (New York, 1973), 444–47; Caroline Barrett White, *Diary,* American Antiquarian Society, Worcester, Mass., December 28, 1861.

13. Ferris, *Trent,* 24, 37–68; Jordan and Pratt, *Europe and Civil War,* 21–42; Crook, *North, South, and Powers,* 124–47; Jenkins, *Britain and War,* vol. 1, chap. 9; Gordon H. Warren, *Fountain of Discontent: The Trent Affair and Freedom of the Seas* (Boston, 1981).

14. Crook, *North, South, and Powers,* 105–10; Ferris, *Trent,* 25–26.

15. Randall, *Lincoln,* vol. 2, 44–51; Nevins, *War for the Union,* vol. 1, 390–94; Seward to Lord Lyons, December 26, 1861, in George E. Baker, ed., *The Works of William H. Seward* (Boston, 1884), vol. 5, 295–309.

16. *London Times* as quoted in Ferris, *Trent,* 193–94.

17. Adams and Seward quoted in Ferris, *Trent,* 203; Rawley, *Turning Points,* 92–95.

D. R. Crook argues that there were also negative lessons from the affair, the main one being the belief of the English that force was the best way to deal with the United States. He also points to the persistence of anti-American feelings among some groups in England, especially workers. Crook's conclusions seem not to take account of the fact that never again would the English send an ultimatum to the United States as they had on releasing Mason and Slidell, and that the growing power of the North as the war continued surely would weaken any British inclination to challenge the Lincoln government. The United States that backed away from war in 1861 was hardly the same power that an enemy would face in the future. Crook, *North, South, and Powers*, 169–70.

18. Duberman, *Adams*, 293–94, 300–3; Frank Merli, *Great Britain and the Confederate Navy* (Bloomington, 1970); Crook, *North, South, and Powers*, 258–62; Adams, *Great Britain and Civil War*, vol. 2, 119–30.

19. Duberman, *Adams*, 302–14; Niven, *Gideon Welles*, 449–51; Crook, *North, South, and Powers*, 322–29. Adams' dispatch to Lord Russell is in Commager, ed., *Blue and Gray*, 558–60; Merli, *Great Britain and Navy*, 179–80; Adams, *Great Britain and Civil War*, 131–51.

20. Russell F. Weigley, *Towards an American Army: Military Thought from Washington to Marshall* (New York, 1962), 1–2, 7–9; James C. Curtis, *Andrew Jackson and the Search for Vindication* (Boston, 1976), 64–65. Robert Shalhope, "The Ideological Origins of the Second Amendment," *Journal of American History* 62 (December 1982): 599–614; Lawrence Cress, "An Armed Community: The Origins and Meaning of the Right to Bear Arms," *Journal of American History* 71 (June 1984): 22–42; Shalhope and Cress, "The Second Amendment and the Right to Bear Arms: An Exchange," *Journal of American History* 71 (December 1984): 587–93; these articles discuss the relationship between citizenship and the militia. They debate whether the right to bear arms is individual or based on community needs.

21. Richard H. Kohn, *Eagle and Sword* (New York, 1975).

22. The early history of the militia is well summarized in Robert Reinders, "Militia and Public Order in Nineteenth-Century America," *Journal of American Studies* 11 (April 1977): 81–86.

23. *Ibid.*, 86–87; Weigley, *Towards an American Army*, 38–39; Samuel P. Huntington, *The Soldier and the State* (Cambridge, Mass., 1957), 203–10; Robert McGraw, "Minutemen of '61: The Prewar Massachusetts Militia," *Civil War History* 15 (June 1969): 101–12; Reinders, *Militia*, 89–91; David Grimsted, "Rioting in Jacksonian Setting," *American Historical Review* 77 (April 1972): 361–97.

24. Marcus Cunliffe, *Soldiers and Civilians* (Boston, 1968), 215–54.

25. Shannon, *Organization*, vol. 1, 28–29; Cunliffe, *Soldiers and Civilians*, 205–12, 388; Alexander H. Meneely, *The War Department in 1861* (New York, 1928), 23–24; McGraw, "Minutemen of '61," 101–12.

26. Robert S. Chamberlain, "The Northern State Militia," *Civil War History* 4 (June 1958): 105–18.

27. *Personal Memoirs of U. S. Grant*, 29–30, 83–84; Cunliffe, *Soldiers and Civilians*, 387–88; James L. Morrison, ed., *Memoirs of Henry Heth* (Westport, Conn., 1974).

28. Weigley, *Towards an American Army*, 38–78; Cunliffe, *Soldiers and Civilians*, 159–72.

29. David Donald, "Refighting the Civil War," in *Lincoln Reconsidered* (New York,

1961), 82–102; Weigley, *Towards an American Army*, 55–57; T. Harry Williams, "The Military Leadership of North and South," in Donald, ed., *Why the North Won, the Civil War* (New York, 1960), 33–54. There is an ongoing debate over Jomini's influence. Herman Hattaway and Archer Jones argue for limited impact, although focusing their discussion on his relationship to Napoleon: *How the North Won: A Military History of the Civil War* (Urbana, 1983), 21–24. See James Morrison, *"The Best School in the World": West Point, The Pre–Civil War Years 1833–1866* (Kent, 1986), for the most recent assessment.

30. Edward Hagerman, "From Jomini to Dennis Hart Mahan: The Evolution of Trench Warfare and the American Civil War," *Civil War History* 13:197–220; Grady McWhiney, "Who Whipped Whom? Confederate Defeat Reexamined," *Civil War History* 11:5–26; Major General J. F. C. Fuller, *Grant and Lee: A Study in Personality and Generalship* (Bloomington, 1982), 43–50. Grady McWhiney and Perry Jameson, *Attack and Die: Civil War Military Tactics and the Southern Heritage* (University, Ala., 1982), discuss this subject at length.

31. Strong, *Diary*, vol. 2, 146–47.

32. Hagerman, "From Jomini," 197–222.

33. *Personal Memoirs of U. S. Grant*, 145; Cunliffe, *Soldiers and Civilians*, 378; Charles F. Elliott, *Winfield Scott: The Soldier and the Man* (New York, 1937), 718–20; Weigley, *Towards an American Army*, 106–7; Williams, "Military Leadership," in Donald, ed., *Why the North Won*, 36.

34. John Hope Franklin, *The Militant South, 1800–1861* (Boston, 1956); Michael C. C. Adams, *Our Masters the Rebels* (Cambridge, Mass., 1978), 27–31. William Taylor, *Cavalier and Yankee* (New York, 1961), notes other images of the Southerner that authors had explored, among them the troubled Hamletlike figure of the slave owner. While this image was clearly known in the North, the picture of the violent Southerner was more common, and certainly more likely to come to mind in times of conflict. See Taylor's discussion, 151–62, "From Hotspur to Hamlet." The best-known Hamletlike Southerner of the prewar period was surely Augustine St. Clare in *Uncle Tom's Cabin*.

35. Cunliffe, *Soldiers and Civilians*, 337–75; Weigley, *Towards an American Army*, 38–53; Adams, *Our Masters*, 54–55, 61–63; T. Harry Williams, "The Attack Upon West Point During the Civil War," *Mississippi Valley Historical Review* 25 (March 1939): 491–504; James L. Morrison, "The Struggle Between Sectionalism and Nationalism at Antebellum West Point," *Civil War History* 19 (June 1973): 138–48. Strong, *Diary*, vol. 3, 128; Strong himself believed that the North had "four advantages, viz., money, numbers, the navy, the sympathy of Christendom." The South had "one vital disadvantage, viz., niggers; and another, the utter want of mechanical skill and educated labor." But he also did not believe that Providence would send the South a great general.

36. Hattaway and Jones, *How the North Won*, 39–47.

37. Trumbull quoted in Nevins, *War for the Union*, vol. 1, 218n; Walt Whitman, "Battle of Bull Run, July 1861," *Specimen Days and Collect* (Philadelphia, 1883); John Russell Young quoted in Frank Moore, ed., *Rebellion Record* (New York, 1863), vol. 2, Documents, 376.

38. William Howard Russell, *My Diary, North and South*, Fletcher Platt, ed. (Gloucester, Mass., 1969), 226, 229.

39. Scott quoted in Adams, *Our Masters*, 80. Stories of officer incompetence are mentioned in newspaper reports in Moore, *Rebellion Record*, 108–18.
40. Officers quoted in Adams, *Our Masters*, 78–80.
41. *Belleville Advocate*, July 27, 1861; *New York Post*, July 26, 1861; Sherman quoted in Rawley, *Turning Points*, 58.
42. Nevins, *War for the Union*, vol. 1, 223–24; Niven, *Connecticut;* James Rawley, *Edwin D. Morgan, 1811–1883* (New York, 1955), 161.
43. Olmstead quoted in Strong, *Diary*, vol. 3, 185.
44. Fredrickson, *Inner Civil War*, 73–77; Strong, *Diary*, vol. 3, 198 (December 31, 1861).

Chapter 3. The Ways of Making War

1. Hattaway and Jones, *How the North Won*, 51–52; Warren Hassler, Jr., *General George B. McClellan: Shield of the Union* (Baton Rouge, 1957). Joseph Harsch, "On the McClellan-Go-Round," *Civil War History* 19 (June 1973): 101–18, is the best survey of the McClellan literature.
2. Burton Bledstein, *The Culture of Professionalism* (New York, 1976), links professionalization to the rise of the middle class. Since being middle class is perhaps *the* American aspiration, his equation obscures early fears of professionalization. For apprehensions, see Daniel Calhoun, *Professional Lives in America* (Cambridge, Mass., 1965), 1–8; Marvin Meyers, *The Jacksonian Persuasion* (New York, 1956); Perry Miller, *The Life of the Mind in America* (New York, 1965), 99–121; Ralph Waldo Emerson, "Napoleon" in *Representative Men.* Collected in Ralph Waldo Emerson, *Essays and Lectures* (New York, Library of America ed., 1983).
3. Stephen Ambrose, *Duty, Honor, Country: A History of West Point* (Baltimore, 1966), 106–24; Huntington, *The Soldier and the State*, 195–204. Huntington argues (74) that professionalization of the army is the best defense a society has against army control. S. E. Finer, *The Man on Horseback* (London, 1962), 24–27, counters that professionalization can breed attitudes that rationalize military manipulation of the political amateurs who 1) don't understand what national security requires, 2) place political selfishness above the good of the nation. Williams, "The Attack on West Point"; "Report of the Secretary of War," Senate Executive Documents, 37th Cong., 1st sess., serial set #1112, 27–28, 46; *Congressional Globe*, 37th Cong., 2d sess., 165.
4. McPherson, *Struggle for Equality*, 70–72, 80–83; *Congressional Globe*, 37th Cong., 2d sess., 15; "Brownson on the Rebellion," in Freidel, ed., *Union Pamphlets*, vol. 1, 138–40.
5. On McClellan as possible dictator, see Adams, *Our Masters*, 110–23; G. W. Smith and Charles Judah, eds., *Life in the North During the Civil War* (Albuquerque, 1966), 90–91. Discussions of McClellan's ambitions for civilian power are also in Nathaniel Hawthorne, "Chiefly About War Matters," *Atlantic Monthly* (July 1862): 51–53; Walter Lowenfels, ed., *Walt Whitman's Civil War* (New York, 1960), 248–50; James Russell Lowell, "General McClellan's Report," in *Political Essays* (Boston, 1899), 94–113.
6. Benjamin Thomas and Harold Hyman, *Stanton: The Life and Times of Lincoln's Secretary of War* (New York, 1962), 232–34; McPherson, *Struggle for Equality*, 192–93; Hans Trefousse, *The Radical Republicans* (New York, 1968), 205–6.

7. Trefousse, *Radical Republicans*, 182–90, 247–49; Thomas and Hyman, *Stanton*, 148–49, 177–78, 184–85, 259–62; W. W. Pierson, Jr., "The Committee on the Conduct of the War Civil," *American Historical Review* 23:574–76.

8. McClellan to Samuel L. M. Barlow, November 8, 1861, July 30, 1862, Barlow Papers, Huntington Library, San Marino, Cal.; G. B. McClellan, *McClellan's Own Story* (New York, 1887), 159–60. Cunliffe, *Soldiers and Civilians*, 19–20, passim, discusses conflict between amateur and professional but does not place it in the context of general attitudes toward professionals in the nineteenth century.

9. George Julian, *Political Recollections* (Chicago, 1884), 210–14.

10. Trefousse, *Radical Republicans*, 182–88. McClellan's staunchest recent defender admits that the general's suspicions that the Committee on the Conduct of the War wanted to discredit him were wrong. See Rowena Reed, *Combined Operations in the Civil War* (Annapolis, 1978), 109.

11. *McClellan's Own Story*, 148–50.

12. *Ibid.*, 57, 64, 83–84, 89, 129.

13. *Ibid.*, 85, 91, 172, 398, 409, 425; Hattaway and Jones, *How the North Won*, 83–85; *Collected Works of Lincoln*, vol. 5, 48–49.

14. T. Harry Williams, *The History of American Wars* (New York, 1981), 248–50; *Official Record*, series 1, vol. 51, part 1, 369–70. These goals, presented in McClellan's letter to Lincoln of July 7, 1862, the "Harrison's Landing Letter," are described and analyzed in Harsch, "On the McClellan-Go-Round," 117–18; Hassler, *General George B. McClellan*, 177–78; Russell Weigley, *The American Way of War: A History of United States Military Strategy and Policy* (New York, 1973), 128–35.

15. Reed, *Combined Operations*, xvi–xix, 34–39; Weigley, *American Way of War*, 134. See discussion of strategy in Hattaway and Jones, *How the North Won*, 82–83, 87–89, 93–94.

16. William T. Sherman, *Memoirs* (New York, 1892), vol. 2, 381–409; Thomas Wentworth Higginson, "Regular and Volunteer Officers," *Atlantic Monthly* 14 (September 1864): 348–51.

17. *Official Record*, series 3, vol. 2, 797; Edward Hagerman, "The Professionalization of George B. McClellan and Early Civil War Field Command," *Civil War History* 21 (June 1975): 121–24.

18. Adams, *Our Masters*, 93–95; Hassler, *General George B. McClellan*, 33; Harsch, "On the McClellan-Go-Round," 115–16.

19. Grant quoted in Hassler, *General George B. McClellan*, 324–25.

20. *Collected Works of Lincoln*, vol. 5, 111 (January 27, 1862).

21. All biographical data on Grant is based on William McFeely, *Grant: A Biography* (New York, 1981).

22. Adams, *Our Masters;* Lloyd Lewis, *Sherman: Fighting Prophet* (New York, 1958), 317; Nevins, *War for the Union*, vol. 2, 154; Hattaway and Jones, *How the North Won*, 86. See also McPherson, *Struggle for Equality*, 478; Shelby Foote, *The Civil War* (New York, 1974), vol. 2, 842–43.

23. *Personal Memoirs of U. S. Grant*, 139–44; Major General J. F. C. Fuller, *The Generalship of Ulysses S. Grant* (New York, 1929), 72–74; Hattaway and Jones, *How the North Won*, 52–53.

24. McFeely, *Grant*, 102–3; Thomas and Hyman, *Stanton*, 173–74; *Collected Works of Lincoln*, vol. 5, 135; Nevins, *War for the Union*, vol. 2, 27; Hattaway and Jones, *How the North Won*, 64–77.

25. Hattaway and Jones, *How the North Won,* are much more favorable to Halleck's overall strategy, insisting on the actual need for the general's cautious organizing: chap. 3. My discussions of battles and campaigns rely heavily on *How the North Won.*

26. McFeely, *Grant,* 118–20; Lewis, *Sherman,* 211–12.

27. *Personal Memoirs of U. S. Grant,* 191–92; McFeely, *Grant,* 111–21; Weigley, *American Way of War,* 148–49.

28. McClellan had been making the same points since late fall of 1861. See McClellan to Barlow, November 8, 1861, as well as same to same, June 23, 1862, Barlow Papers.

29. Trefousse, *Radical Republicans,* chap. 5; Thomas and Hyman, *Stanton,* 192–202.

30. Hassler, *General George B. McClellan,* 165–70; Williams, *History of American Wars,* 278–79; Reed, *Combined Operations,* 133–89.

31. Weigley, *American Way of War,* 133–35; Hattaway and Jones, *How the North Won,* 194–200.

32. *McClellan's Own Story,* 487–89; Herman Belz, *Reconstructing the Union: Theory and Policy During the Civil War* (Ithaca, 1969), 66–83; James Randall, *Constitutional Problems Under Lincoln,* 275–92; Patricia M. Lucie, "Confiscation: Constitutional Crossroads," *Civil War History* 23 (December 1977): 304–22.

33. Gideon Welles, "The History of Emancipation," *Galaxy* (December 1872): 842–43; Stephan Oates, *Our Fiery Trial: Abraham Lincoln, John Brown and the Civil War* (Amherst, 1979), 76–77.

34. Thomas and Hyman, *Stanton,* 217–18; Nevins, *War for the Union,* vol. 2, 150–56.

35. William A. Frassanito, *Antietam: America's Bloodiest Day* (New York, 1978), 288–89.

36. *McClellan's Own Story,* 613–14, 618–19; Nevins, *War for the Union,* vol. 2, 215–31.

37. *McClellan's Own Story,* 614–15; Thomas and Hyman, *Stanton,* 247; Glyndon Van Deusen, *Horace Greeley* (Philadelphia, 1953), 282–85; Fawn Brodie, *Thaddeus Stevens, Scourge of the South* (New York, 1966), 164–65.

38. Randall, *Lincoln the President,* vol. 2, 116–25.

39. Brodie, *Thaddeus Stevens,* 164–65; Van Deusen, *Horace Greeley,* 282–85; *Lincoln and the Civil War in the Diaries of John Hay* (New York, 1939), 218–19; Randall, *Lincoln the President,* vol. 2, 116–25; *New York Tribune,* November 12, 1862; Hattaway and Jones, *How the North Won,* 172–73; Williams, "Attack upon West Point."

Chapter 4. The Dialogue of Politics, 1861–1862

1. Moore, *Rebellion Record,* vol. 2, Documents, 126; Robert W. Johannsen, "The Douglas Democracy and the Crisis of Disunion," *Civil War History* 9 (September 1963): 229–47; Frank Klement, *The Limits of Dissent: Clement L. Vallandigham and the Civil War* (Lexington, Ky., 1970), 61–62; Stewart Mitchell, *Horatio Seymour of New York* (Cambridge, Mass., 1938), 232–35; Joel Silbey, *A Respectable Minority* (New York, 1977), 39–42; John Bigelow, ed., *Letters and Literary Memorials of Samuel J. Tilden* (New York, 1908), vol. 1, 160; Baker, *Affairs of Party,* 330–31.

2. Silbey, *A Respectable Minority,* 40–42; *Tribune Almanac and Political Register for 1862* (New York, 1862), 56–64; Eugene Roseboom, *The Civil War Era,* 338–93; Kenneth Stampp, *Indiana Politics During the Civil War* (Indianapolis, 1949), 83–99; Mitchell, *Horatio Seymour,* 236–37.

3. Hyman, *A More Perfect Union*, 73–77; Niven, *Connecticut*, 299–304; Klement, *The Limits of Dissent*, 75–78; Frank Klement, *Copperheads in the Middle West* (Chicago, 1960), 17–20; Silbey, *A Respectable Minority*, 51–52; Baker, *Affairs of Party*, 158–60.

4. Jean Baker, "A Loyal Opposition: Northern Democrats in the 37th Congress," *Civil War History* 25 (June 1979): 141–44; Edward McPherson, *The Political History of the United States During the Great Rebellion* (Washington, 1865), 195–96.

5. *Statistical History of the United States* (Stamford, Conn., 1965), 688–92; Silbey, *A Respectable Minority*, 18–23.

6. The seminal article on the benefits of the party system in the North is Eric McKitrick, "Party Politics and the Union and Confederate War Efforts," in Walter Burnham and William Chambers, eds., *The Changing American Party Systems* (New York, 1967), 117–51; James Rawley, *Politics and Union: Northern Politics during the Civil War* (Lincoln, Neb., 1974) sustains McKitrick's views at some length. My argument here relies heavily on McKitrick. Party name calling quoted in Silbey, *A Respectable Minority*, 26–27, 46–47, 72–74. Baker, *Affairs of Party*, 132–40, provides the theories of Democrat S. S. Cox on the value of opposition parties to the nation.

7. Mary Boykin Chesnut, *A Diary from Dixie* (Boston, 1949), 230; Nevins, *War for the Union*, vol. 3, 409–10; Louise B. Hill, *Joseph E. Brown and the Confederacy* (Chapel Hill, 1939), 183–86.

8. Hesseltine, *Lincoln and the War Governors*; Bertram Wyatt-Brown, *Southern Honor: Ethics and Behavior in the Old South* (New York, 1982); David Potter, "Jefferson Davis and the Political Factors in the Confederate Defeat," in Donald, ed., *Why the North Won*, 101–12; McKitrick, "Party Politics," 136–41; Harry Carmen and Richard Luthin, *Lincoln and the Patronage* (New York, 1943).

9. Hyman, *A More Perfect Union*, 79; Baker, *Affairs of Party*, 143.

10. Formisano, *Birth of Mass Political Parties*; Michael Holt, *Forging a Majority: The Birth of the Republican Party in Pittsburgh* (New Haven, 1969); Paul Kleppner, *The Cross of Culture: A Social Analysis of Midwestern Politics, 1850–1900* (New York, 1970), 100–3; Silbey, *A Respectable Minority*, 25–26. Vallandigham had stood almost alone in Congress in July 1861 in fighting for the right of rabbis to serve as chaplains in the army; see Bertram W. Korn, "Clement L. Vallandigham's Championship of the Jewish Chaplaincy in the Civil War," *American Jewish Historical Quarterly* 53 (December 1963): 188–91, and Korn, *American Jewry and the Civil War* (Cleveland, 1961), 56–97.

11. James Vallandigham, *Life of Clement Vallandigham* (Baltimore, 1872), 222; Silbey, *A Respectable Minority*, 77–80, 103–4; *Congressional Globe*, 37th Cong., 3d sess., 15; Niven, *Connecticut*, 296–98; Baker, *Affairs of Party*, 148–58; Hyman and Wiecek, *Equal Justice Under Law*, 291.

12. S. S. Cox, *Three Decades of Federal Legislation* (Providence, 1888), 35–36; Edward Ingersoll, "Personal Liberty and Martial Law," in Freidel, ed., *Union Pamphlets*, vol. 1, 255–94.

13. Marvin Meyers, *The Jacksonian Persuasion*; Eric Foner, "The Causes of the American Civil War: Recent Interpretations," *Civil War History* 20 (September 1974): 207–8; Baker, *Affairs of Party*, 147–68. Baker insists that Democratic rhetoric was "more . . . than reactionary carping," but provides an entire chapter showing just how the Democrats focused on the past in their wartime attacks.

14. William Gerald Shade, *Banks or No Banks: The Money Issue in Western Politics 1832–1865* (Detroit, 1972), 248–54; Kelley, *The Cultural Pattern in American Politics*, 235–37. Clement Vallandigham, "The Great Civil War in America," in Freidel, ed., *Union Pamphlets*, vol. 2, 723–30; Paul Kleppner, *The Cross of Culture*, 105; Silbey, *A Respectable Minority*, 74–77; Klement, *Copperheads*, 9–11, 25; Lee Benson, *The Concept of Jacksonian Democracy* (Princeton, 1961), 200–1; Mitchell, *Horatio Seymour*, 257.

15. Newspapers quoted in V. Jacques Voegeli, *Free but Not Equal: The Midwest and the Negro during the Civil War* (Chicago, 1967), 4–6; John H. Hopkins, *Bible View of Slavery* (New York, 1863) in Freidel, ed., *Union Pamphlets*, vol. 2, 658–87. See also *The Lincoln Catechism*, in *Union Pamphlets*, 981–1015, especially 998–1001; Silbey, *A Respectable Minority*, 80–83; George Fredrickson, *The Black Image in the White Mind* (New York, 1971), 170–74; Forrest Wood, *Black Scare: The Racist Response to Emancipation and Reconstruction* (Berkeley, 1968), chap. 4.

16. Baker, *Affairs of Party*, 213–43, provides an excellent description of the minstrel show and its racial dimensions. See Fredrickson, *Black Image*, 93–96, for the suggestion that the dislocations of the mid-nineteenth century helped sustain the racial inequality argument.

17. Formisano, *Birth of Mass Political Parties*, 266–70; Kelley, *The Cultural Pattern in American Politics*, 200–1; Silbey, *A Respectable Minority*, 49–51.

18. Frank Klement, "Economic Aspects of Middle-Western Copperheadism," *Historian* 14 (Fall 1951): 39–40; Baker, *Affairs of Party*, 156–57; James McPherson, *Ordeal by Fire* (New York, 1982), 272–74; Shade, *Banks or No Banks*, 214–15, 222–23.

19. T. J. Barnett to Barlow, late 1861–early 1862, Barlow Papers; Mitchell, *Horatio Seymour*, 247–53; Nevins, *War for the Union*, vol. 2, 302–4, 317–18; Bigelow, ed., *Letters and Memorials of Tilden*, vol. 1, 166–67; Silbey, *A Respectable Minority*, 69–77.

20. John Hope Franklin, *The Emancipation Proclamation* (New York, 1963), 78–80; Silbey, *A Respectable Minority*, 82–86; Voegeli, *Free but Not Equal*; 52–67; Reginald Charles McGrane, *William Allen, A Study in Western Democracy* (Columbus, 1925), 156–57.

21. Trefousse, *Radical Republicans*, 254–57; Voegeli, *Free but Not Equal*, 55–59; Nevins, *War for the Union*, vol. 2, 317–18; Rawley, *Politics and Union*, 96–97.

22. Silbey, *A Respectable Minority*, 143–46.

23. Voegeli, *Free but Not Equal*, 62–64; Horace Greeley, *The American Conflict* (Hartford, 1865–66), vol. 2, 254–55; Theodore Pease and James G. Randall, eds., *Diary of Orville Hickman Browning* (Springfield, Ill., 1925), vol. 1, 582, 588–90; Trefousse, *Radical Republicans*, 259–61.

24. Silbey, *A Respectable Minority*, 67–69; Trefousse, *Radical Republicans*, 259–61.

25. On Democratic loyalty as a function of community tradition, see the description of Hunterdon, New Jersey, in Baker, *Affairs of Party*. Hunterdon was not settled from the South, not significantly poorer than average, had no distinguishing religious faith usually associated with Democrats. "Hunterdon was exceptional only in its politics." (48) For correlation between underdevelopment and democracy, see Richard O. Curry, "The Union as It Was: A Critique of Recent Interpretations," *Civil War History* 13 (March 1967): 32–36.

26. Trefousse, *Radical Republicans*, 260–61; *Tribune Almanac for 1863*, 50–63; Silbey,

A Respectable Minority, 143–45. Paul Kleppner, *The Third Electoral System* (Chapel Hill, 1979), notes the support of "Yankee" areas for egalitarian measures; 53, 57, 83–84. It is possible that diminished Republican voting in New England in 1862 reflects the fact that Democrats campaigned under fusion party labels and thus failed to inspire the combative nature of their rivals. Republicans in New England may have felt that Democrats simply had no hope of winning and so stayed home. In Michigan, however, this explanation does not fit.

27. Voegeli, *Free but Not Equal*, 60–62; Klement, *Copperheads*, 1–39; Thomas and Hyman, *Stanton*, 247–48. The political power of the threat of black immigration to the North can be seen by the effort expended in Republican circles to prove that blacks would never do it. Hours before the 1862 election *Leslies Illustrated Newspaper* was reassuring its readers that blacks were agriculturalists who loved their traditional homes in Dixie. Turning to the offensive, the paper charged that people who used the threat of black invasion were "probably traitors." (November 1, 1862)

28. Hattaway and Jones, *How the North Won*, 94–95, 98–99, 683–84, passim; Weigley, *American Way of War*, 142–44; Reed, *Combined Operations*, 120; Nevins, *War for the Union*, vol. 2, 321–22.

Chapter 5. Congress and the Capitalists

1. Sidney Ratner, James Soltow, and Richard Sylla, *The Evolution of the American Economy* (New York, 1979); Susan Previant Lee and Peter Passell, *A New Economic View of American History* (New York, 1979); Douglas North, Terry Anderson, and Peter Hill, *Growth and Welfare in the American Past* (Englewood Cliffs, N.J., 1983); George Rogers Taylor, *The Transportation Revolution, 1815–1860* (New York, 1951); E. B. Long, *The Civil War Day by Day* (Garden City, N.Y., 1971), 394–96.

2. Pessen, *Riches, Class and Power*, 16–17, 323–35; Lee Soltow, *Men and Wealth*, 112–15.

3. *Collected Works of Lincoln*, vol. 4, 421–41; David Donald, "Whig in the White House," in *Lincoln Reconsidered*; S. Gabor Borritt, *Lincoln and the Economics of the American Dream* (Memphis, 1978), 195–99; Nevins, *War for the Union*, vol. 1, 9–91; John Sherman, *Recollections of Forty Years in the House, Senate and Cabinet* (Chicago, 1895), vol. 4, 236–38. Sherman's work is an excellent survey of the economic legislation of the war, much of it framed by the Ohio senator. See his chaps. 10–12, 14, 16.

4. The idea that President Jackson's attack on the Bank of the United States created economic disaster is argued in Bray Hammond, *Banks and Politics in America, from the Revolution to the Civil War* (Princeton, 1957), and Arthur Schlesinger, Jr., *The Age of Jackson* (Boston, 1945). The argument is challenged by Peter Temin, *The Jacksonian Economy* (New York, 1969). Susan Lee and Peter Passell, *A New Economic View of American History*, 112–29, analyze the more recent evidence.

5. Robert Sharkey, *Money, Class and Party: An Economic Study of Civil War and Reconstruction* (Baltimore, 1959), 194–95, 219–20; Bray Hammond, *Sovereignty and an Empty Purse* (Princeton, 1970), 18–23; *Historical Statistics of the United States* (Washington, 1975), 711; James Willard Hurst, *A Legal History of Money in the United States, 1774–1970* (Lincoln, Neb., 1973), 171–72.

6. Hammond, *Sovereignty and an Empty Purse*, 23–46; John Sherman, *Recollections*, 216–17; Irwin Unger, *The Greenback Era* (Princeton, 1964), 13–15.

7. Shade, *Banks or No Banks*, 248–50; *Congressional Globe*, 37th Cong., 2d sess., 550–51; Hammond, *Sovereignty and an Empty Purse*, 181–83.

8. Ralph Korngold, *Thaddeus Stevens: A Being Darkly Wise and Rudely Great* (New York, 1955), 133–35; Hammond, *Sovereignty and an Empty Purse*, 134–35, 214; Ellis Paxton Oberholtzer, *Jay Cooke: Financier of the Civil War*, 2 vols. (Philadelphia, 1907), vol. 1, 172–73.

9. Hammond, *Sovereignty and an Empty Purse*, 225–29.

10. *Ibid.*; Max Farrand, ed., *Records of the Federal Convention* (New Haven, 1927), 144, 308–10; *United States Statutes at Large*, 12:345. Hammond's assertion that the law went "counter to the principle of the tenth amendment that the federal government possessed only those powers *specifically* [my italics] assigned to it by the Constitution" ignores the wording of that amendment and the action of Congress in removing the word "expressly" from the phrase "The powers not delegated to the United States by the Constitution, nor prohibited by it to the States, are reserved to the States respectively, or to the people." See *McCulloch v. Maryland*, 4 Wheaton 407: *Annals of Congress* (Washington, 1791), 1897.

11. Leonard Curry, *Blueprint for Modern America* (Nashville, 1968), 181–96; Brodie, *Thaddeus Stevens*, 174–75.

12. The success of the greenbacks as the people's currency can be seen in the fact that after the war, former hard money Democrats became the most vocal supporters of increasing the amount of greenbacks in circulation. They were consistent in their hatred of banks and the banking system, but this very consistency was the pivot on which their changed monetary views rested. They came to insist that greenbacks were the money of the people and their government, while other monetary schemes and the older currency were bankers' devices and hence instruments of oppression. See Unger, *The Greenback Era*, passim; Sharkey, *Money, Class and Party,* 194–95, 219–20.

13. Stephen DeCanio and Joel Mokyr, "Inflation and the Wage Lag During the Civil War," *Explorations in Economic History* 14 (October 1977): 315, 324; Ratner, Soltow, and Sylla, *Evolution of American Economy*, 349–51; Wesley Mitchell, *A History of the Greenbacks* (Chicago, 1903), 320, 392; Unger, *The Greenback Era*, 15–25.

14. *Historical Statistics of the United States*, 1118, 1140.

15. Oberholtzer, *Jay Cooke*, vol. 1, 107–20, 132–33; Hammond, *Sovereignty and an Empty Purse*, 324.

16. Oberholtzer, *Jay Cooke*, vol. 1, 134, 143–44.

17. *Ibid.*, 145–59.

18. *Ibid.*, 58–86; *New York Tribune*, March 7, 1865.

19. Sidney Ratner, *Taxation and Democracy* (New York, 1967), 61–64; Curry, *Blueprint*, 154–55; Hammond, *Sovereignty and an Empty Purse*, 52–55; Nevins, *War for the Union*, vol. 2, 214.

20. Hammond, *Sovereignty and an Empty Purse*, 52–59; William Schultz and M. R. Caine, *The Financial Development of the United States* (New York, 1937), 306–7.

21. Harry Scheiber, "Economic Change in the Civil War Era," *Civil War History* 11 (December 1965): 407.

22. James G. Blaine, *Twenty Years of Congress* (Norwich, Conn., 1884), vol. 1, 443; Curry, *Blueprint*, 162–66; *New York Times*, March 3, 1862.

23. *Congressional Globe*, 38th Cong., 1st sess., 1876–77, 1940, 2513–15; Ratner, *Taxation and Democracy*, 83–85.

24. *Report of the Commissioner of Internal Revenue for the Year Ending June 30, 1863;* Ratner, *Taxation and Democracy*, 81–83; Elmer Ellis, "Public Opinion and the Income Tax, 1860–1900," *Mississippi Valley Historical Review* 26 (September 1940): 225–27; Emerson Fite, *Social and Industrial Conditions in the North during the Civil War* (New Haven, 1910), 135–36.

25. *United States Statutes at Large* 13:281–83; Ratner, *Taxation and Democracy*, 86–87.

26. Timothy Shay Arthur, *Growler's Income Tax* (New York, 1864), in Friedel, ed., *Union Pamphlets*, vol. 2, 975–80.

27. *Historical Statistics of the United States*, 1104; Scheiber, "Economic Change in the Civil War Era," 407; James G. Randall and David H. Donald, *The Civil War and Reconstruction* (Lexington, Mass., 1969), 341–48.

28. Reuben Kessel and Armen Alchain, "Real Wages in the North During the Civil War," *Journal of Law and Economics* vol. 2 (1959): 111; Lee and Passell, *A New Economic View*, 229–37; Jeffrey Williamson, "Watersheds and Turning Points: Conjectures on the Long-Term Impact of Civil War Financing," *Journal of Economic History* 34 (September 1974): 652–61; Ratner, *Taxation and Democracy*, 78, 88–89; Fite, *Social and Industrial Conditions*, 168; Philip R. P. Coelho and James F. Shepherd, "Regional Differences in Real Wages: The United States, 1861–1880," *Explorations in Economic History* 13 (1976): 212–17, 223. These authors differ with Kessel and Alchain as to causes of inflation but agree on the decline in real wages.

29. Oberholtzer, *Jay Cooke*, 331; David Gische, "The New York City Banks and the Development of the National Banking System," *American Journal of Legal History* 23 (January 1979): 33–38; Shade, *Banks or No Banks*, 248–52.

30. Hammond, *Sovereignty and an Empty Purse*, 315–17; Borritt, *Lincoln and Economics*, 199–203; Sharkey, *Money, Class and Party*, 224–27; Gische, "The New York City Banks," 35–37.

31. John Sherman, "Speech on the National Banking Bill, February 10, 1863," in Herman E. K"ross, ed., *Documentary History of Banking and Currency in the United States* (New York, 1969), vol. 2, 1312–22; Sharkey, *Money, Class and Party*, 225; Hammond, *Sovereignty and an Empty Purse*, 321–26; John Sherman, *Recollections*, 229–38.

32. Curry, *Blueprint;* McPherson, *Political History of U.S.*, 362–63.

33. See "The National Banking System: A Report to the Legislature of New York," *Bankers Magazine* 18:964–72; Gische, "The New York City Banks," 43–44; Fite, *Social and Industrial Conditions*, 112–13.

34. Gische, "The New York City Banks," 40–48; Oberholtzer, *Jay Cooke*, vol. 1, 345–47.

35. Oberholtzer, *Jay Cooke*, vol. 1, 331–36.

36. Hammond, *Sovereignty and an Empty Purse*, 345–49; Gische, "The New York City Banks," 49–55.

37. Richard Sylla, "Federal Policy, Banking, Market Structure and Capital Formation in the United States," *Journal of Economic History* 29 (December 1969): 657–86; Robert Sharkey, "Commercial Banking," in David Gilchrist and W. David Lewis, eds., *Economic Change in the Civil War Era* (Greenville, Del., 1965), 27–30; Unger, *The Greenback Era*, chaps. 1, 2.

Chapter 6. Congress and the Second "American System"

1. Daniel T. Rodgers, *The Work Ethic in Industrial America, 1850–1920* (Chicago, 1978), 30–33; George Winston Smith, "Antebellum Attempts of Northern Business to 'Redeem' the Upper South," *Journal of Southern History* 11 (May 1945): 177–213; Eric Foner, *Free Soil*, chaps. 1, 2.

2. *Collected Works of Lincoln*, vol. 4, 438; Borritt, *Lincoln and Economics*, 158–62, Richard Hofstadter, *The American Political Tradition and the Men Who Made It* (New York, 1960), observes that "For Lincoln the vital test of a democracy was economic—its ability to provide opportunities for social ascent to those born in its lower ranks. This belief in opportunity for the self-made man is the key to his entire career; it explains his public appeal; it is the core of his criticism of slavery." (105) Borritt documents this observation at length.

3. "Republican Platform of 1860," in Kirk H. Porter and Donald Bruce Johnson, *National Party Platforms, 1840–1960* (Urbana, 1961), 31–33.

4. F. W. Taussig, *The Tariff History of the United States* (New York, 1910), 155–70; Richard Hofstadter, "The Tariff Issue on the Eve of the Civil War," *American Historical Review* 44 (October 1938): 55; Randall and Donald, *Civil War and Reconstruction*, 285–87; Reinhard Luthin, "Abraham Lincoln and the Tariff," *American Historical Review* 49 (July 1944): 622; Sharkey, *Money, Class and Party*, 18.

5. Borritt, *Lincoln and Economics*, 100–17; Sharkey, *Money, Class and Party*, 208–10; McPherson, *Political History of U.S.*, 362; G. W. Smith, *Henry Carey*, 100–3.

6. Stanley Coben, "Northeastern Business and Radical Reconstruction: A Re-examination," *Mississippi Valley Historical Review* 46 (June 1959): 67–90; Sharkey, *Money, Class and Party;* Michael Les Benedict, *A Compromise of Principle* (New York, 1974), 40–51.

7. Randall and Donald, *Civil War and Reconstruction*, 290–91; Nevins, *War for the Union*, vol. 2, 207.

8. Paul W. Gates, *Agriculture and the Civil War* (New York, 1965); Fite, *Social and Industrial Conditions*, 235–36; Nevins, *War for the Union*, vol. 2, 206–8.

9. Peter D. Hall, *The Organization of American Culture, 1700–1900: Private Institutions, Elites and the Origins of American Nationality* (New York, 1982), 223–24; Fite, *Social and Industrial Conditions*, 237–40.

10. Hall, *Organization of American Culture*, 229–33.

11. *Ben Butler's Book* (Boston, 1892), 201–2, as quoted in Robert Bruce, *Lincoln and the Tools of War* (Indianapolis, 1956), 66. See also William R. Brock, *Conflict and Transformation: The United States, 1844–1877* (New York, 1973), 238–39.

12. Foner, *Free Soil;* Joseph Dorfman, *The Economic Mind in American Civilization* (New York, 1966), vol. 2, 799–800; Smith, *Henry Carey*, 22–24.

13. *Collected Works of Lincoln*, vol. 4, 202; Gates, *Agriculture and the Civil War*, 275–83; Paul Gates, *The Farmer's Age: Agriculture, 1815–1860* (New York, 1960), 80.

14. Gates, *Agriculture and the Civil War*, 283–86; *United States Statutes at Large* 12:392.

15. Paul Gates, "The Homestead Law in an Incongruous Land System," *American Historical Review* 41 (July 1936): 652–81.

16. Nevins, *War for the Union*, vol. 2, 208–11; Brodie, *Thaddeus Stevens*, 181–82; Fite, *Social and Industrial Conditions*, 70–71; Howard Russell, *A Long Deep Furrow: Three Centuries of Farming in New England* (Hanover, N.H., 1976), 417–18.

17. Robert S. Henry, "The Railroad Land Grant Legend in American History Texts," *Mississippi Valley Historical Review* 32 (September 1944): 182; Nevins, *War for the Union*, vol. 2, 211n.

18. Fred A. Shannon, "Comments on 'The Railroad Land Grant Legend,'" *Mississippi Valley Historical Review* 32 (March 1946): 572–74; Louis Hartz, "Government and Business Relations," in Gilchrist and Lewis, eds., *Economic Change*, 83–93, argues that the war allowed the Hamiltonian economic program, which involved government in assisting enterprise, to be changed from the program of elites to the program of democracy.

19. George Rogers Taylor, "The National Economy Before and After the Civil War," in Gilchrist and Lewis, eds., *Economic Change*, 1–22.

20. George Miller, *Railroads and the Granger Laws* (Madison, 1971); Michael Cassity, "Modernization and Social Crisis," *Journal of American History* 66 (June 1979): 41–61; Anne Mayhew, "A Reappraisal of the Causes of Farm Protest in the United States, 1870–1900," *Journal of Economic History* 32 (June 1972): 464–75.

21. Alfred Chandler, Jr., *The Visible Hand: The Managerial Revolution in American Business* (Cambridge, Mass., 1977); Chandler, "The Organization of Manufacturing and Transportation," in Gilchrist and Lewis, eds., *Economic Change*, 137–51; Albert W. Niemi, "Structural and Labor Productivity Patterns in United States Manufacturing, 1849–1899," *Business History Review* 46 (Spring 1972): 67–84.

22. George R. Taylor and Irene Neu, *The American Railroad Network* (Cambridge, Mass., 1956), 6, 50–55; Thomas Weber, *The Northern Railroads in the Civil War* (New York, 1952), 7–13; Fite, *Social and Industrial Conditions*, 55–57.

23. Weber, *Northern Railroads*, 152–53, 199–204; W. T. Sherman, *Memoirs*, vol. 2, 398–99.

24. Weber, *Northern Railroads*, 228–32.

25. Ibid., 14–17; *Historical Statistics of the United States*, 427–28.

26. Anna Jacobson Schwartz, "Gross Dividend and Interest Payments by Corporations at Selected Dates in the 19th Century," in *Trends in the American Economy in the Nineteenth Century* (Princeton, 1960), 412; Nevins, *War for the Union*, vol. 3, 249.

27. Thomas and Hyman, *Stanton*, 153–54; Weber, *Northern Railroads*, 94–99.

28. Weber, *Northern Railroads*, 88–99; Nevins, *War for the Union*, vol. 3, 26–27.

29. Wallace Farnham, "The Weakened Spring of Government: A Study in 19th-Century American History," *American Historical Review* 68 (April 1963): 662–80. Farnham points out the connection between lack of regulation and political corruption, but does not note the connection between business and government in winning the war. Republican policy was, of course, also part of the general policy of the government at all levels in the nineteenth century to advance enterprise without significant regulation. See Hurst, *Law and the Conditions of Freedom in the Nineteenth-Century United States*, for a benign picture of the process. See Morton Horwitz, *The Transformation of American Law* (Cambridge, Mass., 1977), for a darker view.

30. *Collected Works of Lincoln*, vol. 8, 151; *Journal of the House of Representatives of the 23rd Central Assembly of the State of Illinois*. See also *Governor's Message* [Kansas 1864] (Topeka, 1864); Thomas Cochran, "Did the Civil War Retard Industrialization?" *Mississippi Valley Historical Review* 48 (September 1961): 197–210; Robert

Gallman, "Commodity Output 1891–1899," in *Trends in the American Economy*, 13–71.

31. Quoted in Victor Clark, "Manufacturing Development During the Civil War," *Military Historian and Economist* 3 (1918): 92–100, as quoted in Ralph Andreano, ed., *The Economic Impact of the American Civil War* (Cambridge, Mass., 1962), 47.

32. Glenn Porter and Harold Livesay, *Merchants and Manufacturers: Studies in the Changing Structure of 19th-Century Manufacturing* (Baltimore, 1971), 116–21.

33. Robert Sharkey, "Commercial Banking," 27–30; Sylla, "Federal Policy, Banking, Market Structure," 657–86; Porter and Livesay, *Merchants and Manufacturers*, 127–29.

34. Fite, *Social and Industrial Conditions*, 86–87; Cochran, "Did Civil War Retard?" 200; Nevins, *War for the Union*, vol. 3, 248–49; Parish, *The American Civil War*, 345; Daniel Walkowitz, "Working-Class Culture in the Gilded Age," Ph.D. diss., University of Rochester, 1977, 187–88.

35. "The Iron Trade for the Year, 1862," *Merchants Magazine and Commercial Review* 49 (December 1863): 463–64; "New Rolling Mills in Pittsburgh," *Scientific American* 10 (March 1864): 200; Pershing Vartanian, "The Cochran Thesis: A Critique in Statistical Analysis," *Journal of American History* 51 (June 1964): 77–80; Scheiber, "Economic Change in the Civil War Era," 396–411.

36. Nevins, *War for the Union*, vol. 3, 251–53; Fite, *Social and Industrial Conditions*, 92–93; Andrew Carnegie, *Autobiography* (Boston, 1920).

37. Dawley, *Class and Community*, 93–96; Nevins, *War for the Union*, vol. 2, 493–94.

38. Harold Williamson, Ralph Andreano, and Carmen Menezes, "The American Petroleum Industry," in *Output, Employment and Productivity in the United States after 1800* (New York, 1966), 383–85; Fite, *Social and Industrial Conditions*, 164–65. *Commercial and Financial Chronicle*, January 13, 1866, quoted in Fite, 165.

39. "Trade and Business of the United States," *New York Times*, January 8, 1865; Gerald Gunderson, *A New Economic History of America* (New York, 1976), 268–69; Gunderson, "The Origin of the American Civil War," *Journal of Economic History* 34 (December 1974).

40. Ratner, Soltow, and Sylla, *The Evolution of the American Economy*, 253.

41. Fredrickson, *Inner Civil War*, 199–216, sees in this era the rise of a social scientific elite who abandoned the romantic illusions of the antebellum era for a more tough-minded elitist approach to problems of the age.

42. Richard Pohlenburg, *War and Society: The United States, 1941–1945* (Philadelphia, 1972), 73–91; John M. Blum, *V was for Victory: Politics and Culture during World War II* (New York, 1976), 117–46; David Kennedy, *Over Here: The First World War and American Society* (New York, 1980), 94–98, 137–43.

Chapter 7. Agriculture and the Benefits of War

1. *Sixteenth Census of the United States* (1940), "Population," vol. 1, 20.

2. *Ibid.*; Gates, *Agriculture and the Civil War*, vii; Robert E. Lipsey, *Price and Quantity Trends in the Foreign Trade of the United States* (Princeton, 1963), 45–52; *Ninth Census of the United States* (1870), "Wealth and Industry," 334–40.

3. Clarence Danhof, *Change in Agriculture: The Northern United States, 1820–1870* (Cambridge, Mass., 1969), 16–17: Gates, *Agriculture and the Civil War*, 130–31.

4. *Prairie Farmer*, January 6, 9, 30, 1864.

5. *Prairie Farmer*, January 9, 1864; Wayne D. Rasmussen, "The Civil War: A Catalyst of Agrarian Revolution," *Agriculture History* 39 (October 1965): 187–95; Charlotte Erickson, *Invisible Immigrants* (London, 1972), 29–30.

6. Quoted in Danhof, *Change in Agriculture*, 22. On the importance of railroads to changing farm conditions, see Danhof, chap. 1; Albert Fishlow, *American Railroads and the Transformation of the Antebellum Economy* (Cambridge, Mass., 1965); Taylor, *The Transportation Revolution*, chap. 4; Gates, *Agriculture and the Civil War*, 131–32.

7. Rasmussen, "The Civil War: A Catalyst," 187–95; Gates, *Agriculture and the Civil War*, 222; Marvin Towne and Wayne Rasmussen, "Farm Gross Product and Gross Investment in the Nineteenth Century," in *Trends in the American Economy*, 260–61.

8. Fred Bateman and Jeremy Atack, "The Profitability of Northern Agriculture in 1860," *Research in Economic History* 4 (1979): 87–125; Clarence Danhof, "The Farm Enterprise: The Northern United States, 1820–1860s," *ibid.*, 127–91.

9. Jeremy Atack, "Farming and Farm-Making Costs Revisited," *Agricultural History* 56 (October 1982): 661–76.

10. David Schob, *Hired Hands and Plowboys* (Urbana, 1976), 266–72; Gates, *The Farmer's Age*; Allan Bogue, *From Prarie to Corn Belt: Farming on the Illinois and Iowa Prairies in the Nineteenth Century* (Chicago, 1963); Margaret Bogue, *Patterns from the Sod: Land Use and Tenure in the Grand Prairie, 1850–1900* (Springfield, Ill., 1969); Donald L. Winters, "Tenant Farming in Iowa, 1860–1900: A Study of the Terms of Rental Leases," *Agricultural History* 48 (October 1974): 130–50; Winters, "Tenancy as an Economic Institution: The Growth and Distribution of Agricultural Tenancy in Iowa, 1850–1900," *Journal of Economic History* 37 (June 1977): 382–408; Robert Swierenga, "Comment," *ibid.*, 151–54.

11. Quoted in Danhof, "The Farm Enterprise," 183–84.

12. Danhof, *Change in Agriculture*, 44–45; *Journal of the [Illinois] House of Representatives*, 23d General Assembly, January 6, 1863, 22.

13. Danhof, *Change in Agriculture*, 46–47; *Ninth Census of the United States* (1870), "Wealth and Industry," 340–41.

14. Lee Benson, *Merchants, Farmers and Railroads: Railroad Regulation and New York Politics, 1850–1887* (Cambridge, Mass., 1955), 17, 18; Sharkey, *Money, Class and Party*, 135–38.

15. Gates, *Agriculture and the Civil War*, 229; Rasmussen, "The Civil War: A Catalyst," 189–90.

16. Robert L. Jones, *Ohio Agriculture during the Civil War* (Columbus, 1962), 5.

17. Gates, *Agriculture and the Civil War*, 229; *Eighth Census of the United States* (1860), "Population," vol. 17; Fite, *Social and Industrial Conditions*, 4; Russell, *A Long Deep Furrow*, 417.

18. "One Farmer's Wife," *The Independent* 58 (February 9, 1905): 294–98, reprinted in Gerda Lerner, ed., *The Female Experience: An American Documentary* (Indianapolis, 1977), 126–29; also available in David Katzman and William Tuttle, eds., *Plain Folk: The Life Stories of Undistinguished Americans* (Urbana, 1982), 62–63; Carl Degler, *At Odds: Women and the Family from the Revolution to the Present* (New York, 1980), 363–64, 405–10; Dr. W. W. Hall, "Health of Farmer's Families," *Report*

of the Commissioner of Agriculture for the Year 1862 (Washington, 1863), 462–63, as quoted in John Mack Faragher, *Women and Men on the Overland Trail* (New Haven, 1979), 59–60; see 53–65 for fuller discussion of women's work. Carolyn Sachs, *"Invisible Farmers": Women in Agricultural Production* (Totowa, N.J., 1983).

19. Gates, *Agriculture and the Civil War*, 242–43.

20. John Mack Faragher, "History from the Inside-Out: Writing the History of Women in Rural America," *American Quarterly* 33 (Winter 1981): 537–57; Robert Swierenga, "Theoretical Perspectives in the New Rural History: From Environmentalism to Modernization," *Agricultural History* 66 (July 1983): 495–502.

21. Gates, *Agriculture and the Civil War*, 214–15; Jones, *Ohio Agriculture*, 9–10; William Leach, *True Love and Perfect Union: The Feminist Reform of Sex and Society* (New York, 1980); Faragher, "History from the Inside-Out," 554–55; Catherine Clinton, *The Other Civil War: American Women in the 19th Century* (New York, 1984), 90–92.

22. Faragher, "History from the Inside-Out," 542–43; James Mohr, ed., *The Cormany Diaries: A Northern Family in the Civil War* (Pittsburgh, 1982), 18, 550, passim; Martha Coffin Wright to Ellen Wright (1855) in Lerner, ed., *The Female Experience*, 21–25; Faragher, *Women and Men on the Overland Trail*, chaps. 4, 5.

23. Gates, *Agriculture and the Civil War*, 238–39; Rasmussen, "The Civil War: A Catalyst," 192–93; *Belleville Democrat*, May 1, 1861.

24. *Prairie Farmer*, January 30, 1864; *Scientific American*, July 4, 1863, as quoted in Fite, *Social and Industrial Conditions*, 7.

25. Gates, *Agriculture and the Civil War*, 238; Frank D. Lewis, "Explaining the Shift of Labor from Agriculture to Industry in the United States, 1869–1899," *Journal of Economic History* 39 (September 1979): 681–98; Stanley Lebergott, *Manpower in Economic Growth: The American Record Since 1800* (New York, 1964), 510–11; *Sixteenth Census of the United States*, "Population," vol. 1, 20.

26. Morton Rothstein, "International Market for Agricultural Commodities, 1850–1873," in Gilchrist and Lewis, eds., *Economic Change in the Civil War Era*, 63–72; Danhof, *Change in Agriculture*, 289–90; Mayhew, "Reappraisal of the Causes of Farm Protest," 464–75. Benson, *Merchants, Farmers and Railroads*; Miller, *Railroads and the Granger Laws*; Dennis Nordin, *Rich Harvest* (Birmingham, Ala., 1974). These works point to the importance of commercial groups in passing legislation to regulate railroads and commercial grain activity. None of them deny the influence of farmers in supporting these measures. All of them fail to take seriously enough the rural character of state legislators' constituencies.

27. Fite, *Social and Industrial Conditions*, 11–12; Gates, *Agriculture and the Civil War*, 241–42, 277.

28. Gates, *Agriculture and the Civil War*, 244.

29. *Ibid.*, 188–99.

30. Hyman, *A More Perfect Union*, 336–41; Gates, *Agriculture and the Civil War*, 190–93.

31. Joe B. Frantz, *Gail Borden, Dairyman to a Nation* (Norman, 1951); Russell, *A Long Deep Furrow*, 420–21; Gates, *Agriculture and the Civil War*, 193–94.

32. Gates, *Agriculture and the Civil War*, 142–56; Jones, *Ohio Agriculture*, 15–16.

33. Gates, *Agriculture and the Civil War*, 184–87; Nevins, *War for the Union*, vol. 3, 234; Russell Weigley, *Quartermaster General of the Army: A Biography of M. C. Meigs* (New York, 1959).

34. Gates, *Agriculture and the Civil War*, 176–84.

35. *Ibid.*, 301–23; Danhof, *Change in Agriculture,* 289–90.
36. Arnold Tilden, *The Legislation of the Civil War Period Considered as a Basis of the Agricultural Revolution in the United States* (Los Angeles, 1937).
37. Gates, *Agriculture and the Civil War,* 272–300. Merle Curti, *The Making of an American Community* (Stanford, 1959), 185, 212–13.
38. Robert Sterling, "Civil War Draft Resistance in the Middle West," Ph.D. diss., Northern Illinois University, DeKalb, 1974, after a thorough survey says that "draft resistance in the Middle West was widespread and severe." (178–70, 648) His evidence suggests that Klement, *Copperheads,* and Eugene Murdock, *One Million Men: The Civil War Draft in the North* (Madison, 1971), both underestimated the extent of the protest.
39. Sterling, "Civil War Draft Resistance," 259–74; Hubert Wubben, *Civil War Iowa and the Copperhead Movement* (Ames, 1980); Murdock, *One Million Men,* 356; Judith Lee Hancock, "The Role of Community in Civil War Desertion," *Civil War History* 29 (June 1983): 125–26; Ella Lonn, *Desertion during the Civil War* (New York, 1928).
40. Quoted in Erickson, *Invisible Immigrants,* 200–2.

Chapter 8. Industrial Workers and the Costs of War

1. Calculated from the *Ninth Census of the United States* (1870), vol. 3, 808–9. This was the first census to list occupations. National occupational figures have been discussed by David Montgomery, *Beyond Equality: Labor and the Radical Republicans* (New York, 1967) 28–29, 448–50; Daniel Rodgers, *The Work Ethic in Industrial America* (Chicago, 1978), 36–37; and Carl Siracusa, *Mechanical People: Perceptions of the Industrial Order in Massachusetts, 1815–80* (Middletown, Conn., 1978). Also helpful is Lebergott, *Manpower in Economic Growth.* See Clyde Griffin, "Occupational Mobility in 19th-Century America: Problems and Possibilities," *Journal of Social History* 5 (Spring 1972): 310–30, for the complexities of determining occupational status.
2. Norman J. Ware, *The Labor Movement in the United States, 1860–1890* (New York, 1929), 1–5; Dawley, *Class and Community,* 101–4; Sylvis, *Life of William Sylvis,* 61–63; John R. Commons et al., *History of Labour in the United States* (New York, 1918), vol. 2, 33–39; Stanley Lebergott, "The American Labor Force," in Lance Davis et al., *American Economic Growth* (New York, 1971), 220.
3. Grossman, *William Sylvis,* 34, 55–67, 72–80; Montgomery, *Beyond Equality,* 223–25.
4. Dawley, *Class and Community,* 86–88, 102–3, 200–2 (Dawley fails to notice this phenomenon, although his evidence clearly reveals it); Herbert Gutman, "Social and Economic Structure and Depression: American Labor in 1873 and 1874," Ph.D. diss., University of Wisconsin, Madison, 1959, xii–xv; Daniel Walkowitz, *Worker City, Company Town* (Urbana, 1978), 12–13; Michael Frisch, *Town into City: Springfield, Massachusetts, and the Meaning of Community* (Cambridge, Mass., 1972) 127–28.
5. Calculated from the *Eighth Census of the United States,* "Manufacturers," 677–701, 705–11, 729–30; Henry Pelling, *American Labor* (Chicago, 1960), 25–26; Gutman, "Social and Economic Structure and Depression," 234–36; Lawrence Costello,

"The New York City Labor Movement, 1861–1873," Ph.D. diss., Columbia University, New York, 1967.

6. *New York Times*, February 22, 1869, 2.

7. Stephen Thernstrom, *Poverty and Progress* (Cambridge, Mass., 1964); Walkowitz, *Worker City, Company Town;* Daniel Walkowitz, "Statistics and the Writing of Working-Class Culture," *Labor History* 15 (Summer 1974): 416–60; Peter Knights, *The Plain People of Boston, 1830–1860: A Study of City Growth* (New York, 1971), 78–102. Knights and Thernstrom, who present the darkest picture of upward mobility, still report upward climbing for even their lowest groups. Two-thirds of the lowest classes in Newburyport who stayed in the town improved their position. See Thernstrom, 149–50. Almost 15 percent of those who stayed in Boston between 1850 and 1860 moved up; 2.8 percent moved down. See Knights, 99. Dawley, *Class and Community*, finds an upward mobility of about 10 percent per decade in Lynn, Massachusetts, between 1860 and 1880. (161–65)

8. Bruce Laurie, Theodore Hershberg, and George Alter, "Immigrants and Industry: The Philadelphia Experience, 1850–1880," *Journal of Social History* 9 (Winter 1975): 219–48.

9. Daniel T. Rogers, "Tradition, Modernity and the American Industrial Worker," *Journal of Interdisciplinary History* 7 (Spring 1977): 655–81; Herbert Gutman, "Work, Culture, and Society in Industrializing America, 1815–1919," *American Historical Review* 78 (June 1973): 531–89. Montgomery, *Beyond Equality*, 14–15, notes the vagueness of class rhetoric. For surveys of the literature of the "new labor history," which emphasizes working class consciousness and the impact of diverse religious and intellectual perspectives on the condition of workers, see David Brody, "Labor History in the 1970s: Toward a History of the American Worker," in Michael Kammen, ed., *The Past Before Us* (Ithaca, 1980); David Brody, "The Old Labor History and the New: In Search of an American Working Class," *Labor History* 20 (Winter 1979); David Montgomery, "To Study the People: The American Working Class," *Labor History* 21 (Fall 1980); Sean Wilentz, "Against Exceptionalism: Class Consciousness and the American Labor Movement, 1790–1920," paper delivered at Organization of American Historians meeting, Los Angeles, 1984. Wilentz especially has tried to link the intellectual and cultural perspectives of workers with their class consciousness. See his *Chants Democratic: New York City and the Rise of the American Working Class* (New York, 1984).

10. Montgomery, *Beyond Equality*, 42–44; Timothy Smith, *Revivalism and Social Reform: American Protestantism on the Eve of Civil War* (New York, 1957), 45–79; Ray Allen Billington, *The Protestant Crusade, 1800–1860* (New York, 1938), 305–7; Kelley, *The Cultural Pattern in American Politics;* Paul Kleppner, "Lincoln and the Immigrant Vote: A Case of Religious Polarization," *Mid-America* 48 (July 1966): 176–95; Ronald P. Formisano, "Ethnicity and Party in Michigan, 1854–1860," in Frederick Luebke, ed., *Ethnic Voters and the Election of Lincoln* (Lincoln, Neb., 1971), 175–95.

11. Dawley, *Class and Community*, 48–52; Robert Cross, "The Changing Image of the

City Among American Catholics," *Catholic Historical Review* 48 (April 1962): 33–52; Montgomery, *Beyond Equality*, 35–38; Mark Sullivan, *The Education of an American* (New York, 1938), 11; Schob, *Hired Hands and Plowboys.*

12. The religious, ethnic, and class differences that divided workers were still generally vague, as were the distinctions between employer and employee. Using cultural analysis to describe the condition of the workers in this period thus "involves a sacrifice of historical complexity for descriptive clarity," in the words of Leonard S. Wallock, "The Limits of Solidarity: Philadelphia's Journeymen Printers in the Mid-Nineteenth Century," paper delivered at OAH meeting, Los Angeles, 1984, 21. See the warning on this point by Bruce Laurie, *Working People of Philadelphia, 1800–1850* (Philadelphia, 1980). Also see Friedrich Lenger, "Class, Culture, and Class Consciousness in Antebellum Lynn: Critique of Alan Dawley and Paul Faler," *Social History* 6 (October 1981): 317–32.

13. *New York Daily Tribune,* January 8, February 16, February 20, 1861. On the complicated issue of German-American support for Lincoln, see Luebke, ed., *Ethnic Voters and the Election of Lincoln.* Most contributors to this volume argue that the German vote was divided, with Lincoln likely to have received the Lutheran votes but very unlikely to have gotten Catholic support. See also David Potter, *The Impending Crisis* (New York, 1976), 435–36.

14. Montgomery, *Beyond Equality*, 92–93; Grossman, *William Sylvis*, 44–46; Terence Powderly, *Thirty Years*, 44; Commons et al., *History of Labour*, vol. 2, 10–12.

15. Gould, *Investigations in Military and Anthropological Statistics,* 5, 10–14, 209–10; Grossman, *William Sylvis*, 46–55; Powderly, *Thirty Years*, 57; Dawley, *Class and Community;* Walkowitz, "Working Class Culture," 186ff. McPherson, *Ordeal by Fire,* disputes the argument that industrial workers served in especially high percentages. (357–59)

16. Borritt, *Lincoln and Economics*, 183–85, 218–21.

17. Montgomery, *Beyond Equality*, 108–10; Dawley, *Class and Community;* Frisch, *Town into City*, 53–55.

18. Samuel Gompers, *Seventy Years of Life and Labour* (New York, 1925), vol. 2, 49; Carl Siracusa, *Mechanical People*, 216–18; George McNeill, *The Labor Movement: The Problem of Today* (New York, 1887), 123–24; Charles Nordhoff, "America for Free Working Men!" (New York, 1865).

19. Fite, *Social and Industrial Conditions*, 125–27, 198–99; Nevins, *War for the Union,* vol. 3, 231; Charles C. Binney, *The Life of Horace Binney* (Philadelphia, 1903); Robert Bremner, *The Public Good: Philanthropy and Welfare in the Civil War Era* (New York, 1980); Commons et al., *History of Labour*, vol. 2.

20. Williamson and Lindert, *American Inequality*, 34, 38–39, 47, 51; Soltow, *Men and Wealth*, 24, 67, 99–103; Gallman, "Professor Pessen on the 'Egalitarian Myth,'" 194–95.

21. Williamson and Lindert, *American Inequality*, 78–81, 100–2.

22. *Ibid.,* 105–9, 122.

23. *Scientific American,* May 21, 1864, quoting the *New York Evening Post.* See also *New York Independent,* June 25, 1864; *New York Herald,* October 6, 1863; Robert

Tomes, "The Fortunes of War," *Harpers Monthly* 29 (July 1864): 230–31; Nevins, *War for the Union*, vol. 3, 264–66; Fite, *Social and Industrial Conditions*, 259–74.

24. Finchers, March 19, April 9, 1864; Costello, "The New York City Labor Movement," 59.

25. Joseph Hernon, *Celts, Catholics, and Copperheads* (Columbus, 1968), 11–12, 38; Thernstrom, *Poverty and Progress*, 174; Long, *Civil War Day by Day*, 707.

26. Willston H. Lofton, "Northern Labor and the Negro during the Civil War," *Journal of Negro History* 34 (July 1949): 251–73.

27. John R. Commons et al., *A Documentary History of American Industrial Society* (Cleveland, 1910), 67–73; Nevins, *War for the Union*, vol. 3, 229–30; Fite, *Social and Industrial Conditions*, 185–87; Montgomery, *Beyond Equality*, 96–97; *Report of the Special Commissioner of Revenue*, 40th Congress, 3d sess., no. 16, 14–20.

28. Charles Loring Brace, *The Dangerous Classes of New York and Twenty Years' Work Among Them* (New York, 1872), 109, 356; Brace, "The Little Laborers of New York City," *Harpers New Monthly* 47 (August 1873): 321–32; Gutman, "Social and Economic Structure," 247; Montgomery, *Beyond Equality*, 33–34. Bremner, *The Public Good*, 85ff. It is difficult to determine the number of children who were employed before 1870. The census of that year was the first to gather data on the ages of workers. Some 765,000 workers between ten and fifteen were listed. This misses, of course, workers under ten. It also does little to show what kind of work they did. At the very least, about 380,000 of these children worked off the farms, if we assume that the division between farm and nonfarm employment in the overall population can be applied. But given the undercounting of urban workers generally in that year, the likelihood that employers would hide the number of children they employed, and the possibility that more people would consider themselves gainfully employed in nonfarm occupations, it seems probable that the number of children at work off the farms in the nation was higher than the estimated 380,000 figure.

29. Quoted in Edith Abbott, "Child Labor in America Before 1870," in Grace Abbot, *The Child and the State* (Chicago, 1938), vol. 1, 275–76.

30. Eric Monkkonen, *Police in Urban America, 1860–1920* (New York, 1981), 78–82; Edith Abbott, "The Civil War and the Crime Wave of 1865–70," *Social Science Review* 1 (June 1927): 219–22; Robert Bremner, ed., *Children and Youth in America: A Documentary History*, vol. 1: *1600–1865* (Cambridge, Mass., 1970), 713–14, 800–1; Robert Ernst, *Immigrant Life in New York City, 1825–1863* (New York, 1949), 205.

31. Bremner, *The Public Good*, 80–83; Fite, *Social and Industrial Conditions*, 301. Fite's statement that "the increase in the work of the children's societies does not indicate any increase in poverty and misery in the cities" is difficult to understand in light of worker protests and the thousands of orphans that war created.

32. Sylvis, *Life of William Sylvis*, 97–115; Grossman, *William Sylvis*, 49–50.

33. As quoted in Commons et al., *History of Labour*, vol. 2, 20. Although statistics on the actual number of union members are notoriously imprecise, it seems a reasonable assumption that by the end of the 1860s, somewhere near 300,000 men belonged to a union of some sort. Assuming an industrial wage-earning population of at least 3,546,000 in the nation as a whole as of 1870, it is clear that the vast majority of these workers were not members of a union.

34. Costello, "The New York City Labor Movement," 283–92; Walkowitz, "Working Class Culture," 189–91; Nevins, *War for the Union*, vol. 3, 265–67; Fite, *Social and Industrial Conditions*, 205–10.
35. Commons et al., *History of Labour*, vol. 2, 21–26; Montgomery, *Beyond Equality*, 160–65, 457–59; McPherson, *Ordeal by Fire*, 376.
36. H. M. Gitelman, "The Labor Force at Waltham Watch during the Civil War Era," *Journal of Economic History* 25 (June 1965): 214–43.
37. Hernon, *Celts, Catholics, and Copperheads*, 15–19; Dennis Clark, *The Irish in Philadelphia* (Philadelphia, 1973), 121–22.
38. Adrian Cook, *The Armies of the Streets: The New York City Draft Riots of 1863* (Lexington, Ky., 1974), 52; Murdock, *One Million Men*; Finchers, July 18, 1863; Grossman, *William Sylvis*, 49–51; Iver Bernstein, "The New York City Draft Riots of 1863 and the Political Crisis of the Middle Decades: Class Relations on the Eve of Industrial Capitalism," paper delivered at OAH meeting, Los Angeles, 1984.
39. Cook, *The Armies of the Streets*; James McCague, *The Second Rebellion* (New York, 1968); Albion Man, "Labor Competition and the New York Draft Riots of 1863," *Journal of Negro History* 36 (October 1951): 375–405.
40. Wayne C. Broehl, *The Molly Maguires* (Cambridge, Mass., 1964), 83–90; Murdock, *One Million Men*, 86–88; *Official Record*, vol. 3, 1004–9; Alexander K. McClure, *Old Time Notes of Pennsylvania* (Philadelphia, 1905), vol. 1, 548–49. James Walter Coleman, *The Molly Maguire Riots: Industrial Conflicts in the Pennsylvania Coal Region* (Richmond, 1936), 40–48.
41. Murdock, *One Million Men*, 54–57.
42. Peter Levine, "Draft Evasion in the North during the Civil War," *Journal of American History* 67 (March 1981): 816–34; Eric Foner, "The Causes of the American Civil War," 197–214; Richard Brown, *Modernization: The Transformation of American Life, 1600–1865* (New York, 1976); Sterling, "Civil War Draft Resistance in the Middle West." Of course, it is impossible to explain any individual decision to fight or evade the draft. However, the evidence is strong that protest against conscription was highly correlated with low economic status, foreign birth, and Catholic religion, the composite of a crucial and large element of the Democratic party. See Silbey, *A Respectable Minority*.
43. Murdock, *One Million Men*, 72–77, 80–82; Broehl, *The Molly Maguires*, 88–90.
44. Larry Nelson, *Bullets, Ballots and Rhetoric: Confederate Policy for the United States Presidential Contest of 1864* (University, Ala., 1980), 2–3; Herman Melville, *Battle Pieces and Aspects of the War*, a fascimile reproduction with an introduction by Sidney Kaplan (Gainesville, 1980), 86–87; Daniel Aaron, *The Unwritten War: American Writers and the Civil War* (New York, 1973), 79–83; Fredrickson, *Inner Civil War*.
45. Montgomery, *Beyond Equality*, 103–7; Cook, *The Armies of the Streets*, 195–96; Grossman, *William Sylvis*, 53–54; Hernon, *Celts, Catholics, and Copperheads*, 20–21; Bernstein, "New York City Draft Riots."
46. Montgomery, *Beyond Equality*, 108–9, 110–11; *Harpers Weekly*, July 18, 1863.
47. Commons et al., *History of Labour*, vol. 2, 26–33; Commons et al., *History of Industrial Society*, vol. 9, 91–116; Montgomery, *Beyond Equality*, 146–47; Joseph Rayback, *A History of American Labor* (New York, 1966), 113–14.
48. Fite, *Social and Industrial Conditions*, 203; Montgomery, *Beyond Equality*, 98–99,

199, 462–69; Grossman, *William Sylvis*, 51–52; *Finchers*, May 14, 21, 28, June 11, 1864; Walkowitz, "Worker City," 249; McNeill, *The Labor Movement.*

49. Soltow, *Men and Wealth*, 99–104; Williamson and Lindert, *American Inequality*, 38–39, 46–48.

Chapter 9. The Meanings of Emancipation

1. Eric Foner, *Free Soil*, 40–43.
2. *Ibid.*, 11–39; Meyers, *The Jacksonian Persuasion;* Rogers, *The Work Ethic*, 1–29.
3. *Collected Works of Lincoln*, vol. 2, 461; G. W. Smith, "Antebellum Attempts of Northern Business," 177–213; Lawrence N. Powell, "The American Land Company and Agency: John A. Andrew and the Northernization of the South," *Civil War History* 21 (December 1975): 293–97; George Winston Smith, "Some Northern Wartime Attitudes Toward the Post–Civil War South," *Journal of Southern History* 10 (August 1944): 255–57; McPherson, *Struggle for Equality*, 47–51; Lyman Abbot, "Lutheran Evangelization," *New Englander* 23 (October 1864): 699–708. See also *New York Times*, "The War as Regenerative of the South," December 5, 1863.
4. Barrington Moore, Jr., *Social Origins of Dictatorship and Democracy: Lord and Peasant in the Making of the Modern World* (Boston, 1967), 142–44; Margaret Shortreed, "The Antislavery Radicals: From Crusade to Revolution," *Past and Present* 16 (November 1959): 65–76. These works offer a simple Marxist view of Republican economic goals for Dixie. For a more complex picture, see W. R. Brock, *An American Crisis: Congress and Reconstruction, 1865–1867* (New York, 1963), 240–49. See also G. W. Smith, "Some Northern Attitudes," 262–67. Foner, *Free Soil;* Willie Lee Rose, *Rehearsal for Reconstruction: The Port Royal Experiment* (New York, 1964); Brock, *An American Crisis;* Borritt, *Lincoln and Economics;* and Lawrence Powell, *New Masters: Northern Planters During the Civil War and Reconstruction* (New Haven, 1980), show the interrelationship between the humanitarian and economic elements in Republican policy.
5. John Eaton, *Grant, Lincoln and the Freedmen* (New York, 1907), 105–6.
6. *New York Times*, January 3, 1863, 4.
7. Rose, *Rehearsal for Reconstruction;* Edwin Hoffman, "From Slavery to Self Reliance," *Journal of Negro History* 56 (January 1956): 10; John G. Sproat, "Blueprint for Radical Reconstruction," *Journal of Southern History* 22 (February 1957): 29.
8. Rose, *Rehearsal for Reconstruction*, 223–38, 420; Paul Cimbala, "The 'Talisman Power': Davis Tillson, The Freedmen's Bureau, and Free Labor in Reconstruction Georgia, 1865–1866," *Civil War History* 28 (June 1982): 153–71; Eric Foner, "Reconstruction and the Crisis of Free Labor," in *Politics and Ideology in the Age of the Civil War* (New York, 1980), 97–127.
9. Rose, *Rehearsal for Reconstruction*, 37–38, 49–50, 217–19, 223–29, 298–311; Foner, "Reconstruction and the Crisis," 107–11; Eric Foner, *Nothing but Freedom: Emancipation and Its Legacy* (Baton Rouge, 1983), 55–57.
10. Eaton, *Grant, Lincoln and the Freedmen*, 85–86; Janet Sharp Herman, *The Pursuit of a Dream* (New York, 1983), 46–47.
11. Herman, *The Pursuit of a Dream*, 56–57. See, for wider Southern picture, Leon Litwack, *Been in the Storm So Long: The Aftermath of Slavery* (New York, 1980), 482–85.

12. *New York Times,* December 4, 1864, as quoted in Herman, *The Pursuit of a Dream,* 61; Rose, *Rehearsal for Reconstruction,* 304–8. Rose notes the actual limitations on the profitability of the free labor system, but does not deny that many Northerners had reason to believe, as Edward Philbrick asserted, that "any just and equitable man can raise cotton or any other product here at far less cost than under any system of compulsory labor." Whitelaw Reid, *After the War: A Tour of the Southern States, 1865–1866* (New York, 1965), 279–87.

13. Joel Grant to "Dear Father," September 3, 1863, Grant Family Papers, Sophia Smith Collection, Smith College, Northampton, Mass.

14. Litwack, *Been in the Storm,* 147–49, notes occasions of slave reprisals. Whites throughout the South had feared slave insurrections with profound horror, and they feared violence by freedmen as well. The army shared such fears. See James E. Sefton, *The United States Army and Reconstruction* (Baton Rouge, 1967), 43.

15. *Personal Memoirs of U. S. Grant,* 221. Louis Gerteis, *From Contraband to Freedman* (Westport, Conn., 1973), emphasizes the oppressive nature of the army contact with freedmen. Litwack, *Been in the Storm,* shows the complexities of the encounter and its meaning for freedmen. McPherson, *Ordeal by Fire,* 394–401, provides a fine summary. Herman Belz, *Emancipation and Equal Rights* (New York, 1978), 57–62, is also excellent on these points.

16. Thomas and Hyman, *Stanton,* 234–37, 241. Dudley Taylor Cornish, *The Sable Arm: Negro Troops in the Union Army, 1861–1865* (New York, 1966).

17. Iowan quoted in Wubben, *Civil War Iowa and the Copperhead Movement,* 99; Winther, ed., *With Sherman to the Sea: Theodore F. Upson,* 55–56, 69, 101; James McPherson, ed., *The Negro's Civil War: How American Negroes Felt and Acted during the War for the Union* (New York, 1965), 163–64; Cornish, *Sable Arm,* 40–51; Bell I. Wiley, *The Life of Billy Yank* (Baton Rouge, 1952).

18. Fredrickson, *Black Image,* 168–71; George Winston Smith, "Broadsides for Freedom: Civil War Propaganda in New England," *New England Quarterly* 21 (September 1948): 303; Fredrickson, *Inner Civil War,* chap. 10.

19. Cornish, *Sable Arm,* 133–47; Peyton McCrary, *Lincoln and Reconstruction* (Princeton, 1978), 142–50; McPherson, *Struggle for Equality,* 192–220.

20. McPherson, *Struggle for Equality,* 202–6.

21. Quoted in McPherson, *Ordeal by Fire.*

22. *Collected Works of Lincoln,* vol. 6, 408–10 (August 26, 1863).

23. *Atlantic* 14 (October 1864): 517; Strong, *Diary,* vol. 3, 344–47; Fredrickson, *Inner Civil War,* 115.

24. Albert Castel, "The Fort Pillow Massacre," *Civil War History* 4 (March 1958): 37–50; Nevins, *War for the Union,* vol. 4, 60; Cornish, *Sable Arm,* 162–65, 173–80.

25. McPherson, *Ordeal By Fire,* 450–56.

26. While most authorities list 2,751 blacks killed in action, Frank Phisterer, *Statistical Record of the Armies of the United States* (New York, 1884), 70, says that there were 1,514 killed in battle and 1,760 who died of wounds and injuries. Cornish, *Sable Arm,* 288; Parish, *The American Civil War,* 259; Mark Boatner, *Civil War Dictionary* (New York, 1959), 584, follow Thomas L. Livermore, *Numbers and Losses in the Civil War in America* (Boston, 1901), 50n. See also McPherson, ed., *The Negro's Civil War,* 237, chaps. 11–16.

27. "Our Soldiers," *North American Review* 99 (July 1864): 172–204 (italics in original); "Harvard Heroes," *Atlantic* 12 (September 1863): 385–88. Fredrickson,

Inner Civil War, chap. 10, focuses on Shaw as martyr to the cause and as symbol for Yankee aristocrats; chap. 2 discusses prewar concerns.

28. *New York Times*, September 25, 1862; "The Rebellion, Its Causes and Consequences," *North American Review* 99 (July 1864): 267.

29. *Bigelow Papers*, 2d ed., as quoted in Martin Duberman, *James Russell Lowell* (Boston, 1966), 221.

30. Leon Litwack, *North of Slavery: The Negro in the Free States, 1790–1860* (Chicago, 1961), 70, 91–99, passim; Voegeli, *Free but Not Equal*, 1–9; McPherson, *Struggle for Equality*, 222–24.

31. *Collected Works of Lincoln*, vol. 5, 534–36.

32. Quoted in McPherson, *Struggle for Equality*, 221–26.

33. Donald, *Charles Sumner*, 192–93; McPherson, *Struggle for Equality*, 225–26; Herman Belz, *A New Birth of Freedom* (Westport, Conn., 1976), 143–44; Allen Bogue, *Earnest Men: Republicans of the Civil War Senate* (Ithaca, 1981), 196–201; Martha Saxton, *Louisa May: A Modern Biography of Louisa May Alcott* (New York, 1977), 277–78.

34. McPherson, *Struggle for Equality*, 224–36; Voegeli, *Free but Not Equal*, 165–67.

35. As quoted in McPherson, ed., *The Negro's Civil War*, 263–64; *Life and Times of Frederick Douglass, Written by Himself* (New York, rev. ed., 1892; reprint, 1962), 365–66; Leech, *Reveille in Washington*, 370. The *New York Times*, March 6, 1865, reported that several Negroes had attended the reception.

36. James C. Mohr, ed., *Radical Republicans in the North: State Politics during Reconstruction* (Baltimore, 1976), 5, 28, 56–57, 68–73, 85–91, 107–11, 125–26, 147–50, 167–93; Voegeli, *Free but Not Equal*, 169–72; William G. Cochran, "Freedom without Equality: A Study of Northern Opinion and the Negro, 1861–1870," Ph.D. diss., University of Minnesota, Minneapolis, 1957; Leslie Fishel, "Northern Prejudice and Negro Suffrage, 1865–1870," *Journal of Negro History* 39 (January 1954): 8–26.

37. Eric McKitrick, *Andrew Johnson and Reconstruction* (Chicago, 1960), 58–59.

38. For one state's experience, see David M. Katzman, *Before the Ghetto: Black Detroit* (Urbana, 1973), 35–50; William Gillette, *The Right to Vote: Politics and the Passage of the Fifteenth Amendment* (Baltimore, 1965); Lawanda Cox and John Cox, "Negro Suffrage and Republican Politics: The Problem of Motivation in Reconstruction Historiography," *Journal of Southern History* 33 (August 1967): 303–30.

39. *Tribune Almanac for 1870*, 22; Hyman and Wiecek, *Equal Justice Under Law*, 222–23; Kenneth M. Stampp, *The Era of Reconstruction* (New York, 1965).

40. Fredrickson, *Inner Civil War*, 116–22; Duberman, *Lowell*, 216–18; McPherson, *Struggle for Equality*, 90–93; *Collected Works of Lincoln*, vol. 7, 132–33.

41. McPherson, *Struggle for Equality*, 90–93; Fredrickson, *Inner Civil War*, 116–22.

42. Lance Davis and John Legler, "The Government in the American Economy, 1815–1902: A Quantitative Study," *Journal of Economic History* 26 (December 1966): 514–51; Mohr, ed., *Radical Republicans;* Frisch, *Town into City*. The enduring power of state rights is explored in Paludan, *A Covenant with Death;* Hyman, *A More Perfect Union;* Belz, *Emancipation and Equal Rights;* Hyman and Wiecek, *Equal Justice Under Law;* and Morton Keller, *Affairs of State: Public Life in Late Nineteenth-Century America* (Cambridge, Mass., 1977).

43. "Education of the Freedmen," *North American Review* 101 (October 1865): 542–

43; Howard quoted in Harold M. Hyman, ed., *The Radical Republicans and Reconstruction* (Indianapolis, 1967), 214–15, and see Hyman's discussion, 189–229. Powell, "The American Land Company and Agency," 293–300; Jacqueline Jones, *Soldiers of Light and Love: Northern Teachers and Georgia Blacks, 1865–1873* (Chapel Hill, 1980), 109–11; James McPherson, *The Abolitionist Legacy: From Reconstruction to the NAACP* (Princeton, 1975), 161–64; McPherson, *Ordeal by Fire*, 399; Eric Foner, "Reconstruction Revisited," *Reviews in American History* 10 (December 1982): 97 n. 15; *Life and Times of Frederick Douglass*, 78–80; Litwack, *Been in the Storm*, 472–76, 500–1; Howard Swint, *The Northern Teacher in the South, 1862–1870* (Nashville, 1941).

44. Brodie, *Thaddeus Stevens*, 166–67; McPherson, *Struggle for Equality*, 252–53; *New York Tribune*, December 21, 1863; Belz, *Emancipation and Equal Rights*, 34–38; John Syrett, "The Confiscation Acts: Efforts at Reconstruction during the Civil War," Ph.D. diss., University of Wisconsin, Madison, 1971, 1–4, 26; Lucie, "Confiscation," 310.

45. McPherson, *Struggle for Equality*, 255–57; *Collected Works of Lincoln*, vol. 6, 457; W. T. Sherman, *Memoirs*, vol. 2, 250–52; Litwack, *Been in the Storm*, 398–404; Rose, *Rehearsal for Reconstruction*, 330; Lawanda Cox, "The Promise of Land to Freedmen," *Mississippi Valley Historical Review* 45 (December 1958): 431–33.

46. McPherson, *Struggle for Equality*, 250–52; Powell, "The American Land Company and Agency," 293–308; Powell, *New Masters*; Rose, *Rehearsal for Reconstruction*, 223–39, 298–313.

47. Litwack, *Been in the Storm*, 403; W. T. Sherman, *Memoirs*, 245–47; McPherson, ed., *The Negro's Civil War*, 293–300; Belz, *A New Birth of Freedom*, 151–52.

48. *Life and Times of Frederick Douglass*, 375–77; Harriet Beecher Stowe, *The Lives and Deeds of Our Self-Made Men* (Boston, 1872); John Cawelti, *Apostles of the Self-Made Man* (Chicago, 1965). Lincoln's 1861 annual address, discussing the war as an effort to preserve free labor, was the focus of an 1865 essay by Charles Eliot Norton on the meaning of the war. The essence of the war, Norton insisted, was the rights of labor. "It is a struggle for the rights of labor, and for the form of government by which alone those rights can be securely maintained." "Abraham Lincoln," *North American Review* 100 (January 1865): 8; Philip Foner, *The Life and Writings of Frederick Douglass*, vol. 4, 158–65. Lawanda Cox, "The Promise of Land for the Freedmen," 413–38; Belz, *A New Birth of Freedom*, 103–4; Lawanda Cox, *Lincoln and Black Freedom: A Study on Presidential Leadership* (Columbia, S.C., 1981), 28–30.

49. For a summary of black economic gains in late nineteenth century, see Roger Ransom and Richard Sutch, *One Kind of Freedom* (New York, 1977); Robert Higgs, *Competition and Coercion: Blacks within American Economy, 1865–1914* (New York, 1977); Phillip S. Paludan, "The American Civil War: Triumph Through Tragedy," *Civil War History* 20 (September 1974).

Chapter 10. The Dialogue of Politics: Loyalty and Unity, 1863–1864

1. *Official Record*, series 2, vol. 2, 277–79; Randall, *Constitutional Problems under Lincoln*, 82–85, 155–56; Harold Hyman, *A More Perfect Union*, 81–89; Nevins, *War for the Union*, vol. 3, 167–72. Frank L. Klement, *Dark Lanterns: Secret Political Societies,*

Conspiracies, and Treason Trials in the Civil War (Baton Rouge, 1984), raises strong doubts about the extent of conspiracy against the government.

2. Smith and Judah, eds., *Life in the North during the Civil War*, 213–17; Sterling, "Civil War Draft Resistance in the Middle West," passim; Broehl, *The Molly Maguires*, 83–90; Murdock, *One Million Men*, 47–82.

3. See Thomas Reed Turner, *Beware the People Weeping: Public Opinion and the Assassination of Abraham Lincoln* (Baton Rouge, 1982), 65–73. Turner focuses only on plots to kill Lincoln, but his evidence suggests the uniqueness of that event. Lamon did speak to people before the assassination and also said that someone had previously shot at Lincoln, hitting his hat. Stanton did provide Lincoln with a mounted guard for his carriage rides, but Lincoln protested that it was useless to try to stop an assassination attempt. The only previous attempt on the life of a president occurred when an insane man tried to kill Andrew Jackson.

4. Arnold M. Shankman, *The Pennsylvania Antiwar Movement, 1861–1865* (Cranbury, N.J., 1980), 107–21; Baker, *Affairs of Party*, 39–41; Wubben, *Civil War Iowa and the Copperhead Movement.*

5. Sterling, "Civil War Draft Resistance in the Middle West," 666–68, passim; Judith Lee Nallock, "The Role of Community in Civil War Desertion," *Civil War History* 29 (June 1983): 123–34; Peter Levine, "Draft Evasion in the North during the Civil War," 816–34; McPherson, *Ordeal by Fire*, 345–48; Parish, *The American Civil War*, 498–505.

6. Seymour speech of July 4, 1863, in Society for The Diffusion of Political Knowledge, *The Constitution* (New York, 1864), 103–5; Voorhees, *Congressional Globe*, 37th Cong., 3d sess., 1062.

7. Bigelow, ed., *Letters and Memorials of Tilden*, vol. 1, 166–67; Turpie speech of February 7, 1863, in *Handbook of the Democracy for 1863–64* (New York, 1864), 4–5.

8. Nevins, *War for the Union*, vol. 3, 159. Adams County, scene of the Battle of Gettysburg, voted Democratic in both 1863 and 1864. See Shankman, *Pennsylvania Antiwar Movement*, 137, 202.

9. *Collected Works of Lincoln*, vol. 6, 265; Sterling, "Civil War Draft Resistance in the Middle West," 663–66; William Whiting, *The War Powers of the President and the Legislative Powers of Congress in Relation to Rebellion, Treason and Slavery* (Boston, 1862); Thomas and Hyman, *Stanton*, 280–81, 375–77; Swisher, *History of Supreme Court*, 901–24; Murdock, *One Million Men*, 91–120; Shankman, *Pennsylvania Antiwar Movement*, 142–44; Klement, *Dark Lanterns.*

10. Nevins, *War for the Union*, vol. 3, 162–67; Frank Freidel, *Francis Lieber, Nineteenth-Century Liberal* (Baton Rouge, 1947); Paludan, *A Covenant with Death*, 89–91.

11. Mark E. Neely, Jr., paper presented at Lincoln Club of Topeka, Kansas, December 4, 1986. Randall, *Constitutional Problems under Lincoln*, 152, provides the figure of 13,535 army arrests that put suspects in military prisons. He also notes that the figure excludes navy and state department arrests and local efforts. Hyman, *A More Perfect Union*, 73–77, describes local energy in suppressing dissenters. Randall reports the estimate of 38,000 made by Alexander Johnston in *Laylors Encyclopedia* in an article, "Habeas Corpus," and noted by James Ford Rhodes in his *History of the United States* (New York, 1892–1906), vol. 4, 230n. Community histories and state studies contain descriptions of local acts of repression against

Democrats who opposed the war efforts. See John Caughey, "Our Chosen Destiny," *Journal of American History* 52:246, for California illustrations; Don Harrison Doyle, *The Social Order of a Frontier Community: Jacksonville, Illinois, 1825–1870* (Urbana, 1978), 235–39, for events in one Illinois town; and Arthur Cole, *The Era of the Civil War*, 301–7, for other Illinois illustrations.

12. Hyman, *A More Perfect Union*, 65–72; Leonard Levy, *Legacy of Suppression* (New York, 1963).

13. *Official Record*, series 2, vol. 2, 495–505. Blair's discretion on excluding newspapers from the mails was extensive. Congress, after investigating cases of exclusion, urged the postmaster general to exercise caution when he acted but nonetheless allowed action against papers that "manifestly tend to the disruption of the government or to the destruction of life or property of its people." Craig D. Tenney, "Major General A. E. Burnside and the First Amendment: A Case Study of Civil War Freedom of Expression," Ph.D. diss., University of Indiana, Bloomington, 1977, provides excellent context, 18–26.

14. Randall, *Constitutional Problems under Lincoln*, chaps. 7, 8. Randall concludes that while there were excesses committed, the context makes administrative action understandable. He is quite tolerant of Lincoln's actions, as are most commentators. See Kennedy to Seward, September 14, 1861, *Official Record*, series 2, vol. 2, for example of successful disciplining of editors by arrest or indictment alone. Tenney, "A. E. Burnside," doubts Lincoln's softness.

15. Phisterer, *Statistical Record of Armies*, 43–51; E. McPherson, *Political History of U.S.*, 161–62; Klement, *The Limits of Dissent*.

16. *Official Record*, series 2, vol. 5, 634–45; John A. Marshall, *American Bastile: A History of the Illegal Arrests and Imprisonment of American Citizens during the Late Civil War* (Philadelphia, 1878), reprints the details of Vallandigham's arrest, relying on the statement of Rev. James Vallandigham.

17. *Collected Works of Lincoln*, vol. 6, 260–69; Thomas and Hyman, *Stanton*, 278–81. Even the latter authors call the administration policy "incredibly harsh." Vallandigham's protest is in Marshall, *American Bastile*, along with the description of the Dayton riot, 725–27. On May 8, 1863, Stanton and Lincoln had written to Burnside promising full support for the general's efforts to suppress "treason" and to uphold the authority of the president. Telegram is noted in Tenney, "A. E. Burnside," 150–51. *Collected Works of Lincoln*, vol. 6, does not reprint this telegram; see Lincoln to Stanton, May 13, 1863, 215n. Burnside responded to an unfound letter from Lincoln, "I thank you for your kind assurance of support and beg to say that every possible effort will be made on my part to sustain the Government of the United States in its fullest authority." Tenney also believes that Lincoln supported Burnside's arrest, and other efforts to stifle dissent; see "A. E. Burnside," ii–iii, 150, 164–66.

18. Swisher, *History of Supreme Court*, 925–30; Randall, *Constitutional Problems under Lincoln*, 176–79. There are legal distinctions between *ex parte Vallandigham* and the later case, *ex parte Milligan*, which would uphold civil over military justice in areas outside the war zone. However, these distinctions are quite refined and posed no major barrier to treating both cases the same way, had the judges been so inclined.

19. Society for the Diffusion of Political Knowledge, *The Constitution; Handbook of the*

Democracy for 1863–4; Klement, *The Limits of Dissent.* "Correspondence Between New York Democrats and President Lincoln" (Erastus Corning Letter), in E. McPherson, *Political History of U.S.,* 162–77, contains protests from New York and Ohio Democrats, and Lincoln's replies.

20. *Harpers Weekly* 7 (1863): 338; Lorraine A. Williams, "Northern Intellectual Reaction to Military Rule during the Civil War," *Historian* 27 (May 1865): 337–38, 352–55; Paludan, *A Covenant with Death,* 130–32, 141–44; *Diary of Orville Hickman Browning,* vol. 1, 586–87; *Leslies Illustrated,* December 20, 1862; *Journal of the Illinois House of Representatives,* January 6, 1863, 44–45.

21. Randall, *Constitutional Problems under Lincoln,* 163–68; Bogue, *Earnest Men,* 263–69; Hyman, *A More Perfect Union,* 245–62.

22. Harold M. Hyman, "The Election of 1864," in Arthur M. Schlesinger, Jr., ed., *History of American Presidential Elections* (New York, 1971), 1155–56.

23. T. Harry Williams, "Voters in Blue: The Citizen Soldiers of the Civil War," *Mississippi Valley Historical Review* 31 (September 1944): 187–204. On the soldiers as voters, see two older works: Josiah Benton, *Voting in the Field* (Boston, 1915); and Oscar Winther, "The Soldier Vote in the Election of 1864," *New York History* 25 (1944): 440–58.

24. Quoted in Silbey, *A Respectable Minority,* 118; Nevins, *War for the Union,* vol. 4, 29–45; William Frank Zornow, *Lincoln and the Party Divided* (Norman, 1954), 105–7; *Collected Works of Lincoln,* vol. 7, 514–15.

25. Silbey, *A Respectable Minority,* 110–12; Mitchell, *Horatio Seymour,* 360–62; Zornow, *Lincoln and the Party Divided,* 125–28.

26. Silbey, *A Respectable Minority,* 115–18; Klement, *The Limits of Dissent,* 135–36; Baker, *Affairs of Party,* 286–87.

27. McPherson, *Political History of U.S.,* 385–86; Silbey, *A Respectable Minority,* 120–30; Hyman, "Election of 1864," 1171–72.

28. McPherson, *Political History of U.S.,* 419–20; Silbey, *A Respectable Minority,* 130–34.

29. Silbey, *A Respectable Minority,* 134–39; McPherson, *Political History of U.S.,* 421–22; Union Executive Congressional Committee, *The Great Surrender to Rebels in Arms* (Washington, 1864), reprinted in Freidel, ed., *Union Pamphlets,* vol. 2, 1016–27.

30. Silbey, *A Respectable Minority;* Mohr, ed., *Radical Republicans;* Brock, *Conflict and Transformation,* 244–45, 272; Keller, *Affairs of State,* 25–27; Baker, *Affairs of Party,* 344–46.

31. Zornow, *Lincoln and the Party Divided,* 35–51; Nevins, *War for the Union,* vol. 4, 66–68; David Donald, "A. Lincoln, Politician," in *Lincoln Reconsidered,* 72–73.

32. Zornow, *Lincoln and the Party Divided,* 72–85; McPherson, *Political History of U.S.,* 410–61; J. McPherson, *Struggle for Equality,* 264–71.

33. McPherson, *Struggle for Equality,* 264–71.

34. On the possibility of a bargain to trade Fremont's withdrawal for Blair's resignation, see Trefousse, *Radical Republicans,* 294–96, who believes that there was a bargain; and Nevins, *War for the Union,* vol. 4, 105–7, who suggests that larger forces were at work.

35. *Collected Works of Lincoln,* vol. 7, 51–56.

36. "The Wade-Davis Bill, July 8, 1864," in Henry Steele Commager, ed., *Documents of American History* (New York, 1949), 435–39. The most extended discussions of the Wade-Davis Bill are Belz, *Reconstructing the Union,* 198–243, and Benedict,

A Compromise of Principle. See also L. Cox, *Lincoln and Black Freedom,* 36–43, and Hyman and Wiecek, *Equal Justice Under Law,* 269–79.

37. Cox, *Lincoln and Black Freedom;* McCrary, *Abraham Lincoln and Reconstruction;* S. Gabor S. Borritt, "Mrs. Cox's Affair with Mr. Lincoln," *Reviews in American History* 11 (March 1983): 20–26.
38. *Collected Works of Lincoln,* vol. 7, 433.
39. E. McPherson, *Political History of U.S.,* 332; Belz, *Reconstructing the Union,* 228–31; Trefousse, *Radical Republicans,* 284–90; Thomas and Hyman, *Stanton.*
40. Trefousse, *Radical Republicans,* 294; Van Deusen, *Horace Greeley,* 317.
41. Cox, *Lincoln and Black Freedom,* 41–43; Hyman and Wiecek, *Equal Justice Under Law,* 273–74; Benedict, *A Compromise of Principle,* 81–83; Belz, *Reconstructing the Union,* 241–42.
42. Hyman, "The Election of 1864," in Arthur Schlesinger, Jr., ed., *History of American Presidential Elections,* vol. 2, 1124–26, 1180–82.
43. David Donald, "The Radicals and Lincoln," in *Lincoln Reconsidered,* 119–27.
44. *Tribune Almanac for 1865,* 46–67; Silbey, *A Respectable Minority,* 153–57. Zornow, *Lincoln and the Party Divided,* 145–47; "Editorial by Benjamin Wade from the Cincinnati *Gazette,* October 25, 1865," in Schlesinger, ed., *History of American Presidential Elections,* vol. 2, 1197–1203.
45. *Collected Works of Lincoln,* vol. 8, 399–405; Belz, *Reconstructing the Union,* 252–55, 294–311; Cox, *Lincoln and Black Freedom,* 36–37; Hyman and Wiecek, *Equal Justice Under Law,* 277–78.
46. Wade's comment quoted in Trefousse, *Radical Republicans,* 208. The large literature on the debate between Lincoln and Congress seems to me to be marked by this either/or conceptualization that I am challenging here. Recent works that emphasize the unity of goals between the two still seem to follow the format. The importance of the process of politics has been clarified for me by Baker, *Affairs of Party,* cited earlier. The consensus view of shared ideals began with Donald, "The Radicals and Lincoln," and is carried on by Trefousse, Hyman, Benedict, Belz, and Cox.
47. Ellen Dubois, *Feminism and Suffrage: The Emergence of an Independent Women's Movement in America, 1848–1869* (Ithaca, 1978); Aileen Kraditor, *The Ideas of the Women Suffrage Movement, 1890–1920* (New York, 1965). Both of these works note the conflict that often emerged between proponents of votes for blacks and those of votes for women. My point is not that the movement for equal suffrage for all was a unity. It is that the ideals of both movements were endorsed and energized by the war. Hyman and Wiecek, *Equal Justice under Law,* 439–72; J. McPherson, *Struggle for Equality,* 310–11, 326–27, 377, 382–83; Trefousse, *Radical Republicans,* 316–18, 301–4, 340, 362; Keller, *Affairs of State,* 158–61; James McPherson, "Abolitionists, Woman Suffrage and the Negro, 1865–1869," *Mid America* 47 (1965): 40–47.

Chapter 11. World Images of War

1. Henry Adams to C. F. Adams, Jr., November 20, 1863, in Worthington Ford, ed., *A Cycle of Adams Letters, 1861–65* (Boston, 1920), vol. 2, 103; Thomas Bailey, *A Diplomatic History of the American People* (New York, 1950), 375.

2. See the fine collection in Commager, ed., *Britain Through American Eyes;* Temperly, "Anglo-American Images," 322; H. C. Allen, *The Anglo-American Relationship Since 1783;* Cushing Strout, *The American Image of the Old World* (New York, 1963), preface.

3. Donald, *Charles Sumner,* 123–24; Greabner, "Northern Diplomacy and European Neutrality," 59–60; Strong, *Diary.* vol. 3, 194–97, 205–9.

4. Wilbur Devereux Jones, "The British Conservatives and the American Civil War," *American Historical Review* 58 (April 1953): 527–43.

5. *Our Old Home* (Boston, 1963), as quoted in Commager, ed., *Britain Through American Eyes,* 333, 335; see 214–21, 282, 293–94, 302–3, for views quoted above. See also Temperly, "Anglo-American Images," for the vision of English industrialism as America's future.

6. John Stuart Mill, "The Contest in America," reprinted in Freidel, ed., *Union Pamphlets,* 336; Crook, *North, South, and Powers,* 272–74; Carlyle quoted in Jordan and Pratt, *Europe and the American Civil War,* 73; Frederick Douglass Papers, vol. 3, 455.

7. For British questions about Northern links to industrial evils, see Royden Harrison, *Before the Socialists: Studies in Labour and Politics, 1861–1881* (London, 1965), 54–57.

8. Harrison, *Before the Socialists,* 54–55; Mary Ellison, *Support for Secession: Lancashire and the American Civil War* (Chicago, 1972), passim. Philip Foner, *British Labor and the American Civil War* (New York, 1981), challenges Ellison's position that British labor in Lancaster especially favored the Southern position. He argues that the masses were pro-North, despite the pro-Confederate position of the labor press. Overall, Foner's position seems the stronger, if the goal is to assess the numbers of British laborers favoring North or South. My point is that evidence existed for Northerners to believe that the British laborer opposed the Northern effort, that evidence being contained in the labor press, which did reflect the position of many workers. Northerners chose the position that put their own struggle in the most comforting light.

9. Ellison, *Support for Secession,* 15; Harrison, *Before the Socialists,* 55.

10. Cobden quoted in Guido de Riggiero, *The History of European Liberalism* (New York, 1927), 126–27; Bright, in R. R. Palmer and Joel Colton, *A History of the Modern World* (New York, 1965), 462. Harrison, *Before the Socialists,* 54–61; E. P. Thompson, *The Making of the English Working Class* (New York, 1963), 807–32; Donald Read, *Cobden and Bright: A Victorian Political Partnership* (London, 1967), 211–12, 222–28.

11. For this element in pro-Union support, see Pole, *Lincoln and the Working Classes,* 22–23. Royden Harrison makes this distinction between skilled and unskilled workers, a view accepted by Melvin Dubofsky, "Myth and History," *Reviews in American History* 1 (September 1973): 396–99.

12. Henry Adams to Charles Francis Adams, Jr., January 27, 1863, in Ford, ed., *A Cycle of Adams Letters,* vol. 1, 251–52; Arthur Silver, ed., "Henry Adams' Diary of a Visit to Manchester," *American Historical Review* 51 (October 1945): 74–89.

13. *Collected Works of Lincoln,* vol. 6, 63–65, 176; Franklin, *The Emancipation Proclamation,* 140–49. Royden Harrison argues that belief in workers' support for the Union came from "middle class observers, many of whom were eager to per-

suade themselves." See his two essays, "British Labour and the Confederacy," *International Review of Social History* 2 (1959): 78–105, and "British Labour and American Slavery," *Science and Society* 25 (1961): 291–319.

14. *New York Times*, October 16, 1862, as quoted in Crook, *North, South, and Powers*, 274. Crook notes the need for endorsement of the Union effort from overseas, but does not note the element of industrial conflict in the need for that support.

15. *Collected Works of Lincoln*, vol. 6, 64 (January 19, 1863); Jenkins, *Britain and the War for the Union*, vol. 2, 213–17. Randall, *Lincoln the President*, vol. 2, 178–79, notes that Manchester was the home of the Manchester school of economic liberalism, but links that to prolabor activity, obscuring thereby important differences between upper and lower classes in England.

16. Edward Spencer Beesley, "The Free Inheritance of Us All," speech in St. James Hall, London, March 26, 1863, in Harrison, *Before the Socialists*, 69–73; Pole, *Lincoln and the Working Classes*, 17–29; Ellison, *Support for Secession*, passim, especially introductory essay by Peter A. Jones, 199–219. This essay traces the literature on worker support for the Union and notes strongest evidence is on the side of worker opposition. This is also the view of J. M. Hernon, Jr., "British Sympathies in the American Civil War," *Journal of Southern History* 33 (August 1967): 356–67.

17. John Bright, *Speeches on the American Question* (Boston, 1865), xii, 177–78.

18. James Kelly, *American Catalogue of Books Published in the United States, January 1861–January 1866* (New York, 1938, 1939, 1941); *New York Times Index*; Pinkney, "France and the Civil War," 97–144; Elizabeth Brett White, *American Opinion of France* (New York, 1927).

19. Pinkney, "France and the Civil War," 97–144; *North American Review* 94 (April 1862): 408–33 and 95 (July 1862): 138–62, 437–62; Crook, *North, South, and Powers*, 273–74; Jordan and Pratt, *Europe and the American Civil War*, 227–44.

20. Thomas Sancton, "The Myth of the French Workers' Support for the North," *French Historical Studies* 11:58–80; *New York Times*, August 28, 1864; White, *American Opinion*, 130ff.

21. Pinkney, *France and the Civil War*, 103–4. Case and Spencer, *The United States and France*, chap. 11, discuss the 1863 efforts.

22. Van Deusen, *William Henry Seward*, 366–67; Henry Blumenthal, *France and the United States: Their Diplomatic Relations, 1789–1914* (Chapel Hill, 1970), 106–16.

23. Van Deusen, *William Henry Seward*, 364–65.

24. *Congressional Globe*, 38th Cong., 1st sess., 1408–9.

25. Crook, *North, South, and Powers*, 336–40; Case and Spencer, *The United States and France*, 550–56.

26. Van Deusen, *William Henry Seward*, 367–70.

27. Bailey, *A Diplomatic History*, 377–91; Alfred J. Hanna and Katharyn A. Hanna, *Napoleon III and Mexico* (Chapel Hill, 1971).

28. Crook, *North, South, and Powers*, 345–46; John A. Williams, "Canada and the Civil War," in Hyman, ed., *Heard Round the World*, 259–69; Winks, *Canada and the United States*, 4–5.

29. Winks, *Canada and the United States*, 209–39.

30. *Ibid.*, 7–10; Williams, "Canada and the Civil War," 269–70.

31. Winks, *Canada and the United States*, 128–29, 209–10, and chap. 6.

32. Van Deusen, *William Henry Seward*, 348–59; Crook, *North, South, and Powers,* 345–52; Williams, "Canada and the Civil War," 280–82; Winks, *Canada and the United States,* chap. 14.

33. Lonn, *Foreigners in the Union Army,* 573–75, passim; Gould, *Investigations in Military Statistics,* 27–28; John Francis Maguire, *The Irish in America* (London, 1868), chap. 29; Carl Wittke, *The Irish in America* (Baton Rouge, 1956), chap. 13.

34. Maguire, *The Irish in America,* chap. 29; Wittke, *The Irish in America,* 136–37; Craig Lee Kautz, "Fodder for Cannon: Immigrant Perceptions of the Civil War—The Old Northwest," Ph.D. diss., University of Nebraska, Lincoln, 1976, 67–71; Lonn, *Foreigners in the Union Army,* 119–21.

35. Kautz, "Fodder for Cannon," passim.

36. Wiley, *The Life of Billy Yank,* 308–9; Wittke, *The Irish in America,* 138–39; Lonn, *Foreigners in the Union Army,* 645–47; Maguire, *The Irish in America,* chap. 26; Hernon, *Celts, Catholics, and Copperheads,* 11–18.

37. Strong, *Diary,* vol. 3, 343; Jay Dolan, *The Immigrant Church* (Baltimore, 1975), 161–62; John Higham, *Strangers in the Land: Patterns in American Nativism, 1860–1925* (Boston, 1973), 12–13.

38. Wittke, *The Irish in America,* 172–73.

39. Lonn, *Foreigners in the Union Army,* 574–75; Leonard Dinnerstein, Roger Nichols, and David Reimers, *Natives and Strangers: Ethnic Groups and the Building of America* (New York, 1979), 99–101; Marcus Lee Hansen, *The Immigrant in American History* (Cambridge, Mass., 1942), 141–42; *Statistical History of the United States,* 56–57.

40. Winks, *Canada and the United States,* 374–81; Crook, *North, South, and Powers,* 379–80.

Chapter 12. Frankenstein and Everyman: Sherman, Grant, and Modern War

1. Lewis, *Sherman,* 134, 137.

2. *Ibid.,* 134.

3. *Ibid.,* 185–207; James T. Merrill, *William Tecumseh Sherman* (Chicago, 1971), 174–94. T. Harry Williams, *McClellan, Sherman and Grant* (Westport, Conn., 1976), 46.

4. Lewis, *Sherman,* 334–36.

5. *Collected Works of Lincoln,* vol. 5, 469n; vol. 6, 43, 83, 142–43, 155, 210, 230, 241, 326.

6. Weigley, *American Way of War,* 139; Williams, *McClellan, Sherman and Grant;* Fuller, *Generalship of U. S. Grant,* 114–57. The following discussion relies heavily on McFeely, *Grant.*

7. Kelly, *American Catalogue of Books;* McFeely, *Grant,* 169–70; Rhodes, *History of the United States,* vol. 4, 436; Strong, *Diary,* vol. 3, 462, July 1, 1864; Julian Larke, *General Grant and His Campaigns* (New York, 1864), 463.

8. Quoted in Williams, *McClellan, Sherman and Grant,* 84.

9. Nevins, *War for the Union,* vol. 3, 141–43.

10. McFeely, *Grant,* 150–53, 172, 176; Larke, *General Grant,* 466; L. P. Brockett, *Our Great Captains: Grant, Sherman, Thomas, Sheridan and Farragut* (New York, 1865), 68–70.

11. Larke, *General Grant,* 43, 77–78, 312; McFeely, *Grant,* 52–55, 132–38, 174.

12. McFeely, *Grant,* xiii; *Collected Works of Lincoln,* vol. 8, 151.

13. Larke, *General Grant,* 3–27; Brockett, *Our Great Captains,* 9–17; *Milwaukee Wisconsin,* January 1864, quoted in Larke, *General Grant,* 42–43.

14. Ralph B. Potter, *War and Moral Discourse* (Richmond, 1969), 58–61; Russell Weigley, *American Way of War,* chaps. 7, 14–18; Bruce Catton, *U. S. Grant and the American Military Tradition* (Boston, 1954), 130–35; Denis Brogan, *The American Character* (New York, 1956), 149–65. James Turner Johnson, *Just War Tradition and the Restraint of War: A Moral and Historical Inquiry* (Princeton, 1981), 259–67, agrees that the Civil War featured a commitment to total war, but challenges the idea that all American wars have sought total victory. Only the Revolution, the Civil War and World War II, especially the fight against Japan, fit that category, he says.

15. Weigley, *American Way of War,* 139–50; Grant to Sherman, August 9, 1864, Sherman to Grant, January 21, 1865, Huntington Library, San Marino, Cal.; McFeely, *Grant,* 118–20, 155–56.

16. The best study of the battle and the context is James Lee McDonough, *Chattanooga—A Death Grip on the Confederacy* (Knoxville, 1984).

17. *Official Record,* vol. 29, part 1, 146–88; Thomas and Hyman, *Stanton,* 286–89; George Turner, *Victory Rode the Rails* (Indianapolis, 1953), 289–94; Taylor and Neu, *The American Railroad Network.*

18. Bruce Catton, "The Generalship of Ulysses S. Grant," in Grady McWhiney, ed., *Grant, Lee, Lincoln and the Radicals* (New York, 1964), 3–29.

19. *New York Herald,* as reported also in Larke, *General Grant,* 405; R. V. Johnson and C. C. Buel, eds., *Battles and Leaders of the Civil War* (New York, 1887–88), vol. 3, 726; Grant, in *Personal Memoirs of U. S. Grant,* 339–40, says that he had in fact ordered Thomas to "either carry the riflepits and ridge directly in front of them, or move to the left as the presence of the enemy may require." Fuller, *Generalship of U. S. Grant,* 176, 390–91.

20. Exchange with Hood is in W. T. Sherman, *Personal Memoirs,* 116–29, and in works by Headley and Senour cited in note 27.

21. W. T. Sherman, *Personal Memoirs,* 116–29.

22. Lewis, *Sherman,* 420; Ford, ed., *A Cycle of Adams Letters,*

23. Michael Walzer, *Just and Unjust Wars* (New York, 1977), 30–31.

24. Quoted in Lewis, *Sherman,* 421.

25. For an effort to equate Sherman's activities with the atrocities of My Lai, see John Bennett Walters, *Merchant of Terror: General Sherman and Total War* (Indianapolis, 1973), xiii; see also James Reston, Jr., *Sherman's March and Vietnam* (New York, 1984).

26. Johnson, *Just War Tradition and the Restraint of War.*

27. S. M. Bowman and R. B. Irwin, *Sherman and His Campaigns* (New York, 1865); Brockett, *Our Great Captains;* David P. Conyngham, *Sherman's March Through the South* (New York, 1865); P. C. Headley, *Life and Military Career of Major General William Tecumseh Sherman* (New York, 1865); G. W. Nichols, *The Story of the Great March* (New York, 1865); Rev. Founteleroy Senour, *Major General William Tecumseh Sherman and His Campaigns* (Chicago, 1865).

28. Sherman quoted in Senour, *Sherman and His Campaigns,* 284. Theodore Lyman, *Meade's Headquarters, 1863–1865,* G. R. Agassiz, ed. (New York, 1922).

29. Quoted in Nevins, *War for the Union*, vol. 4, 26; Brockett, *Our Great Captains*, 86–88, 94, 99, 158; Conyngham, *Sherman's March*, 50–61; Headley, *Life and Military Career of Sherman*, 174, 358.

30. Herman Melville, *Moby-Dick*, Modern Library ed. (New York, 1950), 167.

31. Bruce Catton, *A Stillness at Appomattox* (New York, 1953), 91–92; Horace Porter, *Campaigning with Grant* (New York, 1897), 78–79; *Personal Memoirs of U. S. Grant*, 411.

32. Phisterer, *Statistical Record of Armies*, 216–17; Porter, *Campaigning with Grant*, 174–75; Nevins, *War for the Union*, vol. 4, 45.

33. Porter, *Campaigning with Grant*, 69–70.

34. Quoted in Foote, *The Civil War*, vol. 3, 5.

35. *New York Tribune*, June 6, 8, 1864, as quoted in Nevins, *War for the Union*, vol. 4, 39.

36. Horace Porter, "The Philosophy of Courage," *Century* 36:246–54; John William DeForest, *Miss Ravenel's Conversion from Secession to Loyalty* (New York, 1867), 520; Oliver Wendell Holmes, "The Soldier's Faith," in Max Lerner, ed., *The Mind and Faith of Justice Holmes*, Modern Library ed. (New York, 1943), 20; Herman Melville, "Armies of the Wilderness," in *Battle Pieces*, part 2; Bushnell quoted in Edwin P. Parker, "Ministry at Large," in Mary Bushnell Cheney, ed., *Life and Letters of Horace Bushnell* (New York, 1969), 475. See also Charles Janeway Stille, *How a Free People Conduct a Long War: A Chapter From English History* (Philadelphia, 1862), reprinted in Freidel, ed., *Union Pamphlets*, 382–83; Nevins, *War for the Union*, vol. 6, 58–59.

37. "The President's Policy," *North American Review* (January 1864); Duberman, *Lowell*, 216–18. See Fredrickson, *Inner Civil War*, 166–83.

38. *Collected Works of Lincoln*, vol. 7, 514 (August 23, 1864).

39. As quoted in McPherson, *Ordeal by Fire*, 458.

40. Catton, *A Stillness at Appomattox*, 58; Fuller, *Generalship of U. S. Grant*, 362–63; Adams, *Our Masters*, chap. 9.

41. McFeely, *Grant*, 216–20; *Personal Memoirs of U. S. Grant*, 556; Porter, *Campaigning with Grant*, 472–75; Edmund Wilson, *Patriotic Gore* (New York, 1962), 148.

42. Porter, *Campaigning with Grant*, 472–88; Foote, *The Civil War*, vol. 3, 945–51.

43. "The Editor's Study," *Harper's Monthly* (March, August 1886); Long, introduction to *Personal Memoirs of U. S. Grant*; McFeely, *Grant*, 493–517; Wilson, *Patriotic Gore*, 131–73.

44. "The Editor's Study," *Harper's Monthly* (August 1886).

45. *Personal Memoirs of U. S. Grant*, 3.

Chapter 13. The Scars of War

1. Livermore, *Numbers and Losses in the Civil War;* Phisterer, *Statistical Record of Armies*, 67–72; Long, *Civil War Day by Day*, 709–13.

2. John Nelson, *Worcester County: A Narrative History* (New York, 1934), 454–55.

3. Haven Family Letters, American Antiquarian Society, Worcester, Mass.; Earl Schenck Miers, *Robert E. Lee* (New York, 1956), 120–22; Warren W. Hassler, Jr., *Commanders of the Army of the Potomac* (Westport, Conn., 1979), 97–105.

4. Austin Whipple Papers, Dartmouth College Library, Hanover, N.H., July 1862

to January 1863. Whipple's feeling of being reduced to part of a machine was widespread among Northern soldiers. William Ferry of Michigan spoke for many in telling his wife, "One becomes as though the property of somebody else by a life in the army. We are liable to become mere machines." Another soldier grumbled, "One can make no plans in the army, indulge no hopes in any particular direction, have no independence, no voice in anything. He becomes a mere machine while he stays & if it were not for that spark of hope which lives with nothing to feed upon, he would soon give up everything." Another noted, "The discipline and restraint of the army are unnatural. Man was never made for a machine." Quoted in Jimerson, "A People Divided," 287–90. Jimerson argues that this rhetoric reflected the "burgeoning industrial society" of the North.

5. Albert Ames Papers, New York State Archives, Albany, N.Y.

6. Van Vleck Papers, New York State Archives, Albany, N.Y. (#15433).

7. *American Journal of Medical Science* 43 (April 1862): 432–33.

8. Winther, ed., *With Sherman to the Sea: Theodore F. Upson*, 86; *Medical and Surgical History of the War of the Rebellion* (Washington, 1870), Surgical vol. 2, 468–71, 673, 697, 967, 1019, and vol. 3, 213, 398, 461, 596, 618; George W. Adams, *Doctors in Blue* (New York, 1957), 131; Stewart Brooks, *Civil War Medicine* (Springfield, Ill., 1966), 97–99.

9. *Medical and Surgical History*, Surgical vol. 3, 968.

10. *Ibid.*, Surgical volume 2, 318.

11. Anna Robeson Burr, *Weir Mitchell: His Life and Letters* (New York, 1929), 105, 388.

12. William Walton, ed., *A Civil War Courtship: The Letters of Edwin Weller from Antietam to Atlanta* (Garden City, N.Y., 1980).

13. Augusta Noyes to Mrs. L. H. Putnam, 1861, Ward Family Papers, American Antiquarian Society, Worcester, Mass.; Ellen Wright to Lucy McKim, August 11, 1862, February 12, 1863, Garrison Family Collection, Smith College, Northampton, Mass.

14. Ellen Wright to Lucy McKim, August 11, 1862, February 12, 1863; same to same, January 24, 1863; Ellen Wright to William Beverly Chase, September 1862, Garrison Family Collection.

15. Mohr, ed., *The Cormany Diaries*, 255–58, 282; Walton, ed., *A Civil War Courtship*; Saxton, *Louisa May*, 277–81.

16. John D. Cooper to Ada M. Cooper, Cooper Papers, Dartmouth College, Hanover, N.H. In New York Elijah Penny wrote similarly to his son Charlie, "If you will write me regularly every two weeks and take a little more pains with your writing and spelling, I will answer them. [Be sure to take] great pains to spell every word correctly and write every line as well as you can, taking care that your sheet is kept clean and free from any blots or unnecessary marks," January 23, 1863, Penny Family Papers, New York State Archives, Albany, N.Y.

17. *American Journal of Medical Science* 46 (October 1863): 497–98; William S. Keen and George Morehouse Mitchell, "On Malingering, Especially in Regard to Stimulating Diseases of the Nervous System," *American Journal of Medical Science* 48 (October 1864): 367–94.

18. *Medical and Surgical History*, vol. 1, 639–46; *American Journal of Medical Science* 48 (January 1864): 367–94.

19. *American Journal of Medical Science* 48 (October 1864): 473–74, 488; 50 (July, October 1865): 474–76; 51 (January, April 1866): 218, 488–89.

20. George Beard, *American Nervousness, Its Causes and Consequences* (New York, 1881), vi–vii, 96–97, 101, 186–87; Beard, *A Practical Treatise on Nervous Exhaustion* (New York, 1880), 1–9; David Rothman, *The Discovery of the Asylum: Social Order and Disorder in the New Republic* (Boston, 1971), 109–19; Norman Dain, *Concepts of Insanity in the United States, 1789–1865* (New Brunswick, 1964).

21. Rothman, *Discovery of the Asylum*, 114–19; Fredrickson, *Inner Civil War*, chap. 2.

22. *American Journal of Medical Science* 47 (April, October 1864); 218, 488; 50 (October 1865): 473–74; 51 (January 1866): 217–18.

23. Beard, *American Nervousness*, 101–26.

24. *American Journal of Medical Science* 50 (July 1865): 475; 51 (January 1866): 162–215.

25. J. M. DaCosta, "On Irritable Heart," *American Journal of Medical Science* 61 (January 1871): 17–52; Donald W. Goodwin and Samuel B. Guze, *Psychiatric Diagnosis* (New York, 1979), 52. I am indebted to my colleague C. S. Griffin for calling my attention to this material.

26. David Courtwright, "Opiate Addiction as a Consequence of the Civil War," *Civil War History* 24 (June 1978); 101–11.

27. Ernest P. Earnest, *S. Weir Mitchell: Novelist and Physician* (Philadelphia, 1950), 48–52, 61–63, 85–86; David Rein, *S. Weir Mitchell as a Psychiatric Novelist* (New York, 1952), 13–50; G. M. Beard, "Neurasthenia or Nervous Exhaustion," *Boston Medical and Surgical Journal* 3 (1869): 217; Keen and Mitchell, "On Malingering," 367–94.

Chapter 14. The Coming of the Lord: Religion in the Civil War Era

1. T. Smith, *Revivalism and Social Reform*, 17–21, 39–43; Lewis Vander Velde, *The Presbyterian Churches and the Federal Union, 1861–1869* (Cambridge, Mass., 1932), 5, 22–25; Ann Douglas, *The Feminization of American Culture* (New York, 1977), 23–24; Clifford S. Griffin, *Their Brother's Keepers* (New Brunswick, 1960); Miller, *The Life of the Mind in America*, 67; William G. McLoughlin, ed., *The American Evangelicals, 1800–1900* (New York, 1968), 1; Whitney Cross, *The Burned-Over District: The Social and Intellectual History of Enthusiastic Religion in Western New York* (Ithaca, 1950), 104–9, passim; Smith, *Revivalism and Social Reform*, 22–25, 124; Sidney Ahlstrom, *A Religious History of the American People* (New Haven, 1972), 672.

2. Kelley, *The Cultural Pattern in American Politics*, 187–227; Potter, *The Impending Crisis*, 238–46. For careful assessments of the ethnocultural school of political history, see J. Morgan Kausser, "The New Political History," and Richard B. Latner and Peter Levin, "Perspectives on Antebellum Pietistic Politics," both in *Reviews in American History* 4 (March 1976): 1–14, 15–24.

3. George Marsden, *The Evangelical Mind and the New School Presbyterian Experience* (New Haven, 1970), 185–90; Smith, *Revivalism and Social Reform*, 225–37; Ahlstrom, *Religious History*, 478–81; William McLoughlin, *The Meaning of Henry Ward Beecher* (New York, 1970), 52–53; Ronald G. Walters, *American Reformers, 1815–1860* (New York, 1978).

4. Paul E. Johnson, *A Shopkeeper's Millennium: Society and Revivals in Rochester, New*

York, *1815–1837* (New York, 1978); Dawley, *Class and Community,* 35–39; Wallace, *Rockdale,* chap. 8.

5. Henry Ward Beecher, "Our Blameworthiness," *Patriotic Addresses* (Boston, 1887), 250–52; Fredrickson, *Inner Civil War,* chap. 2.

6. Beecher, "Our Blameworthiness," 257–65.

7. Donald G. Matthews, "The Abolitionists on Slavery: The Critique Behind the Social Movement," *Journal of Southern History* 33 (May 1967): 168; Lewis Perry, *Radical Abolitionism: Anarchy and the Government of God in Antislavery Thought* (Ithaca, 1973); Lawrence J. Friedman, *Gregarious Saints: Self and Community in American Abolitionism, 1830–1870* (New York, 1982); James Brewer Stewart, *Holy Warriors: The Abolitionists and American Slavery* (New York, 1976). Gilbert Barnes, *The Antislavery Impulse* (New York, 1933), was the first major investigation of the power of revivalism in the abolitionist movement.

8. Vander Velde, *The Presbyterian Churches,* 133–34; Stewart, *Holy Warriors,* 114–15; James Hennesey, *American Catholics: A History of the Roman Catholic Community in the United States* (New York, 1981), 143–47; John Tracy Ellis, *American Catholicism* (Chicago, 1969), 89–90; Dolan, *The Immigrant Church,* 121–23.

9. *Harper's New Monthly* 9 (1854): 115–16, and 12 (1856): 841–43; Smith, *Revivalism and Social Reform,* 15–16; Badeau quoted in Clifford Clark, *Henry Ward Beecher* (Urbana, 1978), 136.

10. Ahlstrom, *Religious History,* 462–68; Vander Velde, *The Presbyterian Churches,* 9–15.

11. Vander Velde, *The Presbyterian Churches,* 280–89.

12. Sources quoted in James H. Moorhead, *American Apocalypse: Yankee Protestants and the Civil War, 1860–1869* (New Haven, 1978), 38–41; Paludan, "The American Civil War Considered as a Crisis in Law and Order," 1013–34; Hennesey, *American Catholics,* 148. Vander Velde, *The Presbyterian Churches,* 48–50, 79–80. Horace Bushnell, *The Vicarious Sacrifice, Grounded in Principles of Universal Obligation* (New York, 1866), contains five chapters explaining how order, law, and obedience are fundamental to Christian sacrifice.

13. Vander Velde, *The Presbyterian Churches,* 346–48; Marsden, *The Evangelical Mind,* 204–5; Melville, *Battle Pieces.*

14. Marsden, *The Evangelical Mind;* Peter Brock, *Radical Pacifists in Antebellum America* (Princeton, 1968), 235–40; Darrel Bigham, "American Christian Thinkers and the Function of War, 1861–1920," Ph.D. diss., University of Kansas, Lawrence, 1970, 52–64.

15. William Warren Sweet, *Methodism in American History* (New York, 1933), 283–91; Ralph E. Morrow, *Northern Methodism and Reconstruction* (East Lansing, 1956), 3–17; Moorhead, *American Apocalypse,* 138.

16. Ahlstrom, *Religious History,* 670; Chester Dunham, *The Attitude of the Northern Clergy Toward the South, 1860–1865* (Toledo, 1942), 112; Clark, *Beecher,* 151–52; Hennesey, *American Catholics,* 148–49.

17. Ahlstrom, *Religious History,* 674–78; Vander Velde, *The Presbyterian Churches,* 428–30.

18. Griffin, *Their Brother's Keepers,* 242–59; Vander Velde, *The Presbyterian Churches,* 433–36; Moorhead, *American Apocalypse,* 68–69; Fite, *Social and Industrial Conditions,* 285–86.

19. Laura E. Richards and Maud Howe Elliott, *Julia Ward Howe, 1819–1910* (Boston, 1916), vol. 1, 188–89; Julia Ward Howe, *Reminiscences, 1819–1899* (Boston, 1899), 273–76.

20. Headley, *Life and Military Career of Sherman*, 174, 364; Mary A. H. Gay, *Life in Dixie During the War* (Atlanta, 1892), 79–86, as quoted in Commager, ed. *The Blue and the Gray*, 414–71.

21. Bremner, *The Public Good*, 57–62; Griffin, *Their Brother's Keepers*, 248–50; Ahlstrom, *Religious History*, 678–79; Fredrickson, *Inner Civil War*, 107.

22. Christian Commission for the Army and Navy, *First Annual Report* (Philadelphia, 1863), 5–14, as quoted in Smith and Judah, eds., *Life in the North During the Civil War*, 257–60.

23. Bremner, *The Public Good*, 57–58.

24. Fredrickson, *Inner Civil War*, 98–112; Robert Weibe, *The Search for Order* (New York, 1967); Bremner, *The Public Good*, 57–62; Jane Swisshelm, *Half a Century* (Chicago, 1880).

25. Bremner, *The Public Good*, 65–68; Martha Saxton, *Louisa May;* Ishbell Ross, *Angel of the Battlefield: Clara Barton* (New York, 1956); Griffin, *Their Brother's Keepers*, 252–54.

26. Swisshelm, *Half a Century*, 272–73, 280–95, 308–9.

27. Bremner, *The Public Good;* J. Jones, *Soldiers of Light and Love;* Robert C. Morris, *Reading, 'Riting and Reconstruction: The Education of Freedmen in the South, 1861–1870* (Chicago, 1981).

28. Bigham, "American Christian Thinkers," 93–98, discusses the expectations of liberal Protestants for the war. Bremner, *The Public Good*, 72–90, illustrates the extent of religious involvement in Northern charities without comment on it. McPherson, *Struggle for Equality*, demonstrates the linkage betwen emancipation and the realization of religious faith. Moorhead, *American Apocalypse*, and Fredrickson, *Inner Civil War*, discuss the ideology of religion during the war, but their failure to link activity in charity with the words of faith results in interpretations that undervalue the actual benefits of wartime religious activities.

29. Wendell Phillips, "The Philosophy of the Abolition Movement," in *Speeches, Lectures, and Letters* (Boston, 1863), 106–10.

30. "A Plea for Captain John Brown," in James Redpath, ed., *Echoes of Harper's Ferry* (Boston, 1860), 37–39; Brock, *Radical Pacifists*, 236–37; Perry, *Radical Abolitionism*, 259–87; Alice Felt Tyler, *Freedom's Ferment* (New York, 1962), 396–423.

31. Moncur Conway, *The Rejected Stone; or Insurrection vs. Resurrection in America* (Boston, 1862), 116–17.

32. Brock, *Radical Pacifists*, 258–65; Peter Brock, *Pacifism in the United States: From the Colonial Era to the First World War* (Princeton, 1968), 717–23.

33. Brock, *Pacifism in the United States*, 713–15; Edward Needles Wright, *Conscientious Objectors in the Civil War* (Philadelphia, 1931).

34. Brock, *Pacifism in the United States*, 716–17; *Collected Works of Lincoln*, vol. 7, 535 (September 4, 1864); Wright, *Conscientious Objectors*, 2.

35. Brock, *Pacifism in the United States*, 725–26; *Collected Works of Lincoln*, vol. 7, 536.

36. Brock, *Pacifism in the United States*, 733–34.

37. *The Civil War Diary of Cyrus Pringle* (Wallingford, Pa., 1962); Brock, *Pacifism in the United States*, 751–55.

38. Brock, *Pacifism in the United States*, 758–62.

39. Moorhead, *American Apocalypse*, 42–82; Marsden, *The Evangelical Mind*, 199–211; Ahlstrom, *Religious History*, 670–72; Caroline Barrett White, *Diary*.

40. Beecher quoted in McLoughlin, *The Meaning of Henry Ward Beecher*, 216–20; Furness and Frothingham quoted in Fredrickson, *Inner Civil War*, 82–83.

41. *Collected Works of Lincoln*, vol. 8, 116–17; Ellen Wright to Lucy McKim, January 24, 1863, Garrison Family Collection.

42. Lewis Saum, "Death in the Popular Mind of Pre-Civil War America," *American Quarterly* 26 (December 1974): 477–80, 485–86.

43. *Ibid.*

44. *Ibid.*

45. Caroline Leverett to Mrs. Whipple, January 19 and 23, 1863; Joseph Garrison to Mr. Russell, January 25, 1863. Austin Whipple Papers.

46. James Burn, *Three Years Among the Working Classes* (London, 1865), 112–13; Rebecca Harding Davis, *Bits of Gossip* (New York, 1904), 20, as quoted in Nevins, *War for the Union*, vol. 3, 4.

47. Walt Whitman, *Specimen Days*, 35–36, 79–81; Thomas H. Johnson, ed., *The Complete Poems of Emily Dickinson* (Boston, 1960), poem #502. Dickinson's most creative and prolific years were those of the war, and her most common theme was death. See Richard B. Sewell, *The Life of Emily Dickinson* (New York, 1974), vol. 2, 535–37, 631–32, 646–47.

48. Kelly, *American Catalogue*, vols. 1852–55, 1855–58, 1858–60, 1861–66, 1866–71, 1871–76. Ann Douglas argues that concern about heaven is a constant fact from about 1830 to 1880, but her evidence reveals that the preponderance of writing about the subject is postwar; see "Heaven Our Home: Consolation Literature in the Northern United States, 1830–1880," *American Quarterly* 26 (December 1974): 496–515.

49. See James J. Ferrill, *Inventing the American Way of Death, 1830–1920* (Philadelphia, 1980), 33–35. Two brilliant examples of the power in the new conceptions of death as part of nature are Whitman's section of *Leaves of Grass* beginning, "The child said what is the grass" and Emily Dickinson's, "The gentian weaves her fringes" and, "When roses cease to bloom dear." Indeed the corpus of Dickinson's poetry is filled with this theme. Dickinson's most common noun is "heaven," followed closely by "death." See S. P. Rosenbaum, ed., *Concordance to the Poems of Emily Dickinson* (Ithaca, 1969).

50. Ferrill, *Inventing the American Way of Death*. Ferrell, like every other writer on the subject of death, ignores the possibility that the war that took the lives of over 600,000 men might have had an impact on understanding of the subject. For a parallel discussion of changing ideas about death to the end of the nineteenth century, see David Stannard, *The Puritan Way of Death: A Study of Religion, Culture and Social Change* (New York, 1977). Stannard also ignores the Civil War. For an evocation of meanings of heaven in the war years, see Johnson, ed., *The Complete Poems of Emily Dickinson*, "Going to heaven." Dickinson's discussion of heaven is much more subtle than that of the many writers who sought to domesticate the afterlife. Her mentions of heaven as home and her images of God as "Papa" are counterbalanced with doubts about any sentimental view of heaven. Her poems may be part of a dialogue that was encouraged by the presence of the more

sentimentalized concepts of the age. See also and especially "Arcturas is his other name"; "I noticed people disappeared"; "The life we have is very great"; the bitterly ironic "All men for Honor hardest work"; "Immortal is an ample word"; "My wars are laid away in Books"; "Who has not found the heaven below."

51. Elizabeth Stuart Phelps, *The Gates Ajar* (New York, 1868); Elizabeth Phelps, *Chapters from a Life* (Boston, 1897), 97–98; Douglas, "Heaven Our Home," 497–515.

52. William J. Wolfe, *The Religion of Abraham Lincoln* (New York, 1963), 123; Charles Strozier, *Lincoln's Quest for Union* (New York, 1982), 97–98, 138; Oates, *With Malice Toward None* 313–17; Benjamin Thomas, *Abraham Lincoln* (New York, 1952), 304; Robert V. Bruce, *Lincoln and the Riddle of Death:* The Fourth Annual R. Gerald McMurtry Lecture, Louis Warren Lincoln Library and Museum, Fort Wayne, 1981.

53. Wolfe, *The Religion of Abraham Lincoln,* 169–72; Roy P. Basler, *Abraham Lincoln, His Speeches and Writings* (New York, 1946), 42.

54. *Collected Works of Lincoln,* vol. 8, 332–33, 403; Sidney Mead, "Abraham Lincoln's 'Last Best Hope of Earth': The American Dream of Destiny and Democracy," *Church History* 23 (March 1954): 3–16.

Conclusion

1. This discussion of Upson is based on Winther, ed., *With Sherman to the Sea: Theodore F. Upson.*

2. My discussion of Sylvis is based on Sylvis, *Life of William Sylvis;* Grossman, *William Sylvis;* Montgomery, *Beyond Equality;* and Unger, *The Greenback Era.*

3. The final decades of Mary Livermore's life are best understood in the following: Livermore, *The Story of My Life,* and *My Story of the War* (Hartford, 1891), with background in Dubois, *Feminism and Suffrage;* Ellen Dubois, ed., *Elizabeth Cady Stanton, Susan B. Anthony: Correspondence, Writings, Speeches* (New York, 1981); Robert Reigel, *American Feminists* (Lawrence, 1963); William Leach, *True Love and Perfect Union: The Feminists' Reform of Sex and Society* (New York, 1980); Mary Jo Beuhle, *Women and American Socialism, 1870–1920* (Urbana, 1981).

4. Frederick Douglass' postwar years are described in *Life and Times of Frederick Douglass;* Philip Foner, *The Life and Writings of Frederick Douglass;* Waldo Martin, Jr., *The Mind of Frederick Douglass* (Chapel Hill, 1984); August Meier, *Negro Thought in America, 1880–1915* (Ann Arbor, 1969); Booker T. Washington, *Frederick Douglass* (New York, 1900); and Louis Harlan, *Booker T. Washington: The Making of a Black Leader* (New York, 1972).

5. My discussion of Strong is drawn from his *Diary,* volumes 3 and 4.

Bibliographical Essay

There has not been a single-volume study of the North in the Civil War since Emerson Fite, *Social and Industrial Conditions in the North during the Civil War* (New Haven, 1910). The subject received its fullest attention in Allan Nevins' *The War for the Union*, 4 vols. (New York, 1959–1971), but Nevins emphasized the political and military history of the war years in both North and South and wrote before the "new social and economic history" gathered momentum. He thus paid scant attention to the intellectual history of the conflict and to the images evoked by the conflict in popular culture; his lack of interest in religion was especially notable. Nevins omitted the impact of the war on classes and on women and thus missed analyzing the industrial revolution and its relationship to the war.

One-volume studies of the Civil War in both North and South have been generated for decades. James McPherson's text, cited below, lists the most recent ones. My concern is for those works that best interpret the impact of war on Northern society. The best general guide to Civil War historiography is Thomas Pressley, *Americans Interpret Their Civil War* (Princeton, 1962), which needs updating. The best of the larger recent studies are Peter Parish, *The American Civil War* (New York, 1975), which focuses predominantly on the war years, and James McPherson, *Ordeal by Fire: The Civil War and Reconstruction* (New York, 1982), which encompasses the pre- and postwar eras in addition to its nearly 350 pages on the conflict itself. James G. Randall and David H. Donald, *The Civil War and Reconstruction* (Lexington, Mass., 1969), remains a solid and careful work, especially helpful for its massive bibliography. For interpreting the nature of the war, the best of the smaller general histories are David Potter, *Division and the Stresses of Reunion: 1845–1876* (Glenview, 1973); Robert Cruden, *The War That Never Ended* (Englewood Cliffs, N.J., 1973); David Donald, *Liberty and Union* (Lexington,

Mass., 1978); W. R. Brock, *Conflict and Transformation: The United States, 1844–1877* (New York, 1973); and Arthur Cole, *The Irrepressible Conflict, 1850–1865* (New York, 1934).

Important interpretive essays are included in George Fredrickson, ed., *A Nation Divided: Problems and Issues of the Civil War and Reconstruction* (Minneapolis, 1975); Eric Foner, *Politics and Ideology in the Age of the Civil War* (New York, 1980); and David Donald, *Lincoln Reconsidered,* 2d ed. (New York, 1961). Eric Foner, "The Causes of the American Civil War," *Civil War History* 20 (1974), suggests ways to integrate the new social history and more traditional forms to create new syntheses.

Much has been written on specific elements of the wartime society. George Fredrickson, *The Inner Civil War: Northern Intellectuals and the Crisis of Disunion* (New York, 1965), is a model of this literature. The *Impact of the Civil War* series, begun by Nevins and continued by Harold M. Hyman, contains invaluable volumes on agriculture: Paul Gates, *Agriculture and the Civil War* (New York, 1965); women: Mary Massey, *Bonnet Brigades* (New York, 1966); literature: Daniel Aaron, *The Unwritten War* (New York, 1973); the constitutional system: Harold Hyman, *A More Perfect Union* (New York, 1973); philanthropy and welfare: Robert Bremner, *The Public Good: Philanthropy and Welfare in the Civil War Era* (New York, 1980); and international perspectives: Harold Hyman, ed., *Heard Round the World* (New York, 1969). Robert Bruce, *The Scientific Enterprise in America, 1846–1876* (New York, 1987), appeared too late to be useful here. Edmund Wilson, *Patriotic Gore: Studies in the Literature of the American Civil War* (New York, 1962), contains several intriguing insights despite its simple view of why nations go to war.

There is much to be gained from looking at the Civil War in the context of war generally. The literature on that subject is large, and the best introduction to it is Leon Bramson and George W. Goethals, eds., *War: Studies from Psychology, Sociology and Anthropology* (New York, 1964). Useful perspectives may also be gained by considering the impact of other wars on society. Arthur Marwick, *War and Social Change in the Twentieth Century: A Comparative Study of Britain, France, Russia, and the United States* (London, 1974), presents a very helpful agenda for assessing how war effects transitions in a culture. John U. Nef, *War and Human Progress: An Essay on the Rise of Industrial Society* (Cambridge, England, 1952), focuses on Europe but suggests helpful directions for thinking about the United States. The two major twentieth-century wars and their impact on the United States have been well studied. For World War I the best work is David Kennedy, *Over Here* (New York, 1980). For World War II two fine books are Richard Polenberg, *War and Society* (Philadelphia, 1972), and John M. Blum, *V Was for Victory* (New York, 1976). Robert W. Johannsen, *From the Halls of Montezuma* (New York, 1985), is excellent on the impact of the Mexican War.

Industrialization and Society

The social history of the war era has erupted in the past decade, providing new contexts in which to perceive the changes of the mid-nineteenth century. James Henretta, "Social History as Lived and Written," *American Historical Review* 84 (December 1979), provides a broader context in which to view such writing. The literature is summarized in essays in "The Promise of American History: Progress and Prospects," *Reviews in American History* 10 (December 1982). However, in reacting to the limitations of more traditional history, the "new social historians" have all but ignored the greatest crisis in the nation's history, the Civil War. In part this neglect is the result of a focus on the prewar years in tracing the transitions wrought by industrialization and urbanization. Community studies by Stuart Blumin, *Urban Threshold: Growth and Change in a Nineteenth-Century Community* (Chicago, 1976); Susan Hirsch, *Roots of the American Working Class: The Industrialization of Crafts in Newark, 1800–1860* (Philadelphia, 1978); Bruce Laurie, *Working People of Philadelphia* (Philadelphia, 1980); Peter Knights, *The Plain People of Boston, 1830–1860* (New York, 1971); Thomas Dublin, *Women and Work: The Transformation of Work and Community in Lowell, Massachusetts, 1826–1860* (New York, 1979); Sean Wilentz, *Chants Democratic: New York City and the Rise of the American Working Class, 1790–1850* (New York, 1985); Robert Doherty, *Society and Power: Five New England Towns, 1800–1860* (Amherst, 1977); and Richard Horwitz, *Anthropology Toward History: Culture and Work in a Nineteenth-Century Maine Town* (Middletown, Conn., 1978), all stop before the war, although the changes they describe hardly stopped in 1850 or 1860. Anthony Wallace, *Rockdale: The Growth of an American Village in the Early Industrial Revolution* (New York, 1978), provides a superb picture of one town's experience while it manages to ignore most of the findings of the new social history. His treatment of the war is, however, almost an afterthought. The two pathbreaking studies of social change, Merle Curti, *The Making of an American Community* (Stanford, 1959), and Stephan Thernstrom, *Poverty and Progress* (Cambridge, Mass., 1964), cover chronologically the war years, but neither provides a focus on the conflict's impact, Thernstrom omitting the war from his index and Curti providing only occasional comment. The exceptions to this general description are Michael Frisch, *Town into City: Springfield, Massachusetts, and the Meaning of Community, 1840–1880* (Cambridge, Mass., 1972), and Alan Dawley, *Class and Community: The Industrial Revolution in Lynn* (Cambridge, Mass., 1976), and, to a lesser degree, Don Harrison Doyle, *The Social Order of a Frontier Community: Jacksonville, Illinois, 1825–70* (Urbana, 1978). The insights to be gained from town studies of specific topics are suggested by Emily J. Harris, "Sons and Soldiers: Deerfield, Massachusetts, and the Civil War," *Civil War History* 30 (June 1984).

The economic environment in which industrialization occurred has produced a large literature in recent decades. The best summary is Susan P. Lee and Peter Passell, *A New Economic View of American History* (New York, 1979). *Trends in the American Economy in the Nineteenth Century* (Princeton, 1960) contains several invaluable articles. Two books focusing on changes in transportation outline the subject with great skill: George R. Taylor, *The Transportation Revolution, 1815–1860* (New York, 1951), and Alfred Chandler, *The Visible Hand: The Managerial Revolution in American Business* (Cambridge, Mass., 1977). Introducing the issue of wealth distribution are Lee Soltow, *Men and Wealth in the United States, 1850–1870* (New Haven, 1975); Robert Gallman, "Trends in the Size Distribution of Wealth in the Nineteenth Century: Some Speculations," in Lee Soltow, ed., *Six Papers on the Size Distribution of Wealth and Income* (New York, 1969); and Jeffrey Williamson and Peter Lindert, *American Inequality: A Macroeconomic History* (New York, 1980). These conclusions are challenged by Scott Grosse, "On the Alleged Antebellum Surge in Wage Differentials," *Journal of Economic History* 42 (Winter 1982): 413–18. Williamson and Lindert effectively rebut Grosse in the same volume, 419–22. Studies of urban wealth are led by Edward Pessen, *Riches, Class and Power Before the Civil War* (Lexington, Mass., 1973), whose conclusions are modified by Gallman in "Professor Pessen on the 'Egalitarian Myth,' " *Social Science History* 2 (Winter 1978). Philip Cohelo and James Shepard, "Regional Differences in Real Wages: The United States, 1851–1880," *Explorations in Economic History* 13 (1976): 203–230, can be usefully compared with Stephan Thernstrom and Peter Knights, "Men in Motion: Some Data and Speculations about Urban Population Mobility in Nineteenth-Century America," in Tamara Haraven, ed., *Anonymous Americans* (Englewood Cliffs, N.J., 1971), 17–48, in assessing the mobility induced by industrial change and its consequences. See also section below on labor and previously mentioned community studies.

The broader issue of the extent to which economic change unleashed vast social change is the subject of Richard D. Brown, *Modernization: The Transformation of American Life, 1600–1865* (New York, 1976). James McPherson begins his fine *Ordeal by Fire* with a chapter utilizing Brown's ideas but does not utilize the new social and economic history extensively in exploring the concept. He does provide an excellent bibliographic essay, which mentions many of the important works in the area. Dean C. Tripps, "Modernization Theory and the Comparative Study of Societies: A Critical Perspective," *Comparative Studies in Society and History* 15 (1967): 199–226, provides a critical assessment of modernization theory. Herbert Gutman's pathbreaking essay, "Work, Culture and Society in Industrializing America, 1815–1919," *American Historical Review* 78 (June 1973): 531–88, discusses transformations in work roles with a fine sensitivity to the dialectic between change and tradition. Thomas Bender, *Community and Social Change in America* (Baltimore, 1978), provides an intriguing discussion that is alert to the impact of modernizing forces on small communities. Morton Horwitz, *The Transformation of American Law* (Cambridge, Mass., 1977), describes the legal innovation that implemented nineteenth-century economic change. Charles McClain, "Legal Change and Class Interest: A Review Essay," *California Law Review* 68: 382, challenges Horwitz's argument. Daniel Walker Howe, "American Victorianism as a Culture," *American Quarterly* 27 (December 1975), looks at the cultural dimensions of modernizing American society in the years 1837–1900.

There has been no marriage between literary criticism and history based on a shared interest in modernization. However, the major literary artists of the age all reflected in their works various elements of the transformation that the nation was undergoing. Literary historians and critics have recently begun to place authors into their environments, although without familiarity with new directions in historiography. The two best studies of nineteenth-century literature remain R. W. B. Lewis, *The American Adam: Innocence, Tragedy and Tradition in the Nineteenth Century* (Chicago, 1958), and the monumental F. O. Matthiessen, *American Renaissance: Art and Expression in the Age of Emerson and Whitman* (New York, 1941).

The current work makes no pretense of being based on a deep and extensive reading of literary criticism. For that, the best place to start is the annual volume, *American Literary Scholarship*, which contains reviews of the vast amount of writing on the giants of the mid-nineteenth century. The major figures of nineteenth-century literature are the subject of two works: Floyd Stoval, ed., *Eight American Authors: A Review of Research and Criticism* (New York, 1971), and Robert Rees and Earl Harbert, eds., *Fifteen American Authors before 1900: Bibliographic Essays on Research and Criticism* (Madison, 1971). My understanding of Herman Melville has been enhanced by two studies of his short stories: William Dillingham, *Melville's Short Fiction, 1853–1856* (Athens, Ga., 1977), and, more alert to historical context, Marvin Fisher, *Going Under: Melville's Short Fiction and the American 1850s* (Baton Rouge, 1977). Carolyn Karcher, *Shadow over the Promised Land: Slavery, Race and Violence in Melville's America* (Baton Rouge, 1980), pays little attention to the anxieties provoked by economic and social change, while Michael Paul Rogin's intriguing *Subversive Genealogy: The Politics and Art of Herman Melville* (New York, 1983), concentrates on linking the author's art to personal family experience. The starting point for the important "Paradise of Bachelors and Tartarus of Maids" is Beryl Bowland, "Melville's Bachelors and Maids," *American Literature* 41 (1969): 389–405. Even the allegedly reclusive Emily Dickinson has been placed in the context of the Civil War, which raged during her most productive years. See Shira Wolosky, *Emily*

Dickinson: A Voice of War (New Haven, 1984). The literary reaction to the coming of the machine and industrialization is set forth in two works: Leo Marx, *The Machine in the Garden* (New York, 1964), and John Kasson, *Civilizing the Machine: Technology and Republican Values in America, 1776–1900* (New York, 1977).

Popular literature in America is studied best in two works: Frank Luther Mott, *Golden Multitudes: The Story of Best-Sellers in the United States* (New York, 1947), which looks at the sales and influence of the books over their publishing life, and James D. Hart, *The Popular Book* (New York, 1960), which focuses on popularity immediately following publication. James Kelly, *American Catalogue of Books Published in the United States, January 1861–January 1866* (New York, 1938, 1941), lists all books published in the mid-nineteenth century and beyond. Helen Papashvily, *All the Happy Endings* (Port Washington, N.Y., 1971), and Susan Geary, "Scribbling Women" (Ph.D. diss., Brown University, 1976), describe the women's fiction of the period. Ann Douglas, *The Feminization of American Culture* (New York, 1977), is a fascinating interpretive study of that literature and the culture that spawned it, focusing on New England. Mary Kelley, *Private Woman, Public Stage: Literary Domesticity in Nineteenth-Century America* (New York, 1984), is also helpful.

The prewar social disruptions are interpreted by traditional methods in Fred Somkin, *Unquiet Eagle: Memory and Desire in the Idea of American Freedom, 1815–1860* (Ithaca, 1967); Rowland Berthoff, *An Unsettled People: Social Order and Disorder in American History* (New York, 1971); David Donald, "An Excess of Democracy," in *Lincoln Reconsidered* (New York, 1961); and Stanley Elkins, *Slavery: A Problem in American Institutional and Intellectual Life* (Chicago, 1976). Interweaving social conditions and the questions of slavery and disunion more directly are David B. Davis, *The Slave Power Conspiracy and the Paranoid Style* (Baton Rouge, 1969), and George Forgie, *Patricide in the House Divided: A Psychological Interpretation of Lincoln and His Age* (New York, 1979). David B. Davis, *The Problem of Slavery in the Age of Revolution* (Ithaca, 1975), while dealing with earlier decades in England provides illuminating insights on the relationship between slavery and larger social apprehensions. Davis' outstanding collection of documents for the antebellum era, *Antebellum American Culture* (Lexington, Mass., 1979), illustrates the multiple facets of concern for stability. Works emphasizing elements of stability in the prewar world are Daniel J. Boorstin, *The Americans, The National Experience* (New York, 1965); J. C. Furnas, *The Americans: A Social History* (New York, 1969); and Page Smith, *As A City Upon a Hill: The Town in American History* (New York, 1966). Phillip S. Paludan, "The American Civil War Considered as a Crisis in Law and Order," *American Historical Review* 77 (October 1972), and Lewis Saum, *The Popular Mood of Pre–Civil War America* (Westport, 1980), provide useful insights.

The impact of prewar changes on women is a subject of extensive discussion. Three essays in the December 1982 issue of *Reviews in American History* introduce this literature. See Mary Ryan, "The Explosion in Family History"; Estelle Freedman, "Sexuality in Nineteenth-Century America"; and Elaine Tyler May, "Expanding the Past . . . Women in Politics and Work." Of particular interest for the pre–Civil War years are Barbara Berg, *The Remembered Gate: Origins of American Feminism—the Woman and the City, 1800–1860* (New York, 1978); Nancy Cott, *The Bonds of Womanhood: "Woman's Sphere" in New England, 1780–1835* (New Haven, 1977); Mary Ryan, *Cradle of the Middle Class: The Family in Oneida County, New York, 1790–1865* (New York, 1981); Kathryn Kish Sklar, *Catherine Beecher: A Study in American Domesticity* (New York, 1973); Barbara Welter, "The Cult of True Womanhood," *American Quarterly* 18 (1966); and Gerda Lerner, "The Lady and the Mill Girl: Changes in the Status of Women in the Age of Jackson, 1800–1840," *Midcontinent American Studies Journal* 10 (Spring 1969). G. J. Barker-Benfield, *The Horrors of the Half-Known Life: Male Attitudes Toward Women and Sexuality in Nineteenth-Century America* (New York, 1976), discusses the impact on men of challenges to traditional sex roles.

The changing views of work that the industrializing economy engendered are discussed ably in Daniel T. Rogers, *The Work Ethic in Industrial America* (Chicago, 1978). Two works look at images of men whose hard work allegedly brought success: John Cawalti, *Apostles of the Self-Made Man* (Chicago, 1965), emphasizes images of work more than does Irwin Wyllie, *The Self-Made Man in America: The Myth of Rags to Riches* (New York, 1954). Carl Siracusa, *Mechanical People: Perceptions of the Industrial Order in Massachusetts, 1815–1880* (Middletown, Conn., 1978), analyzes political rhetoric while Francis Gregory and Irene Neu, "The American Industrial Elite in the 1870s: Their Social Origins," in William Miller, ed., *Men in Business* (Cambridge, Mass., 1952), demonstrate who actually got ahead among industrial leaders. Work cited in the above section on community also includes discussion by workers and bosses on the meaning of their work and suggests who lived up to the rhetoric and who did not. Paul Faler, "Cultural Aspects of the Industrial Revolution: Lynn, Massachusetts, Shoemakers and Industrial Morality, 1826–1860," *Labor History* (Summer 1974), is also helpful.

Concern over the meaning of the changing economy for the work ethic can be seen in the discussion over the relationship between free and slave labor. Bernard Mandel, *Labor: Free and Slave, Workingmen and the Antislavery Movement in the United States* (New York, 1955), is a fine starting point for this issue. Marcus Cunliffe, *Chattel Slavery and Wage Slavery: The Anglo-American Context, 1830–1860* (Athens, Ga., 1979), and Betty Fladeland, *Abolitionists and Working-Class Problems in the Age of Industrialization* (Baton Rouge, 1984), provide the most recent assessments. Volume 2 of Davis' study, *The*

Problem of Slavery, cited above, also is instructive on the issue. Eric Foner, "Abolitionism and the Labor Movement in Antebellum America," in his *Politics and Ideology in the Age of the Civil War* (New York, 1980), discusses the much debated issue of the extent to which the labor movement aided abolitionism. Foner's general position on the nature of the antebellum free labor rhetoric is integral to his superb *Free Soil, Free Labor, Free Men: The Ideology of the Republican Party Before the Civil War* (New York, 1970). The postwar encounter between antislavery rhetoric and the costs of industrialization is the major focus of David Montgomery, *Beyond Equality: Labor and the Radical Republicans, 1862–1872* (New York, 1967), which contains an excellent introduction to the context of labor in the mid-nineteenth century. See sections on labor and politics below for additional material.

Abolitionism is a subject of extensive discussion among historians. The best introduction is James B. Stewart, *Holy Warriors: Abolitionists and American Society* (New York, 1976). Leonard Richards, *"Gentlemen of Property and Standing"* (New York, 1970), by looking at the opposition to the movement, places the crusade in the context of its society. Lewis Perry and Michael Fellman, eds., *Abolitionism Reconsidered* (Baton Rouge, 1981), does so on a broad scale. The best illustration of abolitionism as a critique of the entire antebellum culture is Harriet Beecher Stowe, *Uncle Tom's Cabin.* See afterword to the Signet edition of the novel by John William Ward and foreword to the Penguin edition by Ann Douglas. The most recent illustration of the relationship of the novel to larger issues of its day is Isabelle White, "The Uses of Death in *Uncle Tom's Cabin,*" *American Studies* 26 (Spring 1985). Lawrence J. Friedman, *Gregarious Saints: Self and Community in American Abolitionism, 1830–1870* (New York, 1983), provides the most recent insight into the complexities of abolitionism.

The response to abolitionism understood as a critique of the North was offered mainly by George Fitzhugh, who is best studied in his own works: *Sociology for the South* (Richmond, 1854), and *Cannibals All* (Richmond, 1857). Fitzhugh and his influence are assessed in Harvey Wish, *George Fitzhugh: Propagandist of the Old South* (Baton Rouge, 1943), and Eugene Genovese, *The World the Slaveholders Made* (New York, 1969). Richard Hofstadter, *The American Political Tradition and the Men Who Made It* (New York, 1949), describes Calhoun as critic of the industrial process. The South as a counterimage to Northern evils is presented in William Taylor, *Cavalier and Yankee: The Old South and American National Character* (New York, 1961).

The defense of the Northern economy and society finds extensive explanation in Foner's *Free Soil, Free Labor, Free Men,* cited above. His work conveys the Republican perspective—combining criticism of the Southern system with justification for a new vision of the North, freed of the corruptions of slavery. Foner undervalues the anxieties of Northern audiences and of Republicans themselves as they defended their society. An earlier effort to assess the relationship between Northern social goals and the South are two articles by George Winston Smith: "Ante-bellum Attempts of Northern Business Interests to 'Redeem' the Upper South," *Journal of Southern History* 11 (May 1945), and "Some Northern Wartime Attitudes Toward the Post–Civil War South," *JSH* 10 (August 1944). The outstanding spokesman for the Republican position, Henry Carey, has also been studied, most ably in George Winston Smith, *Henry Carey and American Sectional Conflict* (Albuquerque, 1951), and Arnold Green, *Henry Charles Carey: Nineteenth-Century Sociologist* (Philadelphia, 1951). A more recent study is Rodney Morrison, "Henry Carey and American Development," *Explorations in Entreprenuerial History*, series 2, vol. 5 (Winter 1968). The economic and social visions of nineteenth-century political economists out of which Carey and the Republican vision emerged are summarized in two fine works: Joseph Dorfman, *The Economic Mind in American Civilization*, 5 vols. (New York, 1946–1959), especially vol. 2; and Paul K. Conkin, *Prophets of Prosperity: America's First Political Economists* (Bloomington, 1980).

Beginning the War

The immediate reaction to the outbreak of war is best followed in the personal experience of individual diaries and letters. The best guides to these materials are the bibliography of James G. Randall and David Donald, *Civil War and Reconstruction* (Lexington, Mass., 1969); Louis Kaplan et al., *Bibliography of American Autobiographies* (Madison, 1961); and the *National Union Catalogue of Manuscripts* (Washington, 1961–). Every state and local historical society in the nation will contain some collection of letters and/or diaries of Civil War veterans. More illuminating of life behind the lines are the collections of family letters, usually by women, describing day-to-day experience. The local newspapers are full of reactions to the war from Sumter to Appomattox. Far too little use has been made of these invaluable resources. Two guides point the way here: Winifred Gregory, *American Newspapers, 1821–1936: A Union List* (Washington, 1937), and Library of Congress, Union Catalogue Division, *Newspapers on Microfilm*. George W. Smith and Charles Judah, eds., *Life in the North during the Civil War* (Albuquerque, 1966), is a fine collection of documents for the whole war, while Howard Cecil Perkins, ed., *Northern Editorials on Secession* (New York, 1942), provides extensive clues to Northern fears and expectations. Kenneth M. Stampp, *And the War Came: The North and the Secession Crisis* (Baton Rouge, 1950), remains the best description of the reaction of the Union to the outbreak of war. The reasons that the North was willing to go to war have been analyzed in Paludan, "The American Civil War Considered as a Crisis in Law and Order," cited above. Kenneth Stampp, ed., *The Causes of the Civil War* (Englewood Cliffs, N.J., 1974), summarizes discussion on the much larger issue of why the war came.

The intricate subject of nationalism in the war era is explored in Clinton Rossiter, *The American Quest* (Ithaca, 1971); Merle Curti, *The Roots of American Loyalty* (New York, 1946); Paul Nagel, *One Nation Indivisible* (New York, 1964); Hans Kohn, *American Nationalism* (New York, 1957); Yehoshua Arieli, *Individualism and Nationalism in American Ideology* (Cambridge, Mass., 1964); and Major Wilson, *Space, Time, and Freedom* (Westport, 1974). David Potter's brilliant essay, "The Historian's Use of Nationalism and Vice Versa," in his *The South and the Sectional Conflict* (Baton Rouge, 1968), alerts readers to the importance of studies that reveal the interconnection between local and national loyalties. The most valuable of these are Morton Grodzins, *The Loyal and the Disloyal* (Chicago, 1956), and Harold Guetzkow, *Multiple Loyalties* (Princeton, 1955). The studies of community in the mid-nineteenth century cited in the section above illustrate the relevance of writings on loyalty without being aware of those writings.

The relationship between loyalty and the political system is imaginatively discussed in Jean Baker, *Affairs of Party: The Political Culture of Northern Democrats in the Mid-Nineteenth Century* (Ithaca, 1983). Demonstrating the vast involvement of Northerners in their political system are two articles: Walter Dean Burnham, "The Changing Shape of the American Political Universe," *American Political Science Review* 59 (1965), and William Gienapp, "Politics Seem to Enter Into Everything," in Stephan Maizlish, ed., *Essays on American Antebellum Politics, 1840–1860* (Arlington, Tx., 1982). Baker's exploration of the role of schools in nurturing loyalty needs to be supplemented by Lawrence Cremin, *American Education: The National Experience, 1783–1876* (New York, 1980); Michael Katz, *The Irony of Early School Reform* (Boston, 1968); Stanley K. Schultz, *The Culture Factory: Boston Public Schools, 1789–1860* (New York, 1973); Carl Kaestle, *The Evolution of an Urban School System: New York City, 1750–1850* (Cambridge, Mass., 1973); David Tyack and Elisabeth Hansot, *Managers of Virtue: Public School Leadership in America, 1820–1980* (New York, 1982); and Carl Kaestle and Maris Vinovkis, *Education and Social Change in Nineteenth-Century Massachusetts* (Cambridge, Mass., 1980). Peter Hall, *The Organization of American Culture, 1700–1900* (New York, 1982), is also very helpful on higher education, as is Rush Welter, *The Mind of America, 1820–1860* (New York, 1975), on education and culture generally.

Every Northern state has a history of its wartime experience. A good place to begin investigating state government activity is Daniel Elazar, *The American Partnership: Intergovernmental Cooperation in the Nineteenth-Century United States* (Chicago, 1962). William Weeden, *War Government: Federal and State in Massachusetts, New York, Pennsylvania and Indiana, 1861–1865* (Boston, 1906), is still useful for interstate views. William B. Hesseltine, *Lincoln and the War Governors* (New York, 1948), reviews Northern state activities ably. H. C. Hubbart, *The Older Middle West, 1840–1880* (New York, 1936), is excellent on the region, as is Edward Conrad Smith, *The Borderland in the Civil War* (New York, 1927).

The best of the state studies are John Niven, *Connecticut for the Union* (New Haven, 1965); Emma Thornborough, *Indiana in the Civil War Era* (Indianapolis, 1965); Kenneth Stampp, *Indiana Politics during the Civil War* (Bloomington, 1949); Arthur Cole, *The Era of the Civil War, 1848–1870* (Springfield, Ill., 1919); and Eugene Roseboom, *The Civil War Era* (Columbus, 1944). New York is best studied in biographies by Stewart Mitchell, *Horatio Seymour of New York* (New York, 1938), and Alexander Flick, *Samuel Jones Tilden: A Study in Political Sagacity* (New York, 1939), although Mitchell tends to admire his subject too much. William Dusenberre, *Civil War Issues in Philadelphia, 1856–1865* (Philadelphia, 1965), and Margaret Leech, *Reveille in Washington, 1860–1865* (New York, 1945), are indispensable on these two major cities.

For the organization of the Union army the classic is Fred R. Shannon, *The Organization and Administration of the Union Army* (Cleveland, 1928). Confusions in the War Department are shown by A. Howard Meneely, *The War Department, 1861: A Study in Mobilization and Administration* (New York, 1928), and assessed in Benjamin Thomas and Harold Hyman, *Stanton: The Life and Times of Lincoln's Secretary of War* (New York, 1962). Russell Weigley, *Quartermaster General of the Union Army: A Biography of Montgomery C. Meigs* (New York, 1959), reveals the importance of its subject in bringing order to the gathering of supplies. Benjamin A. Gould, *Investigations in the Military and Anthropological Statistics of American Soldiers* (New York, 1869), provides an immense amount of data on the characteristics of the soldiers who enlisted in the army.

The reaction of intellectuals to the outbreak of war is discussed in Fredrickson, *The Inner Civil War,* cited above. Concern for loss of revolutionary purity is seen in Forgie, *Patricide in the House Divided,* also cited above, and in Lincoln's prewar perspective, which is discussed in Phillip Paludan, "Lincoln, the Rule of Law and the American Revolution," *Journal of the Illinois State Historical Society* 70 (February 1977). James McPherson, *Struggle for Equality: The Abolitionists and the Negro in the Civil War and Reconstruction* (Princeton, 1964), is definitive on the abolitionist reaction to the outbreak of war. Walt Whitman's war experience is gathered beautifully in Walter Lowenfels, ed., *Walt Whitman's Civil War* (New York, 1960). John P. McWilliams, Jr., " 'Drum Taps' and *Battle Pieces*: The Blossom of War," *American Quarterly* 23 (1971): 181–201, and Richard Hart Fogle, "Melville and the

Civil War," *Tulane Studies in English* 9 (1959), illuminate the impact of the conflict on these literary giants.

The border state experience is described in E. C. Smith, *The Borderland in the Civil War*, cited above, and in specific state studies: Richard Curry, *A House Divided: A Study of Statehood Politics and the Copperhead Movement in West Virginia* (Pittsburgh, 1964); E. Merton Coulter, *Civil War and Readjustment in Kentucky* (Chapel Hill, 1926); Lowell Harrison, *The Civil War and Kentucky* (Lexington, Ky., 1975); William Parrish, *Turbulent Partnership: Missouri and the Union, 1861–1865* (Columbia, Mo., 1963); Jean Baker, *The Politics of Continuity: Maryland Political Parties from 1858 to 1870* (Baltimore, 1973). Don Bowen, "Guerrilla Warfare in Western Missouri, 1862–1865," *Comparative Studies in Society and History* 14, analyzes the class structure of irregular forces in Missouri. For guerrilla warfare during the conflict, see Albert Castel, "The Guerrilla War," Special Issue of *Civil War Times Illustrated*, October 1974, and Virgil Carrington Jones, *Gray Ghosts and Rebel Raiders* (New York, 1956). These accounts emphasize the dramatic and dashing qualities of the raiders, although Castel deplores the brutality of William Quantrill. A systematic study of this irregular war is needed. A study of one incident and the larger social and cultural context in the South is Phillip Shaw Paludan, *Victims: A True Story of the Civil War* (Knoxville, 1981).

The constitutional dilemmas that arose from the border states and then expanded to the whole North are best described in Hyman's *A More Perfect Union*, cited above, and more recently in Harold Hyman and William Wiecek, *Equal Justice Under Law* (New York, 1982). James G. Randall, *Constitutional Problems Under Lincoln* (Urbana, 1951), is basic on defining the constitutional nature of the war and discussing all major legal issues involved in the conflict. Carl B. Swisher, *History of the Supreme Court of the United States: The Taney Period* (New York, 1974), and Don Fehrenbacher, *The Dred Scott Case* (New York, 1978), provide thorough pictures of Taney's constitutional views. The habeas corpus issue is surveyed in Sydney G. Fisher, "The Suspension of Habeas Corpus during the War of the Rebellion," *Political Science Quarterly* 3 (September 1888). See also Phillip S. Paludan, *A Covenant with Death: The Constitution, Law and Equality in the Civil War Era* (Urbana, 1975). For the events in Baltimore, see Gary Lawson Browne, *Baltimore in the Nation, 1789–1861* (Chapel Hill, 1980), and William Brown, *Baltimore and the Nineteenth of April, 1861* (Baltimore, 1887).

Foreign Images and Affairs

The best study of diplomacy in the war era is D. P. Crook, *The North, the South, and the Powers* (New York, 1974). Older but still useful on public opinion especially is Donaldson Jordan and Edwin Pratt, *Europe and the*

American Civil War (Boston, 1931). Hyman, ed., *Heard Round the World,* cited above, provides valuable essays on the war in foreign eyes. For England the most recent starting point is Brian Jenkins, *Britain and the War for the Union,* 2 vols. (Montreal, 1974), while Kenneth Bourne, *Britain and the Balance of Power in North America, 1815–1908* (London, 1967), provides long-range context. Ephraim Adams, *Great Britain and the American Civil War,* 2 vols. (London, 1925), still remains helpful. Robin Winks, *Canada and the United States: The Civil War Years* (Baltimore, 1960), discusses relations with our northern neighbor. Martin Duberman, *Charles Francis Adams, 1807–1886* (Stanford, 1960), provides a fine discussion of our minister in these crucial years.

William Seward is revealed in Glyndon Van Deusen, *William Henry Seward* (New York, 1967), and his diplomacy in the crucial first year of the war is the focus of Norman Ferris, *Desperate Diplomacy: William Seward's Foreign Policy, 1861* (Knoxville, 1976). Gordon Warren, "Imperial Dreamer: William Henry Seward and American Destiny," in Frank Merli and Theodore Wilson, eds., *Makers of American Diplomacy* (New York, 1974), is illuminating. The *Trent* affair now has two able studies: Norman Ferris, *The Trent Affair* (Knoxville, 1977), and Gordon Warren, *Fountain of Discontent: The Trent Affair and Freedom of the Seas* (Boston, 1981). Stuart Bernath, *Squall Across the Atlantic: The American Civil War Prize Cases and Diplomacy* (Los Angeles, 1970), sets those cases in a valuable context.

The question of British recognition of the Confederacy is discussed in all the above studies but is illuminated more fully in James B. Baxter III, "The British Government and Neutral Rights," *American Historical Review* 34 (October 1928), and Frank Merli and Theodore Wilson, "The British Cabinet and the Confederacy," *Maryland Historical Magazine* 65 (Fall 1970), and especially in Norman Greabner, "Northern Diplomacy and European Neutrality," in David Donald, ed., *Why the North Won the Civil War* (Baton Rouge, 1960).

The complexities of the love-hate relationship between Americans and the English is shown in the fine collection edited by Henry Commager, *Britain Through American Eyes* (New York, 1974). Cushing Strout, *The American Image of the Old World* (New York, 1963), provides a broader view, while Harold Temperly, "Anglo-American Images," in H. C. Allen and Roger Thompson, eds., *Contrast and Connection: Bicentennial Essays in Anglo-American History* (Athens, Ohio, 1976), provides a stimulating discussion of self-definitions through contrasts.

The position of English classes on the Civil War has been the subject of much discussion. Wilbur D. Jones, "The British Conservatives and the American Civil War," *American Historical Review* 58 (April 1953), describes upper-class attitudes. The working-class position is hotly debated. J. M.

Hernon, "British Sympathies in the American Civil War," *Journal of Southern History* 33 (August 1967), and Mary Ellison, *Support for Secession: Lancashire and the American Civil War* (Chicago, 1972), argue that workers were mainly pro-South. Philip Foner, *British Labor and the American Civil War* (New York, 1981), provides effective evidence for an opposing view, confirming an earlier argument for the more traditional position by J. R. Pole, *Abraham Lincoln and the Working Classes of Britain* (London, 1959). Royden Harrison, *Before the Socialists: Studies in Labour and Politics, 1861–1881* (London, 1965), notes distinctions between types of industrial workers whose favor Lincoln sought. Donald Read, *Cobden and Bright: Victorian Partnership* (London, 1967), illuminates Manchester economic liberalism as one element in the pro-Union position, while the monumental E. P. Thompson, *The Making of the English Working Class* (New York, 1963), provides an unforgettable picture of the impact of industrialization on the workers. Gabor S. Borritt, *Lincoln and the Economics of the American Dream* (Memphis, 1978), notes Lincoln's firm commitment to laboring men and women, without noting the political dimension of Lincoln's views. For the perspective of Marx and Engels on the labor question in its Civil War context, see Karl Marx and Friedrich Engels, *The Civil War in the United States,* edited by Richard Enmale (New York, 1937), and Saul Padover, ed., *Karl Marx on America and the Civil War* (New York, 1972). Gerald Runkle, "Karl Marx and the American Civil War," *Comparative Studies in Society and History* 6 (1964), analyzes Marx's insights.

For French diplomacy and the war, see Lynn Case and Warren Spencer, *The United States and France: Civil War Diplomacy* (Philadelphia, 1970), and Henry Blumental, *France and the United States: Their Diplomatic Relations, 1789–1914* (Chapel Hill, 1970). Alfred J. Hanna and Kathryn A. Hanna, *Napoleon III and Mexico* (Chapel Hill, 1971), is the basic work on Maximilian's adventures. Thomas Sancton, "The Myth of French Workers' Support for the North in the American Civil War," *French Historical Studies* 11 (September 1979), questions the "free labor" image of the war in French eyes.

Canada in the war is seen in two basic works: Robin Winks, *Canada and the United States: The Civil War Years* (Baltimore, 1960), and John A. Williams, "Canada and the Civil War," in Hyman ed., *Heard Round the World,* cited above.

The contributions of foreign soldiers to the Union army are discussed in Ella Lonn, *Foreigners in the Union Army and Navy* (Baton Rouge, 1951). Carl Wittke, *The Irish in America* (Baton Rouge, 1956); James Hernon, *Celts, Catholics, and Copperheads* (Columbus, 1968); and John Francis Maguire, *The Irish in America* (London, 1868), focus on the Irish. John Higham, *Strangers in the Land: Patterns of American Nativism, 1860–1925* (Boston, 1973); Marcus Lee Hansen, *The Immigrant in American History* (Cambridge, Mass., 1942);

and Leonard Dinnerstein, Roger Nichols, and David Reimers, *Natives and Strangers: Ethnic Groups and the Building of America* (New York, 1979), provide valuable context.

War, Soldiers, and Society

The present volume is not a military history of the war. Students of that immense topic are directed to Herman Hattaway and Archer Jones, *How the North Won: A Military History of the Civil War* (Urbana, 1980), the standard work. John T. Hubbell, ed., *Battles Lost and Won: Essays from Civil War History* (Westport, 1975), is a useful collection. The historical context for this war is provided by Allen Millett and Peter Mazlowski, *For the Common Defense: A Military History of America* (New York, 1984), and T. Harry Williams, *The History of American Wars* (New York, 1981). For discussions of strategy, Russell Weigley, *Toward an American Army: Military Thought from Washington to Marshall* (New York, 1962), and his *The American Way of War: A History of United States Military Policy and Strategy* (New York, 1973), are indispensable. The role of the army in American society is imaginatively discussed in Marcus Cunliffe, *Soldiers and Civilians: The Martial Spirit in America, 1775–1865* (Boston, 1968), while Richard Kohn, *Eagle and Sword* (New York, 1975), shows the origins of the discussion.

The rise of the professional army, and its role in American society, is linked with the history of West Point. The best books on that institution are Stephen Ambrose, *Duty, Honor, Country: A History of West Point* (Baltimore, 1966), and James Morrison, *"The Best School in the World": West Point, the Pre–Civil War Years, 1833–1866* (Kent, 1986). The larger question of the relationship between the professional soldier and a democratic society is debated in Samuel Huntington, *The Soldier and the State* (Cambridge, Mass., 1957), and S. E. Finer, *The Man on Horseback* (London, 1962). Professionalism in the context of economic and social transformation is best studied in Burton Bledstein, *The Culture of Professionalism* (New York, 1976), and Daniel Calhoun, *Professional Lives in America* (Cambridge, Mass., 1965). The rise of the legal profession is presented in Maxwell Bloomfield, *American Lawyers in a Changing Society, 1776–1876* (Cambridge, Mass., 1976), and its struggle for legitimacy is shown in Perry Miller, *Life of the Mind in America* (New York, 1965). Marvin Meyers, *The Jacksonian Persuasion* (New York, 1956); Leonard White, *The Jacksonians* (New York, 1954); and Richard Hofstadter, *Anti-Intellectualism in American Life* (New York, 1965), all illustrate aspects of the fear of the professional in the prewar era.

The wartime images of the generals can be found in volumes listed in James Kelly, *American Catalogue of Books Published in the United States, January 1861–January 1866* (New York, 1938), as well as in articles in *The United*

States Service Magazine and in articles listed in *Poole's Guide to Nineteenth-Century Literature.*

General George McClellan has inspired much controversy, little of it sensitive to his quality as a symbol of social change. The best survey of the literature is Joseph Harsch, "On the McClellan-Go-Round," *Civil War History* 19 (1973). Rowena Reed, *Combined Operations in the Civil War* (Annapolis, 1978), is a passionate defender, while Michael C. C. Adams, *"Our Masters the Rebels": A Speculation on Union Military Failure in the East, 1861–1865* (Cambridge, Mass., 1978), blames the general for lack of faith in his soldiers and his society. G. B. McClellan, *McClellan's Own Story* (New York, 1887), provides evidence for both theses. Edward Hagerman, "The Professionalization of George B. McClellan and Early Civil War Field Command," *Civil War History* 21 (1975), is a keen interpretation. The most complete defense of McClellan is Warren Hassler, *General George B. McClellan: Shield of the Union* (Baton Rouge, 1957)

The best guide to Grant is his *Personal Memoirs of U. S. Grant* (New York, 1886), and the best biography is William McFeely, *Grant: A Biography* (New York, 1981). Brooks Simpson, "Butcher? Racist? An Examination of William McFeely's *Grant: A Biography,*" *Civil War History* 33 (1987), challenges McFeely insightfully. Major General J. F. C. Fuller, *The Generalship of Ulysses S. Grant* (New York, 1929), assesses Grant's superiority to other Civil War commanders. T. Harry Williams compares the three commanders in *McClellan, Sherman and Grant* (Westport, 1976), and finds Grant superior. Bruce Catton, *Grant Moves South* (New York, 1960); *Grant Takes Command* (New York, 1969); and "The Generalship of Ulysses S. Grant," in Grady McWhiney, ed., *Grant, Lee, Lincoln and the Radicals* (New York, 1964), offer compelling descriptions. Edmund Wilson, *Patriotic Gore,* cited above, discusses the high literary merit of Grant's *Memoirs* and notes Howells' positive assessment as well.

Sherman is revealed in his own autobiography, *Memoirs of General W. T. Sherman,* 2 vols. (New York, 1892). The most persuasive biography is Lloyd Lewis, *Sherman; Fighting Prophet* (New York, 1958). James T. Merrill, *William Tecumseh Sherman* (Chicago, 1971), and Basil Liddell Hart, *Sherman: Soldier, Realist, American* (New York, 1929), are also helpful. John B. Walters, *Merchant of Terror: General Sherman and Total War* (Indianapolis, 1973), provides helpful background on Sherman's pre-Georgia duty but is unfortunately shaped by the Vietnam War environment, a major flaw that also marks James Reston, Jr., *Sherman's March and Vietnam* (New York, 1984). Joseph Glaathar, *The March to the Sea and Beyond: Sherman's Troops in the Savannah and Carolinas Campaigns* (New York, 1985), provides a careful look at Sherman's men.

The battlefield experience of Civil War soldiers has been described ably in two major works: Gerald Linderman, *Embattled Courage: The Experience of Combat in the American Civil War* (New York, 1987), and Bell Wiley, *The Life of Billy Yank* (New York, 1952). Randall Jimerson, "A People Divided: The Civil War Interpreted by Participants" (Ph.D. diss., University of Michigan, 1977), is also helpful. The firsthand reports are listed in Charles Dornbusch, *Regimental Publications and Personal Narratives of the Civil War*, 3 vols. (New York, 1961–1971). Gould, *Investigations in the Military and Anthropological Statistics of American Soldiers*, cited above, contains much valuable data. The multivolume *Medical and Surgical History of the War of the Rebellion* (Washington, 1870), graphically illustrates the murderousness of the battlefield. The statistics on numbers of dead and wounded are in William F. Fox, *Regimental Losses in the American Civil War, 1861–1865* (New York, 1889), and Frederick Phisterer, *Statistical Record of the Armies of the United States* (New York, 1884). The figures are analyzed in Thomas L. Livermore, *Numbers and Losses in the Civil War* (Boston, 1901). William Frassanito, *Gettysburg: A Journey in Time* (New York, 1975), and *Antietam: America's Bloodiest Day* (New York, 1978), provide fascinating photographs of the battlegrounds then and now.

The emotional impact of war is suggested in David Courtwright, "Opiate Addiction as a Consequence of the Civil War," *Civil War History* 24 (1977), and in two studies of S. Weir Mitchell: Ernest P. Earnest, *S. Weir Mitchell: Novelist and Physician* (Philadelphia, 1950), and David Rein, *S. Weir Mitchell as a Psychiatric Novelist* (New York, 1952). George Beard, *American Nervousness, Its Causes and Consequences* (New York, 1881), provides a general context for the postwar age. The *American Journal of Medical Science* for the war years contains the reports of mental institutions as well as occasional articles on "nonphysical" maladies.

The justness of the Civil War is discussed from several perspectives in Michael Walzer, *Just and Unjust Wars* (New York, 1977). James Turner Johnson, *The Just War Tradition and the Restraint of War: A Moral and Historical Inquiry* (Princeton, 1981), and Ralph Porter, *War and Moral Discourse* (Richmond, 1969), provide helpful background on this issue, as does Paul Ramsey, *War and Christian Conscience* (Durham, 1960). Donald A. Wells, "How Much Can a 'Just War' Justify?" *Journal of Philosophy* 66 (1969), is a helpful summary.

Politics and the Constitution

The political environment of the mid-nineteenth century is ably presented in Robert Kelley, *The Cultural Pattern in American Politics* (New York, 1969), which generally accepts the ethnocultural basis for political behavior. This viewpoint is the basis for the new political history written by Michael Holt,

Forging a Majority: The Birth of the Republican Party in Pittsburgh (New Haven, 1969); Ronald Formisano, *The Birth of Mass Political Parties: Michigan, 1827–1861* (Princeton, 1971); Paul Kleppner, *The Cross of Culture: A Social Analysis of Midwestern Politics, 1850–1900;* and Kleppner, *The Third Electoral System . . . 1853–1892* (Chapel Hill, 1979). Lee Benson, *Toward the Scientific Study of History: Selected Essays* (Philadelphia, 1972), sets forth the ideology of such efforts. This position has been challenged on traditional grounds as ignoring the importance of ideology, especially by Foner, *Politics and Ideology*, cited above; by Don Fehrenbacher, "The New Political History and the Coming of the Civil War," in *Lincoln in Text and Context* (Stanford, 1987), for overdependence on statistical methods; on methodological grounds by Morgan Kousser, "The 'New Political History': A Methodological Critique," *Reviews in American History* 4 (1975); and for a combination of these weaknesses by Richard Latner and Peter Levine, "Perspectives on Antebellum Pietistic Politics," *ibid.* Stephan Maizlish and John Kushma, eds., *Essays on American Antebellum Politics, 1840–1860* (College Station, Tex., 1982), provide a fine collection that integrates new and old methodologies. The Democrats and their world views are described ably in Baker, *Affairs of Party*, cited above, and Joel Silbey, *A Respectable Minority: The Democratic Party in the Civil War Era* (New York, 1977). Daniel Walker Howe, *The Political Culture of the American Whigs* (New York, 1979), and Borritt, *Lincoln and the Economics of the American Dream,* also cited above, describe the ideology that would form a crucial part of Republicanism. Foner's *Free Soil, Free Labor, Free Men* sets forth Republican beliefs. William Gienapp, *The Origins of the Republican Party, 1852–56* (New York, 1987), is the standard work, while Dale Baum, *The Civil War Party System: The Case of Massachusetts, 1848–1876* (Chapel Hill, 1984), provides a state-level picture. William Shade, *Banks or No Banks: The Money Issue in Western Politics, 1832–1865* (Detroit, 1972), and Roger Sharp, *The Jacksonians Versus the Banks: Politics in the States After the Panic of 1837* (New York, 1970), focus on a major divisive issue.

Wartime politics can be followed in the state histories cited in the first part of this essay as well as in James Rawley, *The Politics of Union: Northern Politics during the Civil War* (Lincoln, Neb., 1974), and in Nevins' volumes. Edward McPherson, ed., *The Political History of the United States During the Great Rebellion* (Washington, 1865), contains major laws, documents, and votes. Frank Moore, ed., *Rebellion Record* (New York, 1863), is filled with useful material. Frank Freidel, ed., *Union Pamphlets of the Civil War,* 2 vols. (Cambridge, Mass., 1967), provides a very helpful collection of the spectrum of political perspectives.

The best interpretation of the political environment is provided in Eric McKitrick, "Party Politics and the Union and Confederate War Efforts," in Walter Dean Burnham and William Chambers, ed., *The Changing American*

Party Systems (New York, 1967). Michael Holt, "Abraham Lincoln and the Politics of Union," in John Thomas, ed., *Abraham Lincoln and the American Political Tradition* (Amherst, 1986), responds imaginatively to McKitrick's argument. Richard Hofstadter, *The Idea of a Party System* (Berkeley, 1969), describes the development of faith in the political process, providing a balance to the discussions of antiparty feelings evident in Formisano and Holt, discussed above. Baker's fine book is again illuminating on political culture.

The constitutional environment that helped to structure politics and tested civil liberty is the subject of much high-quality discussion. The idea that the system works best as a "conversation" among its various voices is implied in Sotirios Barber, *On What the Constitution Means* (Baltimore, 1984), and in John Hart Ely, *Democracy and Distrust: A Theory of Judicial Review* (Cambridge, Mass., 1980). The constitutional process itself is described from differing perspectives in Randall, *Constitutional Problems Under Lincoln*, cited above, which focuses on legal doctrine, and Hyman, *A More Perfect Union*, also cited above, which expands discussion to political discourse. Paludan, *A Covenant with Death*, already cited, examines constitutional theory in the disunion and reunion crises. Herman Belz, *Emancipation and Equal Rights: Politics and Constitutionalism in the Civil War Era* (New York, 1978), is a subtle and persuasive picture of how the process worked. Hyman and Wiecek, *Equal Justice Under Law*, cited above, combines good coverage with challenging interpretations. Swisher, *History of the Supreme Court*, already cited, is the standard study.

The civil liberties question has inspired extensive discussion beyond that provided in the above works. An older interpretation, which insisted on disloyalty among the copperheads, had been presented by Wood Gray, *The Hidden Civil War* (New York, 1942), and George Fort Milton, *Lincoln and the Fifth Column* (New York, 1942), both works demonstrating their wartime origins. Frank Klement has made the issue of copperhead loyalty his province and has defended them from their accusers; see *The Copperheads in the Middle West* (Chicago, 1960); *The Limits of Dissent: Clement Vallandigham and the Civil War* (Lexington, Ky., 1970); and *Dark Lanterns: Secret Political Societies, Conspiracies and Treason Trials in the Civil War* (Baton Rouge, 1984). Hubert Wubben, *Civil War Iowa and the Copperhead Movement* (Ames, 1982), and Arnold Shankman, *The Pennsylvania Antiwar Movement, 1861–1865* (Cranbury, N.J., 1980), are helpful state studies showing the diversity within the movement. Robert Sterling, "Civil War Draft Resistance in the Middle West" (Ph.D. diss., Northern Illinois University, 1974), is an excellent look at one of the main charges against copperheads. Judith Lee Nallock, "The Role of Community in Civil War Desertion," *Civil War History* 29 (1983), and Peter Levine, "Draft Evasion in the North during the Civil War," *Journal of American History* 67 (1981), provide detailed studies. The arbitrary arrest issue is covered in Randall, *Constitutional Problems Under Lincoln;* Hyman, *A More Perfect Union;* and Hyman and Wiecek, *Equal Justice Under Law;* as well as in Thomas and Hyman, *Stanton: The Life and Times of Lincoln's Secretary of War,* cited above. Craig Tenney, "Major General A. E. Burnside and the First Amendment" (Ph.D. diss., Indiana University, 1977), and Dean Sprague, *Freedom under Lincoln* (Boston, 1965), raise questions about Lincoln's commitment to civil liberty. Herman Belz, *Lincoln and the Constitution: The Dictatorship Question Reconsidered,* Gerald McMurtry Lecture (Fort Wayne, 1984), and Don Fehrenbacher, "Paradoxes of Freedom" and "Lincoln and the Constitution," in *Lincoln in Text and Context,* cited above, place the issue in a wider context. Mark Neely, Jr., has underway a major reinterpretation of the arbitrary arrest issue.

Lincoln's relationship to Congress has focused on the debate over Reconstruction. The starting point for that issue is Herman Belz, *Reconstructing the Union: Theory and Policy during the Civil War* (Ithaca, 1969). Michael Les Benedict, *A Compromise of Principle: Congressional Republicans and Reconstruction, 1863–1869* (New York, 1974), and Hans Trefousse, *The Radical Republicans: Lincoln's Vanguard for Racial Justice* (New York, 1969), provide important material, which rebuts an older view of implacable hostility between the two in T. Harry Williams, *Lincoln and the Radicals* (New York, 1941). Allan Bogue, *The Earnest Men: Republicans of the Civil War Senate* (Ithaca, 1981), provides important evaluations of voting patterns. Lawanda Cox and John Cox, *Politics, Principle and Prejudice, 1865–1866* (New York, 1963), describe the cooperation between Lincoln and Congress in getting the Thirteenth Amendment passed. Louisiana as a test case of the policy is discussed in Peyton McCrary, *Lincoln and Reconstruction: The Louisiana Experiment* (Princeton, 1978), and Lawanda Cox, *Lincoln and Black Freedom* (Columbia, S.C., 1981). David Donald, *The Politics of Reconstruction, 1863–1867* (Baton Rouge, 1967), is sensitive to state political realities, as is James Mohr, ed., *Radical Republicans in the North: State Politics during Reconstruction* (Baltimore, 1976). James G. Randall and Richard Current, *Lincoln the President,* 4 vols. (New York, 1945–1955), provide the fullest picture of the administration. Harry Carmen and Richard Luthin, *Lincoln and the Patronage* (New York, 1943), show Lincoln's manipulation of the Northern political system. Burton J. Hendrick shows how the cabinet operated in *Lincoln's War Cabinet* (New York, 1946), while William B. Hesseltine, *Lincoln and the War Governors* (New York, 1948), shows the integration between state and national war making. The most recent guides to the vast Lincoln literature are Mark Neely, Jr., "The Lincoln Theme Since Randall's Call," in *Papers of the Abraham Lincoln Association* (1979), and Don Fehrenbacher, "The Changing Image of Lincoln," in his *Lincoln in Text and Context,* cited above.

The nominations and the election of 1864 are still covered best in William Zornow, *Lincoln and the Party Divided* (Norman, 1954). Harold M. Hyman, "The Election of 1864," in Arthur Schlesinger, Jr., ed., *History of American Presidential Elections* (New York, 1971), adds insight to this story. The importance of the soldier vote is described in T. Harry Williams, "Voters in Blue: The Citizen Soldiers of the Civil War," *Mississippi Valley Historical Review* 31 (1944); Josiah Benton, *Voting in the Field* (New York, 1915); and Oscar Winther, "The Soldier Vote in the Election of 1864," *New York History* 25 (1944).

The Economic Impact of War

The impact of the Civil War on the economy is much debated. The best guides to that debate are Stanley Engerman, "The Economic Impact of the Civil War," *Explorations in Entrepreneurial History,* 2d series, 3 (1966), and Harry Scheiber, "Economic Change in the Civil War Era: An Analysis of Recent Studies," *Civil War History* 11 (1965). Two collections of essays explore the major topics: Ralph Andreano, ed., *The Economic Impact of the American Civil War* (Cambridge, Mass., 1962), and David Gilchrist and W. David Lewis, eds., *Economic Change in the Civil War Era* (Philadelphia, 1967). Thomas Cochran, "Did the Civil War Retard Industrialization?" *Mississippi Valley Historical Review* 48 (1961), started most of the discussion. Pershing Vartanian, "The Cochran Thesis: A Critique in Statistical Analysis," *Journal of American History* 51 (1964), offers a strong critique.

Bray Hammond's two fine works, *Banks and Politics in America, from the Revolution to the Civil War* (Princeton, 1957), and *Sovereignty and an Empty Purse: Banks and Politics in the Civil War* (Princeton, 1970), provide the basis for discussion of financial changes in the war. Leonard P. Curry, *Blueprint for Modern America: Non-Military Legislation of the First Civil War Congress* (Nashville, 1968), is a helpful general description, while John Sherman, *Recollections of Forty Years in the House, Senate and Cabinet* (Chicago, 1895), provides firsthand analysis by the major author of wartime economic measures. Robert Sharkey, *Money, Class and Power: An Economic Study of Civil War and Reconstruction* (Baltimore, 1959), is an intriguing interpretive study, while Irwin Unger, *The Greenback Era* (Princeton, 1964); James Willard Hurst, *A Legal History of Money in the United States, 1774–1970* (Lincoln, Neb., 1973); and Wesley Mitchell, *A History of Greenbacks* (Chicago, 1903), are basic for understanding money questions.

Taxation is explained in Sidney Ratner, *Taxation and Democracy* (New York, 1967), and Elmer Ellis, "Public Opinion and the Income Tax, 1860–1900," *Mississippi Valley Historical Review* 26 (1940), describes reactions to the new measures. James G. Blaine, *Twenty Years of Congress* (New York,

1884), is an insider's view of the legislation. Herman E. Krooss, ed., *Documentary History of Banking and Currency in the United States* (New York, 1969), provides important documents.

On banking, in addition to Hammond's indispensable works, see David Gische, "The New York City Banks and the Development of the National Banking System," *American Journal of Legal History* 23 (1979), and Richard Sylla, "Federal Policy, Banking, Market Structure and Capital Formation in the United States," *Journal of Economic History* 29 (1969).

Bond selling is best followed in Ellis Paxton Oberholtzer, *Jay Cooke, Financier of the Civil War* (Philadelphia, 1907), and in Hammond's works.

For assessments of the impact of wartime economic legislation, see Reuben Kessel and Armen Alchain, "Real Wages in the North during the Civil War," *Journal of Law and Economics* 2 (1959); Jeffrey Williamson, "Watersheds and Turning Points: Conjectures on the Long-Term Impact of Civil War Financing," *Journal of Economic History* 34 (1974); and Stephen DeCanio and Joel Mokyr, "Inflation and the Wage Lag during the Civil War," *Explorations in Economic History* 14 (1977).

The Second American System

The economic ideals of the Republican party are described in Foner, *Free Soil, Free Labor, Free Men;* Borritt, *Lincoln and the Economics of the American Dream;* and Howe, *American Whigs.* See also Richard Hofstadter, *The American Political Tradition and the Men Who Made It* (New York, 1960), essay on Lincoln, as well as the work on Henry Carey cited in the section on prewar environment.

The tariff is discussed in the above works and in F. W. Taussig, *The Tariff History of the United States* (New York, 1910); Richard Hofstadter, "The Tariff Issue on the Eve of the Civil War," *American Historical Review* 44 (1938); and Reinhard Luthin, "Abraham Lincoln and the Tariff," *American Historical Review* 69 (1944).

The Morrill Land Grant Act is discussed in Paul Gates, *Agriculture and the Civil War* (New York, 1965), and W. B. Parker, *Life and Public Services of Justin Smith Morrill* (Boston, 1924). The relationship between higher education and the war is seen in Peter Hall, *The Organization of American Culture, 1700–1900* (New York, 1982).

Paul Gates has also described the Homestead Act in the above cited book, in "The Homestead Act in an Incongruous Land System," *American Historical Review* 41 (1936), and in *The Farmer's Age* (New York, 1960). See also references cited in the section on agriculture below.

The railroad in the war has received much valuable discussion. Thomas Weber, *The Northern Railroads in the Civil War* (New York, 1952), is the best of these works. George Turner, *Victory Rode the Rails* (Indianapolis, 1953) is also important. Alfred Chandler, *The Visible Hand*, cited above, provides important context, as does George R. Taylor and Irene Neu, *The American Railroad Network* (Cambridge, Mass., 1956). The social costs of the railroad grants are debated in Robert S. Henry, "The Railroad Grant Legend in American History Texts," *Mississippi Valley Historical Review* 32 (September 1945), and several authors, "Comments on 'The Railroad Grant Legend,'" *Mississippi Valley Historical Review* 32 (March 1946).

Glenn Porter and Harold Livesay, *Merchants and Manufacturers: Studies in the Changing Structure of 19th-Century Manufacturing* (Baltimore, 1971), is excellent on how war profits had later impacts. Wallace Farnham, "The Weakened Spring of Government: A Study in Nineteenth-Century History," *American Historical Review* 68 (April 1963), is challenging on government regulation.

Agriculture and the War

The general environment of mid-nineteenth-century agriculture is described in Gates, *Agriculture and the Civil War*, cited above; Clarence Danhof, *Change in Agriculture: The Northern United States, 1820–1870* (Cambridge, Mass., 1969); and Gates, *The Farmer's Age: Agriculture, 1815–1860* (New York, 1960). Wayne Rasmussen, "The Civil War: A Catalyst of Agrarian Revolution," *Agricultural History* 39 (October 1965), places the war within those changes. Robert L. Jones, *Ohio Agriculture during the Civil War* (Columbus, 1962), is a good local study for the Midwest, while Howard S. Russell, *A Long Deep Furrow: Three Centuries of Farming in New England* (Hanover, N.H., 1976), discusses more Eastern trends. Robert Swieringa, "Theoretical Perspectives in the New Rural History: From Environmentalism to Modernization," *Agricultural History* 66 (July 1983), provides an intriguing interpretation of the literature. The more specialized economic literature is listed in the bibliography to chapter 7 in Susan Lee and Peter Passell, *A New Economic View*, cited above.

The question of farm ownership has had much attention. The foundation works are Margaret Bogue, *Patterns from the Sod: Land Use and Tenure in the Grand Prairie, 1850–1900* (Springfield, Ill., 1969); Allan Bogue, *From Prairie to Cornbelt: Farming on the Illinois and Iowa Prairies in the Nineteenth Century* (Chicago, 1963); and two articles by Donald Winters: "Tenant Farming in Iowa, 1860–1900: A Study of the Terms of Rental Leases," *Agricultural History* 48 (October 1974), and "Tenancy as an Economic Institution: The Growth and Distribution of Agricultural Tenancy in Iowa, 1850–1900," *Journal of Economic History* 37 (June 1977). The mobility of farm labor is ably described in David Schob, *Hired Hands and Plowboys* (Urbana, 1976).

The profitability of agriculture is discussed in Fred Bateman and Jeremy Atack, "The Profitability of Northern Agriculture in 1860," *Research in Economic History* 4 (1979); Jeremy Atack, "Farming and Farm-Making Costs Revisited," *Agricultural History* 56 (October 1982); and Clarence Danhof, "The Farm Enterprise: The Northern United States, 1820–1860s," *Research in Economic History* 4 (1979).

Women's role in farming is surveyed in Carolyn Sachs, *"Invisible Farmers," Women in Agricultural Production* (Totowa, N.J., 1983), and in two fine pieces by John Mack Faragher: *Women and Men on the Overland Trail* (New Haven, 1979), and "History from the Inside-Out: Writing the History of Women in Rural America," *American Quarterly* 33 (Winter 1981). See also the work on women in the era by Massey, *Bonnet Brigades,* cited above, as well as Catherine Clinton, *The Other Civil War: American Women in the 19th Century* (New York, 1984), and Carl Degler, *At Odds: Women and the Family from the Revolution to the Present* (New York, 1980), for suggestive insights.

The interconnectedness of the urban-rural marketplace is shown in Taylor, *The Transportation Revolution,* and is a major theme in Lee and Passell, *A New Economic View of American History,* both cited. Albert Fishlow, *American Railroads and the Transformation of the Antebellum Economy* (Cambridge, Mass., 1965), is invaluable. More specialized studies showing the railroad's impact are Lee Benson, *Merchants, Farmers and Railroads* (Cambridge, Mass., 1955); George Miller, *Railroads and the Granger Laws* (Madison, 1971); and Frank Lewis, "Explaining the Shift of Labor from Agriculture to Industry in the United States, 1869–1899," *Journal of Economic History* 39 (September 1979). Joe B. Frantz, *Gail Borden, Dairyman to a Nation* (Norman, 1951), shows that interrelationship in one industry. Charlotte Erikson, *Invisible Immigrants* (London, 1972), is revealing on immigrant farmers.

Industrial Labor and the War

The most complete study of labor in the war era is Montgomery, *Beyond Equality,* cited above. Montgomery's bibliography lists the extant biographies of labor leaders. George R. McNeil, *The Labor Movement: The Problem of Today* (New York, 1887), is valuable for the war experience of postwar leaders. Norman Ware, *The Labor Movement in the United States, 1860–1890* (New York, 1929) and John Commons et al., eds., *History of Labor in the United States* (New York, 1918), vol. 2, can be integrated for a general picture of the labor experience. Major essays in the literature are the pathbreaking Herbert Gutman, "Work, Culture and Society in Industrializing America, 1815–1919," *American Historical Review* 78 (June 1973); Daniel T. Rogers, "Tradition, Modernity and the American Industrial Worker," *Journal of Interdisciplinary History* 7 (Spring 1977); and David Brody's two essays:

"Labor History in the 1970s: Toward a History of the American Worker," in Michael Kammen, ed., *The Past Before Us* (Ithaca, 1980), and "The Old Labor History and the New: In Search of an American Working Class," *Labor History* 21 (Fall 1980). David Montgomery, "To Study the People: The American Working Class," *Labor History* 20 (Winter 1980), is also very useful, as is Daniel Walkowitz, "Statistics and the Writing of Working-Class Culture," *Labor History* 15 (Summer 1974). Clyde Griffin, "Occupational Mobility in Nineteenth-Century America: Problems and Possibilities," *Journal of Social History* 5 (Spring 1972), and Stanley Lebergott, ed., *Manpower in Economic Growth: The American Record Since 1800* (New York, 1964), provide valuable context.

Work on communities in the war era, cited in the "Industrialization and Society" section above, provides the indispensable foundation for understanding the labor experience. Two fine dissertations provide important insights: Herbert Gutman, "Social and Economic Structure and Depression: American Labor in 1873 and 1874" (University of Wisconsin, 1959), and Lawrence Costello, "The New York City Labor Movement, 1861–1873" (Columbia, 1967).

Divisions within the working class are indicated by studies of religion and ethnicity cited in the section on politics, above. In addition, see Paul Kleppner, "Lincoln and the Immigrant Vote," *Mid-America* 48 (July 1966), and essays in Frederick Luebke, ed., *Ethnic Voters and the Election of Lincoln* (Lincoln, Neb., 1971). Hernon, *Celts, Catholics and Copperheads*, cited above, intertwines religion and ethnicity to study disloyalty and Irish feelings during the war.

The impact of the war on women workers is indicated in Massey, *Bonnet Brigades*, cited above. Bremner, *The Public Good*, also cited, describes women as recipients and as welfare workers. The impact on children needs more study. Starting places are the essays in Joseph Hawes and N. Ray Hiner, eds., *American Childhood: A Research Guide and Historical Handbook*, (Westport, 1985); Robert Bremner, ed., *Children and Youth in America: A Documentary History* (Cambridge, Mass., 1970); and Grace Abbott, ed., *The Child and the State* (Chicago, 1938). Edith Abbott, "The Civil War and the Crime Wave of 1865–1870," *Social Science Review* 1 (June 1927), and Erik Monkonnen, *Police in Urban America, 1860–1920* (Cambridge University Press, New York, 1981), reveal elements of the disorder produced by war. Robert Ernst, *Immigrant Life in New York City, 1825–1863* (New York, 1949), is also suggestive here.

The draft riots are best understood in terms of the draft itself, described by Eugene Murdock in *One Million Men: The Civil War Draft in the North* (Madison, 1971). Carol Groneman Pernicone, " 'The Bloody Ould Sixth': A Social Analysis of a New York City Working-Class Community in the

Mid-Nineteenth Century" (Ph.D. diss., University of Rochester, 1973), provides valuable context for the major area of the riots. Adrian Cook, *The Armies of the Streets: The New York City Draft Riots of 1863* (Lexington, Ky., 1974), is the standard work. Albion Man, "Labor Competition and the New York City Draft Riots of 1863," *Journal of Negro History* 36 (October 1951), emphasizes the racial conflict. Wayne C. Broehl, *The Molly Maguires* (Cambridge, Mass., 1964), and J. Walter Coleman, *The Molly Maguire Riots: Industrial Conflicts in the Pennsylvania Coal Region* (Richmond, 1936), provide careful and compelling stories of the Pennsylvania conflicts. Sterling, "Civil War Draft Resistance in the Middle West," cited above, and Craig Lee Kautz, "Fodder for Cannon: Immigrant Perceptions of the Civil War in the Old Northwest" (Ph.D. diss., University of Nebraska, 1976), provide the Western experience of dissent. Peter Levine, "Draft Evasion in the North during the Civil War," *Journal of American History* 67 (March 1981), is a recent assessment.

Emancipation

The works on politics cited above provide imperative background, as do studies of the political economy of the mid-nineteenth century also cited. Works that put emancipation and Reconstruction in the context of free labor ideology most directly are Eric Foner, "Reconstruction and the Crisis of Free Labor," in his *Politics and Ideology in the Age of the Civil War* (New York, 1980); Lawrence Powell, *New Masters: Northern Planters During the Civil War and Reconstruction* (New Haven, 1980); Paul Cimbala, "The 'Talisman Power': David Tilson, The Freedman's Bureau, and Free Labor in Reconstruction Georgia, 1865–1866," *Civil War History* 28 (June 1982); Lawrence Powell, "The American Land Company and Agency: John A. Andrew and the Northernization of the South," *Civil War History* 21 (December 1975); and Edwin Hoffman, "From Slavery to Self-Reliance," *Journal of Negro History* 56 (January 1956). William Messner, *Freedmen and the Ideology of Free Labor: Louisiana, 1862–1865* (Baton Rouge, 1978), applies the concept to a single state.

The present work focuses on Northern experiences but the South set the stage for Northern plans. The process of emancipation and Reconstruction in the South is seen from the freedmen's perspective in Leon Litwack, *Been in the Storm So Long: The Aftermath of Slavery* (New York, 1979), which is subtle and comprehensive. Louis Gerteis, *From Contraband to Freedmen: Federal Policy Toward Southern Blacks, 1861–1865* (Westport, 1973), emphasizes similarities between slavery and freedom. James Sefton, *The United States Army and Reconstruction* (Baton Rouge, 1967), describes the army viewpoint. There are two outstanding local studies of the Reconstruction experience: Willie

Lee Rose, *Rehearsal for Reconstruction: The Port Royal Experiment* (New York, 1964), and Janet Sharp Herman, *The Pursuit of a Dream* (New York, 1983), discussing Davis Bend. Eric Foner, *Nothing But Freedom: Emancipation and Its Legacy* (Baton Rouge, 1983), is a challenging comparative study of possibilities and limitations. Cox, *Lincoln and Black Freedom,* cited above, has a brilliant essay, "The Limits of the Possible."

The best work on the Emancipation Proclamation remains John Hope Franklin, *The Emancipation Proclamation* (New York, 1963). All the Lincoln studies discussed above, of course, consider the act of emancipation. Fredrickson, *The Inner Civil War,* cited above, has an interesting chapter as well. James McPherson, *Struggle for Equality,* cited above, is the standard work. The context of racial thought in which emancipation occurred is provided in George Fredrickson, *Black Image in the White Mind: The Debate on Afro-American Character and Destiny, 1817–1914* (New York, 1971); Leon Litwack, *North of Slavery: The Negro in the Free States, 1790–1860* (Chicago, 1961); and V. Jacques Voegeli, *Free But Not Equal: The Midwest and the Negro during the Civil War* (Chicago, 1967). The perspectives of blacks themselves are documented in James McPherson, ed., *The Negro's Civil War* (New York, 1965). The black soldiers' contributions are best described in Dudley Cornish, *The Sable Arm: Negro Troops in the Union Army, 1861–1865* (New York, 1966). Ira Berlin et al., *Freedom: A Documentary History of Emancipation* (Cambridge, Mass., 1985), provides valuable documentation of the soldiers' and the freedmen's experiences.

State studies cited above provide information on equal rights efforts in the North. In addition, James Mohr, ed., *Radical Republicans in the North,* cited above, is useful. David Donald, *Charles Sumner and the Rights of Men* (New York, 1970), is a superb study of the most eloquent congressional spokesman for equality. The best single state study is David Gerber, *Black Ohio and the Color Line, 1860–1915* (Urbana, 1976). David M. Katzman, *Before the Ghetto: Black Detroit* (Urbana, 1973), is also valuable for its social science perspectives. *The Life and Times of Frederick Douglass, Written by Himself* (New York, 1892), gives the firsthand story of the nation's most prominent black man.

Eric Foner, "Reconstruction Revisited," *Reviews in American History* 10 (December 1982), provides the the fullest bibliographic study. Harold Hyman, ed., *The Radical Republicans and Reconstruction* (Indianapolis, 1967), is a comprehensive collection of documents illustrating the power of free labor and federalist ideals in shaping the process. Jacqueline Jones, *Soldiers of Light and Love: Northern Teachers and Georgia Blacks, 1865–1873* (Chapel Hill, 1980), is an important case study of free labor ideals in Dixie.

The constitutional impediments to equality are discussed in Hyman and Wiecek, *Equal Justice Under Law;* Paludan, *A Covenant with Death;* Benedict,

A Compromise of Principle; and Belz, *Emancipation and Equal Rights,* cited above.

The gains for blacks as a result of war are described in Phillip Paludan, "The American Civil War: Triumph Through Tragedy," *Civil War History* 20 (September 1974), which challenges John S. Rosenberg, "Toward a New Civil War Revisionism," *American Scholar* 38 (Spring 1969). More solid evidence on the issue is provided in Roger Ransom and Richard Sutch, *One Kind of Freedom* (New York, 1977), and Robert Higgs, *Competition and Coercion: Blacks within the American Economy, 1865–1914* (New York, 1977). The beginning point for the property redistribution question is Lawanda Cox, "The Promise of Land for the Freedmen," *Mississippi Valley Historical Review* 45 (December 1958). Wartime debates on confiscation are analyzed in Patricia Lucie, "Confiscation: Constitutional Crossroads," *Civil War History* 23 (December 1977), and John Syrett, "The Confiscation Acts: Efforts at Reconstruction during the Civil War" (Ph.D. diss., University of Wisconsin, 1971).

Religion

The religious environment of the nineteenth century is described in Timothy Smith, *Revivalism and Social Reform: American Protestantism on the Eve of Civil War* (New York, 1957); Lewis Vander Velde, *The Presbyterian Churches and the Federal Union, 1861–1869* (Cambridge, Mass., 1932); George Marsden, *The Evangelical Mind and the New School Presbyterian Experience* (New Haven, 1970); and Whitney Cross, *The Burned-Over District: The Social and Intellectual History of Enthusiastic Religion in Western New York* (Ithaca, 1950). William McLoughlin, *The Meaning of Henry Ward Beecher* (New York, 1970), is especially good on Beecher's enormous influence. Barbara Cross, *Horace Bushnell: Minister to a Changing America* (Chicago, 1958), explains doctrines that influenced the nation. Ann Douglas, *The Feminization of American Culture* (New York, 1977), interprets the decline of Calvinism in the culture. Perry Miller, *The Life of the Mind in America* (New York, 1966), sets revivalism in the context of a search for order. Sidney Ahlstrom, *A Religious History of the American People* (New Haven, 1972), is the standard survey.

The intriguing question of the relationship between religion and the nation's self-image is explored in Russell Richey and Donald Jones, eds., *American Civil Religion* (New York, 1974). See also William A. Clebsche, *From Sacred to Profane America: The Role of Religion in American History* (New York, 1968). Donald Jones, *The Sectional Crisis and Northern Methodism* (Metuchen, N.J., 1970), applies the civil religion paradigm to the war era.

The interrelationship between religion, abolition, and reform is explored in Ronald Walters, *American Reformers, 1815–1860* (New York, 1978). Clifford S. Griffin, *Their Brother's Keepers* (New Brunswick, 1960), remains challenging. Gilbert Barnes, *The Antislavery Impulse* (New York, 1933); Lewis Perry, *Radical Abolitionism: Anarchy and the Government of God in Antislavery Thought* (Ithaca, 1973); Lawrence Friedman, *Gregarious Saints: Self and Community in American Abolitionism, 1830–1870* (New York, 1982); and James Brewer Stewart, *Holy Warriors: The Abolitionists and American Slavery* (New York, 1976), all explore the religious sources of antislavery reform.

The more conservative Catholic Church is described in James Hennesey, *American Catholics* (New York, 1981); John Tracy Ellis, *American Catholics* (Chicago, 1960); and Jay Dolan, *The Immigrant Church* (Baltimore, 1975). Benjamin Bleid, *Catholics and the Civil War* (New York, 1945), is also helpful. Jews in the war era have been studied by Bernard Korn, *American Jewry and the Civil War* (New York, 1951)

The best interpretation of the impact of the war on Protestantism is James Moorhead, *American Apocalypse: Yankee Protestants and the Civil War, 1861–1869* (New Haven, 1978). The December 1960 issue of volume 10 of *Civil War History* is also helpful. Darrell Bigham, "American Christian Thinkers and the Function of War, 1861–1920" (Ph.D. diss., University of Kansas, 1970), contains helpful insights, as does Chester Dunham, *The Attitude of the Northern Clergy Toward the South, 1860–1865* (Toledo, 1942).

The varied social welfare activity of Northern churches is considered in Bremner, *The Public Good*, and Massey, *Bonnet Brigades*, cited above, and in William Quentin Maxwell, *Lincoln's Fifth Wheel: The Political History of the United States Sanitary Commission* (New York, 1956). Fredrickson, *The Inner Civil War*, cited above, has a challenging interpretation of the commission. Isabell Ross, *Angel of the Battlefield: Clara Barton* (New York, 1956), is revealing on Barton's role. Jones, *Soldiers of Light and Love*, cited above, and Robert Morris, *Reading, 'Riting and Reconstruction: The Education of Freedmen in the South, 1861–1870* (Chicago, 1981), describe Southern philanthropy.

Pacifism during the war is best seen in Peter Brock's monumental *Pacifism in the United States from the Colonial Era to the First World War* (Princeton, 1968), and his *Radical Pacifists in Antebellum America* (Princeton, 1968). Edward Needles Wright, *Conscientious Objectors in the Civil War* (Philadelphia, 1931), tells another aspect of the story.

Death in the Civil War has received little attention. The basic books on death in American history are James J. Ferrill, *Inventing the American Way of Death, 1830–1920* (Philadelphia, 1980), and David Stannard, *The Puritan Way of Death: A Study of Religion, Culture and Social Change* (New York, 1977), which is broader than its title indicates. Lewis Saum, "Death in the Popular Mind of Pre–Civil War America," *American Quarterly* 26 (December 1974), and his *The Popular Mood of Pre–Civil War America*, cited above, provide a sensitive picture. Ann Douglas, "Heaven Our Home: Consolation Literature in the Northern United States," *American Quarterly* 26 (December 1974), provides insightful speculation on thought about the afterlife. Wolosky, *Emily Dickinson: Voice of War,* cited above, explores the insights of the nation's most sensitive observer of death in the war.

Lincoln's religious ideas are explored in William J. Wolf, *The Religion of Abraham Lincoln* (New York, 1963); David Hein, "Lincoln's Theology and Political Ethics," in *Essays on Lincoln's Faith and Politics* (Lanthan, Md., 1983); Glen Thurow, *Abraham Lincoln and American Political Religion* (Albany, 1976); Reinhold Niebuhr, "The Religion of Abraham Lincoln," in Allan Nevins, ed., *Lincoln and the Gettysburg Address* (Urbana, 1964); and Sidney Mead, "Abraham Lincoln's 'Last Best Hope of Earth': The American Dream of Destiny and Democracy," *Church History* 23 (March 1954). See David Hein, "Research on Lincoln's Religious Beliefs and Practices: A Bibliographic Essay," *Lincoln Herald* 86 (Spring 1984).

Index

abolitionists: attitudes toward, 4; and black equality, 218–19; and black soldiers, 212; in Canada, 278, 279; and the election of 1864, 251, 252; and emancipation, 200, 201, 224; influence of, 64, 200; and patriotism, 25; and racism, 218–19; and religion, 343, 344, 349; and the Republican party, 380; and the women's movement, 387

Adams, Charles Francis, 39, 40–41, 44–45

Adams, Charles Francis, Jr., 301

Adams, Henry, 263–64, 270

agriculture: and army deserters, 168; commercialization of, 153–54, 161–63; and debts of farmers, 155, 160; demographics concerning, 151–52, 161, 170; diversity in, 152; and exports/tariffs, 130, 161; and farm acquisition, 154; and gender roles, 158, 159–60; growth/strength of Northern, 105, 144, 148, 161–62; and health, 163–64; and immigrants, 162, 176; and industrial workers, 176; and land policies, 130–33, 162, 167–68; and market integration, 152–53, 163–64, 167; mechanization of, 153, 160–61; and middlemen, 155, 162; and the organization of farmers, 162; and the railroads/transportation system, 106, 138,

agriculture *(cont.)*
152, 155; and self-sufficiency, 152, 153, 162–63; and size of farms, 155–56; and social isolation, 158; and subsistence farming, 155; wages in, 155; and the war effort, 150, 156–57, 162, 164–66, 168–69

Agriculture, U.S. Department of, 149, 166–67

Alabama [Confederate ship], 45

Alcott, Louisa May, 219, 330, 355

Allen, William, 98, 247

American party, 175

Ames, Albert, 322–23

amputations, 325–26

Anderson, Adna, 142

Andrew, John, 15–16, 99, 211

Anthony, Susan B., 219, 251, 387

Antietam [battle], 82–83, 102, 283, 292, 316, 363

Appomattox: surrender at, 312–13, 363, 375, 382–83, 392

Arkansas, 254, 257

Army of the Potomac. *See* military; *name of specific battle or commander*

army. *See* military; state/local militia; West Point

Army of Virginia, 80–81, 82

Ashley, James, 257

Aspinwal, William, 121

assassination of Lincoln, 280, 374, 375–76, 383, 392